Windows Azure Platform

TEJASWI REDKAR

Windows Azure Platform

Copyright © 2009 by Tejaswi Redkar

All rights reserved. No part of this work may be reproduced or transmitted in any form or by any means, electronic or mechanical, including photocopying, recording, or by any information storage or retrieval system, without the prior written permission of the copyright owner and the publisher.

ISBN-13 (pbk): 978-1-4302-2479-2

ISBN-13 (electronic): 978-1-4302-2480-8

Trademarked names, logos, and images may appear in this book. Rather than use a trademark symbol with every occurrence of a trademarked name, logo, or image we use the names, logos, and images only in an editorial fashion and to the benefit of the trademark owner, with no intention of infringement of the trademark.

The use in this publication of trade names, trademarks, service marks, and similar terms, even if they are not identified as such, is not to be taken as an expression of opinion as to whether or not they are subject to proprietary rights.

President and Publisher: Paul Manning
Lead Editor: Ewan Buckingham
Technical Reviewer: Fabio Claudio Ferracchiati
Editorial Board: Steve Anglin, Mark Beckner, Ewan Buckingham, Gary Cornell, Jonathan Gennick, Jonathan Hassell, Michelle Lowman, Matthew Moodie, Jeff Olson, Jeffrey Pepper, Frank Pohlmann, Douglas Pundick, Ben Renow-Clarke, Dominic Shakeshaft, Matt Wade, Tom Welsh
Coordinating Editor: Anita Castro
Copy Editors: Heather Lang, Tiffany Taylor, and Mary Ann Fugate
Compositor: Kimberly Burton
Indexer: Toma Mulligan
Artist: April Milne
Cover Designer: Anna Ishchenko

Distributed to the book trade worldwide by Springer Science+Business Media, LLC., 233 Spring Street, 6th Floor, New York, NY 10013. Phone 1-800-SPRINGER, fax (201) 348-4505, e-mail orders-ny@springer-sbm.com, or visit www.springeronline.com.

For information on translations, please e-mail rights@apress.com, or visit www.apress.com.

Apress and friends of ED books may be purchased in bulk for academic, corporate, or promotional use. eBook versions and licenses are also available for most titles. For more information, reference our Special Bulk Sales–eBook Licensing web page at www.apress.com/info/bulksales.

The information in this book is distributed on an "as is" basis, without warranty. Although every precaution has been taken in the preparation of this work, neither the author(s) nor Apress shall have any liability to any person or entity with respect to any loss or damage caused or alleged to be caused directly or indirectly by the information contained in this work.

The source code for this book is available to readers at www.apress.com. You will need to answer questions pertaining to this book in order to successfully download the code.

This book is dedicated to my grandmother Vimal Sharad Redkar. She has been my inspiration for whatever I do. I thank my wife Arohi and my sons Aaryan and Dhruv for supporting me in writng this book. Arohi, I will never forget your sacrifices for making this book happen. I thank my sister, Aasawari for being with me when I needed her in the time of crisis. Finally, I thank my parents for their teachings that has shaped up my life.

Contents at a Glance

Contents

About the Author

 Tejaswi Redkar is a software architect with a passion for writing. He has been working with Windows Azure since its first announcement during PDC 2008.He been working with Windows Azure early adopter customers and the product team for the past one year. He believes that the best way to master a new technology is to either teach it or write a book on it. Tejaswi has designed large-scale cloud as well as on-premise applications in diverse industries ranging from financial, manufacturing, oil & gas, pharmaceutical, retail and technology. In the past, Tejaswi has not only written on conceptual topics like C# and VB.Net Threading, but also on broader topics like MSMQ and Offhore project governance
Tejaswi has a Master's Degree in Computer Engineering from San Jose State University and an MBA from University of Wisconsin, Whitewater.
Tejaswi Redkar resides with his wife, Arohi, and two sons Aaryan and Dhruv, in the beautiful San Francisco Bay Area.. When Tejaswi is not working, he is either engrossed in music or finding out reasons to avoid this week's laundry.

About the Technical Reviewer

Fabio Claudio Ferracchiati is a prolific writer on cutting-edge technologies. Fabio has contributed to more than a dozen books on .NET, C#, Visual Basic, and ASP.NET. He is a .NET Microsoft Certified Solution Developer (MCSD) and lives in Rome, Italy. You can read his blog at http://www.ferracchiati.com.

Acknowledgments

I would like to thank the following individuals for their contributions to my professional life:

- Smt. Laxmi Natarajan, the only school teacher who once told me I had what it takes to be an author

- Prof. M.B Unde from NCL, India for teaching me the importance of teaching and writing in learning new engineering concepts

- Jamal Haider from Microsoft for believing in me and encouraging the author in me

- Ewan Buckingham from Apress for believing in my idea for writing an advanced book on Windows Azure Platform

- Penny Tong, in teaching me that software is not only about development but also about delivery and support.

- My seniors and friends in University of Mississippi (Olemiss) who convinced me to enroll for a Computer Science Master's degree instead of continuing PhD. in Chemical Engineering.

- Justin Smith from Microsoft for providing me the right answers at the right time on some key releases.

- Mark Kottke, Sanjeev Karande, Eric Golpe, Patrick Butler Monterde and all of the Windows Azure OneTAP team for giving me access to Microsoft internal cluster and early adopter customers

- The Microsoft Consulting Services leadership team for fostering an atmosphere promoting the creation of intellectual property.

- Kui Jia for being a mentor and the right person at the right time for encouraging me in joining Microsoft.

- Ed Koch, Dan Hennage and the Coactive Networks leadership team for inspiring the architect in me and teaching the whole telemetry and energy management business.

My professional life is incomplete without a personal network of amazing friends, coworkers, educators and students who have played an important role in shaping my professional as well as personal life. Finally, special thanks to my wife, Arohi. Without Arohi's selfless help and support, this book wouldn't have been possible at all.

CHAPTER 1

■ ■ ■

Introducing Cloud Services

As an introduction to our discussion of cloud services, let's consider a situation that's typical in today's medium to large enterprises. Assume a business unit has an immediate need to deploy and maintain an analytics application that it has built internally. The application will provide the business users with valuable business insight that will make the company much more competitive in the marketplace. The business unit has the budget but not the time to implement the solution, and this deployment needs to happen in the next three months.

The IT hosting team members understand the requirement, but to deploy an application with IT resources requires coordination among hardware, software, operations, and support teams. Perhaps ordering hardware and preparing the enterprise operating system build itself takes two months. After that, IT has to go through its standard testing process and operations procedures to make sure all the support needs are identified. So, the earliest application delivery date would be in six months.

The business owner escalates the urgency of the issue but cannot get past the process boundaries of the enterprise. Ultimately, the business owner establishes an independent IT department funded by the business and delivers the application in three months. Even though the application is delivered, it doesn't have the enterprise support and operations quality.

Now, the CEO and the CTO evaluate the situation at the enterprise level and come to the conclusion that there are too many application instances running redundantly across the enterprise and costing the enterprise millions of dollars in resource and maintenance costs. Therefore, they decide to create a mandate that all the applications need to be migrated to the IT application-hosting infrastructure. Eventually, the business unit ends up creating an exception for its situation and continues running its own IT department, thus costing the overall enterprise on redundant resources.

I see these scenarios on a daily basis, and I don't see a clear solution to the problem unless the entire process and structure in which these organizations operate is revamped, or technology like cloud computing takes off and enterprises embrace it wholeheartedly.

How will cloud computing help in this area? To understand, let's go back to the original business requirement: the business owner has an immediate need to deploy and maintain an analytics application, and the time frame is within three months. The biggest hurdles IT has in deploying this application are not in the application itself but in the dependencies and the process involved in provisioning the infrastructure required to deploy and maintain it. If the cloud computing dream is realized, it will eliminate the need for the application hosting team to be dependent on most of the hardware team requirements, because abstraction of hardware is one of the main tenets of cloud computing, and this abstraction is provided by cloud service providers' data centers. If the servers', load balancers', routers', and switches' dependencies are eliminated, the application hosting team could focus solely on deploying the application in the cloud service of its choice, with business approval. In this case, the overall IT agility will improve and better align with the business goals of the enterprise.

Of course, considering the current state of cloud service providers, I am discounting several facts like security, performance, reliability, political atmosphere, on-going maintenance costs, and overall company culture. But all technologies start slow and with skepticism from large enterprises. Skepticism fades away as early adopters of the technology embrace it and provide valuable feedback, which goes back into the product helping it mature over time. As the technology matures, larger enterprises start embracing it. Some larger enterprises do play parts as early adopters, but very rarely because companies typically become risk averse as they grow in size and their processes become streamlined and mature.

As discussed in the scenario earlier, cloud services platforms relieves you of investing in expensive hardware and IT resources for maintaining a highly available and scalable infrastructure. Cloud platforms are designed to be used on demand. The cost of the platform is directly proportional to its usage. The more you use the platform, the more you pay, and vice a versa. These dynamic capabilities allow you to proportionately balance the service operating costs to its usage and thus make your business more elastic and responsive to change. For example, if you have an e-commerce site that peaks during the Thanksgiving and Christmas seasons and attracts fewer but consistent numbers of users for the rest of the year, then you can dynamically increase the capacity of the underlying platform during the holiday season and reduce it for the rest of the year. This dynamic capability offered by service providers is called *utility computing* and is analogous to your utility service providers' model: they charge you by the amount of energy you use. You can scale back your energy bill by reducing the energy usage, or your energy bill will go up during peak load. If you invest in a highly available and scalable infrastructure on premise, scaling in either direction based on demand is difficult. So, in the long term, cloud platforms are designed to reduce your average operating costs by giving you the flexibility to commission and decommission infrastructure depending on the business needs. Currently, the level of performance, flexibility, and reliability offered by heavily invested on-premise infrastructures may not be matched by the currently available cloud service offerings. But, as the offerings mature, they are expected to provide you with lower total cost of ownership without compromising the service reliability.

Internet itself is a vast phenomenon to be branded as a cloud. "Cloud" is a subset of the Internet. The term specifically means applications, platform, infrastructure and consumer services offered by service providers to build applications for the Internet. Acronyms like software as a service (SaaS), platform as a service (PaaS), software plus service (S + S), and database as a service (DaaS) all represent a piece of cloud services in one way or the other. In this chapter, I will go over the evolution of Internet services into cloud services and look at the offerings from major industry players like Microsoft, Google, Amazon, SalesForce.com, GoGrid, and 3Tera.

There has been a sudden burst of interest in cloud computing not only because of the cost savings it offers but also the quality of infrastructure the cloud service providers promise. The credit should go not only to SalesForce.com for revolutionizing their SaaS platform in the small business market, but also to VMWare who created a new market for operating system and hardware virtualization. I credit VMWare for market awareness they brought around virtualization and its enormous possibilities. Microsoft and Amazon followed the trend by investing heavily in virtualizing not only operating systems and software but also data center assets. Virtualization is a key piece in building low-maintenance platforms for cloud services, because a virtualized platform can be moved and scaled without any dependency on the underlying hardware. It abstracts the operating system from the hardware and applications from operating systems. Virtualization makes the concept of utility computing a reality in terms of cost and manageability. As you read this book, you will learn how virtualization plays an important role in Microsoft's Windows Azure platform infrastructure.

The cloud services platforms are in their infancy and have not yet matured either in business models or technology. But, the addition of software vendors like Amazon, Microsoft, Google, and IBM to the list of cloud service providers adds credibility to its future success. These software vendors are going to drive the cloud services industry by offering their enterprise-grade software products to businesses of all scales. So far, businesses clearly value the cost savings but are still concerned about the security and reliability of their data in the cloud. Cost, control, reliability and security are the four main quality attributes enterprises will evaluate before deciding to adopt a cloud services platform. Enterprises can also adopt hybrid models, where some services are hosted on-premises and others off. For example, the Microsoft Dynamics CRM Online service offers on-premise option that can be switched to off-premise anytime by the enterprise. These kinds of models help enterprises slowly transition a fully on-premise application to an off-premise or a hybrid solution. This helps critical technical resources in the enterprise focus on important strategic initiatives instead of worrying about day-to-day operational issues. After reading this chapter, you will have good understanding about the cloud services industry and some major players in it.

■ **Note** Throughout this book, depending on the context of the conversation, I have used the terms "cloud services" and "cloud applications" interchangeably to generally represent cloud services. A cloud service may be thought of as a collection of cloud applications in some instances, but in the context of this book, both mean the same thing.

Defining Our Terms

Before diving deep into cloud services, I would like to introduce you to the terminology used in this book. "Cloud" is an overloaded word because the platform is not a standardized yet. There are different flavors of interpretations and perspectives about it in the technology industry. To be consistent in this book, I have developed this section for introducing and defining some important terms used herein. Table 1-1 lists the common industry terms and their definitions as they relate to this book.

Table 1-1. Terminology in This Book

Term	Definition
Azure	Microsoft's Windows Azure Platform
Azure Services	The components of Windows Azure Platform (e.g., Windows Azure, SQL Azure, AppFabric, and Live Services)
Cloud	The cloud services platform (e.g., the Windows Azure platform)
Cloud application	An application deployed to a cloud services platform and typically part of a larger cloud service
Cloud platform	A service offering by a cloud service provider for deploying cloud services (e.g. Windows Azure platform offered by Microsoft and EC2 offered by Amazon)

Continued

Table 1-1. *Continued*

Term	Definition
Cloud service	An end-to-end service deployed to the cloud platform that may contain one or more cloud applications
Cloud services platform	The same as a cloud platform, which is defined earlier in this table.
On-premise	Refers to applications or services deployed and managed by an enterprise on its own and at its location
Off-premise	Refers to applications or services in the cloud
Service	When used on its own in this book, refers to the cloud service
Solution	When used on its own, refers to a collection of multiple applications and/or cloud services designed for a specific business purpose (e.g., a payroll solution consisting of three cloud services and four on-premise applications)

Evolution of Cloud Services

The Internet service platform has evolved from a simple dial-up access provider to an enterprise-grade software applications platform. The evolution of its maturity is depicted in Figure 1-1.

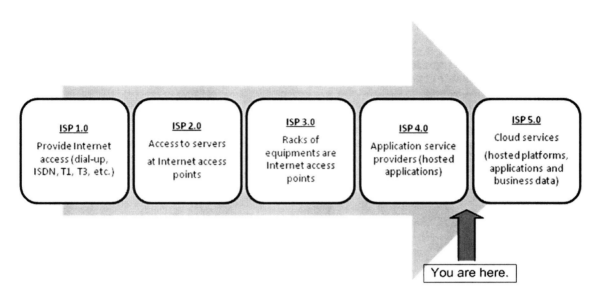

Figure 1-1. *Evolution of ISP into cloud services (Source Data: Forrester Research Inc.)*

The ISP 1.0 era was in the early to mid-1990s, and the focus was on building Internet access networks for consumers and businesses. This era was dominated by companies like AOL, NetZero, Comcast, and Time Warner. Businesses were also heavily involved in building their own internal network infrastructure. In the ISP 2.0 era, the focus shifted to providing access to the servers in the ISP infrastructure. Businesses and consumers could host their web sites on ISP servers with limited capabilities. The ISP 3.0 era brought the colocation concept into the ISP equation. Businesses could host their servers with the ISP, thus leveraging the ISP's massively scalable, efficient, and redundant infrastructure. Companies like Rackspace.com and AT&T were the leaders in this space. Even though ISP 4.0 could achieve economies of scale in the network and power infrastructures, it had to keep up with the technology and business demands to achieve economies of scale at the application and platform levels. This gave rise to the ISP 4.0 era, where the application service providers (ASP) built scalable business software services and abstracted the intricacies of the data centers from the enterprises. Enterprises just had to subscribe to the software services like the CRM services offered by SalesForce.com and Microsoft Dynamics CRM Online without worrying about the underlying data center infrastructure. In this era, the software vendors took the initiative to offer their software services to businesses over the Internet. We have not fully graduated out of the ISP 4.0 era; I would say that we are on the border of ISP 4.0 and ISP 5.0. ISP 4.0 still faces the connectivity, security, and integration challenges between on-premise and cloud services. SalesForce.com, Microsoft Dynamics CRM Online, SharePoint Online, and Exchange Online are viable services that businesses are subscribing to. In the ISP 5.0 era, the ISP infrastructure will mature into a scalable on-demand platform, called the cloud, ripe to be leveraged for building and hosting business applications.

Later in this book, you will see how Microsoft has built an operating system in the cloud comprised of virtually enabled nodes of Windows operating system for building Internet-scale applications. In the ISP 5.0 era, there is complete transparency in application hosting. Enterprises will be able to deploy custom applications into the cloud without worrying about the hardware and platform requirements for the application. This will create transparency between on-premise and cloud applications for businesses, as they will interoperate seamlessly. You will see in future chapters how Windows Azure achieves some level of this transparency.

A critical success factor for ISP 5.0 is the quality of service (QoS) offered by the cloud service providers. Cloud service providers like Amazon, Microsoft, Google, and IBM are in the process of creating massively scalable data center infrastructure, but there is little focus on the QoS for businesses as of yet. Cost, control, reliability, and security will be the determining factors cloud service providers will have to focus on to convince businesses to use their services. The biggest difference between ISP 4.0 and ISP 5.0 is the entire application life cycle hosting support offered by ISP 5.0. This means applications can be planned, developed, stabilized, deployed, and operated around cloud services with little dependence on on-premise infrastructure. Figure 1-2 shows the ISP 5.0 as an application development and deployment platform.

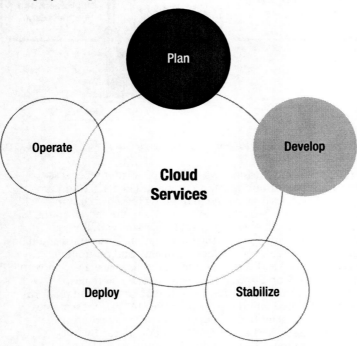

Figure 1-2. *Cloud services application platform (ISP 5.0)*

In Figure 1-2, the planning phase is conducted completely on site, similar to an on-premise application. The deviation from the on-premise application life cycle happens in the development phase, where developers have to work directly with the cloud for unit and functional testing, even though the actual software development may take place on-premise. From the development phase onward, the control of cloud over the service increases and in the deployment and operation phases the cloud is completely in control of the service. The cloud manages the deployment, availability, scalability, and connectivity of the service.

Planning

In the planning phase, you typically envision and plan your cloud service. This may involve designing a new cloud service, migrating an existing on-premise application to the cloud, or creating a hybrid on-premise and cloud service. In this phase, you also decide on the cloud services provider you want to host your service with and open and account with that provider. The most amount of effort in this phase goes into architecting the following attributes of the cloud service:

- Access control
- Network connectivity
- Reliability
- Storage architecture
- Service usage projections

Developing

In this phase, you develop the application in a local development environment provided by the cloud services provider. A *local development environment* is a simulated cloud running on-premise on your development machine used purely for development and functional testing purposes. Development may also involve deploying to the cloud development environment for unit testing.

Stabilizing

In the stabilization phase, the development, testing and the release engineering team iteratively test the application by deploying the service into a testing environment in the cloud. The black box , performance, and business scenarios testing are done in the cloud environment.

Deploying

In the deployment phase, the production version of the application is deployed into the staging environment in the cloud and then further promoted to the production cloud environment for business.

Operating

In the operation phase, the operation logs and usage of the service are evaluated periodically to analyze the usage and health of the service. Usage data is analyzed for billing purposes, and health data is analyzed for improvements to the future versions of the service.

Modeling Cloud Service Offerings

Cloud services offer several different models depending on the industry requirements. For better understanding of the cloud offerings, I have designed a pyramid for categorizing the offerings into four layers: platform, middleware, enterprise services, and consumer services. Figure 1-3 illustrates the four-layered pyramid model of the cloud service offerings.

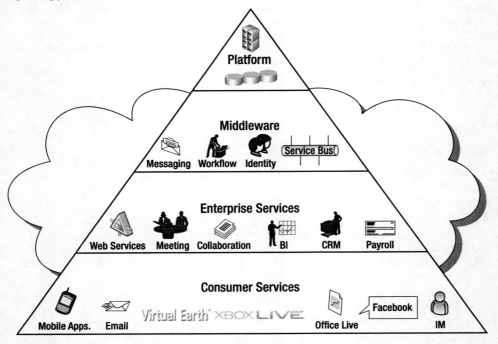

Figure 1-3. *Cloud services offerings pyramid*

Each layer in the pyramid can be considered as a separate offering, but some providers like Microsoft and Google are building complete offering spanning all the layers.

Consumer Services Layer

The consumer services layer represents cloud services that are targeted for the consumers. Some of the services like e-mail, instant messaging, and searching have been available to the consumers from the very beginning of the Internet era, whereas new services like massively multiplayer games, mobile applications, collaboration, social networking, and mapping services have gained significant consumer attention in recent years. The early cloud services like instant messaging and e-mail were developed as dedicated services without any flexibility or abstraction built into their architectures. Every software vendor had its own communication protocol and little effort was made to interoperate across platforms. I call such services as *silos* because each stands on its own, performing a certain function without any cross-platform interoperability. Over the years, these silo architectures have matured with several layers of abstraction and interoperability built in not only the platform but also the infrastructure architecture. These services now support open web services protocols and interoperate across vendor platforms. The consumer layer is built on top the foundation created by the application, infrastructure, and platform layers. Each of these layers has its own software boundaries, and the consumer market has been and will be the broadest market in terms of end users for cloud services.

Enterprise Services Layer

The enterprise services layer represents application platforms that can be leveraged by businesses to host their business-specific applications or enhanced by independent software vendors (ISVs) in building additional functionality. Most of today's SaaS applications fall into this category of cloud services, and SalesForce.com and Microsoft's Dynamics CRM Online are good examples of application platforms in the cloud. They also offer web services application programming interfaces (APIs) for custom development and add-ons on top of their basic CRM functionality. From the business perspective, the upfront cost and risk involved in deploying these services is minimal, because they are completely managed by the service provider. Businesses have to adapt to the new interface and make sure the software satisfies their business requirements. In contrast, it will cost much more to build and maintain such software in-house, because the businesses cannot leverage economies of scale like the service provider. Service providers can share the same platform across multiple customers, thus benefitting from economies of scale and passing on these cost savings to the businesses. This layer is the fastest growing in cloud services offerings because of its flexibility, low risk, and low upfront cost to the businesses.

Middleware Layer

The middleware layer is a direct result of the monetization of large-scale middleware software components already built to support massively scalable consumer services. Some examples of these already existing services are Amazon e-commerce systems, Google Search, and Windows Live services. As the consumer services and matured, the middleware layer was abstracted and service providers decided to monetize this intellectual property (IP) by offering their middleware capabilities directly to the businesses. In the middleware layer, businesses can utilize proven scalable software services and infrastructure platform offered by service providers for hosting custom software services. All businesses have custom software services that are developed internally to suite their own business processes. Such services are expensive to scale internally due to licensing, hardware, and labor costs. By deploying these services in the cloud and leveraging the scalable middleware of the service providers, businesses can scale these custom services on demand. Microsoft's AppFabric falls into this category because it offers software platforms like service bus and Access Control Service businesses can leverage for building and scaling custom services.

Platform Layer

The platform layer forms the core foundation for all the other cloud services offerings in the pyramid. The platform layer represents the computational, data storage, and network platforms ISVs, and software vendors can leverage this layer in building middleware, enterprise, and consumer services. In this layer, virtualization is employed at its optimum for providing platform abstraction and dynamic scalability for the rest of the layers. Provisioning, management, and milling of the operating systems and storage are automated to reduce maintenance and deployment costs. Quality attributes like scalability, performance, reliability, and availability are built right into the architecture of the platform layer. The primary audiences of the platform layer are ISV developers and infrastructure architects interested in leveraging this highly resilient platform in building end-to-end cloud services. Amazon's Elastic

Compute Cloud (EC2), Microsoft Windows Azure, and Microsoft SQL Azure fall into the platform payer of the cloud services pyramid.

▓ **Note** Throughout this book, I will refer to the cloud services pyramid to explain the differences between the cloud services products that we will be working with.

Shifting to the Cloud Paradigm

The move from a traditional on-premise model to an off-premise cloud model is a fundamental paradigm shift for businesses. Usually businesses are in their comfort zone of managing IT internally. With the cloud services model, even though the cost savings become evident, the challenge for businesses is to get out of their comfort zones and make the paradigm shift of moving to cloud services to stay competitive. The shift does not happen overnight; it takes several months of rigorous analysis, planning, and implementation. Depending on the costs, benefits, risks, and security requirements, a business can either stay on-premise, embrace cloud services fully, or settle on a hybrid model yielding cost benefits while keeping core competencies on-site. Figure 1-4 illustrates the ownership of key enterprise assets in on-premise, cloud, and hybrid scenarios.

The recommended migration process is to move step by step, one application at a time. When the offshore software development model became popular in 2000, businesses faced a similar challenge in getting aboard the outsourcing wagon. Now, many businesses have significant offshore investments and clearly see the payoffs. It took time and learning for businesses to make the paradigm shift in off-shore software development projects. For cloud services to succeed, businesses will be required to make a paradigm shift again.

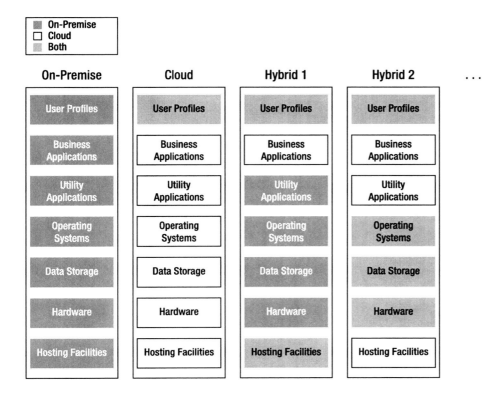

Figure 1-4. On-premise, cloud, and hybrid scenarios

In Figure 1-4, the on-premise and cloud scenarios are fairly easy to understand, because either all the assets are on-premise or in the cloud. The user profiles asset is usually required on both the sides because of single sign-on requirements between on-premise and cloud services. In hybrid models, the businesses and the service provider must negotiate and decide which assets and services are better suited for locations on-premise, in cloud, or both. In the Hybrid 1 scenario in Figure 1-4, the user profiles and hosting facilities are present on both the sides; the business applications are in the cloud, whereas the utility applications, operating systems, data storage, and hardware are on-premise. In the Hybrid 2 scenario, the user profiles, operating systems, data storage, and hardware are present on both the sides, whereas the business applications, utility applications, and hosting facilities are in the cloud. Most of the companies typically choose some hybrid model that best suits them.

Understanding the Cloud Services Ecosystem

The cloud services ecosystem consists of five major roles, as shown in Figure 1-5.

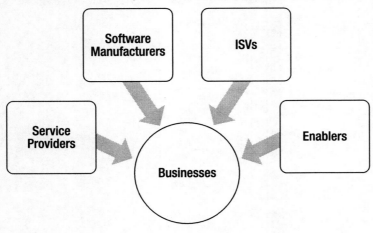

Figure 1-5. *The cloud ecosystem*

Service Providers

The service providers are the companies that provide cloud services to the businesses and to the consumers. These companies run the giant data centers hosting massively virtualized and redundant software and hardware systems. Service providers like Amazon with its EC2 service and Microsoft with its Windows Azure fall into the service providers category. These companies not only have expertise in data center management but also in scalable software management. The service providers may offer services directly to the businesses, consumers, or ISVs.

Software Vendors

Software designed to run on-premise is very different to software designed for cloud services. Even though they both may provide the same business functionality to the end users, architecturally they are not the same. The cloud services must account for multitenancy, scalability, reliability and performance at a much broader scale than on-premise architecture. Cloud services run in data centers offered by cloud service providers. In some cases, there is a significant overlap between the service providers and the software vendors. For example, Microsoft Windows Azure and Google Apps are cloud software running in their own data centers. The software vendors have found it economically feasible to package hardware and software together in the data centers to optimize the service delivery in the cloud.

Independent Software Vendors

Independent software vendors (ISVs) are going to play a key role in the success of cloud services because of their expertise in vertical business applications. ISVs typically build vertical applications on an already existing platform. ISVs identify the business demand for a particular solution in vertical markets and thrive by offering the solution on existing platforms. The cloud offers a great platform for the ISVs to build vertical solutions. For example, an ISV could build a medical billing solution in the cloud and offer the service to multiple doctors and hospitals. The infrastructure required for building multitenant scalable software is already provided by the service providers, so the ISVs have to focus only on building the business solution.

Enablers

Enablers (which are also called *implementers*) are vendors offering services to build end-to-end solutions by integrating software from multiple vendors. Many enterprises purchase software licenses from vendors but never deploy the software because of lack of strategic initiative or availability of product expertise. Enablers fill in the gap by offering consulting services for the purchased software. Companies like Microsoft Consulting Services and IBM Global Services offer customer-specific services regardless of the underlying platform. Enablers play a key role by integrating on-premise and cloud services or building end-to-end cloud services customized for a business. Cloud platform offers enablers an opportunity to expand their service offerings beyond on-premise solutions.

Businesses

Finally, businesses drive the demand for software products and services. If businesses see value or cost savings in a particular solution, they do not hesitate to implement it. To stay competitive in today's market, businesses have to keep their IT and applications portfolios up-to-date and take advantage of economies of scale wherever possible. Cloud service offerings are architected to achieve economies of scale by supporting multiple businesses on a scalable and automated platform. For cloud service offerings to be successful, service providers, software vendors, ISVs and enablers must work together in creating cloud applications and services not only providing cost savings but also a competitive edge to businesses. This search for a competitive edge will drive demand for cloud services.

Cloud Services Drivers and Barriers

Even though cloud computing has gained popularity as the new technology driver, businesses are still evaluating its feasibility for their own business environment. Figure 1-6 shows some of the key business drivers and barriers for cloud services.

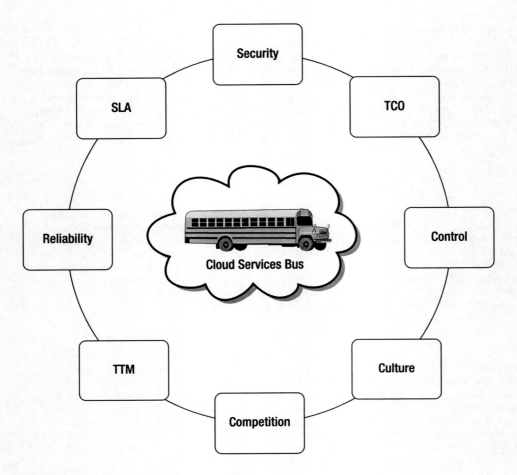

Figure 1-6. *Cloud services drivers and barriers*

Security

Security is a nonnegotiable requirement for a cloud service offering to be successful. Access control and security for business data is of utmost importance. Business data stored in the cloud needs to be encrypted during not only during storage but also transport. Secure data and network channels across application domains in the cloud should be built right into the cloud service infrastructure. Access control prohibits unauthorized access to the data and applications and provides authorization schemes for multiple applications. Businesses already have full-blown access control systems like Active Directory located on-premise and expect to seamlessly integrate cloud services with these systems. Cloud service providers must also provide a secure virtual execution environment that is isolated for other applications running in the same infrastructure.

Overly complex security architecture increases the barriers to entry for businesses to jump on to the cloud services bus. To reduce barriers to entry, the security architecture of a cloud service offering should be easier to integrate and transparent to businesses. One of the advantages of cloud services is the platform and infrastructure security can be totally transparent to the businesses lowering barriers to entry.

Following is the list of security business drivers for cloud services:

- Data storage security

- Data transport security

- Transparent storage and transport security

- Authentication and authorization control

- Single sign-on with other cloud offerings and on-premise systems

- Recommended design patterns and architectures for application access control

- Secure and isolated execution environments

- Easy integration with on-premise security infrastructure (e.g., Active Directory)

Total Cost of Ownership

For any new technology in its infancy, total cost of ownership (TCO) is the first criteria businesses evaluate for finding the return on investment (ROI). If the business is not satisfied with the TCO, the technology or product is shelved until it matures. For businesses to jump on to the cloud services bus, the TCO of the cloud services should be significantly lower than on-premise software. For example, some CRM cloud services charge customers per seat. This pricing structure works out cheaper for small businesses, but for medium to large businesses, it turns out to be expensive because savings from economies of scale are not clearly passed on to the customer. Even if the TCO for on-premise CRM application is within the five percent margin of its cloud counterpart, businesses would prefer the on-premise CRM application because of the flexibility and control an on-premise CRM application offers. Business would consider moving to a cloud service only if its TCO is lower than 15 percent of its on-premise counterpart.

Control

An on-premise application offers businesses significant technological control compared to a cloud service. Control can be in the form of data storage, customizations, security, deployment, operations, and integration with other applications. When evaluating cloud services, businesses assume the loss of control and conduct a trade-off analysis between loss of control and TCO. For some businesses, control of the application is important for customizing specific business processes. Every enterprise has some unique business processes that are not supported by any out-of-box applications. Enterprises then customize applications as per the business requirements before deploying it. So, to reduce the barriers to entry, software vendors must provide a customization platform in the form or an API or a software development kit (SDK) for businesses to customize the software for their specific needs. Software vendors offering cloud services must offer a customization platform and a developer SDK that is comparable to the on-premise applications. So, control is an important business driver for cloud services to be successful in the enterprise.

Culture

Company culture plays a significant role in technology adoption. Some companies' cultures dictate that they remain at least two versions behind the current released version of the product. These companies never evaluate a product unless a competitor has implemented it or it has gained popularity in a particular industry, irrespective of the business value or cost savings it offers. In industry terms, these companies are called *laggards* and are not going to be interested in cloud services anytime soon. Another kind of companies, called *visionaries* are exact opposite of laggards. Being on the leading edge of technology is embedded into the culture of these companies, and they do not hesitate to deploy beta version of a product in production if it offers business value or satisfies key business requirements. Cloud services vendors should market their services to these companies and get them aboard the cloud services bus.

Competition

Competition can force a company to take extreme business decisions to avoid risking its current market position. By saving operating expenses, a company can exert pressure on its competitor's market position by reducing the product prices. Companies are constantly analyzing their competitors' technology stacks to evaluate the operating expenses its competitors may be incurring and find a way to beat those expenses. For example, recently in a consulting project at a Fortune 100 pharmaceutical company, I did a technology stack analysis of its competitor to compare the overall IT portfolios. As a result, my customer found out that the competitor's IT portfolio consists of only 600 applications, whereas my customer's IT portfolio consisted of 10,000 applications. If the business models are the same and revenues, market shares, growth rates are similar, how was the competitor's IT department providing services to its businesses through only 600 applications? This analysis triggered a massive application consolidation effort for reducing my client's IT department's application offerings to less than 1,000 over the next three years.

    If efficient companies embrace cloud services to reduce their operating expenses, competitors will soon follow to remain competitive and avoid risking their relative market position.

Time to Market

Time to market (TTM) is the time required for a particular product to be available in the market once it is conceptualized. TTM is critical for product companies where release of their products is scheduled years in advance and cannot be adjusted because of changes in technology. Cloud service is a platform for product and service companies to build applications on top. Cloud service providers must offer a significantly lower TTM as compared to on-premise software because of the minimal infrastructure and platform investments required by enterprises for cloud service adoption.

Reliability

Reliability is one of the quality attributes businesses look for in any software investment. Reliability encompasses the entire spectrum of quality attributes like availability, stability, scalability, performance, and maintainability. Businesses do not automatically assume the reliability of cloud services platforms because of lack of customer evidence available during the early stages. Cloud services vendors must not only demonstrate the reliability in hosting business critical applications but also outperform their on-premise competitors.

Service Level Agreement

A service level agreement (SLA) is an agreement between the cloud service provider (CSP) and the customer. Even though an SLA is a broader topic than the scope of this book, it is important to understand that an SLA can make or break a deal. A common misconception about SLAs is that they represents the availability of a service. An SLA not only covers the availability of a service, but also other objectives like customer expectations, performance measurements, reporting, quality standards, and relationship management. A successful business driver for cloud services is an SLA addressing the quality of service required by the customer.

Understanding Cloud Architecture

Fundamentally, cloud architectures are based on creation of large data centers with a management fabric defining clear abstraction between server hardware and operations systems. The management fabric automates the deployment of virtualized operating systems images on server hardware. In its simplest form, a typical cloud data center consists of a bank of server hardware and massive storage for storing fully functional operating system images. The management fabric manages the life cycle of the deployment by allocating and decommissioning hardware and operating system images as needed. As a user, when you deploy your service to the cloud, the management fabric provisions the hardware servers, deploys operating system image on those servers, and deploys your service to those servers. Once the service is deployed on the servers, it is ready to be consumed. The number of service instances is configured by the service owner and would typically depend on the demand and high availability requirements of the service. Figure 1-7 illustrates typical cloud data center architecture.

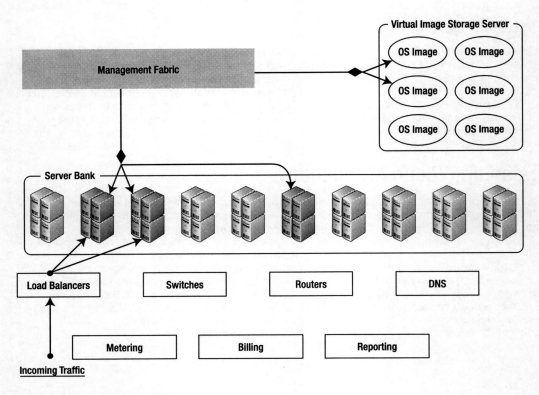

Figure 1-7. *Cloud architecture*

As shown in Figure 1-7, the cloud architecture also consists of some fixed hardware assets like load-balancers, switches, routers, and DNS servers that manage the work load distribution across multiple service instances. A typical cloud infrastructure like Windows Azure consists of several geographically dispersed data centers for providing geo-located services. Finally, the metering, billing and reporting components complement the infrastructure with the ability to measure and report the usage of the service per customer.

▓ **Note** Even though, at a high level, most of the cloud architectures may follow the pattern illustrated in Figure 1-7, my interpretation is heavily influenced by Windows Azure architecture. Different providers may have different implementation and approach to this pattern.

Getting to Know Some Cloud Services Vendors

Cloud services platforms are still in their infancy considering the size of the market, but big players like Microsoft, IBM, Amazon, and Google have made significant investments for the future in offering cloud services in some form or the other. In this section, I will outline the offerings of some cloud services providers and map them to the cloud services pyramid I discussed earlier in this chapter.

Amazon Web Services[1]

Amazon is the largest online retailer in the world, and to support its daily operations, Amazon has one of the most advanced data centers in the world. Processing millions of transactions every hour requires a high-class transactional infrastructure that will not only provide reliability and speed but also reduce the total cost of a transaction. Amazon has achieved this by building a resilient data center infrastructure boasting automated virtualized operating systems and storage servers. Amazon has decided to further monetize its intellectual property by renting this platform and storage services to developers and ISVs for developing and hosting applications. Amazon's cloud services offerings consist of five services:

- Elastic Compute Cloud(EC2)
- SimpleDB
- Simple Storage Service (S3)
- CloudFront
- Simple Queue Service (SQS)
- Elastic MapReduce

Figure 1-8 shows the screenshot of the Amazon Web Services (AWS) home page.

---

[1] Source Data: http://aws.amazon.com/

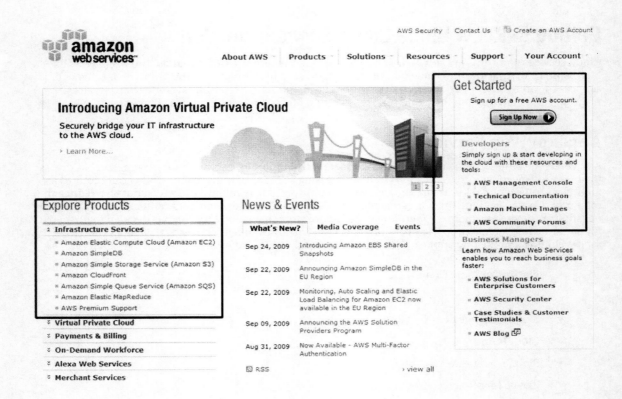

Figure 1-8. *The Amazon Web Services home page*

From a developer's perspective, there are three important sections on the AWS home page: Explore Products, Signup, and Developers. The Infrastructure Services section under Explore Products lists all the core platform services offered by AWS. The Sign Up Now button lets you sign up for the AWS, and the Developers section has links to developer sign-up, technical documentation, the AWS management console, community forums, and the Amazon Machine Images (AMI). AMIs are preconfigured virtual machine images for running in Amazon's web services. Figure 1-9 shows some of the categories of pre-configured AMIs available.

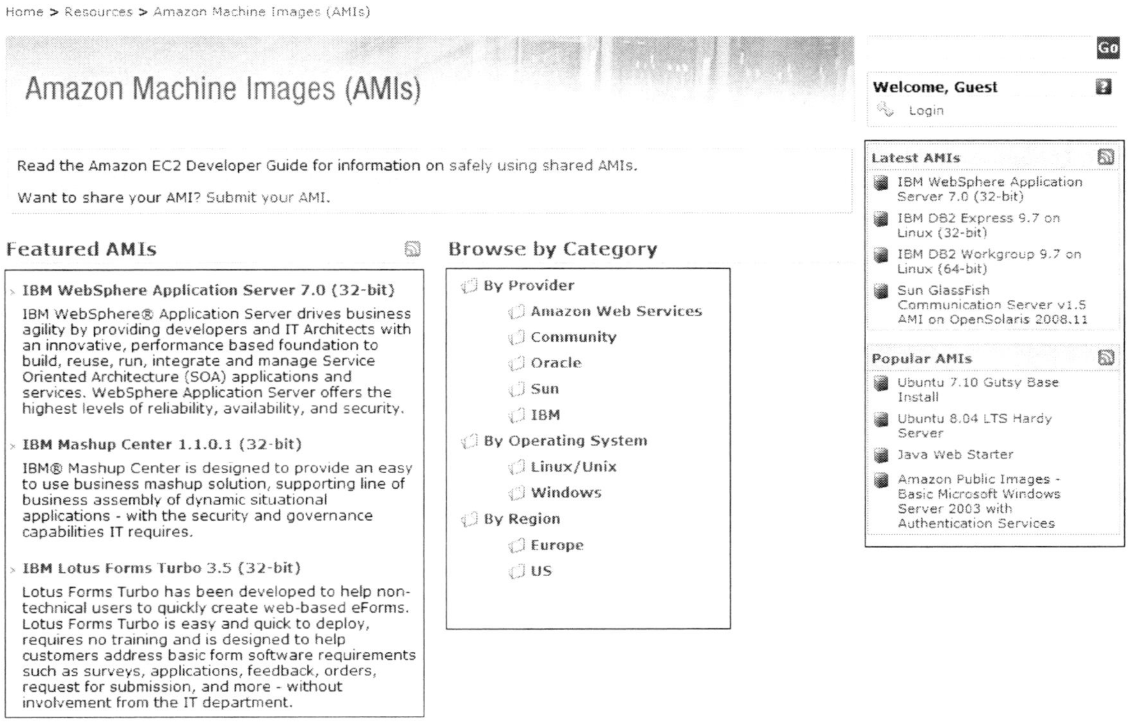

Home > Resources > Amazon Machine Images (AMIs)

Amazon Machine Images (AMIs)

Read the Amazon EC2 Developer Guide for information on safely using shared AMIs.

Want to share your AMI? Submit your AMI.

Welcome, Guest

Login

Latest AMIs

- IBM WebSphere Application Server 7.0 (32-bit)
- IBM DB2 Express 9.7 on Linux (32-bit)
- IBM DB2 Workgroup 9.7 on Linux (64-bit)
- Sun GlassFish Communication Server v1.5 AMI on OpenSolaris 2008.11

Popular AMIs

- Ubuntu 7.10 Gutsy Base Install
- Ubuntu 8.04 LTS Hardy Server
- Java Web Starter
- Amazon Public Images - Basic Microsoft Windows Server 2003 with Authentication Services

Featured AMIs

> **IBM WebSphere Application Server 7.0 (32-bit)**

IBM WebSphere® Application Server drives business agility by providing developers and IT Architects with an innovative, performance based foundation to build, reuse, run, integrate and manage Service Oriented Architecture (SOA) applications and services. WebSphere Application Server offers the highest levels of reliability, availability, and security.

> **IBM Mashup Center 1.1.0.1 (32-bit)**

IBM® Mashup Center is designed to provide an easy to use business mashup solution, supporting line of business assembly of dynamic situational applications - with the security and governance capabilities IT requires.

> **IBM Lotus Forms Turbo 3.5 (32-bit)**

Lotus Forms Turbo has been developed to help non-technical users to quickly create web-based eForms. Lotus Forms Turbo is easy and quick to deploy, requires no training and is designed to help customers address basic form software requirements such as surveys, applications, feedback, orders, request for submission, and more - without involvement from the IT department.

Browse by Category

- By Provider
  - Amazon Web Services
  - Community
  - Oracle
  - Sun
  - IBM
- By Operating System
  - Linux/Unix
  - Windows
- By Region
  - Europe
  - US

Figure 1-9. *Preconfigured AMIs*

Note You can find more information on AMI in the *Amazon EC2 Developer Guide*, http://docs.amazonwebservices.com/AWSEC2/latest/DeveloperGuide/.

Amazon EC2

Amazon EC2 is a virtual computing environment providing resizable computing capacity in the cloud. Developers can create, launch, and terminate virtual machines on-demand. The virtual machines support a variety of operating systems like Red Hat Enterprise, Linux, Windows Server 2003, Oracle Enterprise Linux, OpenSolaris, openSUSE Linux, Ubuntu Linux, Fedora, Gentoo Linux, and Debian. The virtual machines also support a variety of software—Oracle 11g, Microsoft SQL Server 2005 Standard Edition, Apache Web Server, IIS/ASP.NET, Java Application Server, JBoss Enterprise Application Platform, and many more.

Figure 1-10 shows the home page for the Amazon EC2 service.

Amazon Elastic Compute Cloud (Amazon EC2)

Amazon Elastic Compute Cloud (Amazon EC2) is a web service that provides resizable compute capacity in the cloud. It is designed to make web-scale computing easier for developers.

Amazon EC2's simple web service interface allows you to obtain and configure capacity with minimal friction. It provides you with complete control of your computing resources and lets you run on Amazon's proven computing environment. Amazon EC2 reduces the time required to obtain and boot new server instances to minutes, allowing you to quickly scale capacity, both up and down, as your computing requirements change. Amazon EC2 changes the economics of computing by allowing you to pay only for capacity that you actually use. Amazon EC2 provides developers the tools to build failure resilient applications and isolate themselves from common failure scenarios.

This page contains the following categories of information. Click to jump down:

↓ **Amazon EC2 Functionality**	↓ **Pricing**
↓ **Service Highlights**	↓ **Resources**
↓ **Features**	↓ **Detailed Description**
↓ **Instance Types**	↓ **Intended Usage and Restrictions**
↓ **Operating Systems and Software**	

Amazon EC2 Functionality

Amazon EC2 presents a true virtual computing environment, allowing you to use web service interfaces to launch instances with a variety of operating systems, load them with your custom application environment, manage your network's access permissions, and run your image using as many or few systems as you desire.

To use Amazon EC2, you simply:

▪ Create an Amazon Machine Image (AMI) containing your applications, libraries, data and associated configuration settings. Or use pre-configured, templated images to get up and running immediately.

▪ Upload the AMI into Amazon S3. Amazon EC2 provides tools that make storing the AMI simple. Amazon S3

Figure 1-10. *The Amazon EC2 home page*

The Amazon EC2 home page contains links to features, pricing, supported operating systems and software, and developer resources.

▓ **Note** The developer guide for Amazon EC2 service is located at `http://docs.amazonwebservices.com/ AWSEC2/latest/DeveloperGuide/`.

Figure 1-11 illustrates typical developer workflow to get an EC2 instance deployed with a web application.

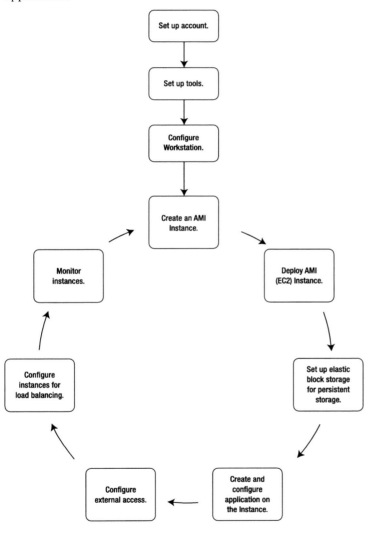

Figure 1-11. *Amazon EC2 developer workflow*

To deploy a web application on an EC2 instance, you have to follow these steps:

1. Set up an account for Amazon Web Services, EC2, and S3 at http://aws.amazon.com.

2. Configure your workstation with the setup tools from Amazon Developer Resource Center.

3. Create an AMI instance from one of the predefined instances, or create a new instance.

4. Deploy the Amazon EC2 instance. Windows users can access the deployed instance using Remote Desktop Connection.

5. Set up the Elastic Block Store (EBS). EC2 instances have volatile storage and may not survive reboots. EBS is a persistent storage volume that can be attached and detached to AMI instances.

6. Create and configure the web application on the deployed instance.

7. Configure external access to the web application by configuring the firewall and creating a friendly URL for it.

8. Create as many instances of the AMI as needed.

9. Monitor instances using the AWS Management Console.

■ **Note** Amazon EC2 fits into the platform category of the cloud services pyramid model discussed earlier in this chapter.

Amazon SimpleDB

Amazon SimpleDB is a cloud database service providing core database functionality of storing indexing and querying data. SimpleDB is not a relational database in the cloud but a storage engine for storing and retrieving structured data. Figure 1-12 shows the home page of Amazon SimpleDB where you can sign up for the service and also access pricing and related resources.

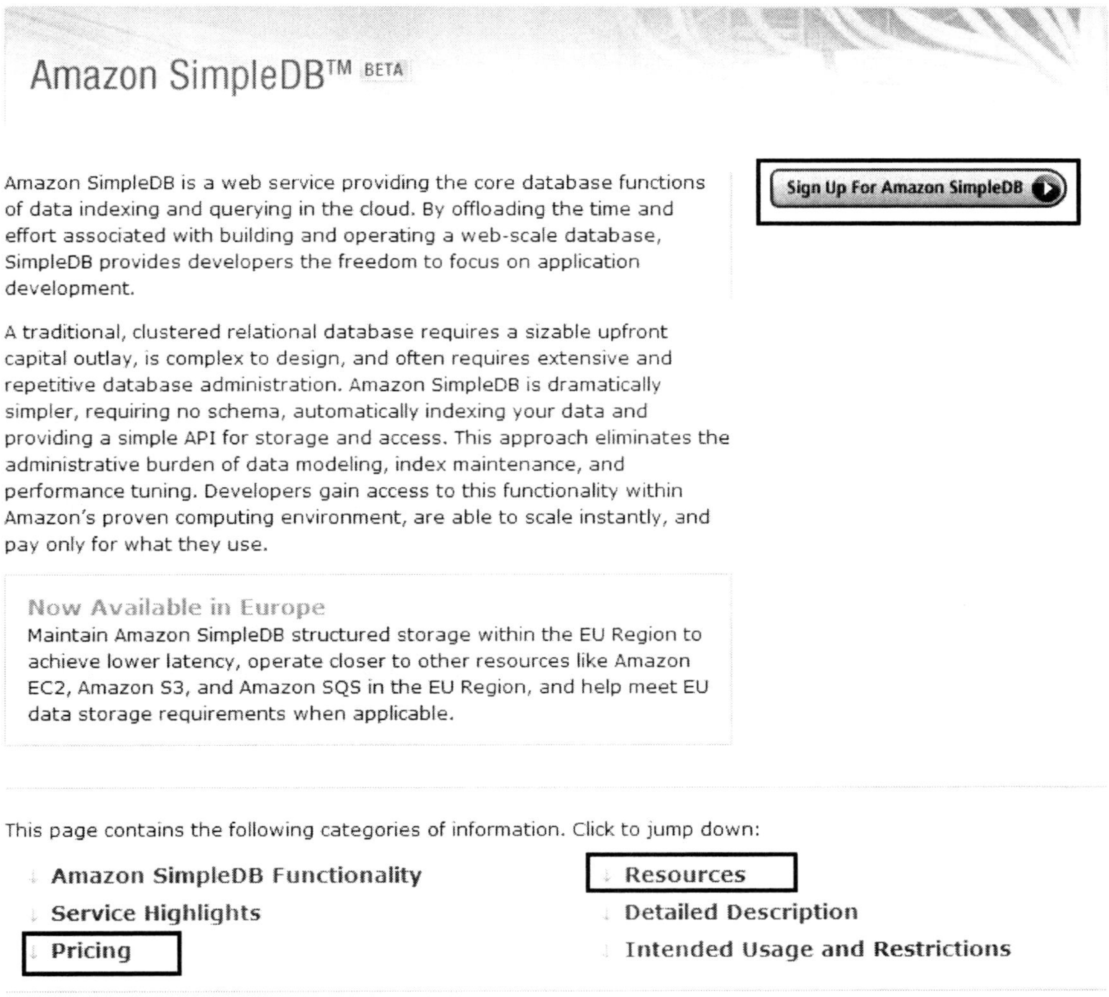

Amazon SimpleDB™ BETA

Amazon SimpleDB is a web service providing the core database functions of data indexing and querying in the cloud. By offloading the time and effort associated with building and operating a web-scale database, SimpleDB provides developers the freedom to focus on application development.

A traditional, clustered relational database requires a sizable upfront capital outlay, is complex to design, and often requires extensive and repetitive database administration. Amazon SimpleDB is dramatically simpler, requiring no schema, automatically indexing your data and providing a simple API for storage and access. This approach eliminates the administrative burden of data modeling, index maintenance, and performance tuning. Developers gain access to this functionality within Amazon's proven computing environment, are able to scale instantly, and pay only for what they use.

Now Available in Europe
Maintain Amazon SimpleDB structured storage within the EU Region to achieve lower latency, operate closer to other resources like Amazon EC2, Amazon S3, and Amazon SQS in the EU Region, and help meet EU data storage requirements when applicable.

This page contains the following categories of information. Click to jump down:

- **Amazon SimpleDB Functionality**
- **Service Highlights**
- **Pricing**
- **Resources**
- **Detailed Description**
- **Intended Usage and Restrictions**

Figure 1-12. The Amazon SimpleDB home page

Figure 1-13 shows a typical developer workflow in an Amazon SimpleDB environment.

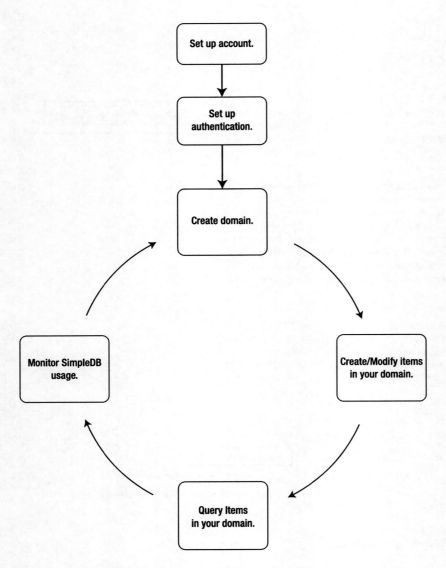

Figure 1-13. *The Amazon SimpleDB developer workflow*

▓ **Note** The developer guide for the Amazon SimpleDB can be found at http://docs.amazonwebservices.com/ AmazonSimpleDB/latest/DeveloperGuide/.

The developer workflow steps for Amazon SimpleDB storage follow:

1. Set up an account with AWS and sign up for the SimpleDB service.

2. Set up authentication with SimpleDB to validate the identity of the party making a request.

3. Create a new domain.

4. Get, put, or delete items in a domain. The data is indexed automatically upon storage.

5. Query the data using the SELECT or QUERY API.

6. Monitor SimpleDB usage, and pay only for the resources that you consume.

■ **Note** SimpleDB falls in the platform category of the cloud services Pyramid.

Amazon Simple Storage Service (S3)

The Amazon S3 is a cloud database that can be used to store and retrieve any amount of data over the Internet. This is the data storage infrastructure on which Amazon runs its own global sites. Developers can leverage the same quality storage infrastructure to store application data. Like all other Amazon web services, S3 provides web services access for applications to interface with. Amazon S3 consists of three storage level concepts: objects, buckets, and keys. An *object* is a fundamental entity in S3, consists of data and metadata, and can be a maximum of 5GB in size. Objects are stored in *buckets*. Buckets give a unique namespace to its contained objects. A *key* is the unique identifier for an object within a bucket. Figure 1-14 shows the home page of Amazon S3 where you can sign up for the service and also access pricing, design, and related resources.

Amazon Simple Storage Service (Amazon S3)

Amazon S3 is storage for the Internet. It is designed to make web-scale computing easier for developers.

Amazon S3 provides a simple web services interface that can be used to store and retrieve any amount of data, at any time, from anywhere on the web. It gives any developer access to the same highly scalable, reliable, fast, inexpensive data storage infrastructure that Amazon uses to run its own global network of web sites. The service aims to maximize benefits of scale and to pass those benefits on to developers.

This page contains the following categories of information. Click to jump down:

↓ **Amazon S3 Functionality**	↓ **Amazon S3 Design Requirements**
↓ **Pricing**	↓ **Amazon S3 Design Principles**
↓ **Transferring Large Amounts** of Data	↓ **Intended Usage and Restrictions**
↓ **Resources**	

Amazon S3 Functionality

Amazon S3 is intentionally built with a minimal feature set.

* Write, read, and delete objects containing from 1 byte to 5 gigabytes of data each. The number of objects you can store is unlimited.
* Each object is stored in a bucket and retrieved via a unique, developer-assigned key.
* A bucket can be located in the United States or in Europe. All objects within the bucket will be stored in the bucket's location, but the objects can be accessed from anywhere.
* Authentication mechanisms are provided to ensure that data is kept secure from unauthorized access. Objects can be made private or public, and rights can be granted to specific users.
* Uses standards-based REST and SOAP interfaces designed to work with any Internet-development toolkit.
* Built to be flexible so that protocol or functional layers can easily be added. Default download protocol is HTTP. A BitTorrent™ protocol interface is provided to lower costs for high-scale distribution. Additional interfaces will be added in the future.
* Reliability backed with the Amazon S3 Service Level Agreement.

Figure 1-14. *The Amazon S3 home page*

■ **Note** The developer guide for Amazon S3 can be found at `http://docs.amazonwebservices.com/AmazonS3/latest/dev/`.

Figure 1-15 shows a typical developer workflow in an Amazon S3 environment.

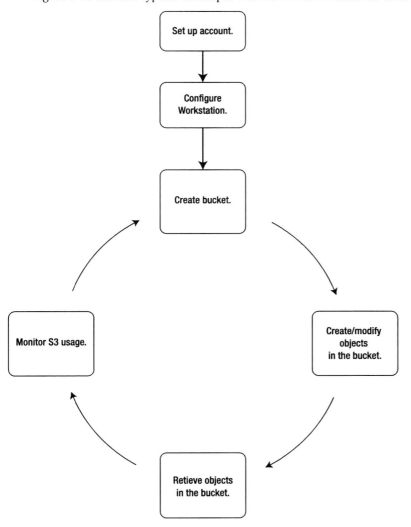

Figure 1-15. *Amazon S3 Developer Workflow*

The developer workflow steps for Amazon S3 storage are:

1. Set up an account with AWS and sign-up for the S3 service.

2. Set up authentication with S3 to validate the identity of the party making a request.

3. Create a new bucket to store objects in S3.

4. Once you have a bucket, you can start adding objects to bucket.

5. Access objects in the bucket using the URL of the object.

6. Monitor S3 usage, and pay only for the resources that you consume.

▓ **Note** The Amazon S3 falls in the platform category of the cloud services pyramid.

Amazon CloudFront

Amazon CloudFront is a data distribution network for content delivery. Amazon CloudFront works in conjunction with Amazon S3 to deliver copies of objects from the nearest location to the calling application. For example, if you have an application running in a data center in Asia, Amazon CloudFront can deliver objects from your Asian location when configured accordingly.

Figure 1-16 shows the home page of Amazon CloudFront where you can sign up for the service and access pricing, design, and related resources.

Amazon CloudFront BETA

Amazon CloudFront is a web service for content delivery. It integrates with other Amazon Web Services to give developers and businesses an easy way to distribute content to end users with low latency, high data transfer speeds, and no commitments.

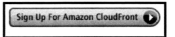

Amazon CloudFront delivers your content using a global network of edge locations. Requests for your objects are automatically routed to the nearest edge location, so content is delivered with the best possible performance. Amazon CloudFront works seamlessly with Amazon Simple Storage Service (Amazon S3) which durably stores the original, definitive versions of your files. Like other Amazon Web Services, there are no contracts or monthly commitments for using Amazon CloudFront – you pay only for as much or as little content as you actually deliver through the service.

This page contains the following categories of information. Click to jump down:

↓ **Amazon CloudFront Functionality**	↓ **Resources**
↓ **Service Highlights**	↓ **Detailed Description**
↓ **Pricing**	↓ **Intended Usage and Restrictions**

Amazon CloudFront Functionality

Amazon CloudFront has a simple, web services interface that lets you get started in minutes. In Amazon CloudFront, your objects are organized into distributions. A distribution specifies the location of the original version of your objects. A distribution has a unique CloudFront.net domain name (e.g. abc123.cloudfront.net) that you can use to reference your objects through the network of edge locations. If you wish, you can also map your own domain name (e.g. images.example.com) to your distribution.

To use Amazon CloudFront, you:

- Store the original versions of your files in an Amazon S3 bucket.

- Create a distribution to register that bucket with Amazon CloudFront through a simple API call.

- Use your distribution's domain name in your web pages or application. When end users request an object using this domain name, they are automatically routed to the nearest edge location for high performance delivery of your content.

- Pay only for the data transfer and requests that you actually use.

Figure 1-16. *The Amazon CloudFront home page*

■ **Note** The developer guide for Amazon CloudFront can be found at `http://docs.amazonwebservices.com/AmazonCloudFront/latest/DeveloperGuide/`.

Figure 1-17 shows a typical developer workflow in an Amazon CloudFront environment.

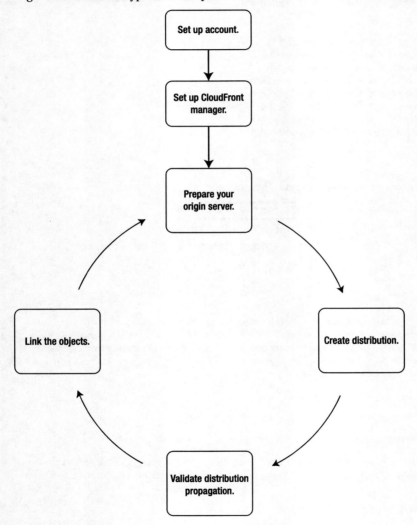

Figure 1-17. *Amazon CloudFront Developer Workflow*

To use Amazon CloudFront, follow these steps:

1. Set up an account with AWS, and sign up for the CloudFront service.

2. Download and install the manager for Amazon CloudFront.

3. Prepare your S3 origin server, and create buckets and objects in the origin server.

4. Create distribution by registering the S3 storage with the CloudFront using a domain name.

5. Validate the status of the propagation of the distribution.

6. Link the object with the domain name for the CloudFront to serve from an appropriate edge location.

Note CloudFront falls in the infrastructure category of the cloud services pyramid.

Amazon Simple Queue Service

Amazon SQS is a cloud queue service for reliable storage of messages. Developers can leverage SQS to share queued data across distributed applications. SQS supports all the basic queue functions like creating, listing, and deleting queues as well as sending, receiving, and deleting messages. You can use Amazon SQS in conjunction with EC2 and S3 to build sophisticated workflows. Figure 1-18 shows the home page of Amazon SQS, where you can sign up for the service and access pricing, design, and related resources.

Amazon Simple Queue Service (Amazon SQS)

Amazon Simple Queue Service (Amazon SQS) offers a reliable, highly scalable, hosted queue for storing messages as they travel between computers. By using Amazon SQS, developers can simply move data between distributed components of their applications that perform different tasks, without losing messages or requiring each component to be always available. Amazon SQS makes it easy to build an automated workflow, working in close conjunction with the Amazon Elastic Compute Cloud (Amazon EC2) and the other AWS infrastructure web services.

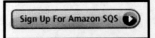

Amazon SQS works by exposing Amazon's web-scale messaging infrastructure as a web service. Any computer on the Internet can add or read messages without any installed software or special firewall configurations. Components of applications using Amazon SQS can run independently, and do not need to be on the same network, developed with the same technologies, or running at the same time.

This page contains the following categories of information. Click to jump down:

↓ **Amazon SQS Functionality**

↓ **Service Highlights**

↓ **Using Amazon SQS with Other AWS Infrastructure Web Services**

↓ **Pricing**

↓ **Resources**

↓ **Detailed Description**

↓ **Previous WSDL Versions**

↓ **Intended Usage and Restrictions**

Amazon SQS Functionality

▪ Developers can create an unlimited number of Amazon SQS queues with an unlimited number of messages.

  ▪ A queue can be created in the United States or in Europe. Queue names and message stores are independent of other regions.

  ▪ The message body can contain up to 8 KB of text in any format.

  ▪ Messages can be retained in queues for up to 4 days.

Figure 1-18. *The Amazon SQS home page*

■ **Note** The developer guide for Amazon SQS can be found at `http://docs.amazonwebservices.com/AWSSimpleQueueService/latest/SQSDeveloperGuide/`.

Figure 1-19 shows a typical developer workflow in an Amazon SQS environment.

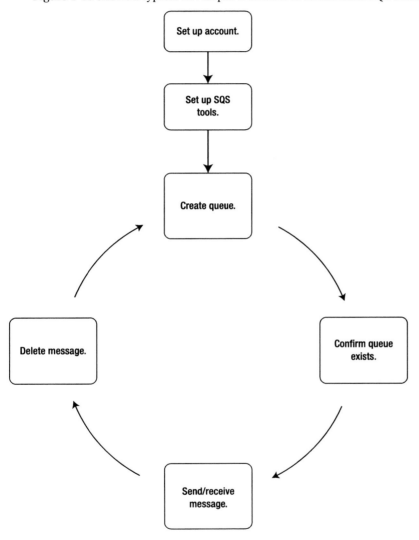

Figure 1-19. *The Amazon SQS developer workflow*

■ **Note** The Amazon SQS service falls in the middleware category of the cloud services pyramid.

These are the steps for using SQS:

1. Set up an account with AWS, and sign up for the SQS service.

2. Configure your programming environment for SQS access. SQS supports HTTP GET/POST and SOAP access.

3. Create a queue using the programming language chosen in step 2.

4. Send a message to the queue after confirming it exists

5. Receive the messages by specifying the maximum number of messages to get.

6. Delete the message to acknowledge the receipt of the message.

Amazon Elastic MapReduce

Amazon Elastic MapReduce is a cloud service designed for performing data-intensive tasks like data mining, analytics data processing, batch processing, data cleanup, and indexing in a parallelized environment. The service enables you to provision a job to be executed in parallel across multiple Amazon EC2 instances and aggregate the final results. You can use Amazon S3 storage service for storing input and output data. Amazon Elastic MapReduce uses the Apache Hadoop framework for processing massive amounts of data in parallel. Hadoop is designed for executing simpler operations on massive amounts of data. For example, you can use Hadoop framework for adding copyright information to ten million documents.

Figure 1-20 shows the home page of Amazon Elastic MapReduce, where you can sign up for the service and access pricing, design, and related resources.

Amazon Elastic MapReduce BETA

Amazon Elastic MapReduce is a web service that enables businesses, researchers, data analysts, and developers to easily and cost-effectively process vast amounts of data. It utilizes a hosted Hadoop framework running on the web-scale infrastructure of Amazon Elastic Compute Cloud (Amazon EC2) and Amazon Simple Storage Service (Amazon S3).

Using Amazon Elastic MapReduce, you can instantly provision as much or as little capacity as you like to perform data-intensive tasks for applications such as web indexing, data mining, log file analysis, machine learning, financial analysis, scientific simulation, and bioinformatics research. Amazon Elastic MapReduce lets you focus on crunching or analyzing your data without having to worry about time-consuming set-up, management or tuning of Hadoop clusters or the compute capacity upon which they sit.

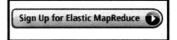

This page contains the following categories of information. Click to jump down:

- **Amazon Elastic MapReduce Functionality**
- **Service Highlights**
- **Instance Types**
- **Pricing**

- **Resources**
- **Detailed Description**
- **Intended Usage and Restrictions**

Amazon Elastic MapReduce Functionality

Amazon Elastic MapReduce automatically spins up a Hadoop implementation of the MapReduce framework on Amazon EC2 instances, sub-dividing the data in a job flow into smaller chunks so that they can be processed (the "map" function) in parallel, and eventually recombining the processed data into the final solution (the "reduce" function). Amazon S3 serves as the source for the data being analyzed, and as the output destination for the end results.

Figure 1-20. *The Amazon Elastic MapReduce home page*

■ **Note** The developer guide for Amazon Elastic MapReduce can be found at
http://docs.amazonwebservices.com/ElasticMapReduce/latest/DeveloperGuide/.

Figure 1-21 shows a typical developer workflow in an Amazon Elastic MapReduce environment

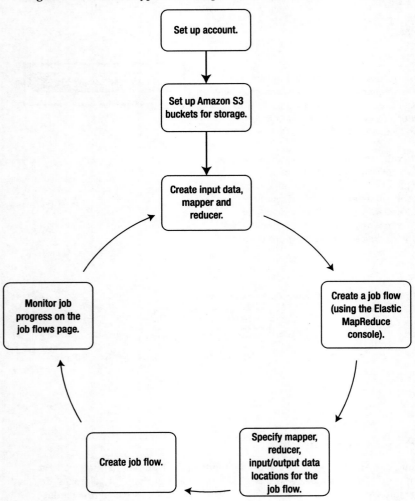

Figure 1-21. *Amazon Elastic MapReduce Developer Workflow*

▧ **Note** Elastic MapReduce falls into either the middleware or platform category of the cloud services pyramid.

As shown in Figure 1-21, the steps for getting started with Amazon Elastic MapReduce service are as follows:

1. Set up an account with AWS, and sign up for the Elastic MapReduce service.

2. Sign up for the Amazon S3 service for storing the input and output data.

3. Create your input data, mapper, and reducer.

▨ **Note** According to the Apache Hadoop tutorial at `http://hadoop.apache.org/common/docs/current/` `mapred_tutorial.html`, a *mapper* maps the input data into intermediate data for processing, and a *reducer* reduces the intermediate values created by the mapper to a smaller set.

---

4. Create an EC2 job using the Elastic MapReduce console.

5. Configure input location, output location, mapper, and reducer.

6. Create the job flow.

7. Finally, you can monitor the job flow from the job flow details page.

▨ **Note** More information on getting started with Amazon Elastic MapReduce can be found at `http://docs.amazonwebservices.com/ElasticMapReduce/latest/GettingStartedGuide/`.

Google

Google is the leader in search services on the Internet and has a significant presence and properties in advertising, collaboration, e-mail, and social networking sites. Google has massively scaled data centers with customized caching algorithms that host the fastest search engine in the world. The company has extended this massively scalable infrastructure for hosting communication and collaboration platform called Google Apps and an application platform called Google AppEngine for developing and deploying web applications.

Google Apps[2]

Google Apps is a collection of messaging and collaboration software services for businesses and schools. Figure 1-22 shows the landing page of Google Apps.

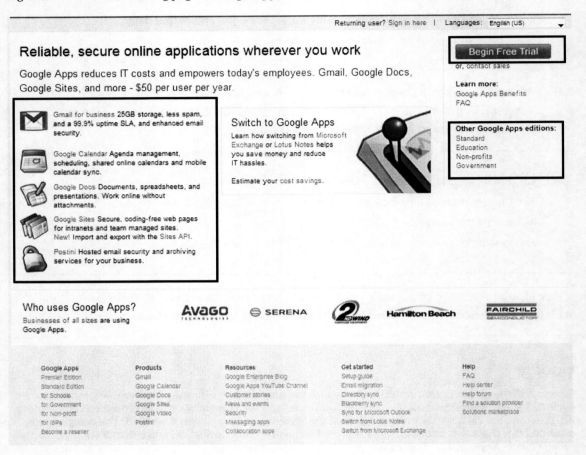

Figure 1-22. *The Google Apps home page*

The main services offered in Google Apps are mail (Gmail), instant messaging (Google Talk), calendar (Google Calendar), document management (Google Docs), and site management (Google Sites). Google Apps guarantees 99.9 percent availability for the Premier edition of its service offering.

---

[2] Source Data: http://www.google.com/apps/intl/en/business/index.html

Google also provides REST-style APIs called Google Data APIs for programming not only for Google Apps but also for other web services offered by Google like Google Maps, Google Health, and YouTube. Figure 1-23 illustrates the services supported by Google Data API.

Google Data Protocol

What is the Google Data Protocol?

The Google Data Protocol is a REST-inspired technology for reading, writing, and modifying information on the web.

Many services at Google provide external access to data and functionality through APIs that utilize the Google Data Protocol. The protocol currently supports two primary modes of access:

- **AtomPub**: Information is sent as a collection of Atom items, using the standard Atom syndication format to represent data and HTTP to handle communication. The Google Data Protocol extends AtomPub for processing queries, authentication, and batch requests.
- **JSON**: Information is sent as JSON objects that mirror the Atom representation.

The following Google products currently offer a Google Data API:

Google Analytics Data Export API

Google Apps APIs

Google Base Data API

Blogger Data API

Google Booksearch Data API

Google Calendar Data API

Google Code Search Data API

Google Contacts Data API

Google Documents List Data API

Google Sites Data API

Google Finance Portfolio Data API

Google Health Data API

Google Maps Data API

Picasa Web Albums Data API

Google Sidewiki Data API

Google Spreadsheets Data API

Google Webmaster Tools Data API

YouTube Data API

Figure 1-23. *The Google Data API*

41

■ **Note** Google Apps falls under the enterprise services category of the cloud services pyramid.

Google App Engine[3]

Google App Engine is an environment for developing and deploying web applications on Google's infrastructure. The App Engine supports Python and Java as the primary programming languages to develop web applications. Developers can develop web applications in Python or Java and deploy those applications in App Engine for automatic scaling and load balancing. App Engine also provides a datastore that supports simple create, retrieve, and delete functions. Developers can access the datastore from within App Engine web applications to store and query data. Google App Engine also provides Google Data APIs for accessing Google Apps components like Mail, Calendar, Search, and Docs.

■ **Note** For more information on Google AppEngine, please visit `http://code.google.com/appengine/`.

Figure 1-24 shows the developer's guide landing page for Google App Engine.

---

[3] Source Data: `http://code.google.com/appengine`

Figure 1-24. *The Google App Engine developer's guide*

■ **Note** You can find the Google AppEngine developer's guide here http://code.google.com/appengine/
docs/python/gettingstarted/

The developer's guide provides developers with APIs and samples to build web applications on Google
App Engine. The App Engine includes all the basic components for building scalable web applications.

■ **Note** The Google App Engine falls under the enterprise category of the cloud services pyramid.

SalesForce.com and Force.com[4]

SalesForce.com is popular as the cloud CRM application and has established a very good user base in small-to-medium businesses. The success of SalesForce.com can be partially attributed to its multitenant architecture that is completely metadata driven and flexible for users to customize. Users can not only customize the user interface but also tailor the CRM business objects their business. SalesForce.com extended the multitenant and metadata-driven architecture to a much more open platform called Force.com, which SalesForce.com refers to as a platform as a service (PaaS) offering.

Force.com is a platform for building business applications like enterprise resource planning (ERP) and supply chain management (SCM). Figure 1-25 illustrates the developer workflow for the Force.com platform.

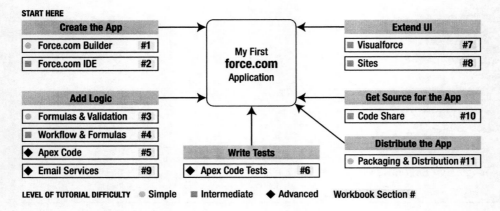

Figure 1-25. *The SalefForce.com developer workflow*

The Force.com developer workflow includes:

- Creation of an application using Force.com Builder, which is a web-based IDE, or the Force.com IDE, which is a plug-in for the Eclipse IDE

- Programming the business logic using formulas, workflows and Apex programming language

- Adding tests to the application

- Extending the user interface using the VisualForce IDE

- Creating public web page using Force.com sites

---

[4] Source Data: http://www.salesforce.com

- Deploying the application

- Distributing the application using the AppExchange on-demand distribution system

---

▨ **Note** The SalesForce.com SaaS falls under the applications category of the cloud services pyramid, and the Force.com PaaS falls under the middleware and enterprise categories.

GoGrid

The GoGrid cloud service offers Windows and Linux virtual machine images preconfigured with the most frequently used software components. It also offers cloud storage and free hardware load-balancing between virtual machine instances using Big IP's F5 load balancer. The service is very similar to the Amazon EC2 service offering with some feature differences.

Figure 1-26 illustrates the cloud hosting features of GoGrid.com.

Figure 1-26. GoGrid.com Cloud Hosting Features

3Tera

3Tera's AppLogic platform is a grid operating system for deploying web applications. AppLogic provides a client interface, shown in Figure 1-27, for virtually designing your cloud application by dragging and dropping virtualized web, application, and database servers on the design surface and connecting them.

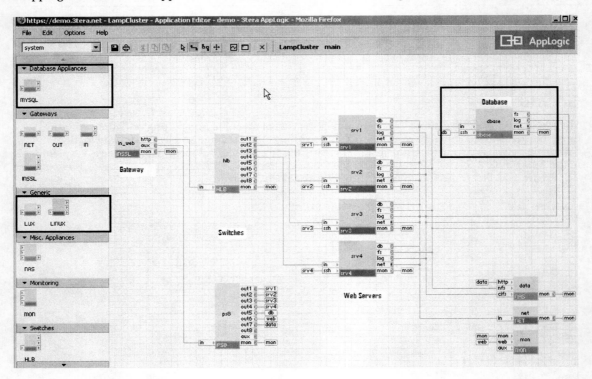

Figure 1-27. *3Tera AppLogic example*

In Figure 1-27, you can drag and drop virtual servers from the toolbox on the left on to the design surface on the right for creating cloud web applications.

Microsoft

In 2008 during the Professional Developer's Conference (PDC), Microsoft announced its official entry into the cloud services arena with the Windows Azure platform (previously known as Azure Services Platform). Even though, the Microsoft Online services called Business Productivity Online Suite (BPOS) have been around for a few years, the Windows Azure platform is an attempt to create an end-to-end cloud service offering in the platform, middleware, enterprise services, and consumer services categories.

Windows Azure is a collection of building blocks for cloud services. Microsoft has been in the cloud business for quite some time with its consumer cloud services like MSN, Xbox Live, and Hotmail. Microsoft has also announced a suite of cloud-based business productivity and collaboration applications called Microsoft Online services that include applications like SharePoint Online, Exchange Hosted Services, and Conferencing Services. Figure 1-28 illustrates the components of the Windows Azure Platform.

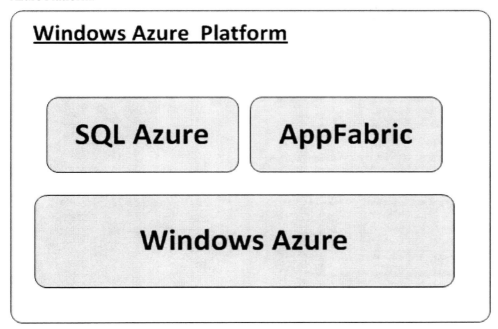

Figure 1-28. *Microsoft Windows Azure Platform (Source: Microsoft Azure Website)*

Figure 1-28 shows that Windows Azure is the core platform for Microsoft's cloud services offerings. It will be the foundation for online services like Windows Live, Office Live, Exchange Online, SharePoint Online, and CRM Online. Windows Azure consists of three main components that I will cover in this book: Windows Azure, SQL Azure, AppFabric (previously known as .NET Services). . Windows Azure is the operating system in the cloud, and it forms the core platform for all the other Azure Services. SQL Azure is the database engine in the Windows Azure Platform. AppFabric is the middleware component that consists of services like ServiceBus and Access Control. Live Services is the building blocks for creating consumer-facing applications. Over the course of one year, Microsoft removed Live Services from the Windows Azure collection of services. So, you will find several versions of Windows Azure platform documentation that includes Live Services. In this book, I will cover only the core Windows Azure platform in detail. I have omitted out Live Services because Microsoft's strategy around it was not clear during the course of writing this book.

■ **Caution** At the time of this writing, Microsoft was implementing many changes in the Windows Azure platform. For example, the workflow services and the developer edition of the Live Services component were recently discontinued. I will not cover workflow services and Live Services in this book. Also, note that SQL Azure is the new name for SQL Services and SQL Server Data Services (SSDS). The .NET Services was renamed to AppFabric. .

Figure 1-29 shows the Windows Azure pricing information available at the time of this writing.

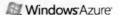

- Compute = $0.12 / hour

- Storage = $0.15 / GB stored / month

- Storage transactions = $0.01 / 10K

- Data transfers = $0.10 in / $0.15 out / GB - ($0.30 in / $0.45 out / GB in Asia)

Windows Azure Service Level Agreement
For compute, we guarantee that when you deploy two or more role instances in different fault and upgrade domains, your internet facing roles will have external connectivity at least 99.95% of the time. For storage, we guarantee that at least 99.9% of the time we will successfully process correctly formatted requests that we receive to add, update, read and delete data. More information on Service Level Agreements.

- Web Edition: Up to 1 GB relational database = $9.99 / month

- Business Edition: Up to 10 GB relational database = $99.99 / month

- Data transfers = $0.10 in / $0.15 out / GB - ($0.30 in / $0.45 out / GB in Asia)

SQL Azure Service Level Agreement
SQL Azure customers will have connectivity between the database and our internet gateway. SQL Azure will maintain a "Monthly Availability" of 99.9% during a calendar month. More information on Service Level Agreements.

AppFabric

- Messages = $0.15/100K message operations, including Service Bus messages, Access Control transactions and service management operations

- Data transfers = $0.10 in / $0.15 out / GB - ($0.30 in / $0.45 out / GB in Asia)

AppFabric Service Level Agreement
Uptime percentage commitments and SLA credits for AppFabric are similar to those specified in the Windows Azure SLA. More information on Service Level Agreements

Figure 1-29. Windows Azure pricing information

■ **Note** You can get the latest pricing information on Windows Azure at http://www.microsoft.com/azure/ pricing.mspx.

Figure 1-30 illustrates a typical developer workflow on the Windows Azure Platform.

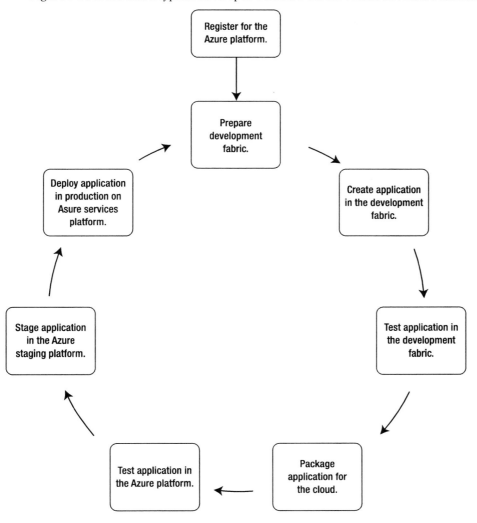

Figure 1-30. *Windows Azure Platform Developer Workflow.*

The typical developer workflow steps for Windows Azure Platform follow:

1. Create a Windows Azure account (i.e., an account for Windows Azure, AppFabric, or SQL Services).
2. Download and prepare the development fabric to create a local cloud platform.
3. Create an application in the development fabric.

4. Test the application in the development fabric.

5. Package the application for cloud deployment.

6. Test the application on Windows Azure in the cloud.

7. Stage the application in the Windows Azure staging environment in the cloud.

8. Deploy the application in the production farm.

The cloud service providers discussed in this section are a subset of a larger cloud service industry. The list is by no means an exhaustive one, but a short-list of the popular vendors. Some of the other vendors making inroads into the cloud services industry are Joyent, IBM (with its Blue Cloud initiative and Amazon partnership), Yahoo, and Cisco.

Figure 1-31 categorizes the cloud services discussed in this chapter in the cloud pyramid layers.

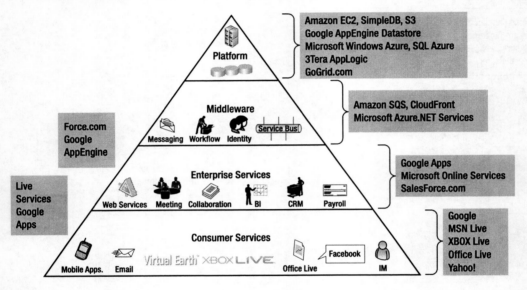

Figure 1-31. *Cloud services Offerings and Pyramid Layers*

Note that some services like Force.com, Google App Engine, Live Services, and Google Apps span multiple layers. The broadest offerings are from Microsoft and Amazon. Amazon has a comprehensive platform and infrastructure offerings, and Microsoft has significant offerings in platform, middleware, enterprise services, and consumer services layers. The Windows Azure platform is the newest but has established its brand name within a very short amount of time in its vast developer community. From the next chapter onward, I will dive deep into Microsoft Azure.

Summary

In this chapter, I gave you a high-level overview of the cloud services industry, its ecosystem, the drivers and barriers for its success, and some of the major cloud services offerings currently available. "Cloud

50

service" is a broad term that can mean different things to different people. Even though one chapter is not enough to clarify this vast nebula of services, I narrowed down the scope of the cloud services definition into a cloud services pyramid model. This pyramid will help you categorize some of the existing and new cloud services by their offerings.

In the next chapter, I will give you an overview of the Microsoft Windows Azure platform, its components and the opportunity it offers to the software developers. You will also learn basic Windows Azure programming in the next chapter.

Bibliography

3Tera. (n.d.). *3Tera AppLogic*. Retrieved from 3Tera: `http://www.3tera.com/`

Apache Software Foundation. (n.d.). *Apache Hadoop*. Retrieved from `http://hadoop.apache.org`

Factor, A. (2001). *Analyzing Application Service Providers*. Prentice Hall.

GoGrid.com. (n.d.). *GoGrid.com*. Retrieved from GoGrid.com: `http://www.gogrid.com`

Google. (n.d.). *Google AppEngine*. Retrieved from Google: `http://code.google.com/appengine`

Google. (n.d.). *Google Apps*. Retrieved from Google Apps:
    `http://www.google.com/apps/intl/en/business/index.html`

Mario Barbacci, M. H. (1995). *Quality Attributes*. Pittsburgh, Pennsylvania 15213: Software Engineering Institute, Carnegie Mellon University.

Microsoft Corporation. (n.d.). *About Windows Azure*. Retrieved from Windows Azure:
    `http://www.azure.com/`

Microsoft Corporation. (n.d.). *Windows Azure Pricing*. Retrieved from Windows Azure:
    `http://www.microsoft.com/azure/pricing.mspx`

Open ID Foundation. (n.d.). Retrieved from `http://openid.net/foundation/`

Staten, J. (2008). *Is Cloud Computing Ready For The Enterprise?* Forrester Research, Inc.

CHAPTER 2

■■■

Windows Azure platform Overview

The Windows Azure platform is Microsoft's cloud computing platform and is a key component of Microsoft's overall Software + Services strategy. Gartner Research has identified Cloud Computing as one of the "top 10 disruptive technologies 2008–2012" (`http://www.gartner.com/it/page.jsp?id=681107`) According to Gartner, a *disruptive technology* is the one that causes major change in the accepted way of doing things. For enterprise architects and developers, the Windows Azure platform does cause a major change in the accepted way of architecting, developing, and deploying software services.

Software development today typically consists one or more of the following types of applications:

- *Rich client and Internet applications*: Examples are Windows Client, Windows Presentation Foundation, and Silverlight.

- *Web services and applications*: Examples are ASP.NET, ASP.NET Web Services, and Windows Communications Foundation.

- *Server applications*: Examples are Windows Services, WCF, message queuing, and database development.

- *Mobile application*: Examples are .NET Compact Framework and placeholder.

Most of these application types are on-premise enterprise applications or consumer applications hosted in data centers. The Windows Azure platform adds a new cloud services type to the list. During planning and architecture phases of a project, architects can now choose to include the Windows Azure platform in the overall service architecture.

The Windows Azure platform supports development and deployment of different types of applications and services, not only in the cloud but also on-premise. It is a collection of building blocks of platform, middleware, enterprise, and consumer services for developers to build cloud services. It provides developers with a cloud operating system called Windows Azure, a cloud database called SQL Azure, infrastructure middleware component called .NET Services and a consumer services component called Live Services. Developers can either build services that span across all these components, or pick and choose the components as needed by the service architecture. The overall concept of Windows Azure platform is to offer developers the flexibility to plug in to the cloud environment as per the architectural requirements of the service.

■ **Note** In this book, I refer to the overall Azure cloud offering from Microsoft that consists of Windows Azure, .NET Services, and SQL Azure as "the Windows Azure platform." Windows Azure is the operating system in the cloud, and it is the core component of the Windows Azure platform. I also use the terms "Azure" and "Windows Azure platform" interchangeably.

Development tools like Visual Studio .NET have matured enough in the past decade to increase developer productivity several folds in application design, development and testing, but there has been little improvement in the infrastructural challenges involved in deploying distributed applications. Organizations frequently require months of planning and coordinated efforts between multiple internal groups like Directory Services, Database Management, Platform Services and Security for deploying distributed enterprise applications. Ultimately, organizations end up spending more time and resources in coordinating activities across multiple groups than the delivery of the application itself.

Windows Azure platform readily provides internet scale infrastructure for deploying distributed applications and services. You can develop a cloud service in Visual Studio .NET and deploy it into the Azure cloud right from on-premise tools. This frees up critical project resources to focus on solution design and delivery instead of managing internal infrastructure dependencies.

In this chapter, I will cover the basics of the Windows Azure platform. I will also cover the development workflows of its components, just enough to get you started with your development environment. At the end of the chapter, I will walk you through a basic Windows Azure example.

Windows Azure Platform Overview

The Windows Azure platform is an end-to-end development and deployment platform for building cloud services. Each component of the Windows Azure platform is designed to provide a specific functionality to cloud services. In this section, we will look at the high-level architecture of the Windows Azure platform.

Windows Azure Platform Architecture

The Windows Azure Platform consists of three main components – Windows Azure, SQL Azure, and .AppFabric. . Figure 2-1 shows a simple illustration of the four Windows Azure platform components.

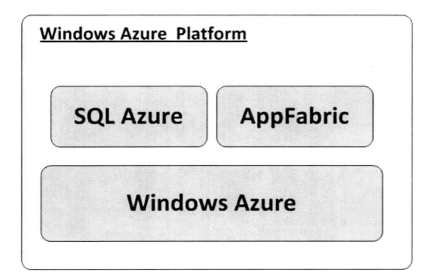

Figure 2-1. *The Windows Azure platform*

░ **Caution** When this book was in progress, Microsoft put the Live Framework and Live Services developer community technology preview on hold indefinitely. The Live Mesh was still running and accessible to end-users. I have not included Live Services in this book.

The Windows Azure Operating System

Windows Azure is the underlying operating system for running your cloud services on the Windows Azure platform. Microsoft brands Windows Azure as the Operating System in the cloud, because it provides all the necessary features for hosting your services in the cloud. It provides a runtime environment that includes a web server, computational services, basic storage, queues, management services, and load-balancers. Windows Azure also provides developers with a local development fabric for building and testing services before they are deployed to Windows Azure in the cloud. Figure 2-2 illustrates the three core services of Windows Azure.

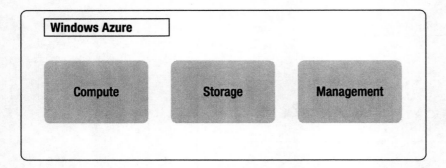

Figure 2-2. *Windows Azure core services*

The three core services of Windows Azure are as follows:

Compute: The compute service offers scalable hosting of services on 64-bit Windows Server 2008 platform with Hyper-V support. The platform is virtualized and designed to scale dynamically based on demand. The platform runs Internet Information Server (IIS) version 7 enabled for ASP.NET Web applications. At the time of this writing, the underlying Windows operating system and other infrastructure components like IIS are not available directly to developers. The abstraction is at the operating system layer. Developers can write managed and unmanaged services for hosting in the Windows Azure Compute cloud without worrying about the underlying operating systems infrastructure.

Storage: There are three types of storage supported in Windows Azure: tables, blobs, and queues. I will cover these storage types later in the book in detail. These storage types support REST-based direct access through REST APIs. Windows Azure tables are not traditional relational database tables like SQL Server tables. Instead, they provide structured data storage capabilities. They have independent data model popularly known as the entity model. Tables are designed for storing terabytes of highly available data like user profiles in a high-volume ecommerce site. Windows Azure blobs are designed to store large sets of binary data like videos, images, and music in the cloud. The maximum allowable size per blob item is 50GB. Windows Azure queues are the asynchronous communication channels for connecting between services and applications not only in Windows Azure but also from on-premise applications. You can also use queues to communicate across multiple Windows Azure role instances. The queue infrastructure is designed to support unlimited number of messages, but the maximum size of each message cannot exceed 8KB. Any account with access to storage can access tables, blobs, and queues.

Management: The management service supports automated infrastructure and service management capabilities to Windows Azure cloud services. These capabilities include automatic commissioning of virtual machines and deploying services in them, as well as configuring switches, access routers, and load balancers for maintaining the user defined state of the service. The management services consist of a fabric controller responsible for maintaining the health of the service. The fabric controller abstracts the underlying virtualized platform infrastructure from the compute and storage services. The fabric controller supports dynamic upgrade of services without incurring any downtime or degradation. Windows Azure management service also supports custom logging and tracing and service usage monitoring.

SQL Azure

SQL Azure is the relational database in the Windows Azure platform. It provides core relational database management system (RDBMS) capabilities as a service, and it is built on the core SQL Server product code base. In the current version (CTP), developers can access SQL Azure using tabular data stream (TDS), which is the standard mechanism for accessing on-premise SQL Server instances through SQL client today. The SQL client can be any client, like ADO.NET, LINQ, ODBC, JDBC, ADO.NET Entity Framework, or ADO.NET Data Services.

■ **Note** ADO.NET Data Services is an independent framework for accessing web-based data services. It can be used not only for consuming web-based data services but also for on-premise data services like SQL Server 2008. For more information on ADO.NET Data Services, please visit the MSDN site `http://msdn.microsoft.com/en-us/data/bb931106.aspx`.

Figure 2-3 illustrates the core components of SQL Azure.

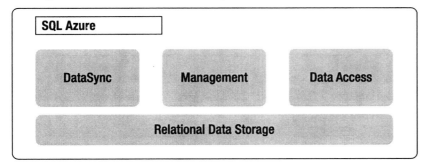

Figure 2-3. *SQL Azure core components*

The core services offered by SQL Azure are as follows:

Relational Data Storage: The relational data storage engine is the backbone of the SQL Azure and is based on the core SQL Server code base. This component exposes the traditional SQL Server capabilities like the tables, indexes, views, stored procedures, and triggers.

Data Sync: The Data Sync capabilities provide the synchronization and aggregation of data to and from SQL Azure to enterprise, workstations, partners and consumers devices using the Microsoft Sync Framework.

■ **Note** The Microsoft Sync Framework is included in the SQL Server 2008 product (http://msdn.microsoft.com/en-us/sync/default.aspx).

Management: The management component provides automatic provisioning, metering, billing, load-balancing, failover and security capabilities to SQL Azure. Depending on the SLA, each database is replicated to one primary and two secondary servers. In case of a failover, the switching between the primary and the secondary server is automatic without interruptions.

Data Access: The Data Access component defines different methods of accessing SQL Azure programmatically. Currently, SQL Azure will support Tabular Data Stream (TDS), which includes ADO.NET, Entity Framework, ADO.NET Data Services, ODBC, JDBC, and LINQ clients. Developers can access SQL Azure either directly from on-premise applications or through cloud services deployed in Windows Azure. You can also locate a Windows Azure compute cluster and a SQL Azure instance together for faster data access. I will discuss SQL Azure in detail later in this book.

.NET Services

.NET Services is the middleware engine of Windows Azure platform providing access control service and service bus.

■ **Note** Later Microsoft may enable Workflow services, which was part of the original AppFabric offering but was discontinued to align it with the Windows Workflow 4.0 release. In this book, I will not cover Workflow Services because its future was uncertain at the time of this writing.

AppFabrichas a service-oriented architecture and allows the creation of federated access control and distributed messaging across clouds and enterprises. I consider AppFabricto be the integration backbone of the Windows Azure platform, because it provides connectivity and messaging capabilities among distributed applications. It also provides capabilities for integrating applications and business processes not only between cloud services but also between cloud services and on-premise applications.

AppFabricalso provides a development environment integrated into Visual Studio .NET 2008 SP1 and beyond. Developers can build WCF-like services in Visual Studio .NET and publish endpoints to the cloud from within Visual Studio .NET design environment. Figure 2-4 illustrates the two core services of .NET Services.

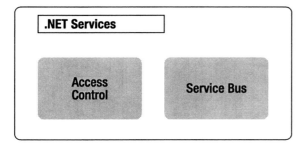

Figure 2-4. *AppFabriccore services*

The two core services of AppFabricare as follows:

> *Access Control*: The access control component provides rules-driven, claims-based access control for distributed applications. You could define claims-based rules and authorization roles in the cloud for accessing on-premise as well as cloud services.

> *Service bus*: The service bus is a generic .NET Internet service bus. It is analogous to the Enterprise Service Bus (ESB) popularly seen in large enterprises. Unlike the ESB, the AppFabricServiceBus is designed for Internet scale and messaging with cross-enterprise and cross-cloud scenarios in mind. The service bus provides key messaging patterns like publish/subscribe, point-to-point, and queues for message exchanges across distributed applications in the cloud as well as on-premise.

I will discuss AppFabricin detail later in this book.

Live Services

Microsoft Live Services is a collection of consumer centric applications and frameworks like Identity Management, Search, Geospatial, Communications, Storage, and Synchronization. Live Services and Live Framework are commonly confused for each other. Live Framework is a unified development model for building applications for Live Services. Live Framework provides the capabilities of building synchronization applications called the Mesh Applications for synchronizing data across multiple desktops and mobile devices seamlessly.

Live Framework also provides a local development environment integrated into Visual Studio .Net and a local runtime environment for on-premise development and testing. Figure 2-5 illustrates the core components of Live Services.

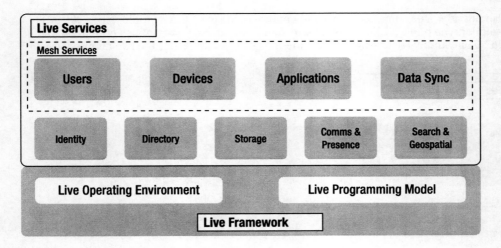

Figure 2-5. *Live Services core components*

The core components of Live Services are as follows:

> *Mesh services*: Mesh services provide programmatic access to users, devices, applications and the data synchronization across them.

- The users service provides management and sharing of resources across devices and other users.

- The devices service provides management, access, sharing and security of user devices across the Internet.

- The applications service provides deployment, configuration, versioning and access control to applications across the Live mesh.

- The data sync service provides synchronization of data and metadata across multiple devices, applications and the Live mesh cloud.

> *Identity services*: the identity service provides identity management and delegated authentication across the Live Services .E.g. Windows Live Identity Provider.

> *Directory Services*: The Directory Services manages the relationships and the graphs of the Users, Identities, Devices, Applications and their connected network. E.g. Relationship between users and devices in Live Mesh.

> *Storage*: The Storage service manages the storage of transient and persistent data for the Users, Devices and Applications in the Mesh. E.g. Windows Live Skydrive and Live Mesh storage

Communications & Presence: The Communication and Presence service provides the communications infrastructure between devices and applications, and manages their presence information for connections and display, for example, Windows Live Messenger and Notifications API.

Search: The Search Service provides search capabilities for users, web sites and applications, for example, Bing.

Geospatial: The Geospatial Service provides rich geo-mapping, location, routing, search, geocoding and reverse geocoding services to web sites and applications, for example, Bing Maps (or Virtual Earth).

Live Framework: Live Framework is a uniform model of programming Live Services across platforms, programming languages and devices. The three core components of the Live Framework are:

- Live Operating Environment (LOE): The LOE is the uniform runtime environment for Live Services objects in the cloud as well as in the local device environment. Developers can connect to the LOE in the cloud or on the local device. LOE gives offline operational capabilities to the Live Mesh. LOE also enables Live Mesh to synchronize offline operational data with the cloud LOE and other devices.

- Resource Model: The Live Framework resource model exposes the LOE resource objects like Data, Applications, Communications, Mesh and Identities via open protocols and formats like HTTP, XML, ATOM and RSS. You can use any programming language supporting these protocols to access LOE resources.

- Live Programming Model: The Live Programming Model provides a common programming model from JavaScript, Silverlight and .NET programming languages. You can build Client, Web and Rich Internet Applications using any of the above mentioned programming languages and deploy them in the Live Mesh. The Live Programming Model provides a uniform resource model across Live Services and exposes these services as REST (Representational State Transfer) resources. The Live Programming model supports open protocols and formats like HTTP, XML, ATOM and RSS for accessing Live Services.

I will discuss Live Services and Live Framework in detail later in this book.

Basic Azure Scenarios

In the previous section, you saw the high-level architectural view of the Windows Azure platform and its core components. In this section, let's take a look at some of the basic scenarios that encompass all of the Windows Azure components. Figure 2-6 illustrates the overall development and runtime architecture of the Windows Azure platform with some embedded scenarios. Let's derive some basic scenarios from this diagram.

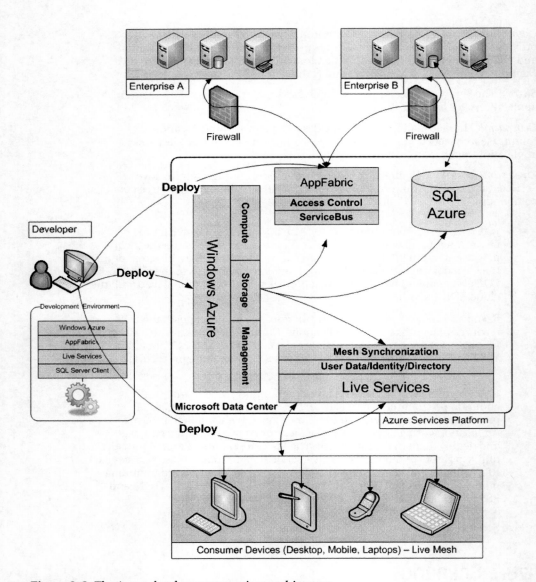

Figure 2-6. *The Azure development runtime architecture*

For the ease of understanding Figure 2-6, let's consider four entities—The Developer, Consumer Devices, the Enterprise and the Cloud (Windows Azure platform); and four scenarios—Windows Azure Software Development, Cross-Enterprise Application Integration, Enterprise Process Offloading and Consumer Services.

Scenario 1: Azure Software Development

In Scenario 1, the developer develops cloud services for Windows Azure, .NET Services, SQL Azure and Live Services on a local development environment and then tests these applications in the local development fabric before deploying them to the Windows Azure platform. The Windows Azure environment can host web as well as background process applications (called Worker) that can communicate with .NET Services, SQL Azure or Live Services depending on the business requirements of the application. Developers can also build services directly targeting each individual Windows Azure platform component. Once the services are deployed in their respective environments in the cloud, enterprises and consumers can start using them. The typical development cycle consists of designing, developing and testing the application in the local development fabric before it is deployed into a cloud staging environment. After testing the application in the cloud staging environment, it is deployed to the cloud production environment for end users to start using it.

Scenario 2: Cross-Enterprise Application Integration

In the Figure 2-6, Enterprise B is a payroll processing company that processes paychecks for Enterprise A. Enterprise A needs to send employee information to Enterprise B for payment processing on a periodic basis. After payment processing, Enterprise B needs to send a consolidated payment report to Enterprise A for accounting purposes. What I want to illustrate here is that there is a two-way financial relationship between the two enterprises and automated data exchange between both the enterprises is a business requirement. Traditionally, to achieve this, the IT departments from both the enterprises would have had to open up Firewall ports for transferring data back and forth from both the enterprises, and create a trust relationship between the directory domains in both the enterprises so the users from one enterprise are recognized in the other.

In the Windows Azure platform, you could achieve this by following these steps:

1. Register trust between the domains in both the enterprises with the AppFabricAccess Control Service.

2. Use the single sign-on capabilities of AppFabricto authenticate users across both the enterprises.

3. Use the ServiceBus network connectivity features to communicate across business applications through the firewall.

4. Optionally, any of the processing applications from both the enterprises could be hosted in the cloud as Windows Azure applications.

Scenario 3: Enterprise Process Offloading

Enterprise B is a payroll processing company that processes payroll calculations and reporting for more than 500 companies. Enterprise B has to generate consolidated payroll reports for all the 500 organizations at the same time, because the payroll date is the same for all the enterprises. After the payroll is processed, Enterprise B has to electronically send the reports to its customers the following day, due to compliance reasons. As Enterprise B is growing, it is not able to keep up with the computing capacity it needs to process reports for all the 500 organizations in a single day. So, Enterprise B decides to offload report processing to the Windows Azure platform by synchronizing the on-premise SQL Server database with SQL Azure, and running the report processing application on Windows Azure platform.

Enterprise B can now scale the report processing application within the cloud, in proportion to the company's growth. Thus, Enterprise B has successfully offloaded a processor intensive application to the Windows Azure platform without worrying about its on-premise infrastructure and processing capacity.

Scenario 4: Consumer Services (Live Mesh Synchronization)

In the fourth scenario, you have a role to play. Assume that in the past decade, the number of devices you and your family owns has increased to seven: one personal computer, three smart phones, and three laptops. Out of these, two laptops are owned by the company you work for.

One day, you decide to write a book on Windows Azure platform, and your company permits you to dedicate 10–15% of your daily time to writing the book. The challenge you are facing is sharing your writings between the enterprise PC at work and home laptop. You also want the ability to write your chapters from the garden next to your house on a perfectly sunny day. You need seamless access to your documents across multiple devices and locations.

You install Live Mesh on all your devices and pick and choose the files that you want to synchronize across them. Now, when you work on the chapters at home, they are automatically synchronized on your work computer. The next day, when you go to work, your work machine is up to date with the new content, and you can start working on the book at work. You can also work on your files from the garden with no network connectivity. When you return home and connect your laptop, Live Mesh automatically synchronizes the documents across all the selected devices for you. Thus, by using Live Mesh, you have created a seamless synchronization network among your own devices for sharing not only documents, but also other artifacts like photos, videos, and files.

Windows Azure Platform for Developers

Windows Azure, SQL Azure, .NET Services, and Live Services all have separate software development kits (SDKs), but Visual Studio .NET and the .NET Framework are the common programming tools used for building applications for all the Windows Azure components. Windows Azure SDK and the Live Framework SDK have local development fabrics that emulate the cloud environment at a miniature scale. Developers can utilize their existing .NET development skills for developing services for Windows Azure platform. In this section, I will cover the developer roles and the technical readiness required for developing Windows Azure platform services.

Developer Roles

The types of developers that may be interested in developing Windows Azure applications follow:

> *Enterprise developers*: Enterprise developers typically work either in the IT or Business departments of an enterprise. They are responsible for developing applications that improve business productivity. The business requirements come directly from the business groups within the enterprise or from strategic IT initiatives. Enterprise developers can then create cloud services on Windows Azure platform for consumption either by the local business units or cross-enterprise business units.

ISV developers: Independent software vendors (ISVs) develop business solutions on an existing platform. ISVs are more focused in vertical markets like financials, manufacturing, oil, gas, and healthcare. ISVs can leverage the Windows Azure platform for deploying services that are targeted for multiple customers in vertical markets. They can design multitenant architectures on top of Windows Azure platform, specifically dedicated for vertical industries they specialize in.

Consumer developers: Consumer developers work for online service companies like MSN Live, Yahoo, Apple, Google, Facebook, and MySpace, and they offer software services like mail, collaboration, social networking, and mobile services directly to the consumers. Consumer developers can build consumer services on Windows Azure platform and offer them to consumers around in the world.

Developer Readiness

Understanding the following technologies and concepts are the primary skills required for developing with Windows Azure:

- Visual Studio .NET 2008/2010
- .NET Framework 3.5
- Windows Communications Foundation
- ADO.NET
- ADO.NET Data Services
- Web services (REST, SOAP)
- XML
- ASP.NET
- .NET security
- SQL Server database development

Essentially, any proficient .NET developer should be able to develop Windows Azure services comfortably. This book assumes that you are comfortable programming in C# using Visual Studio .Net and .NET Framework. Even though all the examples in this book are written in C#, they could easily be ported to any programming language supported by the .NET Framework.

Getting Started

In this section I will cover the prerequisites required for getting started with the Windows Azure platform. As you know by now, Windows Azure is a cloud platform and runs in Microsoft's data centers. To access a particular service in the Windows Azure platform, you need to sign up for an account with

Microsoft. Table 2-1 lists the web sites you can navigate for creating accounts for specific services. You can associate your account with your Windows LiveID.

Table 2-1. *Windows Azure Sign-up Links*

Service Name	Sign-up Web Site
Windows Azure	`https://lx.azure.microsoft.com/`
.NET Services	`http://portal.ex.azure.microsoft.com/`
SQL Azure	`http://portal.ex.azure.microsoft.com/`
Live Services	https://lx.azure.microsoft.com/

Alternatively, you can visit the Windows Azure platform web site `http://www.azure.com`, and navigate to the sign in tab to sign-up for Windows Azure, as shown in Figure 2-7.

Sign In

Already Have an Azure Services Token or Account?

If you have already received a token or an account and are ready to get started, click on one of the links below.

> ▶ **Windows Azure**
> Windows Azure provides compute and essential storage capabilities that allow you to run your code in an on-demand, scalable and reliable environment.
>
> ▶ **SQL Azure**
> Microsoft SQL Azure is part of the Azure Services Platform: an internet-scale cloud computing and services platform hosted in Microsoft data centers. Currently, SQL Azure offers relational database service called SQL Azure Database. We are very excited to announce the availability of the SQL Azure Database Community Technology Preview (CTP) for customers.
>
> ▶ **Microsoft .NET Services**
> .NET Services provides a cloud-based Access Control and Service Bus services.
>
> ▶ **Live Services**
> Live Services is a set of building blocks within the Windows Azure Platform for handling user data and application resources.

Ready to get started? Register for Azure Services
Register for Azure Services here and get started with Azure cloud development today!

Figure 2-7. *The Windows Azure sign-in page*

On the Windows Azure sign in page, you can sign up for each of the four core services—Windows Azure, SQL Azure, Microsoft .NET Services, and Live Services.

■ **Note** Because Live Services will eventually be part of Windows Live, I will not include it in the portal navigation discussions.

Windows Azure Developer Portal

The Windows Azure developer portal is the primary location for developers interested in developing Windows Azure application. You navigate across all the Windows Azure platform components from the portal and then manage your Windows Azure deployments from the web page. Once you sign in with your account, you will be redirected to the Windows Azure developer portal. Figure 2-8 illustrates the Windows Azure developer portal landing page (Summary section).

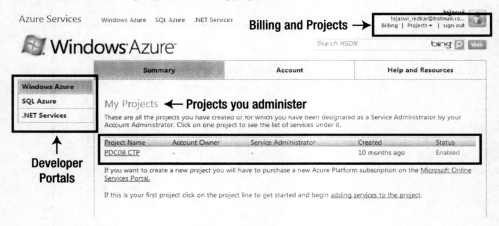

Figure 2-8. *The Windows Azure developer portal*

In the Windows Azure developer portal, there are three top-level navigation options—Summary, Account, and Help. In the Summary page, as shown in Figure 2-8, you can view the list of existing projects that you can administer. If you have not created any projects or are visting the site for the first time, the projects list will be empty. Click one of the listed projects to go to the Windows Azure services list, shown in Figure 2-9.

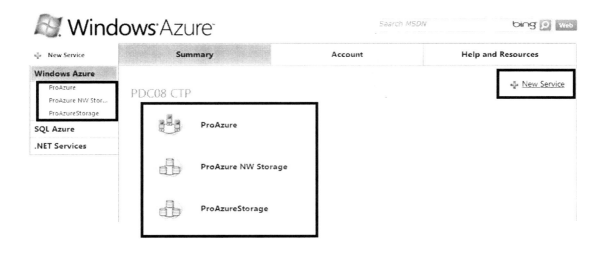

Figure 2-9. *Windows Azure services list*

Click the New Service link to go to the Create a New Service page shown in Figure 2-10.

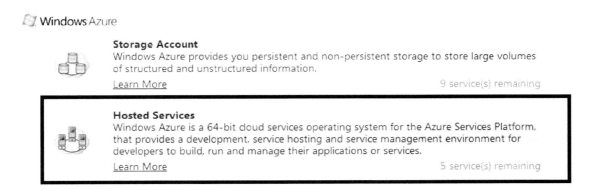

Figure 2-10. *The Create New Service page in the Windows Azure developer portal*

In Figure 2-10, you can create two types of services: Storage Account and Hosted Services Project. I will cover these project types in details in later chapters. You can assume for now that this page is used for creating Windows Azure cloud services. In Figure 2-9, I already have three services created: ProAzure, ProAzure NW Storage, and ProAzureStorage. As the name suggests, ProAzure NW Storage and ProAzure Storage are storage accounts. The ProAzure project is a compute project for hosting web applications and background processing applications. You can click any of the services to go to its respective management page. Figure 2-11 shows the management page for the ProAzureStorage service.

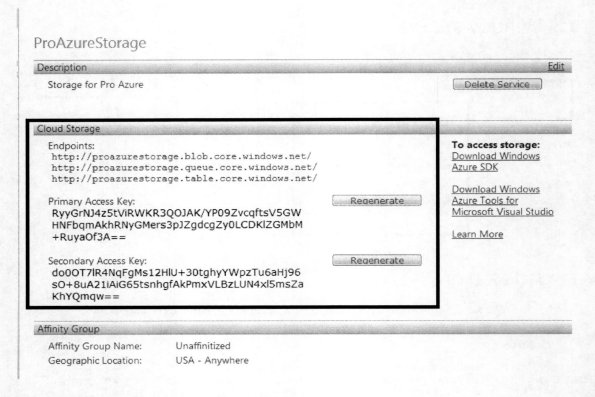

ProAzureStorage

Description   Edit

Storage for Pro Azure   [Delete Service]

Cloud Storage

Endpoints:
http://proazurestorage.blob.core.windows.net/
http://proazurestorage.queue.core.windows.net/
http://proazurestorage.table.core.windows.net/

Primary Access Key: [Regenerate]
RyyGrNJ4z5tViRWKR3QOJAK/YP09ZvcqftsV5GW
HNFbqmAkhRNyGMers3pJZgdcgZy0LCDKlZGMbM
+RuyaOf3A==

Secondary Access Key: [Regenerate]
do0OT7lR4NqFgMs12HlU+30tghyYWpzTu6aHj96
sO+8uA21iAiG65tsnhgfAkPmxVLBzLUN4xl5msZa
KhYQmqw==

To access storage:
Download Windows
Azure SDK

Download Windows
Azure Tools for
Microsoft Visual Studio

Learn More

Affinity Group

Affinity Group Name: Unaffinitized
Geographic Location: USA - Anywhere

Figure 2-11. *The ProAzureStorage management page*

The storage service does not run user-specific applications; instead, it provides URL access points to its storage infrastructure. The storage service management page lists the URL endpoints for the blob, queue, and table services. The page also lists the access keys for securely accessing the storage service and the affinity of the storage service towards a particular geolocation. Figure 2-12 shows the management page for the ProAzure compute service.

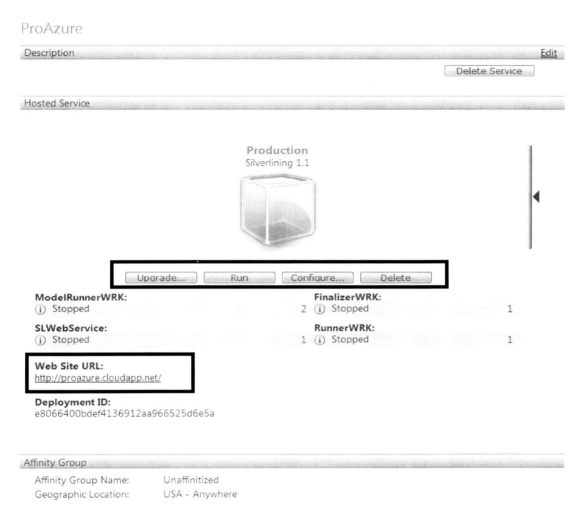

Figure 2-12. *ProAzure management page*

Unlike storage service, the compute service actually runs your applications, so the management page provides upgrade, run, configure, and delete operations on your compute service. In the preceding example, I have four different roles deployed in production. The numbers next to each role indicate the number of instances of each role. The Web Site URL http://proazure.cloudapp.net is the URL of the web application deployed in this service. The service will run only after I click the Run button. On the compute service management page, you have the option of running your application either in the staging environment or the production environment.

Figure 2-13 shows the staging and production environments management page.

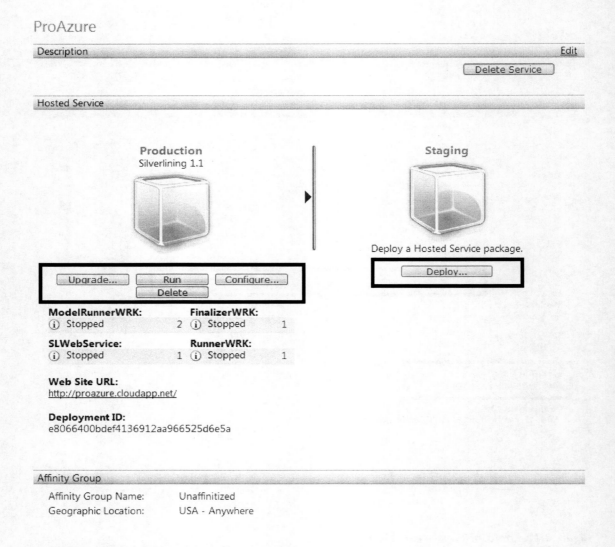

Figure 2-13. *Staging and production environment management*

The staging environment has nothing deployed, because it was swapped to production during the latest release. In any case, it is always a best practice to first test your cloud service in staging before promoting it to production. The Deploy button takes you to the staging deployment page as shown in Figure 2-14.

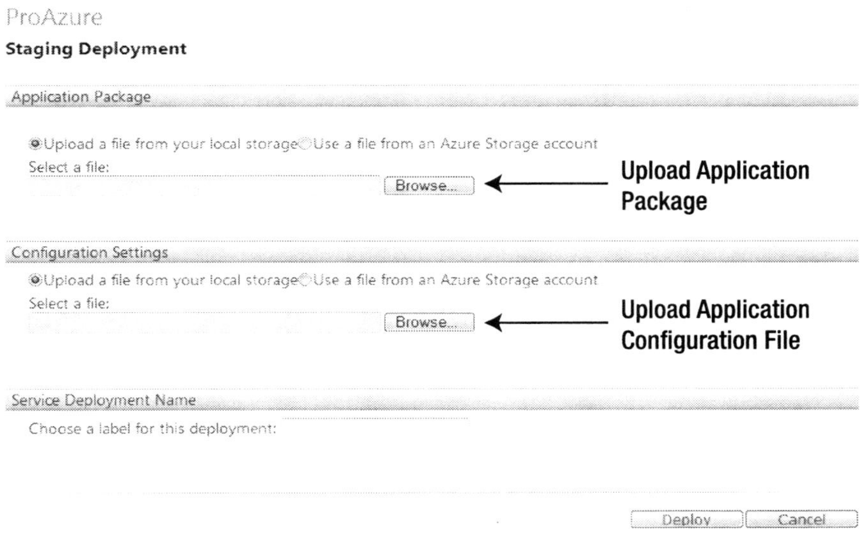

ProAzure

Staging Deployment

Application Package

◉ Upload a file from your local storage ○ Use a file from an Azure Storage account
Select a file:

[Browse...] ◀────── **Upload Application Package**

Configuration Settings

◉ Upload a file from your local storage ○ Use a file from an Azure Storage account
Select a file:

[Browse...] ◀────── **Upload Application Configuration File**

Service Deployment Name

Choose a label for this deployment:

[Deploy] [Cancel]

Figure 2-14. *The Staging Deployment page*

From the deployment page, you can upload your cloud service application package and its associated configuration file. The number of roles and their instances are all contained in the cloud service application package. Later in this chapter, you will build a simple cloud service package for Windows Azure.

Figure 2-15 shows the contents of the Account page of the Windows Azure developer portal.

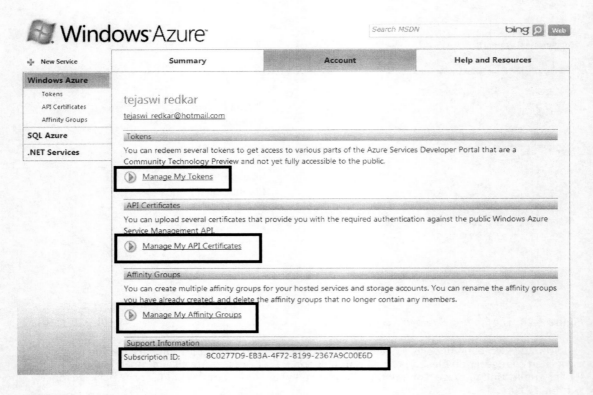

Figure 2-15. *Windows Azure developer portal Account page*

The Account page is generally used for managing account-related information like the invitation tokes received from Microsoft, X.509 API certificates for the Windows Azure Service Management API, and affinity groups for geolocating your services in Windows Azure.

Figure 2-16 illustrates contents of the Help page of the Windows Azure developer portal.

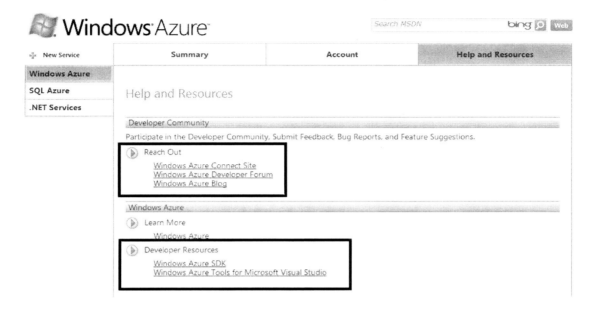

Figure 2-16. *Windows Azure developer portal Help page*

The Help page is a resource page and provides links to software development kits, Windows Azure product blogs, and articles about Windows Azure. The Help page is also the primary feedback page where users can enter product feedback through forums.

AppFabricDeveloper Portal

To navigate to the AppFabricdeveloper portal, click on the AppFabriclink on the Windows Azure portal. The AppFabricsubscription is included in Windows Azure subscription at the time of this writing. The AppFabriclanding page lists the AppFabricsolutions and links to AppFabricSDK, MSDN resources, and forums, as shown in Figure 2-17.

Figure 2-17. *AppFabricLanding Page*

From the AppFabriclanding page, you can add AppFabricsolutions as shown in Figure 2-17. Each solution consists of a solution name, access control service (ACS), service bus registry, and credentials for accessing ACS and ServiceBus endpoints. Each link (ACS, ServiceBus, and Credentials) takes you to their respective management pages. An ACS is a cloud-based claims-mapping service that can be used in cloud-based as well as on-premise applications that use claims-based identity model. ServiceBus is an Internet message bus for sending and receiving messages across the Internet between applications. The Credentials page lets you manage credentials for accessing ACS and ServiceBus services. Figure 2-18 shows the credentials management page from the AppFabricportal.

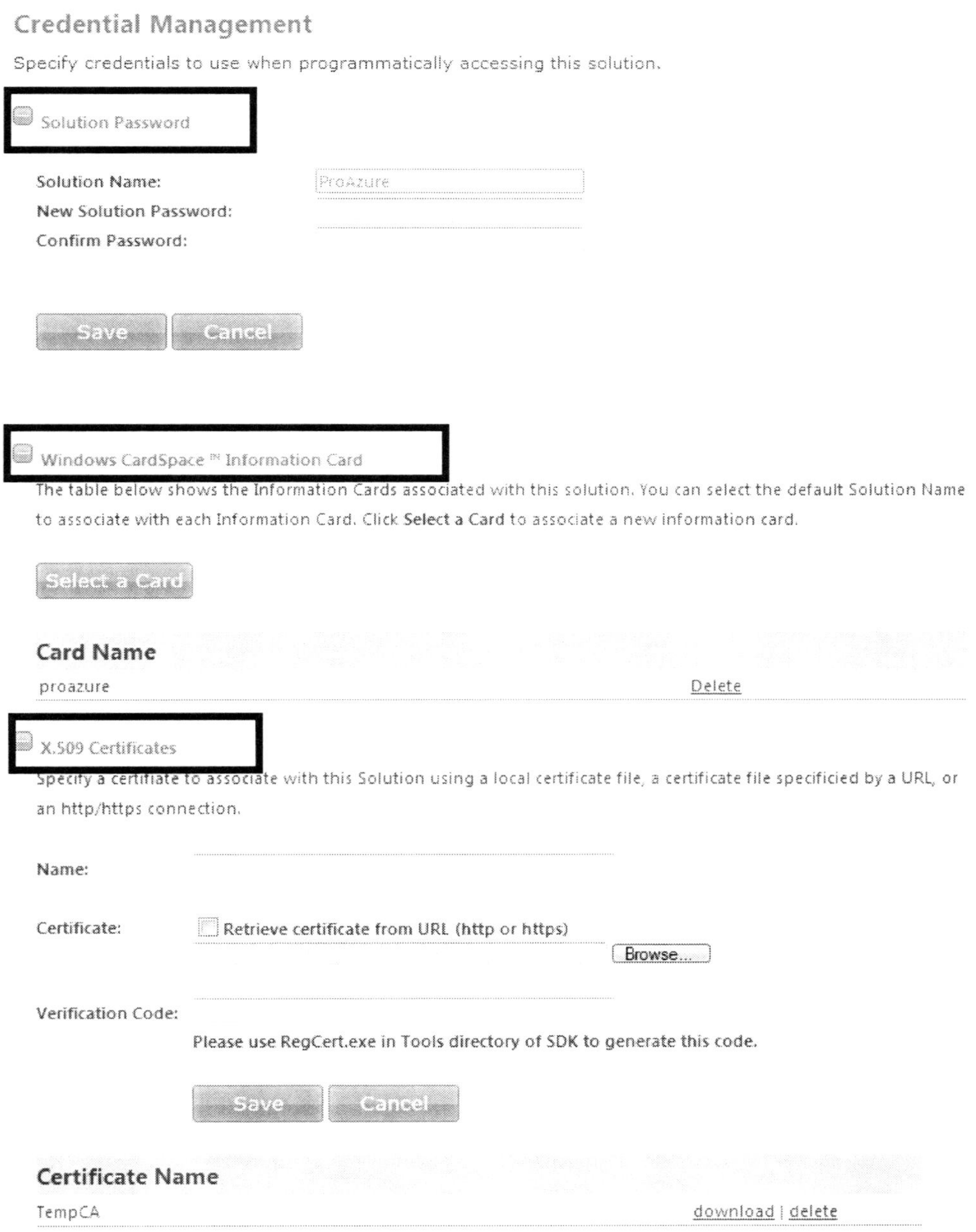

Credential Management

Specify credentials to use when programmatically accessing this solution.

☐ Solution Password

Solution Name: ProAzure

New Solution Password:

Confirm Password:

[Save] [Cancel]

☐ Windows CardSpace ™ Information Card

The table below shows the Information Cards associated with this solution. You can select the default Solution Name to associate with each Information Card. Click **Select a Card** to associate a new information card.

[Select a Card]

Card Name

proazure   Delete

☐ X.509 Certificates

Specify a certificate to associate with this Solution using a local certificate file, a certificate file specificied by a URL, or an http/https connection.

Name:

Certificate: ☐ Retrieve certificate from URL (http or https)

                                     [Browse...]

Verification Code:

    Please use RegCert.exe in Tools directory of SDK to generate this code.

[Save] [Cancel]

Certificate Name

TempCA   download | delete

Figure 2-18. *AppFabricCredentials Management*

You can have three types of credentials for accessing AppFabricendpoints: Solution Password, Windows CardSpace Information Card, and X.509 certificates. You can use any one of the credentials for accessing the AppFabric endpoints.

SQL Azure Developer Portal

To navigate to the AppFabric developer portal, click the SQL Azure link on the Windows Azure portal. If you are logging in for the first time, you may need an invitation token to enter before the portal takes you to the SQL Azure developer portal. From the SQL Azure developer portal, you can manage your projects and create/delete databases. Figure 2-19 shows the list of projects I am allowed to administer in my account.

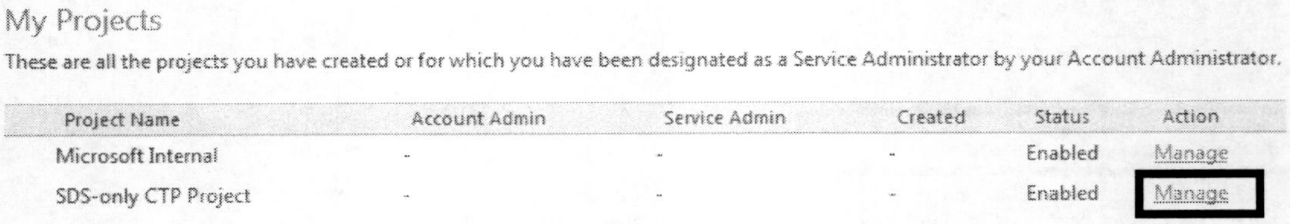

My Projects

These are all the projects you have created or for which you have been designated as a Service Administrator by your Account Administrator.

Project Name	Account Admin	Service Admin	Created	Status	Action
Microsoft Internal	-	-	-	Enabled	Manage
SDS-only CTP Project	-	-	-	Enabled	Manage

Figure 2-19. SQL Azure Projects

Clicking the Manage link will take you to the server administration page, where you can create and delete databases. Figure 2-20 shows the server administration page with five databases. The master database is the SQL Server master database you receive with all the SQL Azure instances.

Figure 2-20. *SQL Azure Project management page*

The Create Database and Drop Database buttons let you create a new database or drop an existing database respectively. The Connection Strings button gives you the format of the database connection string you can use for accessing the database from SQL Server clients.

Building the Development Platform

In this section, I will list the software components recommended for building your own development environment for Windows Azure platform.

▪ **Note** All SDKs for the Windows Azure platform can be downloaded at http://www.microsoft.com/ azure/sdk.mspx.

The following sections list the recommendations for building your own environment for Windows Azure development.

Operating System

You may use Windows Vista SP1 (Home Premium, Enterprise, or Ultimate), Windows 7, or Windows 2008 Server.

Software

I have divided the software requirements for each service into its own section. The "general" section lists the software required for all Windows Azure platform development work.

- General

- Visual Studio .NET 2008/2010 SP+

- .NET Framework 3.5+

- Windows Azure

- Windows Azure SDK: Windows Azure SDK (`http://www.microsoft.com/azure/sdk.mspx`) contains the development fabric, client libraries, tools, samples, and documentation for developing Windows Azure services.

- Windows Azure Tools for Microsoft Visual Studio: Windows Azure Tools for Visual Studio (`http://www.microsoft.com/azure/sdk.mspx`) create cloud services project types you can use for creating and deploying Windows Azure cloud services from within Visual Studio.

- SQL Server 2008 Express or SQL Server 2008 Developer: The development fabric from the Windows Azure SDK depends on SQL Server for creating development storage.

- SQL Azure

- SQL Server 2008 Express or SQL Server 2008 Developer: This is needed for connecting to SQL Azure and executing scripts.

- NET Services

  - Microsoft AppFabric SDK: The AppFabric SDK (`http://www.microsoft.com/azure/sdk.mspx`) integrates the Visual Studio tools. It contains client libraries, tools, samples, and documentation for creating AppFabric applications.

- Live Service

  - Live Framework Tools for Visual Studio and SDK: These are available at `http://dev.live.com/liveframework/`.

  - Live Framework Tools: These are available at `http://dev.live.com/resources/downloads.aspx`.

The installation of all these software components and SDKs is fairly straightforward. In this chapter, we will use only Windows Azure SDK. In later chapters, you will need the AppFabric and Live Framework SDKs.

Getting Started with Windows Azure Platform Development

In this section, I will cover the basics for getting started with developing Windows Azure services. The objectives of this section are to make you comfortable with the concepts discussed and get you started with hands-on experience in building your own cloud services. This section will cover only the basic concepts discussed in the chapter. Later in this book, you will learn advanced concepts through advanced examples in each chapter.

This example assumes you have installed all the prerequisites required for developing Windows Azure services. If you have already setup your development environment, let's get started with a simple Windows Azure service to get you comfortable with Windows Azure development. In this example, you will develop, build and deploy a simple Windows Azure web role service to the cloud. Initially, we will build the complete service in the development fabric and then deploy it to the cloud.

■ **Note** In this example, you will develop a basic Windows Azure web role service to get started on the core Windows Azure services platform. In the rest of book, you will learn to develop more advanced services using other components of the Windows Azure platform.

Setting the Objectives

The objectives of this example follow:

- Understanding the integration of Windows Azure with Visual Studio .NET for developing cloud services

- Exploring different components of a Windows Azure web role

- Understanding the Windows Azure development environment

- Understanding the Windows Azure deployment process

Understanding the Service Architecture

The service architecture consists of a simple Windows Azure web role cloud service developed in the local development environment by the developer and then uploaded to the Windows Azure cloud portal. Figure 2-15 illustrates the service architecture for this example. In Figure 2-21, the developer develops the cloud service on-premise and then deploys it to the Windows Azure cloud platform.

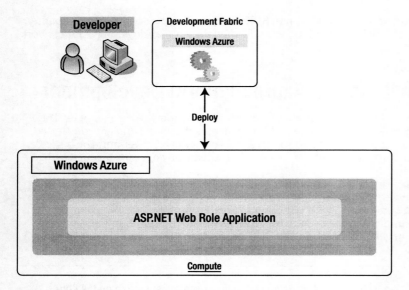

Figure 2-21. *HelloService Architecture*

■ **Note** A web role application is web application you can build in Windows Azure. The cloud service may consist of one or more applications. I will cover the project types in detail in the next chapter. For now, consider a web role as an ASP.NET web application.

Understanding the Developer Workflow

Figure 2-22 illustrates the developer workflow for developing the Windows Azure web role cloud service.

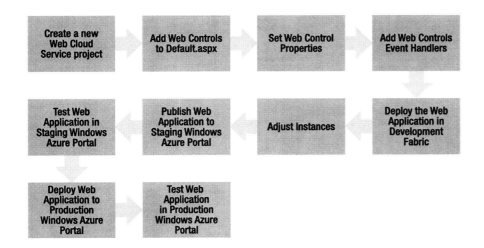

Figure 2-22. *Developer Workflow*

The developer workflow illustrates the steps required to develop, build, and deploy a simple web role cloud service to the cloud.

I have divided the remainder of this example into two separate sections: "Developing the Service" and "Deploying the Service." In the development section, you will develop and test your service locally in the Windows Azure development fabric. In the deployment section, you will deploy the service as a Windows Azure cloud service.

Developing the Service

The step-by-step walkthrough for the Windows Azure Web cloud service example is as follows:

1. Start Visual Studio 2008/2010

▓ **Note** If you have Windows Vista and above, I recommend you right-click Visual Studio in the program menu and select Run as administrator.

---

2. Select File ▶ New ▶ Project.

3. Create a new cloud service project by selecting Cloud Services Project, naming it HelloService, and clicking OK, as shown in Figure 2-23.

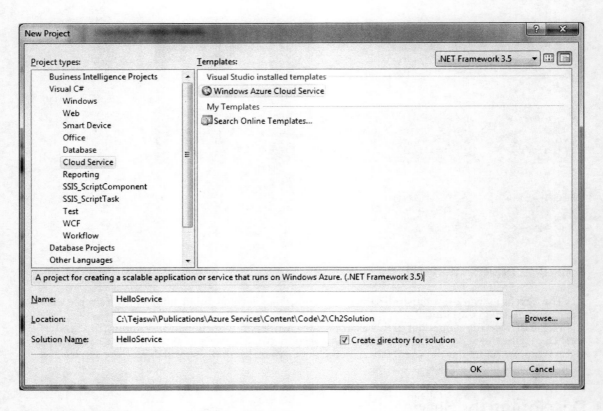

Figure 2-23. *Create a web cloud services project*

    4.   In the New Cloud Service project window, select the ASP.NET Web Role project type from the Roles section, and add it to the Cloud Service solution section. Name the web role HelloAzureCloud, as shown in Figure 2-24.

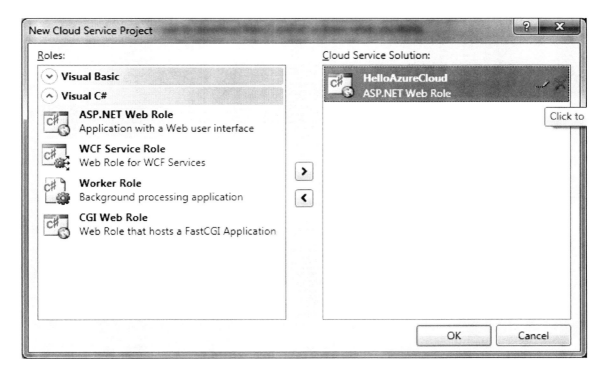

Figure 2-24. *Create a new web role*

The cloud service project creates an ASP.NET project that can be deployed to the Windows Azure cloud. Another type of cloud service template available is the worker role service. The worker role is a background process analogous to a windows service on your personal computer. In the next chapter, you will study each of these Windows Azure roles in detail.

5. Visual Studio creates a new solution consisting of two projects as shown in Figure 2-25.

Figure 2-25. *Cloud services solution*

The HelloService project is the new cloud services project containing configuration and metadata of the Windows Azure cloud service and reference to the web role project. The **Roles** folder holds references to all the roles in the cloud service. The HelloAzureCloud project is the ASP.NET web application, which is called a web role in context of the cloud service. On its own, HelloAzureCloud is a regular ASP.NET web application.

The **ServiceConfiguration.cscfg** file is the configuration file of the cloud service. It contains configuration settings for the service. There are two main sections under the **Role** element—**Instances** and **ConfigurationSettings**, as shown in Listing 2-1.

Listing 2-1. *ServiceConfiguration.cscfg*

```xml
<?xml version="1.0"?>
<ServiceConfiguration serviceName="Ch2Solution"
xmlns="http://schemas.microsoft.com/ServiceHosting/2008/10/ServiceConfiguration">
  <Role name="HelloAzureCloud">
    <Instances count="1" />
    <ConfigurationSettings>
      <Setting name="DiagnosticsConnectionString"
value="UseDevelopmentStorage=true" />
    </ConfigurationSettings>
  </Role>
</ServiceConfiguration>
```

The default configuration setting includes a DiagnosticsConnectionString for instrumentation and logging. For the sake of simplicity, let's not change the default values in the ServiceConfiguration.csfg. The main difference between web.config and ServiceConfiguration.csfg is that Web.config is application specific and ServiceConfiguration.csfg is service specific across multiple instances and roles. The contents of the ServiceConfiguration.csfg can be changed dynamically from the configure section of the deployed cloud service in Windows Azure developer portal.

The ServiceDefinition.csdef contains the metadata information about the service for the Windows Azure Fabric as shown in Listing 2-2.

Listing 2-2. *ServiceDefinition.csdef*

```xml
<?xml version="1.0" encoding="utf-8"?>
<ServiceDefinition name="Ch2Solution"
xmlns="http://schemas.microsoft.com/ServiceHosting/2008/10/ServiceDefinition">
  <WebRole name="HelloAzureCloud">
    <InputEndpoints>
      <InputEndpoint name="HttpIn" protocol="http" port="80" />
    </InputEndpoints>
    <ConfigurationSettings>
      <Setting name="DiagnosticsConnectionString" />
    </ConfigurationSettings>
  </WebRole>
</ServiceDefinition>
```

The file contains information like HTTP input endpoints for the service and configuration information that will apply to all the instances of roles launched by Windows Azure. Next, we're going to set up the web controls for the service.

1. Open Default.aspx in Design mode, and add ASP.NET web controls shown in Listing 2-3.

Listing 2-3. *Default.aspx Controls*

```
<asp:Button ID="btnWhere" runat="server" onclick="btnWhere_Click"
Text="Where are you?" />
<br />
<br />
<asp:Label ID="lblLocation" runat="server" Font-Bold="True" Font-Size="X-Large"
ForeColor="Black"></asp:Label>
```

Figure 2-26 illustrates the Default.aspx page after adding the ASP.NET Web Controls.

Figure 2-26. *Default.aspx Controls*

2. Double-Click btnWhere to open its Click event handler, `btnWhere_Click`. In the `btnWhere_Click` function, set the Text property of lblLocation as shown in Listing 2-4. In Listing 2-4, the `lblLocation.Text` property is set to a static text appended with the server machine name and the host address of the requester.

Listing 2-4. *Code Snippet for btnWhere.Click*

```
protected void btnWhere_Click(object sender, EventArgs e)
{
        lblLocation.Text = String.Format
("I am on Cloud {0}!!. Where are you? {1}",
HttpContext.Current.Server.MachineName,
Request.UserHostAddress);
}
```

3. Build the Solution and then right-click Debug ▶ Start New Instance on HelloService project to start the service in debug mode. If you do this on the ASP.NET project, it will only start the ASP.NET application and not the cloud service. The service initializes the Development Fabric as shown in the Figure 2-27.

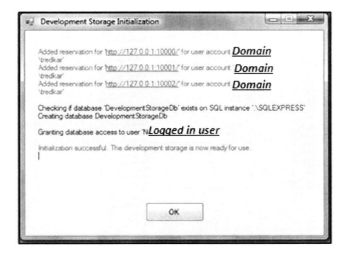

Figure 2-27. *Initialize Development Fabric*

▪ **Caution** The development fabric depends on SQL Server. If your SQL Server Express instance is not running, the Development Fabric will not initialize and produce an error message indicating the SQL Server instance could not be found. To fix the error, go to Start ▶ Run ▶ services.msc to open the Services Management console, and start the SQL Server instances. For initializing a SQL Server instance other than SQLExpress, use the tool DSInit.exe from the Windows Azure SDK's bin directory with the /sqlinstance parameter option. The use for the DSInit tool is DSInit [/sqlinstance:<SQL server instance>] [/forceCreate] [/user:<Windows account name>].

---

4. The Default.aspx page from the Web Application is loaded as shown in Figure 2-28. Click the Where Are You? button to interact with the service.

Figure 2-28. *Run Default.aspx*

89

5. Open Start ▶ All Programs ▶ Windows Azure SDK ▶ Development Fabric to start the development fabric application as shown in Figure 2-29.

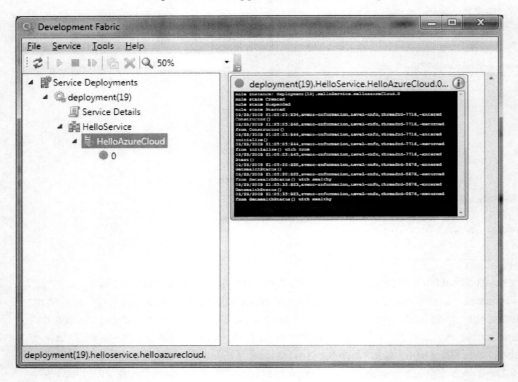

Figure 2-29. *Development fabric*

Alternatively, you could start the development fabric by right-clicking the development fabric system tray icon, as shown in figure 2-30.

Figure 2-30. *System tray development fabric*

6. Observe instance 0 under the web role tree node in Figure 2-29. This is the web role instance that is running the ASP.NET web application. The ASP.NET web application is launched in the development fabric with one instance.

7. Stop the debugging, and open ServiceConfiguration.cscfg file from Solution Explorer. In the Instances node, change the value of the count attribute to 2, as shown in Listing 2-5.

Listing 2-5. *Change Instances*

```xml
<?xml version="1.0"?>
<ServiceConfiguration serviceName="HelloService"
xmlns="http://schemas.microsoft.com/ServiceHosting/2008/10/ServiceConfiguration">
  <Role name="HelloAzureCloud">
    <Instances count="2" />
    <ConfigurationSettings>
    </ConfigurationSettings>
  </Role>
</ServiceConfiguration>
```

8. Run the service again and go to the development fabric application. You will observe, as shown in Figure 2-31, that the development fabric now started two instances of the ASP.NET application as configured in the ServiceConfiguration.cscfg file.

Figure 2-31. *Development Fabric with two instances*

You just started two instances of the same application by just adjusting the Instances count in the ServiceConfiguration.cscfg file. This is a very powerful feature, because it lets you scale the service based on demand, without any infrastructure investments like servers and load-balancers. The Windows Azure Fabric abstracts the infrastructure intricacies from service scalability.

Deploying the Service

So, you have developed and tested your Windows Azure cloud service in the local development fabric. Now, you are ready to deploy the service in the Windows Azure cloud. To do so, you will need to open an account with Windows Azure. In this section, I will show the deployment using my own account, but you should be able to configure the same application using your account details.

1. Go to Visual Studio

2. Right-click the HelloService Project, and select Publish as shown in Figure 2-32.

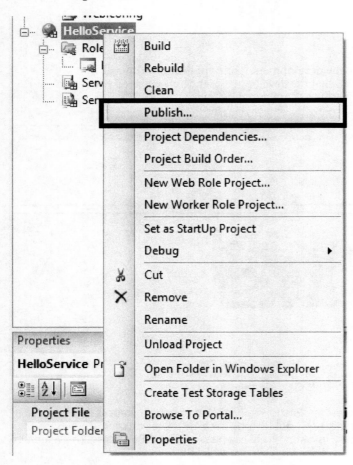

Figure 2-32. Publish HelloService

The Publish action compiles and packages the cloud service into a service package to be deployed to Windows Azure. The package contains all the service components and dependencies required by Windows Azure to run the service in the cloud. For the HelloAzureCloud service, Visual Studio .NET creates a `HelloAzureCloud.cspkg` file and a `ServiceConfiguration.cscfg` file. The `ServiceConfiguration.cscfg` file contains the configuration information for the service instance.

After the publish process is complete, Visual Studio launches a browser window pointing to the Windows Azure developer portal and a Windows Explorer window pointing to the directory containing the service package files, as shown in Figure 2-33.

Name	Date modified	Type	Size
HelloService	9/29/2009 2:17 PM	Service Package file	33 KB
ServiceConfiguration	9/29/2009 2:08 PM	CSCFG File	1 KB

Figure 2-33. Published package files

3. Before navigating to the Windows Azure developer portal, you will be asked to enter your LiveID and password. Enter the same LiveID and password that is associated with the Windows Azure developer portal.

4. On the Windows Azure developer portal, go to the service management page of the desired project, and click the New Service link to go to the Project Types Page.

Tip Take a moment to read the description of the Hosted Services project type, which is used for deploying Windows Azure services.

---

5. Select the Hosted Services service type as shown in Figure 2-34.

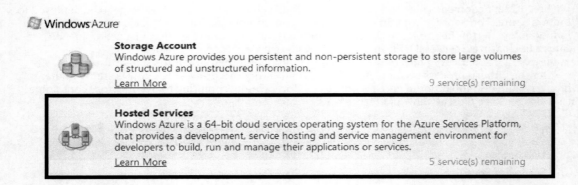

Figure 2-34. *Hosted services project*

6. On the Service Properties page, type **HelloWindowsAzure** as the Project Label and add a Project Description, as shown in Figure 2-35. Then, click Next.

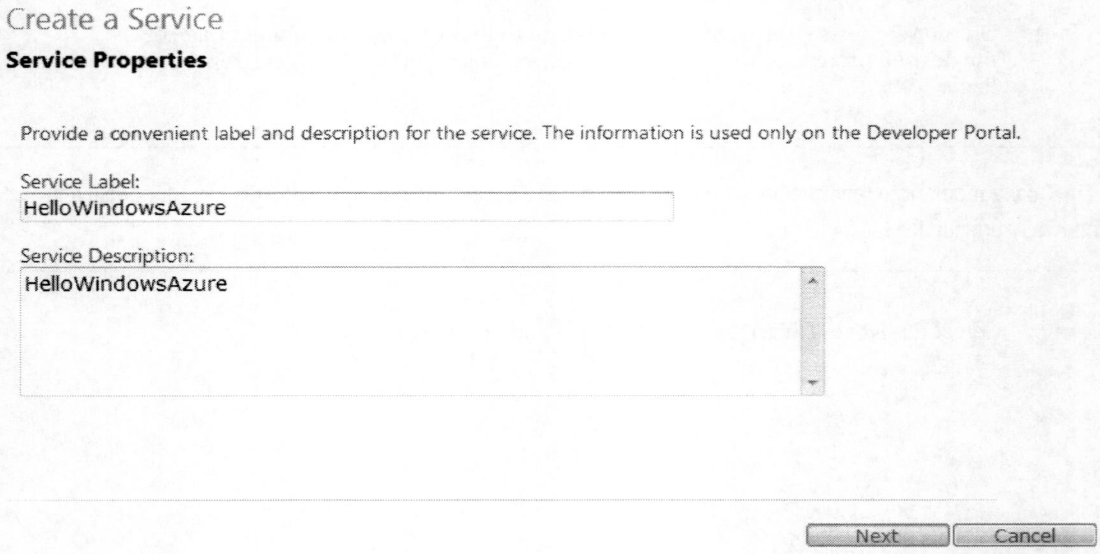

Create a Service

Service Properties

Provide a convenient label and description for the service. The information is used only on the Developer Portal.

Service Label:

HelloWindowsAzure

Service Description:

HelloWindowsAzure

[Next] [Cancel]

Figure 2-35. *Adding a project label and description*

7. On the Hosted Service page, you specify the hosted service URL of the service. Note that you can only enter a globally unique subdomain service name. The domain name `cloudapp.net` is constant and cannot be changed. So, your URL `http://[servicename].cloudapp.net` should be globally unique. You can test the availability of the name by entering your preferred name and then clicking Check Availability button as shown in Figure 2-36. I named the service proazure, and fortunately it was available, but you can choose any name you like as long as it satisfies the URL naming conventions.

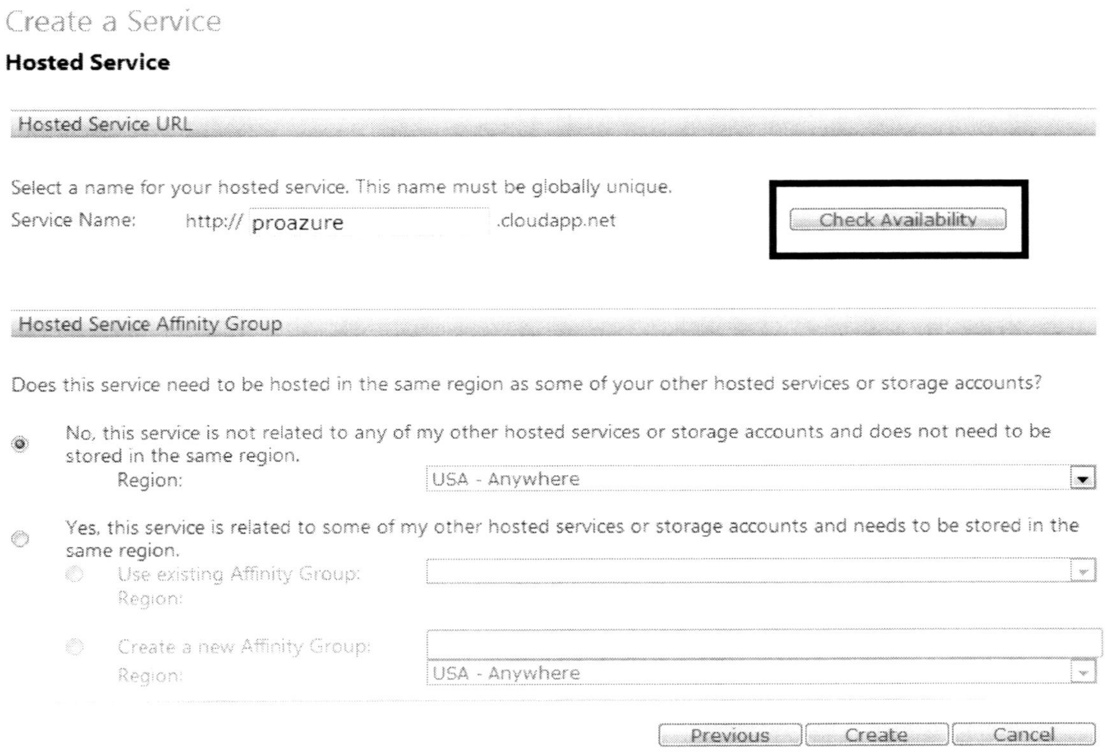

Create a Service

Hosted Service

Hosted Service URL

Select a name for your hosted service. This name must be globally unique.

Service Name: http:// proazure   .cloudapp.net   Check Availability

Hosted Service Affinity Group

Does this service need to be hosted in the same region as some of your other hosted services or storage accounts?

○ No, this service is not related to any of my other hosted services or storage accounts and does not need to be stored in the same region.
      Region: USA - Anywhere ▼

○ Yes, this service is related to some of my other hosted services or storage accounts and needs to be stored in the same region.
   ○ Use existing Affinity Group:
      Region:
   ○ Create a new Affinity Group:
      Region: USA - Anywhere

                                    Previous   Create   Cancel

Figure 2-36. *Choosing a hosted service name*

8. Click Next to create the service. You will be automatically taken to the service management page, which contains two deployment options, Staging and Production, as shown in Figure 2-37.

Figure 2-37. The HelloAzureWorld project page

9. In the staging environment, you will typically test the service for production readiness. After testing the service, you can then synchronize it with the production environment. To deploy the service in the staging environment, click the Deploy button in the Staging section of the page.

10. On the Staging Deployment page, shown in Figure 2-38, browse to the App package that was created when you published the Hello Azure Cloud solution in Visual Studio.

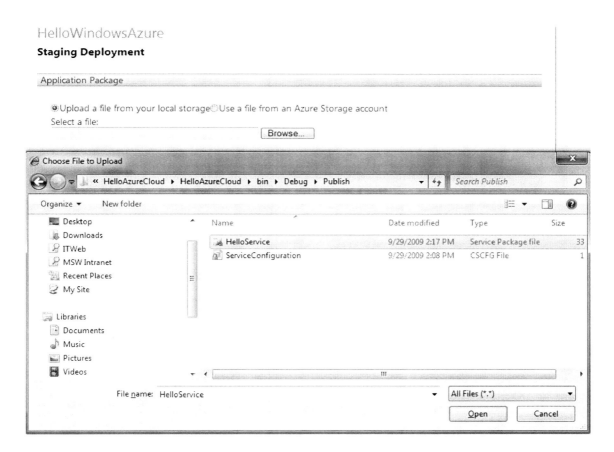

Figure 2-38. *Deploy App Package*

11. Next, browse to the ServiceConfiguration.cscfg file, as shown in Figure 2-39, that was create when you published the Hello Azure Cloud solution in Visual Studio. Typically, it is in the same directory (i.e., bin\Debug\Publish) as the cloud package file in the previous step.

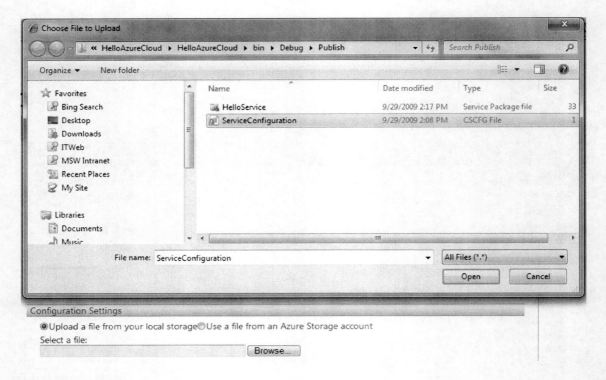

Figure 2-39. *Deploy Configuration Settings*

■ **Note** The `ServiceConfiguration.cscfg` file defines the roles, instances, and configuration information for the cloud service.

---

12. Give the deployment a label and click Deploy to deploy the service in the staging environment

The service package is deployed to the staging environment. During the deployment, Windows Azure extracts all the assemblies and files from the package and also reads the service configuration file to keep the package ready to run. When the deployment of the package completes, the staging cube changes its color from gray to light blue. If there is some problem in the package or any errors in the `ServiceConfiguration.cscfg` file, the deployment may fail changing the cube color to red.

Figure 2-40. Service package deployed

13. Once the service is deployed to staging, you have the following options: update, run, configure, delete, or promote to production using the sync button. Click the Configure option to go to the Service Tuning page shown in Figure 2-41.

Service Tuning

Event Logs

Copy the event logs for this deployment to a storage account: [Copy Logs]

Storage Account: [ProAzure NW Storag ▾]

Container Name: proazure-production

Configuration Settings

Edit the configuration:

```xml
<?xml version="1.0"?>
<ServiceConfiguration serviceName="HelloService"
xmlns="http://schemas.microsoft.com/ServiceHosting/2008/10/ServiceConfigura
tion">
  <Role name="HelloAzureCloud">
    <Instances count="2" />
    <ConfigurationSettings>
    </ConfigurationSettings>
  </Role>
</ServiceConfiguration>
```

Upload a new configuration file:

[_____]   [Browse...] [Upload]

Figure 2-41. *Service tuning page*

On the Service Tuning page, you can edit the service configuration, and thus the number of instances. For the purpose of this example, we will keep the service configuration unchanged with two instances.

14. Go back to the Service Details page, and click the Run button. When you click the Run button, Windows Azure creates virtual machine instances for each of the role mentioned in the service configuration file. In Figure 2-42, note that there are two allocated instances for the web role because in the service configuration file, you had specified two instances. Once the instances are allocated, the service is deployed across these instances and made available for running.

Staging
HelloAzure

Upgrade...   Run   Configure...
Delete

HelloAzureCloud:
ⓘ Allocated   2

Web Site URL:
http://59b5cb3d4c6b4fa8ada0288feffe2641.cloudapp.net/

Deployment ID:
59b5cb3d4c6b4fa8ada0288feffe2641

Figure 2-42. *Staging allocated instances*

When you click the Run button, web role state changes from Allocated to Initializing, and the Run button changes to Suspend button. Initialization may take a few minutes for Windows Azure to configure virtual machines and deploy the service to them. Once the service is initialized, the web role state changes to Started as shown in the Figure 2-43.

HelloAzureCloud:

✓ Started   2

Web Site URL:
http://59b5cb3d4c6b4fa8ada0288feffe2641.cloudapp.net/

Deployment ID:
59b5cb3d4c6b4fa8ada0288feffe2641

Figure 2-43. *Started Staging Application*

Now, you can test your service:

1. To test the service, click on the Website URL in the Staging section of the project. The Website URL in the Staging section is a temporary URL generated for testing the service. Hello Azure Cloud service starts in a new browser window, as shown in Figure 2-44.

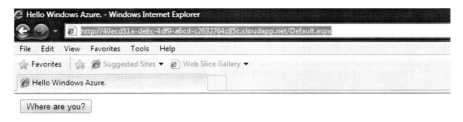

Figure 2-44. *Hello Azure Cloud in Staging*

2.   Even though the Staging environment is for testing, it is still a cloud
     environment. So, you can compare the testing results with the service
     deployed in the development fabric. If you are fine with the results of the
     service testing in the staging environment, you can move the service to
     production by clicking the Sync button between the Staging and the
     Production environment. Click the Sync button to promote the service to
     Production.

     When the service is deployed in production environment successfully, its web
     role status is set to Started, as shown in Figure 2-45.

Figure 2-45. *Deployed to production*

3. In the production environment, note that the Web Site URL is
   `http://proazure.cloudapp.net`. The `proazure` is the subdomain name I chose
   for the cloud service earlier.

4. Click the Website URL in the production environment to launch the Hello
   Azure Cloud service. Congratulations! You are now running the Hello Azure
   cloud service in Windows Azure Production environment.

You successfully developed, tested, and deployed your first Windows Azure cloud service without
purchasing any server or load-balancer hardware.

Example Summary

In this example, you saw how easily an ASP.NET web application can be developed, tested, and deployed
to the Windows Azure cloud as a cloud service. You learned to use Visual Studio .NET tools for
developing Windows Azure cloud service. You also saw how easy it is to start multiple instances of the
same web role application to enhance availability and scalability. Imagine the efforts it would require to
create a multi-instance ASP.NET application across multiple machines in your local or an enterprise
environment. The key idea to take away from this example is how Windows Azure abstracts the
hardware and software complexities of deploying and scaling cloud services in a production
environment. The intricacies involved in commissioning servers, network switches, load balancers, and
network connectivity are abstracted from application developers. With just a few mouse clicks and XML
settings, you can increase or decrease the number of role instances in Windows Azure.

The simplicity of the ASP.NET web application was on purpose to keep the overall solution simple
and take you through the entire life cycle of creating Windows Azure cloud service. You can enhance this
service by adding more complex features like AJAX and external Web Service Access.

Summary

In this chapter, I gave you an overview of Microsoft's Windows Azure platform for developing cloud
applications. You learned the different services offered by the Windows Azure platform and the
capabilities of each service. You also saw some basic Windows Azure scenarios for building cloud
services.

After that, I gave you an overview of the Windows Azure developer portal for managing Windows Azure,
SQL Azure and AppFabric projects. . Finally, you acquired the skills for developing and deploying a
Windows Azure cloud service in this chapter's example. The objective of this chapter was to give you a
high-level overview of the Windows Azure platform and to get you started with a simple cloud service. In
the next chapter, you will learn details about the Windows Azure platform and its components.

Bibliography

Gartner Research. (n.d.). *Gartner Identifies Top Ten Disruptive Technologies for 2008 to 2012*. Retrieved
   from Gartner Newsroom: `http://www.gartner.com/it/page.jsp?id=681107`

Microsoft Corporation. (n.d.). *Windows Azure*. Retrieved from Windows Azure platform:
   `http://www.azure.com`

CHAPTER 3

■■■

Windows Azure

Enterprises today run on several flavors of operating systems like Windows, UNIX, and mainframes. As the business grows, enterprises have to expand their data and processing capacities by buying more servers and operating systems to support capacity. Typically businesses have to plan for growth well in advance to budget the expenses. The tipping point, where investments in server systems may not justify the value they provide for the business growth, is not far away. This is because server systems are expensive to maintain, and before they start providing real value to the business, they may become obsolete. As a result, businesses have a constant struggle of justifying system upgrades to new server systems.

By moving to a cloud operating system, businesses can outsource their server growth to a cloud service provider like Microsoft. Microsoft can manage the server growth for businesses by providing compute, storage, and management capabilities in the cloud. When businesses feel the need to grow or scale back their server capacities, they just buy more or reduce the current capacities in the cloud according to business demand. Microsoft, on the other hand, can provide cloud services to multiple customers and transfer the savings achieved through economies of scale to businesses. Typical on-premise systems are designed and deployed to handle maximum capacity, but with the hardware elasticity offered by the cloud, businesses can deploy their systems to handle minimum capacity and then dynamically scale up as the demand increases.

Microsoft offers computing, storage, and management capabilities to businesses through Windows Azure. Windows Azure runs in Microsoft's data centers as a massively scalable operating system spanning multiple virtualized and actual platforms.

In this chapter, I will discuss Windows Azure architecture and its computational and service management components in detail. In the next chapter, I will cover Windows Azure storage.

Windows Azure Architecture

Windows Azure is the operating system that manages not only servers but also services. Under the hood, Windows Azure runs on 64-bit Windows Server 2008 R2 operating systems with Hyper V support. You can think of Windows Azure as a virtual operating system composed of multiple virtualized servers running on massively scalable but abstracted hardware. The abstraction between the Windows Azure core services and the hardware is managed by Fabric Controller. Fabric Controller manages en-to-end automation of Windows Azure services, from hardware provisioning to maintaining service availability. Fabric Controller reads the configuration information of your services and adjusts the deployment profile accordingly. Figure 3-1 illustrates the role of Fabric Controller in Windows Azure architecture.

105

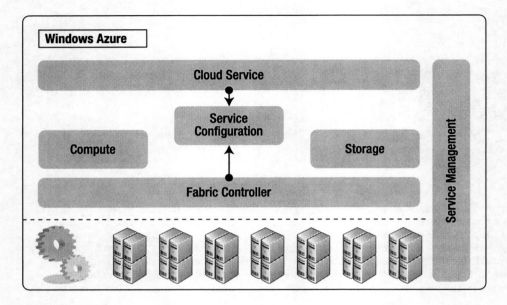

Figure 3-1. *Fabric Controller*

Windows Azure is designed to be massively scalable and available. In Figure 3-1, the Fabric Controller reads the service configuration information provided by the cloud service and accordingly spawns the server virtual machines required to deploy the cloud service. The deployment of cloud services and spawning of virtual instances of servers are transparent to the developer. The developer just sees the status of the cloud service deployment on the Windows Azure developer portal. Once the cloud service is deployed, it is managed entirely by Windows Azure. You just have to specify the end state of the cloud service in its configuration file, and Windows Azure will provision the necessary hardware and software to achieve it. Deployment, scalability, availability, upgrades, and hardware server configurations are managed by Windows Azure for the cloud service.

In the previous chapter, you saw that Windows Azure consists of three main services: Compute, Storage, and Management. The Compute service provides scalable hosting for IIS web applications and .NET background processes. The web application role is called the Web role, and the background process role is called the Worker role. The Worker role is analogous to Windows Services and is designed specifically for background processing. A Windows Azure cloud service comprises of a Web role and/or a Worker role and service definition of the service.

The Storage service in Windows Azure supports three types of services: blobs, queues, and tables. these storage types support local as well as direct access through a REST API. Table 3-1 illustrates the commonalities and differences among the three storage types in Windows Azure.

Table 3-1. *Windows Azure Storage*

Feature	Blob	Queue	Table
URL schema	http://[Storage Account].blob.core.windows.net/[Container Name]/[Blob Name]	http://[Storage Account].queue.core.windows.net/[Queue Name]	http://[Storage Account].table.core.windows.net/[Table Name]?$filter=[Query]
Maximum size	50GB	8K (string)	Designed for terabytes of data
Recommended usage	Large binary data types	Cross-service message communication	Storing smaller structured objects like the user state across sessions
API reference	http://msdn.microsoft.com/en-us/library/dd135733.aspx	http://msdn.microsoft.com/en-us/library/dd179363.aspx	http://msdn.microsoft.com/en-us/library/dd179423.aspx

Even though the Storage service makes it easy for Windows Azure cloud services to store data within the cloud, you can also access data directly from client applications using the REST API. For example, you could write a music storage application that uploads all your MP3 files from you client machine to the blob storage, completely bypassing the Windows Azure Compute service. Compute and Storage services can be used independently of each other in Windows Azure.

The Management service offers the features offered by Windows Azure developer portal as REST API calls. So, you can manage your applications and storage in Windows Azure dynamically by calling the Service Management API over REST interface.

Figure 3-2 illustrates the Windows Azure architecture.

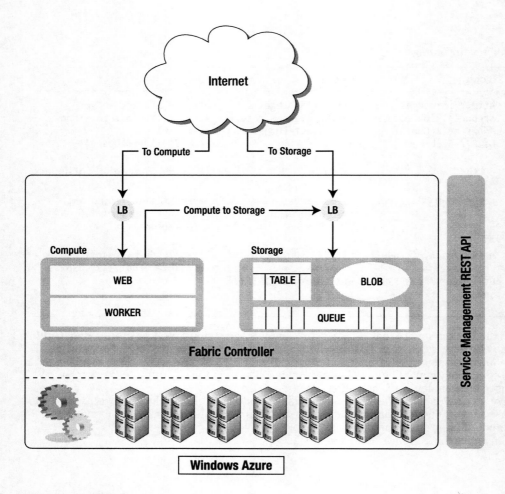

Figure 3-2. *Windows Azure*

In Figure 3-2, Compute and Storage services run as independent services in Windows Azure. The Web and Worker roles run in the Compute Service, and the blob, queue and table services run in the Storage service of Windows Azure. The Fabric Controller abstracts the underlying infrastructure components like virtualized servers, network components, DNS, and load balancers from Compute and Storage services. When a request from the Internet comes for a Windows Azure Web role application, it passes through the load balancer to the Web role of the Compute Service. If a request for a Storage service comes in, it passes through the load balancer to the appropriate Storage service component. Even when a Web or Worker role wants to communicate with the Storage service, it has to use the same REST APIs that other client applications use. Finally, the Compute and Storage services can be managed by the Service Management API.

Let's consider an example of your own media storage system in the cloud. In the past decade, there has been a data explosion due to exponential rise in the amount of digital assets in an individual's life.

These assets are in the form of music, video, pictures, and documents. Individuals face the challenge of storing all this content in one place locally. I personally have three hard drives with a combined capacity of 1TB, and I have almost 700GB full. Web sites like Flickr.com and Shutterfly.com can help manage pictures, and sites like YouTube.com and MSN Videos can manage videos. But what if you want a personal hard drive in the cloud with some backup capabilities and functionality so that you don't have to maintain terabytes of digital assets in your house or scattered over multiple web sites. Maybe you would also like to access these assets from anywhere you are. To resolve the digital asset storage problem, you could build a media storage service for yourself on Windows Azure as shown in Figure 3-3.

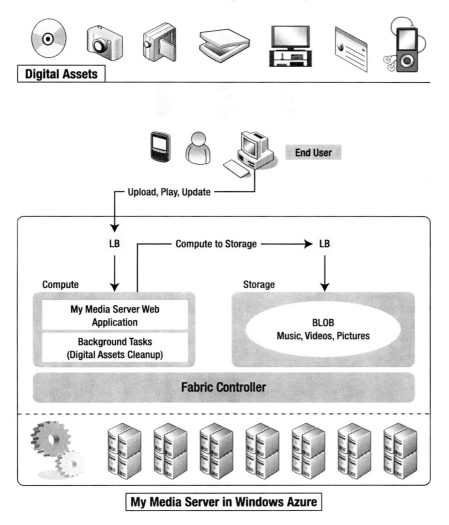

Figure 3-3. A Windows Azure Media Server

Figure 3-3 is a solution specific illustration of Figure 3-2. The Web role is a web application interface for viewing and managing the digital assets stored in Storage services. It also provides some application services like uploading, deleting, updating, and listing of digital assets stored in the Storage service. The Web role application also provides a built-in Silverlight Media Player for accessing the digital assets from your client machine or mobile phone browsers. All the digital assets are stored in the Storage service as blobs. The Worker service does background processing of indexing and cleaning up the digital assets on a periodic basis. Note that this service does not use either tables or queues because the service does not need them.

To keep the discussion simple, I have kept this example at the conceptual, rather than at the physical or logical design, level. In the next section, I will discuss the development environment for Windows Azure so that you can start building your own Windows Azure cloud services like the media storage service discussed here.

Again, the three core services Compute, Storage, and Management combined form the Windows Azure cloud operating system. All the three services abstract the underlying hardware and the operating system infrastructure required for deploying applications in the cloud. The Compute service provides Web and Worker roles that enable running of web and background process applications respectively in Windows Azure. The Storage service offers blob storage, queuing, and table storage capabilities for storing any kind of files, messages, and structured storage in the cloud respectively. The service management interface provides management capabilities to all of your Windows Azure deployments through a single interface. From an architect's perspective, Windows Azure provides most of the features required for designing distributed applications in the cloud.

The Compute Service

As you now know, Compute is one of the core services of Windows Azure. It is also called Hosted Service in Windows Azure portal terminology. In this section, I will cover Windows Azure Compute service and the developer experience associated with it. The Compute service gives you ability to develop and deploy Windows Azure cloud services. The environment consists of an underlying .NET 3.5 Framework (SP1) and IIS 7 running on 64-bit Windows 2008 servers. You can also enable Full Trust in Windows Azure services for developing native applications.

The Windows Azure Compute service is based on a role-based design. To implement a service in Windows Azure, you have to implement one or more roles supported by the service. The current version of Windows Azure supports two roles: Web and Worker.

Web Role

A Web role is a web site or web service that can run in an IIS 7 environment. Most commonly, it will be an ASP.NET web application or a Windows Communications Foundation (WCF) service with HTTP and/or HTTPS endpoints.

■ **Note** Inbound supported protocols are HTTP and HTTPS, and outbound protocols can be any TCP socket. The UDP outbound protocol is not supported at this time in Windows Azure services.

The Web role also supports FastCGI extension module to IIS 7.0. This allows developers to develop web applications in interpreted languages like PHP and native languages like C++. Windows Azure supports Full Trust execution that enables you to run FastCGI web applications in Windows Azure Web role. To run FastCGI applications, you have to set the `enableNativeCodeExecution` attribute of the Web role to `true` in the `ServiceDefinition.csdef` file. In support of FastCGI in the Web role, Windows Azure also introduces a new configuration file called `Web.roleconfig`. This file should exist in the root of the web project and should contain a reference to the FastCGI hosting application, like `php.exe`. In the interest of keeping this book conceptual, I will not be covering FastCGI applications. For more information on enabling FastCGI applications in Windows Azure, please visit the Windows Azure SDK site at `http://msdn.microsoft.com/en-us/library/dd573345.aspx`.

■ **Caution** Even though Windows Azure supports native code execution, the code still runs with Windows user, not administrator, privileges, so some WIN32 APIs that require system administrator privileges will not be accessible

---

Worker Role

The Worker role gives you the ability to run a continuous background process in the cloud. The Worker role can expose internal and external endpoints and also call external interfaces. A Worker role can also communicate with the queue, blob, and table Windows Azure storage services. A Worker role instance runs independently of the Web role instance, even though both of them may be part of the same service. A Worker role runs on a totally different virtual machine than the Web role in the same service. In some Windows Azure services, you may require communication between a Web role and a Worker role. Even though the Web and Worker role expose endpoints for communication among roles, the recommended mode of reliable communication is Windows Azure queues. Web and Worker roles both can access Windows Azure queues for communicating runtime messages. I will cover Windows Azure queues in the next chapter.

A Worker role class must inherit from the `Microsoft.WindowsAzure.ServiceRuntime.RoleEntryPoint` class. `RoleEntryPoint` is an abstract class that defines functions for initializing, starting and stopping the Worker role service. A Worker role can stop either when it is redeployed to another server, or you have executed the Stop action from the Windows Azure developer portal. Figure 3-4 illustrates the sequence diagram for the life cycle of a Worker role.

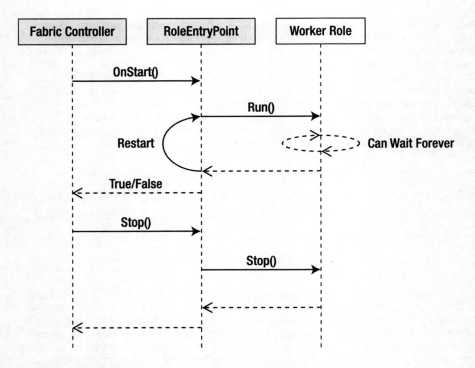

Figure 3-4. *Sequence diagram for a Worker role service*

In Figure 3-4, there are three objects: Fabric Controller, RoleEntryPoint, and a Worker role implementation of your code. Fabric Controller is a conceptual object; it represents the calls that the Windows Azure Fabric Controller makes to a Worker role application. The Fabric Controller calls the Initialize() method on the RoleEntryPoint object. RoleEntryPoint is an abstract class so it does not have its own instance; it is inherited by the Worker role instance to receive calls. The OnStart() method is a virtual method, so it does not need to be implemented in the Worker role class. Typically, you would write initialization code like starting diagnostics service or subscribing to role events in this method. The Worker role starts its application logic in the Run() method. The Run() method should have an continuous loop for continuous operation. If the Run() method returns, the role is restarted by the OnStart() method. If the role is able to start successfully, the OnStart() method returns True to the Fabric Controller; otherwise, it returns False. The Fabric Controller calls the Stop() method to shut down the role when the role is redeployed to another server or you have executed a Stop action from the Windows Azure developer portal.

Windows Azure API Structure

Windows Azure SDK provides a set of APIs to complement the core services offered by Windows Azure. These APIs are installed as a part of Windows Azure SDK and can be used locally for developing

Windows Azure applications. The `Microsoft.WindowsAzure.ServiceRuntime` assembly and namespace consists of classes used for developing applications in the compute service.

The `Microsoft.WindowsAzure.StorageClient` assembly and namespace consists of classes used for developing applications to interact with the storage service. The assembly makes REST calls to the storage service REST interface.

The service management API is exposed as a REST interface, and the `csmanage.exe` application in Windows Azure code samples (`http://code.msdn.microsoft.com/windowsazuresamples`) can be used to call the service management APIs.

Developer Environment

The development environment of Windows Azure consists of two main components: Windows Azure Tools for Visual Studio and the Windows Azure SDK. In this section, I will cover these in detail.

Windows Azure Tools for Visual Studio

Windows Azure Tools for Visual Studio is a Visual Studio extension supporting Windows Azure development. You can download it from the Azure SDK web site `http://www.microsoft.com/azure/sdk.mspx`.

Visual Studio Project Types

The Windows Azure Tools for Visual Studio creates a project type named Cloud Service containing project templates for Web role and Worker role. After you install Windows Azure Tools for Visual Studio, open Visual Studio and create a new Project by selecting File ▸ New ▸ Project. Figure 3-5 shows the New Project Dialog box.

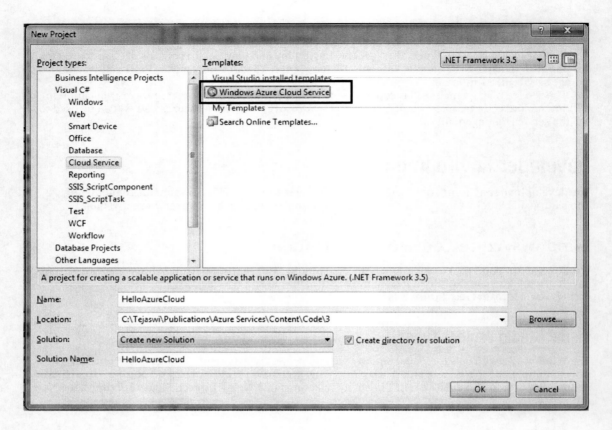

Figure 3-5. *New Project*

The Windows Azure Cloud Service template defines the cloud service project. Click OK to choose from the available roles (see Figure 3-6).

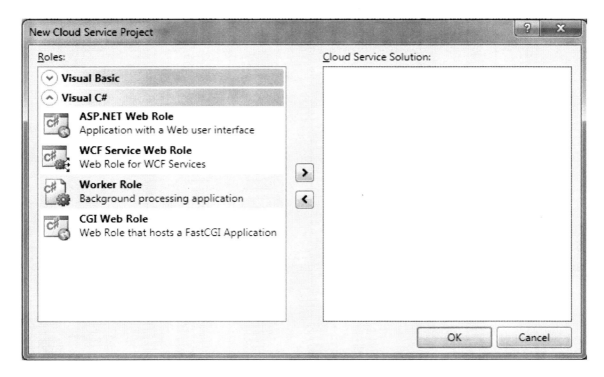

Figure 3-6. *Cloud Service roles*

The available cloud service roles are as follows:

- *ASP.NET Web role*: As the name suggests, this role consists of an ASP.NET project. You can build or migrate any ASP.NET compatible project for deploying to the cloud.

- *WCF Service Web role*: This role consists of a WCF project. You can build or migrate a WCF services in this project for deploying to the cloud.

- *Worker role*: The Worker role project is a background process application. It is analogous to a Windows service. A Worker role has start and stop methods in its superclass and can expose internal and external endpoints for direct access.

- *CGI Web role*: The CGI Web role is a FastCGI-enabled Web role. It does not consist of a Cloud Service project as shown in Figure 3-10.

Choose the roles you want, as shown in Figure 3-7. I have selected a Web role, a WCF Web role, and a Worker role.

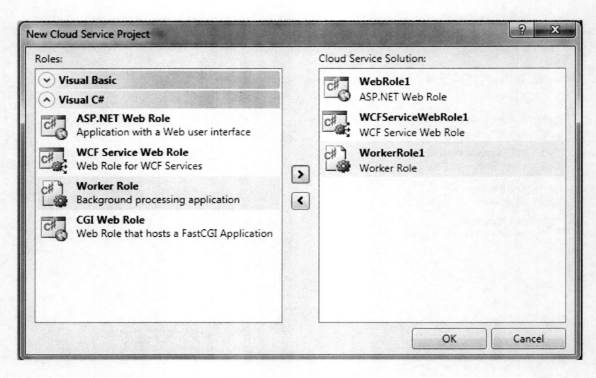

Figure 3-7. *Selected roles*

Click OK to create the cloud service project, as shown in Figure 3-8.

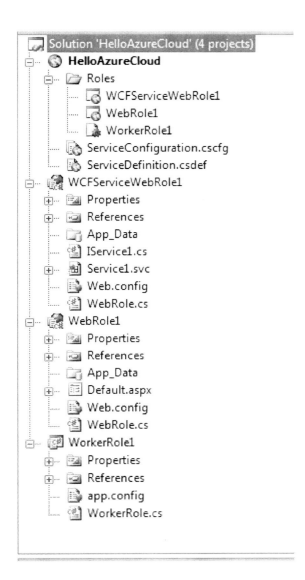

Figure 3-8. Empty cloud service project

In Figure 3-8, the HelloAzueCloud cloud service project holds references in the Roles subfolder to all the role projects in the solution. The cloud service project also contains ServiceDefinition.csdef and ServiceConfiguration.cscfg files that define the configuration settings for all the roles in the cloud service.

The WCF service Web role project includes a sample service and its associated configuration in the we.config file. The WebRole.cs file implements the start and configuration changing events fired by the

Windows Azure platform. This file is created for all the roles with default start and configuration changing event handlers. You can handle additional events like `StatusCheck` and `Stopping` depending on your application needs. The `WebRole` class inherits the `RoleEntryPoint` class from the `Microsoft.WindowsAzure.ServiceRuntime` namespace. The `WebRole.cs` file is analogous to the `Global.asax` file in a traditional ASP.NET application.

The ASP.NET Web role project consists of a `Default.aspx` file and its associated code-behind and `web.config` file.

Finally, the Worker role project consists of `WorkerRole.cs` file and its associated `app.config` file. In addition to inheriting the `RoleEntryPoint` class, it also overrides the `Run()` method in which you add your continuous processing logic. Because a Worker role is not designed to have any external interface by default, it does not contain any ASP.NET or WCF files.

In summary, the cloud service defined in this project consists of a WCF service, an ASP.NET web application, and a Worker role service. The entire package constitutes a Windows Azure cloud service.

■ **Note** In the interest of keeping this book conceptual, I will not be covering FastCGI applications.

Role Settings and Configuration

In the cloud service project, you can configure each role's settings by double-clicking the role reference in the **Roles** subdirectory of the cloud service project. Figure 3-9 shows the role settings page in Visual Studio.

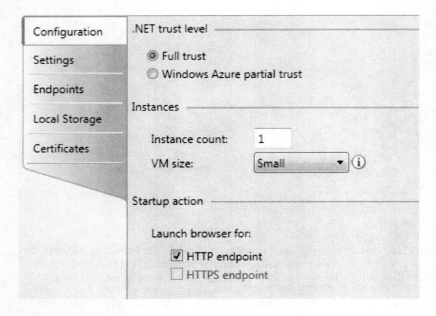

Figure 3-9. Role settings (the default is Configuration)

The role settings page has five tabs: Configuration, Settings, Endpoints, Local Storage, and Certificates.

The Configuration tab is selected by default and displays the following configuration options:

- *.NET Trust Level*: The .NET Trust Level specifies the trust level under which this particular role runs. The two options are Full Trust and Windows Azure Partial Trust. Full Trust options gives the role privileges to access certain machine resources and execute native code. Even in full trust, the role still runs in the standard Windows Azure user's context and not the administrator's context. In the partial trust option, the role runs in a partially trusted environment and does not have privileges for accessing machine resources and native code execution.

- *Instances*: The instance count defines the number of instances of each role you want to run in the cloud. For example, you can run two instances of ASP.NET Web role and one instance of the Worker role for background processing. The two instances of ASP.NET Web role will give you automatic load-balancing across the instances. By default, all the roles run as single instance. This option gives you the ability to scale-up and scale-down your role instances on-demand.

The VM size option gives you the ability to choose from a list of virtual machines preconfigured in the Windows Azure virtual machine pool. You can choose from the following list of predefined virtual machines depending on your deployment needs:

- *Small*: 1 core processor, 1.7GB RAM, 250GB hard disk

- *Medium*: 2 core processors, 3.5GB RAM, 500GB hard disk

- *Large*: 4 core processors, 7GB RAM, 1000GB hard disk

- *Extra large*: 8 core processors, 15GB RAM, 2000GB hard disk

The Web roles have a startup action that defines the endpoint on which the browser should launch. This setting is not a cloud service setting but a project setting for launching the Web role in the development fabric.

The Settings tab, shown in Figure 3-10, defines any custom settings you can add to the role configuration.

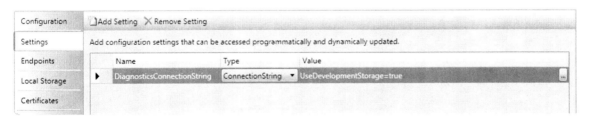

Figure 3-10. *Settings*

These custom name-value pairs are analogous to the name-value `appSettings` in an `app.config` or `web.config` file. You can retrieve the values of these settings in your code by calling the

`RoleEnvironment.GetConfigurationSettingValue.` By default there is a `DiagnosticsConnectionString` setting present which is used for logging from your roles. Do not remove this setting.

The Endpoints tab contains endpoints your role will create when it is deployed. Figure 3-11 shows the Endpoints tab for a Web role and a Worker role respectively.

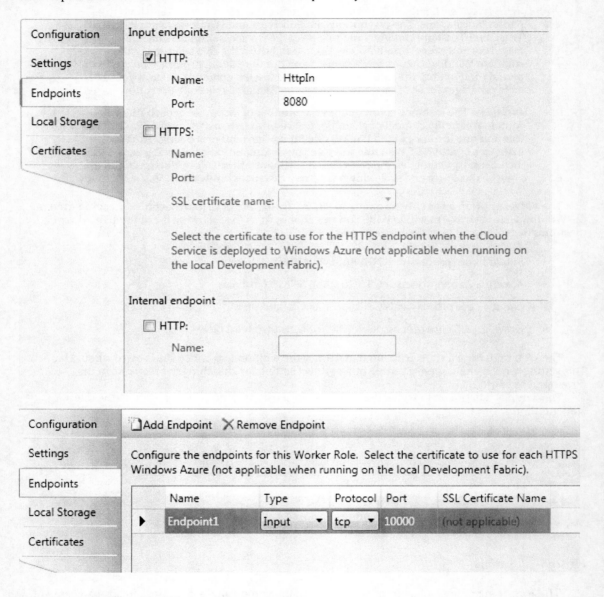

Figure 3-11. *Endpoints tab for Web and Worker roles*

The Web role can have `InputEndpoints` and an internal endpoint. `InputEndpoints` are HTTP or HTTPS endpoints exposed externally. The port number defines the port your will use while accessing the default web page or service in this Web role. In case of an HTTPS endpoint, you can upload the X.509 certificate for accessing the web page or service using an HTTPS encrypted connection.

The internal endpoint is the endpoint accessible to other roles within the cloud service. For example, a Worker role can get a reference to the internal endpoint of a Web role in the same cloud service for making web service method calls to it.

A Worker role has no defined endpoints like a Web role because it is intended to be used as a background process. To define an endpoint, you have to add one to the list and select its type (`input` or `internal`), protocol (tcp, http, https), port, and optionally, an SSL certificate name.

Note that a Web role can have only HTTP or HTTPS endpoints, but a Worker role can have an HTTP, HTTPS, or TCP endpoint.

The LocalStorage tab defines local directories that will be created on the server machine of the role for storing files locally. Figure 3-12 shows the settings on the LocalStorage tab.

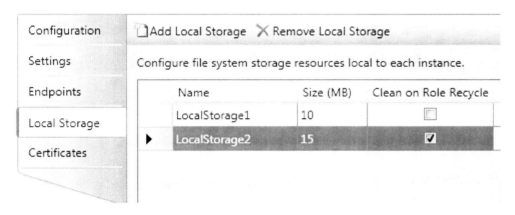

Figure 3-12. *Local storage*

The name of the local storage will be the names of directories created on the server. The size column defines the maximum size of the folder contents and the "Clean on Role Recycle" column defines whether you want the contents of the directory cleaned up when a role recycles. You can use this option for creating sticky storage for maintaining state of the role across reboots and failures. Local storage can be effectively used for temporary caching and session management applications.

The Certificate tab is used for referencing the certificates in your role. At the time of this writing, you still had to use the Windows Azure developer portal or the service management API for uploading the certificate to the server and then reference the certificate in the settings as shown in Figure 3-13.

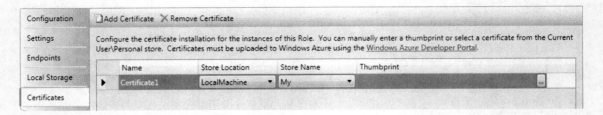

Figure 3-13. *Certificate configuration*

■ **Note** Some of the role settings directly modify the `ServiceDefinition.csdef` and `ServiceConfiguration.cscfg` files, and you can achieve the same configuration effect by directly modifying these files instead.

Visual Studio Project Actions

Once you have created a Windows Azure cloud service project, you can work with the cloud service roles, work with storage services or work on the debug and deployment of the cloud service.

Working with Cloud Service Roles

You can associate an existing Web role or a Worker role from a solution to the cloud service project, or create a new role by right-clicking on the **Roles** subdirectory and selecting Add, as shown in Figure 3-14.

Figure 3-14. *Adding associate roles to cloud service*

By selecting New Web Role or New Worker Role project, you can create a new Web role project in the solution that is associated with the cloud service project. By selecting a Web role or Worker role project in the solution, you can associate an existing project in the solution to the cloud service project. Figure 3-15 shows option for adding a new role to the existing cloud service.

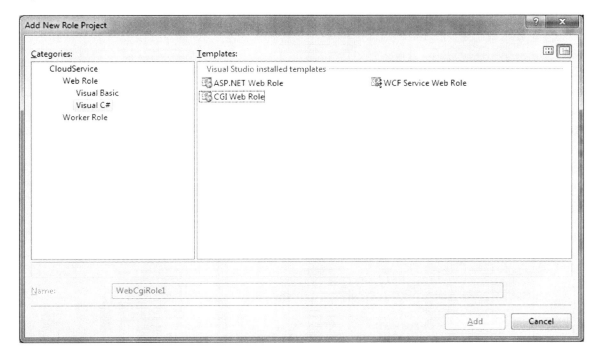

Figure 3-15. *Adding new roles*

Working with Storage Services

The Windows Azure development fabric includes a local storage environment that resembles the cloud storage service. It has development-specific blob, queue, and table services that simulate the ones in the Windows Azure cloud. These services depend on SQL Server 2005 or 2008 database. So, you need to have SQL Server 2005 or 2008 installed on your machine to work with storage services development environment (also called Development Storage).

To start the development storage:

- Select Start ▶ All Programs ▶ Windows Azure SDK ▶ Development Storage, as shown in Figure 3-16.

Figure 3-16. *Development Storage*

When you debug your service within Visual Studio, it starts the development storage, which you can access by right-clicking the Windows Azure system tray icon and selecting Show Development Storage UI. Figures 3-17 and 3-18 illustrate the system tray options and the development storage user interface.

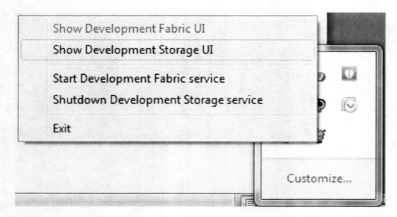

Figure 3-17. *Windows Azure System Tray Options*

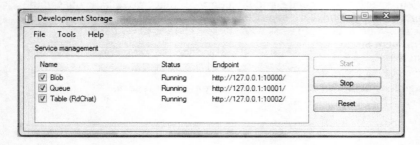

Figure 3-18. *Developer Storage User Interface*

Debugging in Visual Studio .NET

In the Windows Azure Cloud environment, no direct debugging is available. Your only option is logging. But in the development fabric, you can debug by adding breakpoints in the code and by viewing the logging information in the development fabric user interface. Like any typical .NET application, Visual Studio .NET attaches the debugger to the application when run in debug mode in the development fabric. The debugger will break to the breakpoint set in the Web and Worker role projects. In the Windows Azure cloud, Visual Studio debugging environment is not available, so the best option is to log. I will discuss diagnostics and logging later in this chapter. Figure 3-19 illustrates the Development Fabric UI used for logging.

Figure 3-19. *Development Fabric Logging*

■ **Tip** I recommend inserting logging statements to the Windows Azure application right from the beginning. This way, you can debug the application in the development fabric as well as in the Windows Azure cloud without making any code changes.

To enable native code debugging in a Web role project, right-click the Web role project, select Properties, go to the Web tab, and select the "Native code" check box in the Debuggers section, as shown in Figure 3-20.

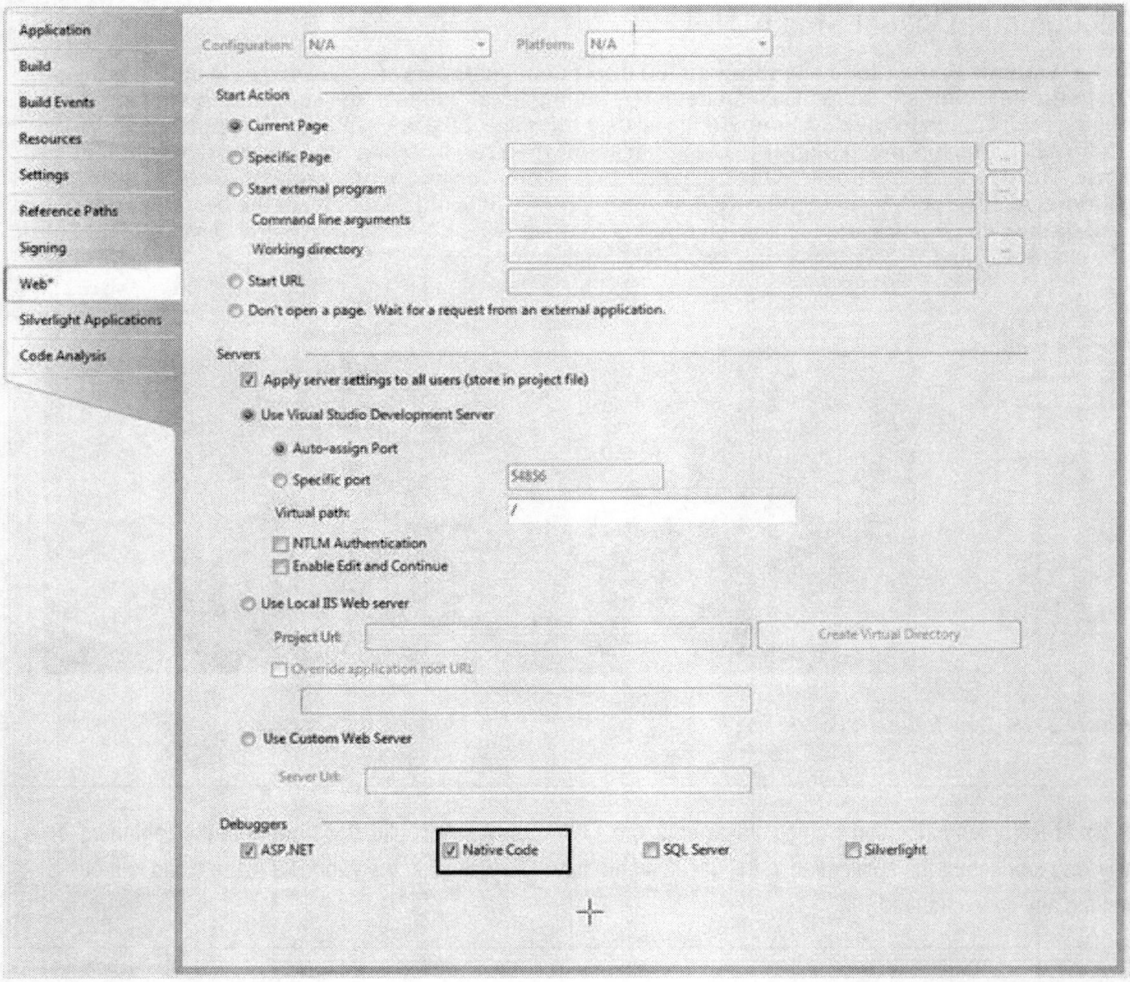

Figure 3-20. Web role unmanaged code debugging

To enable native code debugging in a Worker role project, right-click the Worker role project, select Properties, go to the Debug tab, and select the "Enable unmanaged code debugging" check box, as shown in Figure 3-21.

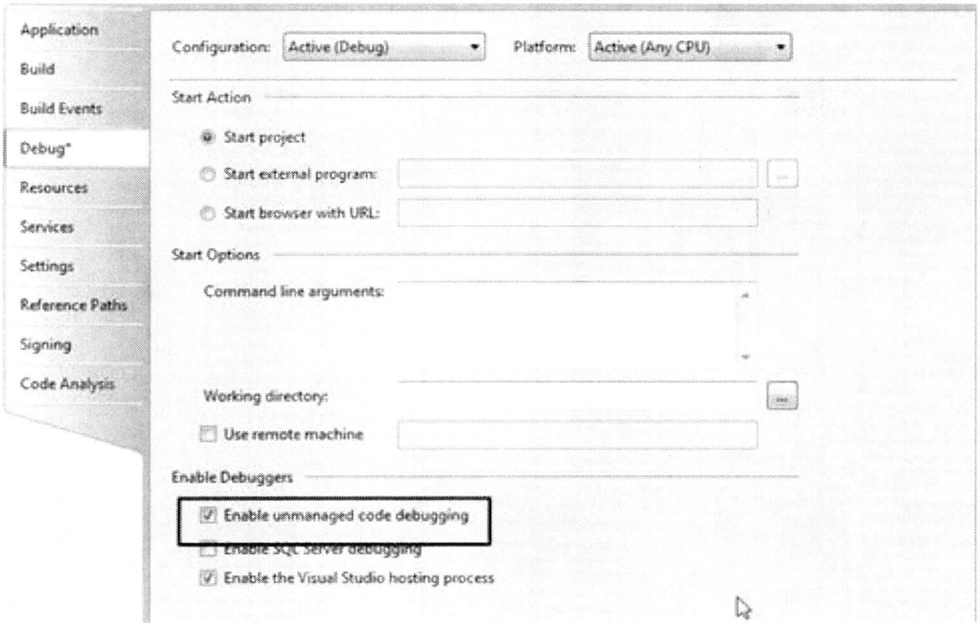

Figure 3-21. Worker role unmanaged code debugging

Packaging the Service

To deploy the Windows Azure cloud service in the cloud, you have to package it into a `.cspkg` file containing all the assemblies and components, and upload the package to Windows Azure developer portal. To package a service, right-click the cloud service project, and select Publish, as shown in Figure 3-22.

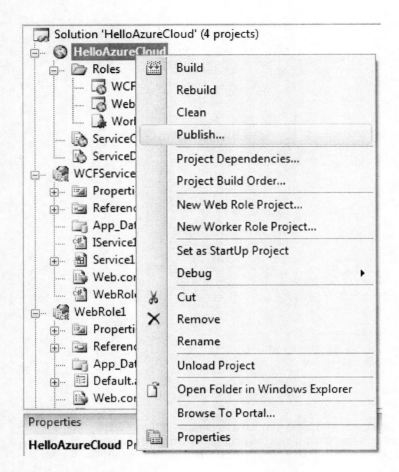

Figure 3-22. *Packaging a Windows Azure service*

When you select Publish, Visual Studio .NET creates two files: `[Service Name].cspkg` and `ServiceConfiguration.cscfg`. It also opens Internet Explorer and takes you to the LiveID sign-in screen to sign into the Windows Azure developer portal. The `[Service Name].cspkg` is the service package containing all the service components required by Windows Azure to run the service in the cloud. The `.cspkg` file is a zip archive, and you can explore its contents by renaming it to `.zip` and extracting it. The `ServiceConfiguration.cscfg` file is the configuration file for the service instances. It is a copy if the `ServiceConfiguration.cscfg` file from the cloud service project.

Windows Azure SDK Tools

The Windows Azure SDK tools are located in the directory `C:\Program Files\Windows Azure SDK\v1.0\bin` for a default Windows Azure installation. Table 3-2 lists the tools included in the Windows Azure SDK.

Table 3-2. Windows Azure SDK Tools

Tool	Description
CSPack.exe	This tool is used to package a service for deployment. It takes in a ServiceDefinition.csdef file and outputs a .cspkg file.
CSRun.exe	This tool deploys a service into the local development fabric. You can also control the run state of the development fabric from this tool. This tool depends on the service directory structure created by the CSPack.exe /copyonly option.
DSInit.exe	This tool initializes the development storage environment. It is automatically called by Visual Studio.NET and DevelopmentStorage.exe when you run a cloud application in the development fabric for the first time.

Service Models

A service model of Windows Azure cloud service consists of two main configuration files: ServiceDefinition.csdef and ServiceConfiguration.cscfg. ServiceDefinition.csdef defines the metadata and configuration settings for the service, and ServiceConfiguration.cscfg sets the values of configuration settings for the runtime instance of the service. The overall service model defines the metadata and configuration parameters and the end state of the service. Windows Azure reads these files when deploying instances of your service in the cloud. You can also modify the service model settings by right-clicking each role in the cloud service project and selecting properties. This is the recommended way of configuring your service manually.

ServiceDefinition.csdef

The ServiceDefinition.csdef files defines the overall structure of the service. It defines the roles available to the service and the service input endpoints. It also defines the configuration settings for the service. The values of these configuration parameters are set in the ServiceConfiguration.cscfg configuration file. Listing 3-1 shows the contents of a ServiceDefinition.csdef file.

Listing 3-1. ServiceDefinition.csdef

```
<?xml version="1.0" encoding="utf-8"?>
<ServiceDefinition name="CloudService1"
xmlns="http://schemas.microsoft.com/ServiceHosting/2008/10/ServiceDefinition">
  <WebRole name="WebRole1">
    <InputEndpoints>
      <InputEndpoint name="HttpIn" protocol="http" port="80" />
    </InputEndpoints>
    <ConfigurationSettings>
      <Setting name="DiagnosticsConnectionString" />
```

```
      </ConfigurationSettings>
    </WebRole>
    <WebRole name="WCFServiceWebRole1">
      <InputEndpoints>
        <InputEndpoint name="HttpIn" protocol="http" port="8080" />
      </InputEndpoints>
      <ConfigurationSettings>
        <Setting name="DiagnosticsConnectionString" />
      </ConfigurationSettings>
      <LocalResources>
       <LocalStorage name="L1" cleanOnRoleRecycle="false" sizeInMB="10" />
      </LocalResources>
      <Certificates>
       <Certificate name="C1" storeLocation="LocalMachine" storeName="My" />
      </Certificates>
  <InternalEndpoint name="InternalHttpIn" protocol="http" />
    </WebRole>
    <WorkerRole name="WorkerRole1" enableNativeCodeExecution="true">
      <ConfigurationSettings>
        <Setting name="DiagnosticsConnectionString" />
      </ConfigurationSettings>
      <Endpoints>
        <InputEndpoint name="Endpoint1" protocol="tcp" port="10000" />
        <InternalEndpoint name="Endpoint2" protocol="tcp" />
      </Endpoints>
      <Certificates>
        <Certificate name="C1" storeLocation="LocalMachine" storeName="My" />
      </Certificates>
    </WorkerRole>
</ServiceDefinition>
```

Listing 3-1 is the service definition for the CloudService1: it has two Web role instances with names WebRole1 and WCFServiceWebRole1, and a Worker role instance with the name WorkerRole1. They also define endpoints, local storage, and certificates. WCFServiceWebRole1 has a <LocalStorage> element that defines the local storage space for the service role. The <ConfigurationSettings> element defines a DiagnosticsConnectionString configuration setting for the service role. The value for the DiagnosticsConnectionString setting is set in ServiceConfiguration.cscfg.

> ▓ **Note** The `ServiceDefinition.csdef` file of a service cannot be changed at run time because it defines the shape and non-changeable parameters of the service. You have to republish the service after changing its `ServiceDefinition.csdef` for the changes to take effect. For more details on the `ServiceDefinition.csdef` schema, please visit `http://msdn.microsoft.com/en-us/library/dd179395.aspx`.

Endpoints

Windows Azure roles can have two types of endpoints: internal and input. The internal endpoints are used for interrole communications within the same cloud service, whereas the input endpoints can be accessed from anywhere. Figure 3-23 illustrates some internal endpoints of Web and Worker roles.

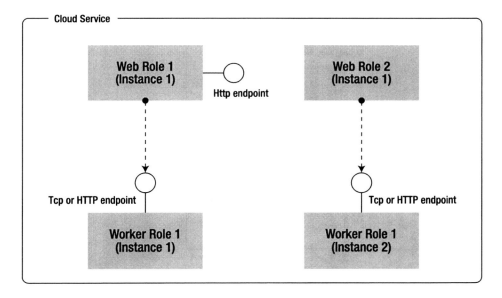

Figure 3-23. Internal endpoints for interrole communication

In Figure 3-23, there are two Web roles with one instance each and two instances of a Worker role. The Worker role exposes an endpoint that is consumed by both the Web roles. Note that each Web role can communicate with the exact instance of the Worker role. The Web role also exposes an HTTP endpoint that can be consumed by any of the roles in the cloud service. The endpoint only publishes the IP address and port of the instance; you still have to write TCP or HTTP code to send and receive requests. You can get a reference to the internal endpoint of an instance as follows:

```
IPEndPoint internale = RoleEnvironment.Roles["HelloWorkerRole"].Instances[0]
.InstanceEndpoints["MyInternalEndpoint"].IPEndpoint;
```

where `HelloWorkerRole` is the name of the Worker role and `MyInternalEndpoint` is the name of the endpoint. You can get the IP address of an internal instance end point in the following manner:

```
string ipaddress = RoleEnvironment.Roles["HelloWorkerRole"].Instances[0]
.InstanceEndpoints["MyInternalEndpoint"].IPEndpoint.ToString();
```

Figure 3-24 illustrates the input endpoints of a Web role and a Worker role.

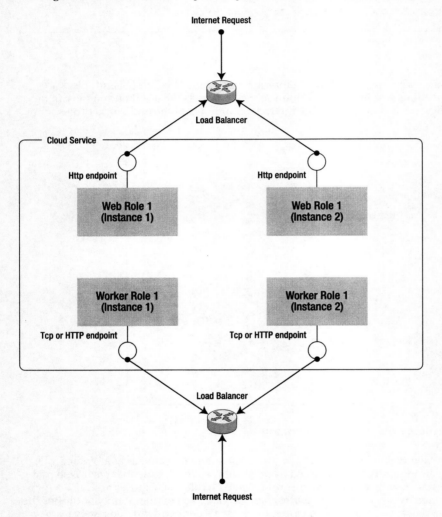

Figure 3-24. Input endpoints for external communication

The Web role instances have default HTTP input endpoints for accepting Internet requests. Windows Azure also allows Worker roles to have HTTP and TCP input endpoints for accepting connections over the Internet. Like the internal endpoint, the access to input endpoint is not limited within the cloud service; any external application can communicate with the input endpoint of the role. In Figure 3-24, Web Role 1 and Worker Role 1 have input endpoints available for communication. Any application can now communicate with endpoints of these roles over the Internet. Because the input endpoints are exposed externally, they are automatically load balanced by Windows Azure between instances. In some documentation, input endpoints are also referred to as external endpoints. You can get a reference to the input endpoint of an instance as follows:

```
IPEndPoint inpute = RoleEnvironment.Roles["HelloWorkerRole"].Instances[0]
.InstanceEndpoints["MyInputEndpoint"].IPEndpoint;
```

where `HelloWorkerRole` is the name of the Worker role and `MyInputEndpoint` is the name of the endpoint. Once you have the `IPEndPoint` object, you can get the IP address and port number of the endpoint to initiate communications.

Local Storage

The `<LocalStorage>` element defines a temporary local storage space for the service role instance on the server running the role instance. It has three attributes: `name`, `cleanOnRoleRecycle`, and `sizeInMb`. The Fabric Controller reserves some space on the server file system of the machine on which the role instance of the service is running. The `name` attribute refers to the directory allocated by the Fabric Controller for storage, and `cleanOnRecycle` specifies whether to clean the contents of the local storage across instance reboots. The `sizeInMb` attribute refers to the amount of space allocated for local storage. The minimum value that `sizeInMb` can take is 1, which is the minimum amount of storage that can be allocated in megabytes. The local storage does not have any relationship with Windows Azure storage services; it is a feature of the Compute service for providing temporary storage space for Web and Worker roles.

Windows Azure runtime provides a static function `LocalResource GetLocalResource (string localResourceName)` in the `Microsoft.WindowsAzure..ServiceRuntime.RoleEnvironment` class to get reference to the `LocalResource` class, which represents the local storage space reserved for the service. The `localResourceName` function parameter is the name of storage space defined as the name attribute of `<LocalStorage>` element. In Listing 3-1, I am allocating a space of 10MB for the storage space named `L1` on local machine of the service role instance. I can now get a reference to the local storage space by calling the function `LocalResource resource = RoleEnvironment.GetLocalResource("L1");`

■ **Caution** Local storage space allocated on the local machine is local for that instance. If the `cleanOnRoleRecycle` attribute is set to `false`, the data from local directory will be lost on role recycle. So, while developing applications, you should consider local storage purely for unreliable caching purposes with data loss checks built into the application.

Full Trust Execution

By default, Windows Azure applications run under full trust in the cloud environment. When running under partial trust, the code has access only to limited resources and libraries. When running under full trust, cloud services can access certain system resources and can call managed assemblies as well as native code. To enable Full Trust in your application, set the enableNativeCodeExecution attribute of the `<WebRole>` or `<WorkerRole>` element in the ServiceDefinition.csdef file to true:

```
<WebRole name="<role name>" enableNativeCodeExecution="true|false">
```

Table 3-3 lists the permissions for a cloud application role running in partial and full trust execution modes.

Table 3-3. *Partial and Full Trust Permissions*

Resource	Partial Trust	Full Trust
Call managed code assemblies	Assemblies with AllowPartiallyTrustedCallers attribute	All assemblies
System registry	No access	Read access to HKEY_CLASSES_ROOT HKEY_LOCAL_MACHINE HKEY_USERS HKEY_CURRENT_CONFIG
32-bit P/Invoke	Not supported	Not supported
64-bit P/Invoke	Not supported	Supported
32-bit native subprocess	Not supported	Supported
64-bit native subprocess	Not supported	Supported
Local storage	Full access	Full access
System root and its subdirectories	No access	No access
Windows (e.g., C:\Windows) and its subdirectories	No access	Read access
Machine configuration files	No access	No access
Service configuration file (ServiceConfiguration.cscfg)	Read access	Read access

---

■ **Note** You can find more information on the Windows Azure partial trust policy in the Windows Azure SDK documentation at `http://msdn.microsoft.com/en-us/library/dd573355.aspx` .

Table 3-3 clearly shows that in partial trust you cannot call native code and the access to the machine resources are limited. Even in full trust execution, the access has been limited to prevent any system-related damage. Partial trust application roles can call only managed code assemblies that have `AllowPartiallyTrustedCallers` attribute, whereas a full trust application role can all any managed code assembly. A partial trust application role cannot make any P/Invoke native calls. A full trust application role can make P/Invoke calls to a 64-bit library. P/Invoke calls to a 32-bit library are not directly supported in Windows Azure. Instead, you could spawn a 32-bit subprocess from your application role and make P/Invoke calls to 32-bit library from within that subprocess. The system root directory (usually `C:\Windows\system32`) is not accessible in Windows Azure. A full trust application role has only read access to the Windows directory (usually `C:\Windows`). Both, full and partial trust roles have full access to the local storage. Local storage is the recommended temporary file and data storage for Windows Azure applications.

■ **Caution** The resource access works differently in the Windows Azure cloud and the development fabric. In the Windows Azure cloud, the application role runs under the privileges of a standard Windows Azure account, whereas the application role in the development fabric runs under the logged-in user account. So, the application role running in the local development fabric may behave differently to the same application role running in the Windows Azure cloud environment.

Certificate Management

In Windows Azure, you can use certificates not only for encrypting the HTTPS endpoints of your web and Worker roles but also for custom message level encryption. You can upload X.509 certificated to your Windows Azure service either from the Windows Azure portal or using the service management API. You can upload any number of certificates for the service and these certificates will be installed in the Windows certificate stores of the role instances.

Once a certificate is uploaded to the service, it can be referenced in the `ServiceDefinition.csdef` and `ServiceConfiguration.cscfg`. The `ServiceDefinition.csdef` defines the name, store location, and store name of the certificate on the instance as shown here:

```
<Certificate name="C1" storeLocation="LocalMachine" storeName="My" />
```

The `ServiceConfiguration.cscfg` file defines the thumbprint and the thumbprint algorithm of the certificate as shown here.

```
<Certificate name="Certificate1" thumbprint="5CA27AF00E1759396Cxxxxxxxxxxxxxxx"
thumbprintAlgorithm="sha1" />
```

ServiceConfiguration.cscfg

The `ServiceConfiguration.cscfg` file contains the values for the configuration parameters that apply to one or more instance of the service. You can have one configuration file per instance of the service or multiple instances can share the same configuration file. Listing 3-2 shows the contents of the `ServiceConfiguration.cscfg` file corresponding to the `ServiceDefinition.csdef` file from Listing 3-1.

Listing 3-2. *ServiceConfiguration.cscfg*

```
<?xml version="1.0"?>
<ServiceConfiguration serviceName="HelloAzureCloud"
xmlns="http://schemas.microsoft.com/ServiceHosting/2008/10/ServiceConfiguration">
  <Role name="WebRole1">
    <Instances count="1" />
    <ConfigurationSettings>
      <Setting name="DiagnosticsConnectionString"
        value="UseDevelopmentStorage=true" />
    </ConfigurationSettings>
  </Role>
  <Role name="WCFServiceWebRole1">
    <Instances count="1" />
    <ConfigurationSettings>
      <Setting name="DiagnosticsConnectionString"
        value="UseDevelopmentStorage=true" />
    </ConfigurationSettings>
    <Certificates>
      <Certificate name="C1" thumbprint="xxxx"
        thumbprintAlgorithm="sha1" />
    </Certificates>
  </Role>
  <Role name="WorkerRole1">
    <Instances count="1" />
    <ConfigurationSettings>
      <Setting name="DiagnosticsConnectionString"
        value="UseDevelopmentStorage=true" />
    </ConfigurationSettings>
    <Certificates>
      <Certificate name="C1"
        thumbprint="xxxx" thumbprintAlgorithm="sha1" />
    </Certificates>
  </Role>
</ServiceConfiguration>
```

In Listing 3-2, there are three roles defined, two Web roles and a Worker role. Each role one has only one instance.

■ **Note** For more details on the `ServiceConfiguration.cscfg` schema, please visit
http://msdn.microsoft.com/en-us/library/dd179389.aspx.

Configuration Settings

If you are a .NET developer, you should be familiar with the `web.config` and `app.config` files for .NET applications. These files define different kinds of runtime settings for the application. In these files, you can also create custom configuration settings, like database connection strings and web service URLs, to avoid hard-coding values. Similarly, Windows Azure allows you to create configuration settings in the `ServiceDefinition.csdef` and `ServiceConfiguration.cscfg` files. In `ServiceDefinition.csdef`, you define the configuration setting names for the entire service, and in `ServiceConfiguration.cscfg`, you set the values for these settings. Therefore, for every `ConfigurationSetting` defined in `ServiceDefinition.csdef`, there should be an equivalent value in the `ServiceConfiguration.cscfg` file. Listing 3-3 shows the definition of the `ConfigurationSettings` in `ServiceDefinition.csdef`, and Listing 3-4 shows the values of `ConfigurationSettings` in `ServiceConfiguration.cscfg`. Note the elements highlighted in bold.

***Listing 3-3.** ConfigurationSettings Definition in ServiceDefinition.csdef*

```
<?xml version="1.0" encoding="utf-8"?>
<ServiceDefinition name=" MyCloudService "
xmlns="http://schemas.microsoft.com/ServiceHosting/2008/10/ServiceDefinition">
  <WebRole name="WebRole">
    <ConfigurationSettings>
      <Setting name="AccountName"/>
      <Setting name="AccountSharedKey"/>
      <Setting name="BlobStorageEndpoint"/>
      <Setting name="QueueStorageEndpoint"/>
      <Setting name="TableStorageEndpoint"/>
      <Setting name="ContainerName"/>
    </ConfigurationSettings>
    <InputEndpoints>
      <InputEndpoint name="HttpIn" protocol="http" port="80" />
    </InputEndpoints>
  </WebRole>
</ServiceDefinition>
```

***Listing 3-4.** ConfigurationSettings Values in ServiceConfiguration.cscfg*

```
<?xml version="1.0"?>
<ServiceConfiguration serviceName="MyCloudService"
xmlns="http://schemas.microsoft.com/ServiceHosting/2008/10/ServiceConfiguration">
  <Role name="WebRole">
    <Instances count="1"/>
    <ConfigurationSettings>
      <Setting name="AccountName" value="devstoreaccount1" />
```

```
        <Setting name="AccountSharedKey" value="Eby8vdM02xNOcqFlqUwJPLlmEtlCDXJ10UzF" />
        <Setting name="BlobStorageEndpoint" value="http://127.0.0.1:10000"/>
        <Setting name="QueueStorageEndpoint" value="http://127.0.0.1:10001"/>
        <Setting name="TableStorageEndpoint" value="http://127.0.0.1:10002/" />
        <Setting name="ContainerName" value="XXXgallery"/>
      </ConfigurationSettings>
    </Role>
</ServiceConfiguration>
```

In Listing 3-3, I have defined six configuration setting names: `AccountName`, `AccoundSharedKey`, `BlobStorageEndPoint`, `QueueStorageEndPoint`, `TableStorageEndPoint`, and `ContainerName` for the `WebRole` service, and in Listing 3-4, I am setting the values of these setting names.

Web.config versus ServiceConfiguration.cscfg

The `web.config` file is the configuration file for an ASP.NET web application. It defines the behavior of the ASP.NET application and also custom configuration setting values. Configuration setting values in `web.config`, or `app.config` for that matter, cannot be dynamically changed at runtime and made available to the application without redeploying the application. Similarly, the ASP.NET behavior defined in a `web.config` file cannot be included in a `ServiceConfiguration.cscfg` file.

`ServiceConfiguration.cscfg` is meant purely for storing configuration setting values used by the service at runtime; it is not meant to define the behavior of the ASP.NET runtime or the .NET Runtime. `ServiceConfiguration.cscfg` is the configuration file for one or more instances of a Windows Azure service deployed in the cloud. You can change the configuration values in `ServiceConfiguration.cscfg` at runtime, and they will be available to the application without redeploying the application to the cloud.

Development Fabric

The development fabric simulates the Windows Azure cloud runtime environment on your local machine. The development fabric is specifically designed for development and testing in your local environment. You cannot attach a development fabric with the Windows Azure cloud service. The development fabric user interface can be started in any of the following manners:

- By debugging or running a cloud service from within Visual Studio.NET
- By running `CSRun.exe` from the command line with valid parameters
- By running `DFUI.exe` from the Windows Azure SDK `bin` directory
- From the Windows Azure SDK programs Start menu

Once the development fabric starts, you can access it from the development fabric system tray icon. Figure 3-25 illustrates the development fabric user interface hosting a cloud service.

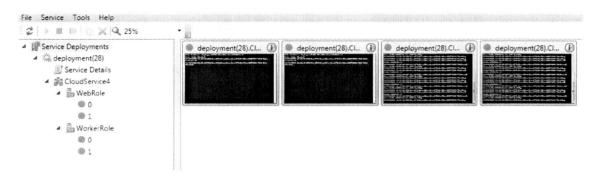

Figure 3-25. *Development fabric UI*

The development fabric UI shows the service deployments in the local environment and allows you to alter the state of a running service. You can run, suspend, restart or remove a service deployment from within the development fabric UI.

Figure 3-25 shows CloudService4 service running with two instances of the Web role and two instances of the Worker role. The console windows on the right-hand side correspond to each instance of the deployed service. The console window depicts the state and health of the instance and displays any logging information that the instance outputs. The Service Details node displays the Service Name, Interface Type, URL, and IP Address for the service. When the development fabric starts a service, it first tries to use the TCP port for the input endpoint mentioned in the `ServiceDefinition.csdef` file, but if the port is not available, it uses the next available TCP port. Therefore, in some cases, the port on which the input endpoint is running may be different to the port in the `ServiceDefinition.csdef` file.

In the development fabric, you can attach a debugger to the running instance at runtime by right-clicking one of the instance and selecting Attach Debugger, as shown in Figure 3-26.

Figure 3-26. *Development fabric's Attach Debugger button*

The development fabric UI will give you the option of selecting the available debuggers on the local machine. It also allows you to set the logging levels at the service, role, and instance levels. The logging levels are accessible either from the Tools menu or by right-clicking the appropriate node. The Tools ➤ Open Local Storage option opens the Local Storage location on the local machine. The name and size of the local storage is optionally specified in the `ServiceDefinition.csdef` file as `<WebRole> <LocalStorage name="<name>" sizeInMb="<n>" /></WebRole>`. The `sizeInMB` is optional and the minimum allocated value is 1MB.

Development Storage

Development storage simulates the Windows Azure blobs, queues, and table storage services on your local computer. The development storage environment is specifically designed for development and testing on the local machine and therefore has several limitations compared to the Windows Azure storage services in the cloud. Development storage provides a user interface to start, stop, reset, and view the local storage services, as shown in Figure 3-27.

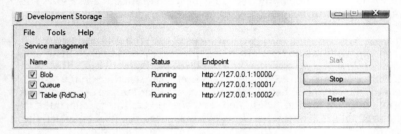

Figure 3-27. *Development storage UI*

Figure 3-27 shows the name of the service, its status, and the endpoint it is listening on. From Tools ▶ Table Service Properties, you can change the database to be used by the table storage service.

The development storage environment depends on the SQL Server 2005/2008 database instance on the local machine and by default is configured for SQL Server Express 2005/2008 databases. You can change the development storage to point to another database using the `DSInit.exe` tool that you saw in Table 3-2, with a `/sqlInstance` parameter.

▓ **Note** Use SQL instance name without the server qualifier or use . (a point) for the default instance. To see all the parameters for `DSInit.exe`, go to the `devstore` directory of the Windows Azure SDK installation, and run `DSInit.exe /?` from the command prompt.

Table 3-4 lists some key limitations of development storage compared to Windows Azure cloud storage.

Table 3-4. *Development Storage Limitations*

Attribute	Limitation
Authentication	Development storage only supports a single fixed developer account with a well-known authentication key. (See below).
Encryption	Development storage does not support HTTPS.
Scalability	Development storage is not designed to support a large number of concurrent clients. You should use development storage only for functional testing, not for performance or stress testing.
Flexibility	In the CTP version of Windows Azure, the development table storage required a fixed schema to be created before using the table service. The cloud table service did not have this constraint. You can use the table service directly without configuring the schema. The development storage does not require fixed schema any more. String properties in the development table cannot exceed 1,000 characters.
Size	The development blob service supports only 2GB of storage, whereas the cloud blob supports 50GB of storage.

In the case of authentication, the account name and account key are as follows:
Account name: `devstoreaccount1`
Account key:
`Eby8vdM02xNOcqFlqUwJPLlmEtlCDXJ1OUzFT50uSRZ6IFsuFq2UVErCz4I6tq/K1SZFPTOtr/KBHBeksoGMGw==`

■ **Caution** Before deploying a storage service application to Windows Azure cloud, please make sure to change the development account information to your cloud account. You should not use the development storage account to access the Windows Azure storage service in the cloud.

Diagnostics

Logging support in the cloud is one of the biggest concerns of the developer community. With highly interactive integrated design environment (IDE) tools like Visual Studio.NET and runtime environments like the .NET Framework, you can pinpoint problems in you code even in deployed environments when applications are running on-premise. However, the Visual Studio.NET domain is limited to the access it has to the application's runtime environment. Visual Studio.NET communicates with the runtime environment of the application to gather debug information of the application. The application needs to have debug symbols loaded in runtime for Visual Studio.NET to debug. The Windows Azure development fabric has access to the local runtime environment, so you can debug your local Windows Azure application like any other .NET application by adding breakpoints.

Unfortunately, the Windows Azure cloud environment is inaccessible to the local Visual Studio.NET environment. Once the service is deployed to Windows Azure, it is totally managed by Windows Azure, and you do not have access to its runtime. The Windows Azure team realized this and has added logging capabilities to the Windows Azure runtime. The diagnostics service runs along with your role instance, collects diagnostics data as per the configuration, and can save the data to your Windows Azure storage service if configured to do so. You can also communicate with the diagnostics service remotely from an on-premise application or configure it to persist the diagnostics data on a periodic basis. The diagnostics service supports logging of the following data types from your cloud service:

- *Windows Azure logs*: These are the application logs that you dump from your application. These can be any messages emitted from your code.

- *Diagnostic monitor logs*: These logs are about the diagnostics service itself.

- *Windows event logs*: These are the Windows event logs generated on the machine on which the role instance is running.

- *Windows performance counters*: These refer to the subscriptions to the performance counters on the machine on which the role instance is running

- *IIS logs and failed request traces*: These are the IIS logs and the IIS failed request traces generated on the Web role instance.

- *Application crash dumps*: These are the crash dumps generated when an application crashes.

The diagnostics gathering model in Windows Azure consists of two fundamental steps—configuration and management. In the configuration step, you configure the diagnostics service with all the data types you are interested in collecting the diagnostics information on, and then the diagnostics service starts collecting the data for the configured data types accordingly. In the management step, you use the diagnostics management API provided by the Windows Azure SDK for changing the configuration of an already running diagnostics service, and the diagnostics service will reconfigure itself for collecting the appropriate data. You can use the diagnostics management API from outside of the Windows Azure cloud environment (e.g., on-premise) to interact with the diagnostics service on your role instance. Next, using the same API, you can perform scheduled or on-demand transfers of the diagnostics information from role instance machines to your Windows Azure storage account.

In this book, I will focus only on the Windows Azure logs data type, because it relates directly to the development of Windows Azure services. I will provide some examples of the rest of the data types, but will not be discussing those in detail in this book. For more information on these data types, please refer to the diagnostics API in Windows Azure SDK documentation. The diagnostics API is present in the `Microsoft.WindowsAzure.Diagnostics` assembly.

■ **Note** You can find more information about the Windows Azure Runtime API at the Windows Azure MSDN reference site: `http://msdn.microsoft.com/en-us/library/dd179380.aspx`.

Logging

Windows Azure Runtime API consists of a managed code library and an unmanaged code library. In this book, I will cover only the managed code library. The managed code library namespace for diagnostics is `Microsoft.WindowsAzure.Diagnostics`. Associating diagnostics with you cloud service is a three step process:

1. Configure the trace listener.

2. Define the storage location for the diagnostics service.

3. Start the diagnostics service.

Configuring the Trace Listener

When you create a new role using the role templates template in Visual Studio.NET, the `app.config` and `web.config` files get created automatically in the role project and it consists of a trace listener provider, as shown in Listing 3-5.

Listing 3-5. *Diagnostics Trace Listener Configuration*

```
<system.diagnostics>
<trace>
 <listeners>
   <add type=
"Microsoft.WindowsAzure.Diagnostics.DiagnosticMonitorTraceListener,
Microsoft.WindowsAzure.Diagnostics, Version=1.0.0.0, Culture=neutral,
PublicKeyToken=31bf3856ad364e35"
name="AzureDiagnostics">
<filter type="" />
      </add>
  </listeners>
 </trace>
</system.diagnostics>
```

The `DiagnosticMonitorTraceListener` enables you to use the .NET Tracing API for logging within the code. You can use the `Write()` and `WriteLine()` methods of the `System.Diagnostics.Trace` class for logging from your code as shown here:

```
Trace.WriteLine("INFORMATION LOG", "Information");
Trace.WriteLine("CRITICAL LOG", "Critical");
```

Defining the Storage Location for the Diagnostics Service

In the `ServiceDefinition.csdef` and `ServiceConfiguration.cscfg` files, you have to define the diagnostics connection string pointing to the storage location of your choice (development storage or cloud storage). Visual Studio automatically generates this configuration for you as shown in Listing 3-6.

Listing 3-6. Diagnostics Connection String Configuration

For development storage:
```
<ConfigurationSettings>
 <Setting name="DiagnosticsConnectionString" value = "UseDevelopmentStorage=true"/>
</ConfigurationSettings>
```
For cloud storage:
```
<ConfigurationSettings>
 <Setting name="DiagnosticsConnectionString" value=
"DefaultEndpointsProtocol=https;AccountName=proazurestorage;AccountKey=[YOURKEY]"/>
</ConfigurationSettings>
```

Starting the Diagnostics Service

Next, you have to start the diagnostics service in your role by passing in the connection string name you defined in step 2. If you create a role using the Visual Studio role templates, the `WebRole.cs/WorkerRole.cs` files contain the code for starting the diagnostics service in the `OnStart()` method, `DiagnosticMonitor.Start("DiagnosticsConnectionString");`.

Once started, the diagnostics monitoring service can start collecting the logged data. You can also choose to further configure the diagnostics service through the `DiagnosticMonitorConfiguration` class, as shown in Listing 3-7.

Listing 3-7. Programmatically Changing the Diagnostics Configuration

```
//Get the default configuration
DiagnosticMonitorConfiguration dmc = DiagnosticMonitor.GetDefaultInitialConfiguration();
//Set the schedule to transfer logs every 10 mins to the storage
dmc.Logs.ScheduledTransferPeriod = TimeSpan.FromMinutes(10);
//Start Diagnostics Monitor with the storage account configuration
DiagnosticMonitor.Start("DiagnosticsConnectionString",dmc);
```

In Listing 3-7, the diagnostics monitor is started with the configuration option to transfer logs to the defined storage every 10 minutes automatically.

▦ **Tip** When designing cloud applications, it is important to design diagnostics and logs reporting right from the beginning. This will save you a lot of debugging time and help you create a high quality application.

Developing Windows Azure Services with Inter-role Communication

In this example, you will learn to develop Windows Azure services in the local development fabric and in the cloud environment. I will also show you how to communicate across roles using the internal endpoints. You will also learn to use your own Configuration Settings in `ServiceDefinition.csdef` and `ServiceConfiguration.cscfg`.

Objectives

The objectives of this example are as follows:

- Understand inter-role communication in Windows Azure cloud services.
- Access local machine resources.
- Understand configuration settings for configuring cloud services.

Adding Diagnostics and Inter-role Communication

In this section, I will guide you through the code for adding diagnostics, configuration and inter-role communication to the Windows Azure services.

1. Open `Ch3Solution.sln` from Chapter 3's source code directory
2. Expand the `HelloService` folder as shown in Figure 3-28.

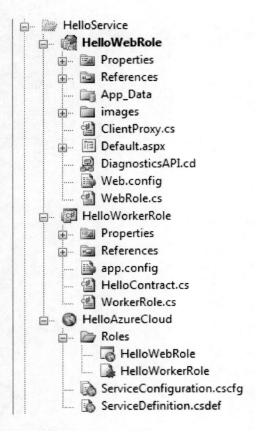

Figure 3-28. HelloService folder

The folder contains one Web role, one Worker role, and one cloud service project: HelloWebRole, HelloWorkerRole, and HelloAzureCloud cloud service respectively.

Service Model

The `ServiceDefinition.csdef` and `ServiceConfiguration.cscfg` file define the service model and configuration values for the service. Listing 3-8 shows the `ServiceDefinition.csdef` for the HelloAzureCloud service.

Listing 3-8. ServiceDefinition.csdef for the HelloAzureCloud Service

```
<?xml version="1.0" encoding="utf-8"?>
<ServiceDefinition name="HelloAzureCloud"
xmlns="http://schemas.microsoft.com/ServiceHosting/2008/10/ServiceDefinition">
  <WebRole name="HelloWebRole" enableNativeCodeExecution="true">
```

```
<LocalResources>
  <LocalStorage name="HelloAzureWorldLocalCache" sizeInMB="10" />
</LocalResources>
  <InputEndpoints>
    <InputEndpoint name="HttpIn" protocol="http" port="80" />
  </InputEndpoints>
  <ConfigurationSettings>
    <Setting name="DiagnosticsConnectionString" />
    <!--This is the current logging level of the service -->
    <Setting name="LogLevel" />
    <Setting name="ThrowExceptions" />
    <Setting name="EnableOnScreenLogging" />
  </ConfigurationSettings>
</WebRole>
<WorkerRole name="HelloWorkerRole" enableNativeCodeExecution="true">
  <Endpoints>
    <!-- Defines an internal endpoint for inter-role communication
that can be used to communicate between worker or Web role instances -->
    <InternalEndpoint name="MyInternalEndpoint" protocol="tcp" />
    <!-- This is an external endpoint that allows a role to listen
 on external communication, this could be TCP, HTTP or HTTPS -->
    <InputEndpoint name="MyExternalEndpoint" port="9001" protocol="tcp" />
  </Endpoints>
  <ConfigurationSettings>
    <Setting name="DiagnosticsConnectionString" />
  </ConfigurationSettings>
</WorkerRole>
</ServiceDefinition>
```

The service model defines an external HTTP endpoint (input endpoint) for the HelloWebRole listening on port 80 and an internal as well as external endpoints for the HelloWorkerRole. HelloWebRole also defines a local storage named HelloAzureWorldLocalCache with maximum size of 10MB. Both the roles define a configuration setting named `DiagnosticsConnectionString` for diagnostics. Listing 3-9 shows the `ServiceConfiguration.cscfg` file for the HelloAzureCloud service.

Listing 3-9. *ServiceConfiguration.cscfg for the HelloAzureCloud Service*

```
<?xml version="1.0"?>
<ServiceConfiguration serviceName="HelloAzureCloud"
xmlns="http://schemas.microsoft.com/ServiceHosting/2008/10/ServiceConfiguration">
  <Role name="HelloWebRole">
    <Instances count="2" />
    <ConfigurationSettings>
      <Setting name="DiagnosticsConnectionString"
value="DefaultEndpointsProtocol=https;AccountName=proazurestorage;AccountKey=Ry " />
      <!--This is the current logging level of the service -->
      <!--Supported Values are Critical,
      Error,Warning,Information,Verbose-->
      <Setting name="LogLevel" value="Information" />
      <Setting name="ThrowExceptions" value="true" />
```

```
      <Setting name="EnableOnScreenLogging" value="true" />
    </ConfigurationSettings>
  </Role>
  <Role name="HelloWorkerRole">
    <Instances count="1" />
    <ConfigurationSettings>
      <Setting name="DiagnosticsConnectionString"
value="DefaultEndpointsProtocol=https;AccountName=proazurestorage;AccountKey=Ry " />
    </ConfigurationSettings>
  </Role>
</ServiceConfiguration>
```

The `ServiceConfiguration.cscfg` file defines the values for the model you defined in
`ServiceDefinition.csdef`. In addition, it also allow you to define the number of instances for you role in
the instances element. In Listing 3-9, two instances of the Web role and one instance of the Worker role
are running. Also note that the diagnostics is pointing to a cloud storage account named
proazurestorage. You must replace this with your own storage account or simple set its value to
`UseDevelopmentStorage=true` to use the development storage.

Worker Role

HelloWorkerRole implements two methods, `OnStart()` and `Run()`. In the `OnStart()` method, it also
subscribes to the role changing event to catch any configuration changes.

■ **Note** In both the Web and the Worker roles, you need to add references to the following assemblies:
`Microsoft.WindowsAzue.ServiceRuntime.dll` and `Microsoft.WindowsAzure.Diagnostics.dll`. And you need
to add the following using statements in code: using `Microsoft.WindowsAzue.ServiceRuntime`; and using
`Microsoft.WindowsAzure.Diagnostics;`.

Listing 3-10 shows the code for the `HelloWorkerRole` class.

Listing 3-10. *HelloWorkerRole*

```
public override void Run()
{
  Trace.WriteLine("HelloWorkerRole entry point called", "Information");
  var internalEndpoint =
RoleEnvironment.CurrentRoleInstance.InstanceEndpoints["MyInternalEndpoint"];
  var wcfAddress = new
Uri(String.Format("net.tcp://{0}",internalEndpoint.IPEndpoint.ToString()));
  Trace.WriteLine(wcfAddress.ToString());
  var wcfHost = new ServiceHost(typeof(HelloServiceImpl), wcfAddress);
  var binding = new NetTcpBinding(SecurityMode.None);
  wcfHost.AddServiceEndpoint(typeof(IHelloService), binding, "helloservice");
```

```
  try
  {
    wcfHost.Open();
    while (true)
    {
      Thread.Sleep(10000);
      Trace.WriteLine("Working", "Information");
    }
  }
  finally
  {
    wcfHost.Close();

  }
}

public override bool OnStart()
{
  //Get the default configuration
DiagnosticMonitorConfiguration dmc = DiagnosticMonitor.GetDefaultInitialConfiguration();
//Set the schedule to transfer logs every 10 mins to the storage
dmc.Logs.ScheduledTransferPeriod = TimeSpan.FromMinutes(10);
//Start Diagnostics Monitor with the storage account configuration
DiagnosticMonitor.Start("DiagnosticsConnectionString",dmc);

  RoleEnvironment.Changing += RoleEnvironmentChanging;
  return base.OnStart();
}

private void RoleEnvironmentChanging(object sender,
RoleEnvironmentChangingEventArgs e)
{
  if (e.Changes.Any(change => change is RoleEnvironmentConfigurationSettingChange))
  e.Cancel = true;
}
```

The OnStart() method starts the diagnostics service with a scheduled log transfer to the storage and also subscribes to the Changing event of the Windows Azure runtime to detect any changes to the configuration. You can use the RoleEnvironmentChanging event to capture the following changes:

- RoleEnvironmentConfigurationSettingChange to detect the changes in the service configuration.

- RoleEnvironmentTopologyChange to detect the changes to the role instances in the service.

In addition, you can remove a role instance from the load-balancer after the service has started by subscribing the RoleEnvironment.StatucCheck event and calling SetBusy() method on the RoleInstanceStatusCheckEventArgs. You can also request a recycle of the role instance on-demand by calling the RoleEnvironment.RequestRecycle() method. For more information on runtime API, please

149

see the `Microsoft.WindowsAzure.ServiceRuntime` namespace in the Windows Azure SDK class documentation.

Because the diagnostics service is configured to save all the logs to the Windows Azure storage, all the `Trace.WriteLine()` statements will be sent to the storage periodically. The `Run()` method gets a reference to the internal endpoint named `MyInternalEndpoint` from the service definition and retrieves its IP address and creates a WCF service host for the `HelloServiceImpl`. Once the WCF host is opened on the internal IP address and port, any role in the service can make WCF method calls. Listing 3-11 shows the code for `IHelloService` and `HelloServiceImpl`.

Listing 3-11. Hello Contract

```
[ServiceContract (Namespace="http://proazure/helloservice")]
    interface IHelloService
    {
        [OperationContract]
        string GetMyIp();
        [OperationContract]
        string GetHostName();


    }
    [ServiceBehavior(AddressFilterMode=AddressFilterMode.Any)]
    public class HelloServiceImpl : IHelloService
    {


        #region IHelloService Members

        public string GetMyIp()
        {
            IPAddress[] ips = null;

            ips = Dns.GetHostAddresses(Dns.GetHostName());

            if (ips != null)
            {
                foreach (IPAddress i in ips)
                {
                    if(i.AddressFamily ==
System.Net.Sockets.AddressFamily.InterNetwork)
                    return i.ToString(); ;
                }

            }

            return "";
        }

        #endregion
```

```
public string GetHostName()
{
    return Dns.GetHostName();
}

}
```

The `IHelloService` interface defines only two methods to retrieve the IP address and the domain name of the machine on which the Worker role is running. `HelloServiceImpl` class implements these two methods.

Web Role

The user interface for the Web role is in `Default.aspx`. The user interface is designed to do a few operations when you click the Get Machine Info button. Figure 3-29 illustrates the user interface design of `Default.aspx` page.

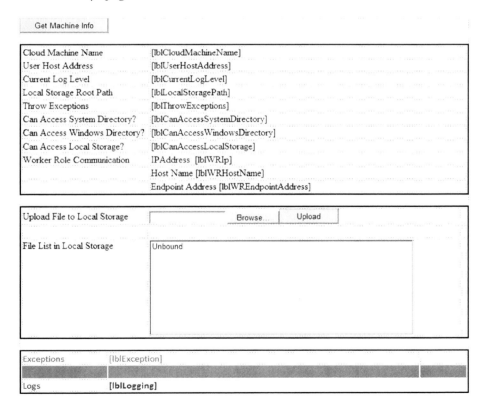

Figure 3-29. *Default.aspx User Interface Design*

When you click the Get Machine Info button, it retrieves the machine name, host address, and local storage and calls the HelloWorkerRole service through an internal endpoint. You can also upload a file to the local storage using the upload file button. All the functions use traditional .NET APIs for retrieving local file and network information of the machine. If you are developing the service from scratch, you will have to add reference to the HelloWorkRole WCF service. In the HelloWebRole project, the reference has already been added for you in the `ClientProxy.cs` file. Listing 3-12 shows the code for calling the HelloWorkerRole WCF service

Listing 3-12. Call Worker Role WCF Service

```
string wrIp =  RoleEnvironment.Roles["HelloWorkerRole"].Instances[0].
InstanceEndpoints["MyInternalEndpoint"].IPEndpoint.ToString();
lblWREndpointAddress.Text = wrIp;
var serviceAddress = new Uri(String.Format("net.tcp://{0}/{1}", wrIp, "helloservice"));
var endpointAddress = new EndpointAddress(serviceAddress);
var binding = new NetTcpBinding(SecurityMode.None);
var client = new ClientProxy(binding, endpointAddress);
lblWRHostName.Text = client.GetHostName();
lblWRIp.Text = client.GetMyIp();
```

In Listing 3-12, the Web role gets reference to the internal endpoint of a Worker role instance and instantiates the `ClientProxy` object to call the `IHelloService` methods `GetHostName()` and `GetMyIp()`.

▦ **Note** An important point to note here is that the endpoints are exposed as IP address of the instance and you still have to build your server in the form of `TcpListener`, WCF service, or HTTP service on that IP address.

Running the HelloAzureCloud Service

To build and run the solution, press F5 on the HelloAzureCloud project to start it in debug mode. Click the Get Machine Info button. Figure 3-30 illustrates the HelloAzureCloud Web role application running on the local machine.

Get Machine Info	
Cloud Machine Name	TREDKARTHINKPAD
User Host Address	127.0.0.1
Current Log Level	Information
Local Storage Root Path	C:\Users\tredkar\AppData\Local\dftmp\s0\deployment(188)\res\deployment(188)\HelloAzureCloud\HelloWebRole.0\directory\HelloAzureWorldLocalCache\
Throw Exceptions	True
Can Access System Directory?	true C:\Windows\system32
Can Access Windows Directory?	true C:\Windows
Can Access Local Storage?	true
Worker Role Communication	IPAddress 192.168.10.58
	Host Name TREDKARTHINKPAD
	Endpoint Address 127.0.0.1:5113

Upload File to Local Storage		Browse...	Upload
File List in Local Storage	0006052cyG7.jpg		

Logs
LOG>On screen logging Setting is True
LOG>Root Path is C:\Users\tredkar\AppData\Local\dftmp\s0\deployment(188)\res\deployment(188).HelloAzureCloud.HelloWebRole.0\directory\HelloAzureWorldLocalCache\
LOG>On screen logging Setting is True
LOG>Root Path is C:\Users\tredkar\AppData\Local\dftmp\s0\deployment(188)\res\deployment(188).HelloAzureCloud.HelloWebRole.0\directory\HelloAzureWorldLocalCache\

Figure 3-30. HelloAzureCloud on local machine

Open the development fabric UI by clicking the development fabric icon in the system tray. Figure 3-31 shows the development fabric UI running two instances of the Web role and one instance of the Worker role.

Figure 3-31. HelloAzureCloud development fabric two instances

153

The information is logged either in the console of instance 0 or instance 1 depending on where the load balancer sends the request. If you click the Get Machine Info button very quickly, you will see that the request gets load balanced across both the instances. Figure 3-32 shows the load-balanced requests across two instances of the Web role application.

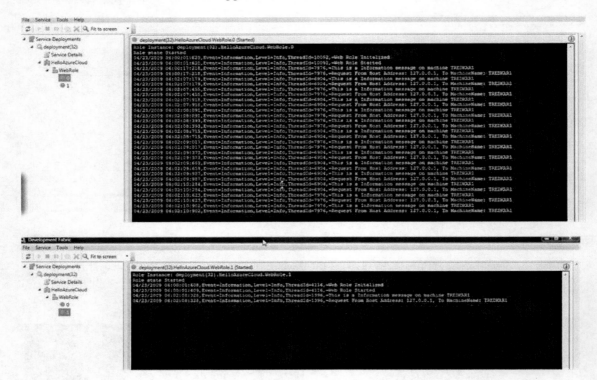

Figure 3-32. *Load Balance across two instances of HelloAzureCloud service*

In Figure 3-32, observe the logs in the consoles of both the instances of HelloAzureCloud Web roles.

Now that you have tested the cloud service in the development fabric, you can deploy it in the Windows Azure cloud. When you deploy the application in the cloud, the consoles that you see in the development fabric are not available to visually view the logs. So, let's see how you can access and view these logs in the cloud.

To deploy HelloAzureCloud service to Windows Azure, right-click on the HelloAzureCloud project, and select Publish to create the service package `HelloAzureCloud.cspkg` as shown in the Figure 3-33.

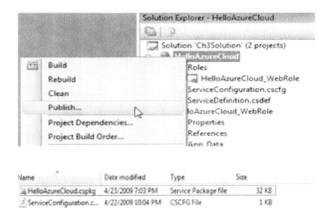

Figure 3-33. *Publish to Windows Azure*

To upload the service package to Windows Azure, you will need to login to Windows Azure developer portal using your LiveID. Once you've logged in, go to the HelloWindowsAzure project that you created in Chapter 2. If you did not create a project in Chapter 2, create a new project by following steps from the Chapter 2 example.

On the project page, click the Deploy button in the staging environment as shown in Figure 3-34.

Figure 3-34. *Deploy to Windows Azure Staging*

On the Staging Deployment page, browse to the `HelloAzureCloud.cspkg` that was created when you published the cloud service from Visual Studio.NET. Next, browse to the `ServiceConfiguration.cscfg` file that was created along with `HelloAzureCloud.cspkg`.

Label the deployment as Hello Azure Service, as shown in Figure 3-35.

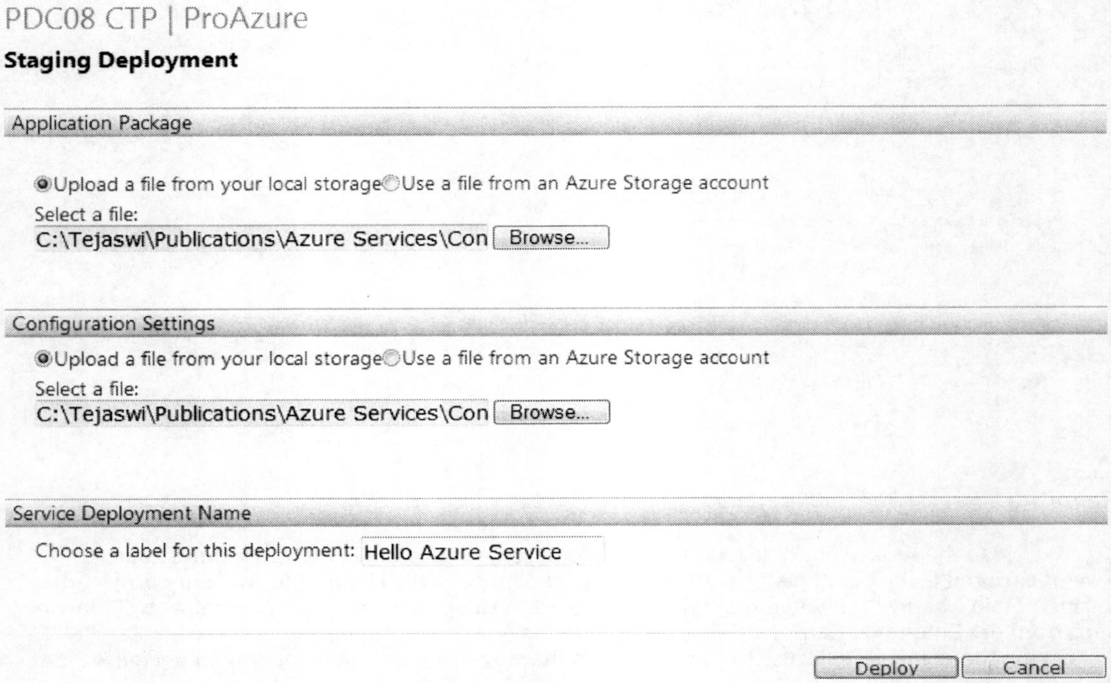

PDC08 CTP | ProAzure
Staging Deployment

Application Package

◉Upload a file from your local storage◯Use a file from an Azure Storage account

Select a file:

C:\Tejaswi\Publications\Azure Services\Con [Browse...]

Configuration Settings

◉Upload a file from your local storage◯Use a file from an Azure Storage account

Select a file:

C:\Tejaswi\Publications\Azure Services\Con [Browse...]

Service Deployment Name

Choose a label for this deployment: Hello Azure Service

[Deploy] [Cancel]

Figure 3-35. *Deploying the service package to staging*

When the package gets deployed, the staging environment cube image will change its color to blue, as shown in Figure 3-36.

Web Site URL:
http://c3b6591b25f54d3fb32c4e8d28467b60.cloudapp.net/

Deployment ID:
c3b6591b25f54d3fb32c4e8d28467b60

Figure 3-36. *Deployed staging environment*

The diagnostic features in Windows Azure allows you to store the logs to a Windows Azure storage or local development storage. The Windows Azure logs generated using the `System.Diagnostics.Trace` class are by default stored in Windows Azure storage tables. In the above example, the logs are configured to be automatically copied to table storage every 10 minutes. To view the logs of your application in Windows Azure table storage, you will need a storage account. You can create a new storage project from the Windows Azure developer portal and configure the diagnostics connection string in the HelloAzureCloud service to point to the storage account.

If you don't have a storage service already created in Windows Azure, go to All Services page, and click New Service as shown in Figure 3-37.

Figure 3-37. Create a new service

On the "Create a new service component" page, select Storage Account, as shown in Figure 3-38.

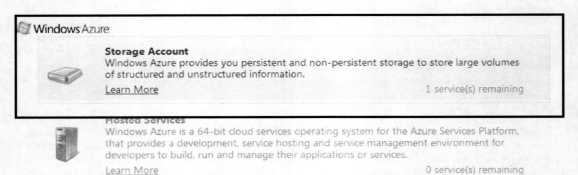

Figure 3-38. Create a new storage account

On the Project Properties page, label the project Pro Azure Storage, give it some description, and click Next, as shown in Figure 3-39.

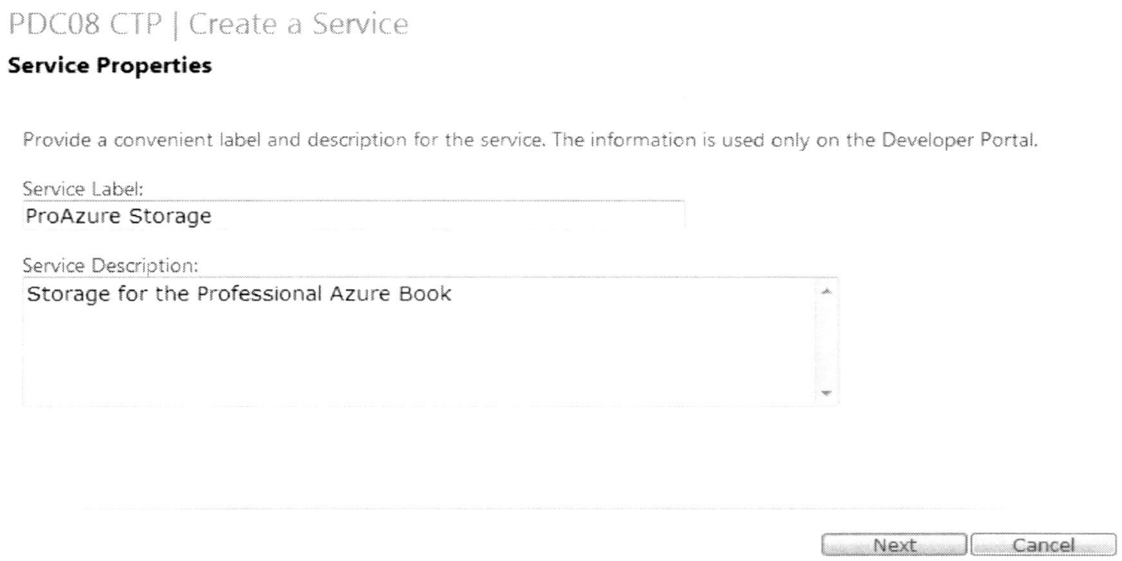

PDC08 CTP | Create a Service

Service Properties

Provide a convenient label and description for the service. The information is used only on the Developer Portal.

Service Label:

ProAzure Storage

Service Description:

Storage for the Professional Azure Book

Next   Cancel

Figure 3-39. *ProAzureStorage Project Properties*

Next create a storage account URL, as shown in Figure 3-40.

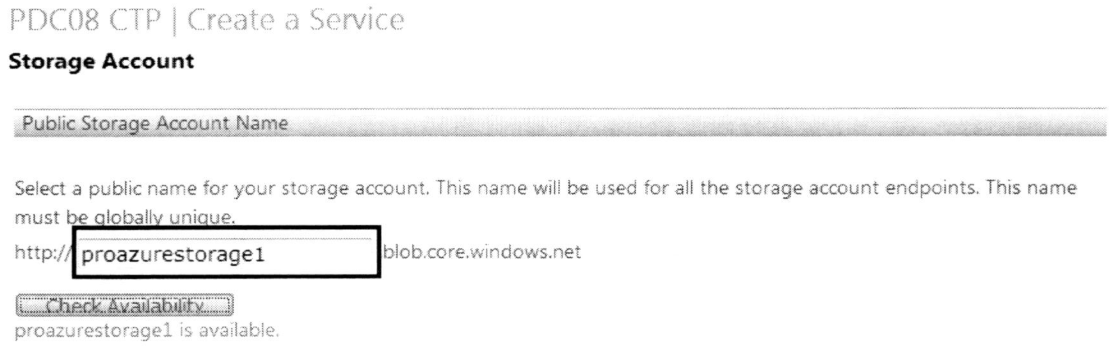

PDC08 CTP | Create a Service

Storage Account

Public Storage Account Name

Select a public name for your storage account. This name will be used for all the storage account endpoints. This name must be globally unique.

http:// proazurestorage1 blob.core.windows.net

Check Availability
proazurestorage1 is available.

Figure 3-40. *Create a storage account URL*

■ **Note** Your name should be globally unique. If there is a project already named proazurestorage, you should choose a different name; you can click Check Availability for its availability.

Once you create the storage account, you will be taken to a page that displays endpoints to blob, queue, and table storage as shown in Figure 3-41. For the purpose of this example, we don't need these URLs.

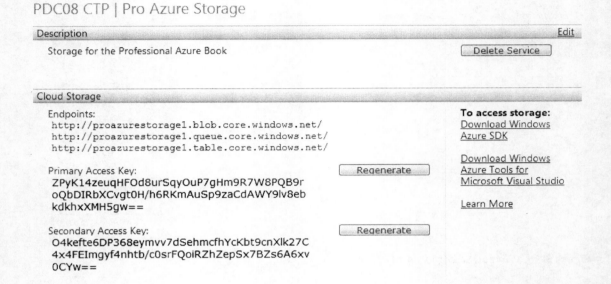

Figure 3-41. *ProAzureStorage Storage Page*

Now that you have the storage created, you can configure the HelloAzureCloud service diagnostics to point to this storage account.

To start the HelloAzure cloud service, go back to the HelloAzureCloud Windows Azure page, and click the Run button in the staging environment to run the web application

When the state of the staging deployment changes from Initializing to Started, click the Web Site URL to test the web application, as shown in Figure 3-42.

Staging
Hello Azure Service

[Upgrade...] [Suspend] [Configure...]
[Delete]

HelloWebRole: **HelloWorkerRole:**
✓ Ready   2 ✓ Ready   1

Web Site URL:
http://c3b6591b25f54d3fb32c4e8d28467b60.cloudapp.net/

Deployment ID:
c3b6591b25f54d3fb32c4e8d28467b60

Figure 3-42. *Start the staging application*

The Default.aspx for the web application shows up in a separate browser window, as shown in Figure 3-43.

Get Machine Info

Cloud Machine Name	RD00155D312B2F
User Host Address	24.130.250.116
Current Log Level	Information
Local Storage Root Path	C:\Resources\directory\c3b6591b25f54d3fb32c4e8d28467b60.HelloWebRole.HelloAzureWorldLocalCache\
Throw Exceptions	True
Can Access System Directory?	true.D:\windows\system32
Can Access Windows Directory?	true.D:\windows
Can Access Local Storage?	true
Worker Role Communication	IPAddress 10.115.99.153
	Host Name RD00155D312542
	Endpoint Address 10.115.99.153:20002

Upload File to Local Storage		Browse...	Upload
File List in Local Storage	0003052cyG7.jpg		

Logs
LOG>On screen logging Setting is True
LOG>Root Path is C:\Resources\directory\c3b6591b25f54d3fb32c4e8d28467b60.HelloWebRole.HelloAzureWorldLocalCache\
LOG>On screen logging Setting is True
LOG>Root Path is C:\Resources\directory\c3b6591b25f54d3fb32c4e8d28467b60.HelloWebRole.HelloAzureWorldLocalCache\
LOG>This is a Information message on machine RD00155D312B2F
LOG>Can access Local Storage?
LOG>Created File C:\Resources\directory\c3b6591b25f54d3fb32c4e8d28467b60.HelloWebRole.HelloAzureWorldLocalCache\proazure.txt
LOG>Wrote in File C:\Resources\directory\c3b6591b25f54d3fb32c4e8d28467b60.HelloWebRole.HelloAzureWorldLocalCache\proazure.txt
LOG>Deleting File C:\Resources\directory\c3b6591b25f54d3fb32c4e8d28467b60.HelloWebRole.HelloAzureWorldLocalCache\proazure.txt
LOG>Deleted File C:\Resources\directory\c3b6591b25f54d3fb32c4e8d28467b60.HelloWebRole.HelloAzureWorldLocalCache\proazure.txt
LOG>Can access System Directory?

Figure 3-43. HelloAzureCloud with Logging

Compare the values generated by the page when you click Get Machine Info with the values generated in the development environment.

■ **Tip** Keep a watch on the machine name as you test your web application. It changes depending on the instance that you request goes to. Currently, the web application is running with two instances.

Now that the logs are copied to the table storage, we should be able to access them using the Windows Azure Table Storage API. There is a nice windows client application called Azure Storage Explorer that I usually use to explore blob storage. The Azure Storage Explorer is free and is available on CodePlex.

■ **Note** Azure Storage Explorer can be downloaded at `http://azurestorageexplorer.codeplex.com/`.

Download, install, and run Azure Storage Explorer using the executable **AzureStorageExplorer.exe**. Go to Tools ▶ Manage Storage Accounts to enter your Account Name and Account Key, and click Save, as shown in the Figure 3-44.

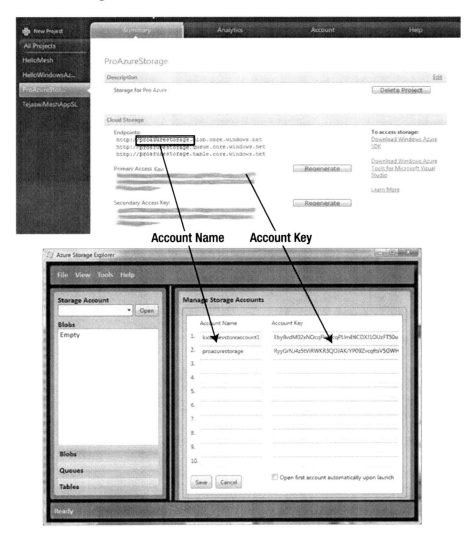

Figure 3-44. Enter account Name in Azure Storage Explorer

The account name is the first word in the blob URL string,
`http://<accountName>.table.core.windows.net`. In Figure 3-44, `proazurestorage` is the account name.

■ **Caution** A common mistake is to enter an account label instead of an account name. Account label is the label of the project. In many cases, the label and name may be the same, depending on how the account was created. However, the account name is always the first word in the blob URL.

Note that the first account in the Accounts list is the local development storage account.

To see the logs in development storage, open development storage in Azure Storage Explorer, click the Tables tab, and click WADLogsTable to see the list of log entries, as shown in Figure 3-45.

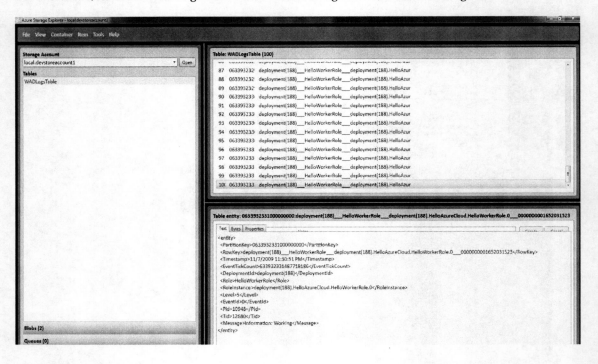

Figure 3-45. Explore logs

Developing a Web Role to Worker Role Message Exchange

In this example, you will develop a Worker role service that calls a Windows Communications Foundation (WCF) service hosted in a Web role. Even though there is interaction between the two roles, I have kept the cloud service at a conceptual level and attempted to cover most of the topics covered in the chapter so far.

Objectives

The objectives of this example are as follows:

- Understand Windows Azure Worker role development.
- Understand configuration settings for Windows Azure applications.
- Work with local storage.
- Host a WCF service in a Web role.
- Call a Web role WCF service from a Worker role.

Service Architecture

The message exchange service between the Web and Worker roles is a role monitoring service. It displays the system properties of the Windows Azure roles running in your Windows Azure cloud service. For example, if your service has two Worker role instances and one Web role instances, then these roles will register with the central Web role application that displays the system properties of all the three roles. Figure 3-46 illustrates the application architecture for this example.

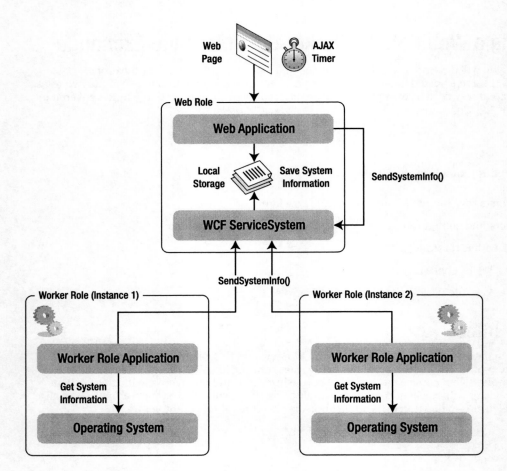

Figure 3-46. *Application architecture*

The service consists of a cloud service project with one Web role application and one Worker role application. The Web role has two logical components—the web application and the SystemInfo WCF service. The SystemInfo WCF service receives system information messages from the Web role instance as well as Worker role instances. The SystemInfo WCF service saves these messages to the local storage of the Web role. The ASP.NET page reads the stored messages from the local storage and displays them in a GridView control. The SystemInfo WCF service and the ASP.NET web application both run in the same Web role instance and thus share the same local storage. The web page has an AJAX timer that refreshes the web page periodically for displaying the latest information from the local storage.

The Worker role has one main logical component, the Worker role service. The Worker role service reads the system information from the underlying operating system it is running on and calls the SystemInfo WCF service in the Web role periodically to send the latest information.

System Information Message

The system information message is the data contract between the Windows Azure roles and the SystemInfo WCF service. The system information message is a dataset object that is exchanged between the Windows Azure roles and the SystemInfo WCF service. Any role instance running in Windows Azure can send a System Information message to the SystemInfo WCF service by calling the WCF method SendSystemInfo(SystemMessageExchange ds). Figure 3-47 illustrates the dataset table schema exchanged between the Windows Azure roles and the SystemInfo WCF service.

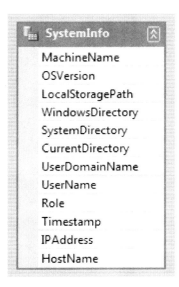

Figure 3-47. *System Information Message*

The system information dataset consists of the fields described in Table 3-5.

Table 3-5. *System Information Dataset Fields*

Field Name	Description
MachineName	This is the name of the underlying machine the role instance is running on. I am using the `System.Environment.MachineName` property for retrieving the machine name.
OSVersion	This is the version of the underlying operating system the role instance is running on. I am using the `System.Environment.OSVersion.VersionString` property for retrieving the version of the operating system.
LocalStoragePath	This is the actual path of the local storage in the underlying operating system. I am using `Microsoft.ServiceHosting.ServiceRuntime.ILocalResource.RootPath` property to retrieve the local storage path.
WindowsDirectory	This is the windows operating system directory. Usually, this maps to `C:\Windows` on most of the operating system installations. I am using the `System.Environment.GetEnvironmentVariable("windir");` method for retrieving the Windows directory path of the underlying operating system instance.
SystemDirectory	This is the system directory of the underlying Windows operating system. I am using the `System.Environment.SystemDirectory` property for retrieving the system directory path of the underlying operating system instance.
CurrentDirectory	The current directory is the path of the current working directory in the underlying Windows operating system. I am using `System.Environment.CurrentDirectory` property for retrieving the current working directory in the underlying operating system instance.
UserDomainName	This is the network domain name associated with the current logged in user. I am using `System.Environment.UserDomainName` property for receiving the user domain name.
UserName	This is the user name of the current logged in user. I am using `System.Environment.UserName` property for retrieving the user name.
Role	This is the role type of the service instance (i.e., Web or Worker).
Timestamp	This is the system message object creation timestamp.

The Components of the Solution

In this section, I will go over the different components of the solution and some key methods.

The Visual Studio.NET solution for this example is called `Ch3Solution.sln`. It can be found in the Chapter 3 source directory. Open the `Ch3Solution.sln` file in Visual Studio.NET. The projects that are referenced in this example are `ProAzureCommonLib`, `WebWorkerExchange`, `WebWorkerExchange_WebRole`, and `WebWorkerExchange_WorkerRole`. Table 3-6 describes the role of each project in the service architecture.

Table 3-6. *Visual Studio.NET Projects*

Project Name	Description
ProAzureCommonLib	This is a class library project that consists of helper classes and methods for logging, configuration, and local storage. It also contains the definition for the `SystemMessageExchange.xsd` dataset for sending system information to the SystemInfo WCF service.
WebWorkerExchange	This is the cloud service project that has the `ServiceDefinition.csdef` and `ServiceConfiguration.cscfg` files. This project also contains references to the Web role and the Worker role projects in the solution.
WebWorkerExchange_WebRole	This is the Web role project that contains the SystemInfo WCF service and the ASP.NET web page for displaying the system information of the role instances.
WebWorkerExchange_WorkerRole	This is the Worker role project that calls the SystemInfo WCF service for sending the System Information.

Figure 3-48 illustrates the four projects in Visual Studio.NET Solution Explorer.

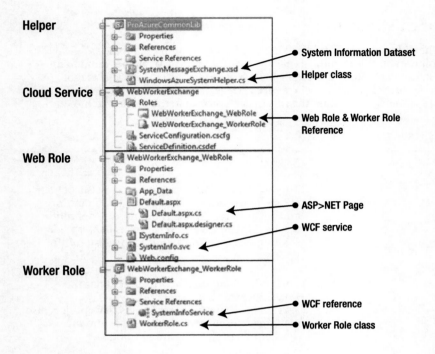

Figure 3-48. *Visual Studio.NET projects*

Now, let's go over each project to explore the implementation of classes and functions.

Creating the ProAzureCommonLib Class Library Project

The **ProAzureCommonLib** project is a class library project containing two main files relevant to this example—WindowsAzureSystemHelper.cs and SystemMessageExchange.xsd. WindowsAzureSystemHelper.cs consists of a class WindowsAzureSystemHelper with all static helper methods. SystemMessageExchange.xsd is the dataset that defines the contract between the role instances and the WCF service. It was discussed previously in the "System Information Message" section. WindowsAzureSystemHelper class has four main sections of helper methods for logging, configuration, local storage, and system information.

Logging

The logging section has two helper methods wrapping over the Trace.WriteLine() function. Listing 3-13 shows the LogError() and LogInfo() helper methods used in the application.

Listing 3-13. Logging Helper Methods

```
public static void LogError(string message)
{
Trace.WriteLine(String.Format("{0} on machine {1}", message,
Environment.MachineName), "Error");

}
public static void LogInfo(string message)
{
Trace.WriteLine(String.Format("{0} on machine {1}", message,
Environment.MachineName), "Information");
}
```

The LogError() and LogInfo() methods accept a string message parameter that is logged using the Trace.WriteLine() method. I also append System.Environment.MachineName property to the message for ease of readability if you are looking at logs from multiple machines.

▪ **Note** You need native code access to read the System.Environment.MachineName property from either the Web or Worker role. In the ServiceDefinition.csdef file, set enableNativeCodeExecution = true for both the roles.

Configuration

The configuration section consists of helper methods for reading the configuration values from SystemConfiguration.cscfg file. The helper methods act as a wrapper over RoleEnvironment.GetConfigurationSettingValue() method and return data type specific values. Listing 3-14 shows the configuration helper method for retrieving a Boolean configuration value.

Listing 3-14. Configuration Helper Method

```
public static bool GetBooleanConfigurationValue(string configName)
{
        try
        {
                bool ret;
                if (bool.TryParse
                (RoleEnvironment.GetConfigurationSettingValue(configName), out ret))
                {
                return ret;
                }
                else
                {
                LogError(String.Format
```

```
                    ("Could not parse value for configuration setting {0}", configName));

                    throw new Exception
                    (String.Format("Could not parse value for configuration setting {0}",
                    configName));
                    }
            }
            catch (Exception ex)
            {
            LogError(ex.Message);
            throw ex;
            }
}
```

The GetBooleanConfigurationValue() method accepts a configuration name and converts the string value returned by RoleEnvironment.GetConfigurationSettingValue() method to a Boolean value. The method also logs errors appropriately if the conversion fails. In the configuration section, there are similar helper functions for retrieving string, integer and double configuration values.

Local Storage

The local storage section contains helper methods for accessing Windows Azure local storage. Local storage is a file system directory on the server on which a particular role instance is running on. The contents of the local storage are not persistent across instance failures and restarts because the role may be redeployed to another virtual machine due to a failure or a restart. Listing 3-15 shows two static helper methods used for accessing the local storage.

Listing 3-15. *Local Storage Access Methods*

```
public static string GetLocalStorageRootPath(string localStorageName)
{
        try
        {
                LocalResource resource = RoleEnvironment.
                GetLocalResource(localStorageName);
                return resource.RootPath;
        }
        catch (Exception ex)
        {
        LogError(String.Format("Error in GetLocalStorageRootPath of {0}. {1}",
        "WindowsAzureSystemHelper", ex.Message));
        throw ex;
        }
}
public static bool CanAccessLocalStorage(string localStorageName)
{
        WindowsAzureSystemHelper.LogInfo("Can access Local Storage?");
        bool ret = false;
        try
```

```
{
string fp = WindowsAzureSystemHelper.
GetLocalStorageRootPath(localStorageName) + "proazure.txt";
using (StreamWriter sw = File.CreateText(fp))
{
        WindowsAzureSystemHelper.LogInfo("Created File " + fp);
        sw.WriteLine("This is a Pro Azure file.");
        WindowsAzureSystemHelper.LogInfo("Wrote in File " + fp);
}//using
string fpNew = WindowsAzureSystemHelper.
GetLocalStorageRootPath(localStorageName) + "proazure2.txt";
File.Copy(fp, fpNew);
string fpNew2 = WindowsAzureSystemHelper.
GetLocalStorageRootPath(localStorageName) + "proazure3.txt";
File.Move(fp, fpNew2);
WindowsAzureSystemHelper.LogInfo("Deleting File " + fpNew2);
File.Delete(fpNew2);
WindowsAzureSystemHelper.LogInfo("Deleted File " + fpNew2);
WindowsAzureSystemHelper.LogInfo("Deleting File " + fpNew);
File.Delete(fpNew);
WindowsAzureSystemHelper.LogInfo("Deleted File " + fpNew);
ret = true;
}
catch (Exception ex)
{
WindowsAzureSystemHelper.LogError("Error in CanAccessSystemDir " + ex.Message);
}
return ret;
}
```

There are two methods defined in Listing 3-12: GetLocalStorageRootPath() and CanAccessLocalStorage(). The GetLocalStorageRootPath() method calls the RoleEnvironment.GetLocalResource() method and returns the root path property of the local storage. The CanAccessLocalStorage() executes a test to check whether the role instance can access the local storage by creating, copying, moving and deleting files. The method returns true if all the tests pass, otherwise it returns false. Both the methods accept local storage name as the parameter defined in the ServiceDefinition.csdef file.

The other two methods in the local storage section are WriteLineToLocalStorage() and ReadAllLinesFromLocalStorage(). The WriteLineToLocalStorage() appends a line of text to the specified file in the local storage. It also creates the file if it does not exist. The writeDuplicateEntries parameter is to specify whether duplicate entries are allowed in the file. The ReadAllLinesfromLocalStorage() method reads all the lines of text from the specified file in the local storage and returns them as an IList<string> data structure. Listing 3-16 shows code for both the methods.

Listing 3-16. *Write and Read Text to Local Storage*

```
public static void WriteLineToLocalStorage
(string fileName, string localStorageName, string message,
bool writeDuplicateEntries)
{
```

```
            LogInfo(message);
            string path = GetLocalStorageRootPath(localStorageName);
            path = Path.Combine(path, fileName);
            string entry = String.Format("{0}{1}", message, Environment.NewLine);
            bool write = true;
            if (!writeDuplicateEntries)
            {
            if (!File.Exists(path))
            {
                    using (StreamWriter sw = File.CreateText(path))
                    {
                    }
            }
            string[] lines = File.ReadAllLines(path, Encoding.UTF8);
            if (lines != null && lines.Length > 0)
            {
                    if (lines.Contains<string>(message))
                    {
                     write = false;
                    }
            }
            }
            if (write)
            {
             File.AppendAllText(path, entry, Encoding.UTF8);
            }
        }

        public static IList<string> ReadAllLinesFromLocalStorage
        (string fileName, string localStorageName)
        {
            List<string> messages = new List<string>();
            string path = Path.Combine(GetLocalStorageRootPath(localStorageName), fileName);
            if (File.Exists(path))
            {
                    using (FileStream stream = File.Open
                    (path, FileMode.Open, FileAccess.Read, FileShare.ReadWrite))
                    {
                            StreamReader reader = new StreamReader(stream, Encoding.UTF8);

                            while (true)
                            {
                                    string line = reader.ReadLine();
                                    if (line == null) break;
                                    messages.Add(line);
                            }
                    }
            }
            return messages;
        }
```

System Information

The system information section contains only one helper method GetSystemInfo() for retrieving the system information and returning the SystemMessageExchange dataset. Listing 3-17 shows the code for GetSystemInfo() method.

Listing 3-17. *GetSystemInfo() Method*

```
public static SystemMessageExchange GetSystemInfo
(string localStorageName, string role)
{
try
{
        SystemMessageExchange ds = new SystemMessageExchange();
        SystemMessageExchange.SystemInfoRow row =
        ds.SystemInfo.NewSystemInfoRow();
        row.CurrentDirectory = Environment.CurrentDirectory;
        try
        {
           row.LocalStoragePath = GetLocalStorageRootPath(localStorageName);
        }
        catch (Exception ex1)
        {
           LogError(ex1.Message);

        }
        row.MachineName = Environment.MachineName;
        row.OSVersion = Environment.OSVersion.VersionString;

        string dir;
        if (CanAccessSystemDir(out dir))
        {
           row.SystemDirectory = dir;

        }

        if (CanAccessWindowsDir(out dir))
        {
           row.WindowsDirectory = dir;
        }
        row.UserDomainName = Environment.UserDomainName;
        row.UserName = Environment.UserName;
        row.Role = role;
        row.Timestamp = DateTime.Now.ToString("s");
        ds.SystemInfo.AddSystemInfoRow(row);

        return ds;
}
catch (Exception ex)
{
```

```
 LogError("GetSystemInfo " + ex.Message);
}

return null;
}
```

The `GetSystemInfo()` method accepts the local storage name and the role name of the instance as the parameters. It then creates an instance of the `SystemMessageExchange` dataset and adds a new row to the `SystemInfo DataTable` in the dataset. The data row is filled with appropriate system information values and added back to the `SystemInfo DataTable` using the `AddSystemInfoRow()` method. The dataset is then returned from the function. Note that this method can be called from either the Web or Worker role to retrieve the system information from the underlying operating system.

WebWorkerExchange Cloud Service Project

This is the cloud service project created using the Web and Worker Cloud Service project template in Visual Studio.NET. It contains the `ServiceDefinition.csdef` and `ServiceConfiguration.cscfg` files. The project also holds references to the Web and Worker role projects. The `Roles` folder in the project contains references to the Web role (`WebWorkerExchange_WebRole`) and the Worker role (`WebWorkerExchange_WorkerRole`) projects from the same solution.

ServiceDefinition.csdef

The `ServiceDefinition.csdef` file defines the service model for the project. Listing 3-18 shows the contents of the `ServiceDefinition.csdef` file.

Listing 3-18. *ServiceDefinition.csdef*

```
<?xml version="1.0" encoding="utf-8"?>
<ServiceDefinition name="WebWorkerExchange"
xmlns="http://schemas.microsoft.com/ServiceHosting/2008/10/ServiceDefinition">
  <WebRole name="WebRole" enableNativeCodeExecution="true">
    <LocalStorage name="SystemInfoWebLocalCache" sizeInMB="10"/>
    <InputEndpoints>
<!-- Must use port 80 for http and port 443 for https when running in the cloud -->
      <InputEndpoint name="HttpIn" protocol="http" port="80" />
    </InputEndpoints>
    <ConfigurationSettings>
     <Setting name="DiagnosticsConnectionString" />
     <!--This is the current logging level of the service -->
     <Setting name="LogLevel"/>
     <Setting name="ThrowExceptions"/>
     <Setting name="EnableOnScreenLogging"/>
    </ConfigurationSettings>
  </WebRole>
  <WorkerRole name="WorkerRole" enableNativeCodeExecution="true">
    <LocalStorage name="SystemInfoWorkerLocalCache" sizeInMB="10"/>
```

```
    <ConfigurationSettings>
     <Setting name="DiagnosticsConnectionString" />
      <!--This is the current logging level of the service -->
      <Setting name="LogLevel"/>
      <Setting name="ThreadSleepTimeInMillis"/>
      <Setting name="SystemInfoServiceURL"/>
    </ConfigurationSettings>
  </WorkerRole>
</ServiceDefinition>
```

In Listing 3-18, a Web role and a Worker role are defined. Both have native code execution enabled for accessing System.Environment properties. Both the roles also define local storage folders. The configuration settings defined in the Web role are mainly related to logging and exception handling. In the Worker role, the ThreadSleepTimeInMillis setting defines the thread sleep time for the worker thread, which corresponds to the time interval for calling the SendSystemInfo() WCF method. The SystemInfoServiceURL is the SystemInfo WCF service URL for sending the system information. The values of these settings are set in the ServiceConfiguration.cscfg file. You have to change the SystemInfoServiceURL value when you deploy the service to the cloud staging and production environments.

ServiceConfiguration.cscfg

The ServiceConfiguration.cscfg file contains the values of the configuration settings defined in ServiceDefinition.csdef. Listing 3-19 shows the contents of the ServiceConfiguration.cscfg file.

Listing 3-19. ServiceConfiguration.cscfg

```
<?xml version="1.0"?>
<ServiceConfiguration serviceName="WebWorkerExchange"
xmlns="http://schemas.microsoft.com/ServiceHosting/2008/10/ServiceConfiguration">
  <Role name="WebRole">
    <Instances count="1"/>
    <ConfigurationSettings>
<Setting name="DiagnosticsConnectionString" value="UseDevelopmentStorage=true" />
      <!--Supported Values are Critical,
      Error,Warning,Information,Verbose-->
      <Setting name="LogLevel" value="Information"/>
      <Setting name="ThrowExceptions" value="true"/>
      <Setting name="EnableOnScreenLogging" value="true"/>
    </ConfigurationSettings>
  </Role>
  <Role name="WorkerRole">
    <Instances count="2"/>
    <ConfigurationSettings>
<Setting name="DiagnosticsConnectionString" value="UseDevelopmentStorage=true" />
      <!--Supported Values are Critical,
      Error,Warning,Information,Verbose-->
        <Setting name="LogLevel" value="Information"/>
      <Setting name="ThreadSleepTimeInMillis" value="5000"/>
```

```
        <Setting name="SystemInfoServiceURL"
value="http://localhost:81/SystemInfo.svc"/>
      </ConfigurationSettings>
    </Role>
</ServiceConfiguration>
```

In Listing 3-19, the values for the configuration settings defined in the `ServiceDefinition.csdef` are set. Note that the Web role has only one instance defined, whereas the Worker role has two instances defined. The `ServiceInfoServiceURL` value points to `SystemInfo` WCF service in the local development fabric, because the testing is done in the development fabric.

Creating the WebWorkerExchange_WebRole Web Role Project

This is the Web role project in the cloud service that defines the `SystemInfo` WCF service (`SystemInfo.svc`) and the ASP.NET Page (`Default.aspx`) for displaying the system information of role instances.

SystemInfo.svc

The `SystemInfo.svc` is a WCF service implements the `ISystemInfo` interface. The `ISystemInfo` interface has only one method `void SendSystemInfo(SystemMessageExchange ds)`.

The method accepts an instance of the `SystemMessageExchange` dataset. Listing 3-20 shows the implementation of the `void SendSystemInfo(SystemMessageExchange ds)` in `SystemInfo` class.

Listing 3-20. SystemInfo.cs

```
public const string LOCAL_STORAGE_NAME = "SystemInfoWebLocalCache";
public const string SYSTEM_INFO_MACHINE_NAMES = "machines.txt";
public const string SYS_INFO_CACHE_XML = "SystemInfoCache.xml";
public static readonly SystemMessageExchange sysDS = new SystemMessageExchange();

public void SendSystemInfo(SystemMessageExchange ds)
{
if (ds != null && ds.SystemInfo.Rows.Count > 0)
{
        string machineName = ds.SystemInfo[0].MachineName;
        string machineLocalStoragePath = ds.SystemInfo[0].LocalStoragePath;
        //Log the message
        WindowsAzureSystemHelper.LogInfo(machineName + ">" + ds.GetXml());

        //Add machine names
        WindowsAzureSystemHelper.WriteLineToLocalStorage
        (SYSTEM_INFO_MACHINE_NAMES,LOCAL_STORAGE_NAME, machineName, false);

        //Copy the file to LocalStorage
        string localStoragePath = WindowsAzureSystemHelper.GetLocalStorageRootPath
        (LOCAL_STORAGE_NAME);
```

```
        try
        {
                string query = String.Format
                ("MachineName = '{0}' AND LocalStoragePath = '{1}'",
                machineName, machineLocalStoragePath);
                WindowsAzureSystemHelper.LogInfo("Query = " + query);
                System.Data.DataRow[] dRows = sysDS.SystemInfo.Select(query);

                if (dRows != null && dRows.Length > 0)
                {
                sysDS.SystemInfo.Rows.Remove(dRows[0]);
                }

                sysDS.SystemInfo.Merge(ds.SystemInfo);
                sysDS.AcceptChanges();
                sysDS.WriteXml(Path.Combine(localStoragePath, SYS_INFO_CACHE_XML));
                WindowsAzureSystemHelper.LogInfo("SystemInfoCache.xml -- " +
                sysDS.GetXml());

        }
        catch (Exception ex)
        {
        WindowsAzureSystemHelper.LogError("SendSystemInfo():" + ex.Message);
        }

}
else
{
WindowsAzureSystemHelper.LogInfo("SendSystemInfo(): null message received");

}
}
```

In Listing 3-20, I define a read-only static instance of the SystemMessageExchange dataset for storing all the requests coming from the WCF clients. When the SendSystemInfo() method is called, a new system information dataset comes in, I read the machine name of the request and write a line to the machines.txt file in the local storage using the call WindowsAzureSystemHelper.WriteLineToLocalStorage(SYSTEM_INFO_MACHINE_NAMES, LOCAL_STORAGE_NAME, machineName, false);.

Next, I query the class instance of the SystemMessageExchange dataset (sysDS) to check whether an entry for this machine name exists. I am using the machine name and the local storage for querying because the same machine may have different roles running with different local storage names. So, my assumption is that the machine name and local storage pair is unique for the purpose of this lab. If a row with the specified parameters already exists in the dataset, I delete it and then merge the received dataset (ds) with the class instance of the dataset (sysDS) for inserting the latest information received from the role instance. In the system information dataset, the timestamp is the only field that will vary with time if the role instance keeps on running on the same underlying virtual machine. Finally, I serialize the dataset (sysDS) to the local storage of the Web role using sysDS.WriteXml() method call. Every time the WCF method is called, the system information file stored in the local storage is updated with the latest information. Once the file is saved to the local storage, it is available to the other objects running in the same Web role instance.

For the sake of simplicity, I am using basicHttpBinding in the web.config file for the SystemInfo WCF service as shown in Listing 3-21.

Listing 3-21. ServiceInfo WCF Binding

```
<services>
<service behaviorConfiguration="WebWorkerExchange_WebRole.SystemInfoBehavior"
name="WebWorkerExchange_WebRole.SystemInfo">
<endpoint address="" binding="basicHttpBinding"
contract="WebWorkerExchange_WebRole.ISystemInfo">
<identity>
<dns value="localhost"/>
</identity>
</endpoint>
<endpoint address="mex" binding="mexHttpBinding" contract="IMetadataExchange"/>
</service>
</services>
```

Default.aspx

The Default.aspx file is the home page for the Web role application. On a periodic basis, the Default.aspx page reads the machines.txt file and the serialized system information dataset from the local storage and displays it to the end user. Figure 3-49 illustrates the design of Default.aspx.

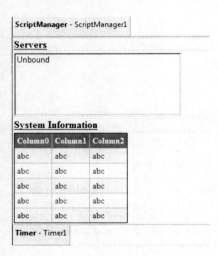

Figure 3-49. Default.aspx

The Default.aspx page has three main controls: an ASP.NET ListBox, a GridView, and an ASP.NET Ajax Timer control. The ListBox is used to display the contents of the messages.txt file from the local storage stored by the SystemInfo WCF service. The GridView is used for displaying the content of the system information dataset file stored in the local storage by the SystemInfo WCF service. The `ListBox` and the `GridView` are both placed on an AJAX update panel. The Timer control refreshes the `UpdatePanel` every 10 seconds. Listing 3-22 shows the `Tick` event of the Timer control in `Default.aspx.cs`.

***Listing 3-22.** Default.aspx.cs*

```
protected void Timer1_Tick(object sender, EventArgs e)
{
        ExecuteExchange();
        ListMachines();
}
private void ListMachines()
{
        try
        {
                IList<string> messages =
                WindowsAzureSystemHelper.ReadAllLinesFromLocalStorage(
                SystemInfo.SYSTEM_INFO_MACHINE_NAMES, SystemInfo.LOCAL_STORAGE_NAME);
                lbMachines.Items.Clear();
                foreach (string message in messages)
                {
                        lbMachines.Items.Add(message);
                }
                string sysInfoPath =
                Path.Combine(WindowsAzureSystemHelper.GetLocalStorageRootPath
                (SystemInfo.LOCAL_STORAGE_NAME), SystemInfo.SYS_INFO_CACHE_XML);
                if (File.Exists(sysInfoPath))
                {
                        string sysInfoFileContents = File.ReadAllText(sysInfoPath);
                        if (!string.IsNullOrEmpty(sysInfoFileContents))
                        {
                                SystemMessageExchange ds = new SystemMessageExchange();
                                ds.ReadXml(new StringReader(sysInfoFileContents));
                                GridView1.DataSource = ds.SystemInfo;
                                GridView1.DataBind();
                        }
                }
        }
        catch (Exception ex)
        {
        WindowsAzureSystemHelper.LogError(ex.Message);
        }
}
```

In Listing 3-22, I am using the helper methods from the `WindowsAzureSystemHelper` class. The first method `WindowsAzureSystemHelper.ReadAllLinesFromLocalStorage()` reads the machine names from `machines.txt` from the local storage. All the retrieved machine names are then added to the list box. Similarly, the dataset method `ds.ReadXml()` deserializes the dataset from the local storage and adds it as a data source to the `GridView`. So, every 10 seconds you will see the timestamp refreshed on the `Default.aspx` page.

Creating the WebWorkerExchange_WorkerRole Worker Role Project

This is the Worker role project for sending continuous system information to the SystemInfo WCF service in the Web role. A Worker role in the Windows Azure cloud is analogous to the Windows Service on a Windows Server system. As discussed earlier in this chapter, the Worker role class must inherit from the RoleEntryPoint abstract class In this example, I have implemented the OnStart() and Run() methods.

Listing 3-23. Worker Role Run() Method

```
public override void Run()
{
        Trace.WriteLine("WebWorkerExchange_WorkerRole entry point called", "Information");
        WindowsAzureSystemHelper.LogInfo("Worker Process entry point called");
        ThreadSleepInMillis =
        WindowsAzureSystemHelper.GetIntConfigurationValue("ThreadSleepTimeInMillis");
        while (true)
        {
        ExecuteExchange();
        Thread.Sleep(ThreadSleepInMillis);
        WindowsAzureSystemHelper.LogInfo("Working");

        }

    }
```

In Listing 3-23, the Run() method has an continuous while loop that executes the WCF method by calling a local method ExecuteExchange() and then goes to sleep for a configured amount of milliseconds. The core logic of the application is in the ExecuteExchange() method shown in Listing 3-24.

Listing 3-24. ExecuteExchange Method

```
private void ExecuteExchange()
{
        try
        {
        SystemMessageExchange ds =
        WindowsAzureSystemHelper.GetSystemInfo(LOCAL_STORAGE_NAME, "Worker");
                if (ds == null)
                {
                        WindowsAzureSystemHelper.LogError
                        ("ExecuteExchange():SystemMessageExchange DataSet is null");
                }
                else
                {

                        WindowsAzureSystemHelper.LogInfo(ds.GetXml());
                        string url = WindowsAzureSystemHelper.GetStringConfigurationValue
                        ("SystemInfoServiceURL");

                        CallSystemInfoService(url, ds);
```

```
        }
    }
    catch (Exception ex)
    {
    WindowsAzureSystemHelper.LogError("ExecuteExchange():" + ex.Message);
    }
}
```

In Listing 3-24, there are two main method calls—WindowsAzureSystemHelper.GetSystemInfo() and CallSystemInfoService(). WindowsAzureSystemHelper.GetSystemInfo() is a helper method that returns the SystemMessageExchage dataset, and CallSystemInfoService() is a private method that calls the SystemInfo WCF service in the Web role. Listing 3-25 shows the code for CallSystemInfoService() method.

Listing 3-25. *CallSystemInfoService() Method*

```
private void CallSystemInfoService(string url, SystemMessageExchange ds)
{
        SystemInfoService.SystemInfoClient client = null;
        BasicHttpBinding bind = new BasicHttpBinding();
        try
        {
                EndpointAddress endpoint = new EndpointAddress(url);
                client = new SystemInfoService.SystemInfoClient(bind, endpoint);
                client.SendSystemInfo(ds);
                WindowsAzureSystemHelper.LogInfo(
                String.Format("Sent message to Service URL {0}", url));


        }
        catch (Exception ex)
        {
        WindowsAzureSystemHelper.LogError("CallSystemInfoService():" + ex.Message);
        }
        finally
        {
                if (client != null)
                {
                        if (client.State == CommunicationState.Faulted)
                        client.Abort();
                        else
                        client.Close();
                }
        }
}
```

In Listing 3-25, I initialize the BasicHttpBinding object and then initialize the EndpointAddress object and pass the URL from the ServiceConfiguration.cscfg passed as a parameter to the method. Next, I instantiate the SystemInfo WCF service proxy class SystemInfoClient and call the

SendSystemInfo() method with the SystemMessageExchange dataset as the parameter. At this time, the WCF method is invoked and the dataset sent to the SystemInfo WCF service in the Web role.

To run the application in the development fabric, press F5 or right-click the WebWorkerExchange project and select Debug ▸ Start new instance.

■ **Note** Make sure that you have added the correct URL of the SystemInfo WCF service in the ServiceConfiguration.cscfg file for the setting name SystemInfoServiceURL.

When the web application starts, it stars the Web role as well as the Worker role instances. The Web role starts a new browser window and loads Default.aspx. The Web role also starts the SystemInfo WCF service. As per the ServiceConfiguration.cscfg, the development fabric starts two instances of the Worker role.

Open the development fabric UI from the system tray icon or by going to All Programs ▸ Windows Azure SDK ▸ Development Fabric. Figure 3-50 illustrates the WebWorkerExchange cloud service running in the Development Fabric.

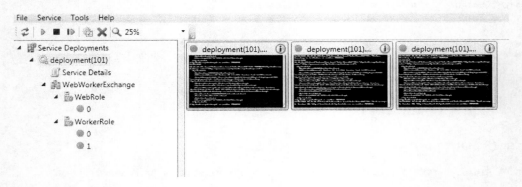

Figure 3-50. *WebWorkerExchange in development fabric*

In Figure 3-50, there are two Worker role instances and one Web role instance. The logs for all the instances are displayed in their respective consoles. You can click one of the green instance nodes to enlarge the console of that instance for more detailed log viewing.

Figure 3-51 illustrates the Default.aspx page with the system information from all the service instances.

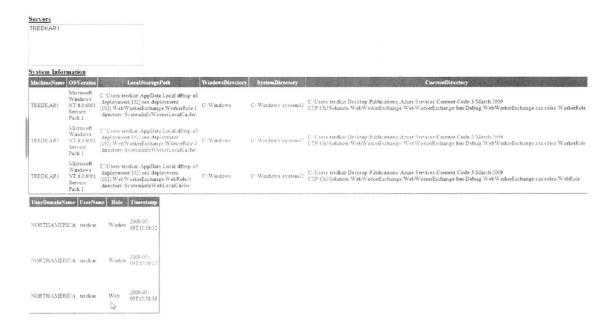

Figure 3-51. *Default.aspx showing system information*

If you observe `Default.aspx`, you will see the Timestamp values change 10 seconds. You will also find it interesting to see the different system properties displayed in the `GridView`. Next, let's deploy the `WebWorkerExchange` cloud service to the Windows Azure cloud. The steps for deploying `WebWorkerExchange` cloud service to Windows Azure are the same as those you say earlier in this chapter:

1. Right-click the `WebWorkerExchange` project, and select Publish.

2. Sign in to the Windows Azure developer portal.

3. In Windows Azure developer portal, select the Windows Azure project you want to deploy the service to or create a new Windows Azure project.

4. Go to the project page, and click Deploy in the Staging section.

5. On the Staging Deployment page, in the App Package section, browse and add the `WebWorkerExchange.cspkg` package.

6. Next, add the `ServiceConfiguration.cscfg` configuration file in the Configuration Settings section.

7. Give the project a name (e.g., Web Worker Exchange).

8. Click Deploy. Windows Azure will read the `ServiceDefinition.csdef` file to provision the Web and Worker roles.

9. Make sure the state of the Web and Worker roles changes to Allocated, so you are ready to run the service.

10. Before running the service, though, you need to configure the `SystemInfoServiceURL` configuration setting in the Worker role to point to the URL of the `SystemInfo` service. Click Configure, and change the `SystemInfoServiceURL` setting to point to your staging environment Web Site URL, as shown in Figure 3-52.

Configuration Settings

Edit the configuration:

```
xmlns:xsd="http://www.w3.org/2001/XMLSchema" serviceName=""
xmlns="http://schemas.microsoft.com/ServiceHosting/2008/10/ServiceConfiguration">
  <Role name="WebRole">
    <ConfigurationSettings>
      <Setting name="LogLevel" value="Information" />
      <Setting name="ThrowExceptions" value="true" />
      <Setting name="EnableOnScreenLogging" value="true" />
    </ConfigurationSettings>
    <Instances count="1" />
  </Role>
  <Role name="WorkerRole">
    <ConfigurationSettings>
      <Setting name="LogLevel" value="Information" />
      <Setting name="ThreadSleepTimeInMillis" value="5000" />
      <Setting name="SystemInfoServiceURL" value="http://fce17bc2-923d-4a11-b3b3-
708876a4eeb2.cloudapp.net/SystemInfo.svc" />
    </ConfigurationSettings>
    <Instances count="2" />
  </Role>
</ServiceConfiguration>
```

Figure 3-52. *Configuring SystemInfoServiceURL*

11. Click the Run button to start the service. Windows Azure now starts the Web and Worker role instances, as shown in Figure 3-53.

Figure 3-53. *WebWorkerExchange in the staging environment*

12. When all roles are in the Started state, click the Web Site URL to open the
Default.aspx page. Figure 3-54 shows the Default.aspx file loaded form the
Windows Azure staging environment.

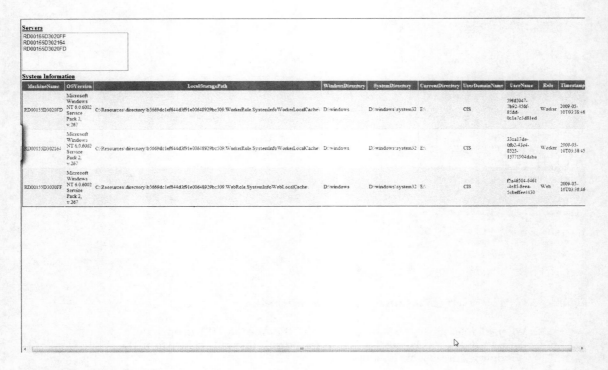

***Figure 3-54.** Default.aspx in the staging environment*

In Figure 3-54, note that all the three instances of the service are provisioned on different underlying servers. Also note the different system information sent by each instance, including the local storage directory, user domain, and user name. The user names under which the instances are run are GUIDs, which makes sense in an automatically provisioned infrastructure. Once you have tested the service in the staging environment, you can swap the staging environment with the production environment for deploying the service in production. Figure 3-55 shows the production deployment of the WebWorkerExchange in Windows Azure.

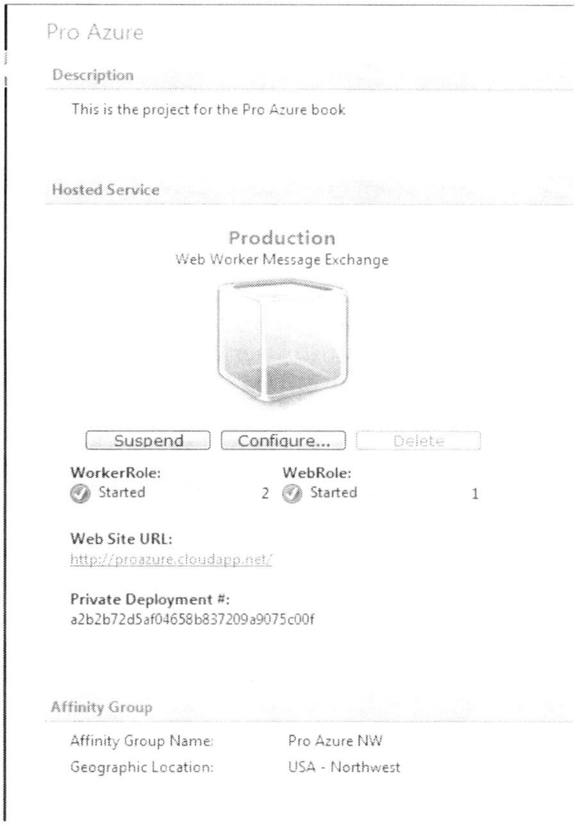

Pro Azure

Description

This is the project for the Pro Azure book

Hosted Service

Production
Web Worker Message Exchange

[Suspend] [Configure...] [Delete]

WorkerRole: **WebRole:**
✓ Started   2   ✓ Started   1

Web Site URL:
http://proazure.cloudapp.net/

Private Deployment #:
a2b2b72d5af04658b837209a9075c00f

Affinity Group

Affinity Group Name: Pro Azure NW
Geographic Location: USA - Northwest

Figure 3-55. *WebWorkerExchange in production*

Geolocation

Windows Azure is already available in multiple data centers within the United States, and going forward, Microsoft plans to expand into data centers around the world. In today's enterprise, as well as consume, applications, the common paint point is to design a globally available service. The service needs to be physically deployed into data centers around the world for business continuity, performance, network latency, compliance, or geopolitical reasons. For example, in one project I had the responsibility for architecting a global deployment of a business critical application for a Fortune 100 company. Even though I did not need to travel around the world, I had to plan and coordinate deployment efforts around five data centers across the world. The effort took six months of rigorous planning and coordination. With geolocation support in Windows Azure, you can choose the geolocation of the storage and the compute host. Table 3-7 lists some of the common geolocation advantages.

Table 3-7. *Geolocation Advantages*

Advantage	Rationale
Business Continuity and Planning	With geolocation features, enterprise data can be replicated across multiple data centers around the world as an insurance shield from natural and political disasters.
Performance and Network Latency	One of the architectural tenets and best practices of cloud services is keeping data close to the application for optimizing performance and end user experience. With geolocation support, a cloud service application can be run in close proximity to the data for improved performance.
Compliance	Compliance laws are different in different countries. Multinational organizations have to deal with compliance regulations in all the countries that they do business in. With Windows Azure, companies can now move data closer to the country offices for adhering to the country specific compliance regulations.
Geopolitical Requirements	Some countries pose restrictions and constraints on enterprises in where they can store enterprise data. Geolocation features can help enterprises better align with such geopolitical requirements

Geolocation support gives you the ability to choose the affinity of the storage and compute services to a particular geo-location.

Enabling Geographic Affinity

When you create a new storage account or a hosted services project, you can specify the location and affinity group for your project. The steps for creating a geographic affinity between a hosted service project and a storage account follow:

1. From the Create a new service component page, create a new Hosted Services project.
2. Give the project a name and a label. I have named my project Pro Azure. Click Next
3. Select a hosted service URL on the Create a Project page. Also, you can check its availability.
4. On the Create a Project page, you will see a Hosted Service Affinity Group section, as shown in Figure 3-56.

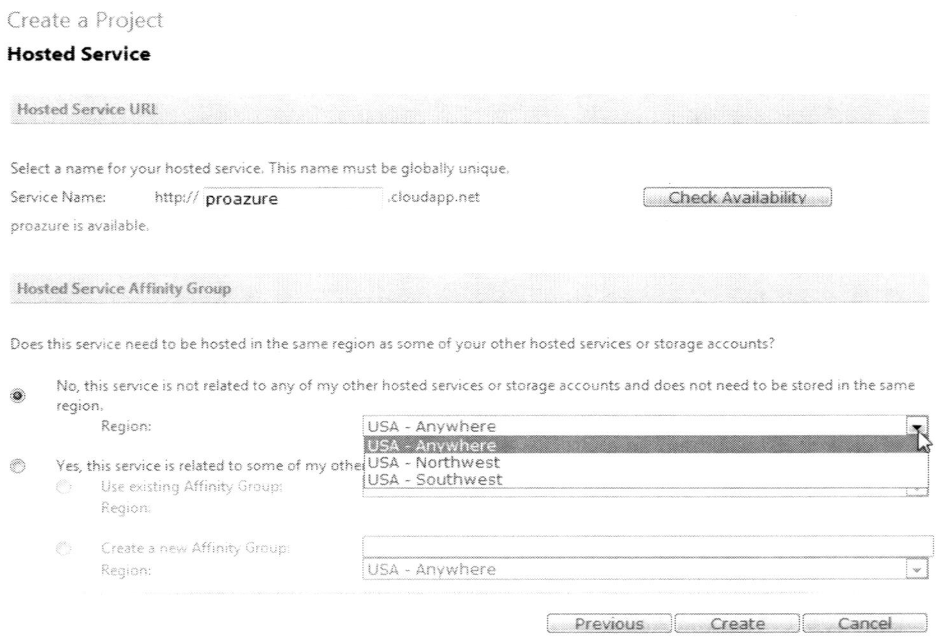

Figure 3-56. *Hosted Service Affinity Group*

5. The Hosted Service Affinity group section starts with the question "Does this service need to be hosted in the same region as some of your other hosted services or storage accounts?"

- If your answer is No, you can just choose a region for your service from the Region drop-down list, and click Create. By default, USA-Anywhere is selected, which does not give you a choice on where the service will be located.

- If your answer is Yes, you have two choices as shown in Figure 3-57: Use an existing affinity group and region or create a new affinity group and region for reusing it across multiple projects.

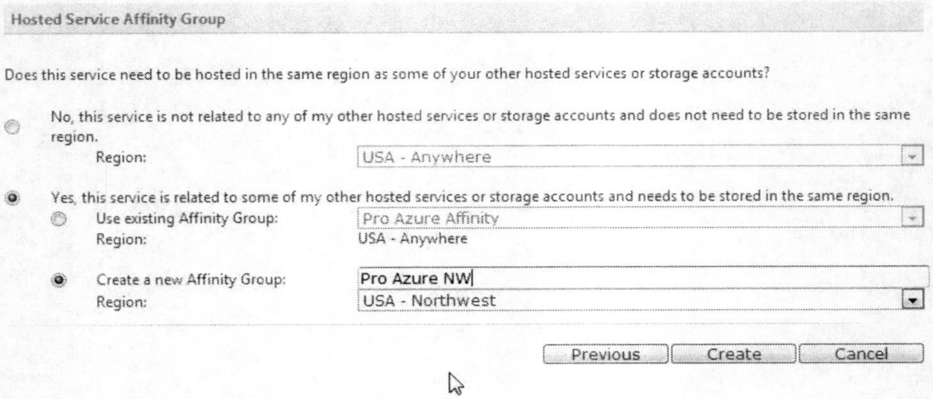

Hosted Service Affinity Group

Does this service need to be hosted in the same region as some of your other hosted services or storage accounts?

○ No, this service is not related to any of my other hosted services or storage accounts and does not need to be stored in the same region.
    Region: [USA - Anywhere   ▾]

◉ Yes, this service is related to some of my other hosted services or storage accounts and needs to be stored in the same region.
    ○ Use existing Affinity Group: [Pro Azure Affinity   ▾]
        Region: USA - Anywhere

    ◉ Create a new Affinity Group: [Pro Azure NW|]
        Region: [USA - Northwest   ▾]

                                        [Previous]   [Create]   [Cancel]

Figure 3-57. *Creating a new affinity group*

6. I will create a new affinity group called Pro Azure NW, and assign it the USA-Northwest geographic location.

7. Click the Create button to create the project.

The new project shows the affinity group and its geographic location, as shown in Figure 3-58.

Affinity Group   Edit

    Affinity Group Name: Pro Azure NW
    Geographic Location: USA - Northwest

Figure 3-58. *Pro Azure NW Affinity group*

Next, let's create a new storage account and specify the same affinity group, so Windows Azure will know to provision the hosted service and the storage account as close to each other as possible for maximizing the bandwidth and lowering the network latency.

1. To create a Storage Account, create a new project of type Storage Account in the Windows Azure developer portal.

2. Give the project a name (e.g., ProAzure NW Storage), and click Next.

3. On Create a Project page, create a storage account name (e.g., **proazuregeostorage**), and check it availability.

4. Next, in the Storage Account Affinity Group section, choose "Use existing Affinity Group" and select Pro Azure NW, or whatever affinity group you created for the hosted services project (see Figure 3-59).

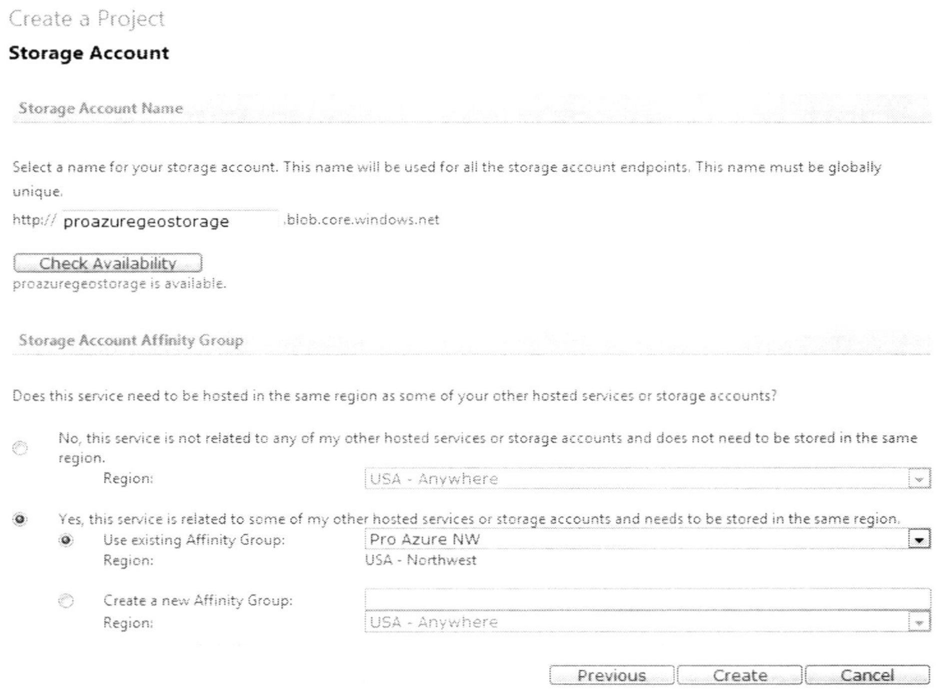

Create a Project

Storage Account

Storage Account Name

Select a name for your storage account. This name will be used for all the storage account endpoints. This name must be globally unique.

http:// **proazuregeostorage**   .blob.core.windows.net

[Check Availability]
proazuregeostorage is available.

Storage Account Affinity Group

Does this service need to be hosted in the same region as some of your other hosted services or storage accounts?

○ No, this service is not related to any of my other hosted services or storage accounts and does not need to be stored in the same region.
    Region: | USA - Anywhere   ▾ |

◉ Yes, this service is related to some of my other hosted services or storage accounts and needs to be stored in the same region.
    ◉ Use existing Affinity Group: | Pro Azure NW   ▾ |
       Region: USA - Northwest

    ○ Create a new Affinity Group: | |
       Region: | USA - Anywhere   ▾ |

[Previous]   [Create]   [Cancel]

Figure 3-59. *Selecting a storage account affinity group*

> Note that the geographic region gets automatically populated and cannot be edited.

5. Click Create to create the storage account project with the same affinity group and region as the hosted services account.

Content Delivery Network

Content Delivery Network (CDN) is a Windows Azure blob replication and caching service that makes your blobs available globally at strategic locations closer to the blob consumers. For example, if your media-heavy web site has media files centrally located in the United States, whereas your users are from all the continents, then there will be performance degradation for the users in distant locations. Windows Azure CDN pushes content closer to the users at several data center locations in Asia, Australia, Europe, South America, and the United States. At the time of this writing, there were 18 locations (or edges) across these continents that provided caching service to the Windows Azure blob storage via CDN. So, if you enable your media files on the Windows blob storage with CDN, they will be automatically available across these locations locally thus improving the performance for the users.

Currently, the only restriction on enabling CDN is the blob containers must be public. This makes CDN extremely useful for e-commerce, news media, social networking, and interactive media web sites.

When you enable a storage account with CDN, the portal creates a unique URL with the following format for CDN access to the blobs in that storage account: `http://<guid>.vo.msecnd.net/`.

This URL is different from the blob storage URL format, `http://<storageaccountname>.blob.core.windows.net/`, because, the blob storage URL is not designed to resolve to CDN locations. Therefore, to get the benefit of CDN, you must use the URL generated by CDN for the blob storage. You can also register a custom domain name for the CDN URL from Windows Azure Developer Portal.

To enable CDN on a storage account, follow these steps:

1. Go to your Windows Azure Developer Portal storage account.

2. Click Enable CDN on the storage account page, as shown in Figure 3-60.

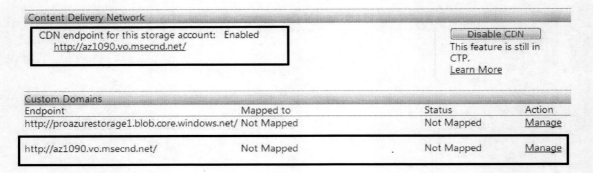

Figure 3-60. *Enabling CDN*

3. The portal provides a CDN endpoint to the storage by creating a CDN URL of the format `http://<guid>.vo.msecnd.net/`.

You can use the CDN endpoint URL for accessing your public containers. The portal also creates a record for the CDN endpoint in the Custom Domains list. To create a custom domain name, you can click on the Manage link for the CDN endpoint in the Custom Domain list and follow the instructions. I will cover Windows Azure storage in the next chapter, but I have covered CDN in this section, because it aligns very well with geographic affinity capabilities of Windows Azure.

Windows Azure Service Management

Unlike on-premise applications, the deployment of a cloud services involves only software provisioning from the developer's perspective. You saw in the earlier examples how hardware provisioning was abstracted from you in the deployment process. In a scalable environment where enterprises may need to provision multiple services across thousands of instances, you need more programmatic control over the provision process rather than configuring services using Windows Azure developer portal. Manually uploading service packages and then starting and stopping services from the portal interface works well for smaller services, but becomes a time-consuming and error-prone process when deploying multiple large-scale services. The Windows Azure Service Management API allows you to programmatically perform most of the provisioning functions via a REST-based interface to your Windows Azure cloud account. Using the Service Management API, you can script your provisioning and deprovisioning process end to end in an automated manner. In this section, I will cover some important functions from the Service Management API and also demonstrate some source code for you to build your own cloud service provisioning process.

Service Management API Structure

The Service Management API provides most of the functions you can perform on the storage services and hosted services from Windows Azure developer portal. The Service Management API categorizes the API operations into three primary sections: storage accounts, hosted services, and affinity groups. Operations on storage accounts mainly cover listing of accounts and generation of the access keys. Operation on hosted services cover listing of services, deploying services, removing services, swapping between staging and production, and upgrading services. The affinity groups operations are limited to listing and getting properties of affinity groups in your account.

■ **Note** You can find the Service Management API reference at http://msdn.microsoft.com/ en-us/library/ee460799.aspx.

The Service Management API uses X.509 client certificates for authenticating calls between the client and the server.

■ **Caution** The source code in the following section is based on early CTP version (released October 10, 2009) of the service management API and its associated client assembly Microsoft.Samples.WindowsAzure .ServiceManagement. You can download the latest version of the assembly from the Windows Azure Code Samples page at http://code.msdn.microsoft.com/windowsazuresamples. Even though the API may change in the future, the concepts used in this section will remain the same past its final release. You may have slightly modify the source code to make it work with the latest available API.

Programming with the Service Management API

To start programming with the Service Management API, you must first create a valid X.509 certificate (or work with an existing one). You can use makecert.exe to create a self-signed certificate

```
makecert -r -pe -a sha1 -n "CN=Windows Azure Authentication Certificate" -ss My -
len 2048 -sp "Microsoft Enhanced RSA and AES Cryptographic Provider" -sy 24
proazureservicemgmt.cer
```

Next, go to the Accounts section of Windows Azure Developer portal and upload the certificate from Manage API certificate section.

Figure 3-61. *Upload the API certificate*

Once the certificate is uploaded, you can call the Service Management REST API by passing the certificate as the `ClientCertificate` property of the `System.Net.HttpWebRequest` object, by using the `csmanage.exe` application from the Service Management API samples, or by building your own application. In Ch3Solution, I have created a sample Windows Application that makes REST calls to the Service Management API. It uses the `Microsoft.Samples.WindowsAzure.ServiceManagement.dll` file from the service management code samples. The `csmanage.exe` uses the same assembly to make the API calls. Eventually, the API assembly may become part of the Windows Azure SDK. Figure 3-62 illustrates the Service Management API windows application.

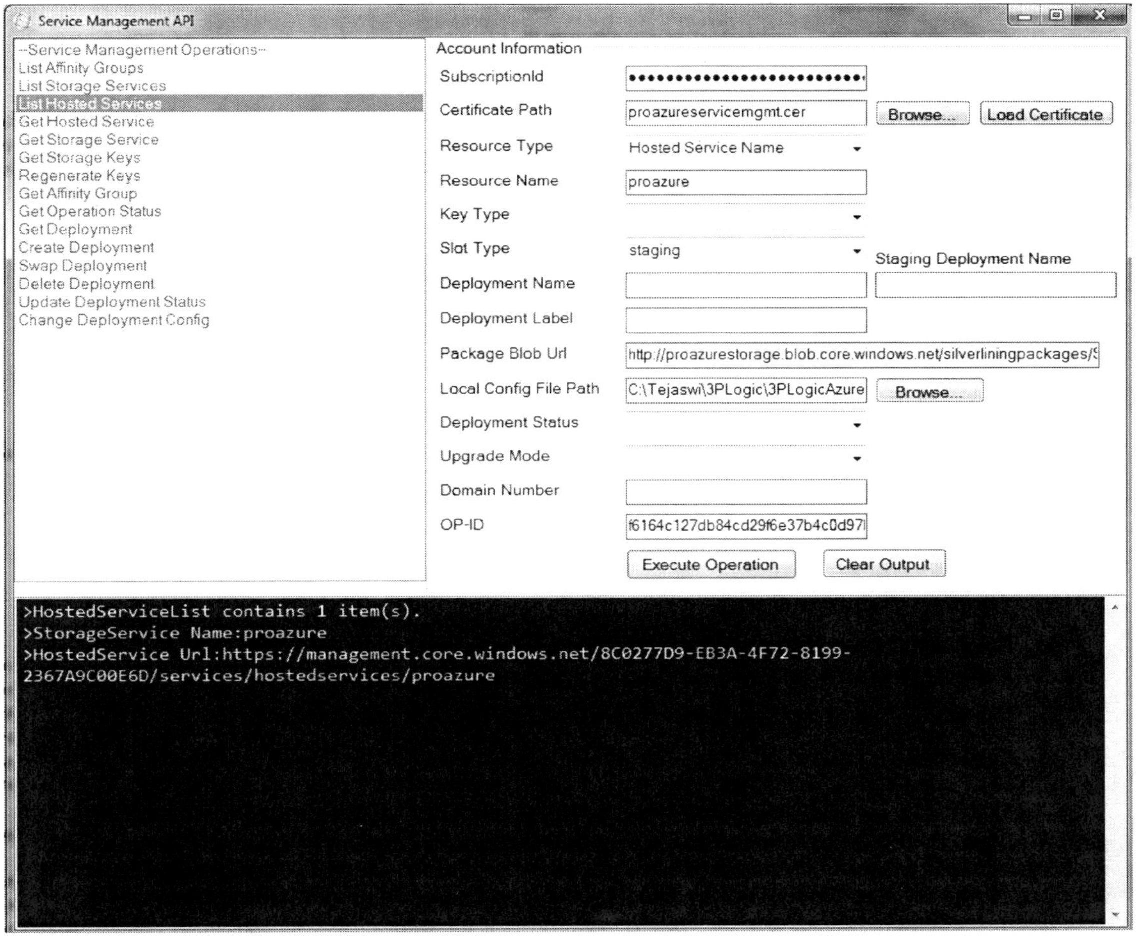

Figure 3-62. *The Service Management API windows application*

In Figure 3-62, The Service Management Operations section lists the operations that you can invoke on the Service Management API. The output textbox prints the output from the operations. The right-hand side of the user interface consists of input parameters. The input parameters are as follows:

- *Subscription Id*: You can get the subscriptionId from the Account page of the developer portal. This parameter is required by all the Service Management API operations.

- *Certificate Path*: This text box points to the API certificate file on the local machine. This certificate must match the one you uploaded to the portal.

- *Resource Type*: This drop-down lists the types of resource you want to access: Hosted Service, Storage Account, or Affinity Group.

- *Resource name*: You should type the name of the resource you want to access (e.g., storage account name, hosted service name, affinity group name).

The remaining input parameters are operation dependant. You can choose an operation from the Service Management operations list, enter input parameters and click Execute Operation. For example, to create a deployment in your hosted service account, you can:

1. Select the Create Deployment operation.

2. Enter your Account SubscriptionId.

3. Select the API certificate from local machine.

4. Select Hosted Service Name as the Resource Type.

5. Enter the name of the Hosted Service you want to deploy your service to in the Resource Name text box.

6. Select the slot type (staging or production).

7. Choose a deployment name.

8. Choose a deployment label.

9. You have to then point to a service package (.cspkg) on a blob storage in the Package Blob URL text box.

10. Select the path to the ServiceConfiguration.cscfg file of the cloud service.

11. Click Execute Operation.

The OP-ID shows the operation ID returned by the method call, which you can use to track the operation status. To check the status of the deploy operation, select the Get Operation Status method, and click Execute Operation. The status gets displayed in the bottom window. Once the deployment is complete, you can run the deployment by selecting the Update Deployment Status method and selecting the "running" option from the deployment status drop-down. Similarly, you can execute other operations from the Service Management API.

Windows Azure Service Life Cycle

The objective of Windows Azure is to automate the service life cycle as much as possible. Windows Azure service life cycle has five distinct phases and four different roles, as shown in Figure 3-60.

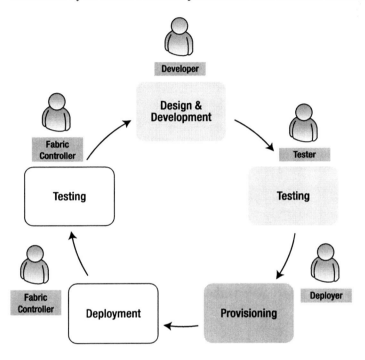

Figure 3-63. *The Windows Azure service life cycle*

The five phases are as follows:

Design and development: In this phase, the on-premise team plans, designs, and develops a cloud service for Windows Azure. The design includes quality attribute requirements for the service and the solution to fulfill them. This phase is conducted completely on-premise, unless there is some proof of concept (POC) involved. The key roles involved in this phase are on-premise stakeholders. For the sake of simplicity, I have combined these on-site design roles into a developer role.

Testing: In this phase, the quality attributes of the cloud service are tested. This phase involves on-premise as well as Windows Azure cloud testing. The tester role is in charge of this phase and tests end-to-end quality attributes of the service deployed into cloud testing or staging environment.

Provisioning: Once the application is tested, it can be provisioned to Windows Azure cloud. The deployer role deploys the cloud service to the Windows Azure cloud. The deployer is in charge of service configurations and makes sure the service definition of the cloud service is achievable through production deployment in Windows Azure cloud. The configuration settings are defined by the developer, but the production values are set by the deployer. In this phase, the role responsibilities transition from on-premise to the Windows Azure cloud. The fabric controller in Windows Azure assigns the allocated resources as per the service model defined in the service definition. The load balancers and virtual IP address are reserved for the service.

Deployment: In the deployment phase, the fabric controller commissions the allocated hardware nodes into the end state and deploys services on these nodes as defined in the service model and configuration. The fabric controller also has the capability of upgrading a service in running state without disruptions. The fabric controller abstracts the underlying hardware commissioning and deployment from the services. The hardware commissioning includes commissioning the hardware nodes, deploying operating system images on these nodes, and configuring switches, access routers, and load-balancers for the externally facing roles (e.g., Web role).

Maintenance: Windows Azure is designed with the assumption that failure will occur in hardware and software. Any service on a failed node is redeployed automatically and transparently, and the fabric controller automatically restarts any failed service roles. The fabric controller allocates new hardware in the event of a hardware failure. Thus, fabric controller always maintains the desired number of roles irrespective of any service, hardware or operating system failures. The fabric controller also provides a range of dynamic management capabilities like adding capacity, reducing capacity and service upgrades without any service disruptions. Figure 3-64 illustrates the fabric controller architecture.

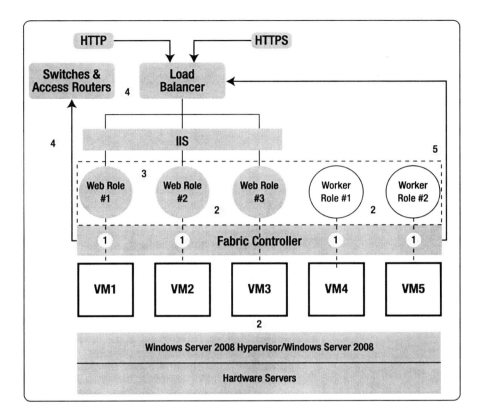

Figure 3-64. *Fabric controller architecture*

In Figure 3-64, the fabric controller abstracts the underlying Windows Server 2008 operating system and the hardware from the service role instances, and it performs the following high-level tasks:

- Allocates the nodes

- Starts operating system images on the nodes

- Configures the settings as per the service model described by the service creator

- Starts the service roles on allocated nodes

- Configures load balancers, access routers, and switches

- Maintains the desired number of role instances of the service irrespective of any service, hardware or operating system failures

Table 3-8 lists the quality attribute requirements for Windows Azure and the description of how it satisfies those.

Table 3-8. Quality Attributes

Quality Attribute	Description
High availability	Windows Azure provides built-in redundancy with access routers, load balancers, and switches. Load balancers are automatically provisioned for external facing roles (e.g. Web roles).
Service isolation	Every service operates within the parameters of its service model. Services can access only the resources declared in the service model configuration. These resources include endpoints, local storage, and local machine resources.
Security	Every service role instance runs in the Windows user context. The instance does not have access to any administrative privileges and limited native execution access when native access is enabled.
Automatic provisioning	The fabric controller automates the service deployment from bare-metal hardware to service role deployment. The service model and the configuration information act as the instruction set for the fabric controller to provision appropriate hardware and virtual machine instances. The fabric controller can also upgrade your service while running without disruptions.

Architectural Advice

Finally, here is a list of some practical advice that should serve you well going forward.

- Clearly separate the functionality of the Web role from the Worker role. Do not use Worker role to perform web functions by exposing HTTP (or HTTPS) endpoints

- Maintaining stateless role interfaces is important for load balancing and fault tolerance. Keep the roles stateless.

- Use internal endpoints only for unreliable communications. For reliable communications, use Windows Azure queues (discussed in the next chapter).

- User Worker roles effectively for batch and background processing.

- Use service management API prudently for commissioning and decommissioning of the role instances. Do not keep instances running idle for a long period of time, because you are using server resources and will be charged for it.

- Do not use local storage for reliable storage; use Windows Azure storage as a reliable storage for storing data from roles.

- Design the system for fault tolerance and always account for failure of role instances.

- Finally, do not deploy your cloud service for maximum capacity; deploy for minimum or optimum capacity, and dynamically provision more instances as demand increases and vice versa.

Summary

In this chapter, we dove deeply into the computational features of Microsoft's Windows Azure cloud operating system. Through the examples, you were exposed to deploying Windows Azure Web role and Worker role instances, not only in the development fabric but also in the Windows Azure cloud. In the examples, you also learned how to access the configuration settings and local storage. Then, I briefly covered the geolocation, CDN, and service management features of Windows Azure. In the examples in this chapter, we were storing and retrieving data from the local storage, which is local and machine dependent. The data will be lost as soon as the underlying machine is rebooted or the service redeployed. Windows Azure storage provides you with persistent storage for storing highly available data that can be accessed from anywhere using REST-based API. In the next chapter, you will learn Windows Azure storage components and their programming APIs in detail.

Bibliography

Mario Barbacci, M. H. (1995). *Quality Attributes.* Pittsburgh, Pennsylvania 15213: Software Engineering Institute, Carnegie Mellon University.

Microsoft Corporation. (n.d.). *Windows Azure SDK.* Retrieved from MSDN:
`http://msdn.microsoft.com/en-us/library/dd179367.aspx`

Microsoft Corporation. (n.d.). *Windows Azure Team Blog.* Retrieved from
`http://blogs.msdn.com/windowsazure`

CHAPTER 4

Windows Azure Storage Part I – Blobs

The previous chapter covered the computational and management features of Windows Azure. In this chapter, you learn about Windows Azure's Storage service feature. Windows Azure Storage is a scalable, highly available, and durable service to store any kind of application data. The Storage service provides you with the ability to store data in three different types of storage types: blobs, queues, and tables. Each storage type has advantages; depending on the application requirements, you can choose the appropriate storage type for your data. You can also use multiple storage types within the same application.

The Blob service is designed to store large binary objects with associated metadata like documents, pictures, videos, and music files. The queue is a reliable asynchronous message delivery and storage type. Cloud services as well as on-premises applications can use queues for asynchronous cross-application communications. The table storage type provides structured storage capability to store billions of lightweight data objects occupying terabytes of data. This chapter covers the details of the blob storage type and equips you with enough information to make the right storage decisions for your applications. Table 4-1 lists the Windows Azure storage types and some of their properties.

Table 4-1. *Windows Azure Storage*

Feature	Blob	Queue	Table
URL schema	`http://[Storage Account].blob.core.windows.net/[Container Name]/[Blob Name]`	`http://[Storage Account].queue.core.windows.net/[Queue Name]`	`http://[Storage Account].table.core.windows.net/[Table Name]?$filter=[Query]`
Max size	50GB/blob	8KB (string)	Designed for terabytes of data
Recommended usage	Designed for large binary data types	Designed for cross-service message communication	Designed to store smaller structured objects like the user state across sessions
API reference	`http://msdn.microsoft.com/en-us/library/dd135733.aspx`	`http://msdn.microsoft.com/en-us/library/dd179363.aspx`	`http://msdn.microsoft.com/en-us/library/dd179423.aspx`

■ **Note** The Windows Azure Storage service is independent of the SQL Services database service offered by the Azure Services Platform.

Storage Service Architecture

The Windows Azure Storage service allows users to store application data in the cloud and access it from anywhere, anytime. The open architecture of the Storage service lets you design your applications and services to store and retrieve data using REST APIs. Each storage type in the Storage service has an independent REST programming API. Figure 4-1 illustrates the Windows Azure storage service architecture.

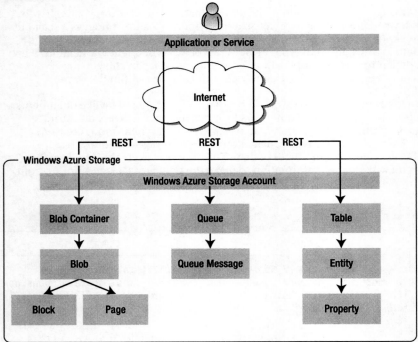

Figure 4-1. *Storage service architecture*

As shown in Figure 4-1, Windows Azure Storage types are scoped at the account level. This means that when you open a storage account, you get access to all the Windows Azure storage services. The Blob, Queue, and Table services all have REST API functions that let you interact with them.

A blob account is a collection of containers. You can create any number of containers in an account. A container consists of number of blobs. A blob can be further composed of a series of blocks.

A queue account is a collection of queues. An account can have any number of queues. A queue is composed of queue messages sent by the message sending applications.

The table storage type supports access via REST as well as the ADO.NET Data Services API. You can create any number of tables in an account. A table consists of a set of entities that represent runtime objects or data. Entities are analogous to the rows of data in a relational database. They have properties, which are analogous to the database fields in a relational database table. The table storage type isn't a relational database table; it follows the entity model, as shown in Figure 4-1.

What is REST?

The term REST was invented by Roy Thomas Fielding in his Ph.D. dissertation[1] "Architectural Styles and the Design of Network-based Software Architectures." Representation State Transfer (REST) is an interface architecture for systems deployed and accessible over the network.

The system entry points are abstracted into web resources. In REST, each resource has metadata and is uniquely identified by a URL. The operations of the resource are also exposed via URL. Each URL interaction with the resource returns a representation that can be any document or a binary object. For example, the URLs for blobs, queues, and tables in table 4-1 represent the REST URLs of these storage type resources. Querying these REST URLs returns appropriate representations from the resources, such as blob files or queue messages. The REST APIs for these storage types also expose operations, which are discussed in detail when I cover the respective storage type.

The URI scheme for addressing the Storage services is

```
<http|https>://<account-name>.<storage service name>.core.windows.net/<resource-path>
```

<http|https> is the protocol used to access Storage services. *<account-name>* is the unique name of your storage account. *<storage service name>* is the name of the storage service you're accessing (blob, queue, or table). And *<resource-path>* is the path of the underlying resource in the storage services that you're accessing. It can be a blob container name, a queue name, or a table name.

You used the Blob service in the previous chapter to store logs. In the next section, you study the Blob service in detail and learn to program against the REST programming API for blobs.

The Blob Service

The Blob service provides scalable and highly available storage for any kind of entities, such as binary files and documents. The Blob service achieves its scalability and high availability by distributing blob files across multiple servers and replicating them at least three times. It provides a REST API to store

---

[1] Roy Thomas Fielding. "Architectural Styles and the Design of Network-based Software Architectures." www.ics.uci.edu/~fielding/pubs/dissertation/top.htm.

named files along with their metadata. The Blob REST API provides consistency-checking features for concurrent operations.

■ **Note** *Windows Azure Blob*, *blob storage*, *Blob service*, and *Blob Storage service* all mean the same thing. The REST API HTTP headers call it the Blob service. Some MSDN documents refer to it as the Blob Storage service, and others call it Windows Azure blob. In this book I have tried to be consistent by calling it the Blob service. The blob object in the Blob service points to the actual file stored in the Blob service.

The Blob service is scoped at the account level. When you create an account on the Azure Services Developer Portal, you get access to the Blob service. Figure 4-2 shows the Azure Services Developer Portal page for the storage account created in the previous chapter and the URL endpoint for the Blob service.

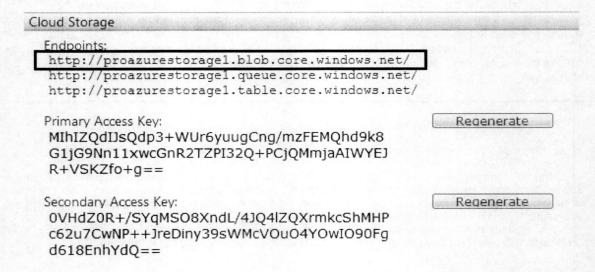

Figure 4-2. Blob endpoint URL

The account endpoint for the Blob service is *<account name>*.blob.core.windows.net, where *<account name>* is the unique name you created for your storage account. The secret key associated with the account provides security for accessing the storage account. You can use the secret key for create an HMAC-SHA256 signature for each request. The storage server uses the signature to authenticate the request.

Note HMAC stands for Hash Message Authentication Code, which is a message-authentication code calculated from the secret key using a special cryptographic hash function like MD5, SHA-1, or SHA256. The Windows Azure Storage service expects a SHA256 hash for the request. SHA256 is a 256-bit hash for the input data.

Blob Limitations and Constraints

Even though the Blob service provides a scalable and highly available service to store large files in the cloud, it has some limitations and constraints that are important to understand before you dive deep into its architecture and programming. The storage limitations of the Blob service are as follows:

- The maximum size of each block blob is 200GB and each page blob is 1TB (per version 2009-09-19 of the storage service API).

- You can upload blobs that are less than or equal to 64MB in size using a single PUT operation. Blobs more than 64MB in size must be uploaded as a set of blocks, with each block not greater than 4MB in size.

- The development Blob service supports blob sizes only up to 2GB.

Blob Architecture

The blob architecture consists of a four-level hierarchical structure: account, containers, blobs, blocks, and pages, as shown in Figure 4-3.

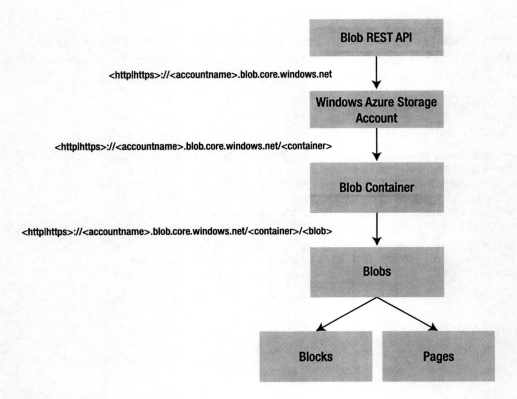

Figure 4-3. *Blob service architecture*

Your Windows Azure storage account is the entry point to the Blob service via the REST API.

Windows Azure Storage Account

The Windows Azure storage account encompasses the blob, queue, and table storage types. The URI scheme to access the Blob service via storage account is

<http|https>://*<account name>*.blob.core.windows.net

where *<account name>* is the unique name you created for your storage account. The *<account name>* must be globally unique.

For example, the Blob service for the storage account created in the previous chapter can be referenced as

<http|https>://proazurestorage.blob.core.windows.net

Containers

A *container* is a logical grouping for a set of blobs. Containers can have metadata in the form of name-value pairs. They can be created as public or private: public containers are visible to all users (anonymous) for read-only purposes without authentication, and private containers are visible only to the account owner. Blob is the only storage type that supports public and private access; the queue and table storage types support only private access.

You can access a container the following URI

`<http|https>://<account name>.blob.core.windows.net/<container>`

where *<container>* is the name of the container you want to access.

For example, if you create a blob container named logs in the proazurestorage account, you can reference it using the following URI:

`<http|https>://proazurestorage.blob.core.windows.net/logs`

The naming constraints on a container are as follows:[2]

- Container names must be unique within an account.

- Container names must start with a letter or a number.

- Container names can't contain any special characters other than the dash (-) character.

- The dash (-) character must be immediately followed by a character or a number.

- All the characters in the container name must be lowercase.

- Container names can't be fewer than 3 or more than 63 characters in length.

If a container name or the URI violates the naming convention, an HTTP status code 400 (Bad Request) is returned by the server.

Blobs

Blobs, which are the actual entities in the Blob service, are stored in containers. A blob name must be unique within the scope of a container. A blob can also have metadata in the form of name-value pairs. The Access Control List (ACL) is set only at the container level, so all the blobs in a public container are visible to everyone for read-only access. You can access a blob using the following URI

`<http|https>://<accountname>.blob.core.windows.net/<container>/<blob>`

---

[2]Source: Windows Azure SDK documentation

where *<blob>* is a unique name of the blob within the specified container. For example, if you create a blob named 200912211752pm-logs in the container named Logs, you can reference it by this URI:

<http|https>`://proazurestorage.blob.core.windows.net/logs/200912211752pm-logs.txt`

A blob name can't be more than 1,024 characters long. Blob doesn't support creation of folder hierarchies to store files; you can store files only in a flat structure. In most applications, the hierarchical organization of files is important for ease of access. To facilitate creation of a virtual folder structure, you to add a delimiter to a blob's name. For example, you can name a blob 2009/december/21/ 1752pm-logs.txt. With this naming scheme, you can add multiple log files in the virtual folder structure 2009/december/21/. For example, 2009/december/21/1752pm-logs.txt, 2009/december/21/1852pm-logs.txt, and 2009/december/21/1952pm-logs.txt can be the log files created on December 21, 2009.

The Blob API provides filtering capabilities based on a delimiter that allows you to retrieve only the log files in a particular virtual structure. For example, you can retrieve only the log files under the virtual folder structure 2009/december/21 by specifying a delimiter when enumerating the blobs. I cover this in the programming exercises later in the chapter. To support this functionality, the blob name can contain any combination of characters. Any reserved URL characters must be appropriately escaped. Some of the well-known URL reserved characters are dollar ($), ampersand (&), plus (+), comma (,), forward slash (/), colon (:), semicolon (;), equals (=), question mark (?), and at symbol (@).

Types of Blobs

In version 2009-09-19 of the storage service API, two types of blobs are available: page blobs and block blobs.

Page Blobs

Page blobs were introduced in the 2009-09-19 version of the storage service API. They're optimized for read/write access and provide you with the ability to copy a series of bytes into a blob. A page is represented by its start offset from the start of the blob. Writes to page blobs are immediately committed to the blob storage. You can store up to 1TB of data per page. Page blobs are ideal for applications requiring quick read/write access to binary data like images, videos, documents, and so on. The Windows Azure Storage Client API provides two operations on page blobs: Put Page and Get Page Regions. This book covers only block blobs in the interest of keeping the discussion conceptual.

Block Blobs

As listed in the blob limitations and constraints earlier, if a file is more than 64MB in size, it can't be uploaded to the Blob service using the PUT blob function. You have to first break the blob file into contiguous blocks and then upload it in the form of smaller chunks of data called *blocks*. Each block can be a maximum of 4MB in size. After all the blocks are uploaded, they can be committed to a particular blob. Note that in Figure 4-3, there is no URI to access blocks in a blob: after blocks are committed to a blob, you can only retrieve that complete blob. So, you can execute the GET operation only to the blob level.

Uploading blocks and committing blocks to a blob are two separate operations. You can upload the blocks in any sequence, but the sequence in which you commit the list of blocks represents the readable blob. You may upload multiple blocks in parallel in any random sequence, but when you execute the commit operation, you must specify the correct list for the block sequence representing the readable blob. Figure 4-4 illustrates the account, container, blob, and block relationships with an example.

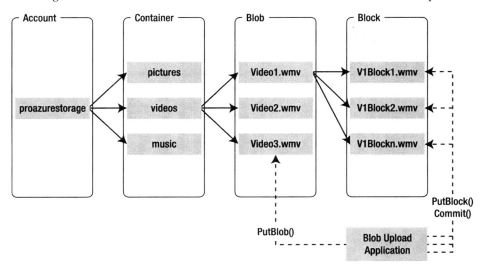

Figure 4-4. *Blob service example*

In Figure 4-4, you have a storage account name proazurestorage. The account has three containers: pictures, videos, and music. In the videos container are three video files: Video1.wmv, Video2.wmv, and Video3.wmv. Video2.wmv and Video1.wmv are less than 64MB in size, so the Blob Upload Application can directly upload these video files as blobs. But Video1.wmv is more than 64MB in size, so the Blob Upload Application has to break it into contiguous blocks and then upload each block. After all the blocks are uploaded, the application can commit the block list by giving the sequential order of the blocks that form the Video1.wmv blob file. Until all the blocks are committed, the blob file isn't available for reading. Any blocks that remain uncommitted due to application errors or network failures are garbage-collected after seven days of inactivity.

I cover the uploading and committing of blocks in a programming example later in the chapter.

REST API

The REST API for the Blob service is available at the account, container, and blob levels. In this section, you learn about the Blob service REST API with specific examples. As a result of the exercise, you also learn to interact with the Blob service programmatically, and you explore the blob methods in the available Storage Client libraries.

The REST API enables you to make HTTP calls to the Blob service and its resources. REST is an HTTP-based protocol that lets you specify the URI of the resource as well as the function you want to execute on the resource. Every REST call involves an HTTP request to the storage service and an HTTP response from the storage service.

■ **Note** Due to frequent changes to the Windows Azure Storage service API, the URL parameters may not be exactly the same as the most recent API version. But conceptually, the variation in the REST API shouldn't be significant. For the exact parameter lists, please refer to the Windows Azure SDK documentation shipped with the SDK.

Request

In the Blob service REST API, the HTTP request components include those outlined next.

HTTP Verb

The HTTP verb represents the action or operation you can execute on the resource indicated in the URI. The Blob service API supports the following verbs: GET, PUT, HEAD, and DELETE. Each verb behaves differently when executed on a different resource.

Request URI

The request URI represents the URI of a resource you're interested in accessing or executing a function on. Example resources in the Blob service API include an account, a container, and a blob. An example URI for creating a container named proazurecontainer in an account named proazurestorage is

PUT `http://proazurestorage.blob.core.windows.net/proazurecontainer`

The HTTP verb PUT instructs the service to create the container, and the URI points to the resource that needs to be created.

URI Parameters

The URI parameters are the extra parameters you specify to fine-tune your operation execution. They may include operation parameters or filter parameters for the results. In the Blob service API, the URI parameters depend on the type of resource and the HTTP verb used. For example, a URI to retrieve a list of containers from an account looks like this:

GET `http://proazurestorage.blob.core.windows.net/?comp=list`

The HTTP verb GET instructs the Blob service to retrieve results, and the parameter ?comp=list instructs that the data requested should be a list of containers.

Shared Access Signatures

Shared Access Signatures are a series of URL parameters specified in the URI of the resources for controlling access privileges to the resources. Shared Access Signatures are available for container and blob resources. In the URL, you can specify the start time when the resource becomes visible, the expiration time after which the Shared Access Signature expires, permissions that are granted to the

URL, the resource that is made available to the URL, and the signature used to authenticate the request to the resource. The available permissions are read (r), write (w), delete (d), and list (l). An example of a blob PUT operation's URL with Shared Access Signatures is as follows:

```
PUT http://proazure.blob.core.windows.net/videos/myvideo.wmv?st=2009-12-21T05%3a52Z&se=2009-
12-31T08%3a49Z&
sr=c&sp=w&si=YWJjZGVmZw%3d%3d&sig=Rcp6gPEIN%GJAI$KAM%PIR$APANG%Ca%IL%O$V%E
you%234so%m$uch2bqEArnfJxDgE%2bKH3TCChIs%3d HTTP/1.1
Host: proazure.blob.core.windows.net
Content-Length: 19

My Name is Tejaswi..
```

In these requests, the Shared Access Signatures are as follows:

- *st (signedstart):* (Optional) This is the start time when the resource becomes available with a valid Shared Access Signature.

- *se (signedexpiry):* (Required) This is the end time when the Shared Access Signature becomes invalid and, as a result, the URL can't access the resource.

- *sr (signedresource):* The parameter can have two values: b to specify access to a specific blob, and c to specify access to any blob in the container and to the list of blobs in the container.

- *sp (signedpermissions):* (Required) This parameter specifies the type of permissions to the resource: read (r), write (w), delete (d), or list (l).

- *si (signedidentifier):* (Optional) This is a unique string with as maximum of 64 characters that correlates to the access policy of the container, thus giving you an additional level of control over the Shared Access Signatures and the ability to revoke the signature.

- sig (signature): This is the signature used to authenticate the request. You can create a signature using the following method:

```
HMAC-SHA256(URL.Decode(UTF8.Encode(string-to-sign)))
```

HMAC-SHA256 is the algorithm used to compute the signature, and string-to-sign is of the format

```
string-to-sign = signedpermissions + "\n"
                 signedstart + "\n"
                 signedexpiry + "\n"
                 canonicalizedresource + "\n"
                 signedidentifier
```

Shared Access Signatures give you the ability to exercise fine-grained access control at the blob and container levels. Shared Access Signatures are very useful in creating time-bound temporary URLs for downloading file(s) from the Blob service.

Request Headers

Request headers follow the standard HTTP 1.1 name-value pair format. Depending on the type of request, the header may contain security, date-time or metadata information, or instructions embedded as name-value pairs. In the Storage Service REST API, the request header must include the authorization information and a Coordinated Universal Time (UTC) timestamp for the request. The timestamp can be in the form of either an HTTP/HTTPS date header or an x-ms-Date header.

The authorization header format is as follows

```
Authorization="[SharedKey|SharedKeyLite] <Account Name>:<Signature>"
```

where SharedKey|SharedKeyLite is the authentication scheme, *<Account Name>* is the storage service account name, and *<Signature>* is a Hash-based Message Authentication Code (HMAC) of the request computed using the SHA256 algorithm and then encoded using Base64 encoding.

To create the signature, you have to follow these steps:

1. Create the signature string for signing.

2. The signature string for the Storage service request consists of the following format:

```
VERB\n
Content - MD5\n
Content - Type\n
Date\n
CanonicalizedHeaders
CanonicalizedResource
```

3. VERB is an uppercase HTTP verb such as GET, PUT, and so on. Content – MD5 is the MD5 hash of the request content. CanonicalizedHeaders is the portion of the signature string created using a series of steps described in the "Authentication Schemes" section of the Windows Azure SDK documentation: http://msdn.microsoft.com/en-us/library/dd179428.aspx. And CanonicalizedResource is the storage service resource in the request URI. The CanonicalizedResource string is also constructed using a series of steps described in the "Authentication Schemes" section of the Windows Azure SDK documentation.

4. Use the System.Security.Cryptography.HMACSHA256.ComputeHash() method to compute the SHA256 HMAC-encoded string.

5. Use the System.Convert.ToBase64String() method to convert the encoded signature to Base64 format.

Listing 4-1 shows an example request header that sets the metadata values of a container.

Listing 4-1. *Request Header*

```
x-ms-date: Thu, 04 Jun 2009 03:58:47 GMT
x-ms-version: 2009-04-14
```

```
x-ms-meta-category: books
x-ms-meta-m1: v1
x-ms-meta-m2: v2
Authorization: SharedKey proazurestorage:88F+32ZRc+FO65+wEiQlDW/
```

The request header consists of x-ms-date, x-ms-version, x-ms-[name]:[value], and Authorization values. The x-ms-date represents the UTC timestamp, and the x-ms-version specifies the version of the storage service API you're using. The x-ms-version isn't a required parameter, but if you don't specify it, you have to make sure the operation you're calling is available in the default version of the Blob service. For example, to use the Copy Blob operation, you must specify the 2009-04-14 version string because the Copy Blob operation was added in this particular version and isn't available in the default version. The x-ms-meta values represent the container metadata name-value pairs that the operation wants to set. The last header value is the Authorization SharedKey used by the Storage service to authenticate and authorize the caller.

The Blob service REST API also supports HTTP 1.1 conditional headers. The conditional headers are used for conditional invocation of operations. For example, consider a scenario where you're working on a document that is stored as a blob. After editing the document, you want to save it back to the Blob service, but you don't know whether someone else on your team modified the document while you were editing it. The Blob service supports four types of conditional headers that act as preprocessing conditions for an operation to succeed. Table 4-2 lists these supported conditional headers.

Table 4-2. *Conditional Headers*

Conditional Header	Description
If-Modified-Since	A DateTime value instructing the storage service to execute the operation only if the resource has been modified since the specified time.
If-Unmodified-Since	A DateTime value instructing the storage service to execute the operation only if the resource has not been modified since the specified time.
If-Match	An ETag value instructing the storage service to execute the operation only if the ETag value in the header matches the ETag value of the resource.
If-None-Match	An ETag value instructing the storage service to execute the operation only if the ETag value in the header doesn't match the ETag value of the resource. You can use a wildcard (*) to instruct the storage service to execute the operation if the resource doesn't exist and fail if it does exists.

Different operations support different conditional headers; I cover conditional headers for specific operations in their respective sections later in the chapter.

Request Body

The response body consists of data returned by the operation. Some operations require a request body and some of them don't. For example, the Put Blob operation request body consists of the contents of the blob to be uploaded, whereas the Get Blob operation requires an empty request body.

Response

The HTTP response of the Blob service API typically includes the components described in the following sections.

Status Code

The status code is the HTTP status code that indicates the success or failure of the request. The most common status codes for the Blob service API are 200 (OK), 400 (BadRequest), 404 (NotFound), and 409 (Conflict).

Response Headers

The response headers include all the standard HTTP 1.1 headers plus any operation-specific headers returned by the Blob service. Typically, when you create or modify a container or a blob, the response header contains an ETag value and a Last-Modified value that can be used in conditional headers for future operations. The x-ms-request-id response header uniquely identifies a request. Listing 4-2 shows an example response header for a List Containers operation.

Listing 4-2. *List Containers Response Header*

```
Transfer-Encoding: chunked
Content-Type: application/xml
Server: Blob Service Version 1.0 Microsoft-HTTPAPI/2.0
x-ms-request-id: 53239be3-4d55-483f-90b9-fc2f2d073215
Date: Thu, 04 Jun 2009 05:28:16 GMT
```

Response Body

The response body consists of data returned by the operation. This data is specific to each operation. For example, the List Container operation returns the list of containers in an account, whereas the Get Blob operation returns the contents of the blob. Listing 4-3 shows an example of the response body for a List Container operation. The response contains three containers and a next marker pointing to the starting point of the remaining containers.

Listing 4-3. *List Containers Response Body*

```
<?xml version="1.0" encoding="utf-8"?>
<EnumerationResults AccountName="http://proazurestorage.blob.core.windows.net/">
<MaxResults>3</MaxResults>
<Containers>
```

```
<Container>
<Name>000000004c00f241-staging</Name>
<Url>http://proazurestorage.blob.core.windows.net/000000004c00f241-staging</Url>
<LastModified>Sun, 26 Apr 2009 15:05:44 GMT</LastModified>
<Etag>0x8CB94979BAAA0F0</Etag>
</Container>
<Container>
<Name>05022009-staging</Name>
<Url>http://proazurestorage.blob.core.windows.net/05022009-staging</Url>
<LastModified>Sun, 03 May 2009 04:50:07 GMT</LastModified>
<Etag>0x8CB99C1C3ECE538</Etag>
</Container>
<Container>
<Name>050320090743-staging</Name>
<Url>http://proazurestorage.blob.core.windows.net/050320090743-staging</Url>
<LastModified>Sun, 03 May 2009 14:44:28 GMT</LastModified>
<Etag>0x8CB9A14CC091F60</Etag>
</Container>
</Containers>
<NextMarker>/proazurestorage/050320091143-staging</NextMarker>
</EnumerationResults>
```

■ **Tip** To test the REST API, I recommend using the Fiddler tool available at `www.fiddler2.com/fiddler2/`. This book uses this tool to trace client/server communications.

Storage Client APIs

Even though the REST API and the operations in the REST API are easily readable, the API doesn't automatically create client stubs like the ones created by WDSL-based web services. You have to create your own client API and stubs for REST API operations. This makes the client programming more complex and increases the barrier to entry for developers. To reduce this barrier to entry, the Windows Azure SDK team has created two client helper libraries: Microsoft.WindowsAzure.StorageClient from the Windows Azure SDK, and the Storage Client code sample. Both libraries are used to invoke the REST APIs of the Windows Azure Storage service. Microsoft.WindowsAzure.StorageClient abstracts this by providing a closed-source interface and therefore is less interesting to developers who want to see the inner workings of the method calls.

In the Windows Azure CTP version, a code sample named Storage Client became the choice of developers for calling Storage services, because Microsoft.WindowsAzure.StorageClient wasn't available and also because it was open source; it gave good insight into building your own storage client library. The Storage Client made it easier to see the end-to-end method calls to the Storage service. This chapter uses the Storage Client code sample in the example applications. I also cover the class structure and calling mechanisms in the Microsoft.WindowsAzure.StorageClient namespace.

The following sections cover the Blob storage APIs from Microsoft.WindowsAzure.StorageClient and the Storage Client code sample.

■ **Note** You don't have to use the StorageClient library to make REST calls to the Storage service. You can create your own client library to make REST operations to the Storage service. In order to keep the book conceptual, I use the StorageClient code sample helper library to interact with the Storage service throughout this book. The source code for StorageClient is available in the samples directory of Windows Azure SDK or from the Windows Azure code samples site, http://code.msdn.microsoft.com/windowsazuresamples.

Windows Azure Storage Client Blob API

The Microsoft.WindowsAzure.StorageClient namespace consists of classes representing the entire Blob hierarchy. Figure 4-5 illustrates the core classes for programming Blob service applications.

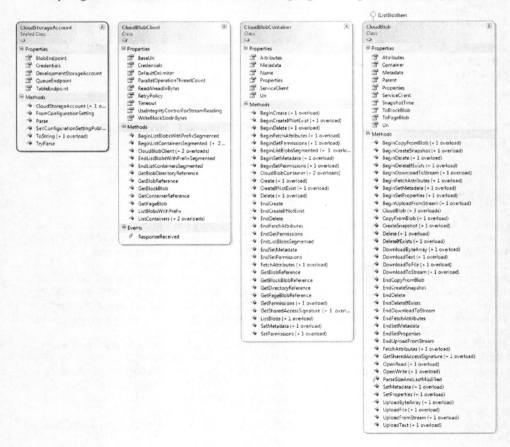

Figure 4-5. *Blob class hierarchy*

As shown in Figure 4-5, four core classes are required for blob operations. Table 4-3 describes these classes.

Tip The Windows Azure Storage Client API is the recommended method for programming storage service applications. The API provides synchronous as well as asynchronous methods for interacting with the Storage service REST APIs.

Table 4-3. *Classes for the Blob Service*

Class Name	Description
CloudStorageAccount	A helper class to retrieve account information from the configuration file or create an instance of the storage account object from account parameters.
CloudBlobClient	A wrapper class for getting references to the core blob objects. The class consists of methods like GetContainerReference() and GetBlobReference().
CloudBlobContainer	A class that consists of container operations like Create(), Delete(), ListBlobs(), and GetBlobReference().
CloudBlob	A class that consists of blob operations like Create(), Copy(), UploadFromFile(), UploadByteArray(), UploadStream(), and so on. This is the class you use the most to interact with blobs.

In addition to these core classes, classes like BlobProperties and BlobContainerProperties represent more details about the blob and the container, respectively. CloudPageBlob and CloudBlockBlob define operations for page blobs and block blobs, respectively.

The steps for programming simple blob applications with these blob classes are as follows:

1. Add the following using statement to your C# class:

```
using Microsoft.WindowsAzure.StorageClient;
```

2. Instantiate the CloudStorageAccount class from the configuration file:

```
CloudStorageAccount  storageAccountInfo =
CloudStorageAccount.FromConfigurationSetting(configurationSettingName);
```

3.   Or, instantiate the CloudStorageAccount class using account information:

```
CloudStorageAccount  storageAccountInfo = new CloudStorageAccount(new
StorageCredentialsAccountAndKey(accountName, accountKey), new Uri(blobEndpointURI), new
Uri(queueEndpointURI), new Uri(tableEndpointURI));
```

4.   Create an instance of CloudBlobClient:

```
CloudBlobClient blobStorageType = storageAccountInfo.CreateCloudBlobClient();
```

5.   When you have an instance of the CloudBlobClient class, you can execute
     operations on the Blob Storage service as follows:

     Get containers:

```
IList<CloudBlobContainer> containers = new
List<CloudBlobContainer>(this.blobStorageType.ListContainers(prefix,
ContainerListingDetails.All));
```

Create a container:

```
blobStorageType.GetContainerReference(containerName).CreateIfNotExist();
```

Create a container with permissions:

```
CloudBlobContainer container = blobStorageType.GetContainerReference(containerName);
BlobContainerPermissions perm = new BlobContainerPermissions();
perm.PublicAccess = accessType;
container.SetPermissions(perm);
container.Metadata.Add(new NameValueCollection());
container.CreateIfNotExist();
```

Create a blob by uploading a byte array:

```
blobStorageType.GetContainerReference(containerName).GetBlobReference(blobName).UploadByteAr
ray(blobContents);
```

Create a blob by uploading text:

```
blobStorageType.GetContainerReference(containerName).GetBlobReference(blobName).UploadText(b
lobContents);
```

Create a blob by uploading a stream:

```
blobStorageType.GetContainerReference(containerName).GetBlobReference(blobName).UploadFromSt
ream(blobContents);
```

Create a blob by uploading a file:

```
blobStorageType.GetContainerReference(containerName).GetBlobReference(blobName).UploadFile(f
ileName);
```

Get a blob by downloading a byte array:

```
blobStorageType.GetContainerReference(containerName).GetBlobReference(blobName).DownloadByte
Array();
```

Get a blob by downloading text:

```
blobStorageType.GetContainerReference(containerName).GetBlobReference(blobName).DownloadText
();
```

Get a blob by downloading a stream:

```
blobStorageType.GetContainerReference(containerName).GetBlobReference(blobName).DownloadToSt
ream(outputStream);
```

Get a blob by downloading a file:

```
blobStorageType.GetContainerReference(containerName).GetBlobReference(blobName).DownloadToFi
le(outputFileName);
```

Storage Client Code Sample: Blob API

The StorageClient library is available along with its source code in the Windows Azure SDK samples directory or on the Windows Azure code samples web site (http://code.msdn.microsoft.com/windowsazuresamples). The StorageClient library consists of several helper classes you can use to interact with the Windows Azure Storage service. These classes abstract the REST API intricacies from you and make it easier to make REST calls to all the storage types. This section covers the blob-specific classes and methods from the StorageClient project.

The StorageClient library has five important classes in the context of the Blob service; see Table 4-4.

Table 4-4. *StorageClient Classes for the Blob Service*

Class Name	Description
StorageAccountInfo	A helper class to retrieve account information from the configuration file.
BlobStorage	An abstract class with properties and methods at the account level of the Blob service hierarchy. It has an AccountName property and the method ListBlobContainers().
BlobStorageRest	A class that extends the BlobStorage class and implements the abstract methods. This class also has a nested class ListContainersResult representing the results returned by the Blob service type.
BlobContainer	An abstract class with signatures for the container and blob operations. Some example method calls are CreateContainer(), CreateBlob(), and ListBlobs().
BlobContainerRest	A class that extends the BlobContainer class and implements the abstract methods. This class also has a nested class ListBlobsResult representing the results returned by the Blob service.

Figure 4-6 illustrates the five classes listed in Table 4-4 and the relationships between them.

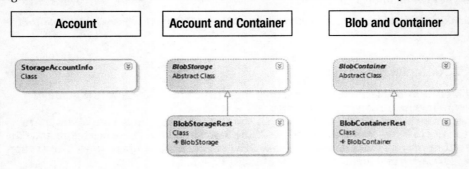

Figure 4-6. *StorageClient classes for the Blob service*

Following are some of the typical steps required to interact with the Blob service using the StorageClient classes:

1. Add your account information in the <appSettings> section of your application configuration file (app.config or web.config):

```
<add key = "AccountName" value="[Your Account Name]"/>
<add key = "AccountSharedKey"
value="[Your Account Shared Key from the Developer Portal]"/>
```

To work with local storage, add "devstoreaccount1" as the AccountName and "Eby8vdM02xNOcqFlqUwJPLlmEtlCDXJ1OUzFT50uSRZ6IFsuFq2UVErCz4I6tq /K1SZFPTOtr/KBHBeksoGMGw==" as the shared key.

2. Add the Blob service endpoint URI in the appSettings section of your application configuration file:

```
<add key="BlobStorageEndpoint" value="http://blob.core.windows.net"/>
```

To work with local storage, add the URI of the local Blob service resource: http://127.0.0.1:10000.

3. Create an instance of the StorageAccountInfo class from the configuration information you entered in the configuration file:

```
StorageAccountInfo account =
StorageAccountInfo.GetDefaultBlobStorageAccountFromConfiguration();
```

4. Create an instance of the BlobStorage class based on the account object:

```
BlobStorage blobStorage = BlobStorage.Create(account);
```

5. Call the ListAllBlobContainers() method on the blobStorage object to get a list of all the containers in the account:

```
blobStorage.ListBlobContainers();
```

6. To access a particular container, call

```
BlobContainer container = blobStorage.GetBlobContainer(containerName);
```

7. When you have a reference to the BlobContainer object, then you can call not only container methods like CreateContainer(), DeleteContainer(), and ListBlobs(), but also blob functions like CreateBlob(), UpdateBlob(), and DeleteBlob().

225

In the next few sections, you learn how to call some of these functions at every level of the Blob service hierarchy.

Account Operations

The storage account provides an entry point to the Blob service via the Blob service endpoint URI. At the account level of the hierarchy, the Blob service supports only one operation: List Containers. The URI of a specific account is of the format `http://<account name>.blob.core.windows.net`. Table 4-5 describes the List Containers operation, and Table 4-6 lists some important characteristics of the List Containers function.

Table 4-5. *Blob Account Operation*

Operation	Description
List Containers	This operation gets a list of all the containers in a storage account. You can limit the number of records returned by specifying a filter on container names and the size of the dataset in the request. Table 4.6 lists all the possible URI parameters for this operation.

Table 4-6. *Blob Account Operation Characterstics*

Operation	HTTP Verb	Cloud URI	Development Storage URI	HTTP Version	Permissions
List Containers	GET	`http://<account name>.blob.core.wind ows.net?comp=list`	`http://127.0.0.1:1 0000/<devstorageac count>?comp=list`	HTTP/1.1	Only the account owner can call this operation.

<account name> is the storage account name, such as proazurestorage, and *<devstorageaccount>* is the account name for the development storage. The HTTP verb used in this operation is GET. The table lists the URI format to access Cloud Blob service as well as the development storage URI. Port 10000 is the default Blob service port in the development fabric.

The URI for the List Containers operation also supports additional optional parameters, as listed in Table 4.7.

Table 4-7. *List Containers URI Parameters*

Parameter	Description	Example
prefix	A filter parameter to return containers starting with the specified prefix value.	http://proazurestorage.blob.core.windows.net /?comp=list&prefix=may returns containers with names starting with the prefix "may".
marker	Used to page container results when not all results were returned by the Storage service either due to the default maximum results allowed (the current default is 5000) or because you specify the maxresults parameter in the URI. The marker prefix is opaque to the client application.	http://proazurestorage.blob.core.windows.net /?comp=list&prefix=may&marker=/proazurestora ge/may0320091132-staging
maxresults	The maximum number of containers the Blob service should return. The default value is 5000. The server returns an HTTP Bad Request (400) code if you specify a maxresults value greater than 5000.	http://proazurestorage.blob.core.windows.net /?comp=list&prefix=may&maxresults=100

The sample REST request for List Containers in raw format looks like Listing 4-4.

Listing 4-4. *List Containers REST Request*

```
GET /?comp=list&prefix=may&maxresults=6&timeout=30 HTTP/1.1
x-ms-date: Wed, 27 May 2009 04:33:00 GMT
Authorization: SharedKey proazurestorage:GCvS8cv4Em6rWMuCVix9YCsxVgssOW62S2U8zjbIa1w=
Host: proazurestorage.blob.core.windows.net
Connection: Keep-Alive
```

The characteristics of the REST request in Listing 4-4 are as follows:

- The parameter comp=list at the account level of the Blob service yields the list of all the containers.

- The prefix=may filters the results by container names starting with "may".

- maxresults=6 returns only six containers.

- x-ms-date is the UTC timestamp of the request.

- The Authorization header contains the SharedKey of the request.

- The Host header points to the Blob service in the cloud.

- Because the request is sending a maxresults parameter, it makes sense to keep the HTTP connection alive because it's highly likely that the user will retrieve the next set of results by making one more call to the Blob service.

Listing 4-5 shows the response for the List Containers request.

Listing 4-5. *List Containers REST Response*

```
HTTP/1.1 200 OK
Content-Type: application/xml
Server: Blob Service Version 1.0 Microsoft-HTTPAPI/2.0
x-ms-request-id: 62ae926f-fcd8-4371-90e1-bdb6d32e31e6
Date: Wed, 27 May 2009 04:34:48 GMT
Content-Length: 1571

<?xml version="1.0" encoding="utf-8"?>
<EnumerationResults AccountName="http://proazurestorage.blob.core.windows.net/">
<Prefix>may</Prefix>
<MaxResults>6</MaxResults>
<Containers>
<Container>
<Name>may022009-01-52-staging</Name>
<Url>http://proazurestorage.blob.core.windows.net/may022009-01-52-staging</Url>
<LastModified>Sat, 02 May 2009 08:54:23 GMT</LastModified>
<Etag>0x8CB991AB99A3DE8</Etag>
</Container>
<Container>
<Name>may022009-01-56-staging</Name>
<Url>http://proazurestorage.blob.core.windows.net/may022009-01-56-staging</Url>
<LastModified>Sat, 02 May 2009 08:58:08 GMT</LastModified>
<Etag>0x8CB991B3F6EECF8</Etag>
</Container>
<Container>
<Name>may031119am-staging</Name>
<Url>http://proazurestorage.blob.core.windows.net/may031119am-staging</Url>
<LastModified>Sun, 03 May 2009 18:21:46 GMT</LastModified>
<Etag>0x8CB9A3326D83577</Etag></Container>
<Container><Name>may0320091132-staging</Name>
<Url>http://proazurestorage.blob.core.windows.net/may0320091132-staging</Url>
<LastModified>Sun, 03 May 2009 18:33:55 GMT</LastModified>
<Etag>0x8CB9A34D97B4CC0</Etag>
</Container>
<Container>
<Name>may0320091413pm-staging</Name>
<Url>http://proazurestorage.blob.core.windows.net/may0320091413pm-staging</Url>
<LastModified>Sun, 03 May 2009 21:14:53 GMT</LastModified>
<Etag>0x8CB9A4B5676BA40</Etag>
</Container>
```

```
<Container>
<Name>may0320091500pm-staging</Name>
<Url>http://proazurestorage.blob.core.windows.net/may0320091500pm-staging</Url>
<LastModified>Sun, 03 May 2009 22:01:55 GMT</LastModified>
<Etag>0x8CB9A51E81571B3</Etag>
</Container>
</Containers>
<NextMarker />
</EnumerationResults>
```

In Listing 4-5, the header consists of the HTTP status (200 OK) indicating the success of the operation. The response body is in XML format with <EnumerationResults /> as the root element. The <Containers /> element contains the retrieved containers. The <ETag> or the entity tag and the <LastModified> values are used to find changes to the content source after it was retrieved. These fields are used to detect concurrency conditions where a resource may change between retrieve and save operations. The empty <NextMarker /> element indicates that all the results have been retrieved.

Programming Example

To help you understand the Blob service programming model, I've created a project named Windows Azure Storage Operations in Ch4Solution.sln. The name of the Windows application project is Windows Azure Storage Operations. The project consists of a Windows Form and uses the StorageClient project from the same solution to make calls to all the Windows Azure Storage. The StorageClient project is shipped with the Windows Azure SDK. I've also created a helper class named WindowsAzureStorageHelper in the ProAzureCommonLib project, to wrap the StorageClient methods. You can replace the StorageClient methods with the Windows Azure SDK Storage Client methods so the application doesn't need a code change when shifting APIs. Figure 4-7 shows the user interface for the Windows Azure Storage Operations.exe application as it pertains to the account operations of the Blob service.

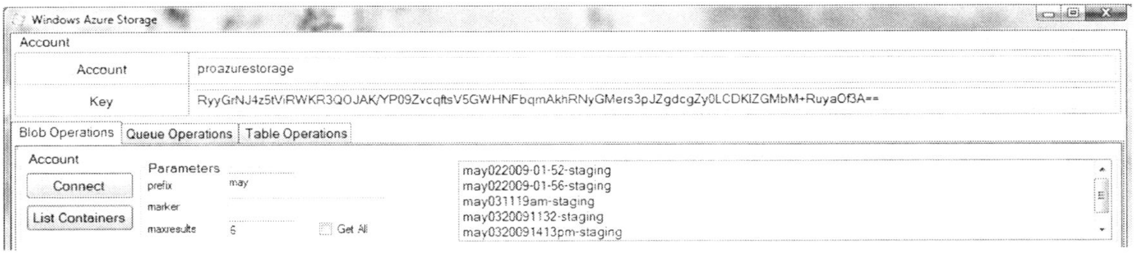

Figure 4-7. *Windows Azure Storage Operations blob account operations*

In Figure 4-7, the top Account section displays the Account name and SharedKey of the storage account. When the Windows Azure Storage Operations application starts, it loads the account information from the configuration file. Listing 4-6 shows the account configuration in the project's app.config file.

Listing 4-6. App.config

```xml
<?xml version="1.0" encoding="utf-8" ?>
<configuration>
  <appSettings>
    <add key ="AccountName" value="proazurestorage"/>
    <add key ="AccountSharedKey" value="RyyGrNJ4z5tViRWKR3QOJAK"/>
    <add key="BlobStorageEndpoint" value="http://blob.core.windows.net"/>
    <add key="QueueStorageEndpoint" value="http://queue.core.windows.net"/>
    <add key="TableStorageEndpoint" value="http://table.core.windows.net"/>
    <add key="LocalStorageAccountName" value="devstoreaccount1"/>
  </appSettings>
</configuration>
```

The AccountName and AccountSharedKey values are loaded when the application starts; the application displays these values in the Account and Key text fields, respectively. When you start the application, make sure to enter the account name and shared key of your own storage account or change then in the app.config file before building the project. The account information is used to initialize the WindowsAzureStorageHelper class, as shown here:

```
StorageHelper = new WindowsAzureStorageHelper(txtAccountName.Text,
                    txtKey.Text, IsLocal,
                    blobStorageEndPoint,
                    queueStorageEndpoint,
                    tableStorageEndpoint);
```

The BlobStorageEndpoint is the URI of the Blob service.

The WindowsAzureStorageHelper class in the ProAzureCommonLib project has two overloaded GetContainers() methods to retrieve container names. Listing 4-7 shows the code for these two methods.

Listing 4-7. GetContainers() Methods

```
public IEnumerable<BlobContainer> GetContainers()
{
return this.BlobStorageType.ListBlobContainers();
}
 public IList<BlobContainer> GetContainers
(string prefix, int maxResults, ref string marker)
{
return this.BlobStorageType.ListBlobContainers(prefix, maxResults, ref marker);
}
```

Both methods call the ListBlobContainers() method on the BlobStorageType object. BlobStorageType is a property that points to an instance of the BlobStorage class from the StorageClient project. The first ListBlobContainers() method returns all the containers from the account; therefore it doesn't accept any filtering parameters. The second ListBlobContainers() method accepts prefix, maxresults, and marker parameters. The marker field is used to page results. Whenever you pass maxresults, the returned response consists of a marker (the XML element name in the response is NextMarker) that points to the next available record that wasn't retrieved from storage because of the maxresults filter. Therefore, it represents the (maxresults + 1) record. You can call the same method again and pass the marker to retrieve the results beginning from the marker records. The results returned from these methods are displayed in the list box in the Account section of the Windows Azure Storage Operations.exe application, as shown in the Figure 4-8.

Figure 4-8. *List Containers*

When you click the List Containers button, the application retrieves containers from the Blob service and displays the names of containers in the list box. In the Parameter section, you can specify the prefix and the maxresults for the result set. Marker is a read-only text box that displays the marker to the next record, if it exists. The Marker text box is empty if all the records have been retrieved. Click the List Containers button again to retrieve the remaining results until the Marker field is empty.

Figure 4-9 illustrates the sequence of method calls across different objects and assemblies to retrieve the result from the Blob service.

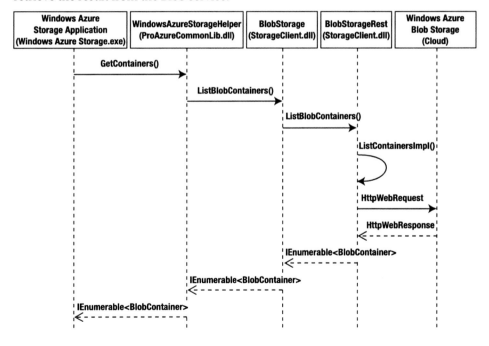

Figure 4-9. *List Containers sequence diagram*

In Figure 4-9, the Windows Azure Storage Operations application calls the GetContainers() method on the WindowsAzureStorageHelper object in the ProAzureCommonLib assembly. The helper object then calls the ListBlobContainers() method on the BlobStorage and BlobStorageRest objects. BlobStorage is an abstract class, and BlobStorageRest inherits and implements the abstract methods from BlobStorage. The ListBlobContainers() method in turn calls the private method ListContainersImpl(). Finally, the actual logic to make the HTTP request to the Blob service is in the ListContainerImpl() method. The Blob service returns the list of containers in an HTTP response, which is parsed and propagated back to the Windows Azure Storage Operations application for display.

▨ **Note** The StorageClient that comes with SDK includes only one signature for the ListBlobContainers() method. This method retrieves all the containers at once. But in reality, you want to page the results by specifying the maxresults parameter. So, I've added a new overloaded method IEnumerable<*BlobContainer*> ListBlobContainers(string prefix, int maxResults, ref string marker) to the BlobStorage and BlobStorageRest classes, to filter the containers you want to retrieve from the Blob service.

Container Operations

The URI of a specific container is of the format <account name>.blob.core.windows.net/<container name>. Containers support several operations, as listed in Table 4-8.

Table 4-8. Container Operations

Operation	Description
Create Container	Creates a new container under the given account. You can specify metadata and access control for the container during creation.
Get Container Properties	Returns the user-defined metadata values and the system properties of the container. The ETag and Last-Modified values are examples of system generated container properties.
Set Container Metadata	Sets the user-defined metadata values of a container. This operation sets or overwrites all the metadata values at once. You can't change specific name-value pairs of a container. The ETag value of a container changes when this operation executes successfully.

Continued

Operation	Description
Get Container ACL	Returns a container's access control bit value. It returns False if a container is private and True if public.
Set Container ACL	Sets a container's access control bit value. You can set the value of the header parameter x-ms-prop-publicaccess to True for a public container or False for a private container.
Delete Container	Marks a container for deletion. The delete operation doesn't delete the container instantly; it's deleted during the next garbage-collection cycle. So, if you delete a container and immediately try to create another container with the same name, you may receive an error if the container hasn't been garbage-collected. When a container is deleted, all the blobs in that container are also deleted.
List Blobs	Retrieves blobs from a particular container. Similar to the List Containers operation, you can specify maxresults and prefix parameters to filter your results. This operation also supports a delimiter parameter that you can use to group blobs in a virtual path structure. For example, if there are two blobs named mydocuments/docA.docx and mydocuments/docB.docx, then if you specify the delimiter as / in your HTTP Request, the HTTP response will contain a <BlobPrefix >mydocuments/</BlobPrefix> element as a virtual group for docA.docx and docB.docx.

Table 4-9 lists some of the important characteristics of the container operations listed in Table 4-8.

Table 4-9. *Container Operation Characterstics*

Operation	HTTP Verb	Cloud URI	Development Storage URI	HTTP Version	Permissions
Create Container	PUT	http://<account name>.blob.core.wind ows.net/<container name>	http://127.0.0.1: 10000/<devstorage account>/<contain erName>	HTTP/1.1	Only the account owner can call this operation.
Get Container Properties	GET/HEAD	http://<account name>.blob.core.wind ows.net/<container name>	http://127.0.0.1: 10000/<devstorage account>/<contain erName>	HTTP/1.1	Any client may call this operation on a public container. *Continued*

Table 4-9. *Continued*

Operation	HTTP Verb	Cloud URI	Development Storage URI	HTTP Version	Permissions
Set Container Metadata	PUT	`http://<account name>.blob.core.wi ndows.net/<contain er name>?comp=metadat a`	`http://127.0.0.1 :10000/<devstora geaccount>/<cont ainerName>?comp= metadata`	HTTP/1.1	Only the account owner can call this operation.
Get Container ACL	GET/ HEAD	`http://<account name>.blob.core.wi ndows.net/<contain er name>?comp=acl`	`http://127.0.0.1 :10000/<devstora geaccount>/<cont ainerName>?comp= acl`	HTTP/1.1	Only the account owner can call this operation.
Set Container ACL	PUT	`http://<account name>.blob.core.wi ndows.net/<contain er name>?comp=acl`	`http://127.0.0.1 :10000/<devstora geaccount>/<cont ainerName>?comp= acl`	HTTP/1.1	Only the account owner can call this operation.
Delete Container	DELETE	`http://<account name>.blob.core.wi ndows.net/<contain er name>`	`http://127.0.0.1 :10000/<devstora geaccount>/<cont ainerName>`	HTTP/1.1	Only the account owner can call this operation.
List Blobs	GET	`http://<account name>.blob.core.wi ndows.net/<contain er name>?comp=list`	`http://127.0.0.1 :10000/<devstora geaccount>/<cont ainerName>?comp= list`	HTTP/1.1	Only the account owner can call this operation.

<account name> is the storage account name in the cloud, and *<devstorageaccount>* is the development storage account. note that only one operation, Get Container Properties, can be called by all the users on a public container. All other operations can only be called by the owner of the container.

The following sections discuss some of the operations from Table 4-9 in detail. Even though the operations are different, the programming concepts behind them are similar. To keep the book at a conceptual level, I discuss Create Container, Set Container Metadata, and List Blobs operations, because they cover most of the discussed concepts. By studying these three operations in detail, you can understand the programming concepts behind all the container operations. The Windows Azure Storage Operations.exe application included with this chapter's source code contains implementations of all the container operations.

Create Container

The Create Container operation is used to create a container in an account. The URI for Create Container is of the format `http://<account name>.blob.core.windows.net/<container name>`. You can think of a container as a bucket for holding similar blobs, although it's not a requirement that blobs in a container be similar. For example, if you want to store all your media files as Azure blobs, you can create a container for each media type, such as Music, Video, and Pictures. Then, you can store your media blobs under each category. This gives you easy access to particular media types. The Create Container REST request looks like Listing 4-8.

Listing 4-8. *Create Container REST Request*

```
PUT /myfirstcontainer?timeout=30 HTTP/1.1
x-ms-date: Fri, 05 Jun 2009 02:31:10 GMT
x-ms-meta-creator: tejaswi
x-ms-meta-creation-date: 06042009
x-ms-prop-publicaccess: true
Authorization: SharedKey proazurestorage:mQfgLwFfzFdDdMU+drg5sY2LfGKMSfXQnWrxrLPtzBU=
Host: proazurestorage.blob.core.windows.net
Content-Length: 0
Connection: Keep-Alive
```

Listing 4-8 shows the request to create a container named myfirstcontainer. x-ms-meta-[name]:[value] represents the metadata values for the container. x-ms-prop-publicaccess:true indicates that the container has public visibility.

For the Create Container operation, the Blob service responds with a status code of HTTP/1.1 201 Created or HTTP/1.1 409 Conflict if a container with the same name already exists. The Create Container response is shown in Listing 4-9.

Listing 4-9. *Create Container REST Response*

```
HTTP/1.1 201 Created
Last-Modified: Fri, 05 Jun 2009 02:32:43 GMT
ETag: 0x8CBB39D0A486280
Server: Blob Service Version 1.0 Microsoft-HTTPAPI/2.0
x-ms-request-id: a0ea17df-5528-4ad3-985c-20664b425c7b
Date: Fri, 05 Jun 2009 02:32:43 GMT
Content-Length: 0
```

In Listing 4-9, the first line represents the status code of the operation. The ETag and the Last-Modified values can be used in conditional headers while modifying or deleting the container. The Create Container operation doesn't support any conditional headers, but the Set Container Metadata and Delete Container operations, discussed later, do support conditional headers. x-ms-request-id represents a unique request identifier that you can use for debugging or tracing.

Figure 4-10 shows the working of the Create Container operation in the Windows Azure Storage Operations application.

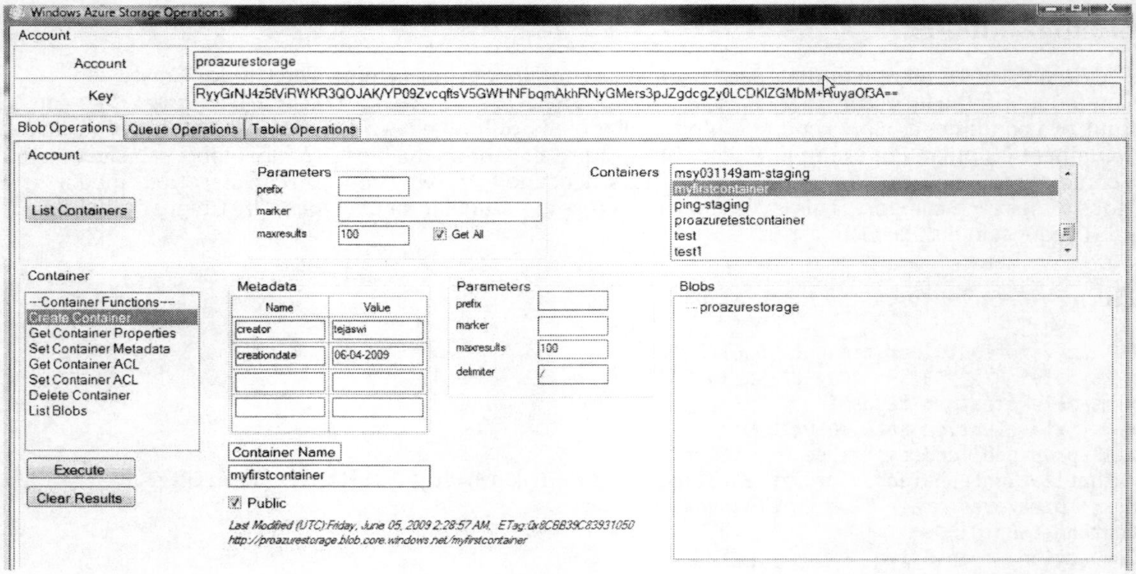

Figure 4-10. *Create Container from the Windows Azure Storage Operations application*

As shown in Figure 4-10, you follow these steps to create a container:

1. Enter a container name (such as myfirstcontainer) in the Container Name text field.
2. Check the Public check box if the container is public (accessible to everyone).
3. Enter any metadata for the container in the Metadata section of the container.
4. Select Create Container Function in the Container Functions list box.
5. Click the Execute button.

After the container is created, the Containers list box in the Account section is refreshed and displays the newly created container's name. To better understand the programming model of the Create Container operation, open the Visual Studio Solution Chapter4.sln from the Chapter 4 source directory. The WindowsAzureStorageHelper class in ProAzureCommonLib contains a helper function called CreateContainer, as shown in Listing 4-10.

Listing 4-10. *CreateContainer Method in the WindowsAzureStorageHelper Class*

```
public void CreateContainer
(string containerName, ContainerAccessControl accessType,
NameValueCollection metadata)
{
BlobContainer container = BlobStorageType.GetBlobContainer(containerName);
container.CreateContainer(metadata, accessType);
```

}

The CreateContainer() method calls the GetBlobContainer() method to get a reference to the BlobContainer object. The BlobContainer object is a local instance of the container object. This instance doesn't create a container when you instantiate it. To create a container, you have to call the CreateContainer() method on the BlobContainer object. The BlobContainer object is used by the StorageClient to create accurate URI and metadata headers and send them to the Blob service. The NameValueCollection object named metadata represents the metadata values of the container you're creating. The ContainerAccessControl enumeration represents the access control for the container. It can be either Public or Private (the default is Private). Figure 4-11 illustrates the sequence of method calls across different objects and assemblies for the Create Container operation.

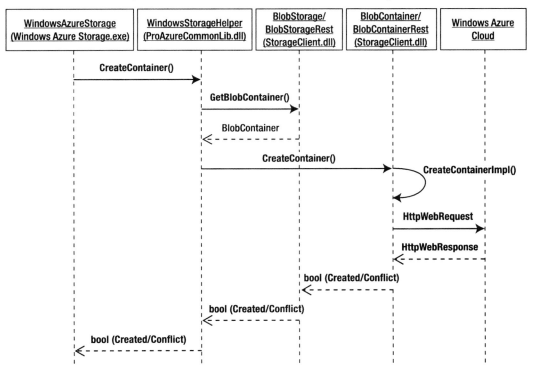

Figure 4-11. *Create Container sequence diagram*

As shown in Figure 4-11, the Windows Azure Storage Operations application calls the CreateContainer() method on the WindowsStorageHelper object in ProAzureCommonLib.dll. The WindowsStorageHelper object calls the GetBlobContainer() method on the BlobStorage object to get an instance of the BlobContainer object. The WindowsStorageHelper object then calls the CreateContainer() method on the BlobContainer object. The BlobContainer object calls a private method CreateContainerImpl(), which creates the REST message and sends it synchronously to the Windows Azure Blob service to create the container. It uses System.Net.HttpWebRequest to send the REST message over HTTP. Upon the success or failure of the operation, the Windows Azure Blob service returns an HTTP status code: HTTP/1.1 201 for success or HTTP/1.1 409 for conflict or failure. The CreateContainerImpl() method translates the HTTP status code into true for success and false for failure or conflict. The Boolean value is passed all the way to the Windows Azure Storage Operations.exe application as a return parameter of the CreateContainer() method.

Set Container Metadata

Containers contain name-value pairs of metadata values. You can store values like time of creation, creator, last modified by user, and so on in a container's metadata fields. The size of the metadata can be 8KB per container. The Set Container Metadata operation sets the metadata of a container independently. The URI for the Set Container Metadata operation is of the format `http://<account name>.blob.core.windows.net/<container name>?comp=metadata`. The Set Container Metadata REST request looks like Listing 4-11.

Listing 4-11. Set Container Metadata REST Request

```
PUT /myfirstcontainer?comp=metadata&timeout=30 HTTP/1.1
x-ms-date: Fri, 05 Jun 2009 05:44:21 GMT
x-ms-meta-creator: tejaswi
x-ms-meta-creation-date: 06042009
x-ms-meta-last-updated-by: arohi
Authorization: SharedKey proazurestorage:hC5t3QscO9kINOzRCRN2vcgTIyPR97ay7WZRzwgbKBI=
Host: proazurestorage.blob.core.windows.net
Content-Length: 0
Connection: Keep-Alive
```

In Listing 4-11, the HTTP verb used is PUT. Note the URI parameter ?comp=metadata; it instructs the Blob service to set the container metadata instead of creating the container. The Create Container operation doesn't have this parameter. The x-ms-meta.[name]:[value] entries represent the metadata name-value pairs you want to set on the container.

▓ **Caution** The Set Container Metadata operation replaces all the existing metadata of the container. It doesn't update individual metadata entries. For example, if a container has two metadata values Creator and Creation-Time, and you call Set Container Metadata with only one metadata value LastUpdatedBy, then the Creator and Creation-Time values will be deleted and the container will have only one metadata value LastUpdatedBy. To avoid this side effect, always set all the metadata values again along with any new values you want to add to the container's metadata.

The Set Container Metadata operation also supports the conditional header If-Modified-Since, which isn't shown in Listing 4-11. The If-Modified-Since header carries a date-time value instructing the Blob service to set the metadata values only if they have been modified since the supplied date in the request header.

The response from the Blob service consists of one the following HTTP status codes:

- HTTP/1.1 200 OK if the operation is successful

- HTTP/1.1 412 PreconditionFailed if the precondition If-Modified-Since fails

- HTTP/1.1 304 NotModified if the condition specified in the header isn't met

Figure 4-12 illustrates the execution of the Set Container Metadata operation in the Windows Azure Storage Operations application.

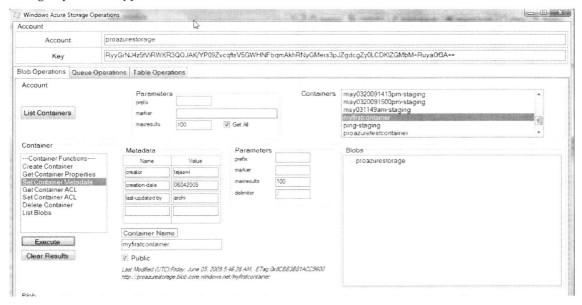

Figure 4-12. *Set Container Metadata in the Windows Azure Storage Operations application*

As shown in Figure 4-12, you follow these steps to execute the Set Container Metadata operation:

1. In the Account section, click the List Containers button to get a list of containers in your account.

2. Select one of the containers from the list (such as myfirstcontainer).

3. Make sure the Container Name text box in the Container section displays the name of the selected container.

4. In the Container section, select the Set Container Metadata operation from the list of container operations.

5. In the Containers section, enter metadata name-value pairs in the Metadata section.

6. Click the Execute button to execute the operation.

7. To verify the success of the operation, click the Clear Results button in the Containers section, and re-select the container from the Containers list in the Account section to the newly set metadata values.

To better understand the programming model of the Set Container Metadata operation, open the Visual Studio Solution Chapter4.sln from the Chapter 4 source directory. The WindowsAzureStorageHelper class in ProAzureCommonLib contains a helper function called SetContainerMetadata(), as shown in Listing 4-12.

Listing 4-12. *SetContainerMetadata Method in the WindowsAzureStorageHelper Class*

```
public bool SetContainerMetadata
(string containerName, NameValueCollection metadata)
{

BlobContainer container = BlobStorageType.GetBlobContainer(containerName);
return container.SetContainerMetadata(metadata);
}
```

In Listing 4-12, the SetContainerMetadata method accepts the name of the container and a System.Collection.Specialized.NameValueCollection object populated with metadata name-value pairs. The container name is used to create a local instance of the BlobContainer object. The code then calls the SetContainerMetadata() method on the BlobContainer object to set the metadata values for the container. If the metadata is set successfully, a Boolean value of true is returned to the caller; otherwise, a false value is returned. Figure 4-13 illustrates the sequence of method calls across different objects and assemblies for the Set Container Metadata operation.

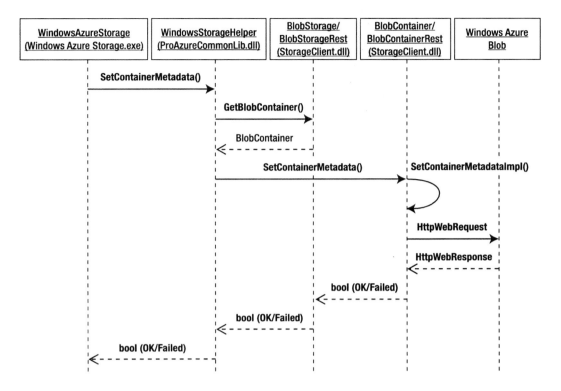

Figure 4-13. *Set Container Metadata sequence diagram*

As shown in Figure 4-13, the Windows Azure Storage Operations application calls the SetContainerMetadata() method on the WindowsStorageHelper object in ProAzureCommonLib.dll. The WindowsStorageHelper object calls the GetBlobContainer() method on the BlobStorage object to get an instance of the BlobContainer object. The WindowsStorageHelper object then calls the SetContainerMetadata() method on the BlobContainer object. The BlobContainer object calls a private method SetContainerMetadataImpl(), which creates the REST message and sends it synchronously to the Windows Azure Blob service to set the container metadata. It uses the System.Net.HttpWebRequest to send the REST message over HTTP. Upon the success or failure of the operation, the Windows Azure Blob service returns an HTTP status code: HTTP/1.1 200 for success or HTTP/1.1 412 or 304 for a precondition failure. The SetContainerMetadataImpl() method translates the HTTP status code into true for success and false for failure. The Boolean value is passed all the way to the Windows Azure Storage Operations application as a return parameter of the SetContainerMetadata() method.

List Blobs

Containers are typically used to logically group and store blobs. The URI for the List Blobs operation is of the format http://<account name>.blob.core.windows.net/<container name>?comp=list. At the container level of the Blob service hierarchy, you can get a list of blobs in a container by calling the List

241

Blobs operation. The List Blobs operation also provides paging capabilities with maxresults and prefix parameters, similar to the List Containers operation discussed earlier. The container and blob hierarchy is a single-level hierarchy, but in real-world applications you want to create deeper hierarchies with folder structures to store blob files. For example, there may be a scenario where you would want to create a multilevel folder structure for your music files in the music container, as shown in Figure 4-14.

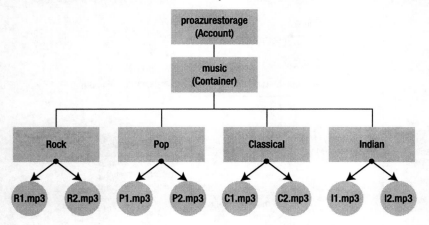

Figure 4-14. *Music container hierarchy*

In Figure 4-14, the *.mp3 files represent the blob files you want to store in the music container, but you want an intermediate folder structure to organize the blob files by the genre of the music file. The Blob service hierarchy doesn't allow you to create folders in containers to create folder structures, but the blob naming convention is relaxed so that you can add a delimiter in the name of the blob file to create a virtual folder structure within the name of the blobs. To create a virtual folder structure as shown in Figure 4-14, you can name the blobs as follows:

> Rock/R1.mp3
>
> Rock/R2.mp3
>
> POP/P1.mp3
>
> POP/P2.mp3
>
> Classical/C1.mp3
>
> Classical/C2.mp3
>
> Indian/I1.mp3
>
> Indian/I2.mp3

When you store a blob to the container, you specify the folder structure in the file name. When you retrieve the blob structure, you specify the delimiter character (/ in this example) as the parameter in the URI of the List blob operation. The Blob service sends you a BlobPrefix XML element specifying the folder structure that groups blobs with similar names together. You see an example of this in a few paragraphs.

The URI for the List Blobs operation also supports additional optional parameters, as listed in Table 4.10.

Table 4-10. *List Blobs URI Parameters*

Parameter	Description	Example
prefix	A filter parameter to return files starting with the specified prefix value.	http://proazurestorage.blob.core.windows.net/music?comp=list&prefix=kishore returns containers with names starting with the prefix "kishore".
delimiter	A character or a string that represents the separation of different tokens present in the name of a blob.	If the name of a blob is rock/R1.mp3, you can specify / as a delimiter to separate the string tokens rock and R1.mp3.
marker	Pages blob results when all results weren't returned by the Storage service either due to the default maximum results allowed (the current default is 5000) or because you specify the maxresults parameter in the URI. The marker prefix is opaque to the client application.	http://proazurestorage.blob.core.windows.net/music/?comp=list&prefix=kishore&marker=/proazurestorage/kishore0320091132.mp3.
maxresults	The maximum number of blobs the Blob service should return. The default value is 5000. The Server returns an HTTP Bad Request (400) code if you specify a maxresults value greater than 5000.	http://proazurestorage.blob.core.windows.net/music/?comp=list&prefix=kishore&maxresults=100.

Assume that the blob hierarchy from Figure 4-14 exists in the Blob service. To retrieve all the blobs in the music container, you have to execute two REST requests for each blob file. In the first request, you pass the delimiter (such as /) as one of the URI parameters. The Blob service response gets the first token of the blob name separated by the delimiter (for example, Classical/) as a BlobPrefix element in the response body. The first token doesn't represent the end of the blob name, so you have to make one more request to the Blob service by passing the first token as a prefix parameter to the Blob service URI (for example, prefix=Classical/). Now, because the next token represents the end of the blob name, the Blob service sends the blob properties in the response. If the blob name has more tokens, you must keep on querying the Blob service until you reach the end of blob name to retrieve the blob properties you're interested in.

Note If the blob name doesn't contain a delimiter, or if you want to retrieve the blob name along with the delimiter, then you don't have to pass a delimiter—the first response retrieves all the blob properties in the specified container.

In the first REST request, you specify the container name, maxresults (optional), and delimiter (/ in the music example), as shown in Listing 4-13.

Listing 4-13. *List Blobs First REST request*

```
GET /music?comp=list&delimiter=%2f&maxresults=100&timeout=30 HTTP/1.1
x-ms-date: Sun, 07 Jun 2009 05:53:37 GMT
Authorization: SharedKey proazurestorage:7euawYh5wNOGFJZGnvrn9vyR4y
Host: proazurestorage.blob.core.windows.net
```

The Blob service responds to this request with the list of <BlobPrefix> values tokenized by the delimiter at the next level of the folder hierarchy. In the music example, the next level of the folder hierarchy consists of Genres values like Classical, Indian, POP, and Rock. The response from the Blob service is shown in Listing 4-14.

Listing 4-14. *List Blobs First Response*

```
HTTP/1.1 200 OK
Content-Type: application/xml
Server: Blob Service Version 1.0 Microsoft-HTTPAPI/2.0
x-ms-request-id: 7c490b17-8c99-43fa-ab8b-bde4cef032d7
Date: Sun, 07 Jun 2009 05:54:41 GMT
Content-Length: 408

<?xml version="1.0" encoding="utf-8"?>
<EnumerationResults
ContainerName="http://proazurestorage.blob.core.windows.net/music">
<MaxResults>100</MaxResults>
<Delimiter>/</Delimiter>
<Blobs>
<BlobPrefix>
<Name>Classical/</Name>
</BlobPrefix>
<BlobPrefix>
<Name>Indian/</Name>
</BlobPrefix>
<BlobPrefix>
<Name>POP/</Name>
</BlobPrefix>
<BlobPrefix>
<Name>Rock/</Name>
</BlobPrefix>
</Blobs>
<NextMarker />
</EnumerationResults>
```

Next, for each <BlobPrefix> value, you send a request to the Blob service to get the next string token separated by the delimiter at the next level of hierarchy. In this request, the prefix URI parameter must contain the <BlobPrefix> value, e.g. prefix=Classical, prefix=Indian, prefix=POP, or prefix=Rock. In the music hierarchy, the next token is the last token representing the file name of the music file. For example, under the Classical folder are C1.mp3 and C2.mp3 files. The response from the Blob service contains the properties of the C1.mp3 and C2.mp3 files. The sample request for the List Blobs operation at the Genre folder structure level looks like Listing 4-15.

Listing 4-15. *List Blob Second REST Request*

```
GET /music?comp=list&
prefix=Classical%2f&delimiter=%2f&
maxresults=100&timeout=30 HTTP/1.1
x-ms-date: Sun, 07 Jun 2009 05:53:38 GMT
Authorization: SharedKey proazurestorage:EOV9XEPvs9J5zejMOHD+d3+3Lc2+B816HS9Vu2NwkaE=
Host: proazurestorage.blob.core.windows.net
```

In Listing 4-15, the prefix parameter is set to the <BlobPrefix> value sent in the response for the first REST request. Listing 4-16 represents the response from the Blob service to get the next level of hierarchy elements. The <Prefix> element contains the value of the prefix parameter passed in the URI.

Listing 4-16. *List Blob Second REST Response*

```
HTTP/1.1 200 OK
Content-Type: application/xml
Server: Blob Service Version 1.0 Microsoft-HTTPAPI/2.0
x-ms-request-id: 6ad95e46-652d-4e4c-a50b-68c14dd2bd74
Date: Sun, 07 Jun 2009 05:54:41 GMT
Content-Length: 863

<?xml version="1.0" encoding="utf-8"?>
<EnumerationResults ContainerName="http://proazurestorage.blob.core.windows.net/music">
<Prefix>Classical/</Prefix>
<MaxResults>100</MaxResults>
<Delimiter>/</Delimiter>
<Blobs>
<Blob><Name>Classical/C1.mp3</Name>
<Url>http://proazurestorage.blob.core.windows.net/music/Classical/C1.mp3</Url>
<LastModified>Sun, 07 Jun 2009 05:47:18 GMT</LastModified>
<Etag>0x8CBB54A8D83F750</Etag>
<Size>4055168</Size>
<ContentType>audio/mpeg</ContentType>
<ContentEncoding /><ContentLanguage />
</Blob>
<Blob><Name>Classical/C2.mp3</Name>
<Url>http://proazurestorage.blob.core.windows.net/music/Classical/C2.mp3</Url>
<LastModified>Sun, 07 Jun 2009 05:47:38 GMT</LastModified>
<Etag>0x8CBB54A99E42600</Etag>
<Size>4055168</Size><ContentType>audio/mpeg</ContentType>
<ContentEncoding />
<ContentLanguage />
</Blob>
</Blobs>
```

```
<NextMarker />
</EnumerationResults>
```

Repeat the same procedure for the other three genres—Indian, POP, and Rock—to get the blobs in those containers.

The Windows Azure Storage Operations application supports the retrieving of blobs with delimiters. In the Container section of the application, the TreeView control on the right side displays the results from the List Blobs operation. The Parameters group box contains text boxes for prefix, marker, maxresults, and delimiter. Figure 4-15 illustrates the List Blobs operation executed on a music container. Note the delimiter and the tree structure that are created in the TreeView control.

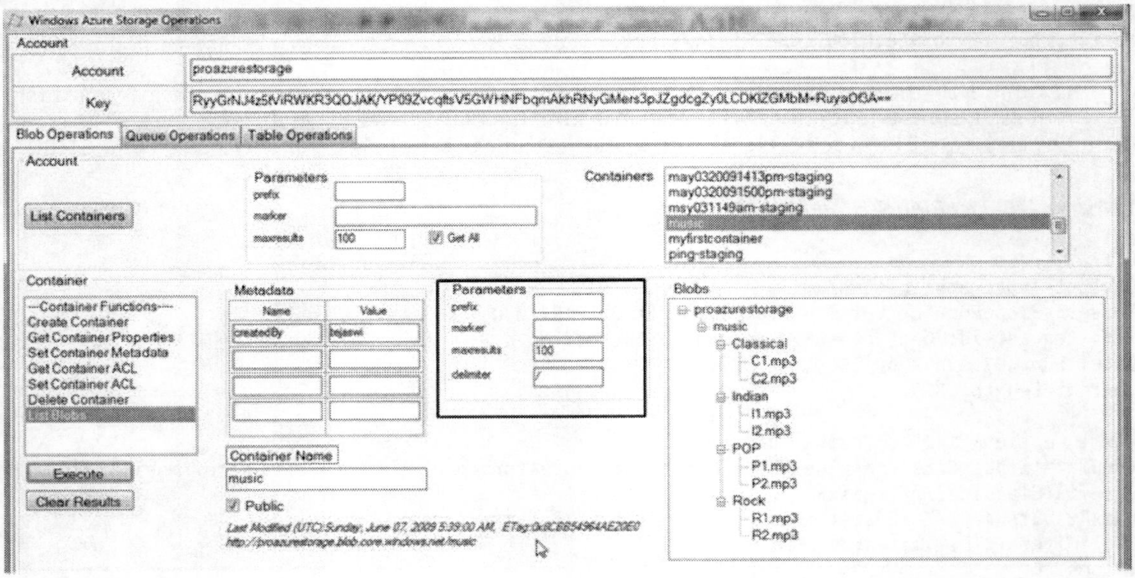

Figure 4-15. *List Blobs in Windows Azure Storage Operations.exe*

As shown in Figure 4-15, the List Blobs operation is called on the music container. The Delimiter text field contains the / delimiter character. The TreeView shows the virtual folder hierarchy of the blobs in the music container.

To help you understand the programming model of the List Blobs operation, open the Visual Studio Solution Chapter4.sln from the Chapter 4 source directory. The WindowsAzureStorage.cs file in the Windows Azure Storage Operations project consists of a ListBlobs() method, as shown in Listing 4-17.

Listing 4-17. *List Blobs in WindowsAzureStorage.cs*

```
private void ListBlobs
(string containerName, string blobPrefix, string delimiter,
int maxResults, ref string marker, TreeNode tn)
{
IList<object> blobList = new List<object>(StorageHelper.ListBlobs
```

```
(txtContainerName.Text, blobPrefix, delimiter, maxResults, ref marker));
foreach (object o in blobList)
{
if (o is BlobProperties)
{
BlobProperties bp = (BlobProperties)o;
string[] structureArr = bp.Name.Split(char.Parse(delimiter));
if (structureArr != null && structureArr.Length > 0)
{
if (tn != null)
{
TreeNode t2 = tn.Nodes.Add(structureArr[structureArr.Length - 1]);
t2.ToolTipText = bp.Name;
}
}
}
else if (o is string)
{
string bPrefix = (string)o;
string[] structureArr = bPrefix.Split(char.Parse(delimiter));

if (structureArr != null && structureArr.Length > 0)
{
string node = string.Empty;
TreeNode t1 = null;
if (structureArr.Length > 1)
{
node = structureArr[structureArr.Length - 2];
t1 = tn.Nodes.Add(node);
}
else
{
node = structureArr[0];
t1 = tn.Nodes.Add(node);
}
                        ListBlobs(containerName, bPrefix, delimiter, maxResults, ref marker,
                        t1);

}
}
}
}
```

As shown in Listing 4-17, the ListBlobs() method is recursive and calls the ListBlobs() method in the WindowsAzureStorageHelper class. For each blob object returned by the Blob service, the method checks if it's of the type BlobProperties or string. If the object is of the string type, then it's a string token separated by the delimiter; if the object is of type BlobProperties, it represents the blob file information. The blobProperties object is always the last item retrieved in a tokenized blob name because it represents the properties of the actual blob file stored in the container. During the recursive process, the function also populates the tree nodes of the TreeView control. Figure 4-16 illustrates the sequence diagram for the List Blobs operation.

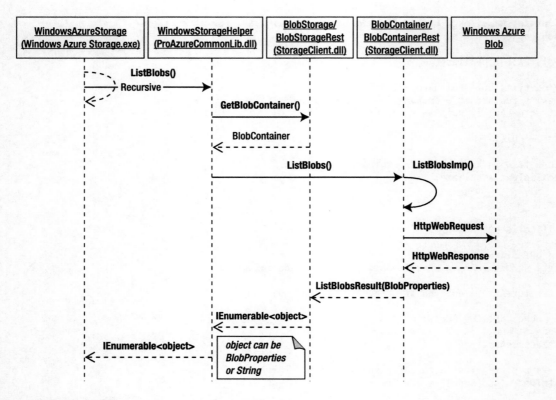

Figure 4-16. *List Blobs sequence diagram*

As shown in Figure 4-16, the ListBlobs() operation makes a recursive call to retrieve the list of blob properties from the container. The recursion is called only if the delimiter is passed as a method parameter. If the delimiter isn't present, a single call to the ListBlobs() method returns a list of all the blob properties in the specified container. The ListBlobs() method in the Windows Azure Storage Operation calls the ListBlobs() method in the WindowsAzureStorageHelper object. The WindowsStorageHelper object calls the GetBlobContainer() method on the BlobStorage object to get an instance of the BlobContainer object. The WindowsStorageHelper object then calls the ListBlobs() method on the BlobContainer object. The BlobContainer object calls a private method ListBlobsImpl(), which creates the REST message and sends it synchronously to the Windows Azure Blob service to retrieve a collection of BlobProperties objects. It uses the System.Net.HttpWebRequest to send the REST message over HTTP. The response from the Blob service is in XML format, which the StorageClient converts into ListBlobsResult object. The ListBlobsResult contains a collection of string or BlobProperties objects, depending on whether a delimiter was passed as a URI parameter. The BlobProperties and/or string collection is passed all the way to the Windows Azure Storage Operation application for display. For a string value, the application makes a recursive call to retrieve the BlobProperties of all the blobs.

Blob Operations

The URI of a specific blob is of the format `http://<account name>.blob.core.windows.net/<container name>/<blob name>`. Blobs support several operations, as listed in Table 4-11.

Table 4-11. Blob Operations

Operation	Description
Put Blob	Creates a new blob under the given container or updates an existing blob. Updates complete overwrite a blob's contents and metadata. You can upload a blob up to 64MB in size using the Put Blob operation. If it's bigger than 64MB, see the Put Block operation.
Get Blob	Retrieves the blob, its metadata, and its properties from the blob service. The operation times out if the download takes more than 2 minutes per megabyte.
Get Blob Properties	Retrieves the blob's system properties, HTTP properties, and user-defined metadata.
Get Blob Metadata	Retrieves only the user-defined metadata of the specified Blob.
Set Blob Metadata	Sets the user-defined metadata of the specified blob.
Put Block	Used to upload blobs larger than 64MB. Split the file into multiple blocks of 4MB each, and upload multiple blocks using this operation.
Get Block List	Gets the list of blocks uploaded by the Put Block operation. The operation supports the listing of committed as well as uncommitted blocks.
Put Block List	Commits a list of uploaded blocks to a blob. The operation accepts a list of block IDs of successfully uploaded blocks. Uncommitted blocks are garbage-collected.
Copy Blob	Copies a blob from a source to a destination within the Blob service.
Delete Blob	Marks a specified blob for deletion. The actual deletion takes place during the garbage-collection cycle.

Table 4-12 lists some of the important characteristics of the blob operations.

Table 4-12. *Blob Operation Characterstics*

Operation	HTTP Verb	Cloud URI	Development Storage URI	HTTP Version	Permissions
Put Blob	PUT	http://<account name>.blob.core.wind ows.net/<container name>/<blob name>	http://127.0.0.1:1 0000/<devstorageac count>/<containerN ame>/<blob name>	HTTP/1.1	Only the account owner can call this operation.
Get Blob	GET	http://<account name>.blob.core.wind ows.net/<container name>/<blob name>	http://127.0.0.1:1 0000/<devstorageac count>/<containerN ame>/<blob name>	HTTP/1.1	Any client may call this operation on a blob in the public container.
Get Blob Properties	HEAD	http://<account name>.blob.core.wind ows.net/<container name>/<blob name>	http://127.0.0.1:1 0000/<devstorageac count>/<containerN ame>/<blob name>	HTTP/1.1	Any client may call this operation on a blob in the public container.
Get Blob Metadata	GET/ HEAD	http://<account name>.blob.core.wind ows.net/<container name>/<blob name>?comp=metadata	http://127.0.0.1:1 0000/<devstorageac count>/<containerN ame>/<blob name>?comp= metadata	HTTP/1.1	Only the account owner can call this operation.
Set Blob Metadata	PUT	http://<account name>.blob.core.wind ows.net/<container name>/<blob name>?comp=metadata	http://127.0.0.1:1 0000/<devstorageac count>/<containerN ame>/<blob name>?comp=metadat a	HTTP/1.1	Only the account owner can call this operation.
Put Block	PUT	http://<account name>.blob.core.wind ows.net/<container name>/<blob name>?comp=block&blo ckid=id	http://127.0.0.1:1 0000/<devstorageac count>/<containerN ame>/<blob name>?comp=block&b lockid=id	HTTP/1.1	Only the account owner can call this operation.

Continued

250

Operation	HTTP Verb	Cloud URI	Development Storage URI	HTTP Version	Permissions
Get Block List	GET	http://<account name>.blob.core.wind ows.net/<container name>/<blob name>?comp=blocklist &blocklisttype=[comm itted|uncommitted| all]	http://127.0.0.1:100 00/<devstorageaccoun t>/<containerName>/< blob name>?comp=blocklist &blocklisttype=[comm itted|uncommitted| all]	HTTP/1.1	Any client may call this operation on a blob in the public container.
Put Block List	PUT	http://<account name>.blob.core.wind ows.net/<container name>/<blob name>?comp=blocklist	http://127.0.0.1:100 00/<devstorageaccoun t>/<containerName>/< blob name>?comp=blocklist	HTTP/1.1	Only the account owner can call this operation.
Copy Blob	PUT	http://<account name>.blob.core.wind ows.net/<container name>/<blob name>	http://127.0.0.1:100 00/<devstorageaccoun t>/<containerName>/ <blob name>	HTTP/1.1	Only the account owner can call this operation.
Delete Blob	DELETE	http://<account name>.blob.core.wind ows.net/<container name>/<blob name>	http://127.0.0.1:100 00/<devstorageaccoun t>/<containerName>/ <blob name>	HTTP/1.1	Only the account owner can call this operation.

<account name> is the storage account name in the cloud, and <devstorageaccount> is the development storage account. <container name> is the name of the container in which the blob is stored, and <blob name> is the name of the blob object.

The following sections discuss some of the operations from Table 4-12 in detail. Even though the operations are different, the programming concepts behind them are similar. To keep the book at a conceptual level, I discuss the Put Blob, Get Blob, and Copy Blob operations because they cover most of the discussed concepts. By studying these three operations in detail, you cab understand the programming concepts behind all the blob operations. The Windows Azure Storage Operations application included with this chapter's source code contains implementations of most of the blob operations.

Put Blob

The Put Blob operation is used to upload blob objects to the Blob service. A blob must be stored in a container, so the URI is of the format http://<account name>.blob.core.windows.net/<container name>/<blob name>, where the <container name> must be referenced before a <blob name>. You can upload a blob file up to 64MB using a single Put Blob operation. The Put Blob REST request looks like Listing 4-18.

Listing 4-18. *Put Blob REST Request*

```
PUT /pictures/toucan.jpg?timeout=30 HTTP/1.1
x-ms-date: Wed, 10 Jun 2009 05:32:42 GMT
Content-Type: image/jpeg
If-None-Match: *
Authorization: SharedKey proazurestorage:GvjnSO2oBj8nS1FjhODOnOwDhvG6ak32VlPHZNp6qc8=
Host: proazurestorage.blob.core.windows.net
Content-Length: 33624
Expect: 100-continue
```

In Listing 4-18, a toucan.jpg file is uploaded to the pictures container in the Blob service. Note that the conditional header If-None-Match has a * value associated with it. This conditional header instructs the Blob service to upload the file only if the ETag value of the destination is different to the ETag value of the source. Because this file is a fresh upload, the conditional header doesn't matter. Also note that the Content-Length of the HTTP request body is only 33,624 bytes. Because this is less than 64MB, a single Put Blob operation can upload this file to the Blob service. Listing 4-19 shows the response from the Blob service.

Listing 4-19. *Put Blob REST Response*

```
HTTP/1.1 201 Created
Content-MD5: df6MtpHeFTI4oChTKxil1A==
Last-Modified: Wed, 10 Jun 2009 05:34:43 GMT
ETag: 0x8CBB7A44AEB70B0
Server: Blob Service Version 1.0 Microsoft-HTTPAPI/2.0
x-ms-request-id: 7a898dd6-4458-439e-8895-003584810d7c
Date: Wed, 10 Jun 2009 05:34:19 GMT
Content-Length: 0
```

The Blob service responds with an HTTP/1.1 201 Created status code for a successful blob upload. Figure 4-17 shows the working of the Put Blob operation in the Windows Azure Storage Operations application.

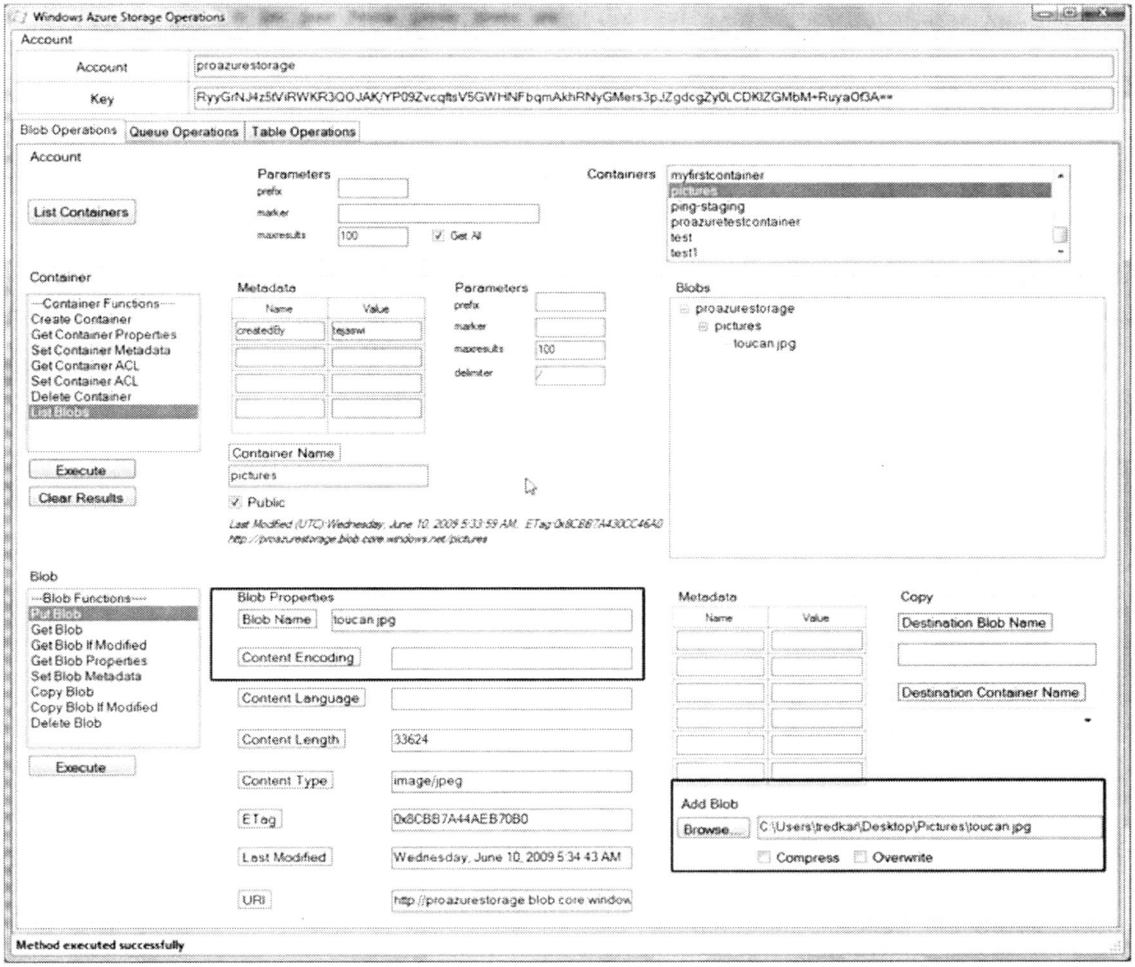

Figure 4-17. *Put Blob in Windows Azure Storage Operations.exe*

As illustrated in Figure 4-17, you can upload a blob to the Blob service from the Windows Azure Storage Operations application. The steps to upload are as follows:

1. Create a new container (called pictures).

2. Select the new container from the list box.

3. In the Blob section on the right side, under Add Blob, select an image from your file system.

253

4.   If you wish, rename the file in the Blob Name text field.

5.   You can also create a virtual folder structure (such as pictures/toucan.jpg) in the path name in the Blob Name text field.

6.   Select the Put Blob function from the Blob functions list box.

7.   Execute the function to upload the blob to the pictures container.

8.   Execute the List Blobs function to refresh the blobs list and display the newly added blob.

To help you understand the programming model of the Put Blob operation, open the Visual Studio Solution Chapter4.sln from the Chapter 4 source directory. The WindowsAzureStorage.cs file in the Windows Azure Storage Operations project consists of a PutBlob() method, as shown in Listing 4-20.

Listing 4-20. *PutBlob() Method in WindowsAzureStorage.cs*

```
private bool PutBlob(string containerName, string blobName,
string fileName, bool overwrite, bool gZipCompression,
NameValueCollection metadata)
{
BlobProperties blobProperties = new BlobProperties(blobName);
blobProperties.ContentType =
WindowsAzureStorageHelper.GetContentTypeFromExtension
(Path.GetExtension(fileName));
blobProperties.Metadata = metadata;
BlobContents blobContents = null;
if (gZipCompression)
{
blobProperties.ContentEncoding = "gzip";
blobContents = WindowsAzureStorageHelper.GZipCompressedBlobContents(fileName);
}
else
{
FileInfo fn = new FileInfo(fileName);
blobContents = new BlobContents(fn.OpenRead());
}
return StorageHelper.CreateBlob(containerName, blobProperties, blobContents, overwrite);
}
```

As shown in Listing 4-20, the PutBlob() method creates a new BlobProperties object to set the content type, content encoding, and metadata of the blob. Optionally, you can also use GZip compression to compress the blob contents. This can be useful if you're uploading heavy web pages and you want to access these pages directly from the browser. (Browsers can decompress GZip files and displaying the contents.) Finally, the method reads the contents of the file a FileInfo object and passes the FileStream object returned by the Fileinfo.Open() method to the BlobContents constructor. Finally, the method calls the StorageHelper.CreateBlob() method from the WindowsAzureStorageHelper class, which in turn calls the CreateBlob() method of the BlobContainer object from the StorageClient assembly. Figure 4-18 illustrates the sequence diagram for the Put Blob operation.

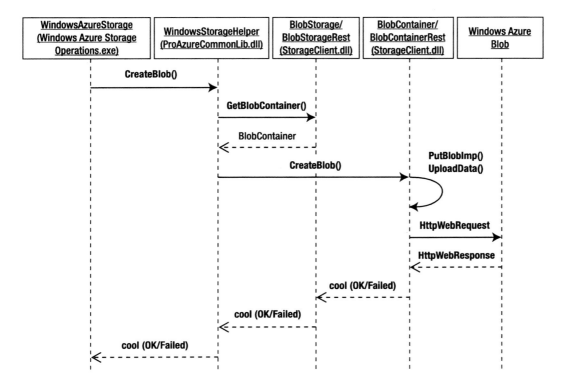

Figure 4-18. *Put Blob sequence diagram*

As shown in Figure 4-18, the Windows Azure Storage Operations application calls the CreateBlob() method on the WindowsStorageHelper object in ProAzureCommonLib.dll. The WindowsStorageHelper object calls the GetBlobContainer() method on the BlobStorage object to get an instance of the BlobContainer object. The WindowsStorageHelper object then calls the CreateBlob() method on the BlobContainer object. The BlobContainer object calls a private method PutBlobImpl(), which checks if the blob qualifies as a large blob that would require you to use the Put Block operation. If the blob doesn't qualify as a large blob, it calls the private method UploadData, which creates the REST message and sends the entire blob synchronously to the Windows Azure Blob service. It uses the System.Net.HttpWebRequest to send the REST message over HTTP. Upon the success or failure of the operation, the Windows Azure Blob service returns an HTTP status code: HTTP/1.1 201 Created for success or HTTP/1.1 412 or 304 for a precondition failure. The UploadData() method translates the HTTP code into true for success or false for failure. The Boolean value is passed all the way to the Windows Azure Storage Operations application as a return parameter of the CreateBlob() method.

Put Block and Put Block list Operations

To upload files larger than 64MB, break the blob into smaller contiguous files (Blocks) that are maximum of 4MB each, and then upload these blocks using the Put Block operation. You can commit uploaded blocks to a blob using the Put Block List operation. Before uploading a block, you have to assign a blockid that is unique within a blob. Blocks in different blobs can have the same blockid because blockids are unique only within the scope of a blob. You can upload blocks in parallel or in any order, as long as the Put Block List operation commits all the blocks to a blob in the correct contiguous order. An uploaded block doesn't become part of a blob unless it's committed using the Put Block operation. Uncommitted blocks are stored for seven days before they're garbage-collected by the system.

Ideally, from an end-user perspective, the Put Block operation should be transparent. The application should upload the blob as contiguous blocks and commit the Blocklist transparently for the end user. The end user should only be given the status of the blob upload. The StorageClient API abstracts the Put Block operation from the end user. To test the Put Block and Put Block List operations, upload an image file larger than 64MB from the Windows Azure Storage Operations application. Listing 4-21 shows four separate REST requests of the Put Block operations to upload a music file R3.mp3 to the music container.

Listing 4-21. *REST Requests for Put Block Operations*

```
PUT /music/Rock/R3.mp3?comp=block&blockid=AAAAAA%3d%3d&timeout=30 HTTP/1.1
x-ms-date: Thu, 11 Jun 2009 04:12:14 GMT
Content-Type: audio/mpeg
If-None-Match: *
Authorization: SharedKey proazurestorage:UE3slooBGXZewrAHTXj7efzdA33ozPoElVs/5NWNoy8=
Host: proazurestorage.blob.core.windows.net
Content-Length: 1048576
Expect: 100-continue

PUT /music/Rock/R3.mp3?comp=block&blockid=AQAAAA%3d%3d&timeout=30 HTTP/1.1
x-ms-date: Thu, 11 Jun 2009 04:12:17 GMT
Content-Type: audio/mpeg
If-None-Match: *
Authorization: SharedKey proazurestorage:BOHjZPkvSN1IZWNJ7VGhrOppe7DAxSvjkV5l6xgGOWQ=
Host: proazurestorage.blob.core.windows.net
Content-Length: 1048576
Expect: 100-continue

PUT /music/Rock/R3.mp3?comp=block&blockid=AgAAAA%3d%3d&timeout=30 HTTP/1.1
x-ms-date: Thu, 11 Jun 2009 04:12:18 GMT
Content-Type: audio/mpeg
If-None-Match: *
Authorization: SharedKey proazurestorage:Fo+V+kdv6cEbBsOCLIMIdQ+lzLfHX7Dit8lqAEkwqeI=
Host: proazurestorage.blob.core.windows.net
Content-Length: 1048576
Expect: 100-continue

PUT /music/Rock/R3.mp3?comp=block&blockid=AwAAAA%3d%3d&timeout=30 HTTP/1.1
x-ms-date: Thu, 11 Jun 2009 04:12:20 GMT
Content-Type: audio/mpeg
If-None-Match: *
Authorization: SharedKey proazurestorage:uwPvdQyf6RMZOi6fYtVmzlRRZxXu3L1SLvXoTGLpCY8=
Host: proazurestorage.blob.core.windows.net
Content-Length: 909440
Expect: 100-continue
```

As shown in Listing 4-21, the blob is uploaded in four contiguous blocks. Note the unique blockid of each REST request.

After uploading blocks to the Blob service, you need to commit them to the blob using the Put Block List operation. Listing 4-22 shows the REST request for the Put Block List operation to commit the uploaded blocks to the Rock/R3.mp3 blob.

Listing 4-22. *REST Request for the Put Block Operation*

```
PUT /music/Rock/R3.mp3?comp=blocklist&timeout=30 HTTP/1.1
x-ms-date: Thu, 11 Jun 2009 04:12:21 GMT
Content-Type: audio/mpeg
If-None-Match: *
Authorization: SharedKey proazurestorage:OXOlXUegzNFcyuwbIcRSoon/CgB8jAOwrEQaMDFGGlk=
Host: proazurestorage.blob.core.windows.net
Content-Length: 156
Expect: 100-continue

<?xml version="1.0" encoding="utf-8"?>
<BlockList>
<Block>AAAAAA==</Block>
<Block>AQAAAA==</Block>
<Block>AgAAAA==</Block>
<Block>AwAAAA==</Block>
</BlockList>
```

The blob Rock/R3.mp3 is created when the four blocks in Listing 4-21 are committed by the Put Block List operation in Listing 4-22. The name of the blob is part of the operation URI, even though the blob doesn't exist before Put Block List is executed. The blob is created only after the Put Block List operation is successfully executed.

Get Blob

The Get Blob operation is used to download the blob contents and its properties and metadata from the Blob service. The URI for the Get Blob operation is of the format `http://<account name>.blob.core.windows.net/<container name>/<blob name>`. Listing 4-23 shows the REST API request for the Get Blob operation.

Listing 4-23. *Get Blob REST Request*

```
GET /pictures/birds/toucan.jpg?timeout=30 HTTP/1.1
x-ms-date: Thu, 11 Jun 2009 05:14:10 GMT
If-Match: 0x8CBB8550DF72BC0
x-ms-range: bytes=0-51086
Authorization: SharedKey proazurestorage:EVXgpmvaiEtyJlmBgupxLi2VebXK4XQk6/HsPF9O3EI=
Host: proazurestorage.blob.core.windows.net
```

In Listing 4-23, the URI points to the blob birds/toucan.jpg. The If-Match conditional header instructs the Blob service to check the specified ETag before downloading the blob. The x-ms-range value represents the range of bytes to be retrieved from the Blob service. This value is usually transparent to the end user; you can use it to download the blobs in batches of bytes. Listing 4-24 shows the REST API response from the Blob service for the Get Blob operation.

Listing 4-24. Get Blob REST Response

```
HTTP/1.1 206 Partial Content
Content-Length: 33624
Content-Type: image/jpeg
Content-Range: bytes 0-51086/51087
Last-Modified: Thu, 11 Jun 2009 02:40:02 GMT
ETag: 0x8CBB8550DF72BC0
Server: Blob Service Version 1.0 Microsoft-HTTPAPI/2.0
x-ms-request-id: 374e2072-106d-4841-b51c-45f25e9e6596
x-ms-meta-createdBy: tejaswi
Date: Thu, 11 Jun 2009 05:15:21 GMT
```

Listing 4-24 shows the HTTP header of the Get Blob operation. The HTTP response body consists of the contents of the blob. Figure 4-19 shows the working of the Get Blob operation in the Windows Azure Storage Operations application.

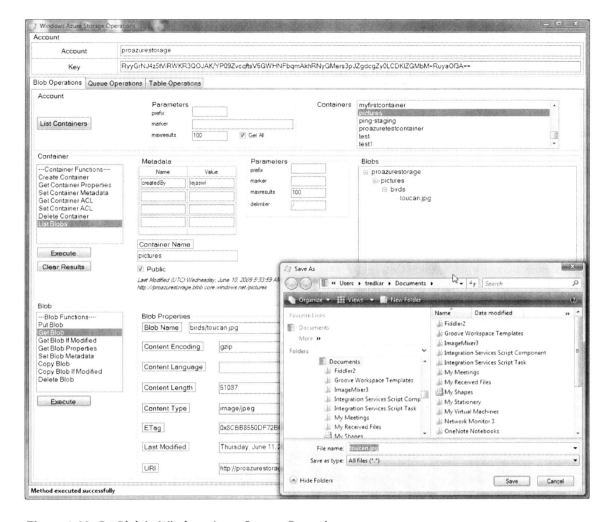

Figure 4-19. *Get Blob in Windows Azure Storage Operations.exe*

As illustrated in Figure 4-19, you can download a blob from the blob service using Windows Azure Storage Operations. The steps for downloading are as follows:

1.   In the Containers list box, select a container (such as pictures) that has blobs.

2.   In the Containers section, execute the List Blobs operation to get a list of blobs in the container (for example, birds/toucan.jpg).

3.   Select a blob (such as birds/toucan.jpg) from the Blobs TreeView control.

4. In the Blobs section, execute the Get Blob operation.

5. A Save As dialog box pops up, where you can choose the local folder in which to store the blob.

6. When you click Save, the blob is stored on your local machine in the specified folder.

To help you understand the programming model of the Get Blob operation, open the Visual Studio Solution Chapter4.sln from the Chapter 4 source directory. The WindowsAzureStorage.cs file in the Windows Azure Storage Operations project consists of a GetBlob() method, as shown in Listing 4-25.

Listing 4-25. GetBlob() Method in WindowsAzureStorage.cs

```
private BlobProperties GetBlob
(string containerName, string blobName, bool transferAsChunks,
out BlobContents blobContents)
{

blobContents = new BlobContents(new MemoryStream());
return StorageHelper.GetBlob(containerName, blobName, blobContents, transferAsChunks);
}
```

The GetBlob() method creates a new BlobContents object that is populated by the StorageHelper.GetBlob() method. StorageHelper.GetBlob() calls the GetBlob() method of the BlobContainer object from the StorageClient assembly. Figure 4-20 illustrates the sequence diagram for the Get Blob operation.

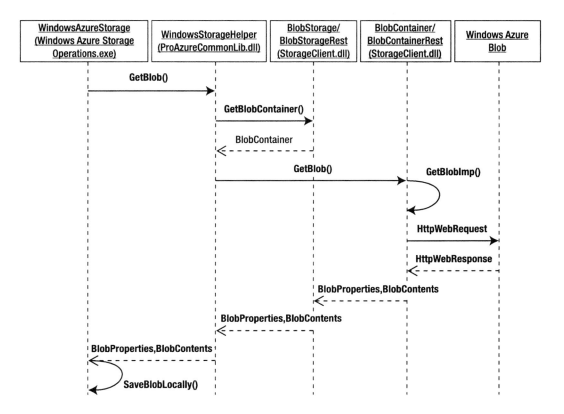

Figure 4-20. *Get Blob sequence diagram*

As shown in Figure 4-20, the Windows Azure Storage Operations application calls the GetBlob()
method on the WindowsStorageHelper object in ProAzureCommonLib.dll. The WindowsStorageHelper
object calls the GetBlobContainer() method on the BlobStorage object to get an instance of the
BlobContainer object. The WindowsStorageHelper object then calls the GetBlob() method on the
BlobContainer object. The BlobContainer object calls a private method GetBlobImpl() to download the
blob contents from the Windows Azure Blob service. Upon the success or failure of the operation, the
Windows Azure Blob service returns an HTTP status code: HTTP/1.1 200 OK for success or HTTP/1.1 412
or 304 for a precondition failure. The body of the HTTP response contains the contents of the blob
object. The contents of the blob object are packaged into the BlobContents object that you passed in
Listing 4-25. Finally, the Windows Azure Storage Operations application saves the blob locally by calling
the SaveBlobLocally() private method. This method writes the contents of the blob to the user-specified
file on the local machine.

■ **Note** The Blob service supports blob concurrency on Get and Put operations via snapshot isolation. A Get Blob operation sees only a single version of the blob. If the blob is updated during the Get Blob operation, you receive a "connection closed" error. You can then follow up the error with an If-Modified conditional Get Blob operation.

Copy Blob

The Copy Blob operation is used to copy a source blob and its properties and metadata to a destination blob within the storage account. If you don't specify metadata values for the destination blob, then the source blob metadata values are copied. If you specify metadata values for the destination blob, the source blob metadata values aren't copied to the destination. The URI for the Copy Blob operation is of the format `http://<account name>.blob.core.windows.net/<destination container name>/<destination blob name>`. Listing 4-26 shows the REST API request for the Copy Blob operation.

Listing 4-26. Copy Blob REST Request

```
PUT /test/birds/toucan-copy.jpg?timeout=30 HTTP/1.1
x-ms-date: Mon, 15 Jun 2009 15:49:56 GMT
x-ms-version: 2009-04-14
x-ms-meta-createdBy: tejaswi
x-ms-copy-source: /proazurestorage/pictures/birds/toucan.jpg
Authorization: SharedKey proazurestorage:FqssEZkcIUjlVrQhHOaLdt+rtEmvgjNOtu9XZO6iRKw=
Host: proazurestorage.blob.core.windows.net
Content-Length: 0
```

In Listing 4-26, the URI points to the destination blob birds/toucan.jpg in the test container. The x-ms-version value specifies the version of the Storage REST API to use. The Copy method wasn't available in the earlier CTP versions of the Storage REST API; you can use it beginning with version 2009-04-14. The x-ms-copy-source value specifies the source blob for the copy operation. Listing 4-27 shows the REST API response from the Blob service for the Copy Blob operation.

Listing 4-27. Copy Blob REST Response

```
HTTP/1.1 201 Created
Last-Modified: Mon, 15 Jun 2009 15:52:27 GMT
ETag: 0x8CBBBE86B023C10
Server: Blob Service Version 1.0 Microsoft-HTTPAPI/2.0
x-ms-request-id: ee93e063-9256-443b-b6cb-536dd4012863
Date: Mon, 15 Jun 2009 15:51:28 GMT
Content-Length: 0
```

Listing 4-27 shows the HTTP header of the Copy Blob operation. The HTTP response body is similar to the Put Blob operation response body you saw earlier in the chapter. Figure 4-21 shows the working of the Copy Blob operation in the Windows Azure Storage Operations.exe application.

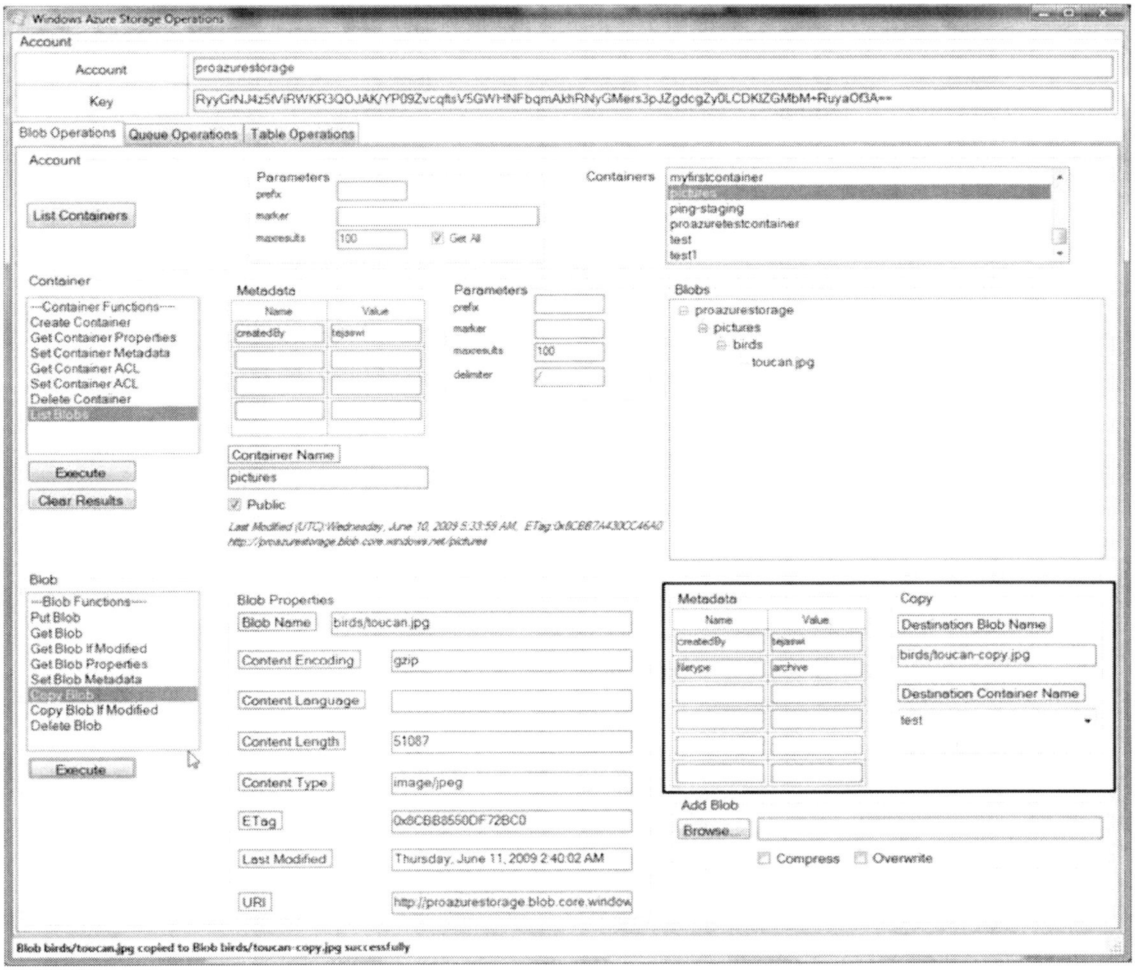

Figure 4-21. *Copy Blob in Windows Azure Storage Operations.exe*

As illustrated in Figure 4-21, you can copy a blob from a source blob to a destination blob within the same storage account from Windows Azure Storage Operations. The steps for copying a blob are as follows:

1. In the Containers list box, select a container (such as pictures) that has blobs.

2. In the Containers section, execute the List Blobs operation to get a list of blobs in the container (for example, birds/toucan.jpg).

3. Select a blob (such as birds/toucan.jpg) from the Blobs TreeView control.

4. In the Blobs section, enter a name for the destination blob in the Destination Blob Name text box.

5. Also select a destination container (such as test) for the blob from the Destination Container Name drop-down list.

6. A Save As dialog box pops up where you can choose the local folder in which to store the blob.

7. Enter metadata, if any, in the Metadata text fields in the Blob section.

8. Select the Copy Blob operation in the Blob operations list box, and click the Execute button to execute the Copy Blob operation.

9. The status bar message indicates the success or failure of the operation.

10. You can execute the List Blobs operation on the destination container to see the copied blob.

To help you understand the programming model of the Copy Blob operation, open the Visual Studio Solution Chapter4.sln from the Chapter 4 source directory. The WindowsAzureStorage.cs file in the Windows Azure Storage Operations project consists of a CopyBlob() method, as shown in Listing 4-28.

Listing 4-28. CopyBlob() Method in WindowsAzureStorage.cs

```
private bool CopyBlob
(string accountName, string sourceContainerName, string blobName, string
destinationContainerName, string destinationBlobName)
        {
            BlobProperties sourceBlobProperties =
StorageHelper.GetBlobProperties(sourceContainerName, blobName);
            sourceBlobProperties.Metadata = GetMetaDataFromControls();
            blobName = String.Format
("/{0}/{1}/{2}", accountName, sourceContainerName, blobName);
            return StorageHelper.CopyBlob
(destinationContainerName, sourceBlobProperties,
blobName, destinationBlobName, "2009-04-14");
        }
```

As shown in Listing 4-28, the CopyBlob() method creates a new BlobProperties object and passes the metadata entered by the user to its Metadata property. The source blob name must be of the format /<*account name*>/<source container name>/<source blob name>. Next, the method calls the StorageHelper.CopyBlob() method, which in turn calls the CopyBlob() method of the BlobContainer object from the StorageClient assembly. Figure 4-22 illustrates the sequence diagram for the Copy Blob operation.

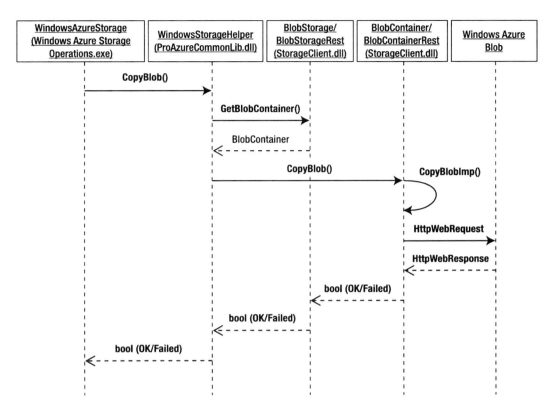

Figure 4-22. *Copy Blob sequence diagram*

As shown in Figure 4-22, the Windows Azure Storage Operations application calls the CopyBlob() method on the WindowsStorageHelper object in ProAzureCommonLib.dll. The WindowsStorageHelper object calls the GetBlobContainer() method on the BlobStorage object to get an instance of the BlobContainer object. The WindowsStorageHelper object then calls the CopyBlob() method on the BlobContainer object. The BlobContainer object calls a private method CopyBlobImpl() to copy the specified source blob to the specified destination blob in the Windows Azure Blob service. Upon the success or failure of the operation, the Windows Azure Blob service returns an HTTP status code: HTTP/1.1 201 Created for success or HTTP/1.1 412 or 304 for a precondition failure.

Blob Summary

The Blob service is a scalable and highly available cloud storage designed to store any kind of file. It has a REST API that you can use to program applications to interact with the Blob service in the cloud. The Windows Azure SDK also provides a local Blob service with a 2GB storage limit. You can use the Windows Azure Storage Operations.exe application to test Blob service scenarios. The next chapter covers Windows Azure queues.

Bibliography

MSDN. (n.d.). ADO.NET Data Services Specification. Retrieved from MSDN Developer's Network: http://msdn.microsoft.com/en-us/library/cc668808.aspx.

MSDN. (2009, May). Windows Azure Blob — Programming Blob Storage. Retrieved from MSDN: http://go.microsoft.com/fwlink/?LinkId=153400.

MSDN. (2009, May). Windows Azure Queue — Programming Queue Storage. Retrieved from MSDN: http://go.microsoft.com/fwlink/?LinkId=153402.

MSDN. (2009, May). Windows Azure SDK. Retrieved from MSDN: http://msdn.microsoft.com/en-us/library/dd179367.aspx.

MSDN. (2009, May). Windows Azure Table — Programming Table Storage. Retrieved from MSDN: http://go.microsoft.com/fwlink/?LinkId=153401.

CHAPTER 5

■■■

Windows Azure Storage
Part II – Queues

The Windows Azure Queue service is an Internet-scale message queuing system for cross-service communications. Even though the service is called a queue, the messages aren't guaranteed to follow the First In First Out (FIFO) pattern. The design focus of the Queue service is on providing a highly scalable and available asynchronous message communication system that's accessible anywhere, anytime. The Queue service provides a REST API for applications to use the large-scale Queue service infrastructure.

The Queue service is scoped at the account level. So, when you create an account on the Azure Services Developer Portal, you get access to the Queue service. Figure 5-1 illustrates the Azure Services Developer Portal page for the storage account that I created in the previous chapter and URL endpoint for the Queue service.

Figure 5-1. Queue endpoint URL

The account endpoint for the Queue service is `<account name>.queue.core.windows.net`, where *<account name>* is the unique name you created for your storage account. The secret key associated with the account provides security for accessing the storage account. You can use the secret key to create a Hash-based Message Authentication Code (HMAC) SHA256 signature for each request. The storage server uses the signature to authenticate the request.

■ **Note** HMAC is a message-authentication code calculated from the secret key using a special cryptographic hash function like MD5, SHA-1, or SHA256. The Windows Azure Storage service expects the SHA256 hash for the request. SHA256 is a 256-bit hash for the input data.

Queue Limitations and Constraints

Even though the Queue service provides a scalable and highly available infrastructure for asynchronous message communications in the cloud, it has some limitations and constraints that are important to understand before diving deep into architecture and programming. The limitations of the Queue service are as follows:

- The Queue service supports an unlimited number of messages, but individual messages in the Queue service can't be more than 8KB in size.

- The FIFO behavior of the messages sent to the Queue service isn't guaranteed.

- Messages can be received in any order.

- The Queue service doesn't offer *guaranteed-once delivery*. This means a message may be received more than once.

- Messages sent to the Queue service can be in either text or binary format, but received messages are always in the Base64 encoded format.

- The expiration time for messages stored in the Queue service is seven days. After seven days, the messages are garbage-collected.

Queue Service Architecture

The Queue service architecture consists of a three-level hierarchy: accounts, queues, and messages, as shown in Figure 5-2.

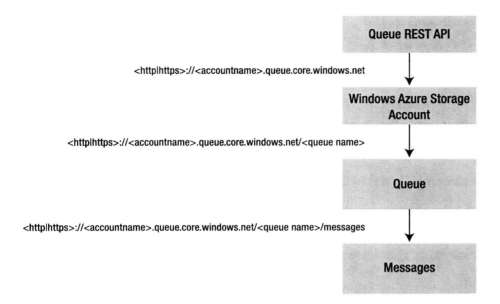

Figure 5-2. *Queue service architecture*

Your Windows Azure storage account is the entry point to the Queue service via the REST API.

Windows Azure Storage Account

A Windows Azure storage account encompasses the Blob, Queue, and Table services. The URI scheme for accessing the Queue service via your storage account is

```
<http|https>://<account name>.queue.core.windows.net
```

where *<account name>* is the unique name you created for your storage account. The *<account name>* must be globally unique.

For example, the Queue service for the storage account that I created in the previous chapter can be referenced as

```
<http|https>://proazurestorage.queue.core.windows.net
```

Queues

A *queue* is a logical destination for sending messages. There can be any number of queues in an account in the Queue service. A queue stores messages and makes them available to applications via the REST API. Queues can have metadata in the form of name-value pairs up to 8KB in size per queue. The Queue service support only private access; that means you need to have account privileges in order to access queues in a Queue service.

You can access a queue using the URI

`<http|https>://<account name>.queue.core.windows.net/<queue name>`

where *<queue name>* is the name of the queue you want to access.

For example, if you create a queue named logsqueue in the proazurestorage account, you can reference it using the following URI:

`<http|https>://proazurestorage.queue.core.windows.net/logsqueue`

The naming constraints for a queue are as follows:[1]

- The queue name must be a valid DNS name.

- Queue names must be unique within an account.

- Queue names must start with a letter or a number.

- Container names can't contain any special characters other than the dash (-) character.

- The dash (-) character must be immediately followed by a character or a number.

- All the characters in the queue name must be lowercase.

- Queue names can't be less than 3 or more than 63 characters in length.

If a queue name or the URI violates the naming convention, an HTTP status code 400 (Bad Request) is returned by the server.

Messages

Messages are stored in queues. There is no limit to the number of messages that can be stored in a queue, but the size of each individual message can't exceed 8KB. To communicate large object messages, you can put the large object in a blob and then send the URI of that object as a message to a queue.

When you send a message, it can be in either text or binary format; but when you receive a message from the queue, it's always in Base64-encoded format. A GUID MessageID assigned by the Queue service uniquely identifies a message in the queue.

A message has the following attributes:

- *MessageID:* Uniquely identifies a message in a queue and is created by the Queue service when you send the message to the Queue service.

---

[1]Source: Windows Azure SDK documentation

- *PopReceipt:* –An attribute of the message used for deleting or popping the message out from the queue.

- *Visibilitytimeout:* An integer value representing the visibility of the message in seconds after it's received by a receiving application. The default visibilitytimeout value is 30 seconds, which means that after a message is received, it remains invisible to other applications for 30 seconds (unless it's deleted by the receiving application). The maximum visibilitytimeout value is 2 hours. The visibilitytimeout value is passed to the Queue service while a message is being retrieved from a queue.

- *Messagettl:* An integer value representing the time-to-live value in seconds. When you send a message to a queue, you can specify the messagettl, which instructs the Queue service to keep the message only for the specified number of seconds. The default value for messagettl is 7 days. That means if you don't specify a messagettl value, the Queue service keeps the message for 7 days before it's garbage-collected.

You can access messages in a queue using the following URI

```
<http|https>://<account name>.queue.core.windows.net/<queue name>/messages
```

where *<queue name>* is the unique name of the queue within the scope of the account specified in the URI, and messages is a constant string representing all the messages in the specified queue. For example, if you create a queue named logsqueue, you can get messages from it by calling the following URI:

```
<http|https>://proazurestorage.queue.core.windows.net/logsqueue/messages
```

REST API

The REST API for the Queue service is available at the account, queue, and message levels. In this section, you learn about the Queue service REST API with specific examples. You also learn to interact with the Queue service programmatically, and you explore the queue methods in the available storage client libraries.

The REST API enables you to make HTTP calls to the Queue service and its resources. REST is an HTTP-based protocol that lets you specify the URI of the resource as well as the function you want to execute on the resource. Every REST call involves an HTTP request to the storage service and an HTTP response from the storage service.

▮ **Note** Due to frequent changes to the Windows Azure Storage service API, the URL parameters may not be exactly the same as the most recent API version. But conceptually, the variation in the REST API shouldn't be significant. For the exact parameter lists, please refer to the Windows Azure SDK documentation shipped with the SDK.

Request

The Queue service REST API's HTTP request components are described in the following sections.

HTTP Verb

The HTTP verb represents the action or operation you can execute on the resource indicated in the URI. The Queue service REST API supports the following verbs: GET, PUT, POST, HEAD, and DELETE. Each verb behaves differently when executed on a different resource.

Request URI

The request URI represents the URI of a resource you're interested in accessing or executing a function on. Example resources in the Queue service include accounts, queues, and messages. An example URI for creating a queue named logsqueue in an account named proazurestorage is

```
PUT http://proazurestorage.queue.core.windows.net/logsqueue
```

The HTTP berb PUT instructs the service to create the queue, and the URI points to the resource that needs to be created.

URI Parameters

The URI parameters are the extra parameters you specify to fine-tune your operation execution. They may include operation parameters or filter parameters for the results. In the Queue service API, the URI parameters depend on the type of resource and the HTTP verb used. For example, a URI for retrieving a list of queues from an account looks like this:

```
GET http://proazurestorage.queue.core.windows.net/?comp=list
```

The HTTP verb GET instructs the Queue service to retrieve results, and the parameter ?comp=list specifies that the data requested is a list of queues.

Request Headers

Request headers follow the standard HTTP 1.1 name-value pair format. Depending on the type of request, the header may contain security, date/time, metadata, or instructions embedded as name-value pairs. In the Storage service REST API, the request header must include the authorization information and a Coordinated Universal Time (UTC) timestamp for the request. The timestamp can be in the form of either an HTTP/HTTPS Date header or the x-ms-Date header.

The authorization header format is as follows:

```
Authorization="[SharedKey|SharedKeyLite] <Account Name>:<Signature>"
```

Where SharedKey|SharedKeyLite is the authentication scheme, *<Account Name>* is the storage service account name, and *<Signature>* is an HMAC of the request computed using the SHA256 algorithm and then encoded by using Base64 encoding.

To create the signature, you follow these steps:

1. Create the signature string for signing. The signature string for the Storage service request consists of the following format:

```
VERB\n
Content - MD5\n
Content - Type\n
Date\n
CanonicalizedHeaders
CanonicalizedResource
```

where VERB is the uppercase HTTP verb such as GET, PUT, and so on; *Content—* MD5 is the MD5 hash of the request content; *CanonicalizedHeaders* is the portion of the signature string created using a series of steps described in the "Authentication Schemes" section of the Windows Azure SDK documentation (http://msdn.microsoft.com/en-us/library/dd179428.aspx); and *CanonicalizedResource* is the storage service resource in the request URI. The *CanonicalizedResource* string is also constructed using a series of steps described in the "Authentication Schemes" section of the Windows Azure SDK documentation.

2. Use the System.Security.Cryptography.HMACSHA256.ComputeHash() method to compute the SHA256 HMAC-encoded string.

3. Use the System.Convert.ToBase64String() method to convert the encoded signature to Base64 format.

Listing 5-1 shows an example request header that sets the metadata values of a queue.

Listing 5-1. *Request Header*

```
PUT /myfirstazurequeue?comp=metadata&timeout=30 HTTP/1.1
x-ms-date: Wed, 17 Jun 2009 04:33:45 GMT
x-ms-meta-createdBy: tejaswi
x-ms-meta-creationDate: 6/16/2009
Authorization: SharedKey proazurestorage:
    spPPnadPYnH6AJguuYT9wP1GLXmCjnOI1S6W2+hzyMc=
    Host: proazurestorage.queue.core.windows.net
Content-Length: 0
```

In listing 5-1, the request header consists of x-ms-date, x-ms-version, x-ms-[name]:[value] and Authorization values. x-ms-date represents the UTC timestamp, and x-ms-version specifies the version of the storage service API you're using. x-ms-version isn't a required parameter, but if you don't specify, you have to make sure the operation you're calling is available in the default version of the Queue service. Before making the REST call, be sure you match the operation you're calling with the API version it's supported in. It's always safe to match the operation with the version to get the expected results. The x-ms-meta values represent the queue metadata name-value pairs the operation should set. The last header value is the Authorization SharedKey used by the Storage service to authenticate and authorize the caller.

■ **Note** Unlike the Blob service REST API, the Queue service REST API doesn't support HTTP 1.1 conditional headers.

Request Body

The request body consists of the contents of the request operation. Some operations require a request body, and some don't. For example, the Put Message operation request body consists of the message data in XML format, whereas the Get Messages operation requires an empty request body.

Response

The HTTP response of the Queue service API typically includes the following components.

Status Code

The status code is the HTTP status code that indicates the success or failure of the request. The most common status codes for the Queue service API are 200 (OK), 201 (Created), 204 (No Content), 400 (BadRequest), 404 (NotFound), and 409 (Conflict).

Response Headers

The response headers include all the standard HTTP 1.1 headers plus any operation-specific headers returned by the Queue service. The x-ms-request-id response header uniquely identifies a request. Listing 5-2 shows an example response header for a List Queues operation.

Listing 5-2. List Queues Response Header

```
HTTP/1.1 200 OK
Transfer-Encoding: chunked
Content-Type: application/xml
Server: Queue Service Version 1.0 Microsoft-HTTPAPI/2.0
x-ms-request-id: ccf3c21c-7cca-4386-a636-7f0087002970
Date: Tue, 16 Jun 2009 04:47:54 GMT
```

Response Body

The response body consists of data returned by the operation. This data is specific to each operation. For example, the List Queues operation returns the list of queues in an account, whereas the Get Messages operation returns the messages in a queue. Listing 5-3 shows an example of the response body for a List Queues operation. The response contains four queues.

Listing 5-3. *List Queues Response Body*

```
<?xml version="1.0" encoding="utf-8"?>
<EnumerationResults AccountName="http://proazurestorage.queue.core.windows.net/">
<MaxResults>50</MaxResults>
<Queues>
<Queue>
<QueueName>testq</QueueName>
<Url>http://proazurestorage.queue.core.windows.net/testq</Url>
</Queue>
<Queue>
<QueueName>testq1</QueueName>
<Url>http://proazurestorage.queue.core.windows.net/testq1</Url>
</Queue>
<Queue>
<QueueName>testq2</QueueName>
<Url>http://proazurestorage.queue.core.windows.net/testq2</Url>
</Queue>
<Queue>
<QueueName>testq3</QueueName>
<Url>http://proazurestorage.queue.core.windows.net/testq3</Url>
</Queue>
</Queues>
<NextMarker />
</EnumerationResults>
```

■ **Tip** To test the REST API, I recommend using the Fiddler Tool available at `www.fiddler2.com/fiddler2/`. In this book, I use this tool to trace client/server communications.

Storage Client APIs

Even though the REST API and the operations in the REST API are easily readable, the API doesn't automatically create client stubs like the ones created by WDSL-based web services. You have to create your own client API and stubs for REST API operations. This makes the client programming more complex and increases the barrier to entry for developers. To reduce this barrier to entry, the Windows Azure SDK team has created two client helper libraries: Microsoft.WindowsAzure.StorageClient from Windows Azure SDK, and the Storage Client code sample. Both libraries are used to invoke REST APIs of the Windows Azure Storage service. The Microsoft.WindowsAzure.StorageClient library abstracts this by providing a closed-source interface and therefore is less interesting to developers who want to see the inner workings of the method calls.

In the Windows Azure CTP version, a code sample named Storage Client became the choice of developers for calling storage services because the Microsoft.WindowsAzure.StorageClient wasn't available and also because it was open source. It provided good insight into building your own storage client library. The Storage Client made it easier to see the end-to-end method calls to the Storage service. This chapter uses the Storage Client code sample in sample applications and covers the class structure and calling mechanisms in the Microsoft.WindowsAzure.StorageClient namespace.

The following sections cover the queue storage APIs from Microsoft.WindowsAzure.StorageClient and the Storage Client code sample.

■ **Note** You don't have to use the Storage Client to make REST calls to the Storage service. You can create your own client library for making REST operations to the Storage service. In order to keep the book conceptual, I use the Storage Client code sample helper library to interact with the Storage service throughout this book. The source code for Storage Client is available in the samples directory of the Windows Azure SDK or from the Windows Azure code samples site, `http://code.msdn.microsoft.com/windowsazuresamples`.

Windows Azure Storage Client Queue API

The Microsoft.WindowsAzure.StorageClient namespace consists of classes representing the entire queue hierarchy. Figure 5-3 illustrates the core classes for programming Queue service applications.

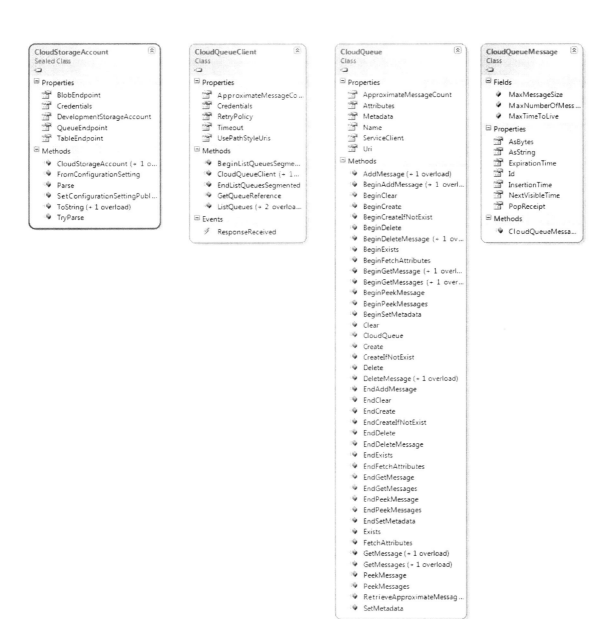

Figure 5-3. *Queue class hierarchy*

As shown in Figure 5-3, four core classes are required for queue operations. Table 5-1 lists these classes and a short description of each of them.

■ **Tip** The Windows Azure Storage Client API is the recommended method for programming Storage service applications. The API provides synchronous as well as asynchronous methods for interacting with the Storage service REST API.

Table 5-1. *Classes for the Queue Service*

Class Name	Description
CloudStorageAccount	A helper class for retrieving account information from the configuration file or creating an instance of the storage account object from account parameters.
CloudQueueClient	A wrapper class for getting references to the core queue objects. The class consists of methods like GetQueueReference() and ListQueues().
CloudQueue	Consists of queue operations like Create(), Delete(), AddMessage(), and GetMessage().
CloudQueueMessage	Represents a queue message with properties like InsertionTime, ExpirationTime, NextVisibleTime, Id, and PopReceipt.

In addition to these core classes, classes like QueueAttributes and QueueErrorCodeStrings represent more details about the queue.

The steps for programming simple queue applications with the queue classes listed in Table 5-1 are as follows:

1. Add the following using statement to your C# class:

```
using Microsoft.WindowsAzure.StorageClient;
```

2. Instantiate the CloudStorageAccount class from the configuration file:

```
CloudStorageAccount  storageAccountInfo =
CloudStorageAccount.FromConfigurationSetting(configurationSettingName);
```

Or, instantiate the CloudStorageAccount class using account information:

```
CloudStorageAccount  storageAccountInfo = new CloudStorageAccount(new
StorageCredentialsAccountAndKey(accountName, accountKey), new Uri(blobEndpointURI), new
Uri(queueEndpointURI), new Uri(tableEndpointURI));
```

3. Create an instance of CloudQueueClient:

```
CloudQueueClient queueStorageType = storageAccountInfo. CreateCloudQueueClient ();
```

When you have an instance of the CloudQueueClient class, you can execute operations on the queue storage service as follows:

List queues:

```
IEnumerable<CloudQueue> queues = queueStorageType.ListQueues();
Create Queue
queueStorageType.GetQueueReference(queueName).Create();
Delete Queue
queueStorageType.GetQueueReference(queueName).Delete();
```

Add a message:

```
public void AddMessage(string queueName, CloudQueueMessage queueMessage)
{
queueStorageType.GetQueueReference(queueName).AddMessage(queueMessage);
}
```

Get messages:

```
queueStorageType.GetQueueReference(queueName).GetMessages(numberofMessages,
TimeSpan.FromSeconds(visibilityTimeoutInSecs));
```

Peek messages:

```
queueStorageType.GetQueueReference(queueName).PeekMessages(numberofMessages);
```

Delete a message:

```
public void DeleteMessage(string queueName, CloudQueueMessage queueMessage)
{
queueStorageType.GetQueueReference(queueName).DeleteMessage(queueMessage);
}
```

Set queue metadata:

```
public void SetQueueMetadata(string queueName, NameValueCollection queueProps)
{

CloudQueue queue = queueStorageType.GetQueueReference(queueName);
queue.Attributes.Metadata = queueProps;
queue.SetMetadata();
}
```

The call to SetMetadata() method calls the method on the queue service API in the cloud.

Storage Client Code Sample Queue API

The Storage Client project consists of five important classes in the context of the Queue service. Table 5-2 lists these classes and a short description of each of them.

Table 5-2. *Storage Client classes for the Queue Service*

Class Name	Description
StorageAccountInfo	A helper class for retrieving account information from the configuration file.
QueueStorage	An abstract class that has properties and methods at the account level of the Queue service hierarchy. It has an AccountName property and the method ListQueues().
QueueStorageRest	A class that extends the QueueStorage class and implements the abstract methods. This class also has a nested class ListQueueResult, representing the results returned by the Queue service.
MessageQueue	An abstract class with signatures for the queue and message operations. Some example method calls are CreateQueue(), PutMessage(), and GetMessages().
QueueRest	A class that extends the MessageQueue class and implements the abstract methods.

Figure 5-4 illustrates the five classes listed in Table 5-2 and the relationships between them.

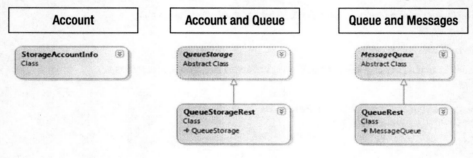

Figure 5-4. *StorageClient classes for the Queue service*

Following are some of the typical steps required to interact with the Queue service using Storage Client classes.

1. Add your account information in the *<appSettings>* section of your application configuration file (app.config or web.config):

```
<add key = "AccountName" value="[Your Account Name]"/>
<add key = "AccountSharedKey"
value="[Your Account Shared Key from the Developer Portal]"/>
```

To work with local storage, add "devstoreaccount1" as the AccountName and
"Eby8vdM02xNOcqFlqUwJPLlmEtlCDXJ1OUzFT50uSRZ6IFsuFq2UVErCz4I6tq/K
1SZFPTOtr/KBHBeksoGMGw==" as the shared key.

2. Add the Queue service endpoint URI in the appSettings section of your
    application configuration file:

```
<add key="QueueStorageEndpoint" value="http://blob.core.windows.net"/>
```

To work with local storage, add the URI of the local Queue service resource,
`http://127.0.0.1:10001`.

3. Create an instance of the StorageAccountInfo class from the configuration
    information you entered in the configuration file:

```
StorageAccountInfo account =
StorageAccountInfo.GetDefaultQueueStorageAccountFromConfiguration();
```

4. Create an instance of the QueueStorage class based on the account object:

```
QueueStorage queueStorage = QueueStorage.Create(account);
```

5. Call the ListQueues() method on the queueStorage object to get a list of all
    the queues in the account:

```
queueStorage.ListQueues();
```

6. To access a particular queue, call

```
MessageQueue messageQueue = queueStorage.GetQueue(queueName);
```

When you have a reference to the message queue object, then you can
call not only queue methods like CreateQueue(), DeleteQueue(), and
ListQueues(), but also message functions like PutMessage(),
GetMessages(), and DeleteMessage().

In the next few sections, you learn how to call some of these functions at every level of the Queue
service hierarchy.

Account Operations

The storage account provides an entry point to the Queue service via the Queue service endpoint URI. At
the account level of the hierarchy, the Queue service supports only one operation: List Queues. The URI
of a specific account is of the format <account name>.queue.core.windows.net. Table 5-3 describes the
List Queues operation, and Table 5-4 lists some important characteristics of the List Queues function.

Table 5-3. *Queue Account Operation*

Operation	Description
List Queues	This operation gets the list of all the queues in a storage account. You can limit the number of records returned by specifying a filter on queue names and the size of the data set in the request. Table 5-4 lists all the possible URI parameters for this operation.

Table 5-4. *Queue Account Operations Characterstics*

Operation	HTTP Verb	Cloud URI	Development Storage URI	HTTP Version	Permissions
List Queues	GET	account name>.queue.core. windows.net?comp= list	http://127.0.0.1 :10001/<*devstora geaccount*>?comp= list	HTTP/1.1	Only the account owner can call this operation.

<*account name*> is the storage account name, such as proazurestorage; and <*devstorageaccount*> is the account name for the development storage. The HTTP verb used in this operation is GET. The table lists the URI format for accessing the cloud Queue service as well as the development storage URI. Port 10001 is the default Queue service port in the development fabric.

The URI for the List Queues operation supports additional optional parameters, as listed in Table 5-5.

Table 5-5. *List Queues URI Parameters*

Parameter	Description	Example
prefix	A filter parameter for returning queues starting with the specified prefix value.	`http://proazurestorage.queue.core.windows.net/?comp=list&prefix=may` returns queues with names starting with the prefix "may".
marker	Used for paging queue results when all results aren't returned by the Storage service either due to the default maximum results allowed (the current default is 5000), or because you specify the maxresults parameter in the URI. The marker prefix is opaque to the client application.	`http://proazurestorage.queue.core.windows.net/?comp=list&prefix=may&marker=/proazurestorage/testq`
maxresults	The maximum number of queues the Queue service should return. The default value is 5000. The server returns HTTP Bad Request (400) code if you specify a maxresults value greater than 5000.	`http://proazurestorage.queue.core.windows.net/?comp=list&prefix=may&maxresults=10`

The sample REST request for List Queues in raw format looks like Listing 5-4.

Listing 5-4. *List Queues REST Request*

```
GET /?comp=list&prefix=test&maxresults=50&timeout=30 HTTP/1.1
x-ms-date: Wed, 27 May 2009 04:33:00 GMT
Authorization: SharedKey proazurestorage:GCvS8cv4Em6rWMuCVix9YCsxVgssOW62S2U8zjbIa1w=
Host: proazurestorage.queue.core.windows.net
Connection: Keep-Alive
```

The characteristics of the REST request in Listing 5-4 are as follows:

- The parameter comp=list at the account level of the Queue service yields the list of all the queues.
- The prefix=test filters the results by queue names starting with "test".
- The maxresults=50 returns 50 queues or less.
- The x-ms-date is the UTC timestamp of the request.

283

- The Authorization header contains the SharedKey of the request.

- The Host header points to the Queue service in the cloud.

Because the request is sending a maxresults parameter, it makes sense to keep the HTTP connection alive because it's highly likely that the user will retrieve the next set of results by making another call to the Queue service.

Listing 5-5 shows the response for the List Queues request.

Listing 5-5. *List Queues REST Response*

```
HTTP/1.1 200 OK
Content-Type: application/xml
Server: Queue Service Version 1.0 Microsoft-HTTPAPI/2.0
x-ms-request-id: dde8c8bd-121d-4692-a578-d8fac08e4525
Date: Wed, 17 Jun 2009 01:24:45 GMT
Content-Length: 648

<?xml version="1.0" encoding="utf-8"?>
<EnumerationResults AccountName="http://proazurestorage.queue.core.windows.net/">
<Prefix>test</Prefix>
<MaxResults>50</MaxResults>
<Queues>
<Queue>
<QueueName>testq</QueueName>
<Url>http://proazurestorage.queue.core.windows.net/testq</Url>
</Queue>
<Queue>
<QueueName>testq1</QueueName>
<Url>http://proazurestorage.queue.core.windows.net/testq1</Url>
</Queue>
<Queue>
<QueueName>testq2</QueueName>
<Url>http://proazurestorage.queue.core.windows.net/testq2</Url>
</Queue>
<Queue>
<QueueName>testq3</QueueName>
<Url>http://proazurestorage.queue.core.windows.net/testq3</Url>
</Queue>
</Queues>
<NextMarker />
</EnumerationResults>
```

In Listing 5-5, the header consists of the HTTP status (200 OK) indicating the success of the operation. The response body is in XML format with <EnumerationResults /> as the root element. The <Queues /> element contains the retrieved queues. The Queue element encompasses queue attributes like the queue name and the queue URI. An empty <NextMarker /> element indicates that all the results have been retrieved.

To help you understand the Queue service programming model, open the Windows Azure Storage Operations project from Ch4Solution.sln. The project consists of a Windows form and uses the StorageClient project from the same solution for making calls to all the Windows Azure storage. The

StorageClient project is shipped with the Windows Azure SDK. I also created a helper class named WindowsAzureStorageHelper in the ProAzureCommonLib project for wrapping the StorageClient methods. Figure 5-5 shows the user interface for the Windows Azure Storage Operations application as it pertains to the Operations account of the Queue service.

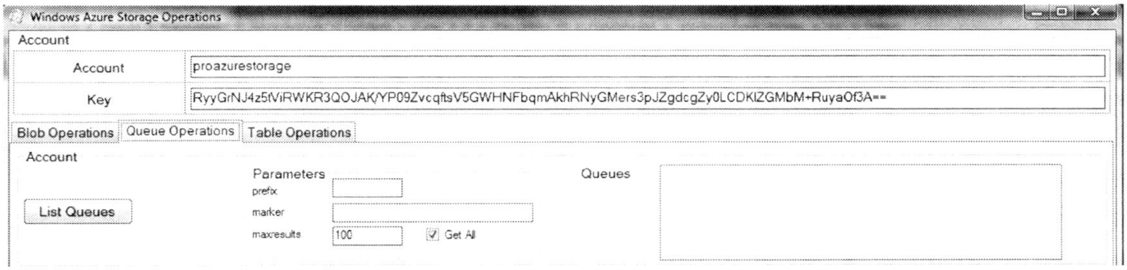

Figure 5-5. *Windows Azure storage Queue service account operations*

In Figure 5-5, the top Account section displays the account name and SharedKey of the storage account. When the Windows Azure Storage Operations.exe application starts, it loads the account information from the configuration file. Listing 5-6 shows the account configuration in the project's app.config file.

Listing 5-6. *App.config*

```xml
<?xml version="1.0" encoding="utf-8" ?>
<configuration>
  <appSettings>
    <add key ="AccountName" value="proazurestorage"/>
    <add key ="AccountSharedKey" value="RyyGrNJ4z5tViRWKR3QOJAK"/>
    <add key="BlobStorageEndpoint" value="http://blob.core.windows.net"/>
    <add key="QueueStorageEndpoint" value="http://queue.core.windows.net"/>
    <add key="TableStorageEndpoint" value="http://table.core.windows.net"/>
    <add key="LocalStorageAccountName" value="devstoreaccount1"/>
  </appSettings>
</configuration>
```

The AccountName and AccountSharedKey values are loaded when the application starts and displays these values in the Account and Key text fields, respectively. When you start the application, make sure to enter the account name and shared key of your storage account. The QueueStorageEndpoint is the URI of the Queue service.

The WindowsAzureStorageHelper class in ProAzureCommonLib project has a ListQueue() method for retrieving queue names. Listing 5-7 shows the code for ListQueues() method.

Listing 5-7. *ListQueues() Method*

```
public IEnumerable<MessageQueue> ListQueues(string prefix)
{
        if (string.IsNullOrEmpty(prefix))
```

```
{
 return this.QueueStorageType.ListQueues();
}
else
{
 return this.QueueStorageType.ListQueues(prefix);
}

}
```

In Listing 5-7, the ListQueues() method calls the ListQueues() method on the QueueStorageType object, which is of type QueueStorage from the StorageClient assembly. In the QueueStorage class, there are two overloaded ListQueues() methods. The first one returns all the queues in an account, whereas the second one accepts a prefix as a filter term for filtering the queues by names. Figure 5-6 illustrate the execution of the ListQueues operation in the Windows Azure Storage Operations application.

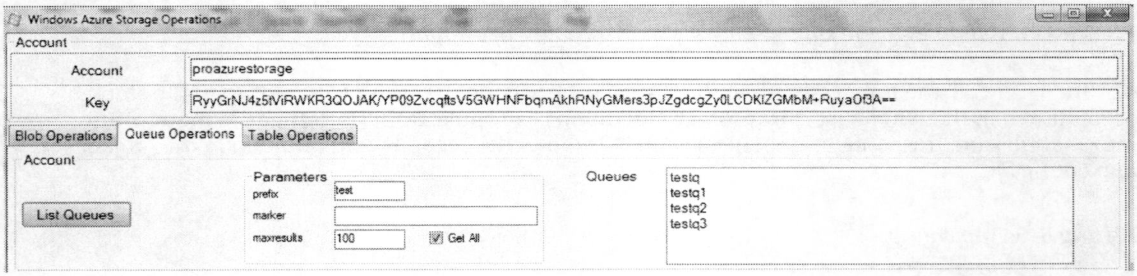

Figure 5-6. *List Queues operation*

When you click the List Queues button, the application retrieves queues from the Queue service and displays the names of queues in the Queues ListBox. In the parameter section, you can specify the prefix. Figure 5-7 is a sequence diagram for the ListQueues() method.

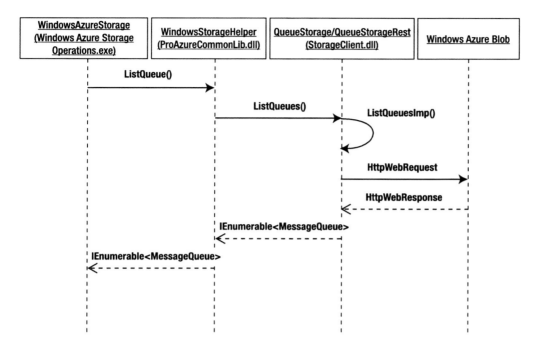

Figure 5-7. *List Queues sequence diagram*

In Figure 5-7, the Windows Azure Storage Operations application calls the ListQueues() method on the WindowsAzureStorageHelper object in the ProAzureCommonLib assembly. The helper object then calls the ListQueues() method on the QueueStorage and QueueStorageRest objects. QueueStorage is an abstract class, and QueueStorageRest inherits and implements the abstract methods from QueueStorage. The ListQueues() method in turn calls the private method ListQueuesImpl(). Finally, the actual logic for making the HTTP request to the Queue service is in the ListQueuesImpl() method. The Queue service returns the list of queues in an HTTP response, which is parsed and propagated back to the Windows Azure Storage Operations application for display.

Queue Operations

Queues support several operations, as listed in Table 5-6.

Table 5-6. *Queue Operations*

Operation	Description
Create Queue	Creates a new queue under the given account. You can specify metadata for the queue during creation.
Delete Queue	Marks the specified queue for deletion. The garbage collector deletes marked queues on a periodic basis. So, if you delete a queue and try to create it immediately, the Queue service complains that the queue already exists.
Get Queue Metadata	Gets the user-defined queue metadata and other queue properties. The metadata is retrieved in the form of name-value pairs.
Set Queue Metadata	Sets the metadata values of the specified queue. Set Queue Metadata replaces all the metadata of the specified queue with new values.

Table 5-7 lists some of the important characteristics of the queue operations listed in Table 5-6.

Table 5-7. *Queue Operations Characterstics*

Operation	HTTP Verb	Cloud URI	Development Storage URI	HTTP Version	Permissions
Create Queue	PUT	http://<account name>.queue.core.windows.net/<queue name>	http://127.0.0.1:10001/<devstorageaccount>/<queue name>	HTTP/1.1	Only the account owner can call this operation.
Delete Queue	DELETE	http://<account name>.queue.core.windows.net/<queue name>	http://127.0.0.1:10001/<devstorageaccount>/<queue name>	HTTP/1.1	Only the account owner can call this operation.
Get Queue Metadata	GET/HEAD	http://<account name>.queue.core.windows.net/<queue name>?comp=metadata	http://127.0.0.1:10001/<devstorageaccount>/<queue name>?comp=metadata	HTTP/1.1	Only the account owner can call this operation.
Set Queue Metadata	PUT	http://<account name>.queue.core.windows.net/<queue name>?comp=metadata	http://127.0.0.1:10001/<devstorageaccount>/<queue name>?comp=metadata	HTTP/1.1	Only the account owner can call this operation.

Table 5-7 lists the HTTP verb, cloud URI, development storage URI, HTTP version, and access control for the queues. The *<account name>* is the storage account name in the cloud, and the *<devstorageaccount>* is the development storage account. Observe that unlike blob containers, all the operations can be called only with the account owner privileges.

The following sections discuss some of the operations from Table 5-7 in detail. Even though the operations are different, the programming concepts behind them are similar. To keep the book at a conceptual level, I discuss just the Create Queue and Set Queue Metadata operations. By studying these operations in detail, you can understand the programming concepts behind all the queue operations. The Windows Azure Storage Operations application included with this chapter's source code contains an implementation of all the queue operations.

Create Queue

The Create Queue operation creates a queue in a storage account. The URI for the Create Queue operation is of the format account name>.queue.core.windows.net/*<queue name>*. You can think of Queue as a message queuing system in the cloud. For example, if you want to send and receive messages across diverse applications in different domains, Windows Azure Queue may fit your requirement. Because of its standard REST interface and Internet scale, you can send and receive queue messages anywhere, anytime, and in any programming language that supports Internet programming. The Create Queue REST request looks like Listing 5-8.

Listing 5-8. *Create Queue REST Request*

```
PUT /myfirstazurequeue?timeout=30 HTTP/1.1
x-ms-date: Wed, 17 Jun 2009 03:16:12 GMT
Authorization: SharedKey proazurestorage:aOEQSlfMdXfFrP/wwdfCUVqMYiv4PjXesFOJp4d71DA=
Host: proazurestorage.queue.core.windows.net
Content-Length: 0
```

Listing 5-8 shows the request for creating a queue named myfirstazurequeue. The PUT HTTP verb instructs the Queue service to create a queue. There is no metadata information for the queue, so the queue is created without any metadata. You can add x-ms-meta-[name]:[value] to the header to create metadata values. For the Create Queue operation, the Queue service responds with a status code of HTTP/1.1 201 Created, or HTTP/1.1 409 Conflict if a queue with the same name already exists. The Create Queue response is shown in Listing 5-9.

Listing 5-9. *Create Queue REST Response*

```
HTTP/1.1 201 Created
Server: Queue Service Version 1.0 Microsoft-HTTPAPI/2.0
x-ms-request-id: 8b4d45c8-2b5d-46b8-8e14-90b0d902db80
Date: Wed, 17 Jun 2009 03:17:57 GMT
Content-Length: 0
```

In Listing 5-9, the first line represents the status code of the operation. The x-ms-request-id represents a unique request identifier that can be used for debugging or tracing.

Figure 5-8 shows the working of the Create Queue operation in the Windows Azure Storage Operations application.

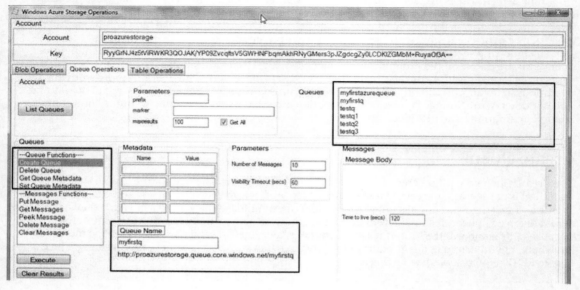

Figure 5-8. *Create Queue from Windows Azure Storage Operations.exe*

As shown in Figure 5-8, to create a queue, you need to do the following:

1. Go to the Queue Operations tab.

2. Enter a queue name (such as myfirstazurequeue) in the Queue Name text field.

3. Select the Create Queue operation from the Operations list box.

4. Click the Execute button. After the queue is created, the queues list box in the Account section is refreshed with the newly created queue name in it.

To help you understand the programming model of the Create Queue operation, open the Visual Studio Solution Chapter4.sln from the Chapter 4 source directory. The WindowsAzureStorageHelper class in the ProAzureCommonLib contains a helper function called CreateQueue, as shown in Listing 5-10.

Listing 5-10. *Create Queue Method in the WindowsAzureStorageHelper Class*

```
public bool CreateQueue(string queueName, out bool alreadyExists)
{
alreadyExists = false;
MessageQueue q = QueueStorageType.GetQueue(queueName);
```

```
return q.CreateQueue(out alreadyExists);
}
```

As shown in Listing 5-10, the CreateQueue() method calls the GetQueue() method to get a reference to the MessageQueue object. The MessageQueue object is a local instance of the Queue object. This instance doesn't create a queue when you instantiate it. To create a queue, you have to call the CreateQueue() method on the MessageQueue object. The MessageQueue object is used by the StorageClient to create accurate URI and metadata headers and send them to the Queue service. Figure 5-9 illustrates the sequence of method calls across different objects and assemblies for the Create Queue operation.

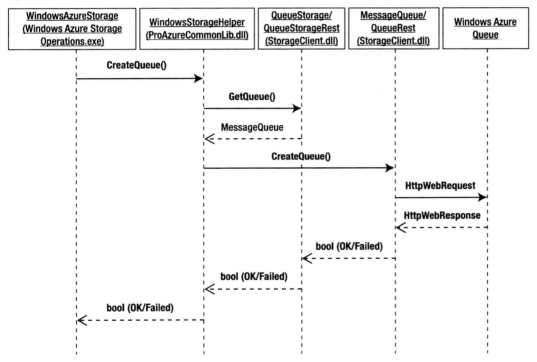

Figure 5-9. *Create Queue sequence diagram*

As shown in Figure 5-9, the Windows Azure Storage Operations application calls the CreateQueue() method on the WindowsStorageHelper object in the ProAzureCommonLib.dll. The WindowsStorageHelper object calls the GetQueue() method on the QueueStorage object to get an instance of the MessageQueue object. The WindowsStorageHelper object then calls the CreateQueue() method on the MessageQueue object. The CreateQueue() method creates the REST message and sends it synchronously to the Windows Azure Queue service to create the queue. It uses the System.Net.HttpWebRequest to send the REST message over HTTP. Upon success or failure of the operation, the Windows Azure Queue service returns an HTTP status code: HTTP/1.1 201 for success or HTTP/1.1 409 for conflict or failure. The CreateQueue() method translates the HTTP status code into true for success and false for failure or conflict. The Boolean value is passed all the way to the Windows Azure Storage Operations application as a return parameter of the CreateQueue() method.

Set Queue Metadata

Queues can contain name-value pairs of metadata values. You can store values like the time of creation, creator, last modified by user, and so on in the metadata fields of a container. The size of the metadata can be 8KB per queue. The Set Queue Metadata operation sets the metadata of a queue independently. The URI for the Set Queue Metadata operation is of the format `account name>.queue.core.windows.net/<queue name>?comp=metadata`. The Set Queue Metadata REST request looks like Listing 5-11.

Listing 5-11. *Set Queue Metadata REST Request*

```
PUT /myfirstazurequeue?comp=metadata&timeout=30 HTTP/1.1
x-ms-date: Wed, 17 Jun 2009 04:33:45 GMT
x-ms-meta-createdBy: tejaswi
x-ms-meta-creationDate: 6/16/2009
Authorization: SharedKey proazurestorage:spPPnadPYnH6AJguuYT9wP1GLXmCjnOI1S6W2+hzyMc=
Host: proazurestorage.queue.core.windows.net
Content-Length: 0
```

In Listing 5-11, the HTTP verb used is PUT, and the URI parameter is ?comp=metadata. This parameter instructs the Queue service to set the queue metadata instead of creating the queue. The Create Queue operation doesn't have this parameter. The x-ms-meta.[name]:[value] entries represent the metadata name-value pairs you want to set on the queue.

■ **Caution** Set Queue Metadata operation replaces all the existing metadata of the queue. It doesn't update individual metadata entries. For example, if a queue has two metadata values Creator and Creation-Time, and you call Set Queue Metadata with only one metadata value LastUpdatedBy, then the Creator and Creation-Time values will be deleted and the queue will have only one metadata value: LastUpdatedBy. To avoid this side effect, always set all the metadata values again along with any new values you want to add to the queue's metadata.

Figure 5-10 illustrates how to execute the Set Queue Metadata operation in Windows Azure Storage Operations application.

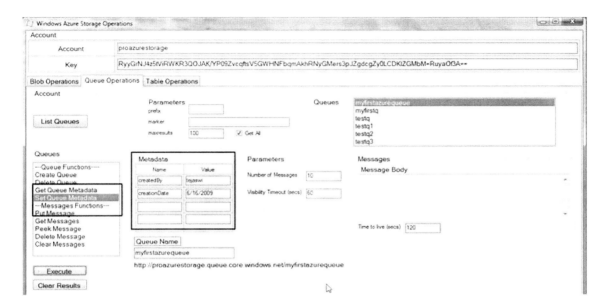

Figure 5-10. *Set Queue Metadata in the Windows Azure Storage Operations application*

As shown in Figure 5-10, to execute the Set Queue Metadata operation, you do the following:

1. Go to the Queue Operations tab.

2. In the Account section, click the List Queues button to get a list of queues in your account.

3. Select one of the queues from the list (such as myfirstazurequeue).

4. Make sure the Queue Name text box in the Queues section displays the name of the selected queue.

5. In the Queues section, select the Set Queue Metadata operation from list of queue operations.

6. In the Queues section, enter metadata name-value pairs in the Metadata section.

7. Click the Execute button to execute the operation.

8. To verify the success of the operation, click the Clear Results button in the Queues section, and re-select the queue from the Queues list in the Account section to retrieve the newly set metadata values.

To help you understand the programming model of the Set Queue Metadata operation, open the Visual Studio Solution Chapter4.sln from the Chapter 4 source directory. The WindowsAzureStorageHelper class in the ProAzureCommonLib contains a helper function called SetQueueProperties(), as shown in Listing 5-12.

293

Listing 5-12. SetQueueProperties Method in the WindowsAzureStorageHelper Class

```
public bool SetQueueProperties(string queueName, QueueProperties queueProps)
{
MessageQueue q = QueueStorageType.GetQueue(queueName);

return q.SetProperties(queueProps);
}
```

In Listing 5-12, the SetQueueProperties() method accepts the name of the queue and a QueueProperties object populated with metadata name-value pairs. The QueueProperties class has a property Metadata of type System.Collections.Specialized.NameValueCollection, which represents the metadata name-value pairs. The queue name is used to create a local instance of the MessageQueue object. The code then calls the SetProperties() method on the MessageQueue object to set the metadata values for the queue. If the metadata is set successfully, a Boolean value of true is returned back to the caller; otherwise, a false value is returned. Figure 5-11 illustrates the sequence of method calls across different objects and assemblies for the Set Queue Metadata operation.

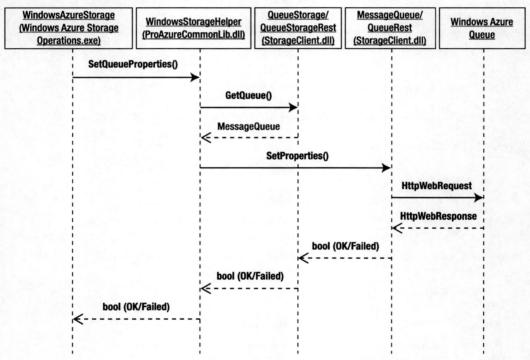

Figure 5-11. Set Queue Metadata sequence diagram

As shown in Figure 5-11, the Windows Azure Storage Operations application calls the SetQueueProperties() method on the WindowsStorageHelper object in the ProAzureCommonLib.dll. The WindowsStorageHelper object calls the GetQueue() method on the QueueStorage object to get an instance of the MessageQueue object. The WindowsStorageHelper object then calls the SetProperties() method on the MessageQueue object. The SetProperties() method creates the REST message and sends it synchronously to the Windows Azure Queue service to set the queue metadata values. It uses the System.Net.HttpWebRequest to send the REST message over HTTP. Upon success or failure of the operation, the Windows Azure Queue service returns an HTTP status code: HTTP/1.1 200 for success or HTTP/1.1 204 (No content). The SetProperties() method translates the HTTP status code into true for success and false for failure. The Boolean value is passed all the way to the Windows Azure Storage Operations application as a return parameter of the SetQueueProperties() method.

Message Operations

Messages support several operations, as listed in Table 5-8.

Table 5-8. Messages Operations

Operation	Description
Put Message	En-queues a message at the end of the specified queue. The message can't be more than 8KB in size.
Get Messages	Dequeues one or more messages from the front of the specified queue. The maximum number of messages that can be retrieved in a single call is 32. The messages received are marked invisible until the visibilitytimeout property of the message expires. The default visibilitytimeout is 30 seconds, and the maximum value is 2 hours.
Peek Messages	Reads one or more messages from the front of the specified queue. This method doesn't alter the visibilitytimeout property of a message, so the messages are visible to other applications at the same time.
Delete Message	Deletes the specified message from the queue. The Queue service marks the message for deletion, and the message is deleted during the next garbage-collection cycle. The delete operation requires the MessageId and PopReceipt of the message to be passed to the Queue service.
Clear Messages	Deletes all messages from the specified queue.

Table 5-9 lists some of the important characteristics of the message operations.

Table 5-9. *Message Operations Characterstics*

Operation	HTTP Verb	Cloud URI	Development Storage URI	HTTP Version	Permissions
Put Message	POST	http://<*account name*>.queue.core.win dows.net/<*queue name*>/messages	http://127.0.0.1:1 0001/<*devstorageac count*>/<*queue name*>/messages	HTTP/1.1	Only the account owner can call this operation.
Get Messages	GET	http://<*account name*>.queue.core.win dows.net/<*queue name*>/messages	http://127.0.0.1:1 0001/<*devstorageac count*>/<*queue name*>/messages	HTTP/1.1	Only the account owner can call this operation.
Peek Messages	GET	http://<*account name*>.queue.core.win dows.net/<*queue name*>/messages?peeko nly=true	http://127.0.0.1:1 0001/<*devstorageac count*>/<*queue name*>/messages?pee konly=true	HTTP/1.1	Only the account owner can call this operation.
Delete Message	DELETE	http://<*account name*>.queue.core.win dows.net/<*queue name*>/<*messageid*>?po preceipt=[pop receipt value]	http://127.0.0.1:1 0001/<*devstorageac count*>/<*queue name*>/<*messageid*>? popreceipt=[pop receipt value]	HTTP/1.1	Only the account owner can call this operation.
Clear Messages	DELETE	http://<*account name*>.queue.core.win dows.net/<*queue name*>/messages	http://127.0.0.1:1 0000/<*devstorageac count*>/<*queue name*>/messages	HTTP/1.1	Only the account owner can call this operation.

The <*account name*> is the storage account name in the cloud, and the <*devstorageaccount*> is the development storage account. The <*queue name*> is the name of the queue in which messages are stored. The following sections discuss some of the operations from Table 5-9 in detail. Even though the operations are different, the programming concepts behind them are similar. To keep the book at a conceptual level, I discuss just the Put Message and Get Messages operations. By studying these two operations in detail, you can understand the programming concepts behind all the message operations. The Windows Azure Storage Operations application included with this chapter's source code contains implementations of most of the message operations.

Put Message

The Put Message operation en-queues (puts) a message at the end of the queue. The URI of a Put Message operation is of the format `account name>.queue.core.windows.net/<queue name>/messages`. You can send a message with size up to 8KB. To send larger files, you can save the message as a blob and send the URI of the blob to the queue. The body of the message while sending can be text or binary, but it should support inclusion in an XML body with UTF-8 encoding. This is because a message received from the queue is always returned in Base64-encoded format within an XML response body. You see this in the Get Messages operation. The URI for the Put Message operation supports an additional optional parameter, listed in Table 5-10.

Table 5-10. Put Message URI Parameter

Parameter	Description	Example
messagettl	This is an integer value of seconds representing the time-to-live for a message in the queue before it's retrieved or deleted. The default and the maximum value for messagettl is 7 days, after which the message is garbage-collected.	`account name>.queue.core.windows.net/<queuename>/messages?messagettl=60`

The Put Message REST request looks like Listing 5-13.

Listing 5-13. Put Message REST Request

```
POST /myfirstazurequeue/messages?messagettl=120&timeout=30 HTTP/1.1
x-ms-date: Thu, 18 Jun 2009 05:52:00 GMT
Authorization: SharedKey proazurestorage:Ahv5yhR9xOrHiMTnq3fBcaBKL8KeUFQ3r
Host: proazurestorage.queue.core.windows.net
Content-Length: 84
Expect: 100-continue

<QueueMessage>
<MessageText>bXlmaXJzdGF6dXJlbWVzc2FnZQ==</MessageText>
</QueueMessage>
```

In Listing 5-13, a string message "myfirstazuremessage" is sent to the queue named myfirstazurequeue. The time-to-live seconds for the message is 120, which means if the message isn't received or deleted by an application within 120 seconds in the queue, the message will be marked for deletion and won't be visible to any applications. The request body consists of the message content wrapped in the <QueueMessage> element. Note that the content of the message within the <MessageText /> element is in Base64-encoded format. Listing 5-14 shows the response from the Queue service.

Listing 5-14. *Put Message REST Response*

```
HTTP/1.1 201 Created
Server: Queue Service Version 1.0 Microsoft-HTTPAPI/2.0
x-ms-request-id: e724cc82-3d21-4253-9317-3b3964374be7
Date: Thu, 18 Jun 2009 05:53:32 GMT
Content-Length: 0
```

As shown in Listing 5-14, the Queue service responds with an HTTP/1.1 201 Created status code for a successful Put Message operation. Figure 5-12 shows the working of the Put Message operation in the Windows Azure Storage Operations application.

Figure 5-12. *Put Message in Windows Azure Storage Operations.exe*

As illustrated in Figure 5-12, you can send a text message using the Windows Azure Storage Operations application. The steps for sending a message to a queue are as follows:

1. Create a new queue (called myfirstazurequeue).

2. Select the new queue from the Queues List Box in the Accounts section.

3. Add some text to the Message Body text box in the Queues section.

4. Select the Put Message operation from the Operations text box.

5. Make sure the Queue Name text box is populated with the selected queue name.

6. Optionally, you can specify the time-to-live in the "Time to live (secs)" text box.

7. Click the Execute button to execute the Put Message operation.

To help you understand the programming model of the Put Message operation, open the Visual Studio Solution Chapter4.sln from the Chapter 4 source directory. The WindowsAzureStorage.cs file in the Windows Azure Storage Operations project consists of a PutMessage() method, as shown in Listing 5-15.

Listing 5-15. PutMessage() Method in WindowsAzureStorage.cs

```
private void PutMessage()
        {
            string messageBody = string.Empty;
            if (txtMessageBody.Text.Length > 0)
            {
                messageBody = txtMessageBody.Text;

            }
            else
            {
                messageBody = String.Format
("Message from Windows Azure Storage Operations",
System.Guid.NewGuid().ToString("N"));
            }
            int ttlsecs = 300;
            if(txtTimeToLive.Text.Length > 0)
            {
                ttlsecs = int.Parse(txtTimeToLive.Text);
            }
            if (StorageHelper.PutMessage(txtQueueName.Text, new
Microsoft.Samples.ServiceHosting.StorageClient.Message(messageBody), ttlsecs))
            {
                statusLabel.Text = String.Format
("Message {0} sent successfully to queue {1}", messageBody, txtQueueName.Text);

            }
        }
```

As shown in Listing 5-15, the PutMessage() method calls the PutMessage() operation on the WindowsAzureStorageHelper (StorageHelper object). The message body and the time-to-live values are parsed appropriately from the server controls and passed as parameters to the method. If you don't enter a message in the Message Body text box, the application automatically creates a default message for you. Figure 5-13 shows the sequence of Put Message operation from the application to the Queue service as it passes through various assemblies and objects.

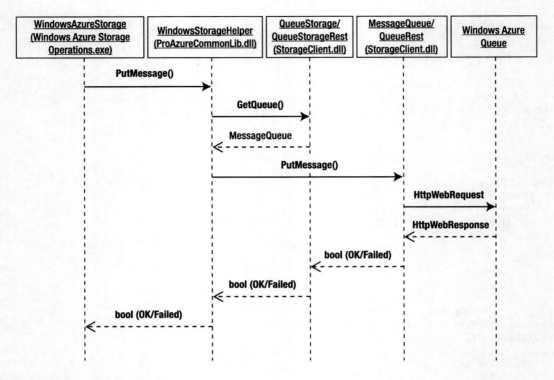

Figure 5-13. *Put Message sequence diagram*

As shown in Figure 5-13, the Windows Azure Storage Operations application calls the PutMessage() method on the WindowsStorageHelper object in the ProAzureCommonLib.dll. The WindowsStorageHelper object calls the GetQueue() method on the QueueStorage object to get an instance of the MessageQueue object. The WindowsStorageHelper object then calls the PutMessage() method on the MessageQueue object. The PutMessage() method of the MessageQueue object creates the REST message request and sends it synchronously to the Queue service. It uses the System.Net.HttpWebRequest to send the REST message over HTTP. Upon the success of the operation, the Queue service returns an HTTP status code: HTTP/1.1 201 Created. The PutMessage() method translates the HTTP code into true for success and false for failure. The Boolean value is passed all the way to the Windows Azure Storage Operations application as a return parameter of the PutMessage() method.

Get Messages

In the previous section, you learned to send messages to queues in the Queue service. In this section, you learn to retrieve these messages using the Get Messages operation. The URI for the Get Messages operation is of the format account name>.queue.core.windows.net/<queue name>/messages. The URI for the Get Messages operation supports additional optional parameters, as listed in Table 5-11.

Table 5-11. *Get Messagse URI Parameters*

Parameter	Description	Example
numofmessages	An integer value specifying the total number of messages you want retrieved. You can retrieve a maximum of 32 messages in a single call. By default, the operation retrieves only one message at a time.	account name>.queue.core.windows.net/ <*queue name*>/messages?numofmessages= 10
visibilitytimeout	An integer value representing the visibility of the message in seconds after it's received by a receiving application. The default visibilitytimeout value is 30 seconds, which means that after a message is received, it will remain invisible to other applications for 30 seconds, unless it's deleted by the receiving application. The maximum visibilitytimeout value is 2 hours.	account name>.queue.core.windows.net/ <*queue name*>/messages?visibilitytime out=60

Listing 5-16 shows the REST API request for the Get Messages operation.

Listing 5-16. *Get Messages REST Request*

```
GET /myfirstazurequeue/messages?numofmessages=10&visibilitytimeout=60&timeout=30_
  HTTP/1.1
x-ms-date: Thu, 18 Jun 2009 05:34:13 GMT
Authorization: SharedKey proazurestorage:qB9P717GTC6nd6rX4Ed16r6QkxO2QwJxLcr
Host: proazurestorage.queue.core.windows.net
```

In Listing 5-16, the URI points to the myfirstazurequeue queue. numofmessages=10 instructs the Queue service to retrieve only 10 messages. visibilitytimeout=60 instructs the Queue service to make the retrieved messages invisible to other applications for 60 seconds, unless the receiving application deletes them. Listing 5-17 shows the REST API response from the Queue service for the Get Messages operation.

Listing 5-17. *Get Messages REST Response*

```
HTTP/1.1 200 OK
Content-Type: application/xml
Server: Queue Service Version 1.0 Microsoft-HTTPAPI/2.0
x-ms-request-id: c10542ae-fa9e-45fd-b036-3f0b77ed611e
Date: Thu, 18 Jun 2009 05:35:43 GMT
Content-Length: 3900

<?xml version="1.0" encoding="utf-8"?>
<QueueMessagesList>
```

```
<QueueMessage>
<MessageId>ba16723c-8b4c-48dd-9d80-d5d2731bcbd8</MessageId>
<InsertionTime>Thu, 18 Jun 2009 05:36:43 GMT</InsertionTime>
<ExpirationTime>Thu, 18 Jun 2009 05:37:28 GMT</ExpirationTime>
<PopReceipt>AgAAAEAAAAAAAAAIBeHw9bvyQE=</PopReceipt>
<TimeNextVisible>Thu, 18 Jun 2009 05:36:43 GMT</TimeNextVisible>
<MessageText>bXlmaXJzdGF6dXJlbWVzc2FnZQ==</MessageText>
</QueueMessage>
<QueueMessage>
<MessageId>c0d92c72-2f9f-4c15-a177-7cf988c2532d</MessageId>
<InsertionTime>Thu, 18 Jun 2009 05:36:43 GMT</InsertionTime>
<ExpirationTime>Thu, 18 Jun 2009 05:37:28 GMT</ExpirationTime>
<PopReceipt>AgAAAEAAAAAAAAAIBeHw9bvyQE=</PopReceipt>
<TimeNextVisible>Thu, 18 Jun 2009 05:36:43 GMT</TimeNextVisible>
<MessageText>bXlmaXJzdGF6dXJlbWVzc2FnZQ==</MessageText>
</QueueMessage>
<QueueMessage>
<MessageId>f3ae9ccd-b97c-4bae-bc22-744cadd2c9c0</MessageId>
<InsertionTime>Thu, 18 Jun 2009 05:36:43 GMT</InsertionTime>
<ExpirationTime>Thu, 18 Jun 2009 05:37:28 GMT</ExpirationTime>
<PopReceipt>AgAAAEAAAAAAAAAIBeHw9bvyQE=</PopReceipt>
<TimeNextVisible>Thu, 18 Jun 2009 05:36:43 GMT</TimeNextVisible>
<MessageText>bXlmaXJzdGF6dXJlbWVzc2FnZQ==</MessageText>
</QueueMessage>
</QueueMessagesList>
```

Listing 5-17 shows the HTTP header and body of the Get Messages operation response. For the sake of brevity, only three messages are shown. The HTTP response body consists of a list of messages in XML format. Every <QueueMessage /> element represents a message. When you retrieve a message, the MessageId and the PopReceipt properties of the message are important for deletion purposes. The recommended pattern is to receive the message, process it, and then delete it before it becomes visible to other applications when the visibilitytimeout period expires. The TimeNextVisible value specifies the expiration time of the visibilitytimeout period. The ExpirationTime specifies the time when the message will be marked for deletion if not retrieved and/or deleted by a receiving application. This value was set when the message was sent to the queue. Figure 5-14 shows the working of the Get Messages operation in the Windows Azure Storage Operations.exe application.

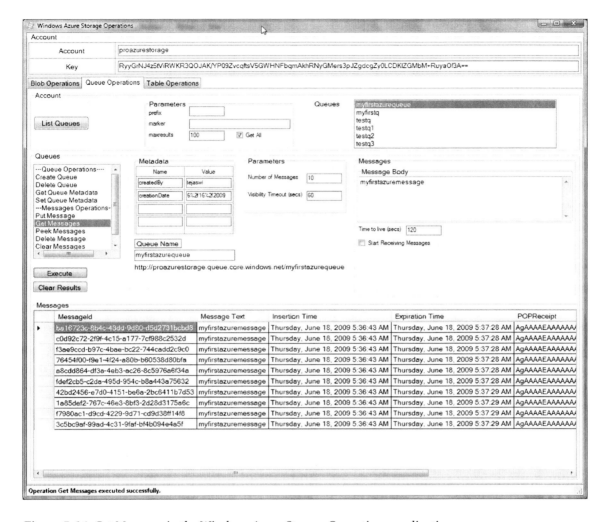

Figure 5-14. *Get Messages in the Windows Azure Storage Operations application*

As illustrated in Figure 5-14, you can use the Get Messages operation for a queue using the Windows Azure Storage Operations application. The steps for retrieving messages are as follows:

1. Select a queue (such as myfirstazurequeue) that already contains some messages.

2. In the Queues section, select the Get Messages operation.

3.   Click the Execute button to get a list of messages from the selected queue.

4.   Optionally, you can specify the Number of Messages and Visibility Timeout in the Parameters section.

The retrieved messages are populated in the DataGridView control in the Messages section. Each message is represented by a row in the DataGridView control. The control displays all the properties of the retrieved messages. To delete a message, select a row in the DataGridView and press the Delete button on your keyboard.

To help you understand the programming model of the Get Messages operation, open the Visual Studio Solution Chapter4.sln from the Chapter 4 source directory. The WindowsAzureStorage.cs file in the Windows Azure Storage Operations project consists of a GetMessages() method, as shown in Listing 5-18.

Listing 5-18. *GetMessages() Method in WindowsAzureStorage.cs*

```
private void GetMessages()
{
dgvMessages.Rows.Clear();
IEnumerable<Microsoft.Samples.ServiceHosting.StorageClient.Message> msgs =
StorageHelper.GetMessages(txtQueueName.Text, int.Parse(txtNumberOfMessages.Text),
int.Parse(txtVisibilityTimeoutSecs.Text));

if (msgs != null)
{
IList<Microsoft.Samples.ServiceHosting.StorageClient.Message> messages =
new List<Microsoft.Samples.ServiceHosting.StorageClient.Message>(msgs);
PopulateMessagesDataGridView(messages);

}
}
```

As shown in Listing 5-18, the GetMessages() method calls the GetMessages() method of WindowsAzureStorageHelper (StorageHelper object). The numofmessages and visibilitytimeout parameters are parsed appropriately into integer values and passed as parameters to the GetMessages() method. The returned messages are then packaged into a list and passed to the PopulateMessagedataGridView() method for display. Figure 5-15 illustrates the sequence diagram for the Get Messages operation.

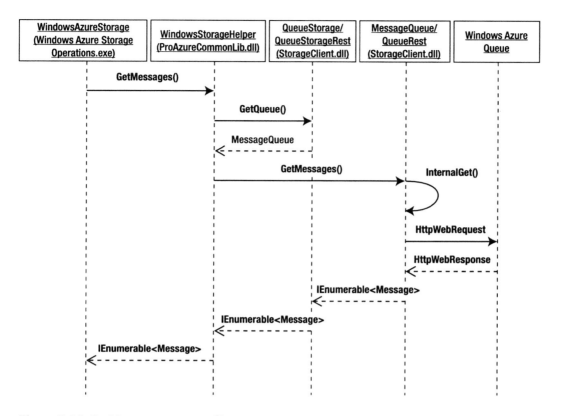

Figure 5-15. *Get Messages sequence diagram*

As shown in Figure 5-15, the Windows Azure Storage Operations application calls the GetMessages() method on the WindowsStorageHelper object in the ProAzureCommonLib.dll. The WindowsStorageHelper object calls the GetQueue() method on the QueueStorage object to get an instance of the MessageQueue object. The WindowsStorageHelper object then calls the GetMessages() method on the MessageQueue object. The MessageQueue object calls a private method InternalGet() to retrieve the messages from the specified queue. The body of the HTTP response contains messages in XML format. The XML contents are parsed and packaged into an IEnumerable<Message> collection and passed as a return parameter to the GetMessages() operation. Finally, the Windows Azure Storage Operations application displays these messages in a DataGridView control, as shown earlier in this section.

Message Event

The StorageClient API also supports an event-driven model for retrieving messages from a queue. The MessageQueue class defines an event called MessageReceived that you can subscribe to. The MessageQueue class also defines two methods StartReceiving() and StopReceiving() that start and stop the event subscription, respectively. The property PollInterval specifies the polling interval in milliseconds. Based on the PollInterval value, a thread calls the Get Messages operation periodically and returns the messages as parameters of the event delegate.

The steps for implementing an event-driven approach to the Get Messages operation are as follows.

1. Create an instance of the MessageQueue object:

```
Microsoft.Samples.ServiceHosting.StorageClient.MessageQueue mq =
StorageHelper.GetQueue(txtQueueName.Text);
```

2. Create an event handler for the MessageReceived event:

```
mq.MessageReceived += new MessageReceivedEventHandler(mq_MessageReceived);
```

1. The event handler method signature for mq_MessageReceived has MessageReceivedEventArgs as one of the parameters, which has a Message property representing the retrieved message.

3. Set the PollInterval property of the MessageQueue object to the desired polling interval in milliseconds:

```
mq.PollInterval = 10000;
```

4. Start receiving messages by calling the StartReceiving() method:

```
mq.StartReceiving();
```

5. To stop receiving messages, call the StopReceiving() method:

```
mq.StopReceiving()
```

■ **Note** The even-driven model is a purely client-side implementation for ease of client programming. In the background, the event is fired periodically and calls the same Get Messages operation discussed in this section. The REST API for the Queue service doesn't offer asynchronous invocations.

Queue Scenarios

In the previous sections, you saw the details of working with the Windows Azure Queue service. This section covers some of the basic application communication scenarios that can use the Windows Azure Queue service.

Scenario 1: Windows Azure Web and Worker Role Communications

Consider a scenario in which you're designing an ecommerce web application in Windows Azure with a Web Role front end and several Worker Roles for back-end processing work. The Web Role instances continuously send purchase order information to the Worker Roles for order processing. In this scenario, you can use the Windows Azure Queue service to queue purchase order messages for the Worker Roles, as shown in Figure 5-16.

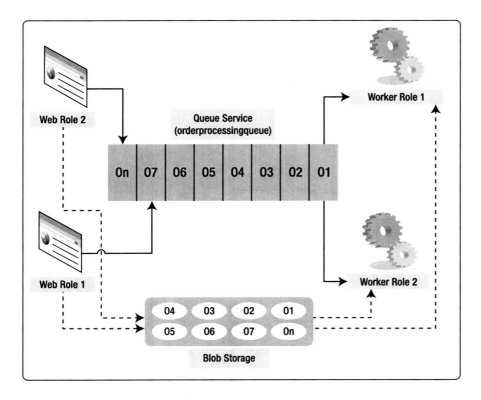

Figure 5-16. *Web Role/Worker Role communication using the Queue service*

In Figure 5-16, Web Role instances 1 and 2 send orders to the order-processing queue. Worker Roles 1 and 2 dequeue the order messages and process the orders. Because not all orders have to be processed immediately, Worker Roles can pick up from the queue only the orders that are ready to be processed. This way, you can create an effective message communication system between Web Roles and Worker Roles, taking advantage of the scalable and highly available Queue service infrastructure. If the order message size exceeds 8KB, you can store the message body in the Blob service and pass a link to the blob as a queue message, as shown in Figure 5-16. When the Worker Role dequeues the message, it can retrieve the contents of the order from the Blob service.

Scenario 2: Worker Role Load Distribution

Continuing Scenario 1, depending on the volume of messages, you can either adjust the number of queues or the number of instances of Worker Roles for processing orders. For example, if you identify during your testing phase that one Worker Role can process only ten orders at a time, you can configure Worker Roles to pick up only ten messages from the queue. If the number of messages in the queue keeps increasing beyond the number that Worker Roles can process, you can create more instances of Worker Roles on demand and increase the order-processing capacity. Similarly, if the queue is under-utilized, you can reduce the Worker Role instances for processing orders.

In this scenario, the Queue service plays the role of capacity indicator. You can think of the queues in the Queue service as indicators of the system's processing capacity. You can also use this pattern to process scientific calculations and perform business analysis. Figure 5-17 illustrates the Worker Role load-distribution scenario.

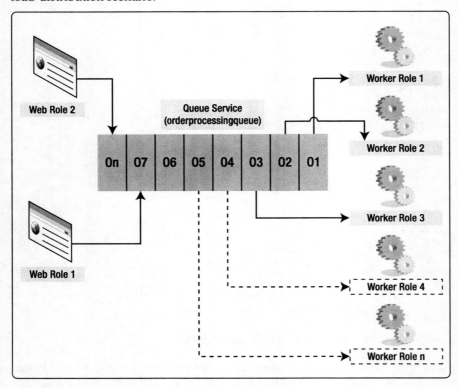

Figure 5-17. *Worker Role load distribution*

In Figure 5-17, Worker Roles 1 through 3 can process average order loads. When the number of orders backs up into the queue, you can spawn more Worker Roles (4 through *n*) depending on demand and the need for overall order-processing capacity.

Scenario 3: Interoperable Messaging

Large enterprises use applications from different vendors, and these applications seldom interoperate with each other. An enterprise may end up buying an expensive third-party tool that acts as the interoperability bridge between these applications. Instead, the enterprise could use the Queue service to send messages across the applications that don't interoperate with each other naturally. The Queue service exposes a REST API based on open standards. Any programming language or application capable of Internet programming can send and receive messages from the Windows Azure Queue service using the REST API. Figure 5-18 illustrates the use of the Queue service to interoperate between a Java-based Sales application and a .NET-based CRM application.

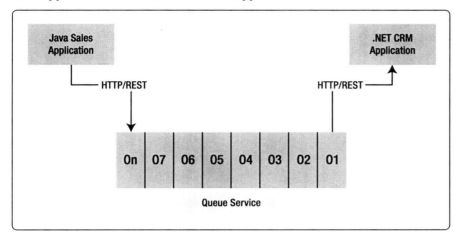

Figure 5-18. *Interoperable messaging*

Scenario 4: Guaranteed Processing

In Scenario 1, every order needs guaranteed processing. Any loss in orders can cause financial damage to the company. So, the Worker Roles and the Queue service must make sure every order in the queue is processed. You can implement guaranteed processing using four simple principles:

- Set the visibilitytimeout parameter to a value large enough to last beyond the average processing time for the messages.

- Set the visibilitytimeout parameter to a value small enough to make the message visible if message processing fails in a consumer (Worker Role) or a consumer crashes.

- Don't delete a message until it's processed completely.

- Design the message consumers (Worker Roles) to be idempotent (that is, they should account for handling the same message multiple times without an adverse effect on the application's business logic).

Figure 5-19 illustrates guaranteed message processing in the context of the order-processing example discussed in Scenario 1.

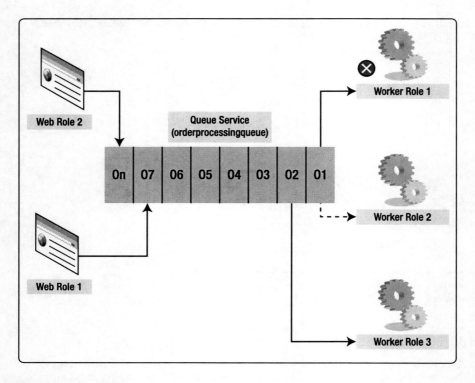

Figure 5-19. *Guaranteed processing*

In Figure 5-19, two Web Roles create orders, and three Worker Roles process orders. Consider the following steps:

1. Worker Role 1 reads order O1 for processing. Worker Roles typically take 15 seconds to process an order. The visibilitytimeout for messages is set to 60 seconds.

2. Worker Role 1 starts processing order O1. At this point, O1 isn't visible to other Worker Roles for 60 seconds.

3. Worker Role 1 crashes after 10 seconds.

4. After 60 seconds, O1 becomes visible again because Worker Role 1 wasn't able to delete it.

5. Worker Role 2 reads O1 and processes it.

6. After processing is complete, Worker Role 2 deletes O1 from the queue.

The important points to note here are that Worker Role 1 didn't delete the message from the queue before processing was complete, and the visibilitytimeout was set to an appropriate time window to exceed the processing time of an order.

Queue Summary

The Queue service provides a scalable and highly available store and delivery mechanism for exchanging messages across distributed applications. It provides reliable message delivery from message producers to message consumers. The Queue service exposes a REST API, making it easily accessible across multiple platforms and programming languages. In the previous section, you saw some of the important operations and scenarios for using the Queue service. The next chapter covers Windows Azure tables.

Bibliography

MSDN. (n.d.). *ADO.NET Data Services Specification*. Retrieved from MSDN Developer's Network: http://msdn.microsoft.com/en-us/library/cc668808.aspx.

MSDN. (2009, May). *Windows Azure Blob — Programming Blob Storage*. Retrieved from MSDN: http://go.microsoft.com/fwlink/?LinkId=153400.

MSDN. (2009, May). *Windows Azure Queue — Programming Queue Storage*. Retrieved from MSDN: http://go.microsoft.com/fwlink/?LinkId=153402.

MSDN. (2009, May). *Windows Azure SDK*. Retrieved from MSDN: http://msdn.microsoft.com/en-us/library/dd179367.aspx.

MSDN. (2009, May). *Windows Azure Table — Programming Table Storage*. Retrieved from MSDN: http://go.microsoft.com/fwlink/?LinkId=153401.

CHAPTER 6

■■■

Windows Azure Storage Part III – Tables

The Windows Azure Table service provides structured storage in the cloud. Windows Azure tables aren't relational database tables as seen in traditional databases. The Table service follows a simple yet highly flexible model of entities and properties. In the simplest of terms, tables contain entities, and entities have properties. The Table service is designed for massive scalability and availability, supporting billions of entities and terabytes of data. It's designed to support high volume, but smaller structured objects. For example, you can use the Table service to store user profiles and session information in high-volume Internet sites. But if you also want to store the photos of users, you should store the images in a Blob service and save the link to the photo in Table service.

There is no limit on the number of tables and entities you can create in a Table service. There is also no limit on the size of the tables in your account. Figure 6-1 illustrates the Azure Services Developer Portal page for the storage account and URL endpoint for the Table service.

Figure 6-1. Table service endpoint URL

Table Service Architecture

The Table service architecture consists of a four-level hierarchical structure: Account, Table, Entity, and Properties, as shown in Figure 6-2.

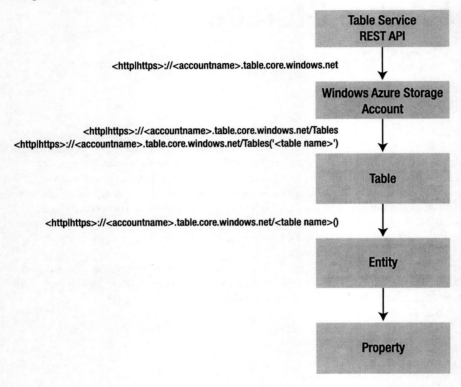

Figure 6-2. Table service architecture

Your Windows Azure storage account is the entry point to the Table service via the REST API.

Windows Azure Storage Account

The Windows Azure storage account encompasses the Blob, Queue, and Table services. The URI scheme for accessing the Table service via a storage account is

<httplhttps>://*<account name>*.table.core.windows.net

where *<account name>* is the globally unique name you created for your storage account. For example, the Table service for the storage account that I created in chapter 4 can be referenced as

<http|https>://proazurestorage.table.core.windows.net

Table

A table is a container for storing data. Data is stored in tables as collection of entities. There can be any number of tables in an account in the Table service. A table stores entities and makes them available to applications via the REST API and .NET client-side libraries like ADO.NET Data Services and LINQ. The Table service supports only private access, which means you must have account privileges to access tables in the Table service.

You can access a table with the following URI

<http|https>://*<accountname>*.table.core.windows.net/Tables('*<table name>*')

where *<table name>* is the name of the table you want to access. You can access all the tables in an account with the following URI:

<http|https>://*<account name>*.table.core.windows.net/Tables

For example, if you create a table named userprofiles in the proazurestorage account, you can reference it using the following URI:

<http|https>://proazurestorage.table.core.windows.net/Tables('userprofiles')

The naming constraints on a table are as follows:[1]

- Table names must be valid DNS names.
- Table names must be unique within an account.
- Table names must contain only alphanumeric characters.
- Table names must begin with an alphabetical character.

---

[1]Source: Windows Azure SDK documentation

- Table names are case sensitive.

- Table names can't be fewer than 3 or more than 63 characters in length.

If a table name or the URI violates the naming convention, the server returns an HTTP status code 400 (Bad request).

Entity

Entities are stored in tables. They're analogous to rows in a relational database table. There is no limit on the number of entities that can be stored in a table. You can retrieve all the entities in a table with the following URI

<http|https>://<*account name*>.table.core.windows.net/<*table name*>()

Where <*table name*> is the name of the table you want to access, and the parentheses instructs the Table service to retrieve the entities in the specified table.

Property

An entity consists of a set of name-value pairs called *properties*. Properties are analogous to columns in a relational database table. An entity must have three mandatory properties: PartitionKey, RowKey, and Timestamp. PartitionKey and RowKey are of string data type, and Timestamp is a read-only DateTime property maintained by the system. The combination of PartitionKey and RowKey uniquely identifies an entity. You must design PartitionKey and RowKey as part of your table design exercise.

The Table service organizes data into several storage nodes based on the entities' PartitionKey property values. Entities with same PartitionKey are stored on a single storage node. A *partition* is a collection of entities with the same PartitionKey. A RowKey uniquely identifies an entity within a partition.

The Table service provides a single index in which entity records are sorted first by PartitionKey and then by RowKey. All the entities in a single partition have the same PartitionKey, so you can safely assume that all the entities in a partition are lexically sorted by RowKey. Figure 6-3 illustrates the design of an example PartitionKey and RowKey for a table.

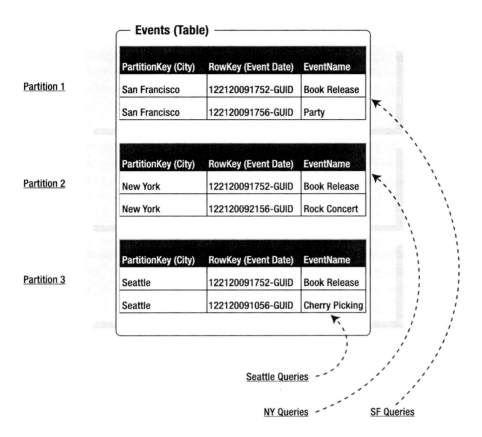

Figure 6-3. *PartitionKey and RowKey*

In Figure 6-3, imagine you're designing an event management web site. On your web site, the most dominant user query is "Give me today's events in my city." So, the application queries the Events table for all the events on a particular day sorted with the most recent event at the top. The example in Figure 6-3 illustrates the Events table with its PartitionKey, RowKey and EventName properties.

Because the most dominant query retrieves all the events from a city, as an architect of the system, you want the dominant query to execute on a single partition (or storage node) for maximum query performance. If a San Francisco user comes to the web site, the application retrieves all the San Francisco events from a single partition. As explained earlier, the Table service groups entities with the same PartitionKey on the same partition. To achieve the desired distribution of entities, you define City as the PartitionKey for the entity; doing so groups all the events in a particular city on a single partition, as shown in Figure 6-3.

The table spans three partitions: the events "Book Release" and "Party" in San Francisco are stored on Partition 1, and New York and Seattle events are stored on Partition 2 and Partition 3. respectively. The distribution of a table across multiple partitions is opaque to the application.

317

The next part of the dominant query involves sorting events by date and time. Remember that the RowKey uniquely identifies an entity within a partition, and the entities are sorted by RowKey within a partition. So, you want all the events in a city (or partition) sorted by date and time. To sort the entities in a partition by date and time, you define RowKey as a function of date and time. You can achieve this by subtracting (`DateTime.MaxValue.Ticks` – `EventTime.Ticks`), where EventTime is the date and time of the event.

The combination of PartitionKey and RowKey uniquely identifies an entity within a table, so you can't have a duplicate PartitionKey and RowKey pair. There can't be two events in the same city starting at the exact same date and time. To create a unique PartitionKey and RowKey pair, you can append the RowKey with a GUID or any unique identifier of your choice. Because there can be only one PartitionKey and one RowKey in an entity, you must concatenate strings to create a PartitionKey and RowKey for every table design. In the future, when the Table service supports multiple indexes and RowKeys, the partitioning and sorting design will be more refined.

If the dominant query was "Get me today's Book Releases (Event Type) across all the Cities." the PartitionKey would be a function of time and Event Type, because you would want all the events of the same type across all the cities partitioned together. But you would also have to consider the impact of the volume of data on the query. The previous examples assume the number of entities on each partition are low enough for the query to perform optimally. If there are millions of events in a particular city, you would further refine the PartitionKey to reduce the load on the query.

While you're designing PartitionKeys, consider a tradeoff between scalability and performance. Depending on the capacity requirements and usage volume of your application, the PartitionKey may play an important role in scalability and performance. Having more partitions distributed over multiple storage nodes makes the table more scalable, whereas narrowing entities on a single partition may yield better performance, assuming the number of entities on a partition is low enough for the query to perform optimally.

■ **Tip** Design your PartitionKeys and RowKeys in an iterative manner. Stress- and performance-test your design for every iteration. Then, choose an optimum PartitionKey that satisfies your application's performance and scalability requirements.

Table 6-1 lists the supported data types for property values and their Common Language Runtime (CLR) counterparts.

Table 6-1. *Property Value Data Types*

Data Type	Corresponding CLR Data Type
Binary	byte[]
Boolean	bool
DateTime	DateTime
Double	Double
Guid	Guid
Int32	int or Int32
Int64	long or Int64
String	string

The following are some of the characteristics of and constraints on entities and properties:

- Tables support flexible schema. This means a table can contain entities that have property values of different data types. For example, in a UserProfiles table, you can have an entity record representing a ZipCode property with an integer data type ("ZipCode", 94582) and another entity record with a string data type for the same property ("ZipCode", "CK45G").

- An entity can contain at the most 255 properties (including the PartitionKey, RowKey, and Timestamp properties, which are mandatory).

- The total size of an entity including all the property names and values can't exceed 1MB.

- Timestamp is a read-only value maintained by the system.

- PartitionKey and RowKey can't exceed 1KB in size each.

- Property names can contain only alphanumeric characters and the underscore (_) character. The following characters aren't supported in property names: backslash (\), forward slash (/), dash (-), number sign (#), and question mark (?).

REST API

The REST API for the Table service is available at the table and entity levels of the hierarchy. The Table service API is compatible with the ADO.NET Data Services REST API. The differences between the Table service API and the ADO.NET Data Services API are highlighted in the Table services API section of the Windows Azure SDK documentation.[2] In this section, you learn about the Table service REST API with specific examples. You also learn to interact with the Table service programmatically, using the .NET Client Library and the Storage Client libraries from the Windows Azure SDK. The REST API enables you to send HTTP messages to the Table service and its resources.

REST is an HTTP-based protocol; you specify the URI of the resource as well as the function you want to execute on the resource. Every REST call involves an HTTP request to the storage service and an HTTP response from the storage service. The programming examples in this section use the .NET Client library and/or Storage Client library to access the Table service. Both of them ultimately result in REST API calls to the Table service, but I used them to keep the examples at a conceptual level. You can choose to program the Table service directly using the REST API.

■ **Note** ADO.NET Data Services provides a REST API for accessing any data service on the Web. You can find the specification for the ADO.NET Data Services at `http://msdn.microsoft.com/en-us/library/cc668808.aspx`.

Request

The following sections describe the Table service REST API's HTTP request components.

HTTP Verb

The HTTP verb represents the action or operation you can execute on the resource indicated in the URI. The Table service REST API supports the following verbs: GET, PUT, MERGE, POST, and DELETE. Each verb behaves differently when executed on a different resource.

---

[2] See `http://msdn.microsoft.com/en-us/library/dd135720.aspx/`

Request URI

The request URI represents the URI of a resource you're interested in accessing or executing a function on. Example resources in the Table service include table and entity. An example URI to create a table named Events in an account named proazurestorage is

```
POST http://proazurestorage.table.core.windows.net/Tables
```

Note that unlike in the Blob and Queue services, the URI doesn't include the name of the table (Events). The request body includes the details of the table to be created. The HTTP verb POST instructs the service to create the table, and the request body points to the resource that needs to be created.

URI Parameters

Typically, URI parameters are the extra parameters you specify to fine-tune your operation execution. They may include the operation parameters or filter parameters for the results. In the Table service API, the URI parameters support the ADO.NET Data Service Framework query options $filter and $top, as described in the ADO.NET Data Service specification at `http://msdn.microsoft.com/en-us/library/cc668809.aspx`.

The $filter parameter retrieves only the tables and entities that match the filter criteria specified in the URI. The following URI shows a sample usage of the $filter parameter:

```
http://proazurestorage.table.core.windows.net/ProAzureReader()?
    $filter=PurchaseDate%20eq%20datetime'2009-06-20T00:00:00'
```

ProAzureReader is the name of the table, and ProAzureReader() retrieves all the entities from the table. The URI further applies a filter "PurchaseDate eq datetime'2009-06-20T00:00:00'" for restricting the number of returned entities.

The $top parameter retrieves only Top(n) number of tables or entities specified in the URI. The following URI shows a sample usage of the $top parameter:

```
http://proazurestorage.table.core.windows.net/ProAzureReader()?$top=3
```

Again, ProAzureReader is the name of the table, and ProAzureReader() retrieves all the entities from the table. The $top parameter instructs the Table service to retrieve only the top three entities from the table.

Request Headers

Request headers follow the standard HTTP 1.1 name-value pair format. Depending on the type of request, the header may contain security information, date time information, or instructions embedded as name-value pairs. In the Storage Service REST API, the request header must include the authorization information and a Coordinated Universal Time (UTC) timestamp for the request. The timestamp can be in the form of either an HTTP/HTTPS Date header or an x-ms-Date header.

The authorization header format is as follows

Authorization="[SharedKey|SharedKeyLite] *<Account Name>*:*<Signature>*"

Where SharedKey|SharedKeyLite is the authentication scheme, *<Account Name>* is the storage service account name, and *<Signature>* is a Hash-based Message Authentication Code (HMAC) of the request computed using the SHA256 algorithm and then encoded by using Base64 encoding.

To create the signature, follow these steps:

1. Create the signature string for signing. The signature string for the Storage service request consists of the following format:

   VERB\n
   Content - MD5\n
   Content - Type\n
   Date\n
   CanonicalizedHeaders
   CanonicalizedResource
   VERB is the uppercase HTTP verb such as GET, PUT, and so on. Content – MD5 is the MD5 hash of the request content. CanonicalizedHeaders is the portion of the signature string created using a series of steps described in the "Authentication Schemes" section of the Windows Azure SDK documentation: `http://msdn.microsoft.com/en-us/library/dd179428.aspx`. CanonicalizedResource is the storage service resource in the request URI. The CanonicalizedResource string is also constructed using a series of steps described in the "Authentication Schemes" section of the Windows Azure SDK documentation.

2. Use the System.Security.Cryptography.HMACSHA256.ComputeHash() method to compute the SHA256 HMAC encoded string.

3. Use the System.Convert.ToBase64String() method to convert the encoded signature to Base64 format.

Listing 6-1 shows an example request header for an entity GET operation.

Listing 6-1. *Request Header*

```
User-Agent: Microsoft ADO.NET Data Services

x-ms-date: Sat, 20 Jun 2009 22:42:54 GMT
x-ms-version: 2009-04-14
Authorization: SharedKeyLite
    proazurestorage:qWuBFkungfapSPIAFsrxeQ+j1uVRHyMUyEPiVOC832A=
```

```
Accept: application/atom+xml,application/xml
Accept-Charset: UTF-8
DataServiceVersion: 1.0;NetFx
MaxDataServiceVersion: 1.0;NetFx
Host: proazurestorage.table.core.windows.net
```

In Listing 6-1, the request header consists of x-ms-date, x-ms-version, and Authorization values. The x-ms-date represents the UTC timestamp, and the x-ms-version specifies the version of the storage service API you're using. The header also specifies the version of the ADO.NET Data Service API. The Authorization SharedKey header value is used by the Storage service to authenticate and authorize the caller.

The Table service REST API also supports the HTTP 1.1 If-Match conditional header. The If-Match conditional header is a mandatory header sent by the ADO.NET Data Service API. For update, merge, and delete operations, the Table service compares the specified ETag value with the ETag value on the server. If they don't match, an HTTP 412 (PreCondition Failed) error is sent back in the response. You can force an unconditional update by specifying a wildcard (*) for the If-Match header in the request.

Request Body

The request body consists of the contents of the request operation. Some operations require a request body, and some don't. For example, the Create Table operation's request body consists of an ADO.NET entity in the form of an Atom feed, whereas the Query Table operation requires an empty request body. Atom is an application-level protocol for publishing and editing web resources[3] defined by the Internet Engineering Task Force (IETF). You see other request body examples later in this chapter.

■ **Note** For more information about the Atom format in ADO.NET Data Services messages, visit the "Atom Format" section in the ADO.NET Data Services specification at http://msdn.microsoft.com/en-us/library/cc668811.aspx.

Response

The HTTP response of the Table service API typically includes the components described in the following sections.

---

[3] Source: ADO.NET Data Services Framework, http://msdn.microsoft.com/en-us/library/cc668811.aspx

Status Code

The status code is the HTTP status code that indicates the success or failure of the request. The most common status codes for the Table service API are 200 (OK), 201 (Created), 400 (BadRequest), 404 (NotFound), 409 (Conflict), and 412 (PreCondition Failed).

Response Headers

The response headers include all the standard HTTP 1.1 headers plus any operation-specific headers returned by the Table service. The x-ms-request-id response header uniquely identifies a request. Listing 6-2 shows an example response header for a Query Entities operation.

Listing 6-2. Query Entities Response Header

```
HTTP/1.1 200 OK

Cache-Control: no-cache
Transfer-Encoding: chunked
Content-Type: application/atom+xml;charset=utf-8
Server: Table Service Version 1.0 Microsoft-HTTPAPI/2.0
x-ms-request-id: a1eccc1c-8c1f-4fca-8ca9-69850684e553
Date: Sat, 20 Jun 2009 22:43:45 GMT
```

Response Body

The response body consists of values returned by the operation. These values are specific to each operation. For example, the Query Entity operation returns an ADO.NET entity set, which is in the form of an Atom feed. Listing 6-3 shows an example of the response body for the following entity query:

```
GET http://proazurestorage.table.core.windows.net/ProAzureReader()?$
    filter=PartitionKey%20eq%20'06202009'
```

The response consists of two entities.

Listing 6-3. Query Entity Response Body

```
<?xml version="1.0" encoding="utf-8" standalone="yes"?>

<feed xml:base=http://proazurestorage.table.core.windows.net/
xmlns:d=http://schemas.microsoft.com/ado/2007/08/dataservices
xmlns:m=http://schemas.microsoft.com/ado/2007/08/dataservices/metadata
xmlns="http://www.w3.org/2005/Atom">
  <title type="text">ProAzureReader</title>
```

```
    <id>http://proazurestorage.table.core.windows.net/ProAzureReader</id>
    <updated>2009-06-20T22:43:46Z</updated>
    <link rel="self" title="ProAzureReader" href="ProAzureReader" />
    <entry m:etag="W/&quot;datetime'2009-06-20T13%3A01%3A10.5846Z'&quot;">
      <id>http://proazurestorage.table.core.windows.net/ProAzureReader
(PartitionKey='06202009',RowKey='12521567980278019999')</id>
      <title type="text"></title>
      <updated>2009-06-20T22:43:46Z</updated>
      <author>
        <name />
      </author>
      <link rel="edit" title="ProAzureReader"
href="ProAzureReader(PartitionKey='06202009',RowKey='12521567980278019999')" />
      <category term="proazurestorage.ProAzureReader"
scheme="http://schemas.microsoft.com/ado/2007/08/dataservices/scheme" />
      <content type="application/xml">
        <m:properties>
          <d:PartitionKey>06202009</d:PartitionKey>
          <d:RowKey>12521567980278019999</d:RowKey>
          <d:Timestamp m:type="Edm.DateTime">2009-06-20T13:01:10.5846Z
</d:Timestamp>
          <d:City>mumbai</d:City>
          <d:Country>india</d:Country>
          <d:EntryDate m:type="Edm.DateTime">2009-06-20T12:59:32.198Z
</d:EntryDate>
          <d:Feedback>Good Book :). But don't write again.</d:Feedback>
          <d:PurchaseDate m:type="Edm.DateTime">2009-06-20T00:00:00Z
</d:PurchaseDate>
          <d:PurchaseLocation>web</d:PurchaseLocation>
          <d:PurchaseType>New</d:PurchaseType>
          <d:ReaderName>tredkar</d:ReaderName>
          <d:ReaderUrl></d:ReaderUrl>
          <d:State>maharashtra</d:State>
          <d:Zip>400028</d:Zip>
        </m:properties>
      </content>
    </entry>
    <entry m:etag="W/&quot;datetime'2009-06-20T11%3A40%3A24.834Z'&quot;">
      <id>http://proazurestorage.table.core.windows.net/ProAzureReader
(PartitionKey='06202009',RowKey='12521568028370519999')</id>
      <title type="text"></title>
      <updated>2009-06-20T22:43:46Z</updated>
      <author>
        <name />
```

```
    </author>
    <link rel="edit" title="ProAzureReader"
href="ProAzureReader(PartitionKey='06202009',
RowKey='12521568028370519999')" />
    <category term="proazurestorage.ProAzureReader"
scheme="http://schemas.microsoft.com/ado/2007/08/dataservices/scheme" />
    <content type="application/xml">
      <m:properties>
        <d:PartitionKey>06202009</d:PartitionKey>
        <d:RowKey>12521568028370519999_</d:RowKey>
        <d:Timestamp m:type="Edm.DateTime">2009-06-20T11:40:24.834Z</d:Timestamp>
        <d:City></d:City>
        <d:Country></d:Country>
        <d:EntryDate m:type="Edm.DateTime">2009-06-20T11:39:22.948Z</d:EntryDate>
        <d:Feedback>Good Book :). But don't write again.</d:Feedback>
        <d:PurchaseDate m:type="Edm.DateTime">2009-06-20T00:00:00Z
</d:PurchaseDate>
        <d:PurchaseLocation></d:PurchaseLocation>
        <d:PurchaseType>New</d:PurchaseType>
        <d:ReaderName></d:ReaderName>
        <d:ReaderUrl></d:ReaderUrl>
        <d:State></d:State>
        <d:Zip></d:Zip>
      </m:properties>
    </content>
  </entry>
</feed>
```

■ **Tip** To test the REST API, I recommend using the Fiddler Tool available at http://www.fiddler2.com/fiddler2/. In this book, I use this tool to trace client/server communications.

ADO.NET Data Services Library (.NET Client Library)

The Table service API provides a subset of the ADO.NET Data Service API, so you can use the ADO.NET Data Services client library to work with tables and entities in the Table service. The System.Data.Services.Client assembly consists of the ADO.NET Data Services and .NET Client library classes.

▒ **Note** For more information about the Table service's support for the ADO.NET Data Services .NET Client library, visit the latest Table services API MSDN documentation at `http://msdn.microsoft.com/en-us/library/dd894032.aspx`.

You don't have to use the ADO.NET Data Services library to interact with tables and entities in the Table service. You may choose to work directly at the REST API level by constructing REST messages on your own.

▒ **Note** For more information about the ADO.NET Data Services .NET client library, visit `http://msdn.microsoft.com/en-us/library/cc668789.aspx`.

If you're using .NET Client library, the Table service lets you use a subset of Language Integrated Queries (LINQ) to interact with tables and entities. For more information about LINQ support in the Table service, visit the "Summary of Table Service Functionality" (`http://msdn.microsoft.com/en-us/library/dd135720.aspx`) and "Writing LINQ Queries" `http://msdn.microsoft.com/en-us/library/dd894039.aspx`) sections in the Table service API Windows Azure SDK documentation.

In this book, I use some of the ADO.NET Data Services .NET client library constructs as an alternative to using the Table service's REST API directly.

Storage Client APIs

Even though the REST API and the operations in the REST API are easily readable, the API doesn't automatically create the client stubs like those created by WSDL-based web services. You have to create your own client API and stubs for REST API operations. This makes the client programming more complex and increases the barrier to entry for developers. To reduce this barrier to entry, the Windows Azure SDK team has created two client helper libraries: Microsoft.WindowsAzure.StorageClient from Windows Azure SDK, and the Storage Client code sample. Both libraries are used to invoke REST APIs of the Windows Azure Storage service. The Microsoft.WindowsAzure.StorageClient library abstracts this by providing a closed-source interface and therefore is less interesting to developers who want to see the inner workings of the method calls.

In the Windows Azure CTP version, a code sample named Storage Client became the choice of developers to call Storage services because the Microsoft.WindowsAzure.StorageClient wasn't available and also because it was open source and thus gave good insight into building your own storage client library. The Storage Client makes it easier to see the end-to-end method calls to the Storage service. In this chapter, I use the Storage Client code sample in the sample applications. I also cover the class structure and calling mechanisms in the Microsoft.WindowsAzure.StorageClient namespace.

In the following sections, I cover the table storage APIs from Microsoft.WindowsAzure.StorageClient and the Storage Client code sample.

■ **Note** You don't have to use any of the StorageClient library to make REST calls to the Storage service; you can instead create your own client library. In order to keep the book conceptual, I use the StorageClient code sample helper library to interact with the Storage service throughout this book. The source code for StorageClient is available in the samples directory of Windows Azure SDK or from the Windows Azure code samples site (http://code.msdn.microsoft.com/windowsazuresamples).

Windows Azure StorageClient Table API

The Microsoft.WindowsAzure.StorageClient namespace consists of classes representing the entire blob hierarchy. Figure 6-4 illustrates the core classes for programming Table service applications.

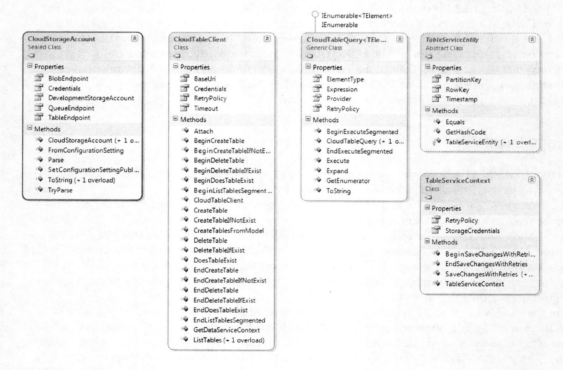

Figure 6-4. *Table class hierarchy*

As shown in Figure 6-4, five core classes are required for table operations. Table 6-2 lists these classes and describes each of them.

Tip The Windows Azure StorageClient API is the recommended method for programming storage service applications. The API provides synchronous as well as asynchronous methods to interact with the Storage service REST APIs.

Table 6-2. Classes for the Table Service

Class Name	Description
CloudStorageAccount	A helper class for retrieving account information from the configuration file or creating an instance of the storage account object from account parameters.
CloudTableClient	A wrapper class to interact with the Table service. It has methods like CreateTable(), DeleteTable(), GetDataServiceContext(), and ListTables().
TableServiceContext	Inherits from the System.Data.Services.Client.DataServiceContext class. It adds additional authentication functionality required by the Table service.
TableServiceEntity	An abstract class representing an entity(row) in a table. It has the mandatory properties (PartitionKey, RowKey, and Timestamp) defined in it. You may inherit your entity class from this class and provide additional properties.
CloudTableQuery<TElement>	Can be used to work with continuation tokens in Table service. A continuation token is similar to the NextMarker property you saw in the Blob and Queue services. It's a pointer to the next object available that wasn't retrieved due to the limit set on the results retrieved either by the application or the Table service itself.

The steps for programming simple table applications with these table classes are as follows:

1. Add the following using statement to your C# class :

```
using Microsoft.WindowsAzure.StorageClient;
```

2. Instantiate the CloudStorageAccount class from configuration file:

```
CloudStorageAccount  storageAccountInfo =
CloudStorageAccount.FromConfigurationSetting(configurationSettingName);
```

Or, instantiate the CloudStorageAccount class using account information:

```
CloudStorageAccount  storageAccountInfo = new CloudStorageAccount(new
StorageCredentialsAccountAndKey(accountName, accountKey), new Uri(blobEndpointURI), new
Uri(queueEndpointURI), new Uri(tableEndpointURI));
```

3.   Create an instance of CloudTableClient:

```
CloudTableClient tableStorageType = storageAccountInfo. CreateCloudTableClient ();
```

4.   When you have an instance of the CloudTableClient class, you can execute
     operations on the table storage service as follows:

```
Create Table
tableStorageType.CreateTable(tableName);
Delete Table
tableStorageType.DeleteTable(tableName);
Get Tables
IEnumerable<string> tables = tableStorageType.ListTables();
```

StorageClient Table Service API

The StorageClient library provides helper classes for using the ADO.NET Data Services and .NET Client
libraries. The StorageClient project consists of six important classes in the context of the Table service.
Table 6-3 lists these classes.

Table 6-3. *StorageClient Classes for the Table Service*

Class Name	Description
StorageAccountInfo	A helper class for retrieving account information from the configuration file.
TableStorage	The entry point to the Table service StorageClient API. It has an AccountName property and table-level methods like CreateTable(), ListTables(), and DeleteTable()
TableStorageTable	A generic table class representing local instance of tables in the Table service.
TableStorageEntity	An abstract class representing an entity(row) in a table. It has the mandatory properties (PartitionKey, RowKey, and Timestamp) defined in it. You may inherit your entity class from this class and provide additional properties.
TableStorageDataServiceContext	Inherits from the System.Data.Services.Client.DataServiceContext class. It adds authentication functionality required by the Table service.
TableStorageDataServiceQuery<TElement>	Can be used to work with continuation tokens in the Table service.

Figure 6-5 illustrates the six classes listed in Table 6-3 and the relationships between them.

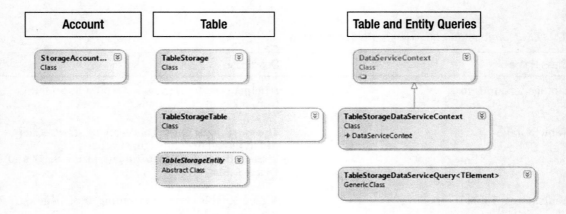

Figure 6-5. *StorageClient classes for the Table service*

The following are some of the typical steps required to interact with the Table service using StorageClient classes:

1. Add your account information in the <appSettings> section of your application configuration file (app.config or web.config):

```
<add key = "AccountName" value="[Your Account Name]"/>
<add key = "AccountSharedKey"
value="[Your Account Shared Key from the Developer Portal]"/>
```

To work with local storage, add "devstoreaccount1" as the AccountName and "Eby8vdM02xNOcqFlqUwJPLlmEtlCDXJ1OUzFT50uSRZ6IFsuFq2UVErCz4I6tq/K1SZFPTOtr /KBHBeksoGMGw==" as the shared key.

2. Add the Table service endpoint URI in the appSettings section of your application configuration file:

```
<add key="TableStorageEndpoint" value="http://table.core.windows.net"/>
```

To work with local storage, add the URI of the local Table service resource, http://127.0.0.1:10002.

3. Define a schema modeling your tables in the table storage. This includes defining an entity class (optionally inherited from TableStorageEntity class) and a DataServiceContext class (optionally inherited from TableStorageDataServiceContext class). For development storage, you must run the DevTableGen.exe tool on these classes to generate SQL Server database tables.

4. Create an instance of the StorageAccountInfo class from the configuration information you entered in the configuration file:

```
StorageAccountInfo account =
StorageAccountInfo.GetDefaultQueueStorageAccountFromConfiguration();
```

5. Create tables in the Table service:

```
TableStorage.CreateTablesFromModel
(typeof(ProAzureReaderDataContext), accountInfo);
```

ProAzureReaderDataContext is a custom class that inherits from the TableStorageDataServiceContext class.

6. Create an instance of the TableStorage class based on the account object:

```
TableStorage tableStorage = TableStorage.Create(account);
```

7. Call the ListTables() method on the tableStorage object to get a list of all the tables in the account:

```
tableStorage.ListTables();
```

In the next few sections, you learn how to call some of these functions at every level of the Table service hierarchy.

Example Table Model

The Table service is quite different from the Blob and Queue services because the tables you create in the Table service are custom and depend on the application's data storage requirements. Unlike Table service, the Queue and Blob services don't require custom schemas to be created. In this section you create a simple application with a one-table custom schema. The purpose of this exercise is to demonstrate a broader overview of the Table service's features.

The application you create is called Pro Azure Reader Tracker. (You can go to the Pro Azure Reader Tracker web site and provide feedback.) The application has only one table, called ProAzureReader. Figure 6-6 illustrates the ProAzureReader class representing the table schema (or the entity).

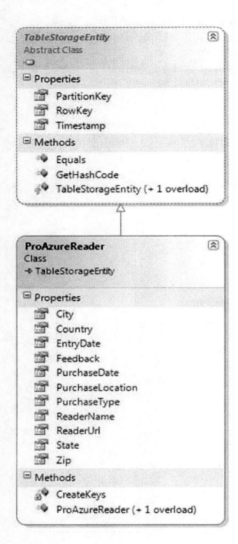

Figure 6-6. *ProAzureReader schema*

As shown in Figure 6-6, the ProAzureReader class inherits from the TableStorageEntity class from the StorageClient library. The TableStorageEntity class defined the mandatory entity properties required by the Table service: PartitionKey, RowKey, and Timestamp. The ProAzureReader class defines the properties required to capture reader information and feedback:

- The Feedback property represents the reader's feedback.

- The EntryDate property represents the data-entry date.

- The PurchaseDate property represents the date the book was purchased by the reader.

- The PurchaseLocation property represents the location where the book was purchased by the reader.

- The PurchaseType property represents whether the purchase was a new or used book.

- The rest of the properties represent user information including name, address, and personal URL.

The ProAzureReader class also creates the PartitionKey and RowKey for the entity record. Figure 6-7 illustrates how the ProAzureReaderDataContext class inherits from the TableStorageDataServiceContext class, which in turn inherits from the System.Data.Services.Client.DataServiceContext class of the ADO.NET Data Services .NET client library.

▓ **Note** You can use the same programming model with the table classes from the Microsoft.WindowsAzure .StorageClient namespace.

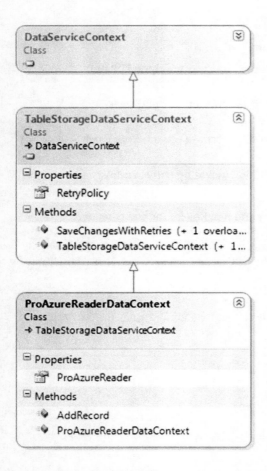

Figure 6-7. ProAzureReaderDataContext class

The DataServiceContext class represents the runtime context of ADO.NET Data Services. The context is a client-side construct and maintains the client-side state of invocations for update management between the client and the service.

Finally, the ProAzureReaderDataSource class is a utility class used to bind the data with client-side controls. See Figure 6-8.

Figure 6-8. *ProAzureReaderDataSource class*

As illustrated in Figure 6-8, the ProAzureReaderDataSource class consists of methods for inserting an entity into the table and retrieving entities from the table.

To design the PartitionKey, first you need to find out the most dominant query in the application. The application lists all the feedback entered by readers on a particular day. When you go the web page, you see all the feedback entries for the day. As a result, the most dominant query in the application can be phrased as, "Get all the entities entered today." If you design the PartitionKey as the same as the entity's EntryDate property, all the entries with the same EntryDate are placed in the same partition by the Table service. This executes the query locally on the partition and yields better query performance.

The query should list the results sorted by time with the most recent entry at the top. To achieve this, the RowKey must be a function of EntryDate. Listing 6-4 shows the code for the ProAzureReader class and the ProAzureReaderDataContext class.

Listing 6-4. ProAzureReader schema classes

ProAzureReader.cs

```
public class ProAzureReader : TableStorageEntity
    {
        public ProAzureReader()
        {
            CreateKeys();
        }
        public DateTime PurchaseDate
        { get; set; }
        public DateTime EntryDate
        { get; set; }
        public string Country
        { get;set;}
        public string State
        { get; set; }
        public string City
        { get; set; }
        public string Zip
        { get; set; }
        public string PurchaseLocation
        { get; set; }
        public string PurchaseType
        { get; set; }
        public string ReaderName
        { get; set; }
        public string ReaderUrl
        { get; set; }
        public string Feedback
        { get; set; }

        private void CreateKeys()
        {
         EntryDate = DateTime.UtcNow;
//By Entry Date: [Query: Get records entered today]
            PartitionKey = EntryDate.ToString("MMddyyyy");

            RowKey = string.Format("{0:10}_{1}",
DateTime.MaxValue.Ticks - EntryDate.Ticks, Guid.NewGuid());

        }
    }
```

ProAzureReaderDataContext.cs

```
public class ProAzureReaderDataContext : TableStorageDataServiceContext
    {
        public ProAzureReaderDataContext(StorageAccountInfo info)
            : base(info)
        { }

        public IQueryable<ProAzureReader> ProAzureReader
        {
            get
            {
                return this.CreateQuery<ProAzureReader>("ProAzureReader");
            }
        }

        public void AddRecord(
            DateTime purchaseDate,
            string country,
            string state,
            string city,
            string zip,
            string purchaseLocation,
            string purchaseType,
            string readerName,
            string readerUrl,
            string feedback)
        {
            ProAzureReader pa = new ProAzureReader(city);
            pa.Country = country;
            pa.Feedback = feedback;
            pa.PurchaseDate = purchaseDate;
            pa.PurchaseLocation = purchaseLocation;
            pa.PurchaseType = purchaseType;
            pa.ReaderName = readerName;
            pa.ReaderUrl = readerUrl;
            pa.State = state;
            pa.Zip = zip;

            this.AddObject("ProAzureReader", pa);
            this.SaveChanges();
        }
    }
```

As shown in Listing 6-4, the CreateKeys() methods in the ProAzureReader class sets the values of the PartitionKey and the RowKey. The CreateKeys method is called by the constructor of the class. The PartitionKey and RowKey are a function of the EntryDate property. The RowKey has a GUID associated with it to take into account multiple entities with the same EntryDate. If the dominant query of the application was "Get all the records from a City," you could design the PartitionKey as a function of the City property.

The ProAzureReaderDataContext class defines an AddRecord method for adding a new entity to the table. The method uses the AddObject() and SaveChanges() methods of the base class to save the entity to the table.

Next, you see how to use this schema model in executing table and entity operations.

■ **Note** The code for these schema objects is in the ProAzureTableStorageClasses project in WindowsAzureStorageSolution.sln.

Account Operations

The storage account provides an entry point to the Table service via the Table service endpoint URI. There are no methods at the Account level in the Table service hierarchy. The URI endpoint of a specific account is of the format http://<*account name*>.table.core.windows.net.

Table Operations

The Table service defines three methods at the table level of the hierarchy: Create Table, Delete Table, and Query Tables. Table 6-4 lists and describes the three operations, and Table 6-5 lists some important characteristics of these methods.

Table 6-4. Table Operations

Operation	Description
Create Table	Creates a new table under the given storage account. The table is actually created as an entity in a master Tables table.
Delete Table	Marks the specified table and its contents for deletion. The garbage collector deletes marked tables on a periodic basis. So, if you delete a table and try to create it immediately, the Table service complains that the table already exists.
Query Tables	Gets a list of tables from the specified storage account.

Table 6-5. Table Operations Characterstics

Operation	HTTP Verb	Cloud URI	Development Storage URI	HTTP Version	Permissions
Create Table	POST	http://<account name>.table.core.win dows.net/Tables	http://127.0.0.1: 10002/<devstorage account>/Tables	HTTP/1.1	Only the account owner can call this operation.
Delete Table	DELETE	http://<account name>.table.core.win dows.net/Tables('<ta ble name>')	http://127.0.0.1: 10002/<devstorage account>/Tables(' <table name>')	HTTP/1.1	Only the account owner can call this operation.
Query Tables	GET	http://<account name>.table.core.win dows.net/Tables()	http://127.0.0.1: 10002/<devstorage account>/Tables	HTTP/1.1	Only the account owner can call this operation.

The *<account name>* is the storage account name in the cloud, and the *<devstorageaccount>* is the development storage account. Observe that unlike with blob containers, the operations can be called only with account owner privileges. The following sections discuss some of the operations from Table 6-5 in detail. Even though the operations are different, the programming concepts behind them are similar. To keep the book at a conceptual level, I discuss the Create Table and Query Tables operations, because they cover most of the discussed concepts. Studying these operations in detail will enable you to understand the programming concepts behind all the table operations. The ProAzureReaderTracker_WebRole web role included with this chapter's source code contains the implementation of the table operations.

Create Table

The Create Table operation creates a table in the storage account. Behind the scenes, the Table service creates an entity with the specified name in the master table Tables.

The URI for the Create Table operation is of the format `http://<account name>.table.core.windows.net/Tables`. Tables give you a structured storage data structure in the cloud. Because of the standard REST interface and Internet scale, you can create tables anywhere, anytime, and in any programming language that supports Internet programming. The Create Table REST request looks like Listing 6-5.

Listing 6-5. Create Table REST Request

```
POST /Tables HTTP/1.1

User-Agent: Microsoft ADO.NET Data Services
```

```
x-ms-date: Sun, 21 Jun 2009 18:42:29 GMT
Authorization: SharedKeyLite proazurestorage:
pwFouPw+BPWzlaQPyccII+K8zb+v6qygxZhp9fCdqRA=
Accept: application/atom+xml,application/xml
Accept-Charset: UTF-8
DataServiceVersion: 1.0;NetFx
MaxDataServiceVersion: 1.0;NetFx
Content-Type: application/atom+xml
Host: proazurestorage.table.core.windows.net
Content-Length: 499
Expect: 100-continue
<?xml version="1.0" encoding="utf-8" standalone="yes"?>
<entry xmlns:d=http://schemas.microsoft.com/ado/2007/08/dataservices
xmlns:m=http://schemas.microsoft.com/ado/2007/08/dataservices/metadata
xmlns="http://www.w3.org/2005/Atom">
  <title />
  <updated>2009-06-21T18:42:29.656Z</updated>
  <author>
    <name />
  </author>
  <id />
  <content type="application/xml">
    <m:properties>
      <d:TableName>MyFirstAzureTable</d:TableName>
    </m:properties>
  </content>
</entry>
```

Listing 6-5 shows the request to create a table named MyFirstAzureTable. The POST HTTP verb instructs the Table service to create a table. The request body consists of an ADO.NET entity set in Atom feed format. For the Create Table operation, the Table service responds with a status code of HTTP/1.1 201 Created or HTTP/1.1 409 Conflict if a table with the same name already exists. The Create Table response is shown in Listing 6-6.

Listing 6-6. *Create Table REST Response*

```
HTTP/1.1 201 Created

Cache-Control: no-cache
Content-Type: application/atom+xml;charset=utf-8
Location: http://proazurestorage.table.core.windows.net/Tables('MyFirstAzureTable')
Server: Table service Version 1.0 Microsoft-HTTPAPI/2.0
x-ms-request-id: 7347b966-9efb-4958-bcf5-d3616563fb28
Date: Sun, 21 Jun 2009 18:44:29 GMT
```

```
Content-Length: 836

<?xml version="1.0" encoding="utf-8" standalone="yes"?>
<entry xml:base=http://proazurestorage.table.core.windows.net/
xmlns:d=http://schemas.microsoft.com/ado/2007/08/dataservices
xmlns:m=http://schemas.microsoft.com/ado/2007/08/dataservices/metadata
xmlns="http://www.w3.org/2005/Atom">
  <id>http://proazurestorage.table.core.windows.net/Tables('MyFirstAzureTable')
</id>
  <title type="text"></title>
  <updated>2009-06-21T18:44:29Z</updated>
  <author>
    <name />
  </author>
  <link rel="edit" title="Tables" href="Tables('MyFirstAzureTable')" />
  <category term="proazurestorage.Tables"
scheme="http://schemas.microsoft.com/ado/2007/08/dataservices/scheme" />
  <content type="application/xml">
    <m:properties>
      <d:TableName>MyFirstAzureTable</d:TableName>
    </m:properties>
  </content>
</entry>
```

In Listing 6-6, the first line represents the status code of the operation. The x-ms-request-id represents a unique request identifier that can be used for debugging or tracing. The response body also contains an ADO.NET entity set in Atom feed format.

Figure 6-9 illustrates the Create Table operation in the ProAzureReaderTracker_WebRole web role.

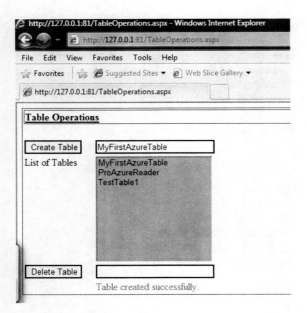

Figure 6-9. *Create Table operation from the ProAzureReaderTracker_WebRole web role*

As shown in Figure 6-9, to create a table, you must do the following:

1. Run the ProAzureReaderTracker_WebRole web role locally or in the cloud.
2. Make sure the appropriate table storage endpoint is specified in the ServiceConfiguration.cscfg file of the ProAzureReaderTracker cloud service.
3. Make TableOperations.aspx the default start page.
4. Run ProAzureReaderTracker cloud service.
5. Enter a table name (such as MyFirstAzureTable) in the text field next to the Create Table button.
6. Click the Create Table button to create the table in the Table service. If the table is created successfully, it appears in the List of Tables list box.

There is one more way to create a table using the schema model you created earlier in this section. To create a table using the schema model, go to TableOperations.aspx and click the Create ProAzureReader Table link button to create the ProAzureReader table from the schema.

To help you understand the programming model of the Create Table operation, open the Visual Studio Solution Chapter4.sln from the Chapter 4 source directory. The WindowsAzureStorageHelper class in the ProAzureCommonLib contains a helper function called CreateTable(), as shown in Listing 6-7.

Listing 6-7. *CreateTable() Method in the WindowsAzureStorageHelper Class*

```
public void CreateTable(string tableName)

{

   TableStorageType.CreateTable(tableName);

}
```

The CreateTable() method calls the CreateTable() method on the TableStorageType object of class TableStorage from the StorageClient library. The project ProAzureTableStorageClasses contains the schema objects for the ProAzureReader table. The project also contains the data source helper class ProAzureReaderDataSource to work with the ProAzureReader table. The ProAzureReaderDataSource class contains a static method CreateTable() specifically to create the ProAzureReader table, as shown in Listing 6-8.

Listing 6-8. *Create ProAzureReader Table*

```
public static void CreateTable(StorageAccountInfo accountInfo)

 {
    TableStorage.CreateTablesFromModel
(typeof(ProAzureReaderDataContext), accountInfo);
 }
```

The CreateTable() method in the ProAzureReaderDataSource class calls the static method CreateTablesFromModel() of the TableStorage class from the StorageClient library. The method accepts the type of DataServiceContext class as the parameter. In the schema model from the Pro Azure Reader Tracker example, the ProAzureReaderDataContext class represents an extension of the DataServiceContext class and can be passed to the CreateTablesFromModel() method. Figure 6-10 illustrates the sequence diagram of the Create Table operation for the ProAzureReader table.

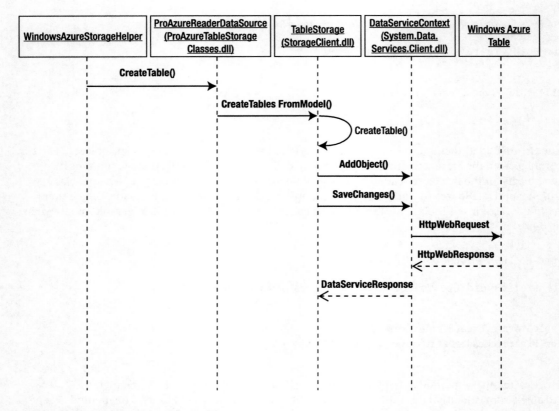

Figure 6-10. *Create Table sequence diagram*

As shown in Figure 6-10, the TableOperations.aspx page calls the static method CreateTable() on the ProAzureReaderDataSource class in the ProAzureTableStorageClasses.dll. The ProAzureReaderDataSource object calls the static method CreateTablesFromModel() on TableStorage. The TableStorage class internally calls the CreateTable() method. The CreateTable() method then calls the AddObject() and SaveObject() methods of the DataServiceContext object. The CreateTablesFromModel() method internally calls the AddObject() and SaveChanges() methods of the System.Data.Services.Client.DataServiceContext class. The AddObject() method adds the object to the local collection of objects DataServiceContext is tracking. The SaveChanges() methods saves the collection of tracked objects to storage.

Query Tables

The Query Tables operation returns a list of all the tables in a storage account. The Table service returns a maximum of 1,000 items in a single query. But similar to the NextMarker element you saw in the Blob and Queue services, the Table service returns a pointer x-ms-continuation-NextTableName. You can send a follow-up request to the Table service to retrieve the remaining items by passing x-ms-continuation-NextTableName as a URI parameter. The Query Tables REST request looks like Listing 6-9.

Listing 6-9. *Query Tables REST Request*

```
GET /Tables()?$top=50 HTTP/1.1

User-Agent: Microsoft ADO.NET Data Services
x-ms-date: Sun, 21 Jun 2009 18:42:10 GMT
Authorization: SharedKeyLite proazurestorage:
hZTV+6FS1lWguxB4vBiDvbubPMALt2kK+kIpVmrYme8=
Accept: application/atom+xml,application/xml
Accept-Charset: UTF-8
DataServiceVersion: 1.0;NetFx
MaxDataServiceVersion: 1.0;NetFx
Host: proazurestorage.table.core.windows.net
Connection: Keep-Alive
```

In Listing 6-9, the HTTP verb used is GET. Note the URI parameter $top=50; this parameter instructs the Table service to return a maximum of 50 items for this call. Listing 6-10 shows the response from the Table service for the Query Tables operation.

Listing 6-10. *Query Tables REST Response*

```
HTTP/1.1 200 OK

Cache-Control: no-cache
Content-Type: application/atom+xml;charset=utf-8
Server: Table Service Version 1.0 Microsoft-HTTPAPI/2.0
x-ms-request-id: d3ca497d-65d2-4fb6-a51e-3babec57e525
Date: Sun, 21 Jun 2009 18:44:09 GMT
Content-Length: 1630

<?xml version="1.0" encoding="utf-8" standalone="yes"?>
<feed xml:base=http://proazurestorage.table.core.windows.net/
xmlns:d="http://schemas.microsoft.com/ado/2007/08/dataservices"
xmlns:m=http://schemas.microsoft.com/ado/2007/08/dataservices/metadata
xmlns="http://www.w3.org/2005/Atom">
  <title type="text">Tables</title>
  <id>http://proazurestorage.table.core.windows.net/Tables</id>
  <updated>2009-06-21T18:44:10Z</updated>
  <link rel="self" title="Tables" href="Tables" />
  <entry>
```

```xml
    <id>
        http://proazurestorage.table.core.windows.net/Tables('ProAzureReader')
    </id>
    <title type="text"></title>
    <updated>2009-06-21T18:44:10Z</updated>
    <author>
      <name />
    </author>
    <link rel="edit" title="Tables" href="Tables('ProAzureReader')" />
    <category term="proazurestorage.Tables"
scheme="http://schemas.microsoft.com/ado/2007/08/dataservices/scheme" />
    <content type="application/xml">
      <m:properties>
        <d:TableName>ProAzureReader</d:TableName>
      </m:properties>
    </content>
  </entry>
  <entry>
    <id>
        http://proazurestorage.table.core.windows.net/Tables('TestTable1')
    </id>
    <title type="text"></title>
    <updated>2009-06-21T18:44:10Z</updated>
    <author>
      <name />
    </author>
    <link rel="edit" title="Tables" href="Tables('TestTable1')" />
    <category term="proazurestorage.Tables"
scheme="http://schemas.microsoft.com/ado/2007/08/dataservices/scheme" />
    <content type="application/xml">
      <m:properties>
        <d:TableName>TestTable1</d:TableName>
      </m:properties>
    </content>
  </entry>
</feed>
```

As shown in Listing 6-10, the Query Tables response contains two tables ProAzureReader and TestTable1. Figure 6-11 illustrates the Query Tables operation in the ProAzureReaderTracker_WebRole web role.

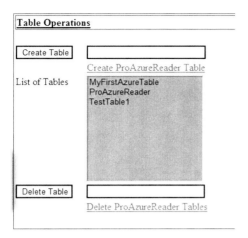

Figure 6-11. *Query Tables operation in the ProAzureReaderTracker_WebRole web role*

As illustrated in Figure 6-11, the TableOperations.aspx loads all the tables from the storage account in the list box.

To help you understand the programming model of the Query Tables operation, open the Visual Studio Solution Chapter4.sln from the Chapter 4 source directory. The WindowsAzureStorageHelper class in ProAzureCommonLib contains a helper method called ListTables(), as shown in Listing 6-11.

Listing 6-11. *ListTables() Method in the WindowsAzureStorageHelper Class*

```
public IEnumerable<string> ListTables()

{

    return TableStorageType.ListTables();

}
```

In Listing 6-11, the ListTables() method calls the ListTables() method on the TableStorageType object from StorageClient library. The TableStorage object utilizes the System.Data.Services.Client.DataServiceQuery object to retrieve a list of tables from the Table service.

Figure 6-12 illustrates the sequence diagram for the Query Tables operation.

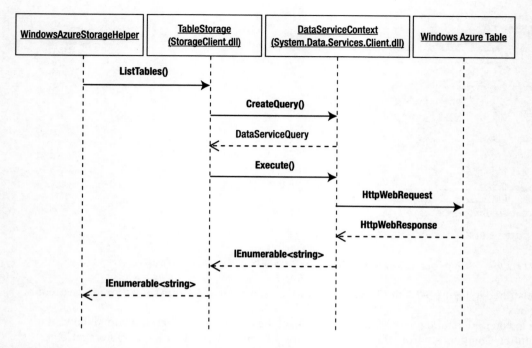

Figure 6-12. List Tables sequence diagram

As illustrated in Figure 6-12, the WindowsAzureStorageHelper object calls the ListTables() method on the TableStorage object from the StorageClient library. The TableStorage object utilizes the DataServiceContext object to create an instance of the DataServiceQuery class. TableStorage then calls the Execute() method on the DataServiceQuery object to retrieve the list of tables from the Table service. The Table service returns a list of all the table names from the storage account.

Entity Operations

Entities support several operations, as listed in Table 6-6.

Table 6-6. *Entity Operations*

Operation	Description
Query Entities	Queries for a list of entities in a table.
Insert Entity	Adds a new entity to the table.
Update Entity	Updates or replaces an entire entity in the table.
Merge Entity	Only updates the properties of an entity in the table. Properties with null values are ignored by this operation.
Delete Entity	Deletes an existing entity from a table

Table 6-7 lists some of the important characteristics of the entity operations listed in Table 6-6.

Table 6-7. *Entity Operations Characterstics*

Operation	HTTP Verb	Cloud URI	Development Storage URI	HTTP Version	Permissions
Query Entities	GET	`http://<account name>.table.core.win dows.net/<table name>()?$filter=<que ry-expression>`	`http://127.0.0.1: 10002/<devstorage account>/<table name>()?$filter=< query-expression>`	HTTP/1.1	Only the account owner can call this operation.
Insert Entity	POST	`http://<account name>.table.core.win dows.net/<table name>`	`http://127.0.0.1: 10002/<devstorage account>/<table name>`	HTTP/1.1	Only the account owner can call this operation.

Continued

Table 6-7. Continued

Operation	HTTP Verb	Cloud URI	Development Storage URI	HTTP Version	Permissions
Update Entity	PUT	`http://<account name>.table.core.w indows.net/<table name>(PartitionKey ="x", RowKey="y")`	`http://127.0.0.1: 10002/<devstorage account>/<table name>(PartitionKe y="x", RowKey="y")`	HTTP/1.1	Only the account owner can call this operation.
Merge Entity	MERGE	`http://<account name>.table.core.w indows.net/<table name>(PartitionKey ="x", RowKey="y")`	`http://127.0.0.1: 10002/<devstorage account>/<table name>(PartitionKe y="x", RowKey="y")`	HTTP/1.1	Only the account owner can call this operation.
Delete Entity	DELETE	`http://<account name>.table.core.w indows.net/<table name>(PartitionKey ="x", RowKey="y")`	`http://127.0.0.1: 10002/<devstorage account>/<table name>(PartitionKe y="x", RowKey="y")`	HTTP/1.1	Only the account owner can call this operation.

The *<account name>* is the storage account name in the cloud, and the *<devstorageaccount>* is the development storage account. The *<table name>* is the name of the table you want to query on. The following sections discuss some of the operations from Table 6-7 in detail. Even though the operations are different, the programming concepts behind them are similar. To keep the book at a conceptual level, I discuss the Query Entities, Insert Entity, and Merge Entity operations, because they cover most of the discussed concepts. By studying these three operations in detail, you can understand the programming concepts behind all the entity operations.

Query Entities

The URI for the Query Entities operation is of the form `http://<account name>.table.core.windows.net/<table name>()?$filter=<query-expression>` or `http://<account name>.table.core.windows.net/<table name>(PartitionKey="x", RowKey="y ")`. Entities are analogous to rows in a relational table. So, you need a flexible mechanism to specify query parameters and filter criteria for the query. The URL parameters for the Query Entities operation support the ADO.NET Data

Services query options as defined in the ADO.NET Data Service Specifications.[4] The $filter and $top URL parameters discussed earlier in this section are the most commonly used criteria for querying entities in a table.

You can use LINQ to query entities in a table. When you enumerate over a LINQ statement, the query is created and sent to the server, and results are retrieved. Listing 6-12 shows an example Query Entities REST request.

Listing 6-12. *Query Entities REST Request*

```
GET /ProAzureReader()?$top=2 HTTP/1.1

User-Agent: Microsoft ADO.NET Data Services
x-ms-date: Mon, 22 Jun 2009 02:35:26 GMT
Authorization: SharedKeyLite
    proazurestorage:K+P5VD/AIhS22b6yuiO4LR1kxx1V4v4/Cy5rc+5nIrO=
Accept: application/atom+xml,application/xml
Accept-Charset: UTF-8
DataServiceVersion: 1.0;NetFx
MaxDataServiceVersion: 1.0;NetFx
Host: proazurestorage.table.core.windows.net
```

Listing 6-12 shows the request for querying the ProAzureReader table with a $top=2 criteria to retrieve top two items. The Query Entities operation can return only 1,000 items in a single call. If the number of items that fit the filter criteria is greater than 1,000 or the query times out, the Table services sends two continuation tokens:- x-ms-continuation-NextPartitionKey and x-ms-continuation-NextRowKey in the response. Similar to the NextMarker token you saw in the Blob and Queue services, these tokens point to the first item in the next data set. Listing 6-13 shows the REST response from the Table service for the Query Entities operation.

Listing 6-13. *Query Entities REST Response*

```
HTTP/1.1 200 OK

Cache-Control: no-cache
Content-Type: application/atom+xml;charset=utf-8
Server: Table Service Version 1.0 Microsoft-HTTPAPI/2.0
x-ms-request-id: ab64434d-9a8d-4090-8397-d8a9dad5da8a
x-ms-continuation-NextPartitionKey: 1!12!MDYyMDIwMDk-
```

---

[4] ADO.NET Data Services Query Options: http://msdn.microsoft.com/en-us/library/cc668809.aspx

```
x-ms-continuation-NextRowKey: 1!76!MTI1MjE1NjgwMjgzNzA1MTk5OTlfM
Date: Mon, 22 Jun 2009 02:38:19 GMT
Content-Length: 3592

<?xml version="1.0" encoding="utf-8" standalone="yes"?>
<feed xml:base=http://proazurestorage.table.core.windows.net/
xmlns:d="http://schemas.microsoft.com/ado/2007/08/dataservices"
xmlns:m="http://schemas.microsoft.com/ado/2007/08/dataservices/metadata"xmlns="http://www.w3
.org/2005/Atom">
  <title type="text">ProAzureReader</title>
  <id>http://proazurestorage.table.core.windows.net/ProAzureReader</id>
  <updated>2009-06-22T02:38:19Z</updated>
  <link rel="self" title="ProAzureReader" href="ProAzureReader" />
  <entry m:etag="W/&quot;datetime'2009-06-20T23%3A30%3A15.251Z'&quot;">
    <id>http://proazurestorage.table.core.windows.net/
ProAzureReader(PartitionKey='06202009',RowKey='12521567602930729999')
</id>
    <title type="text"></title>
    <updated>2009-06-22T02:38:19Z</updated>
    <author>
      <name />
    </author>
    <link rel="edit" title="ProAzureReader"
href="ProAzureReader(PartitionKey='06202009',RowKey='12521567602930729999')" />
    <category term="proazurestorage.ProAzureReader"
scheme="http://schemas.microsoft.com/ado/2007/08/dataservices/scheme" />
    <content type="application/xml">
      <m:properties>
        <d:PartitionKey>06202009</d:PartitionKey>
        <d:RowKey>
         12521567602930729999
        </d:RowKey>
        <d:Timestamp m:type="Edm.DateTime">2009-06-20T23:30:15.251Z</d:Timestamp>
        <d:City></d:City>
        <d:Country></d:Country>
        <d:EntryDate m:type="Edm.DateTime">2009-06-20T23:28:26.927Z</d:EntryDate>
        <d:Feedback>Good Book :). But don't write again.</d:Feedback>
        <d:PurchaseDate m:type="Edm.DateTime">2009-06-20T00:00:00Z</d:PurchaseDate>
        <d:PurchaseLocation></d:PurchaseLocation>
        <d:PurchaseType>New</d:PurchaseType>
        <d:ReaderName></d:ReaderName>
        <d:ReaderUrl></d:ReaderUrl>
        <d:State></d:State>
        <d:Zip></d:Zip>
```

```
        </m:properties>
      </content>
  </entry>
  <entry m:etag="W/&quot;datetime'2009-06-20T13%3A01%3A10.5846Z'&quot;">
    <id>http://proazurestorage.table.core.windows.net/
ProAzureReader(PartitionKey='06202009',RowKey='12521567980278019999')
</id>
    <title type="text"></title>
    <updated>2009-06-22T02:38:19Z</updated>
    <author>
      <name />
    </author>
    <link rel="edit" title="ProAzureReader"
href="ProAzureReader(PartitionKey='06202009',RowKey='12521567980278019999')" />
    <category term="proazurestorage.ProAzureReader"
scheme="http://schemas.microsoft.com/ado/2007/08/dataservices/scheme" />
    <content type="application/xml">
      <m:properties>
        <d:PartitionKey>06202009</d:PartitionKey>
        <d:RowKey>12521567980278019999</d:RowKey>
        <d:Timestamp m:type="Edm.DateTime">2009-06-20T13:01:10.5846Z</d:Timestamp>
        <d:City>mumbai</d:City>
        <d:Country>india</d:Country>
        <d:EntryDate m:type="Edm.DateTime">2009-06-20T12:59:32.198Z</d:EntryDate>
        <d:Feedback>Good Book :). But don't write again.</d:Feedback>
        <d:PurchaseDate m:type="Edm.DateTime">2009-06-20T00:00:00Z</d:PurchaseDate>
        <d:PurchaseLocation>web</d:PurchaseLocation>
        <d:PurchaseType>New</d:PurchaseType>
        <d:ReaderName>tredkar</d:ReaderName>
        <d:ReaderUrl></d:ReaderUrl>
        <d:State>maharashtra</d:State>
        <d:Zip>400028</d:Zip>
      </m:properties>
    </content>
  </entry>
</feed>
```

In Listing 6-13, the first line represents the status code of the operation. The response body consists of ADO.NET entity set in Atom feed format. The body shows two items retrieved. The x-ms-continuation-NextPartitionKey and x-ms-continuation-NextRowKey indicate pointers to the first item from the next data set. To retrieve the remaining items, you can pass the two tokens as the NextPartitionKey and NextRowKey URL parameters of a subsequent call. The x-ms-continuation-NextPartitionKey and x-ms-continuation-NextRowKey are used to page on Query Entity results.

In the Pro Azure Reader Tracker application, you can implement the following queries:

- Get all the entries entered today (the dominant query).

- Get entries by city, state, or country.

- Get the Top(*n*) entries.

- Get entries by purchase date.

Listing 6-14 shows the implementation of each of these queries using LINQ. The methods are implemented in the ProAzureReaderDataSource class.

Listing 6-14. *Query Entities in the ProazureReaderDataSource Class*

```
// Get all the entries entered today (The dominant query)

public IEnumerable<ProAzureReader> Select()
 {
var results = from g in dContext.ProAzureReader
where g.PartitionKey == DateTime.UtcNow.ToString("MMddyyyy")
select g;
var r = results.ToArray<ProAzureReader>();
return r;
 }
//Get entries by City
public IEnumerable<ProAzureReader> SelectByCity(string city)
{
var results = from g in dContext.ProAzureReader
where g.PartitionKey == DateTime.UtcNow.ToString("MMddyyyy")
&& g.City == city
select g;
var r = results.ToArray<ProAzureReader>();
return r;
}
//Get entries by State
public IEnumerable<ProAzureReader> SelectByState(string state)
{
var results = from g in dContext.ProAzureReader
where g.PartitionKey == DateTime.UtcNow.ToString("MMddyyyy")
&& g.State == state
select g;
var r = results.ToArray<ProAzureReader>();
return r;
}
//Get entries by Country
public IEnumerable<ProAzureReader> SelectByCountry(string country)
```

```
{
var results = from g in dContext.ProAzureReader
where g.PartitionKey == DateTime.UtcNow.ToString("MMddyyyy")
&& g.Country == country
select g;
var r = results.ToArray<ProAzureReader>();
return r;
}

//Get entries by Purchase Date
public IEnumerable<ProAzureReader> SelectByPurchaseDate(DateTime purchaseDate)
{
var results = from g in dContext.ProAzureReader
where g.PurchaseDate.Equals(purchaseDate )
select g;
var r = results.ToArray<ProAzureReader>();
return r;
}
//Get Top(n) entries
public IEnumerable<ProAzureReader> SelectTopN(int topNumber)
{
var results = dContext.ProAzureReader.Take(topNumber);
var r = results.ToArray<ProAzureReader>();
return r;
}
```

In Listing 6-14, each method implements a LINQ query for Query Entities on the ProAzureReader table. On the Default.aspx page of the ProAzureReaderTracker_WebRole web role is a link button for each of the queries; see Figure 6-13.

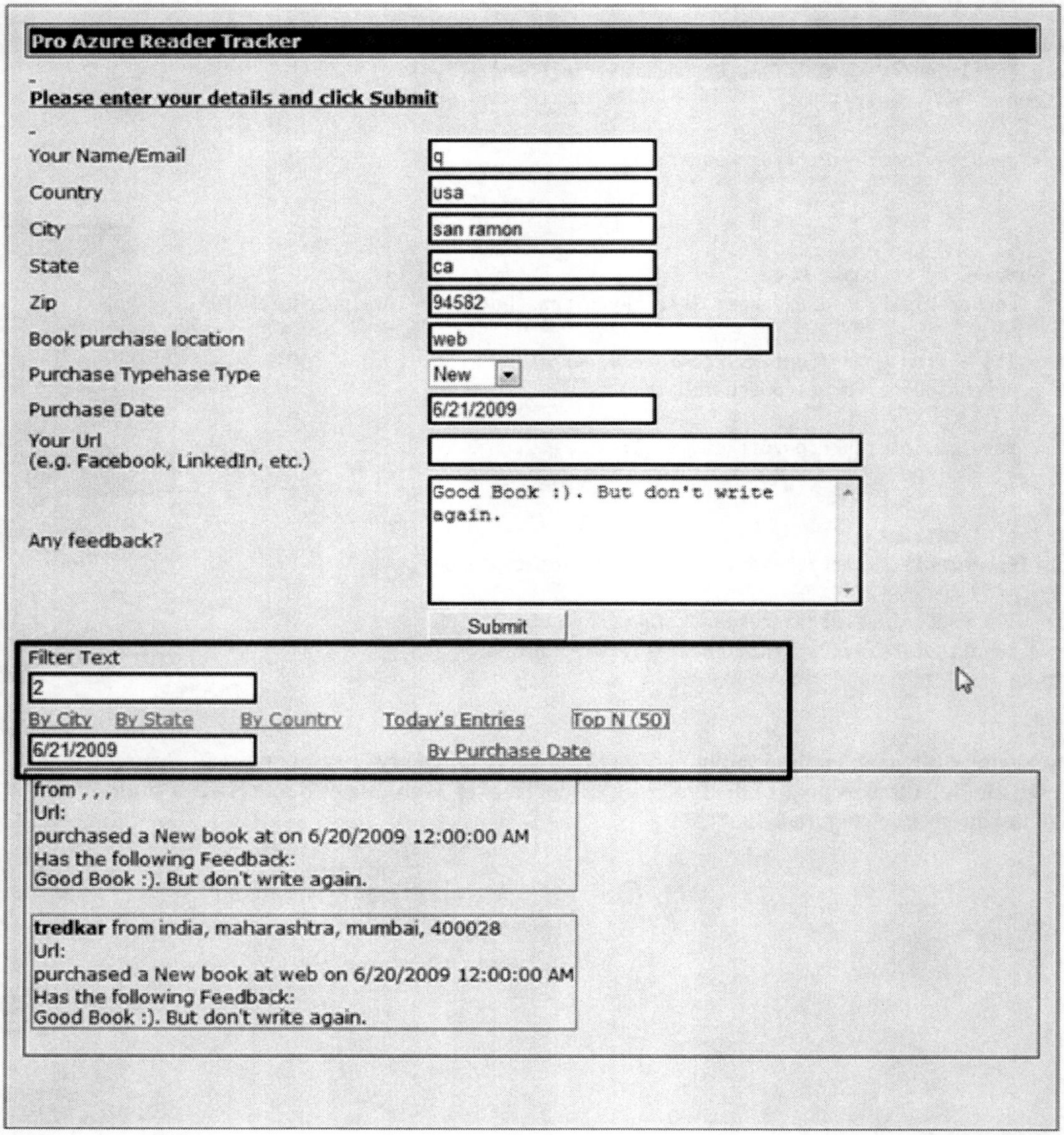

Figure 6-13. *Query entities in the ProAzureReaderTracker_WebRole web role*

As shown in Figure 6-13, you can specify filter criteria in the filter text box and click one of the link buttons to execute the query.

▦ **Tip** If you're running the web application on the local machine, you can run the Fiddler trace tool and capture the request and response contents of each query.

Insert Entity

The Insert Entity operation inserts an entity into the specified table. This operation requires the PartitionKey and RowKey to be specified. The URI for the insert Entity operation is of the format `http://<account name>.table.core.windows.net/<table name>`. A typical Insert Entity REST request looks like Listing 6-15.

Listing 6-15. *Insert Entity REST Request*

```
POST /ProAzureReader HTTP/1.1

User-Agent: Microsoft ADO.NET Data Services
x-ms-date: Mon, 22 Jun 2009 03:25:47 GMT
Authorization: SharedKeyLite proazurestorage:
    mazZ5pykdE1CmH5+SDe7fqWDLQpnWDcK1pgWDvyzxss=
Accept: application/atom+xml,application/xml
Accept-Charset: UTF-8
DataServiceVersion: 1.0;NetFx
MaxDataServiceVersion: 1.0;NetFx
Content-Type: application/atom+xml
Host: proazurestorage.table.core.windows.net
Content-Length: 1178
Expect: 100-continue

<?xml version="1.0" encoding="utf-8" standalone="yes"?>
<entry xmlns:d=http://schemas.microsoft.com/ado/2007/08/dataservices
xmlns:m=http://schemas.microsoft.com/ado/2007/08/dataservices/metadata
xmlns="http://www.w3.org/2005/Atom">
  <title />
  <updated>2009-06-22T03:25:47.469Z</updated>
  <author>
    <name />
  </author>
  <id />
  <content type="application/xml">
    <m:properties>
      <d:City>san ramon</d:City>
      <d:Country>usa</d:Country>
```

```
            <d:EntryDate m:type="Edm.DateTime">2009-06-22T03:25:46.976Z</d:EntryDate>
            <d:Feedback>Excellent Book</d:Feedback>
            <d:PartitionKey>06222009</d:PartitionKey>
            <d:PurchaseDate m:type="Edm.DateTime">2009-06-21T00:00:00</d:PurchaseDate>
            <d:PurchaseLocation>amazon.com</d:PurchaseLocation>
            <d:PurchaseType>New</d:PurchaseType>
            <d:ReaderName>tejaswi</d:ReaderName>
            <d:ReaderUrl m:null="false" />
            <d:RowKey>12521566596530239999_7e9f46ea</d:RowKey>
            <d:State>ca</d:State>
            <d:Timestamp m:type="Edm.DateTime">0001-01-01T00:00:00</d:Timestamp>
            <d:Zip>94582</d:Zip>
        </m:properties>
    </content>
```

In Listing 6-15, the HTTP verb used is POST, to instruct the Table service that this is an insert operation. The request body contains an ADO.NET entity set. The m:properties element defines the property names and values of the entity. In reality, it represents a serialized ProAzureReader object discussed earlier in this chapter. The m:type attribute specifies the data type of the property. The default property is Edm.String if the property is omitted. After the entity is created successfully, the response header consists of an HTTP 1.1 201 (Created) status code. The response body also contains the same ADO.NET entity set that was part of the request body.

The Submit button on the Default.aspx page in the ProAzureReaderTracker_WebRole project is tied to an Insert Entity operation because it inserts a new entity into the ProAzureReader table. Figure 6-14 shows the Default.aspx page.

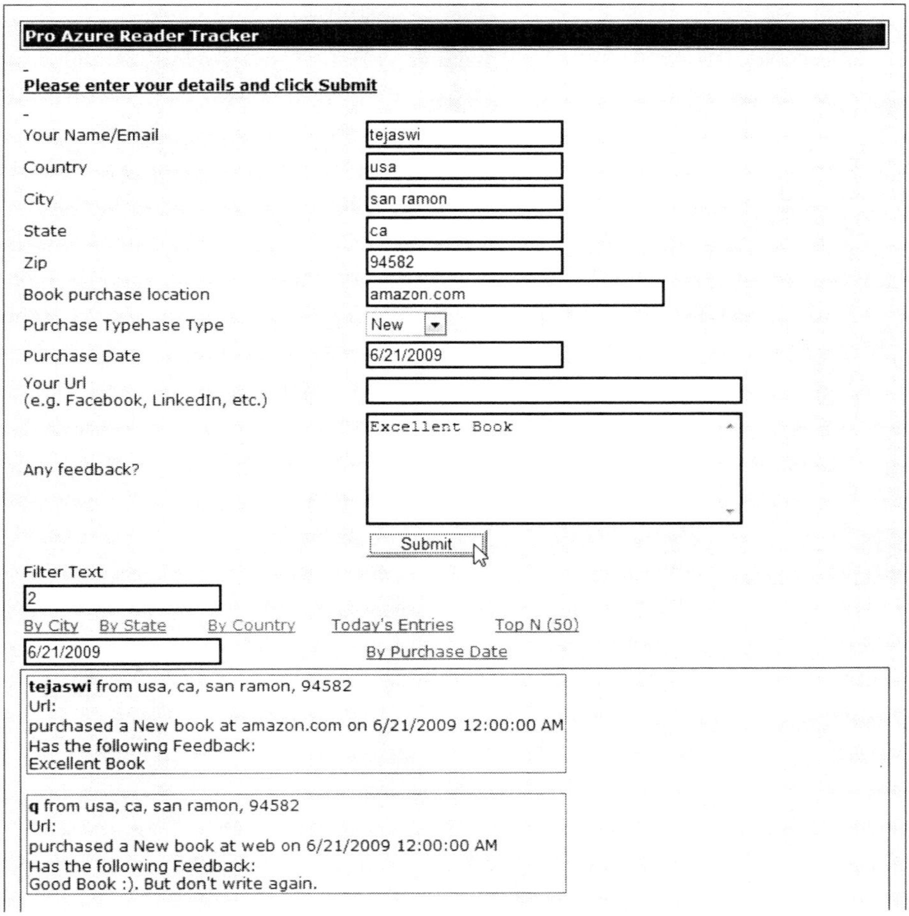

Pro Azure Reader Tracker

Please enter your details and click Submit

Your Name/Email	tejaswi
Country	usa
City	san ramon
State	ca
Zip	94582
Book purchase location	amazon.com
Purchase Typehase Type	New ▾
Purchase Date	6/21/2009
Your Url (e.g. Facebook, LinkedIn, etc.)	
Any feedback?	Excellent Book

Submit

Filter Text

2

By City   By State   By Country   Today's Entries   Top N (50)

6/21/2009   By Purchase Date

tejaswi from usa, ca, san ramon, 94582
Url:
purchased a New book at amazon.com on 6/21/2009 12:00:00 AM
Has the following Feedback:
Excellent Book

q from usa, ca, san ramon, 94582
Url:
purchased a New book at web on 6/21/2009 12:00:00 AM
Has the following Feedback:
Good Book :). But don't write again.

Figure 6-14. Default.aspx in the ProAzureReaderTracker_WebRole web role

In Figure 6-14, when you enter all the reader properties and click Submit, a new entity is created and the data list is refreshed, showing the new entity at the top. Listing 6-16 shows the code for the btnSubmit_Click event from the Default.aspx.cs file. Listing 6-16 also shows the AddProAzureReader() method from the ProAzureReaderDataSource class, which is called by the btnSubmit_Click method to insert a new entity.

Listing 6-16. Insert Entity

```
//Default.aspx
protected void btnSubmit_Click(object sender, EventArgs e)
```

```
{
 try
 {
  ProAzureReader newReader = new ProAzureReader()
  {
   City = txtCity.Text,
   Country = txtCountry.Text,
   Feedback = txtFeedback.Text,
   PurchaseDate = DateTime.Parse(txtPurchaseDate.Text),
   PurchaseType = ddlPurchaseType.SelectedItem.Text,
   PurchaseLocation = txtPurchaseLocation.Text,
   ReaderName = txtName.Text,
   ReaderUrl = txtUrl.Text,
   State = txtState.Text,
   Zip = txtZip.Text


  };
  ProAzureReaderDataSource ds = new ProAzureReaderDataSource();
  ds.AddProAzureReader(newReader);
 }
 catch (Exception ex)
 {

  lblStatus.Text = "Error adding entry " + ex.Message;
 }
}

//ProAzureDataSource.cs
public void AddProAzureReader(ProAzureReader newItem)
 {
        dContext.AddObject(ENTITY_SET_NAME, newItem);
        dContext.SaveChangesWithRetries(SaveChangesOptions.None);
 }
```

As shown in Listing 6-16, the AddProAzureReader() method calls the AddObject() and SaveChangesWithRetries() methods on the ProAzureReaderDataContext object. SaveChangesOptions is an ADO.NET Data Services enumeration with four possible values:

- *None* specifies that the operation is non-batch and should stop if any error occurs.

- *Batch* specifies that multiple changes are packaged into one change set and sent to the server in a single call.

- *ContinueOnError* specifies that subsequent operations are attempted even if an error occurs in one of the operations.

- *ReplaceOnUpdate* replaces all the properties of an entity on the server with the new ones specified.

Figure 6-15 illustrates the sequence diagram for the Insert Entity operation.

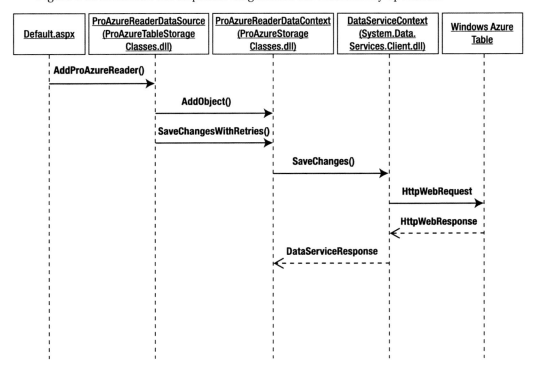

Figure 6-15. *Insert Entity sequence diagram*

As shown in Figure 6-15, the Default.aspx page calls the AddProAzureReader() method on the ProAzureReaderDataSource object. Default.aspx gathers the user input, creates a new ProAzureReader object, and passes it as a parameter to the AddProAzureReader() method. The AddProAzureReader() method calls the AddObject() and SaveChangesWithRetries() methods on the ProAzureReaderDataSourceContext object, which in turn calls the SaveChanges() method on its parent class (DataServiceContext) object. The SaveChanges() method sends the HTTP request and receives the response from the Table service.

> **Note** The Table service supports ACID transactions for batch operations on multiple entities on a single partition (with the same PartitionKey).[5] The constraints are as follows: same PartitionKey, one transaction per entity in the batch, no more than 100 transactions in the batch, and the total batch payload size should be less than 4MB.

Merge Entity

The Merge Entity operation updates the properties of an entity without replacing an entity from the specified table. It requires the PartitionKey and RowKey to be specified. The URI for the Merge Entity operation is of the format `http://<account name>.table.core.windows.net/<table name>(PartitionKey="x", RowKey="y")`. A typical Merge Entity REST request looks like Listing 6-17.

Listing 6-17. Merge Entity REST Request

```
MERGE /ProAzureReader(PartitionKey='06222009',RowKey='12521566596530999') HTTP/1.1

User-Agent: Microsoft ADO.NET Data Services
x-ms-date: Mon, 22 Jun 2009 07:02:04 GMT
Authorization: SharedKeyLite proazurestorage:motXsCh9vzZZpNLbJ8xsNgmO95
Accept: application/atom+xml,application/xml
Accept-Charset: UTF-8
DataServiceVersion: 1.0;NetFx
MaxDataServiceVersion: 1.0;NetFx
Content-Type: application/atom+xml
If-Match: W/"datetime'2009-06-22T07%3A01%3A13.043Z'"
Host: proazurestorage.table.core.windows.net
Content-Length: 1355
Expect: 100-continue

<?xml version="1.0" encoding="utf-8" standalone="yes"?>
<entry xmlns:d=http://schemas.microsoft.com/ado/2007/08/dataservices
xmlns:m=http://schemas.microsoft.com/ado/2007/08/dataservices/metadata
xmlns="http://www.w3.org/2005/Atom">
  <title />
  <updated>2009-06-22T07:02:04.948Z</updated>
```

---

[5] Performing Entity Group Transactions: http://msdn.microsoft.com/en-us/library/dd894038.aspx

```
<author>
  <name />
</author>
<id>http://proazurestorage.table.core.windows.net/ProAzureReader
(PartitionKey='06222009',RowKey='12521566596530239999')
</id>
<content type="application/xml">
  <m:properties>
    <d:City>san ramon</d:City>
    <d:Country>usa</d:Country>
    <d:EntryDate m:type="Edm.DateTime">2009-06-22T03:25:46.976Z</d:EntryDate>
    <d:Feedback>Excellent Book</d:Feedback>
    <d:PartitionKey>06222009</d:PartitionKey>
    <d:PurchaseDate m:type="Edm.DateTime">2009-06-21T00:00:00Z</d:PurchaseDate>
    <d:PurchaseLocation>amazon.com</d:PurchaseLocation>
    <d:PurchaseType>New</d:PurchaseType>
    <d:ReaderName>tejaswi</d:ReaderName>
    <d:ReaderUrl>http://www.bing.com</d:ReaderUrl>
    <d:RowKey>12521566596530239999_7e9f46ea-4230-4abb-bbd1</d:RowKey>
    <d:State>ca</d:State>
    <d:Timestamp m:type="Edm.DateTime">2009-06-22T07:01:13.043Z</d:Timestamp>
    <d:Zip>94582</d:Zip>
  </m:properties>
</content>
</entry>
```

In Listing 6-17, the HTTP verb specified is MERGE, to instruct the Table service that this is a Merge operation. The request body contains an ADO.NET entity set. The m:properties element define the property names and values of the entity. In the example, it represents a serialized ProAzureReader object as discussed earlier in this chapter. The If-Match header is a required condition the server checks before performing a conditional update. The ETag value of the entity is checked before making the update. For an unconditional update, its value should be a wildcard (*). A successful entity update returns an HTTP 1.1 204 (No Content) status code.

The data list in the Default.aspx page in the ProAzureReaderTracker_WebRole project has an UpdateUrl button that update the ReaderUrl property of an entity. Figure 6-16 shows the Default.aspx page.

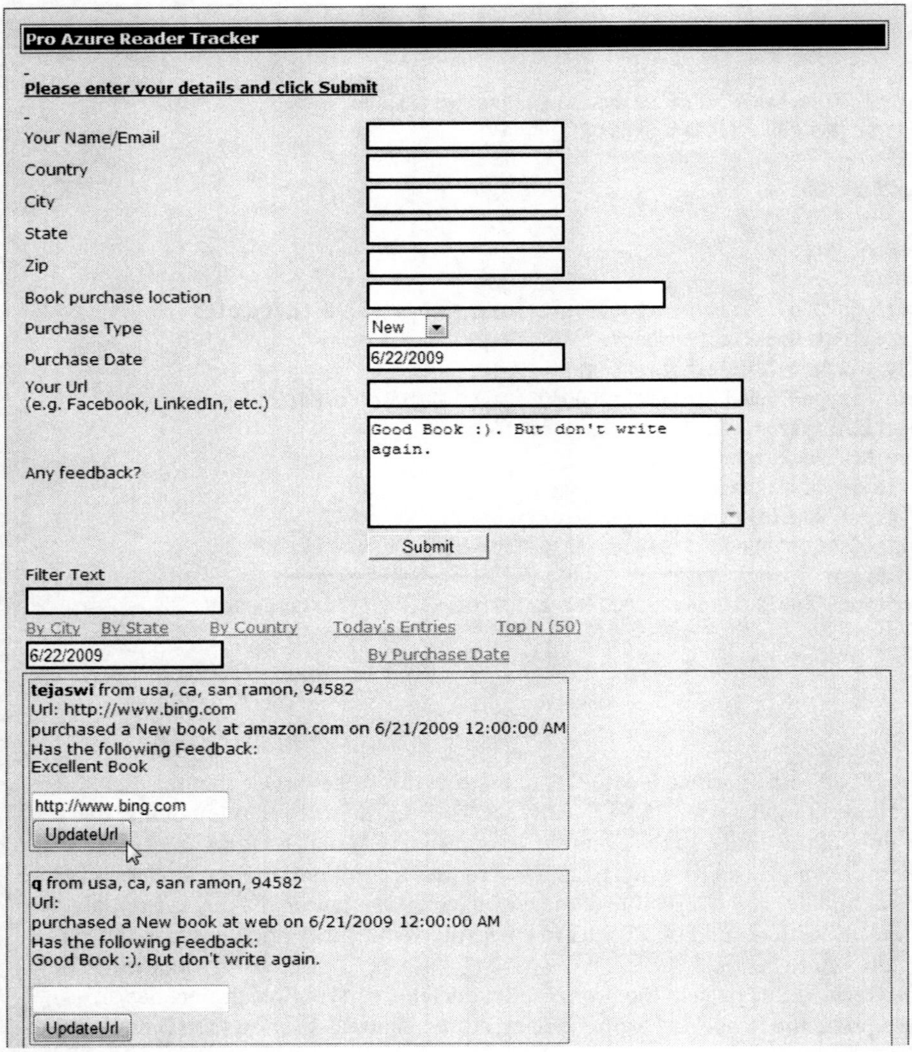

Pro Azure Reader Tracker

-
Please enter your details and click Submit
-

Your Name/Email
Country
City
State
Zip
Book purchase location
Purchase Type   New
Purchase Date   6/22/2009
Your Url
(e.g. Facebook, LinkedIn, etc.)

Good Book :). But don't write
again.

Any feedback?

Submit

Filter Text

By City   By State   By Country   Today's Entries   Top N (50)
6/22/2009   By Purchase Date

tejaswi from usa, ca, san ramon, 94582
Url: http://www.bing.com
purchased a New book at amazon.com on 6/21/2009 12:00:00 AM
Has the following Feedback:
Excellent Book

http://www.bing.com
UpdateUrl

q from usa, ca, san ramon, 94582
Url:
purchased a New book at web on 6/21/2009 12:00:00 AM
Has the following Feedback:
Good Book :). But don't write again.

UpdateUrl

Figure 6-16. *Default.aspx in the ProAzureReaderTracker_WebRole web role for the Merge Entity operation*

In Figure 6-16, you can update the ReaderUrl property of the ProAzureReader entity. The code for Merge Entity is in the UpdateUrl() method in the ProAzureReaderDataSource class, as shown in Listing 6-18.

Listing 6-18. *UpdateUrl() Method*

```
public void UpdateUrl(string PartitionKey, string RowKey, string url)
    {
      var results = from g in dContext.ProAzureReader
                    where g.PartitionKey == PartitionKey
                    && g.RowKey == RowKey
                    select g;
      var e = results.FirstOrDefault<ProAzureReader>();
      e.ReaderUrl = url;
      dContext.MergeOption = MergeOption.PreserveChanges;
      dContext.UpdateObject(e);
      dContext.SaveChanges();
    }
```

As shown in Listing 6-18, the UpdateUrl() method retrieves the appropriate entity using a LINQ query. Then, it sets the merge option to PreserveChanges and calls the UpdateObject() and SaveChanges() methods of the DataServiceContext object. The merge option instructs the DataServiceContext object to track entities in a specific manner locally. The possible options are as follows.

- *AppendOnly* instructs the DataServiceContext object to append entities to already-existing entities in the local cache. The existing entities in the cache aren't modified. This is the default option.

- *NoTracking* instructs the DataServiceContext object that entities aren't tracked locally. As a result, objects are always loaded from the server. The local values are overwritten with the server values.

- *OverwriteChanges* instructs the DataServiceContext object that server values take precedence over client values even if they have changed.

- *PreserveChanges* instructs the DataServiceContext object to preserve the local changes even if changes are detected on the server. The DataServiceContext object doesn't overwrite the property values but updates the ETag value with the server ETag value. Any properties not changed locally are updated with latest values from the server. In this option, the local changes to the properties aren't lost.

Figure 6-17 illustrates the sequence diagram for the Merge Entity operation.

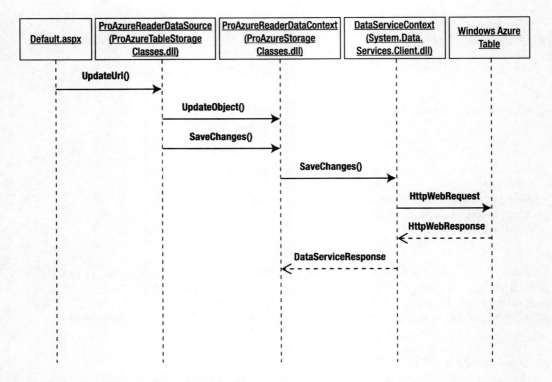

Figure 6-17. *Merge Entity sequence diagram*

As shown in Figure 6-17, the Default.aspx page calls the UpdateUrl() method on the ProAzureReaderDataSource object. The UpdateUrl() method calls the UpdateObject() and SaveChanges() methods on the ProAzureReaderDataSourceContext object.

Table Service Summary

In this chapter, you learned the details of interacting with the Windows Azure Table Storage service. The Table service provides with structured storage that you can use from anywhere, anytime. If you've already worked with REST, the ADO.NET Data Services Framework, or the ADO.NET Entity Framework, you should find the Table service concepts easy to understand and program with. The knowledge you've acquired from learning Table service REST API, ADO.NET Data Services Client library, Windows Azure SDK StorageClient, and Storage Client code sample library should enable you to build your own Table service applications.

Windows Azure Storage Summary

This concludes a series of three intense chapters covering the wide range of features and functionality offered by the Blob, Queue, and Table services. You learned in detail about the three types of storage services offered by Windows Azure. The demonstrations and API discussions in these chapters should enable you to use the concepts in your own storage applications. You also are better prepared to choose the right combination of storage services for your solution.

The next few chapters cover the Middleware layer of the Windows Azure Platform (a.k.a. .AppFabric as it relates to the Cloud Services Pyramid discussed in Chapter 1.

Bibliography

MSDN. (n.d.). *ADO.NET Data Services Specification.* Retrieved from MSDN Developer's Network: `http://msdn.microsoft.com/en-us/library/cc668808.aspx`.

MSDN. (2009, May). *Windows Azure Blob — Programming Blob Storage.* Retrieved from MSDN: `http://go.microsoft.com/fwlink/?LinkId=153400`.

MSDN. (2009, May). *Windows Azure Queue — Programming Queue Storage.* Retrieved from MSDN: `http://go.microsoft.com/fwlink/?LinkId=153402`.

MSDN. (2009, May). *Windows Azure SDK.* Retrieved from MSDN: `http://msdn.microsoft.com/en-us/library/dd179367.aspx`.

MSDN. (2009, May). *Windows Azure Table — Programming Table Storage.* Retrieved from MSDN: `http://go.microsoft.com/fwlink/?LinkId=153401`.

CHAPTER 7

■■■

AppFabric: Access Control Service

What is your digital identity? I personally have at least 15 different identities, and it's tedious as well as insecure to maintain usernames and passwords for every application. You can categorize such identities as critical, important, and less important based on the impact they may have not only on your digital life but also on your real life if you lose them. The critical ones are enterprise identities you may have with your company or partner companies (such as an Active Directory account) and financial identities with financial service providers like the firm that manages your 401K or IRA, online banks, and so on. The important ones are personal e-mail identities like Hotmail, Yahoo Mail, and Gmail. The less-important identities belong to social-networking and other web portal sites and can be reestablished without any effect if necessary.

Where do these identities come from, and how are they maintained? You create an identity when you register with an identity provider. For example, when you join a company, the IT department creates an identity for you in their Active Directory. The identity is maintained in the Active Directory until you leave the company, and sometimes even after you leave. Similarly, when you register for a 401K plan, the plan provider creates a new identity for you that is maintained in the plan provider application. When you create a Hotmail or a Windows Live account, you get a LiveID to share across multiple Microsoft portals and applications online. Even in the same enterprise, most applications maintain their own identity provider within the application domain. This results in identity silos across organizations that are difficult to maintain. When a person leaves a company, the IT department has to not only delete their identity across all the applications, but also maintain these deletion records for compliance reasons. Partner companies also have to delete the user's identity from their extranet identity system.

As an application developer, often you have to design identity providers within applications; and if these applications are extranet or Internet facing, then the complexity of authentication and authorization increases significantly. As a developer, you end up spending more effort on authentication and authorization design instead of the application's business logic. Ideally, you're given a standard interface for identity management that is consistent across all applications. The identity-management architecture needs to be abstracted from the application architecture to focus your time on business logic and reduce the costs involved in maintaining the identity-management infrastructure across multiple applications and identity providers.

Microsoft .NET Access Control Service (ACS) is a cloud service that abstracts the orchestration of authentication and authorization for your application. ACS follows a claims-based architecture where users acquire their claims from ACS based on their identity and present the claims to the application. The application is configured to trust ACS and thus gives appropriate entry to users. In simple terms, ACS is a claims-transformation service in the cloud that relieves you of building a role-based authorization system within your application.

A *claim* is any user or application attribute a service application expects. For example, you may have an application that expects e-mail address, phone number, password, and role attributes for an end user as claims for appropriate access control. You can configure your ACS project to provide these user claims to your application independent of the user's authentication, identity, or provider. Figure 7-1 illustrates a simple view of ACS.

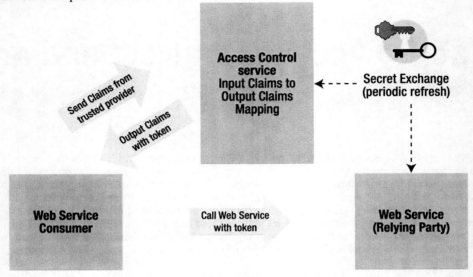

Figure 7-1. *A simple view of the Access Control Service*

The pattern illustrated in Figure 7-1 is called a *claims-based identity model* because the claims tie together the relying party, ACS, the identity provider, and the end user. The primary function of ACS is to transform input claims into output claims. First, you configure ACS and the identity provider to trust each other. Then, you configure ACS and your service (a.k.a. relying party) to trust each other with a signing key. Next, you configure ACS with rules for mapping input claims to output claims that your application expects. In the real world, these tasks are done by system and/or security administrators.

When an application wants to consume the web service, it sends the required claims to ACS in a request for a token. ACS transforms input claims into output claims based on the mapping rules you created while configuring ACS. Next, ACS issues a token with output claims to the consumer application. The consumer application sends the token in the request header to the web service. The web service validates the claims in the token and provides appropriate access to the end user.

■ **Note** Active Directory doesn't support a claims-based identity model. You need Active Directory Federation Services 2.0 (a.k.a. Geneva Server) to provide claims-based identity support to Active Directory.

The important information to learn from this example is the fact that ACS abstracts multiple token providers from the relying party (web service) by always issuing the same type of token. The relying party has to only consider the output claims in its authorization logic to provide appropriate access to the end user. As a result, you as a developer only have to program your application or service against a set of output claims independent of input claims from multiple identity providers. You can reuse these output claims across multiple applications within the enterprise, cross enterprise, and even over the Internet. The relying party can be a web application or a web service. I cover each step discussed in Figure 7-1 in more detail later in the chapter.

Concepts and Terminology

Before diving deep into a technical discussion, you should understand some key concepts and terminology that are extremely important for understanding the design and architecture of ACS. This section introduces some new terms and redefines some existing terms in the ACS context.

Identity Provider

An identity provider manages your identity and provides an authentication service for client applications. Identity providers authenticate users and issue Security Assertions Markup Language (SAML) tokens (defined in a moment). SAML tokens contain user IDs and other identity properties of the user (claims). Examples of some identity providers are Windows Live ID, Geneva Server, Google Accounts, Yahoo ID, and Sun.

Relying Party

The relying party is the application that relies on the claims issued by ACS to authorize a user and release appropriate access to the user. As a developer, you're primarily concerned with developing a relying party application that receives a SAML token filled with claims from ACS. You then process these claims in the relying party to provide appropriate access to the end user.

Security Token (SAML token)[1]

A SAML token is an XML message consisting of sets of claims digitally signed by the issuing authority. The token is issued by a Secure Token Service (STS). The ACS and relying party both process claims from SAML tokens.

Secure Token Service (STS)

An STS is a subsystem responsible for building, signing, validating, cancelling, renewing, and issuing SAML tokens. An STS may support one or more of these features. It typically implements the protocol defined in the WS-Trust specification. Identity providers and ACS both have STS capabilities.

---

[1] You can find the SAML token profile at the WS-I web site: www.ws-i.org/deliverables/workinggroup.aspx?wg=samltoken.

An R-STS is a resource STS that acts as an intermediate claims-transformation service to transform input claims from a partner STS to output claims specific to your application. This model is popular in extranet and cross-enterprise applications. ACS is an R-STS because it transforms input claims from identity providers to output claims. You can build your own STS and R-STS using Microsoft's Geneva Framework.

Request for Security Token (RST)

Every relying party requires a unique set of claims it can process. RST is the request made to an STS to acquire these claims to an STS. For example, a requestor may make this request to ACS to acquire claims for a relying party.

Request Security Token Response (RSTR)

The response sent by an STS to the RST is called an RSTR. This request contains the SAML token with claims signed by the STS.

Claim

A claim consists of information about the user or role interested in accessing an application (or relying party). A claim can have any information about the user depending on the configuration of the identity provider and ACS. A typical ACS scenario involves three kinds of claims:

- User claims: When a user sends a request for a security token to ACS, the request contains claims like the username, password, domain name, and so on, which are usually required for authentication.

- Input claims: When the user is authenticated with the identity provider, the identity provider issues a SAML token. The SAML token usually contains input claims to the ACS. These input claims may contain user claims as well as additional claims introduced by the identity provider in the SAML token.

- Output claims: ACS examines the input claims from the SAML token issued by the identity provider and maps them to output claims. ACS translates input claims into application- (or relying party–) specific output claims and includes them in the token that the relying party can use to authorize users and give appropriate access. For example, an input claim "Username: tejaswi_redkar" may map to an output claim "Role: Domain User." The relying party reads the Role as Domain User and provides Domain User privileges to the user. Input claims are mapped to output claims as a part of ACS configuration exercise covered later in this chapter.

Identity Federation

Identity federation is a set of mechanisms, standards, and patterns that define different ways of sharing identity information between domains. It reduces identity-maintenance costs and also simplifies software development because you don't have to design and maintain a separate identity store within the application. Federated identities also ease single sign-on between applications running in different domains and/or enterprises.

Windows Identity Foundation (Geneva Framework)

The Windows Identity Foundation is a Microsoft product used to create claims-based applications and services. You can build your own STS using the Windows Identity Framework if existing products don't fulfill your application requirements. The Windows Identity Framework simplifies the development of cross-domain security scenarios. It provides a framework for building passive (web browser-based) as well as active (Windows Communications Foundation) clients that support identity federation across a wide variety of clients and servers. ACS uses the Geneva Framework to provide STS capabilities. Geneva Server, Microsoft's next-generation claims-based identity federation server, is also built using the Geneva Framework.

Active Directory Federation Server (ADFS 2.0) (Geneva Server)

Geneva Server is a Microsoft product that provides STS functionality to Active Directory or any identity provider. It's the next version of Active Directory Federation Services (ADFS) and supports a claims-based identity model. It enables the creation of single sign-on between on-premises and cloud applications using the claims-based identity model. By definition, Geneva Server implements the protocol defined in the WS-Trust specification and so provides interoperability with other products like Sun OpenSSO and Novell Access Manager. Geneva Server supports not only passive clients like web browsers but also active stand-alone clients built using the Windows Communications Foundation (WCF).

Web Resource Authorization Protocol (WRAP) and Simple Web Token (SWT)

ACS implements the REST-friendly Web Resource Authorization Protocol (WRAP) that defines the Simple Web Token standard. The token issued by ACS adheres to the SWT specification, which you can find in the WRAP profiles on the OAuth web site at `http://groups.google.com/group/oauth-wrap-wg`. SWT tokens are HTTP form encoded key-value pairs signed with an HMAC-SHA256 cryptographic key. ACS always emits an SWT for different types of input tokens (such as SAML), so the relying party can always expect an SWT from ACS.

Claims-Based Identity Model

This section goes over the details of the claims-based identity model in ACS. Specifically, I expand on the discussion from Figure 7-1. Figure 7-2 illustrates the interaction between different components in a claims-based identity model. With the terminology defined, it will be much easier for you to understand the flow of information between different parties in this model.

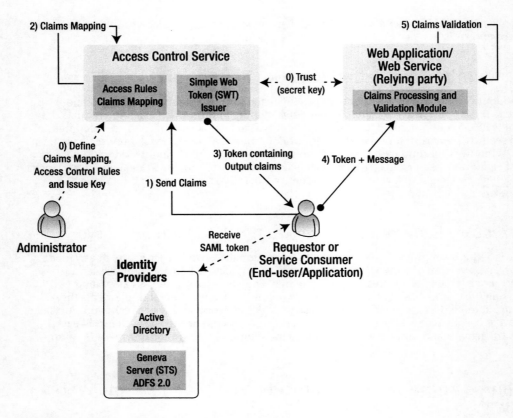

Figure 7-2. ACS claims-based identity message flow

As illustrated in Figure 7-2, several messages and tokens are passed back and forth between the key parties in a claims-based identity model. Before the interaction starts, prerequisites (listed as step 0) are required in order to make the end-to-end scenario work. The following steps describe the flow of information from the requesting user or application to the relying party:

> *Step 0:* Two important prerequisites for claims-based identity to work are completed in this step. First, trust is established between the relying party (web service), ACS, and identity providers. The trust relationships are refreshed on a periodic basis. The trust between ACS and the relying party is established using a signing key. Second, an administrator creates an issuer to identify service consumers and defines the mapping rules between input claims and output claims in the form of rules in ACS. The issuer key material is distributed to the service consumer.

Step 1: When ACS, the relying party, and identity providers are configured for the claims-based identity model to work seamlessly, the service consumer must use the issuer key material to acquire a token from ACS in order to call the web service. In the current version (November 2009 CTP), the ACS supports three types of token requests:

- *Plain text:* The service consumer sends an issuer key directly to ACS to authenticate the request.

- *Signed:* The service consumer creates an SWT, signs the token, and sends the token to ACS for authentication. In this method, unlike with the plain text request, the service consumer doesn't need to send an issuer key directly to ACS. Typically, the signed token from the consumer includes input claims that are then mapped to output claims by ACS and included in the output token emitted by ACS.

- *SAML:* The service consumer acquires a signed SAML token from ADFS 2.0 or a similar identity provider that emits SAML tokens, and sends it to ACS for authentication. Intended primarily for ADFS 2.0 integration, this approach requires that a signed SAML bearer token be acquired and sent to ACS for authentication.

Step 2: Based on the claims-mapping rules configured in ACS, ACS maps the input claims received in the service consumer token to output claims specific to the web service. The ACS then issues an SWT [2] consisting of output claims to the service consumer. ACS signs the token using the key registered in Step 0. The mapping of input claims to output claims makes ACS an R-STS. ACS abstracts the token-issuing party from the token-consuming party by always emitting an SWT containing output claims the web service expects.

Step 3: Regardless of the method used to acquire the input token, ACS creates a SWT and sends it to the service consumer. This SWT contains output claims that the web service expects.

Step 4: The service consumer packages the SWT into an HTTP header and sends it to the web service along with the message payload.

Step 5: The web service validates the token based on the secret key exchange established in Step 0. The web service also validates the required claims and grants or denies access to the resource based on the validation outcome. There is no direct communication between the web service and ACS during the method invocation. The only communication happens during the periodic refresh of the secret key exchange.

---

[2] Simple Web Token specification: `http://groups.google.com/group/oauth-wrap-wg`

Figure 7-2 may look complex initially, but when you go through the steps, the claims-based identity is easy to understand. The next section puts the claims-based identity model into an enterprise scenario perspective.

Access Control Service Usage Scenarios

Now that you understand the claims-based identity and ACS concepts, some real-world scenarios provide more clarity about these concepts. This section presents three real-world scenarios. Scenario 1 shows how an enterprise cloud application can benefit from ACS. Scenario 2 illustrates the use of ACS in a cross-enterprise scenario, and finally scenario 3 shows an ISV cloud service using ACS across multiple enterprise customers.

Scenario 1: Enterprise Cloud Application

For this scenario, consider a news organization named T-Press Inc., similar to the Associated Press or Reuters. T-Press has a large workforce of journalists and technicians based around the world, investigating, planning, and creating news events. Usually, journalists and technicians can be either employees or contractors, but for the purpose of this scenario, assume that the journalists are employees and the technicians are contractors. Currently, T-Press has a newsroom-management web application called T-Room. T-Room is a globally deployed application and can be used by all journalists and technicians in the field. The T-Room web application is deployed in the cloud and federated with T-Press's Active Directory using Geneva Server. The availability of T-Room in the cloud makes it accessible from anywhere in the world with Internet access. Journalists can view all the T-Press news items, but technicians can view only the news items they're assigned to. The current pain point from an identity-management perspective is as follows.

Technicians are typically hired for a short period of time covering the lifetime of a single new event. After the contract expires, the technician rolls off and may or may not join the workforce for another news event. Currently, whenever a technician is hired, an account is created in T-Press's Active Directory. Due to the short contract periods, identity management has become expensive, and T-Press has decided not to create Active Directory accounts for technicians. Instead, T-Press wants to support any technician's existing digital ID (such as a Windows Live ID or Yahoo ID) to access T-Room. T-Press needs help designing an access control system that can not only support any digital ID but also give immediate access to the T-Room application from anywhere in the world. I recommend that T-Press design a claims-based identity model for T-Room and use ACS to abstract a technician's identity provider from T-Room. The design is illustrated in Figure 7-3.

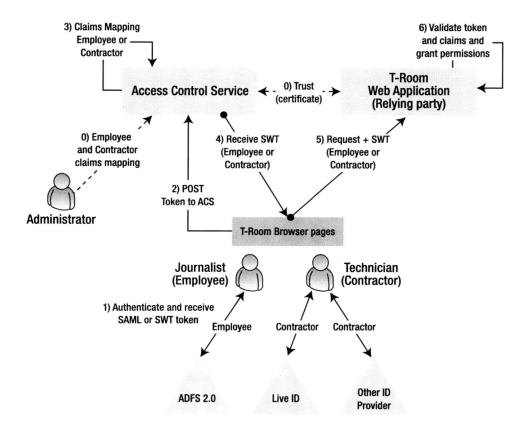

Figure 7-3. Enterprise cloud application scenario

The following steps describe the flow of information from the browser to the T-Room web application:

> *Step 0:* The T-Room system administrator completes all the prerequisites to make ACS work for the T-Room application. In Figure 7-3, the important steps are establishing trust between the T-Room web application and ACS using a shared key, which is refreshed on a periodic basis; configuring ACS with the supported identity providers (such as ADFS 2.0, Windows LiveID, and Yahoo ID); and defining the mapping between input claims and output claims in the form of rules for employees and contractors. This is where the administrator can define different claims for employees and contractors. The ACS can be configured to process employee authentication with Geneva Server, whereas contractors can be authenticated using external identity providers.

Step 1: When a requestor (employees or contractor) signs into the T-Room web application, the requestor acquires the appropriate authentication token (SAML, SWT, and so on) from the appropriate identity provider. For example, an employee acquires a SAML token from the ADFS 2.0, whereas a contractor may acquire a SAML or SWT from the contractor's identity provider (such as Windows LiveID).

Step 2: The requestor posts the acquired token to ACS for claims mapping.

Step 3: ACS is an important piece of the identity federation orchestration because the SAML or SWT token is sent to ACS to transform input claims to output claims.

Step 4: ACS returns an SWT token to the requestor.

Step 5: The requestor packages the SWT token along with the payload and sends it to the relying party or the T-Room web application.

Step 6: The T-Room application processes these claims in a claims-processing module and determines the level of access the requestor is entitled to. The claims-processing module doesn't depend on any identity provider but only refers to the claims in SWT.

In Figure 7-3, the introduction of ADFS 2.0 and ACS into T-Press's existing application infrastructure simplifies the identity management of a cloud application like T-Room that supports users from outside of the organization. The T-Press system administrators don't have to manage the identities of technicians in T-Press systems—technicians use their existing identities to access the T-Press application. Administrators can configure input to output claims mappings in ACS as per the business requirements. The T-Press developers only have to focus on building a claims-processing module for ACS-forwarded claims; they don't have to write separate modules for each identity provider as before. Thus, for T-Press, ACS successfully abstracts claims from multiple identity providers into a single coherent view of output claims for the T-Room web application.

Scenario 2: Cross-Enterprise Application

In this scenario, two partner enterprises would like to collaborate on each other's collaboration platforms. Enterprise A is a software company that manufactures operating system software. Enterprise A has partner companies (OEMs) that customize these operating systems, install those systems on their hardware, brand the integrated platform, and sell the product to consumers through their sales channels. The end product may be a personal computer, a laptop, or even a cell phone. For this example, Enterprise B is an OEM of Enterprise A. To launch a particular product in time, Enterprise B needs early access to some of the software releases and documentation associated with those releases. Enterprise A, on the other hand, needs information about sales of the end product to use for sales and revenue tracking of its own product.

Enterprise A has a dedicated web application named PartnerAccess in its extranet for OEM partners. The PartnerAccess web application supports role-based authorization for different roles in multiple partner enterprises. Some example partner roles are Partner_Manager, Partner_Employee, and Partner_Contractor.

Enterprise B has a list of users configured in Enterprise A's Active Directory who have access to the early release operating system software through the web application in Enterprise A's extranet. Enterprise B users log in to this application using their Enterprise A credentials. Enterprise A's administrators find it difficult to track and maintain users of Enterprise B and other partners because the administrators have to delete or modify partner users when they quit their company or are promoted to another position. The total number of partner users numbers hundreds of thousands across multiple OEM partners. Maintaining these partner user identities has become expensive for Enterprise A, and the company is looking forward to reducing its identity-management costs for the PartnerAccess web application.

On the other side of the equation, Enterprise B has a similar problem maintaining Enterprise A identities for thousands of Enterprise A employees and contractors in its SalesAccess software. The SalesAccess software provides sales information to Enterprise A. Enterprise A users log in to the SalesAccess software using their Enterprise B credentials, to acquire real-time sales information from Enterprise B. Other partner companies also have similar applications providing sales data access capabilities.

As an architect, I recommend that Enterprise A design a claims-based identity model for its PartnerAccess web application and use ACS to abstract the partner's identity provider from PartnerAccess. The partner enterprise (such as Enterprise B) owns the responsibility of authenticating its users. The recommended design is illustrated in Figure 7-4.

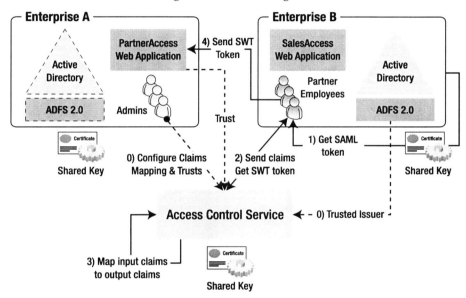

Figure 7-4. *Cross-enterprise scenario*

The following steps describe the flow of information for the PartnerAccess web application:

Step 0: The PartnerAccess web application completes all the prerequisites required to make ACS work for the application. In Figure 7-4, the important steps are establishing trust between PartnerAccess and ACS using a shared key, which is refreshed on a periodic basis; having the PartnerAccess administrator and Enterprise B administrator configure ACS to trust Enterprise B's Geneva-federated identity provider to generate STS for Enterprise B users; and having PartnerAccess define the mapping between input claims from Enterprise B's Geneva Server–generated SAML tokens and output claims in the form of rules specific to the PartnerAccess application. This is where the administrator can define different claims for different roles for Enterprise B employees.

Step 1: When an Enterprise B employee wants to sign in to the PartnerAccess web application, the employee is authenticated with Enterprise B's Active Directory, and the ADFS 2.0 generates a SAML token for ACS. Because Enterprise B is in control of its employee identities, and Enterprise A trusts Enterprise B's authentication process, it makes sense to delegate the authentication of Enterprise B's employees to Enterprise B.

Step 2: The SAML token generated by Enterprise B's ADFS 2.0 is sent to ACS. The SAML token consists of input claims to ACS.

Step 3: ACS maps the input claims from the SAML token to output claims specific to the PartnerAccess web application and packages them into an SWT token.

Step 4: The SWT token with output claims is sent to the PartnerAccess web application for processing. The PartnerAccess application processes these claims in a claims-processing module and determines the level of access the Enterprise B employee is entitled to. The PartnerAccess web application doesn't need to authenticate Enterprise B users in the Enterprise A environment because it trusts SWT tokens generated by ACS.

The introduction of ACS into Enterprise A's environment and federating Enterprise B identities using Geneva simplifies the management of the partner accounts. Enterprise A can reuse this configuration for all the partners accessing the PartnerAccess web application, whereas Enterprise B can reuse Geneva Server to federate identities across multiple partner companies. Note that the PartnerAccess web application isn't dependent on the identity providers of partner companies. As long as a trust is established between ACS and the partner identity provider, the PartnerAccess application does the necessary claims processing for any partner.

For the SalesAccess web application, Enterprise B can implement the same pattern by introducing ACS in the architecture and letting Enterprise A employees authenticate and generate SAML tokens using Enterprise A's own ADFS 2.0. With the same pattern implemented in Enterprise B's architecture, Enterprise A and Enterprise B can access each other's applications seamlessly by removing the identity-management burden from the partner company. The identity management remains with the company that owns the identities.

Scenario 3: ISV Cloud Service

In this scenario, an independent software vendor (ISV) named My Energy has an energy-management cloud service that it offers to multiple utility companies. The service performs data collection from power meters on houses and commercial buildings and offers this data to utility companies for reporting and processing. Currently, the ISV service has its own identity-management database and for every utility company. Due to resource constraints, maintaining identities of all the utility partner companies has turned into an expensive process. Every time an employee of a utility company quits, My Energy has to remove the employ from the database. My Energy wants to reduce its identity-management costs because it's turning out to be a significant portion of the company's support operating expenses. Assuming that utility companies have an identity federation infrastructure, I recommend that My Energy implement a claims-based identity model using ACS as the claims-transformation engine. My Energy can use ACS to map claims issued by a utility company's identity federation server (such as ADFS 2.0) to claims required by the My Energy service.

The recommended design is illustrated in Figure 7-5.

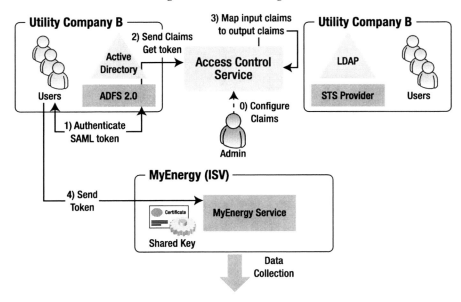

Figure 7-5. *ISV cloud service scenario*

The following steps describe the flow of information for the My Energy web application:

Step 0: In this step, similar to previous scenarios, the My Energy administrator establishes trust relationships between My Energy, ACS, and the identity providers of utility companies. Then, the My Energy administrator configures ACS by mapping input claims from the identity providers to output claims specific to the My Energy application.

Step 1: When a utility company employee wants to sign in to the My Energy service, the employee authenticates with the utility company's identity federation server and receives a SAML token.

Step 2: The SAML token is sent to ACS. Because ACS is configured to trust the company's identity federation server, ACS can accept input claims from the issuer. The SAML token consists of input claims to ACS.

Step 3: ACS maps the input claims from the SAML token to output claims specific to the My Energy service and packages them into a secondary SWT.

Step 4: The SWT with output claims is sent to the My Energy service for processing. The My Energy service processes these claims and determines the level of access the utility company's employee is entitled to.

Using ACS, the My Energy service can support multiple utility companies without managing their identities in its own identity store. The identity costs involved mainly involve claims mapping and establishing trust between identity providers and ACS; but these are one-time efforts per utility company. After trust is established and claims are configured, the claims-based identity process will work seamlessly for My Energy. The My Energy service no longer maintains a separate identity-management store, because users are authenticated against the utility company's identity store. My Energy is configured only to process output claims coming from ACS.

The three scenarios discussed identify the following ACS advantages:

- ACS federates between wide varieties of identity providers because of its standards-based interface.

- ACS abstracts identity management from your application or service.

- ACS abstracts out authorization management from your application or service.

- ACS can help achieve single sign-on across diverse systems because of its standards-based API.

- ACS works with web browsers and web applications (passive participants) as well as smart clients and web services (active participants).

- ACS provides an STS for issuing SWT tokens containing output claims. Every mapping scope can be considered to have its own virtual STS.

Retrieving Tokens from ACS

You can retrieve an SWT token from ACS three ways: using plain text, by sending an SWT, or by sending a SAML token. ACS supports only SSL transmission of the tokens over HTTP POST. ACS always issues an SWT output token that consists of output claims the relying party expects. Figure 7-6 illustrates these token-retrieving methods.

Figure 7-6. *Retrieving tokens from ACS*

In the plain text method, the issuer key is directly sent to ACS. In the SWT method, the client application creates an SWT token to authenticate with ACS and sends the token to ACS. In the SAML token method, a client acquires the SAML token from a SAML token provider like ADFS v2.0 or a custom STS and sends it to ACS for requesting an output SWT token.

Access Control Service Management Portal

The ACS Management Portal provides limited functionality for creating and managing service namespaces and AC resources for service namespaces. A service namespace defines the namespace for your AC resources. Because of the limited functionality available in the portal as of the PDC 2009 release, you can only use the portal to create service namespaces, view management keys, and view URIs for your service namespace. You can also perform all these tasks programmatically through the Management service API. Figure 7-7 shows the Management Portal interface for an already-created account.

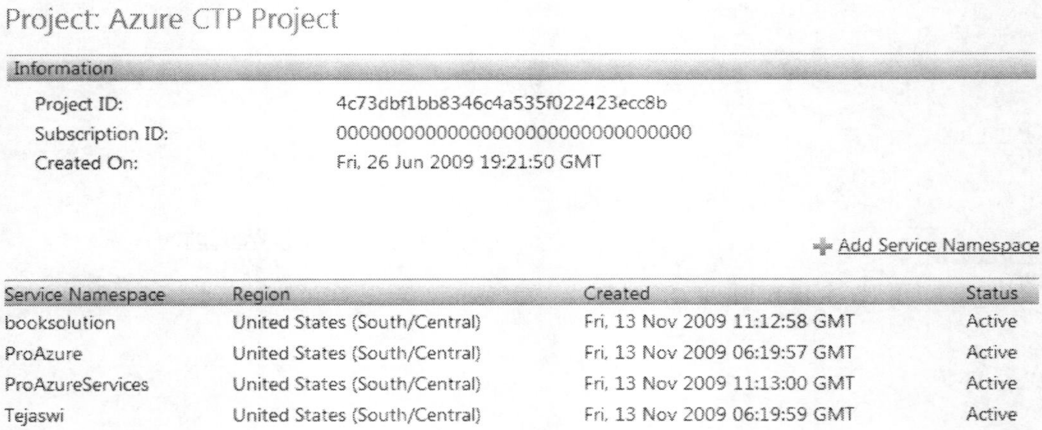

Project: Azure CTP Project

Information	
Project ID:	4c73dbf1bb8346c4a535f022423ecc8b
Subscription ID:	00000000000000000000000000000000
Created On:	Fri, 26 Jun 2009 19:21:50 GMT

✚ Add Service Namespace

Service Namespace	Region	Created	Status
booksolution	United States (South/Central)	Fri, 13 Nov 2009 11:12:58 GMT	Active
ProAzure	United States (South/Central)	Fri, 13 Nov 2009 06:19:57 GMT	Active
ProAzureServices	United States (South/Central)	Fri, 13 Nov 2009 11:13:00 GMT	Active
Tejaswi	United States (South/Central)	Fri, 13 Nov 2009 06:19:59 GMT	Active

Figure 7-7. *Management Portal*

In Figure 7-7, the home page for my AppFabric account lists the project information and the service namespaces that already exists in my account. You can create a new service namespace by clicking the Add Service Namespace link. Figure 7-8 shows the Create New Service Namespace screen.

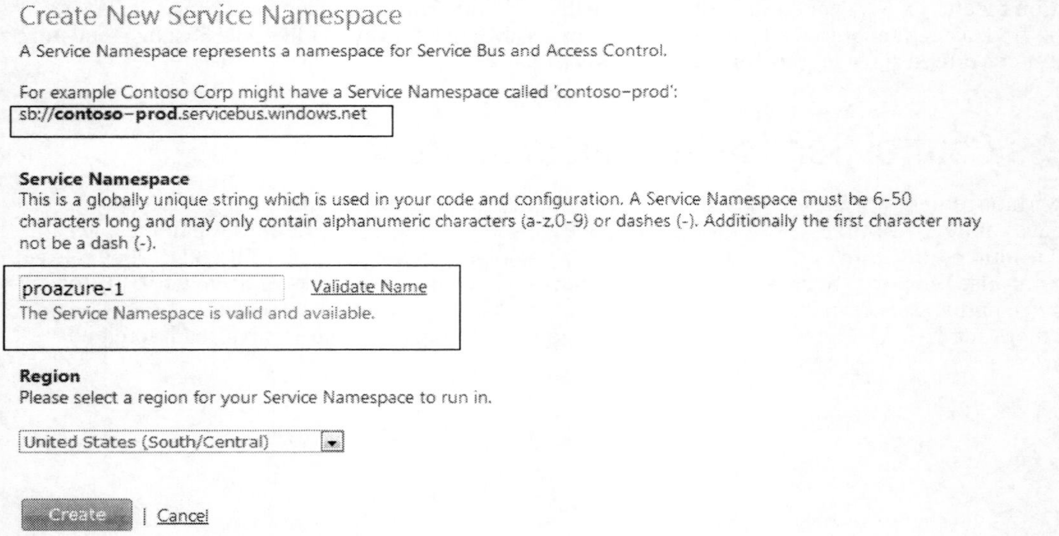

Create New Service Namespace

A Service Namespace represents a namespace for Service Bus and Access Control.

For example Contoso Corp might have a Service Namespace called 'contoso-prod':

sb://**contoso-prod**.servicebus.windows.net

Service Namespace
This is a globally unique string which is used in your code and configuration. A Service Namespace must be 6-50 characters long and may only contain alphanumeric characters (a-z,0-9) or dashes (-). Additionally the first character may not be a dash (-).

proazure-1   Validate Name
The Service Namespace is valid and available.

Region
Please select a region for your Service Namespace to run in.

United States (South/Central) ▼

Create | Cancel

Figure 7-8. *Create a new namespace*

You must select a unique name for your service namespace and the region in which you want the service namespace to run. If you're building a Windows Azure distributed application, you can choose a common location for the Windows Azure services, SQL Azure database, and AppFabric service namespace so that all the Windows Azure components run in close proximity to each other and yield better performance. Figure 7-9 shows an example service namespace screen.

Service Namespace: ProAzure

Manage

Status:	Active
Delete:	Delete Service Namespace
Management Key Name:	owner
Current Management Key:	xHr5CBf/6WJf.02HCETa/A.6YTpps4DIg4gNwcN+X2==
Previous Management Key:	xHr5CBf/6WJf.02HCETa/A.fHTpps4DIg4gNwcN+X23=
	Generate New Key

Service Bus

Registry URL:	https://proazure.servicebus.windows.net/
STS Endpoint:	https://proazure-sb.accesscontrol.windows.net/WRAPv0.8
Management Endpoint:	https://proazure-sb.accesscontrol.windows.net/mgmt/
Management STS Endpoint:	https://proazure-sb-mgmt.accesscontrol.windows.net/WRAPv0.8
Default Issuer Name:	owner
Default Issuer Key:	xHr5CBf/6WJf.02HCETa/A.fHTpps4DIg4gNwcN+X2==

Access Control Service

STS Endpoint:	https://proazure.accesscontrol.windows.net/WRAPv0.8
Management Endpoint:	https://proazure.accesscontrol.windows.net/mgmt/
Management STS Endpoint:	https://proazure-mgmt.accesscontrol.windows.net/WRAPv0.8

Information

Project ID:	4c73dbf1bb8346c4a535f022423ecc8b
Created On:	Fri, 13 Nov 2009 06:19:57 GMT
Region:	United States (South/Central)

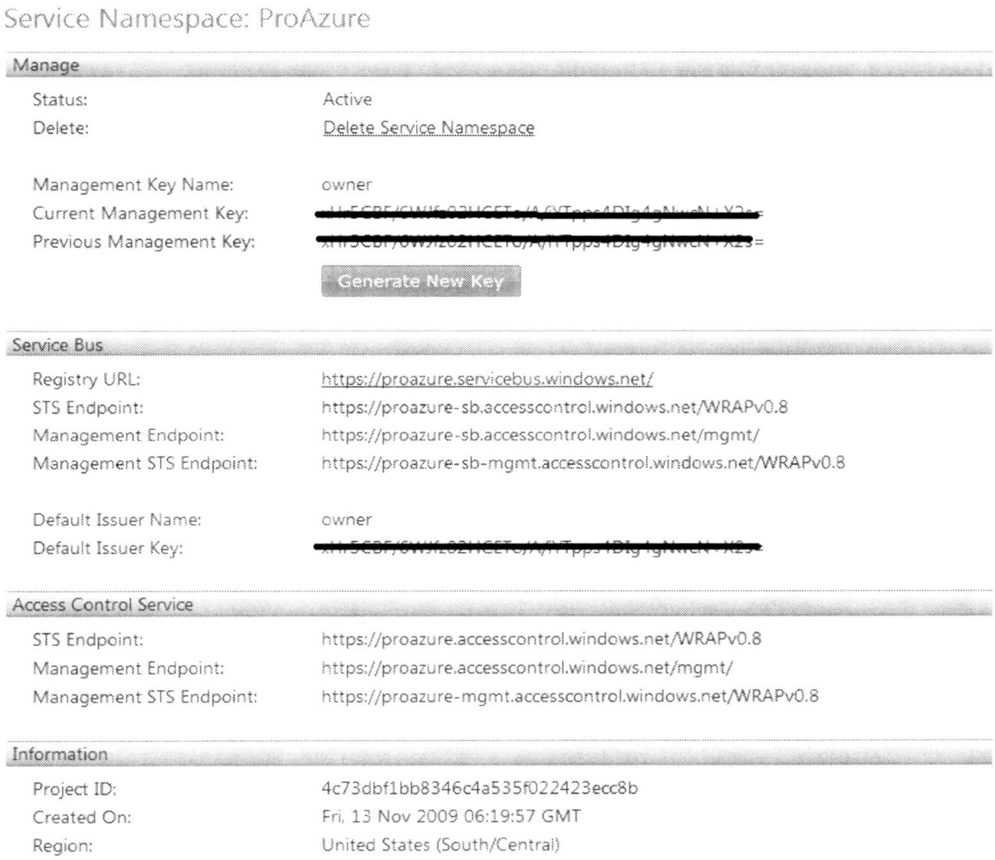

Figure 7-9. *Service namespace screen*

The service namespace page consists of four sections: Manage, Service Bus, Access Control Service, and Information. The Manage section contains the management key information you can use to interact with the Management service interface. The Service Bus section contains service bus endpoints and issuer information for using the AppFabric Service Bus. (I cover the AppFabric Service Bus in the next chapter.) The Access Control Service section contains the STS endpoint, Management endpoint, and Management STS endpoint. The Information section consists of project information and the region where the service namespace is located.

Managing Access Control Service Resources

Access Control resources are defined in your service namespace and are used to define the federation schemes, rules, token issuers, and policies that help realize claims-based identity federation and mapping in the cloud. This section covers ACS resource concepts and the tools required to interact with these resources.

Acm.exe is a command-line tool shipped with the AppFabric SDK. You can perform CREATE (C), READ (R), UPDATE (U), and DELETE (D) operations on your namespace's ACS resources (scopes, issuers, token policy, and rules). Acm.exe uses the management API to interact with the ACS. The source code for ACM.exe is included in the SDK. You can use the source code as a starting point to build your own web or executable application to interact with ACS. You can find the Acm.exe usage options in the AppFabric ACS documentation at `http://msdn.microsoft.com/en-us/library/ee706706.aspx`. Some developers at Microsoft have also released a sample Windows client application called ACS Management Browser, which is available at `http://code.msdn.microsoft.com/acmbrowser`.

ACS resources have a hierarchical structure, with your account at the top of the hierarchy. The ACS hierarchy is illustrated in Figure 7-10.

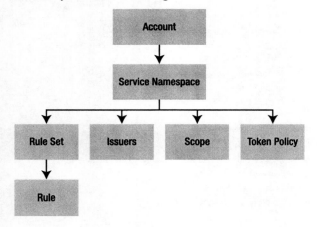

Figure 7-10. *ACS hierarchy*

The ACS hierarchy consists of three main levels: AppFabric account, service namespace, and resources.

Service Namespace

A *service namespace* is a collection of ACS resources like rules sets, issuers, scope, and token policy. From a resources perspective, the service namespace is the root of the resource tree. An account can contain many service namespaces. All the resources under the service namespace can belong to only one single service namespace—you can't share resources across multiple service namespaces. You can create a service namespace from the management portal by clicking the Add Service Namespace link, as shown earlier.

Token Policy

A token policy defines the token expiration and signature key of ACS-issued tokens. This policy can be associated with more than one scope. Typical parameters for a token policy are as follows:

- *DefaultTokenLifetimeInSeconds:* The number of seconds for which the token remains valid

- *SigningKey:* The signing key that ACS uses to sign tokens

You can create a token policy using the Acm.exe tool, as follows:

```
acm.exe create tokenpolicy -name:<Token Policy Name> -autogeneratekey -
host:accesscontrol.windows.net -service:<Service Namespace> -mgmtkey:<Management Key>
```

<Token Policy Name> is an alphanumeric name for the token policy. You can get the service namespace and the management key from the Management Portal. When you execute the command, ACS returns a token policy ID that you can use as a parameter in other operations such as deleting a token policy or creating a scope.

You can also use the Access Control Management browser to create token policies. Figure 7-11 shows the user interface to create token policies.

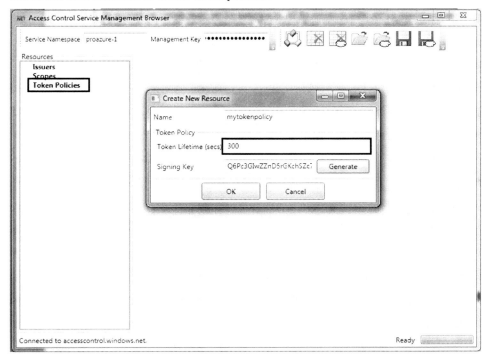

Figure 7-11. *Creating a token policy*

Scope

A *scope* is a collection of rules used by ACS to map input claims to output claims. ACS uses the scope URI to group rules. When you submit a request to the scope URI, ACS checks for the applies_to parameter and generates output claims if both the URIs matches. One service namespace can contain many scopes. The typical parameters required to interact with the scope resource are as follows:

- *AppliesTo:* The URI of the resource to which this scope applies

- *RuleSets/Id:* The ID of the rule set for the scope

- *TokenPolicyId:* The ID of the token policy associated with the scope

To create a scope with the Acm.exe tool, use the following command:

```
acm.exe create scope -name:<Scope Name> -appliesto:<Applies To> -tokenpolicyid:<Token Policy
Id> -host:<Host> -service:<Service Namespace> -mgmtkey:<Management Key>
```

Host is the host name of the management service (most likely accesscontrol.windows.net), -mgmtkey is the management key from the Management Portal, and -tokenpolicyid is the token policy ID returned when you created a token policy.

When you create a scope, ACS returns a scope ID that you should record for further operations like deleting a scope and creating rules. You can also use the Access Control Management browser to create scopes. Figure 7-12 shows the user interface to create scopes.

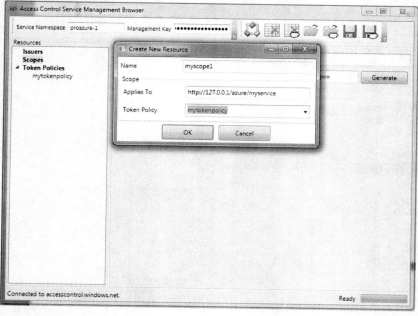

***Figure 7-12.** Creating a scope*

Issuer

An *issuer* is the issuer of an input token to ACS. In ACS, an issuer consists of a set of cryptographic key materials that service consumers use when authenticating with ACS. The cryptographic keys can be either a pair of Base64-encoded 32-byte keys or an X.509 certificate. X.509 certificates are specifically used to authenticate SAML tokens created by ADFS 2.0. One service namespace can contain many issuers.

To create an issuer with the Acm.exe tool, use the following command:

```
acm.exe create issuer -name:<Friendly Issuer Name> -issuername:<Issuer Name> -
autogeneratekey  -host:<Host> -service:<Service Namespace> -mgmtkey:<Management Key>
```

<Friendly Issuer Name> is a display name for the issuer, and *<Issuer Name>* is the value used by the STS to validate the input issuer value. After an issuer is created, ACS returns an IssuerID that you should record for further operations like deleting an issuer and creating rules. You can use other parameters to specify the algorithm, certificate, and key.

You can also use the Access Control Management browser to create an issuer. Figure 7-13 shows the user interface to create issuers.

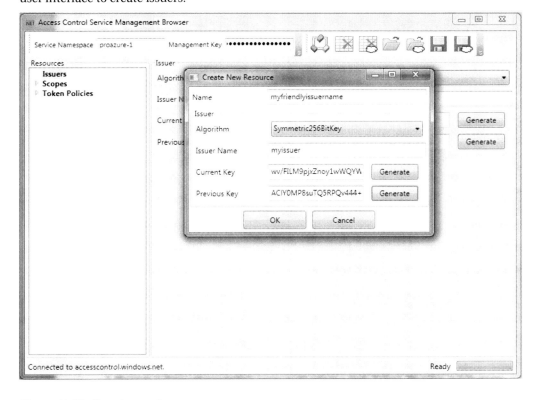

Figure 7-13. *Creating an issuer*

Ruleset

Rulesets are collections of rules. Every scope contains exactly one ruleset. In the current (AppFabric November 2009 CTP) release, a ruleset resource is automatically created and associated with a scope. You can't create rulesets using the management service API in this release.

Rule

The ACS rules engine is the core differentiator of the ACS from any technology currently available in the cloud. The rules define the mapping between input claims and output claims and as a result abstracts the input claims coming from different token providers into a single view in the form of an SWT token. The output claims are included in the final SWT token created by ACS. A rule must be associated with a ruleset. In the current release (AppFabric November 2009 CTP), a ruleset is automatically associated with a scope and shares a common identifier.

To create a rule with the Acm.exe tool, use the following command:

```
acm.exe create rule -name:<Rule Name> -scopeid:<Scope ID> -inclaimissuerid:<Issuer ID> -
inclaimtype:<Input Claim Type> -inclaimvalue:<Input Claim Value> -outclaimtype:<Output Claim
Type> -outclaimvalue:<Output Claim Value> -host:accesscontrol.windows.net -service:<Service
Namespace> -mgmtkey:<Management Key>
```

The parameters are as follows:

- *scopeid:* The scope in which this rule belongs. The scopeid is output by ACS when you create a new scope using Acm.exe.

- *inclaimissuerid:* The ID of the input claims issuer. An input claims is defined as a type/value pair. The issuer ID is output by ACS when you create a new Issuer.

- *inclaimtype:* The type of the claim included in the token by the token issuer (such as ADFS v.2.0). The ACS maps inclaimtype to outclaimtype.

- *inclaimvalue:* The value of the input claim type defined by the inclaimtype parameter. This value is included as part of the token issued by the issuer and sent to ACS.

- *outclaimtype:* The type of claim issued by ACS in the SWT.

- *outclaimvalue:* The value of the claim defined in the outclaimtype. This value is included by ACS in the SWT it issues.

- *passthrough:* Optional. If included, the ACS includes input claims as output claims in the issued token.

You can also use the Access Control Management browser to create a rule. Figure 7-14 shows the user interface to create rules.

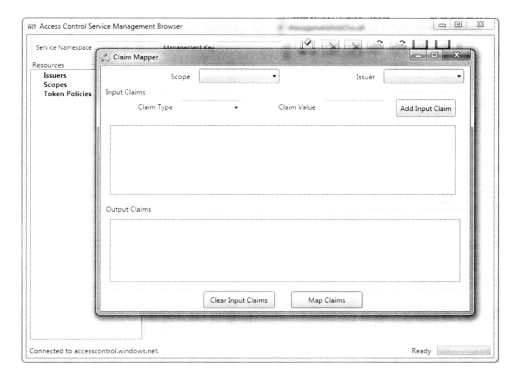

Figure 7-14. Creating a rule

In this section, you saw how to create resources in ACS that can be used for claims-based authentication and authorization in federated scenarios. The next section covers the programming aspects of using ACS in your solution.

Programming Access Control Service

This section discusses some end-to-end examples of configuring and using ACS in web applications and web services. I will cover the following scenarios:

- Creating an ACS solution using SWT

- Integrating ACS with a SAML token provider (such as ADFS v2.0)

- Deploying an ACS protected Web Service in Windows Azure

In a typical ACS solution, the development workflow is as follows:

1. Provision your ACS account.

2.   Create a service namespace.

3.   Design the relying party claims.

4.   Design ACS rules for mapping input claims to output claims.

5.   Create ACS resources (token policy, scope, issuer, and rules).

6.   Create/Modify a relying party for accepting SWT from ACS.

7.   Create/Modify a consumer application that creates or acquires an input token, sends the token to ACS in exchange for an SWT token, and forwards the SWT to the web service relying party for authentication.

▓ **Note** Some of the examples in this section require Windows Identity Foundation (WIF). Before running the examples, please install the WIF Release Candidate and the WIF SDK.

Creating an ACS solution Using SWT

In this example, you learn to use ACS to protect access to a REST web service. Consider an example in which you're exposing a web service named ACSMachineInfo that returns simple machine information to the clients. You want to offer this web service to as wide an audience as possible without worrying about maintaining authentication and authorization for each user. But because this service is part of an enterprise offering, you want the users accessing the service to be authenticated and authorized. ACS can abstract the authentication and authorization logic for your service by offering a generic claims-mapping engine between identity providers and your web service. Your web service is authentication provider agnostic and only accepts SWT tokens and claims issued by ACS to your web service. You web service is configured to trust tokens issued by ACS and only authorizes users adhering to the claims issued by ACS. Figure 7-15 illustrates the high-level architecture of the interaction between your web service, ACS, and the service consumer client.

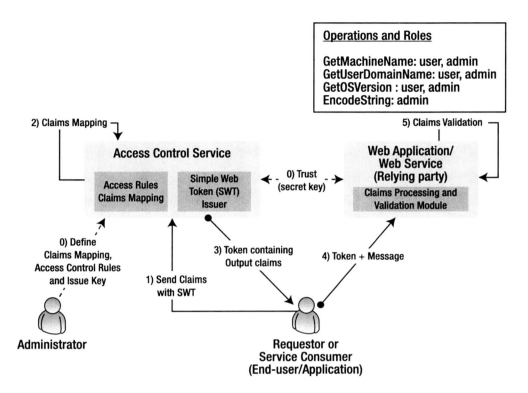

Figure 7-15. *ACS with SWT architecture*

Figure 7-15 is common architecture for using ACS with web services. The code for this example is in the Ch7Solution Visual Studio solution and in the ACSusingSWT solution folder, as shown in Figure 7-16.

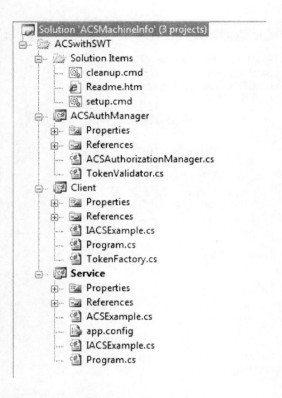

Figure 7-16. *ACS using SWT solution folder*

In Figure 7-16, the service project represents the web service that is protected by ACS, the client project is the web service consumer, and the ACSAuthManager is a utility class library project with utility classes for validating tokens in WCF.

The operations supported by the web service and the roles that can access them are listed in Table 7-1.

Table 7-1. *Web Service Operations and Roles*

Operation	Roles That Can Access the Operation
GetMachineName()	User, Administrator
GetUserDomainName()	User, Administrator
GetOSVersion()	User, Administrator
EncodeString()	Administrator

Only Administrators are allowed to access EncodeString(). All other methods can be accessed by the User and Administrator roles. After you've designed the authorization scheme for your web service, you can proceed with the standard steps required to integrate your web service with ACS and make it available to consumer applications.

Provisioning Your ACS Account

To use ACS, you have to first create an ACS account from the AppFabric developer portal at http://netservices.azure.com. The provisioning process has changed over the past year from limited early adopter access through tokens to direct commercial access. The AppFabric developer portal directs you appropriately to create new accounts. For the purpose of this exercise, I'm using my own account; but for you to use ACS, you must create your own ACS account. During the provisioning process, you may be asked to create a new project in your account.

Creating a Service Namespace

In the new ACS account, you can create a new service namespace. In the following examples, I use a namespace named proazure-1 that I created at the beginning of the chapter. You must create your own service namespace and modify the code accordingly to make it work with your ACS account. Figure 7-17 shows the service namespace page for the proazure-1 service namespace.

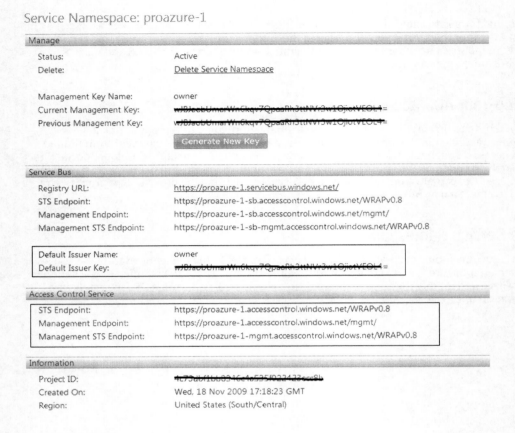

Figure 7-17. *Proazure-1 service namespace*

Designing the Relying Party Claims

When you design a claims-based identity model, one of the important design tasks you must complete is designing claims for the relying party. The relying party is the web service or web application that you want to protect using a claims-based identity model. Most web services and web applications already have some kind of role-based authorization model that defines privileges for end users. In most cases, the role-based authorization model can be easily transformed into a claims-based model by converting the roles to claims; you can keep the privileges the same as in the role-based authorization model. One advantage of moving to the claims-based identity model is that you can remove the end user authentication from your web application. Your web service or web application processes the tokens issued by ACS and validates the claims issued by ACS regardless of the authentication method used to authenticate the end user.

For the ACSMachineInfo web service, Table 7-1 defined the claims expected in the token when an end user accesses the web service. Only two roles are defined: User and Administrator. The

Administrator can access all the methods, whereas the User can access only three out of four methods. The web service should not allow any User role to access the EncodeString() method.

■ **Note** In the interest of keeping the example conceptual to ACS, it's very simple. You can enhance this example to provide more complex web service scenarios.

Designing ACS Rules to Map Input Claims to Output Claims

After you design the claims for your web service, you need to design the input and output claims for ACS. In this example, I use only one input token issuer, so the design of the mapping is simple; complex scenarios can mave multiple input claims from multiple issuers that need to be mapped to a single set of output claims expected by the relying party. This example maps the input claim type group to the output claim type action. Table 7-2 lists the input claim types and values with their corresponding output claim types and values.

Table 7-2. *Claims Mapping*

Input Claim Type	Input Claim Value	Output Claim Type	Output Claim Value
group	user	action	getmachinename
group	user	action	getuserdomainname
group	user	action	getosversion
group	admin	action	encodestring

If you're using multiple input token issuers, you have one table for each provider that maps input claims to output claims.

Creating ACS Resources (Token Policy, Scope, Issuer, and Rules)

After you've identified the claims, you can create the ACS objects using the ACS Management service. You can either use Acm.exe or the AC Management browser tool. To use Acm.exe, first configure the Acm.exe.config file to point to your service namespace. If you don't do that, then you must specify the service namespace and the management key for every Acm.exe execution.

Open Acm.exe.config, and configure the service namespace and management key as shown in Listing 7-1.

Listing 7-1. Acm.exe.config

```xml
<?xml version="1.0" encoding="utf-8" ?>
<configuration>
  <appSettings>
    <add key="host" value="accesscontrol.windows.net"/>
    <add key="service" value="{Enter your service namespace name here}"/>
    <add key="mgmtkey" value="{Enter your management key here}"/>
  </appSettings>
</configuration>
```

After configuring Acm.exe, you can use it to create ACS resources. When you configure ACS resources for the first time, you must create the resources in the following order because of their dependencies on each other: token policy, scope, issuer(s), rules.

Creating a Token Policy

A token policy defines the ACS token-issuing policy. You can create the token policy for the ACSMachineInfo example using Acm.exe as follows:

```
acm.exe create tokenpolicy -name:acsexample -autogeneratekey -service:%acsolution% -
mgmtkey:%acmgmtkey% -simpleout
```

I'm using the default token lifetime of 28888 seconds (8 hours). The autogeneratekey parameter indicates that I'm relying on ACS to autogenerate an HMAC-SHA256 signed key for issuing tokens. One service namespace can contain many token policies.

Creating a scope

A scope is used to group settings of a particular resource. When you create a scope, you assign a token policy ID to it. The Acm.exe command to create a scope in the ACSMachineInfo example is as follows:

```
acm.exe create scope -name:acsexample -appliesto:http://localhost/acsexample/ -
tokenpolicyid:%tokenpolicyid% -service:%acsolution% -mgmtkey:%acmgmtkey% -simpleout
```

This command defines a scope named acsexample. The appliesto parameter specifies the URI of the resource for which you want to specify the access control rules. Note that it accepts the tokenpolicyid created by the previous command.

Creating an Issuer

An issuer describes the cryptographic key material that a web service client uses to acquire ACS tokens. In the ACSMachineInfo example, the web service client creates an SWT token and then sends that token to ACS to acquire another SWT token to send to the web service. In this case, the web service client becomes an issuer of the first SWT token. The Acm.exe command to create an issuer in the ACSMachineInfo example is as follows:

```
acm.exe create issuer -name:acsexample -issuername:acsexample -autogeneratekey -
service:%acsolution% -mgmtkey:%acmgmtkey% -simpleout
```

In this command, the web service client needs to identify itself as the acsexample issuer client when requesting an SWT from ACS. The default algorithm used to generate a key is Symmetrick256Key and X.509. This example uses the default value because typically, the X.509 value is used to issu SAML tokens from ADFS v2.0.

Creating Rules

After the token policy, scope, and issuer are configured, you can create rules that map the input claims coming from the token issued by the issuer to output claims ACS creates in the token it issues back to the caller. A rule is the logic that needs to be executed on a certain set of input claims to produce a set of output claims. These output claims are validated by the web service (relying party) while granting appropriate access to the caller. As discussed earlier, in the ACSMachineInfo example, four rules need to be configured. The Acm.exe commands to create the required rules are shown in Listing 7-2.

Listing 7-2. *Creating Rules*

```
acm.exe create rule -name:acsexamplegetmachinename -scopeid:%scopeid% -
inclaimissuerid:%issuerid% -inclaimtype:group -inclaimvalue:user -outclaimtype:action -
outclaimvalue:getmachinename -service:%acsolution% -mgmtkey:%acmgmtkey% -simpleout

acm.exe create rule -name:acsexamplegetuserdomainname -scopeid:%scopeid% -
inclaimissuerid:%issuerid% -inclaimtype:group -inclaimvalue:user -outclaimtype:action -
outclaimvalue:getuserdomainname -service:%acsolution%
-mgmtkey:%acmgmtkey% -simpleout

acm.exe create rule -name:acsexamplegetosversion -scopeid:%scopeid% -
inclaimissuerid:%issuerid% -inclaimtype:group -inclaimvalue:user -outclaimtype:action -
outclaimvalue:getosversion -service:%acsolution% -mgmtkey:%acmgmtkey% -simpleout

acm.exe create rule -name:acsexampleencodestring -scopeid:%scopeid% -
inclaimissuerid:%issuerid% -inclaimtype:group -inclaimvalue:admin -outclaimtype:action -
outclaimvalue:encodestring -service:%acsolution% -mgmtkey:%acmgmtkey% -simpleout
```

The create rule parameter of Acm.exe creates a rule that defines the name of the rule, the input claim type and value, and the output client type and value. For each mapping defined, ACS includes the output claim in the token it issues.

Creating or Modifying the Relying Party to Accept an SWT from ACS

After you configure ACS, ACS can issue tokens for the web service. But you must still modify the web service to recognize and validate the token and the rules issued in the token. The web service code must do the following things to be compatible with ACS:

1. Verify the presence of the token issued by ACS.
2. Check if the token is signed with the appropriate key.

3. Verify that the token contains the claims it expects.

4. Grant appropriate access to the user depending on the claims.

The Service project in the Visual Studio solution represents the web service implementation. Because the ACSMachineInfo web service is based on WCF, you can create a custom authorization manager inheriting from the ServiceAuthorizationManager class and inject the necessary logic to validate token content automatically. Listing 7-3 shows the implementation of ACSAuthorizationManager.

Listing 7-3. *ACSAuthorizationManager*

```
using System;
using System.Collections.Generic;
using System.Linq;
using System.Net;
using System.ServiceModel;
using System.ServiceModel.Web;

    public class ACSAuthorizationManager : ServiceAuthorizationManager
    {
        TokenValidator validator;
        string requiredClaimType;

        public ACSAuthorizationManager(string acsHostName, string trustedSolution,
    string trustedAudienceValue, byte[] trustedSigningKey, string requiredClaimType)
        {
            this.validator = new TokenValidator(acsHostName, trustedSolution,
    trustedAudienceValue, trustedSigningKey);
            this.requiredClaimType = requiredClaimType;
        }

        protected override bool CheckAccessCore(OperationContext operationContext)
        {
            // get the authorization header
            string authorizationHeader = WebOperationContext.Current.IncomingRequest
    .Headers[HttpRequestHeader.Authorization];

            if (string.IsNullOrEmpty(authorizationHeader))
            {
                WebOperationContext.Current.OutgoingResponse.StatusCode =
    HttpStatusCode.Unauthorized;
                return false;
            }

            // validate the token
            if (!this.validator.Validate(authorizationHeader))
            {
                WebOperationContext.Current.OutgoingResponse.StatusCode =
    HttpStatusCode.Unauthorized;
                return false;
```

```
        }

        // check for an action claim and get the value
        Dictionary<string, string> claims = this.validator.
GetNameValues(authorizationHeader);

        // use the operation name to determine the requried action value
        string requiredActionClaimValue = WebOperationContext.Current.
IncomingRequest.UriTemplateMatch.RelativePathSegments.First();

        string actionClaimValue;
        if (!claims.TryGetValue(this.requiredClaimType, out actionClaimValue))
        {
            WebOperationContext.Current.OutgoingResponse.StatusCode =
HttpStatusCode.Unauthorized;
            return false;
        }

        // check for "," delimited values
        string[] actionClaimValues = actionClaimValue.Split(',');

        // check for the correct action claim value
        if (!actionClaimValues.Contains(requiredActionClaimValue))
        {
            WebOperationContext.Current.OutgoingResponse.StatusCode =
HttpStatusCode.Unauthorized;
            return false;
        }

        return true;
    }
}
```

The CheckAccessCore method validates the token, gets the list of claims in the token, and then checks if the claims are valid for executing the particular operation. The TokenValidator class contains a method to validate the token. The ACSAuthorizationManager class instantiates TokenValidator in its constructor and then calls the Validate() method to validate the token. The TokenValidator class also returns the claims from the GetNameValues() method. The CheckAccessCore() method then checks if the claims contain the action corresponding to the method being called by the user. If the claims contain the action being called, the method returns true; otherwise, the method returns false.

Listing 7-4 shows the code for the TokenValidator constructor.

Listing 7-4. *TokenValidator Constructor*

```
public TokenValidator(string acsHostName, string trustedSolution,
string trustedAudienceValue, byte[] trustedSigningKey)
    {
        this.acsHostName = acsHostName;
        this.trustedSigningKey = trustedSigningKey;
```

```
            this.trustedTokenIssuer = new Uri(string.Format(
                CultureInfo.InvariantCulture,
                "https://{0}.{1}/WRAPv0.8",
                trustedSolution,
                acsHostName));

            this.trustedAudienceValue = new Uri(trustedAudienceValue);
        }
```

In Listing 7-4, trustedSolution represents your ACS service namespace, trustedAudienceValue represents the destination URL where the ACS token will be sent, and trustedSigningKey represents the token policy key associated with the token issuer your trust. In this case, the authority is ACS. Listing 7-5 shows the code for the Validate() method used to validate the token issued by ACS.

Listing 7-5. *TokenValidator Validate Method*

```
public bool Validate(string token)
{
    if (!this.IsHMACValid(token, this.trustedSigningKey))
    {
        return false;
    }

    if (this.IsExpired(token))
    {
        return false;
    }

    if (!this.IsIssuerTrusted(token))
    {
        return false;
    }

    if (!this.IsAudienceTrusted(token))
    {
        return false;
    }

    return true;
}
```

The Validate() method checks the token validity, token expiration, issuer validity, and intended audience for the token. If all the checks pass, the method returns true. The utility functions IsHMACValid(), IsExpired(), IsIssuerTrusted(), and IsAudienceTrusted() drill down into the SWT token format to examine the respective validity of the token.

The Program.cs file in the Service project includes the startup logic for the web service. Listing 7-6 shows the web service startup code.

Listing 7-6. *Web Service Startup Code*

```
class Program
{
const string serviceNamespace = "proazure-1";
const string trustedTokenPolicyKey = "peCRAARL9t/oji4/CWvVKLNcS2KOMiRnHscdcw5HDJQ=";

const string acsHostName = "accesscontrol.windows.net";
const string trustedAudience = "http://localhost/acsexample";
const string requiredClaimType = "action";

        static void Main()
        {
            WebHttpBinding binding =
new WebHttpBinding(WebHttpSecurityMode.None);

            Uri address = new Uri(trustedAudience);

            WebServiceHost host = new WebServiceHost(typeof(ACSExample));
            host.AddServiceEndpoint(typeof(IACSExample), binding, address);

            host.Authorization.ServiceAuthorizationManager =
new ACSAuthorizationManager(
                acsHostName,
                serviceNamespace,
                trustedAudience,
                Convert.FromBase64String(trustedTokenPolicyKey),
                requiredClaimType);

            host.Open();

            Console.WriteLine("The ACSExample Service is listening");
            Console.WriteLine("Press <ENTER> to exit");
            Console.ReadLine();

            host.Close();
        }
    }
```

In Listing 7-6, trustedTokenPolicyKey is the token policy key created when you create the token policy. requiredClaimType is the claim type that the web service expects from the SWT issued by ACS. Note that the ServiceAuthorizationManager property of the host.Authorization object is set to the custom class ACSAuthorizationManager. When you set this property, the method call to the web service is automatically intercepted for validation purposes. The web service is now ready to accept and process SWT tokens from ACS. Listing 7-7 shows the interface of the web service.

Listing 7-7. *ACSMachineInfo Interface*

```
[ServiceContract]
    public interface IACSExample
    {
        [OperationContract]
        [WebGet(UriTemplate = "getmachinename")]
        string GetMachineName();

        [OperationContract]
        [WebGet(UriTemplate = "getuserdomainname")]
        string GetUserDomainName();

        [OperationContract]
        [WebGet(UriTemplate = "getosversion")]
        string GetOSVersion();


        [OperationContract]
        [WebGet(UriTemplate = "encodestring?data={data}")]
        byte[] EncodeString(string data);

    }
```

The UriTemplate property represents the value that is returned when you call the WebOperationContext.Current.IncomingRequest.UriTemplateMatch.RelativePathSegments.First() method in the TokenValidator.CheckAccessCore() method.

Creating the Web Service Consumer

The web service client creates an SWT token with input claims and sends it to ACS to acquire an SWT token with output claims. The web service client packages this token into the header of the web service method call. The Client project in the Visual Studio solution contains the implementation of the web service client. Listing 7-8 shows the main method from Program.cs in the Client project.

Listing 7-8. *Main Method in Program.cs from the Web Service Client*

```
static void Main()
{
Console.WriteLin("Enter your solution name, then press <ENTER>");
serviceNamespace = Console.ReadLine();

Console.WriteLine();
Console.WriteLine("Enter your issuer key, then press <ENTER>");
issuerKey = "K9GJNT96CQTL37OTUnCyATOruMbnHVCLvb3RXOog3z4=";
// create a token with a group=user claim
string userToken = GetUserToken();
```

```
// send the token to ACS
string acsIssuedToken = SendSWTToACS(userToken, "http://localhost/acsexample");

// perform the calculator operations
Console.WriteLine();
Console.WriteLine("Calling calculator with 'group=user' claim");
DoOperations(acsIssuedToken);

// create a token with a group=user,executive claim
string executiveToken = GetUserAdminToken();

// send the token to ACS
acsIssuedToken = SendSWTToACS(executiveToken, "http://localhost/acsexample");

// perform the calculator operations
Console.WriteLine();
Console.WriteLine("Calling ACS Example with 'group=user,admin' claim");
DoOperations(acsIssuedToken);

Console.WriteLine();
Console.WriteLine("Done. Press <ENTER> to end");
Console.ReadLine();
}
```

The GetUserToken() method creates an SWT token representing a user group and then calls the SendSWTToACS() method to get the SWT token from ACS that's specific to the user group. The code then calls the DoOperations() method, which calls all the operations on the ACSMachineInfo web service. Then, the GetUserAdminToken() method creates an SWT token that is sent to ACS to get an ACS-issued token for the admin group. The code then calls the DoOperations() method with the ACS-issued token. The output of the method calls should indicate when the particular group has enough permissions to call a web service method. The TokenFactory class contains the necessary logic to create an SWT token to be sent to ACS. Listing 7-9 shows the code to create an SWT token.

Listing 7-9. *Creating an SWT Token*

```
public string CreateToken(Dictionary<string, string> claims)
{
// check for dup claimtypes
Dictionary<string, string> claimList = this.RemoveDuplicateClaimTypes(claims);

// build the claims string
StringBuilder builder = new StringBuilder();
foreach (KeyValuePair<string, string> entry in claimList)
{
builder.Append(entry.Key);
builder.Append('=');
builder.Append(entry.Value);
builder.Append('&');
}
```

```
// add the issuer name
builder.Append("Issuer=");
builder.Append(this.issuerName);
builder.Append('&');

// add the Audience
builder.Append("Audience=");
builder.Append(string.Format("https://{0}.{1}/WRAPv0.8&", this.solutionName, this.acsHost));

// add the expires on date
builder.Append("ExpiresOn=");
builder.Append(GetExpiresOn(20));

string signature = this.GenerateSignature(builder.ToString(), this.signingKey);
builder.Append("&HMACSHA256=");
builder.Append(signature);

return builder.ToString();
}
```

You can see that creating an SWT token is very simple because you create only certain name/value pairs and POST them to the service namespace.

Running the Examples

The steps required to run the example are as follows:

1. Run the setup.cmd script from the command prompt with Administrator privileges, as shown in Figure 7-18.

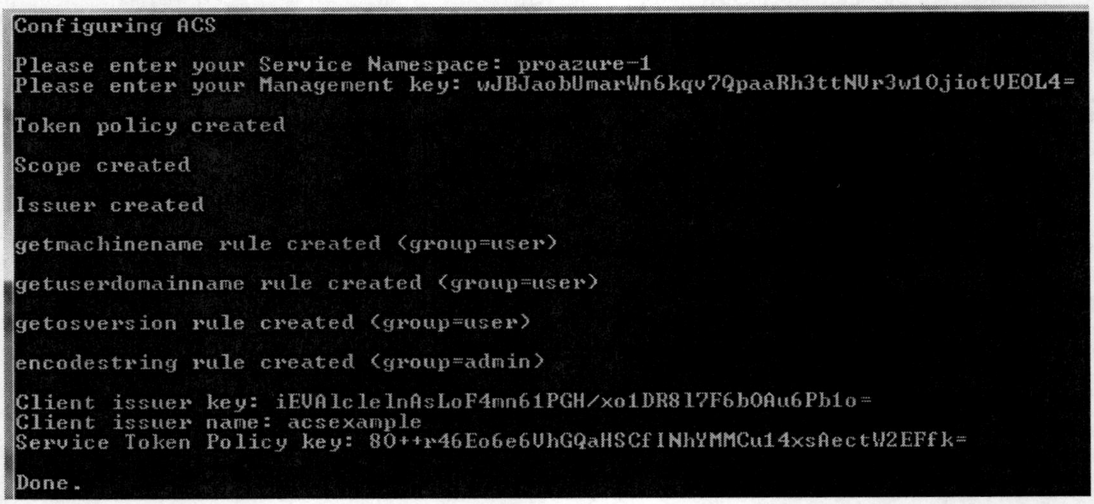

```
Configuring ACS

Please enter your Service Namespace: proazure-1
Please enter your Management key: wJBJaobUmarWn6kqv7QpaaRh3ttNUr3w10jiotUEOL4=

Token policy created

Scope created

Issuer created

getmachinename rule created (group=user)

getuserdomainname rule created (group=user)

getosversion rule created (group=user)

encodestring rule created (group=admin)

Client issuer key: iEUAlcleInAsLoF4mn61PGH/xo1DR817F6bOAu6Pb1o=
Client issuer name: acsexample
Service Token Policy key: 80++r46Eo6e6UhGQaHSCfINhYMMCu14xsAectU2EFfk=

Done.
```

Figure 7-18. *Running setup.cmd*

2. On successful completion of the command, the setup.cmd script outputs the token policy key and the issuer key required by the web service and the web service client, respectively. The web service requires the token policy key to validate the trusted source of the SWT token. The web service client requires the issuer key to register itself as the issuer of input SWT tokens. In the Program.cs file in the Service project, copy and paste the token policy key into the trustedTokenPolicyKey:

```
const string trustedTokenPolicyKey = "8O++r46Eo6e6VhGQaHSCfINhYMMCu14xsAectW2EFfk=";
```

3. Similarly, copy and paste the issuer key into the issuerKey variable in Program.cs file in the Client project:

```
issuerKey = "iEVAlclelnAsLoF4mn61PGH/xo1DR8l7F6bOAu6Pb1o=";
```

4. Start the service application (see Figure 7-19).

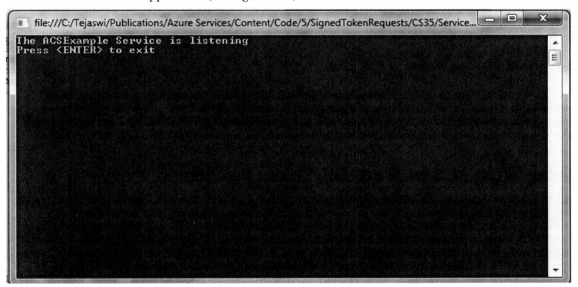

Figure 7-19. *Starting the service*

5. Start the client application (see Figure 7-20).

409

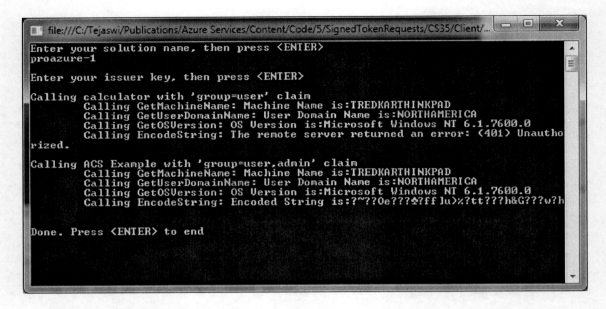

Figure 7-20. *Client application*

As shown in Figure 7-20, the call to EncodeString() fails with an unauthorized exception when executed in the context of a User role as a group claim, whereas all the methods are executed when executed in the context of an Administrator role as a group claim. This demonstrates the claims-based identity model with ACS as the claims-transformation engine between the client and the web service.

Integrating ACS with a SAML Token Provider

In the previous example, the web service consumer creates an SWT token with input claims locally with the User and Administrator roles. But in real-world enterprise applications, user authentication is typically provided by enterprise identity providers like Active Directory. An Active Directory with an ADFS v2.0 instance can create SAML tokens and input claims that can be processed by ACS. ADFS v2.0 can be configured to be a trusted issuer of tokens to ACS. The web service client then sends SAML token issued by ADFS v2.0 instead of locally created SWT tokens. In this section, you see an example of integrating ACS with ADFS v2.0 to protect a web service. Figure 7-21 illustrates the architecture of integrating ACS with a SAML provider.

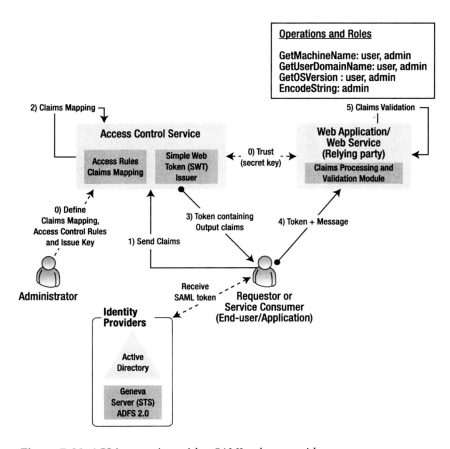

Figure 7-21. ACS integration with a SAML token provider

The overall architecture is very similar to the previous example. The main difference is that the input token to ACS is issued by ADFS v2.0 and is of type SAML instead of SWT. In this section, you learn to modify a web service client to obtain a SAML token from a SAML token provider and use it to request an SWT token from ACS. You use the same relying party web service you used in the previous example. This way, you see how ACS provides abstraction between multiple token providers.

The following are the prerequisites for running the example in this section:

- Microsoft Windows Identity Foundation Runtime

- Microsoft Windows Identity Foundation SDK (`http://msdn.microsoft.com/en-us/evalcenter/dd440951.aspx`)

- Identity Developer Training Kit (PDC 2009) (`www.microsoft.com/downloads/details.aspx?displaylang=en&FamilyID=c3e315fa-94e2-4028-99cb-904369f177c0`)

Download and install all these prerequisites. The Identity Developer Training Kit consists of some labs and sample code that I use in this example. The code for ACS integration with a SAML token provider is in the Visual Studio solution for this chapter. Figure 7-22 shows the projects in the ACSwithSAML solution folder that I discuss in this example.

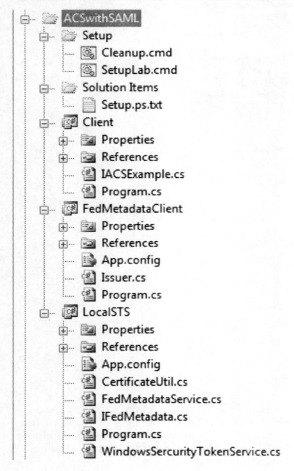

Figure 7-22. ACSwithSAML solution structure

The steps for integrating ACS with a SAML token provider are outlined in the following sections.

■ **Note** ADFS v2.0 is a SAML token provider, but it requires you to install Active Directory and other infrastructure components. With the WIF SDK, you can create your own identity provider. This example uses the LocalSTS server, which is available as part of the Introduction to Access Control lab in the following folder: C:\IdentityTrainingKit\Labs\IntroAccessControlService\Source\Ex02-UsingACSWithSAMLTokens\Assets.

Configuring ACS to Accept SAML Tokens

In the previous example, you created a service namespace, token policy, and scope in ACS for processing SWT tokens generated by the web service consumer client. This example uses the same service namespace and token policy and only configures ACS to process the SAML token issued by the custom STS. If you don't have the token policy ID from the previous example, you can get all the token policies from the service namespace by executing the following command:

```
Acm.exe getall tokenpolicy
```

Figure 7-23 shows the output of the getall token policy command.

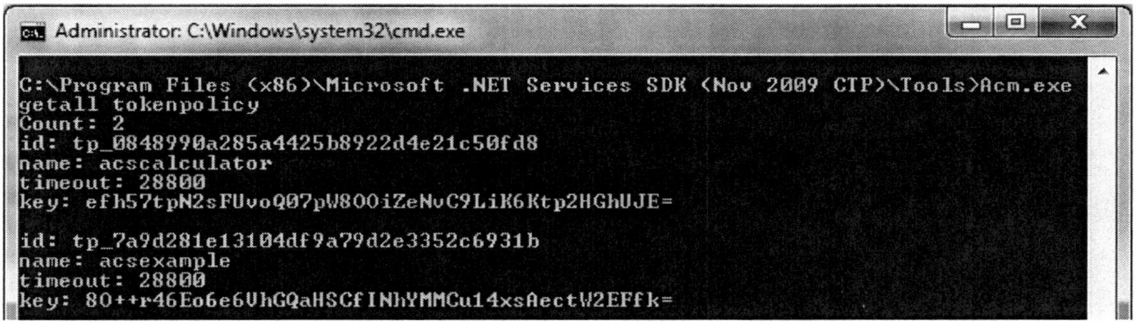

Figure 7-23. *Get all token policy*

Figure 7-23 shows that there are two token policies in the service namespace. Your service namespace may have only one token policy. Note down the token policy ID of the token policy named acsexample. The value of your ID will be different than the one in this example.

Next, you have to register the SAML token issuer with ACS. If you've installed the Identity Developer's Kit, run Setup.cmd for the Introduction to Access Control Service lab from the following directory: C:\IdentityTrainingKit\Labs\IntroAccessControlService\Source\Setup.

On successful installation, open the LocalSTS.sln solution. In WindowsSecurityTokenService.cs, replace "Pilot" with "domainadmin" in the GetOutputClaimsIdentity function, as shown in Listing 7-10.

Listing 7-10. *GetOuputClaimsIdentity*

```
protected override IClaimsIdentity GetOutputClaimsIdentity
(IClaimsPrincipal principal, RequestSecurityToken request, Scope scope)
        {
            IClaimsIdentity callerIdentity = (IClaimsIdentity)principal.Identity;

            IClaimsIdentity outputIdentity = new ClaimsIdentity();

            Claim nameClaim =
new Claim(System.IdentityModel.Claims.ClaimTypes.Name, callerIdentity.Name);
            Claim groupClaim =
new Claim("http://schemas.xmlsoap.org/claims/Group", "domainadmin");

            outputIdentity.Claims.Add(nameClaim);
            outputIdentity.Claims.Add(groupClaim);

            return outputIdentity;
}
```

Compile the LocalSTS project. Then, Run LocalSTS.exe from C:\IdentityTrainingKit\Labs\IntroAccessControlService\Source\Ex02-UsingACSWithSAMLTokens\Assets (see Figure 7-24). LocalSTS.exe is a SAML token issuer that simulates the token-generation function of ADFS v2.0.

Figure 7-24. *Running LocalSTS.exe*

The X.509 certificate path and the STS URL are configured in LocalSTS.exe.config, as shown in Listing 7-11.

Listing 7-11. LocalSTS.exe.config

```xml
<?xml version="1.0" encoding="utf-8" ?>
<configuration>
  <appSettings>
    <add key="signingCertName" value="CN=localhost"/>
    <add key="stsBaseAddress" value="localhost/localsts"/>
    <add key="stsPath" value="Trust/13/UserName"/>
  </appSettings>
</configuration>
```

■ **Note** I'm using the Identity Developer Kit to run LocalSTS in the interest of keeping the book conceptual. To build an enterprise-grade ACS solution, you need to learn Windows Identity Foundation. The Identity Developer Training Kit is the best way to learn the WIF.

The Introduction to Access Control Service lab in the Identity Developer Training Kit also consists of a client utility named FedMetadataClient.exe located in the C:\IdentityTrainingKit\Labs\IntroAccessControlService\Source\Ex02-UsingACSWithSAMLTokens\Assets directory for creating LocalSTS as a trusted issuer in ACS.

Configure the FedMetadataClient.exe tool in FedMetadataClient.exe.config to point to your service namespace, management key, and the relying party URL, as shown in Listing 7-12.

Listing 7-12. FedMetadataClient.exe.config

```xml
<?xml version="1.0" encoding="utf-8" ?>
<configuration>
  <appSettings>
    <add key="stsBaseAddress" value="localhost/localsts"/>
    <add key="stspath" value="Trust/13/UserName"/>
    <add key="serviceNamespace" value="{Enter your service namespace}"/>
    <add key="acsHostName" value="accesscontrol.windows.net"/>
    <add key="applies_to" value="{Enter URL of the Relying Party or web service"/>
    <add key="mgmtKey" value="{Enter management key of your service namespace"/>
  </appSettings>
</configuration>
```

Run the FedMetaDataClient tool from the command line. The FedMetaDataClient tool reads the metadata of the LocalSTS and calls the ACS management service API to register a new token issuer.

Run the "Acm.exe getall issuer" command to retrieve all the registered issuers in the service namespace, as shown in Figure 7-25.

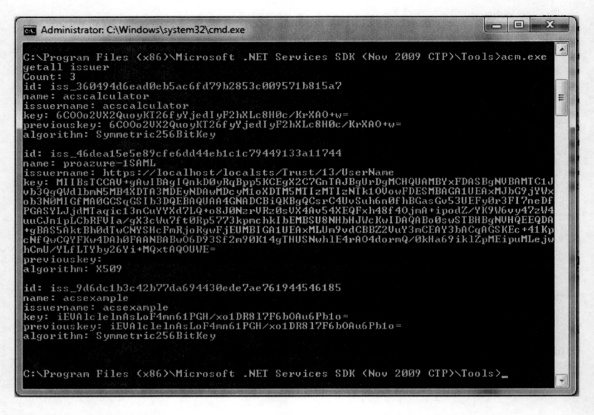

Figure 7-25. *Getting all issuers*

You should see the newly created issuer with the name format {service namespace}SAML. Copy and save the ID of the issuer, which is of the format id:iss_XXX. You use this issuer ID to create a new rule later.

Get the scope ID by executing the "acm.exe getall scope" command. This lists all the scopes in your service namespace, as shown in Figure 7-26.

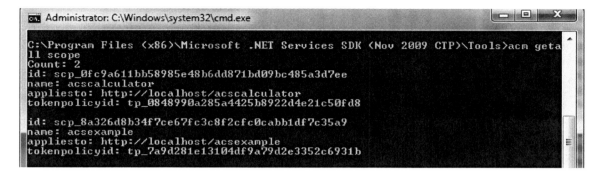

Figure 7-26. *Getting all scopes*

This example uses the same scope (acsexample) you used in the previous example. Copy and save the scope ID of the acsexample scope. The scope ID is of the format id:scp_XXX.

When you have the issuer ID and the scope ID, you can create the rule for mapping input claims from the SAML token to the output claims in the SWT token issued by ACS. Because you're using the same web service (ACSMachineInfo) from the previous example, the output claims remain similar to the previous example, but the input claims change to reflect the claims generated by the LocalSTS. In this example, Table 7-3 lists the mapping between input claims and output claims.

Table 7-3. *Claims Mapping for SAML Token Claims*

Input Claim Type	Input Claim Value	Output Claim Type	Output Claim Value
`http://schemas.xmlsoap.org/claims/Group`	domainadmin	action	encodestring

The SAML token should include an input claim type `http://schemas.xmlsoap.org/claims/Group` with a value of domainadmin. This input claim is mapped to the output claim type of action with a value of encodestring. This means that all the users in the domainadmin group can call the EncodeString() function in the ACSMachineInfo web service. The command to create a new rule is as follows:

```
.\acm.exe create rule
-scopeid:scp_8a326d8b34f7ce67fc3c8f2cfc0cabb1df7c35a9
 -inclaimissuerid:iss_46dea15e5e89cfe6dd44eb1c1c79449133a11744
-inclaimtype:http://schemas.xmlsoap.org/claims/Group
-inclaimvalue:domainadmin
-outclaimtype:action
-outclaimvalue:encodestring
-name:domainadminencodestring
```

When executing the command, you need the scope ID and issuer ID you retrieved from ACS earlier. Figure 7-27 shows the output of the create rule command.

```
C:\Program Files (x86)\Microsoft .NET Services SDK (Nov 2009 CTP)\Tools>acm.exe
create rule -scopeid:scp_8a326d8b34f7ce67fc3c8f2cfc0cabb1df7c35a9 -inclaimissuer
id:iss_9d6dc1b3c42b77da694430ede7ae761944546185 -inclaimtype:http://schemas.xmls
oap.org/claims/Group -inclaimvalue:domainadmin -outclaimtype:action -outclaimval
ue:encodestring -name:domainadminencodestring
Object created successfully (ID:'rul_5c99d067bda2a3b9dc0ebf2d258c3a237043d1dbe66
c0e90ce2b75711946c332dd79af7a1dceabb8')

C:\Program Files (x86)\Microsoft .NET Services SDK (Nov 2009 CTP)\Tools>_
```

Figure 7-27. *Creating a rule*

Configuring a Web Service Client to Acquire and Send SAML Tokens

In this section, you see the client application that acquires a SAML token from LocalSTS and sends it to ACS. Listing 7-13 shows the code in the main function of the Program.cs file from the Client project.

Listing 7-13. *Program.cs in Client Project*

```
private const string ServiceNamespace = "proazure-1";
private const string AcsHostName = "accesscontrol.windows.net";
private const string StsBaseAddress = "localhost/localsts";
private const string StsPath = "Trust/13/UserName";
        public static void Main(string[] args)
        {
            string stsAddress = string.Format("https://{0}/{1}", StsBaseAddress, StsPath);
            string acsSTSAddress = string.Format
("https://{0}.{1}/WRAPv0.8", ServiceNamespace, AcsHostName);

            string samlAssertion = GetSamlAssertion(stsAddress, acsSTSAddress);
            string acsToken = GetACSToken(samlAssertion);

            // create the binding and address to communicate with the service
            WebHttpBinding binding =
          new WebHttpBinding(WebHttpSecurityMode.None);
            Uri address = new Uri(@"http://localhost/acsexample");

            WebChannelFactory<IACSExample> channelFactory =
          new WebChannelFactory<IACSExample>(binding, address);

            IACSExample proxy = channelFactory.CreateChannel();

            using (new OperationContextScope(proxy as IContextChannel))
            {
                string authHeaderValue = "WRAPv0.8" + " "
                + HttpUtility.UrlDecode(acsToken);

                WebOperationContext.Current.OutgoingRequest.Headers
            .Add("authorization", authHeaderValue);
```

```
            // call the service and get a response
            try
            {
                Console.Write("\tCalling GetMachineName: ");
                Console.WriteLine("Machine Name is:"
              + proxy.GetMachineName());

                Console.Write("\tCalling GetUserDomainName: ");
                Console.WriteLine("User Domain Name is:"
                + proxy.GetUserDomainName());

                Console.Write("\tCalling GetOSVersion: ");
                Console.WriteLine("OS Version is:" + proxy.GetOSVersion());
                Console.Write("\tCalling EncodeString: ");
                Console.WriteLine("Encoded String is:"
+ Encoding.UTF8.GetString(proxy.EncodeString("Welcome to ProAzure.")));
            }
            catch (MessageSecurityException ex)
            {
                if (ex.InnerException != null)
                {
                    WebException wex = ex.InnerException as WebException;
                    if (wex != null)
                    {
                        Console.WriteLine("Error: {0}", wex.Message);
                    }
                }
                else
                {
                    throw;
                }
            }
        }

        ((IClientChannel)proxy).Close();

        channelFactory.Close();

        Console.ReadLine();
    }
```

The GetSamlAssertion() function retrieves the SAML token from LocalSTS, and GetACSToken() sends the SAML token to ACS and returns an ACS token. Listing 7-14 shows the code for the GetSamlAssertion() and GetACSToken() functions.

Listing 7-14. *GetSamlAssertion and GetACSToken*

```
private static string GetSamlAssertion(string stsAddress, string acsStsAddress)
{
        WSTrustChannelFactory trustChannelFactory = new WSTrustChannelFactory(
            new WindowsWSTrustBinding
          (SecurityMode.TransportWithMessageCredential),
            new EndpointAddress(new Uri(stsAddress)));
        trustChannelFactory.TrustVersion = TrustVersion.WSTrust13;

        RequestSecurityToken rst =
      new RequestSecurityToken(WSTrust13Constants.RequestTypes.Issue,
          WSTrust13Constants.KeyTypes.Bearer);
        rst.AppliesTo = new EndpointAddress(acsStsAddress);
        rst.TokenType = Microsoft.IdentityModel.Tokens.
        SecurityTokenTypes.Saml2TokenProfile11;

        WSTrustChannel channel =
(WSTrustChannel)trustChannelFactory.CreateChannel();
        GenericXmlSecurityToken token =
 channel.Issue(rst) as GenericXmlSecurityToken;

        return token.TokenXml.OuterXml;
    }

    private static string GetACSToken(string samlAssertion)
    {
        WebClient tokenClient = new WebClient();
        tokenClient.BaseAddress =
string.Format("https://{0}.{1}", ServiceNamespace, AcsHostName);

        NameValueCollection values = new NameValueCollection();
        values.Add("wrap_SAML", samlAssertion);
        values.Add("applies_to", "http://localhost/acsexample");

        byte[] responseBytes = tokenClient.UploadValues("WRAPv0.8", values);
        string response = Encoding.UTF8.GetString(responseBytes);

        return response
            .Split('&')
            .Single(value => value.StartsWith
("wrap_token=", StringComparison.OrdinalIgnoreCase))
            .Split('=')[1];
    }
```

To run the example, do the following:

1.   Run the Service project.

2.   Run the client from the ACSwithSAML solution folder.

Deploying the Web Service in Windows Azure

Once you have tested the claims-based authentication and authorization for the ACSMachineInfo web service, you can package and deploy the web service as a Windows Azure cloud service. The steps required for packaging and deploying the ACSMachineInfo web service as a Windows Azure cloud service are as follows:

1. Create a new Windows Azure cloud service project

2. Create a new Worker Role with external endpoint in the cloud service

3. Add the code from ACSMachineInfo to the Worker Role

4. Test ACSMachineInfo web service in Development Fabric

5. Deploy ACSMachineInfo web service in Windows Azure cloud

6. Test ACSMachineInfo web service in Windows Azure cloud

The source code solution for this chapter includes a cloud service for the ACSMachineInfo web service. Figure 7-28 shows the project structure for the cloud service and the worker role projects.

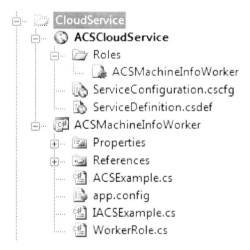

Figure 7-28. *Cloud Service Project Structure*

The ACSCloudService project is a Windows Azure cloud service project and the ACSMachineInfoWorker is the worker role that contains the implementation of the service. The movement of the service from regular WCF to a worker role cloud service should have minimal impact on the client because the web service Url remains the same.

Because the worker role does not have a default external (or input) endpoint, you need to create an external http endpoint for the worker role on port 80, so that all the http requests to the web service Url

421

are received by the web service. Figure 7-29 shows the configuration setting for the external endpoint on port 80.

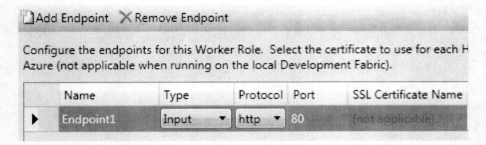

Figure 7-29. *External Endpoint on port 80*

The external endpoint configuration makes port 80 available to the web service for exposing external interface. The web service still needs to create a service on that port. Listing 7-15 shows the code for the Run() method in the worker role. The ACSMachineInfo web service is initialized on port 80 of the cloud service in this method.

Listing 7-15. *Worker Role Run method*

```
const string serviceNamespace = "proazure-1";
const string trustedTokenPolicyKey = "8O++r46Eo6e6VhGQaHSCfINhYMMCu14xsAectW2EFfk=";

const string acsHostName = "accesscontrol.windows.net";
const string trustedAudience = "http://localhost/acsexample";
const string requiredClaimType = "action";

public override void Run()
{

    WebHttpBinding binding = new WebHttpBinding
(WebHttpSecurityMode.None);

    Uri address = new Uri(trustedAudience);

    WebServiceHost host =
new WebServiceHost(typeof(ACSExample));
    host.AddServiceEndpoint(typeof(IACSExample),
binding, address);

    host.Authorization.ServiceAuthorizationManager =
new ACSAuthorizationManager(
        acsHostName,
        serviceNamespace,
        trustedAudience,
        Convert.FromBase64String(trustedTokenPolicyKey),
```

```
        requiredClaimType);

    try
    {
        host.Open();
        while (true)
        {
            Thread.Sleep(10000);
        }
    }
    finally
    {
        host.Close();

    }
}
```

The code for initializing the web service is tan exact replica of the code from the WCF service that we deployed earlier in the chapter. Observer the Url for the web service does not change and because external endpoint is available on port 80, the service will be available publicly for consumption, provided the client gets authenticated by ACS.

To test the cloud web service in development fabric, select ACSCloudService and press F5 to run the web service in debug mode. Figure 7-30 shows the ACSMachineInfo web service running as worker role in development fabric.

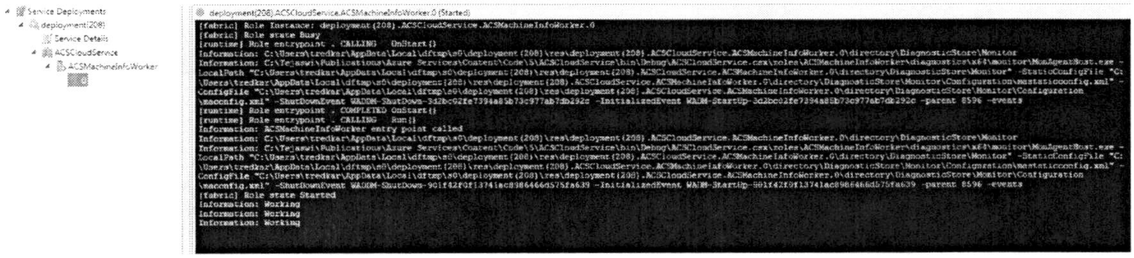

Figure 7-30. ACSMachineInfo Web Service as Worker Role

Next, to test the client access, you can either run the client that generates SWT or client that acquires SAML token from a local STS. Figure 7-31 shows the command line output from the client that generates SWT locally and then calls ACS for authentication before calling the web service.

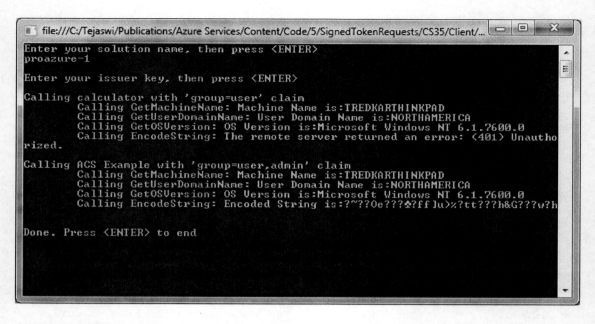

Figure 7-31. *Web Service Client calling cloud web service with ACS authentication*

Creating Your Own Certificates

In a claims-based identity model, X.509 certificates are used by all the participating parties: STS, ACS, and the relying party. X.509 certificates are used to encrypt and/or decrypt SAML tokens and also to validate claims sent from one party to another. Most of the examples in MSDN and training kits use a predefined set of certificates that can cause conflicts when used by multiple developers and testers in the same environment. The following are the steps you can use to create your own certificates so you don't have to rely on the prepackaged certificates in sample applications:

1. Start the Visual Studio command prompt as an administrator.

2. Run the following command to create a temporary certificate:

```
makecert -n "CN=ProAzure" -r -sky exchange -sv ProAzure.pvk ProAzure.cer
```

3. Run the following command to create a certificate that is digitally signed and authorized by ProAzure:

```
makecert -sk ProAzureSignedCA -sky exchange -iv ProAzure.pvk -n "CN=ProAzureSignedCA" -ic ProAzure.cer ProAzureSignedCA.cer -sr localmachine -ss My
```

4. Use MMC to Import the ProAzure.cer certificate into the Trusted Root Certificate Authorities folder of the local machine certificate store. You can start MMC from Start ▸ Run ▸ mmc.exe. Then, choose File ▸ Add/Remove Snap-In ▸ Certificates.

5. From MMC, import ProAzureSignedCA.cer into the certificates personal folder of the local machine certificate store.

6. Export the certificate to distribute it to the outside world, using the pvk2pfx.exe tool from the Visual Studio .NET\Tools\bin folder:

```
pvk2pfx.exe -pvk ProAzure.pvk -spc ProAzure.cer
```

7. If you're hosting your service in IIS and would like to give permissions to certificates to specific accounts, see the WinHttpCertCfg.exe certificate configuration tool at http://msdn.microsoft.com/en-us/library/aa384088(VS.85).aspx.

After the certificate is created, you can use it in any application that requires X.509 certificates. You can also share the same certificate across multiple applications.

The AppFabric ACS doesn't support WS-Trust and WS-Federation. As you saw from the examples, the protocol is REST-based and so can be easily used from multiple platforms. The core functionality of ACS is to map input claims to output claims by abstracting multiple input claims from multiple sources to a consistent set of output claims expected by the relying party. The relying party doesn't have knowledge of the input claim source; it trusts the output claims issued by ACS. The ACS management service API provides functions to create these mappings.

Summary

Microsoft is investing heavily in its products to support a claims-based identity model. The Windows Identity Foundation SDK, ADFS v2.0, WCF, and ACS are good evidence of the direction Microsoft is taking. In cloud applications, currently there is no unified programming model for managing authentication and authorization across multiple applications and platforms. Enterprises rely on identity federation services like ADFS, and consumer applications build custom identity providers within the service. ACS fills this gap by abstracting the claims-transformation logic in the cloud and presenting a unified view of claims issued by identity providers to the claims required by applications.

In this chapter, you learned how ACS achieves this through simple configurations of input and output claims. You also examined different scenarios that ACS supports. Through examples, you gained hands-on knowledge about implementing claims-based identity models using ACS. ACS is a core piece of the overall Azure Services Platform and is actively used in other Azure technologies like the AppFabric Service Bus. In the next chapter, you learn about the communication and messaging possibilities offered by the AppFabric Service Bus in the cloud.

Bibliography

Federated Identity Primer. (n.d.). Retrieved from sourceid.org: `www.sourceid.org/content/primer.cfm`.

Microsoft Corporation. (2009, 11 17). *Identity Developer Training Kit (PDC 2009)*. Retrieved from Microsoft Download Center: `www.microsoft.com/downloads/` `details.aspx?displaylang=en&FamilyID=c3e315fa-94e2-4028-99cb-904369f177c0`.

Microsoft Corporation. (n.d.). *Identity Management (Geneva Framework)*. Retrieved from MSDN: `http://msdn.microsoft.com/en-us/security/aa570351.aspx`.

Microsoft Corporation. (n.d.). *MSDN .NET Services Center*. Retrieved from MSDN: `http://msdn.microsoft.com/en-us/azure/netservices.aspx`.

Microsoft Corporation. (2009, 11 16). *Windows Identity Foundation*. Retrieved from Microsoft Download Center: `www.microsoft.com/downloads/details.aspx?familyid=EB9C345F-E830-40B8-A5FE-AE7A864C4D76&displaylang=en`.

Microsoft Corporation. (2009, 11 16). *Windows Identity Foundation SDK*. Retrieved from Microsoft Download Center: `www.microsoft.com/downloads/details.aspx?familyid=C148B2DF-C7AF-46BB-9162-2C9422208504&displaylang=en`.

Smith, J. (2009, November 14). *ACS SAML / ADFS v2 Sample*. Retrieved from Justin Smith's Blog: `http://blogs.msdn.com/justinjsmith/default.aspx`.

CHAPTER 8

■■■

AppFabric Service Bus

In the past decade, enterprises have invested heavily in upgrading their enterprise architecture by implementing several enterprise software patterns like Service Oriented Architecture and Enterprise Service Bus (ESB). These software patterns make application infrastructure loosely coupled and compatible across software boundaries. For example, Microsoft SharePoint server can integrate with Lotus Domino or EMC Documentum. You can also build custom business applications that can take advantage of these loosely coupled architectures. To make such integrations possible, Microsoft has defined four tenets[1] as guidance:

- Services have explicit boundaries.

- Services are autonomous and deployed, versioned, and managed independently.

- Services share schema and contracts.

- Service compatibility is achieved by appropriate policy configuration.

These tenets are by no means comprehensive, but they give a good high-level framework for service-oriented enterprise architectures.

The ESB pattern is designed to offer service-oriented brokered communications of enterprise objects across enterprise applications. The design and implementations of ESBs varies in different organizations because by definition, ESB is a pattern and not a product. For example, I consulted with an enterprise where the ESB had an FTP interface. You could configure and schedule the ESB on the kind of data the subscriber systems needed from a publisher system. The ESB then queried the publisher system and provided an FTP endpoint to the subscriber systems. The architecture worked like a charm because the contract at the data level was defined in a set of enterprise schema, and the data communication medium was FTP, a well-known public protocol.

Even though these architectures work well in an enterprise environment, they can't easily cross enterprise boundaries and aren't designed for Internet scale. As applications move into the cloud, they still need to decouple themselves to keep the architectural tenets of the enterprise intact and make applications seamlessly accessible not only in the cloud but also on-premises.

---

[1] John Evdemon. The Four Tenets of Service Orientation. Business Architectures and Standards, Microsoft Architecture Strategy Team, Thursday, May 19, 2005.

Microsoft's attempt to create an Internet-scale Service Bus is an Azure Platform Service called AppFabric Service Bus. AppFabric Service Bus runs in the cloud and seamlessly connects cloud, enterprise, and consumer applications. In this chapter, you learn details of the AppFabric Service Bus architecture. After reading this chapter, you should be able to use the AppFabric Service Bus in your own architectures.

■ **Note** During the Professional Developer's Conference (PDC) 2009, .NET Services was rebranded AppFabric. Because most of the content in this book was written much before PDC 2009, some references may refer to .NET Service Bus instead of AppFabric Service Bus. Conceptually, both products represent the same Service Bus service.

Enterprise Service Bus (ESB)

There is no generic architecture for an ESB because it's a pattern and can be built as add-on for already-existing Microsoft products like BizTalk Server, MSMQ, Windows Communications Foundation (WCF), and SQL Server. Every company that makes a product conforming to the ESB pattern has a different definition of ESB. I define the ESB pattern as follows: "ESB is an enterprise architecture pattern that defines the connectivity, contracts, and communication of business objects across enterprise applications."

The definition is depicted in Figure 8-1.

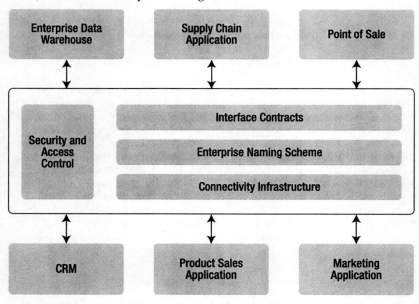

Figure 8-1. *Enterprise Service Bus pattern*

As in my definition, an ESB offers four core services.

Security and Access Control

The Security and Access Control service offers communication as well as message-level security for interacting with ESB endpoints. An ESB usually integrates with the enterprise identity providers but may have an integrated identity provider. All he applications have to pass through this layer before interacting with the ESB.

Connectivity Infrastructure

The connectivity infrastructure defines the mechanisms and endpoints of an ESB to communicate business objects across enterprise applications. These endpoints may be any public or private protocols conforming to enterprise standards. In enterprises, I have seen ESBs with a connectivity infrastructure based on protocols like FTP, HTTP, TCP-Sockets, SOAP, and even REST.

Enterprise Naming Scheme

To communicate business objects across enterprise applications, you need an enterprise standard for defining naming schemes for objects. For example, a Product object must have a single schema across the enterprise. The URI scheme for accessing these objects in an ESB should also be standardized.

ESB can define the URI scheme for accessing business objects. For example, the URI of a specific product object may be of the format `/MyEnterprise/MyProducts/T-Shirts["ProductId"]`. ESB can translate this schema and make it usable across any connectivity infrastructure. For example, in an HTTP-based interface, you can access the product using the URI `http://mysystem/MyEnterprise/MyProducts/T-Shirts["ProductId"]`, whereas in an FTP-based interface, you can access the serialized object in a file /MyEnterprise/MyProducts/T-Shirts/["ProductId"].xml. Enterprise schemes not only define a uniformed way of accessing business object but also offer simple business rules and filters within the scheme.

Interface Contracts

ESB acts a broker of business objects across business applications. One business application can access methods and objects of another business application in a loosely coupled manner. The ESB interface contracts define the standard contracts for invoking methods on the ESB as well as other business systems. For example, I have a marketing reporting application that needs access to daily sales data on a periodic basis, but sometimes I also want to know real-time sales figures by accessing real-time sales data on demand. ESB can define interface contracts that the source and destination systems can adhere to while making asynchronous and synchronous invocations.

Evolution of the Internet Service Bus (ISB)

ESB clearly has challenges in the cloud as well as in cross-organization scenarios. Current ESBs aren't designed to offer the scalability and availability required by cloud applications. In cross-organization scenarios, ESB may somehow integrate the connectivity infrastructure and interface contracts, but it faces significant challenges in integrating security and enterprise naming schemes. Porting enterprise schemes becomes difficult across enterprises, and most applications need to be rewritten to work with different enterprise schemes. To make the security service in ESB work across organizations, ESB needs to integrate with the security provider of another enterprise. ESBs aren't designed to work across security realms and thus usually aren't recommended to be used across enterprises. With the enterprise push toward cloud services, it's important to offer a Service Bus in the cloud that can be used by enterprises as well as consumer applications at an Internet scale.

Some years back, I designed an Internet Service Bus (ISB) specifically to collect data from energy devices in homes and commercial buildings. At that time, I called it Energy Bus, but essentially it was an ISB with some limitations. I deployed this ISB as part of an overall service in a data center. The service was designed for high scalability and availability with multiple clustered nodes at the infrastructure as well as database level. The business purpose of the service was to collect energy data from thousands of homes and commercial buildings and offer energy-management services to end users through utility companies. For example, you as a home owner could control your home devices like lighting, security, HVAC, and coffee maker over the Internet. At the same time, devices in the house could call the energy service in the cloud to send energy usage logs (kWh values) and alarms (fire alarm, burglar alarm, and so on). The entire architecture was build around the concept of an Internet Service Bus with Microsoft Message Queuing (MSMQ) as its backbone communications engine. Figure 8-2 illustrates the high-level architecture of the ISB.

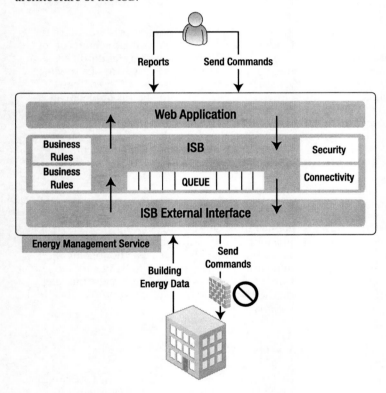

Figure 8-2. Energy management service ISB

As shown in Figure 8-2, end users could generate reports on their energy data and also get and set values of energy-consuming devices in buildings and apartments. The ISB provided the connectivity and interfaces between the devices in the buildings and cloud. Two of the biggest challenges I faced in designing the service were as follows:

- *Connectivity:* Because of the nature of the service, one of its core functions was providing real-time connectivity between devices and the service. Most of the time, devices were behind firewalls or network address translation (NAT) routers. Even though communication from the device to the service was seamless, communication from the service to the device was always challenging. Opening firewall ports to the devices wasn't an option in many cases due to customers' security policies. So, ISB communication couldn't penetrate the firewall, and communications failed. As a workaround, the developers had to tunnel communications through only the ports that were allowed through the firewall, or build a proxy server on the customer site that polled the cloud service on a periodic basis to receive commands from ISB.

- *User profiles:* Customers wanted their existing user profile stores to synchronize with the cloud securely rather than creating all the user profiles from scratch. As a workaround, I ended up building a profile import and synchronization server that periodically synchronized the user profiles from the customer's Active Directory with the service database in the cloud. Because the service was deployed in the cloud and was available for multiple customers, it couldn't directly integrate with any identity providers.

If Microsoft's AppFabric Service Bus had been available at the time, both these challenges would have been non-existent because the Service Bus is designed to address these exact challenges. The AppFabric Service Bus provides access control, naming, service registry, messaging, and connectivity services at Internet scale. It enables bidirectional communications between on-premises and cloud application through relay service capabilities. The relay service runs in the cloud, and interested parties register themselves with it to communicate with each other. The Service Bus determines the best connectivity method by either using outbound bidirectional sockets connections from the service to the Service Bus when a firewall is present, or establishing a direct connection between the client and the service when there is no firewall.

Some of the applications you use today may already support bidirectional communication through NAT traversal. Internet client applications like Windows Live Messenger, Kazaa, BitTorrent, Xbox Live, some Universal Plug and Play clients (UPnP), and so on can traverse through firewalls using Relay Service.

Relay Service

A *relay service* is a central service running in the cloud that provides a rendezvous connection point between the client and the service. In networking terms, the *rendezvous address* is a common meeting point for two connections. Figure 6-3 shows typical relay service communications between client and service.

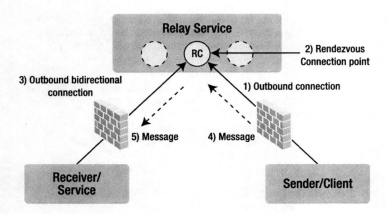

Figure 8-3. *Relay service*

As shown in Figure 6-3, the relay service runs in the cloud and offers connection endpoints to the message client and service. A client opens an outbound connection to the relay service. The service opens a bidirectional outbound connection to the relay service and receives a rendezvous connection endpoint that is shared with the service. The outbound bidirectional connection from the service makes it possible for the service to receive messages on an outbound connection without opening inbound ports in the firewall or NAT routers. The client sends a message to the relay service that is routed by the rendezvous connection point to the service over the outbound connection. Thus, the relay service makes it possible for clients and services to communicate through firewalls.

With the advancements in networking APIs in frameworks like the .NET Framework, it isn't difficult to build a relay service and bidirectional sockets in your applications. The real challenge is to build a relay service at Internet scale for applications around the world. In this chapter, you see how the AppFabric Service Bus provides an Internet scale Service Bus with relay capabilities.

Introduction to the AppFabric Service Bus

Microsoft's AppFabric Service Bus is an Internet-scale Service Bus that offers scalable and highly available connection points for application communication. The AppFabric Service Bus is designed to provide connectivity, queuing, and routing capabilities not only for the cloud applications but also for on-premises applications. It also integrates with the Access Control Service (ACS) to provide secure relay and communications. Figure 8-4 illustrates the architecture of the AppFabric Service Bus.

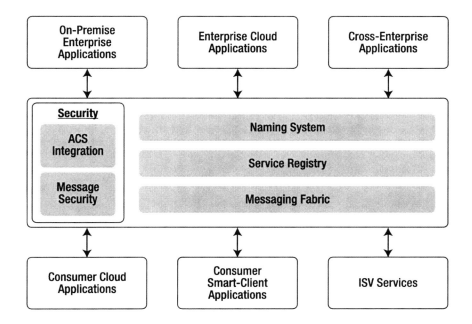

Figure 8-4. *AppFabric Service Bus architecture*

As shown in Figure 8-4, the AppFabric Service Bus consists of four main services that can be used by different kinds of on-premises as well as cloud services:

- Security
- Naming service
- Service registry
- Messaging fabric

Security

As you read in Chapter 1, one of the biggest concerns of enterprises in moving applications to the cloud is security. At Internet scale, where millions of frauds and hacks occur on a daily basis, secure communication across applications is absolutely necessary for enterprises. An on-premises environment is governed and controlled by corporate policies, and prevention is preferred to cure. In the cloud, systems, applications, and data are exposed and prone to not only external but also internal threats. To overcome this barrier, the AppFabric Service Bus offers two main options for securing the transport of messages from clients to services:

- Access Control Service (ACS) integration
- End-to-end security

ACS Integration (Relay Authentication)

Microsoft has integrated the AppFabric Service Bus with ACS to provide relay authentication and authorization. The message sender and message receiver have to pass security checks before connecting to the AppFabric Service Bus. Services (or receivers) must be authenticated either by ACS or an identity provider trusted by ACS before establishing a connection to the AppFabric Service Bus. By default, the clients (or senders) require relay authentication but can be optionally exempted from authentication by services. The client authentication type may be different than the service authentication type. For example, a client can authenticate using a shared secret, whereas a service can authenticate using a SAML token. Three types of authentication are currently available with ACS: shared secret, SAML token, and simple web tokens (SWTs). Figure 8-5 illustrates the Service Bus integration with ACS.

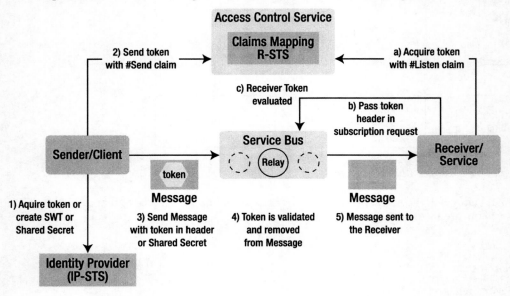

Figure 8-5. *AppFabric Service Bus and ACS integration*

As shown in Figure 8-5, the client and service both have must be authenticated with ACS before connecting to the Service Bus. The authentication for client and service takes place separately and isn't dependent on the other. The client authentication process is as follows:

1. The client acquires a SAML token from a SAML token provider or creates an SWT token or uses a shared secret to authenticate with Service Bus.

2. The client sends an authentication request to ACS and acquires a #Send claim from ACS. After it is authenticated, the client receives a token containing the #Send claim. AppFabric Service Bus is preconfigured to validate only the #Send claim from a client application.

⬛ **Note** For more information about ACS, please refer to Chapter 7.

3. The token with the #Send claim is embedded into the header of the message sent to the Service Bus relay service.

4. The relay service validates the token and removes it from the message header. Because AppFabric Service Bus is the relying party in this scenario, as seen in the previous chapter, ACS encrypts the token with a public key, and Service Bus decrypts the token with a private key. During solution provisioning, trust between ACS solution and Service Bus is already established by the AppFabric portal.

5. The relay service sends the message (without the token) to the service.

The service also has to authenticate itself with ACS before connecting to the AppFabric Service Bus. The service authentication process is as follows:

1. The service sends an authentication request to ACS and acquires the #Listen claim from ACS. Similar to the client, the service can authenticate with any identity provider trusted by ACS.

2. The token with the #Listen claim is embedded in the subscription request to the AppFabric Service Bus relay service.

3. The relay service validates the token and lets the service open a bidirectional outbound connection to the relay service.

Optionally, you can turn off the client authentication by specifying it in the service binding configuration as shown in Listing 8-1.

Listing 8.1. Turning Off Client Authentication

```
<binding name="default">
    <security relayClientAuthenticationType="None" />
</binding>
```

The RelayClientAuthenticationType.None value specifies that clients of the service aren't required to present any token issued by the ACS. Usually, you set the RelayClientAuthenticationType.None value if you want the service to authenticate and authorize the clients and the AppFabric Service Bus authentication is adding unnecessary overhead to the service without adding any value. The default value for the relayAuthenticationType attribute is RelayAccessToken.

TransportClientEndpointBehavior is a class in the Microsoft.ServiceBus namespace that describes the WCF behavior of a particular endpoint registered with the Service Bus. The CredentialType property of the TransportClientEndpointBehavior class specifies the type of authentication you use for the endpoint. AppFabric Service Bus API offers TransportClientCredentialType enumeration with four different values for relay authentication, as shown in Table 8-1.

Table 8-1. *TransportClientCredentialType Values*

TransportClientCredentialType	Description
Saml	Suggests that the client is authenticated using a Security Assertions Markup language (SAML) tokens. The SAML token is sent over the SSL protocol, and you're required to create your own SSL credential server.
SharedSecret	Refers to the issuer and issuer key created in ACS from the ACS management portal. The Service Bus has a dedicated issuer name and issuer key created by default when you create a service namespace in ACS.
SimpleWebToken	Suggests that the client is authenticated using an SWT token that is self-issued by the client and registered with ACS.
Unauthenticated	Doesn't require clients to authenticate to connect to the Service Bus. Clients must set this option explicitly in code if it's exempted from authentication by the service. When this option is used, the AppFabric Service Bus sends the message without acquiring a token from ACS.

The services and clients can choose authenticate using any of the configured types. In the examples later in the chapter, I show you how to implement these options in your code.

As you read in the previous chapter on ACS, ACS creates dedicated Service Bus endpoints in your service namespace. Figure 8-6 shows the Service Bus section from the service namespace page of your account.

Service Namespace: proazure-1

Manage

Status:	Active
Delete:	Delete Service Namespace
Management Key Name:	owner
Current Management Key:	wJBJaobUmarWn6kqv7QpaaRh3ttNVr3w1OjiotVEOL4=
Previous Management Key:	wJBJaobUmarWn6kqv7QpaaRh3ttNVr3w1OjiotVEOL4=

Generate New Key

Service Bus

Registry URL:	https://proazure-1.servicebus.windows.net/
STS Endpoint:	https://proazure-1-sb.accesscontrol.windows.net/WRAPv0.8
Management Endpoint:	https://proazure-1-sb.accesscontrol.windows.net/mgmt/
Management STS Endpoint:	https://proazure-1-sb-mgmt.accesscontrol.windows.net/WRAPv0.8
Default Issuer Name:	owner
Default Issuer Key:	wJBJaobUmarWn6kqv7QpaaRh3ttNVr3w1OjiotVEOL4=

Access Control Service

STS Endpoint:	https://proazure-1.accesscontrol.windows.net/WRAPv0.8
Management Endpoint:	https://proazure-1.accesscontrol.windows.net/mgmt/
Management STS Endpoint:	https://proazure-1-mgmt.accesscontrol.windows.net/WRAPv0.8

Information

Project ID:	4c73dbf1bb8346c4a535f022423ecc8b
Created On:	Wed, 18 Nov 2009 17:18:23 GMT
Region:	United States (South/Central)

Figure 8-6. *Service Bus solution in ACS*

You can map incoming and outgoing claims in ACS to authenticate your clients and/or services. Thus, ACS integration provides The AppFabric Service Bus with the ability to authenticate with any identity provider and participate in a claims-based identity model for authorization.

Message Security

Relay authentication is geared toward authenticating clients and services to communicate with the AppFabric Service Bus. But a true enterprise solution is incomplete without security of the message the travels between the communicating parties. Message security refers to the security of the message that travels from the source through the AppFabric Service Bus to the destination. The AppFabric Service Bus offers four options for securing messages between the clients and services. The enumeration Microsoft.ServiceBus.EndToEndSecurityMode in the AppFabric Service Bus API defines four security modes, as shown in Table 8-2.

Table 8-2. *Message Security Values*

Message Security Type	Description
None	Security for the message is disabled. The message is sent as-is from the client to the service.
Transport	The message is sent through a secure channel (such as HTTPS) to and from the relay service. The movement of the message within the AppFabric Service Bus isn't secure. The message doesn't contain any client credentials. This is the recommended and the default mode for most applications where messages don't contain sensitive information.
Message	In this security type, you can encrypt the body of the message using an X.509 certificate provided by your service. Because the message is encrypted, the movement of the message within the .NET Service Bus is secure. The message may contain client credentials, and the service must authenticate the client credentials if present in the message. Use this option only if you need client credentials in your service for authorization purposes.
TransportWithMessageCredentials	This security type is a combination of the Transport and Message security types. The transport between the relay service and applications is secured using a secure channel, and the message is moved from the client all the way to the service in encrypted format. The message is secure as it travels through the AppFabric Service Bus. The message may also contain client credentials. This security type is recommended only when sending sensitive messages over the Internet.

▦ **Note** Message security is independent of relay security. Relay security is used to connect with the AppFabric Service Bus, whereas message security refers to the security of the message that traverses through the AppFabric Service Bus.

Naming Service

The Naming service allows you to assign DNS-capable names to your service, which makes the service easily resolvable over the Internet. The Internet is based on the Domain Name System (DNS) where every resource on the Internet can be resolved using names. For example, in the URL www.microsoft.com, microsoft.com is the registered domain name for Microsoft's web site. HTTP is the protocol used for accessing the web site. Similarly, http://msdn.microsoft.com is the registered domain name for MSDN site. The msdn part of the URL is called a subdomain of microsoft.com, and microsoft.com itself is called a root domain. DNS follows a hierarchical structure where one root domain can consist of many subdomains to form a tree structure. For example, `social.msdn.microsoft.com` adds one more level (social) under msdn to the `microsoft.com` domain hierarchy.

The Internet DNS system was designed for reference to static resources like web pages and web sites where the application may change but the domain name remains the same. In the cloud services world, there can be multiple unique cloud services and subservices that can register and unregister themselves from the DNS depending on the cloud service requirements. Companies can use the AppFabric Service Bus on-premises as well as off-premises. In case of on-premises services, companies can register unique domain names for services; but for off-premises services, companies must invest in infrastructure and internal naming schemes for identifying these services uniquely on the Internet.

The AppFabric Service Bus offers a DNS-compatible naming system for assigning unique Internet URIs to cloud as well as on-premises services. The AppFabric Service Bus defines a root domain name that can be resolved through the Internet DNS, but offers a service namespace-based naming hierarchy below the root. For example, in the Service Bus naming system, `servicebus.windows.net` is the root domain of the Service Bus. If you have ten service namespaces you want to register with the Service Bus, all ten service namespaces automatically receive URIs for cloud as well as on-premises services. If you name your namespaces solution1, solution2, …, solution10, then each solution has its own URI name:

> solution1.servicebus.windows.net
>
> solution2.servicebus.windows.net
>
> ….
>
> solution10.servicebus.windows.net

Figure 8-7 shows an example hierarchical naming tree structure in the AppFabric Service Bus.

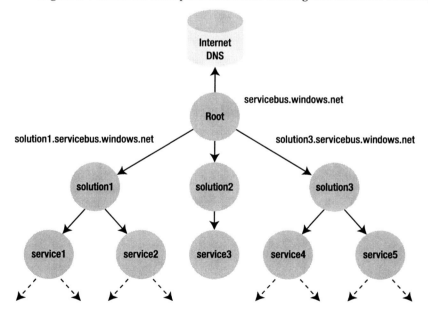

Figure 8-7. Hierarchical naming structure

You, the service namespace owner, have complete control over the naming hierarchy under the Service Bus root node. The naming scheme for the URI formation is

```
[scheme]://[solution-name].servicebus.windows.net/[name]/[name]/...
```

where [scheme] is the protocol for accessing the service. AppFabric Service Bus supports two URI schemes: http and sb. http is used for all HTTP-based communications between clients and services, whereas sb is used for all TCP-based communications between clients and services. [solution-name] is the unique solution name across the entire AppFabric Service Bus namespace. Because this name is the subdomain under the AppFabric Service Bus root domain, this needs to be unique across the entire AppFabric Service Bus namespace. You can choose any solution name while creating the account. For example, the solution I use in this chapter is the ProAzure solution. The name ProAzure is unique across the entire AppFabric Service Bus namespace. You can reference the ProAzure namespace in AppFabric Service Bus as `http://proazure.servicebus.windows.net` or `sb://proazure.servicebus.windows.net`.

[name] is the user-defined virtual name for a service or a hierarchical structure pointing to a service. You can create any hierarchical structure using the user-defined namespace. For example, if you're offering an energy management service in different cities around the world, and you have deployed different instances of you service, you can assign unique names to these service instances based on the names of the cities as follows:

```
http://proazure.servicebus.windows.net/sanfrancisco/energy
```

```
http://proazure.servicebus.windows.net/newyork/energy
```

```
http://proazure.servicebus.windows.net/london/energy
```

```
http://proazure.servicebus.windows.net/singapore/energy
```

```
http://proazure.servicebus.windows.net/mumbai/energy
```

You can also further extend the hierarchy by offering subservices like

```
http://proazure.servicebus.windows.net/sanfrancisco/energy/reports
```

```
http://proazure.servicebus.windows.net/sanfrancisco/energy/realtime
```

```
http://proazure.servicebus.windows.net/sanfrancisco/energy/logs
```

All these URIs point to endpoints of services hosted in these cities. The physical location of these URIs is transparent not only to applications but also to each other. The http://proazure.servicebus.windows.net/sanfrancisco/energy/reports service may be hosted in a totally separate location from the `http://proazure.servicebus.windows.net/sanfrancisco/energy/realtime` service. The AppFabric Service Bus internally resolves the actual location of the service endpoints at runtime. Thus, the AppFabric Service Bus allows you to create an infinitely deep hierarchical naming structure referencing endpoints of cloud as well as on-premises services. It also abstracts the DNS registration and resolution for your services and applications calling these services.

Service Registry

The AppFabric Service Bus provides a registration and discovery service for service endpoints called the service registry. The service endpoints can be in the cloud or on-premises. The service registry offers an Atom feed to your solution. You can register a service endpoint into the Atom Feed using either the Atom Publishing Protocol (APP)[2] or WS-Transfer[3] references. APP and WS-Transfer both support publishing, listing, and removing the service endpoints. The client application can then discover your service endpoint references by simply navigating Atom 1.0 feed of your solution. The Atom 1.0 feed exposes a tree-like structure you can manually or programmatically navigate to get to the leaf node of the service endpoint. You can also programmatically register a service endpoint for public discovery by setting the DiscoveryMode property of the Microsoft.ServiceBus.ServiceRegistrySettings object to Public and associating it with the service endpoint behavior as shown in Listing 8-2. In this approach, the AppFabric Service Bus relay service automatically registers the service endpoint for you in the service registry.

Listing 8-2. Associating ServiceRegistrySettings

```
class Program
{
    static void Main(string[] args)
    {

        ServiceHost host = new ServiceHost(typeof(EnergyManagementService));
        ServiceRegistrySettings settings = new ServiceRegistrySettings();
        settings.DiscoveryMode = DiscoveryType.Public;
        foreach(ServiceEndpoint s in host.Description.Endpoints)
            s.Behaviors.Add(settings);
        host.Open();
        Console.WriteLine("Press [Enter] to exit");
        Console.ReadLine();
        host.Close();
    }
}
```

The default setting for the public discovery is set to private, so if you don't set the discovery type to public, your service won't be discoverable publicly. After you register the service endpoint, you can view the Atom feed of your Service Bus registry by navigating to the AppFabric Developer portal subscriptions page, and clicking the Service Bus Registry link as shown in Figure 8-8.

[2] Atom Publishing Protocol Reference: www.ietf.org/rfc/rfc5023.txt.

[3] WS-Transfer Specification: www.w3.org/Submission/WS-Transfer/.

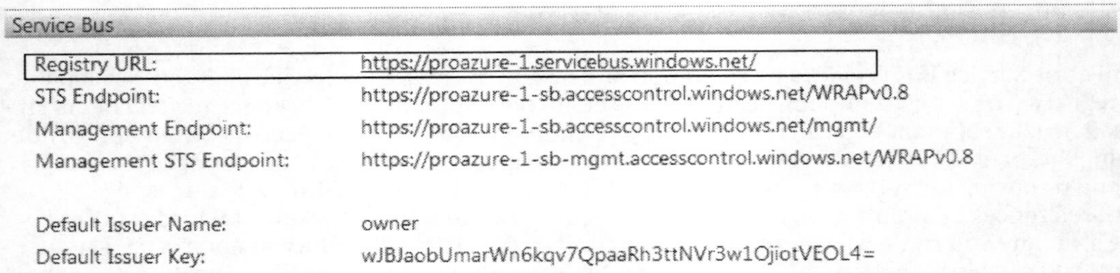

Service Bus	
Registry URL:	https://proazure-1.servicebus.windows.net/
STS Endpoint:	https://proazure-1-sb.accesscontrol.windows.net/WRAPv0.8
Management Endpoint:	https://proazure-1-sb.accesscontrol.windows.net/mgmt/
Management STS Endpoint:	https://proazure-1-sb-mgmt.accesscontrol.windows.net/WRAPv0.8
Default Issuer Name:	owner
Default Issuer Key:	wJBJaobUmarWn6kqv7QpaaRh3ttNVr3w1OjiotVEOL4=

Figure 8-8. Service Bus registry link

Figure 8-9 shows the Atom feed for the publicly listed services in the ProAzure solution.

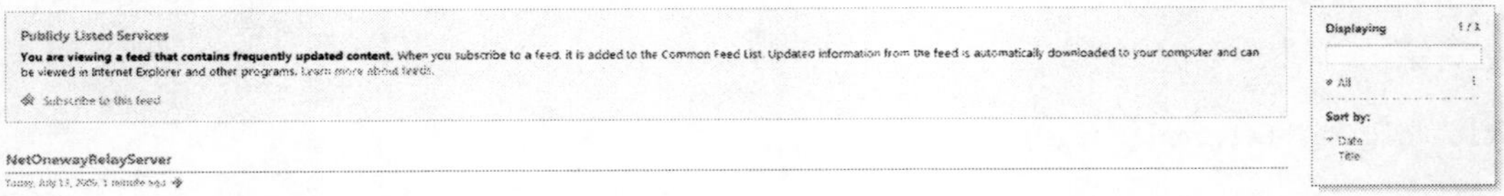

Figure 8-9. Service Bus registry for the ProAzure solution

The Service Bus registry shows only one registered service. I revisit the Service Bus Registry later in the examples in this chapter.

Messaging Fabric

The messaging fabric enables the relaying and communication of messages between clients and services. The messaging fabric makes it possible to expose your service endpoints into the cloud for on-premises as well as cloud deployed services. The messaging fabric also integrates with ACS to provide message level security.

The relay service is the core component of the AppFabric Service Bus messaging fabric. The relay service makes it possible for the client and services to communicate behind firewalls and NAT routers. As the name suggests, the relay service plays the role of relaying messages from clients to the services by assuming the responsibility of receiving the messages from the clients and delivering it to the services. The services can be running in the cloud or on-premises. As long as the endpoints of the services are registered in the service registry of the AppFabric Service Bus and are reachable, the relay service forwards the message. In simple terms, the relay service is like a postman who delivers the message from the client to the service. As long as the services address is valid and in the USPS registry, the postman delivers the mail. The only difference is that the postman is an asynchronous communication whereas the relay service defines a synchronous communication. This means the relay service requires the server to be available in most of the cases when the client sends a message.

The relay service supports the following types of communications between the clients and the services:

442

- One-way communications
- Publish/Subscribe messaging
- Peer-to-peer communications
- Multicast messaging
- Direct connections between clients and services

Figure 8-10 illustrates the communication process that takes place between the client, the service, and the AppFabric Service Bus relay service.

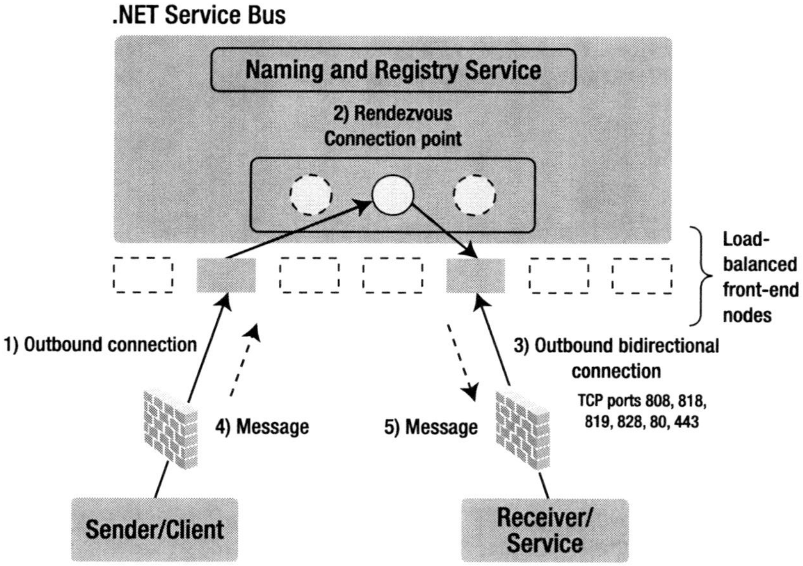

Figure 8-10. AppFabric Service Bus relay service

As shown in Figure 8-10, the service opens an outbound connection with a bidirectional socket to the AppFabric Service Bus relay service. The service registry registers the listener's endpoint in its naming tree for client applications to resolve. Most the AppFabric Service Bus listener bindings require the following TCP ports opened on firewall or the NAT router for outbound communication: 808, 818, 819, 828, 80, and 443.[4]

---

[4] Port information available in the AppFabric SDK: http://msdn.microsoft.com/en-us/library/dd582710.aspx.

Note that you don't need to open any inbound ports in your firewall or NAT router for the end-to-end communication to work when using the AppFabric Service Bus. Therefore, the listener application can be running behind a firewall, NAT router, and even with a dynamic IP address. The client application initiates an outbound connection to the relay service with the appropriate service address that can be resolved from the service registry. The AppFabric Service has a load-balanced array of nodes that provide the necessary scalability to the client and service communications. When the client sends a message to the service, the message is relayed by the relay service to the appropriate node that is holding reference to the listener's endpoint. Finally, the relay service sends the message to the service over the listener's outbound bidirectional socket.

The AppFabric Service Bus URI naming scheme restricts listeners from registering more than one listener on a URI scope. For example, if you have a service with the URI /energy/california, you can't register any listener with a URI suffix of /energy/California—/energy/california/sanfrancisco, /energy/california/sanramon, and so on. You can register a service with the same URI root address, such as /energy/sanfrancisco or /energy/sanjose. The AppFabric Service Bus uses the longest-prefix match algorithm to relay messages to the services. The longest URI under URI scope is evaluated and used to relay the message. So, in your service, you can process the entire URI suffix directory for query processing or filtering.

AppFabric Service Bus Bindings

The AppFabric Service Bus SDK comes with an API for programming AppFabric Service Bus applications. The namespace for AppFabric Service Bus classes is Microsoft.ServiceBus. The AppFabric Service Bus supports bindings similar to Windows Communications Foundation (WCF) bindings. Microsoft architected the AppFabric Service Bus with the vision of supporting the existing WCF programming model so that WCF developers can design and develop services for AppFabric Service Bus with their existing skill sets. The fundamental difference between AppFabric Service Bus bindings and WCF bindings is at the transport level, which is completely opaque to the programming model. The AppFabric Service Bus API provides binding classes that can be used in your WCF applications for binding to the AppFabric Service Bus relay service.

In traditional WCF applications, the service runs with specified bindings on local or remote servers, and client applications connect to the services directly. In traditional WCF, the notion of a relay service doesn't exist. Most of the standard WCF bindings have a direct match in the AppFabric Service Bus bindings. Table 8-3 lists the WCF bindings and the AppFabric Service Bus bindings side by side.

Table 8-3. *WCF and AppFabric Service Bus Bindings*

WCF Binding	AppFabric Service Bus Relay Binding	Description
BasicHttpBinding	BasicHttpRelayBinding	Both bindings use simple HTTP transport. BasicHttpRelayBinding uses the HTTP transport channel to the relay service.
WebHttpBinding	WebHttpRelayBinding	Both bindings support HTTP, XML, and raw binary encodings like base64. Popularly used in REST-style interfaces.

WCF Binding	AppFabric Service Bus Relay Binding	Description
WS2007HttpBinding	WS2007HttpRelayBinding	Both bindings support the Organization for the Advancement of Structured Information Standards (OASIS) standard versions of ReliableSession and Security. WS2007HttpRelayBinding doesn't support atomic TransactionFlow protocols because the MSDTC isn't available between your service and the AppFabric Service Bus.
WSHttpContextBinding	WSHttpRelayContext Binding	Both bindings support context-enabled binding. WSHttpRelayContextBinding enables context-enabled binding between your service and the relay service. You can use SOAP headers for exchanging context.
NetTcpBinding	NetTcpRelayBinding	These bindings are the TCP counterpart of the WSHttp bindings you saw earlier. The NetTcpRelayBinding uses binary message encoding and TCP for message delivery between your service and the relay service.
NetTcpContextBinding	NetTcpRelayContext Binding	NetTcpRelayContextBinding binding uses a context-enabled binding between your service and the relay service. You can use SOAP headers to exchange context.
N/A	NetOnewayRelayBinding	The NetOnewayRelayBinding is available only in the AppFabric Service Bus and doesn't have any corresponding binding in WCF. This binding supports only one-way messages between your service and the relay service.
N/A	NetEventRelayBinding	The NetOnewayRelayBinding is available only in the AppFabric Service Bus and doesn't have any corresponding binding in WCF. The NetEventRelayBinding enables one-way multicast eventing between multiple publishers and subscribers. This binding is used in Internet-scale publish-subscribe scenarios.

The AppFabric Service Bus Relay bindings offer you a complete spectrum of choices when you're selecting a high-performance binding like the NetTcpRelayBinding or a more interoperable and flexible binding like the WSHttpRelayBinding. All the bindings depend on the relay service to decide the message communication path between the clients and the services.

Message Buffer

The AppFabric Service Bus bindings for the WCF-style communications are designed for synchronous communications between the sender and the receiver. This means the receiver must be running to receive the message sent by the sender; otherwise, the message will get lost. The relay service doesn't contain a message store for storing and forwarding messages sent by senders to receivers. At Internet scale, the existence of the senders and receivers 100% of the time is an unrealistic expectation because senders and receivers depend on external and internal dependencies like server availability, on-premises network resources, network availability, bandwidth, and so on, that pose a significant availability risk for synchronous communications.

The AppFabric Service Bus offers a message buffer service for storing messages in a temporary cache for asynchronous communication between clients and servers. The AppFabric Service Bus buffers expose the REST API for applications to create a message buffer, send messages to the message buffer, and retrieve messages from the message buffer. The messages stored in a message buffer on the server don't survive server reboots. The message buffers themselves are replicated across multiple servers to provide redundancy, but messages stored in message buffer are stored in the server memory and are lost when the server reboots or crashes. When you design your application to use a message buffer, you have to design redundancy into the application. If you need redundancy for your messages in the server, you should consider using either Windows Azure Queue storage or SQL Azure. The message buffer also uses ACS authentication to authenticate client applications.

Programming with the AppFabric Service Bus

This section dives into programming applications with the AppFabric Service Bus. The AppFabric Service Bus API provides WCF-like bindings for senders to send messages to receivers via the relay service. The job of the relay service is to receive messages from the sender(s) and relay those messages to the appropriate receiver(s). The AppFabric Service Bus bindings you saw in the previous sections consist of all the communication logic to communicate with the relay service. From a programmer's perspective, you must understand the limitations of and differences between WCF bindings and AppFabric Service Bus bindings in order to program AppFabric Service Bus applications. The WCF-like programming model reduces the barriers to entry for .NET developers and also enables easy porting of existing WCF applications to the AppFabric Service Bus.

The steps to create an AppFabric Service Bus application are as follows:

1. Create an AppFabric solution at `https://netservices.azure.com/`.

2. Design AppFabric contracts between the servers and the clients.

3. Implement the service contracts.

4. Design a bindings plan between the servers and clients for complex services using multiple bindings. This plan lists the AppFabric Service Bus bindings used for every message communication.

5. Create a security plan for relay- and message-level security between the clients and the servers. Some of the popularly used security scenarios include the following:

    - X.509 certificates for message security

    - ACS integration with a third-party identity provider (Windows Identity Foundation, ADFS v2.0, LiveID, and so on)

    - ACS integration with a client generated SWT token

    - ACS integration with a shared issuer key

    - Custom message security

6. Design endpoints for the service.

7. Design service hosting. This design includes whether the service will be hosted on-premises or in the cloud.

8. Design the scalability and availability for the service.

9. Design client applications for the service contract.

The relay bindings are the core concepts for programming AppFabric Service Bus applications. This section covers relay bindings, queues, and routers. For the purpose of demonstration, I use a simple energy-management service that puts the AppFabric Service Bus's capabilities in a business context.

ProAzure Energy Service Example

ProAzure Energy is a sample service I use in most of the demonstrations in this chapter. The ProAzure Energy service offers utility companies energy-related data from consumer and commercial buildings. For the purpose of this demo, assume that the ProAzure Energy service offers the following three services to the utility companies:

- *Energy meter monitoring:* A control gateway device monitors the energy meters in buildings and sends energy meter values to the ProAzure Energy head-end software periodically. The utility companies can then access these values through a subscription service.

■ **Note** Assume the head-end software is either in the cloud or on-premises at the ProAzure Energy company site. It definitely isn't on the customer's site where the actual device monitoring takes place. Also assume there is one gateway per building that can monitor different types of energy devices.

- *Lighting monitoring and control:* A control gateway device in buildings monitors the light switches using a control network protocol. The gateway device accepts ON/OFF commands from the ProAzure head-end software to turn the lights on and off, respectively. The gateway device also send real-time light-switch values to the head-end software when an ON or OFF switch event takes place on the switch either manually or programmatically.

■ **Note** Assume that the control gateway device is control-network-protocol agnostic. That means it supports all control network protocols over power lines to communicate with the energy devices. The gateway has Internet connectivity on one side and control network connectivity on another.

- *Heating Ventilation Air Conditioning (HVAC) monitoring and control:* A control gateway device in buildings monitors the HVAC devices using a control network protocol. The gateway device accepts the following HVAC commands:

  - *SETPOINT:* Changes the set point of the HVAC to the specified value in degrees Fahrenheit (°F)

  - *HEAT:* Sets the HVAC value to heating mode

  - *COOL:* Sets the HVAC value to the cooling mode

  - *OFF:* Sets the HVAC value to the OFF mode

    The control gateway device also sends the set-point value, temperature, and heat/cool HVAC value to the ProAzure head-end software when it changes locally or on a periodic basic.

Figure 8-11 illustrates the high-level architecture of the ProAzure Energy service.

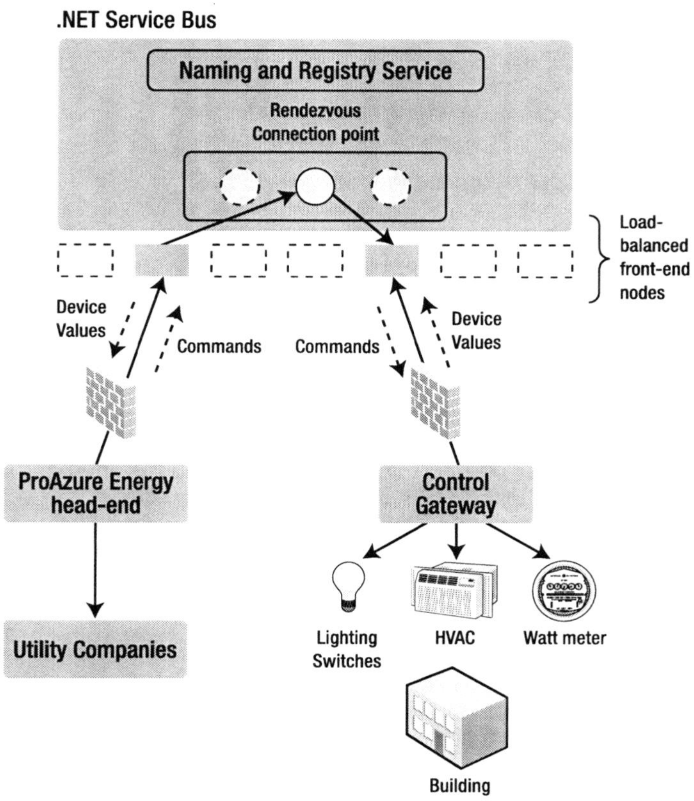

.NET Service Bus

Figure 8-11. *ProAzure Energy service architecture*

Some of the important characteristics of the ProAzure Energy Service are as follows:

- The service monitors thousands of control gateways, which in turn manage energy devices in buildings.

- The control gateways communicate with the AppFabric Service Bus relay service to send and receive messages.

- The control gateways are clients of the head-end server as well as servers to receive commands from the head-end server.

- The control gateways may be behind firewalls.

- The ProAzure head-end server can be hosted either in the cloud in Windows Azure or on-premises at the ProAzure Energy service data center.

- The ProAzure Energy service head-send server uses the AppFabric Service Bus relay service to send and receive messages.

In addition to the device commands, the control gateway also supports the following commands for its own configuration and monitoring:

- *ONLINE:* Periodically, the control gateway sends an online message to let the head-end know of its continued availability.

- *UPLOAD_SOFTWARE:* This command is used to upload the software on the control gateway.

In the following sections, you learn how to leverage different AppFabric Service Bus bindings, queues, and routers to implement the ProAzure Energy service.

NetOnewayRelayBinding

NetOnewayRelayBinding supports one-way messages from client to the server. The method signatures for one-way methods in the service contract must not return any values. One-way methods are optimized for one-way TCP communications between the senders to the relay service and then to the receivers. The default size of the message is set to 65,536 bytes. The receiver using the NetOnewayRelayBinding opens a bidirectional TCP connection on outbound TCP port 828 for an SSL connection and TCP port 808 for a non-SSL connection. If the TCP outbound ports are unavailable due to environmental policies or port conflicts, you can configure the AppFabric Service Bus to use the HTTP protocol instead. The HTTP protocol polls the relay service through outbound ports 443 for SSL and 80 for non-SSL communications.

Figure 8-12 illustrates the workings of NetOnewayRelayBinding.

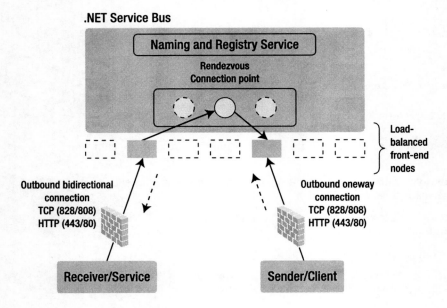

Figure 8-12. *NetOnewayRelayBinding*

For the purpose of demonstrating NetOnewayRelayBinding, in this section you design part of the ProAzure Energy sample service. Based on the requirements discussed in the previous section, you use the following communications from the control gateway to the head-end server to use the NetOnewayRelayBinding:

- Sending energy meter value (kWh) to the head-end server periodically

- Sending light switch value (ON/OFF) to the head-end server when the state of the switch changes

- Sending the HVAC set-point value to the head-end server when the set point changes

- Sending the HVAC mode value (OFF/COOL/HEAT) to the head-end server when the HVAC mode changes

The service project for this example is NetOnewayRelayServer, and the client project is NetOnewayRelayClient.

AppFabric Contract

The service contract represents the interface contract between the client and the server. The contract abstracts the interface of the server from its implementation. For the four communication requirements defined in the previous section, you design four methods in a service contract interface named IOnewayEnergyServiceOperations, as shown in Listing 8-3.

Listing 8-3. *Service Contract IOnewayEnergyServiceOperations*

```
[ServiceContract(Name = "IOnewayEnergyServiceOperations.",
Namespace = "http://proazure/ServiceBus/energyservice/headend")]
    public interface IOnewayEnergyServiceOperations
    {
        [OperationContract(IsOneWay=true)]
        void SendKwhValue(string gatewayId, string meterId,
double kwhValue, DateTime utcTime);
        [OperationContract(IsOneWay = true)]
        void SendLightingValue(string gatewayId, string switchId,
int lightingValue, DateTime utcTime);
        [OperationContract(IsOneWay = true)]
        void SendHVACSetPoint(string gatewayId, string hvacId,
int setPointValue, DateTime utcTime);
        [OperationContract(IsOneWay = true)]
        void SendHVACMode(string gatewayId, string hvacId,
int mode, DateTime utcTime);
    }

    public interface IOnewayEnergyServiceChannel : IOnewayEnergyServiceOperations,
IClientChannel { }
```

The IOnewayEnergyServiceOperations define four operations you implement in the head-end server for the control gateway to call to send the values. Note the IsOneWay=true property of the OperationContract attribute, and also note that none of the one-way methods return any values. This is a requirement for all one-way methods in the AppFabric Service Bus.

■ **Tip** Always explicitly define the name and namespace for the service contract as a best practice. Doing so ensures a unique namespace for your contract and avoids any conflicts with default values.

The IOnewayEnergyServiceChannel defines a channel for client communications that inherits from the IOnewayEnergyServiceOperations and IClientChannel interfaces.

■ **Note** All the code for the interfaces is available in the EnergyServiceContract project in the Ch8Solution.sln Visual Studio.NET solution. Before opening the solution, download the latest Windows Azure AppFabric SDK, also known as the AppFabric SDK. The projects in this book are built with the November 2009 CTP release of the AppFabric SDK.

Service Implementation

After the contract is designed, the next step is to implement the contract in the head-end server. In the interest of keeping the book conceptual, you create a simple implementation of the contract that prints out the received messages to the console. Listing 8-4 shows the implementation of the IOnewayEnergyServiceOperations interface.

Listing 8-4. IOnewayEnergyServiceOperations Implementation

```
[ServiceBehavior(Name = "OnewayEnergyServiceOperations",
Namespace = "http://proazure/ServiceBus/energyservice/headend")]
    public class OnewayEnergyServiceOperations :
EnergyServiceContract.IOnewayEnergyServiceOperations
    {
      public void SendKwhValue(string gatewayId, string meterId,
double kwhValue, DateTime utcTime)
      {
         Console.WriteLine(String.Format
("{0}>Energy Meter {1} value:{2:0.00} kWh @ {3}",
 gatewayId, meterId, kwhValue, utcTime.ToString("s")));
      }
      public void SendLightingValue(string gatewayId, string switchId,
int lightingValue, DateTime utcTime)
      {
```

```
            Console.WriteLine(String.Format
("{0}>Changed lightbulb state of switch {1} to {2}",
gatewayId, switchId, ((lightingValue == 1) ? "ON" : "OFF")));
        }
        public void SendHVACSetPoint(string gatewayId, string hvacId,
int setPointValue, DateTime utcTime)
        {
            Console.WriteLine(String.Format
("{0}>HVAC {1} has SETPOINT value:{2:0} F @ {3}",
 gatewayId, hvacId, setPointValue, utcTime.ToString("s")));
        }
        public void SendHVACMode(string gatewayId, string hvacId,
int mode, DateTime utcTime)
        {
            Console.WriteLine(String.Format
("{0}>HVAC {1} MODE is set to {2} @ {3}", gatewayId,
hvacId, GetHVACModeString(mode), utcTime.ToString("s")));
        }
```

Note that all the concepts applied until now are the same as any WCF service implementation.

Service Binding

Bindings define the transport, encoding, and protocol required by the WCF services and clients to communicate with each other. A binding configuration is applied to the endpoint to represent the transport, encoding, and protocol used for communication between client and services. NetOnewayRelayBinding is an AppFabric Service Bus binding that defines one-way communication between the client, relay server, and service. Listing 8-5 shows the binding configuration in App.config for the OnewayEnergyServiceOperations service implementation.

Listing 8-5. *Service Binding for OnewayEnergyServiceOperations*

```
<bindings>
      <netOnewayRelayBinding>
        <binding name="default" />
      </netOnewayRelayBinding>
 </bindings>
```

The bindings section defines the netOnewayRelayBinding. You can define multiple bindings in the bindings section and then later apply one to the service endpoint. The netOnewayRelayBinding makes a TCP outbound connection on port 828 by default, which is on a secure connection. For a non-secure TCP connection, it uses port 808. In most enterprises, no outbound connections other than HTTP on port 80 or SSL on port 443 are allowed due to corporate security policies. In such scenarios, you can configure netOnewayRelayBinding to establish an HTTP connection with the relay service over port 80 or 443. The AppFabric Service Bus environment supports a ConnectivityMode property you can set to one of these enum values: AutoDetect, TCP, or HTTP, as listed in Table 8-4.

Table 8-4. *ConnectivityMode Values*

ConnectivityMode	Description
AutoDetect	This option automatically detects the communication options between TCP and HTTP depending on the availability of TCP and HTTP. If both are available, it chooses TCP over HTTP.
TCP	This is the default mode of communication. If the TCP option is selected, the application opens a TCP connection with the relay service on outbound TCP port 828 for secure TCP connections.
HTTP	If the HTTP option is selected, the application opens an HTTP connection with the relay service on port 443 for SSL communications and port 80 for non-SSL communications. The HTTP connection on the receiver side polls the relay service for messages. Use this option only if you don't have TCP outbound connections restricted, because the HTTP option has a performance impact due to the polling mechanism.

You can set the ConnectivityMode of the netOnewayRelayBinding using

```
ServiceBusEnvironment.SystemConnectivity.Mode = ConnectivityMode.AutoDetect;
```

SystemConnectivity.Mode sets the value of ConnectivitySettings that represents the AppFabric Service Bus connectivity. The default connectivity mode between the AppFabric Service Bus and the service is TCP. If you're running your service behind a firewall, you can use the HTTP binding. If you aren't sure about the network constraints, use AutoDetect mode, where the Service Bus selects TCP by default but automatically switches to HTTP if TCP connectivity isn't available.

You can configure end-to-end security between the client and the server as shown in Listing 8-6.

Listing 8-6. *Binding Security for netOnewayRelayBinding*

```
<netOnewayRelayBinding>
<binding name="default" >
<security mode="Transport" relayClientAuthenticationType="None" />
</binding>
</netOnewayRelayBinding>
```

The mode attribute supports four values, as listed in Table 8-5.

Table 8-5. *End to End Security Values*

Security Mode Value	Description
Message	Provides SOAP message security
Transport	Provides transport-level security like SSL
TransportWithMessageCredential	Provides transport-level security like SSL along with message-level client security
None	Provides no security between client and server

Relay Security

The AppFabric Service Bus integrates with ACS to provide the authentication and authorization required for accessing and creating service endpoints in the AppFabric Service Bus. Even though ACS can be configured to use an external identity provider like ADFS v2.0 or Windows Live ID, this example uses a shared secret to authenticate with ACS for both the service and the client. Listing 8-7 shows the code to pass an issuer name and issuer key as credentials to authenticate with the AppFabric Service Bus.

Listing 8-7. *Shared Secret Authentication*

```
TransportClientEndpointBehavior sharedSecretServiceBusCredential =
new TransportClientEndpointBehavior();
          sharedSecretServiceBusCredential.CredentialType =
TransportClientCredentialType.SharedSecret;
          sharedSecretServiceBusCredential.Credentials.SharedSecret.IssuerName =
 issuerName;
          sharedSecretServiceBusCredential.Credentials.SharedSecret.IssuerSecret =
issuerKey;
ServiceHost Host = new ServiceHost(serviceType);
Host.Description.Endpoints[0].Behaviors.Add(behavior);
```

In Listing 8-7, you create a TransportClientEndpointBehavior object and select the credential type SharedSecret to use the issuer and issuer key as the authenticating credentials.

Figure 8-13 shows the service namespace page with Service Bus credentials. You can use the default issuer name and default issuer key in the shared secret values while connecting to the Service Bus.

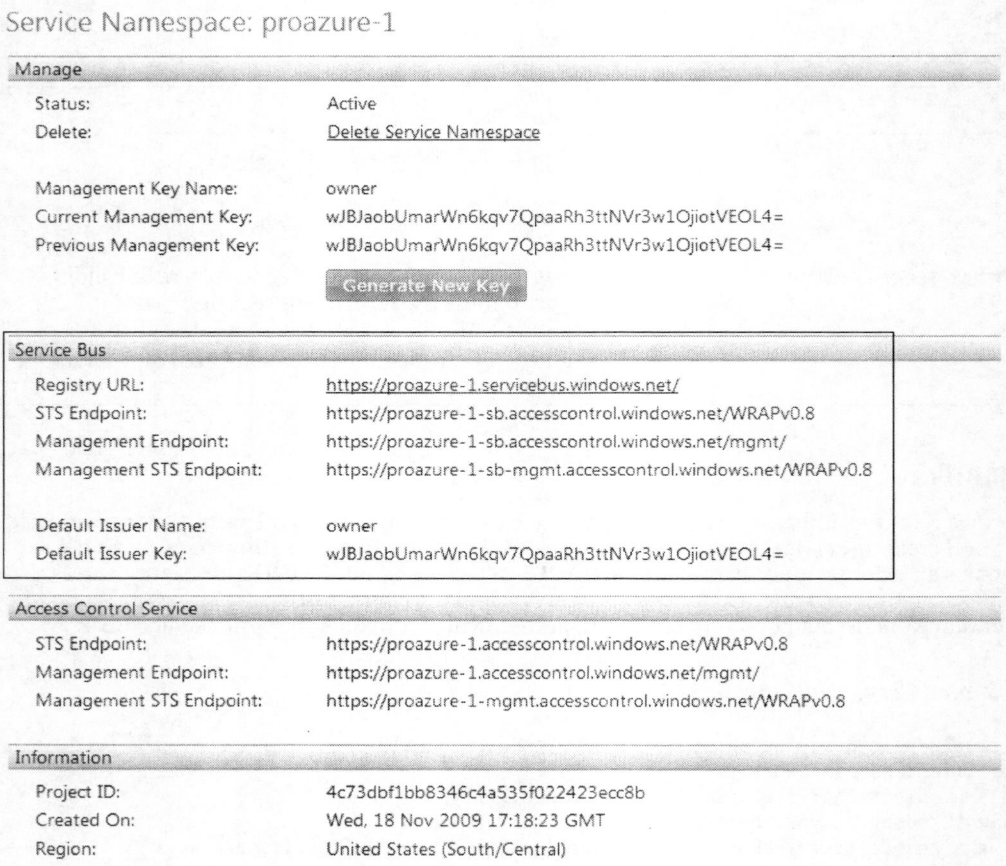

Service Namespace: proazure-1

Manage

Status:	Active
Delete:	Delete Service Namespace

Management Key Name:	owner
Current Management Key:	wJBJaobUmarWn6kqv7QpaaRh3ttNVr3w1OjiotVEOL4=
Previous Management Key:	wJBJaobUmarWn6kqv7QpaaRh3ttNVr3w1OjiotVEOL4=

Generate New Key

Service Bus

Registry URL:	https://proazure-1.servicebus.windows.net/
STS Endpoint:	https://proazure-1-sb.accesscontrol.windows.net/WRAPv0.8
Management Endpoint:	https://proazure-1-sb.accesscontrol.windows.net/mgmt/
Management STS Endpoint:	https://proazure-1-sb-mgmt.accesscontrol.windows.net/WRAPv0.8
Default Issuer Name:	owner
Default Issuer Key:	wJBJaobUmarWn6kqv7QpaaRh3ttNVr3w1OjiotVEOL4=

Access Control Service

STS Endpoint:	https://proazure-1.accesscontrol.windows.net/WRAPv0.8
Management Endpoint:	https://proazure-1.accesscontrol.windows.net/mgmt/
Management STS Endpoint:	https://proazure-1-mgmt.accesscontrol.windows.net/WRAPv0.8

Information

Project ID:	4c73dbf1bb8346c4a535f022423ecc8b
Created On:	Wed, 18 Nov 2009 17:18:23 GMT
Region:	United States (South/Central)

Figure 8-13. *Credentials Management page*

You can also define the shared secret in app.config, as shown in Listing 8-8. If you define credentials as your service behavior and assign it to the service endpoint, then you don't need to initialize transport client credentials in the code.

Listing 8-8. *SharedSecret Declaration*

```
<?xml version="1.0" encoding="utf-8" ?>
<configuration>
  <system.serviceModel>
  <behaviors>
     <endpointBehaviors>
       <behavior name="sharedSecretClientCredentials">
```

```
                <transportClientEndpointBehavior credentialType="SharedSecret">
                   <clientCredentials>
                      <sharedSecret issuerName="owner"
issuerSecret="wJBJaobUmarWn6kqv7QpaaRh3ttNVr3w1OjiotVEOL4=" />
                   </clientCredentials>
                </transportClientEndpointBehavior>
             </behavior>
          </endpointBehaviors>
       </behaviors>
       <bindings>
          <!-- Application Binding -->
          <netOnewayRelayBinding>
             <binding name="default" />
          </netOnewayRelayBinding>
       </bindings>
       <services>
          <service name="EnergyServiceContract.OnewayEnergyServiceOperations">
             <endpoint address="sb://proazure-
1.servicebus.windows.net/OnewayEnergyServiceOperations/"
                       binding="netOnewayRelayBinding"
                       behaviorConfiguration="sharedSecretClientCredentials"
                       bindingConfiguration="default"
                       name="RelayEndpoint"
                       contract="EnergyServiceContract.IOnewayEnergyServiceOperations" />
          </service>
       </services>
    </system.serviceModel>
</configuration>
```

In Listing 8-8, the transport client behavior is defined under the sharedSecretClientCredentials element, which is assigned as the behaviorConfiguration of the service endpoint.

Message Security

Message security refers to the security of the message as it travels from client to service via the AppFabric Service Bus. As discussed earlier, the AppFabric Service Bus API offers four options for message security in the enumeration Microsoft.ServiceBus.EndToEndSecurityMode: None, Transport, Message, and TransportWithMessageCredentials. netOnewayRelayBinding doesn't support TransportWithMessageCredentials. If you want to use a certificate in the client, you have to explicitly configure the service certificate in the client; in a one-way message, there is no direct connection between the client and service. When the client sends a message, the service may not be available, and so the client can't negotiate the certificate with the service.[5]

---

[5] Juval Lowy. Securing The .NET Service Bus. MSDN. http://msdn.microsoft.com/en-us/magazine/dd942847.aspx.

The netOnewayRelayBinding example provides configuration files for default (AppBasic.config), Transport (AppTransport.config), Message without client credentials (AppMsgSecNoClientCreds.config), and Message with username credentials (AppMsgSecUsernameClientCreds.config). Figure 8-14 shows the client (NetOnewayRelayClient) and service (NetOnewayRelayServer) projects.

Figure 8-14. *NetOnewayRelayBinding example*

To use any particular message security, copy and paste the contents of the appropriate configuration file into App.config for the project in both client and service, and recompile the project. The examples use the TempCA.cer X.509 certificate for the service identity, which you can find in the code directory of Ch8Solution. Listing 8-9 shows the contents of AppMsgSecNoClientCreds.config for the service, and Listing 8-10 shows the contents of AppMsgSecNoClientCreds.config for the client.

Listing 8-9. *AppMsgSecNoClientCreds.config for the Service*

```xml
<?xml version="1.0" encoding="utf-8" ?>
<configuration>
  <system.serviceModel>
<behaviors>
    <serviceBehaviors>
      <!--Configure certificate for service identity-->

      <behavior name = "CertificateProtection">
        <serviceCredentials>
          <serviceCertificate
            findValue       = "TempCA"
```

```
              storeLocation = "LocalMachine"
              storeName     = "My"
              x509FindType  = "FindBySubjectName"
                  />
        </serviceCredentials>
      </behavior>
    </serviceBehaviors>
    <endpointBehaviors>
      <behavior name="sharedSecretEndpointBehavior">
        <transportClientEndpointBehavior credentialType="SharedSecret">
          <clientCredentials>
            <sharedSecret issuerName="ISSUER_NAME" issuerSecret="ISSUER_SECRET" />
</clientCredentials>
        </transportClientEndpointBehavior>
      </behavior>
    </endpointBehaviors>
  </behaviors>
  <bindings>
    <!-- Application Binding -->
    <netOnewayRelayBinding>
      <binding name = "OnewayMessageSecurity">
        <security mode = "Message">
          <message clientCredentialType = "None"/>
        </security>
      </binding>
    </netOnewayRelayBinding>
   </bindings>
   <!--Configure certificate for message security-->

   <services>
     <service name="EnergyServiceContract.OnewayEnergyServiceOperations"
              behaviorConfiguration = "CertificateProtection">
       <endpoint address=
"sb://proazure.servicebus.windows.net/OnewayEnergyServiceOperations/"
          binding="netOnewayRelayBinding"
          bindingConfiguration="OnewayMessageSecurity"
          name="RelayEndpoint"
          contract="EnergyServiceContract.IOnewayEnergyServiceOperations"
behaviorConfiguration="sharedSecretEndpointBehavior" />
     </service>
   </services>
 </system.serviceModel>
</configuration>
```

Listing 8-10. *AppMsgSecNoClientCreds.config for the Client*

```
<?xml version="1.0" encoding="utf-8" ?>
<configuration>
  <system.serviceModel>
    <bindings>
      <netOnewayRelayBinding>
```

```xml
        <binding name = "OnewayMessageSecurity">
          <security mode = "Message">
            <message clientCredentialType = "None"/>
          </security>
        </binding>
      </netOnewayRelayBinding>
    </bindings>
<behaviors>
    <endpointBehaviors>
      <behavior name = "ServiceCertificate">
        <transportClientEndpointBehavior credentialType="SharedSecret">
          <clientCredentials>
            <sharedSecret issuerName="ISSUER_NAME" issuerSecret="ISSUER_SECRET" />
          </clientCredentials>
        </transportClientEndpointBehavior>
        <clientCredentials>
          <serviceCertificate>
            <scopedCertificates>
              <add targetUri = "sb://{your service
namespace}.servicebus.windows.net/OnewayEnergyServiceOperations/"
                   findValue       = "TempCA"
                   storeLocation   = "LocalMachine"
                   storeName       = "My"
                   x509FindType    = "FindBySubjectName"
                   />
            </scopedCertificates>
          </serviceCertificate>
        </clientCredentials>
      </behavior>
    </endpointBehaviors>
  </behaviors>
  <client>
    <!-- Service Endpoint -->
    <endpoint name="RelayEndpoint"
              contract="EnergyServiceContract.IOnewayEnergyServiceOperations"
              binding="netOnewayRelayBinding"
              bindingConfiguration="OnewayMessageSecurity"
              address=
"sb://proazure.servicebus.windows.net/OnewayEnergyServiceOperations/"
              behaviorConfiguration = "ServiceCertificate"
              >
      <identity>
        <dns value = "TempCA"/>
      </identity>
    </endpoint>
  </client>
</system.serviceModel>
</configuration>
```

The TempCA X.509 certificate is configured in the service as well as the client in the behavior section of the configuration file. In production applications, you have to use a production certificate issued by a certificate authority. Note that the behavior elements in both the client and server configuration include the transport client endpoint behavior set to shared secret. You can also initialize the TransportClientEndpointBehavior class in the client and server code. In production applications, you should encrypt the issuer credentials wherever they're stored. The X.509 certificate is used.

Service Endpoints

A WCF service endpoint defines how a client can communicate with the WCF service. The endpoint consists of four main attributes: the address of the endpoint, a binding that defines what protocol a client can use to communicate with the endpoint, a service contract that defines the operations available for the client to call, and a set of behaviors defining the local behavior of the endpoint. AppFabric Service Bus endpoints are similar to WCF endpoints. The only difference is the specific bindings used to communicate with the relay service.

Endpoints can be configured in application configuration files or programmatically. For the netOnewayRelayBinding example, Listing 8-11 shows the service endpoint definition from the App.config file.

Listing 8-11. *netOnewayRelayBinding Endpoint*

```
<!-- Service Endpoint -->
<endpoint
                address="sb://{your service namespace}
.servicebus.windows.net/OnewayEnergyServiceOperations/"
                behaviorConfiguration="sharedSecretClientCredentials"
                binding="netOnewayRelayBinding"
                bindingConfiguration="default"
                name="RelayEndpoint"
                contract="EnergyServiceContract.IOnewayEnergyServiceOperations" />
```

In Listing 8-11, the binding is set to netOnewayRelayBinding, and the bindingConfiguration and behaviorConfiguration are pointers to the sections within the same configuration file. The address refers to the URI of the service endpoint. You can also create the URI of the service using the static method call

```
ServiceBusEnvironment.CreateServiceUri("sb", serviceNameSpace, servicePath);
```

where servicePath is the part of the URI after `sb://proazure.servicebus.windows.net`. In this example, it's OnewayEnergyServiceOperations. The "sb" represents the scheme used to communicate with the AppFabric Service Bus. The scheme can be either "http" or "sb" depending on the binding you're using. For netOnewayRelayBinding, you must use the "sb" scheme.

Service Hosting

After you've defined the service contract, service implementation, bindings, and endpoints, you can create a host for the service, as shown in Listing 8-12.

Listing 8-12. Hosting the AppFabric Service Bus Service

```
TransportClientEndpointBehavior behavior =
ServiceBusHelper.GetUsernamePasswordBehavior(issuerName, issuerKey);
Host = new ServiceHost(typeof(OnewayEnergyServiceOperations));
Host.Description.Endpoints[0].Behaviors.Add(behavior);
Host.Open();
```

As shown in Listing 8-12, the System.ServiceModel.ServiceHost is used to host the service. The TransportClientEndpointBehavior object is created from the issuer name/issuer key and passed to the defined endpoint. Finally, the Host.Open() method opens the service for communication. If you define the issuer name and issuer key in the configuration file, then you don't have to initialize it programmatically. In this example, you define the transport client endpoint behavior in the configuration file.

Client Design

You can find the client application in the NetOnewayRelayClient Visual Studio .NET project. From the business requirements perspective, the client application is the control gateway application that connects to the head-end server to send messages. Figure 8-15 illustrates the user interface for the NetOnewayRelayClient client application.

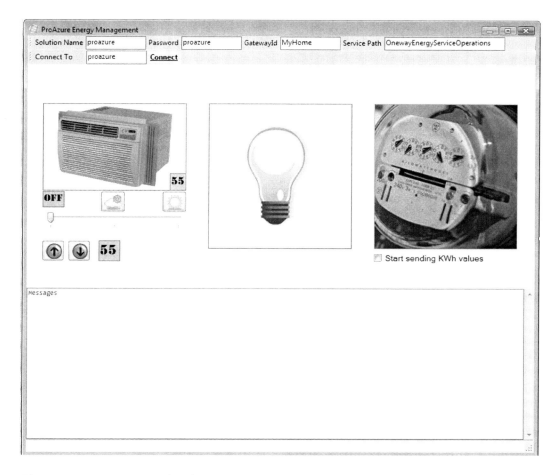

Figure 8-15. *NetOnewayRelayClient application Design View*

The client user interface has four main sections: configuration, HVAC operations, light switch operations, and meter reading, as discussed in the original requirements of the application. In the configuration section at the top of the form, you should enter your solution name and solution password. The Connect button establishes a connection to the AppFabric Service Bus. Any change to the HVAC set point or mode is sent to the head-end server by calling the SendHVACSetPoint() and SendHVACMode() methods on the server. Clicking the light bulb button turns the light switch on and off. Any change to the state of the light switch is sent to the server by calling the SendLightingValue() method on the head-end server. If you click on the energy meter button, a random kWh value is sent to the server by calling the SendKwhValue() method on the head-end server. If you check the "Start sending kWh values" check box, a random kWh value is sent to the head-end server every 10 seconds.

Listing 8-13 shows the code to initialize the channel to communicate with the server. The credentials are defined in the app.config file so they don't need to be initialized in the code.

Listing 8-13. Client Communication Initialization

```
Uri address = ServiceBusEnvironment.CreateServiceUri
("sb", serviceNamespaceDomain, "OnewayEnergyServiceOperations");

ChannelFactory<IOnewayEnergyServiceChannel> netOnewayChannelFactory = new
ChannelFactory<IOnewayEnergyServiceChannel>("RelayEndpoint", new EndpointAddress(address));

IOnewayEnergyServiceChannel netOnewayChannel = channelFactory.CreateChannel();

channel.Open();
```

After the channel is opened successfully, you can call the methods on the service as follows:
```
netOnewayChannel.SendLightingValue(gatewayId, switchId, lightingValue, DateTime.UtcNow);
        netOnewayChannel.SendKwhValue(gatewayId, meterId, kWhValue, DateTime.UtcNow);
```

■ **Note** In a real-world application, the control gateway polls the actual energy meter and sends kWh values to the head-end server. This example uses random numbers to simulate a real-world environment.

Running the Application

The steps required to run the end-to-end application are as follows:

1. Open App.config for the server and client, and configure them to represent your service namespace and issuer credentials.

2. Open a command prompt as Administrator, and navigate to the bin\Debug directory of the NetOnewayRelayServer project.

3. Run NetOnewayRelayServer.exe.

4. Enter the service namespace to start the service.

5. Open Windows Explorer, and navigate to the bin\Debug directory of the NetOnewayRelayClient project.

■ **Note** Make sure the configuration for the server and the client match in terms of address and security

---

6. Double-click NetOnewayRelayClient.exe to start the client application.

7. Click the Connect button to connect to the relay service. If the connection is successful, the text box displays success messages.

8. You can interact with the application by changing the state of HVAC, Light switch or the meter reading button. The client application calls the appropriate methods on the head-end server, and as a result the NetOnewayRelayServer.exe command prompt displays the received method calls.

Figure 8-16 illustrates a running instance of the client application, and Figure 8-17 illustrates the messages received on the server command prompt.

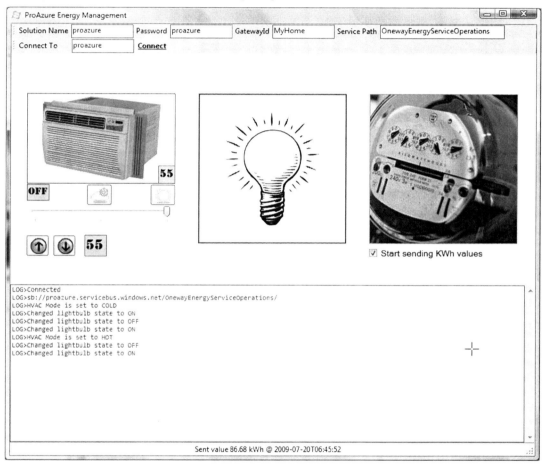

Figure 8-16. *NetOnewayRelayClient application*

```
C:\Users\tredkar\Desktop\Publications\Azure Services\Content\Code\6\.NETServices July2009 CTP\...
Please enter the Solution name to use for this sample:proazure
Your Solution Password: ********
ServiceUri:sb://proazure.servicebus.windows.net/OnewayEnergyServiceOperations/
Service registered for public discovery.
Scheme:sb
Security Mode:Transport
Security RelayAuthType:RelayAccessToken
Security Transport.ProtectionLevel:EncryptAndSign
Press [Enter] to exit
MyHome>Changed lightbulb state of switch LightSwitch-1 to OFF
MyHome>Changed lightbulb state of switch LightSwitch-1 to ON
MyHome>HVAC HVAC-1 MODE is set to HOT @ 2009-07-20T06:44:48
MyHome>Energy Meter Meter-1 value:30.80 kWh @ 2009-07-20T06:44:50
MyHome>Changed lightbulb state of switch LightSwitch-1 to OFF
MyHome>Energy Meter Meter-1 value:92.84 kWh @ 2009-07-20T06:45:02
MyHome>Energy Meter Meter-1 value:18.15 kWh @ 2009-07-20T06:45:12
```

Figure 8-17. *NetOnewayRelayServer application*

■ **Tip** If you want to observe the ports open or trace messages sent back and forth between the client and the service, you can use Microsoft's Network Monitor (netmon.exe), available at http://www.microsoft.com/downloads/details.aspx?displaylang=en&FamilyID=983b941d-06cb-4658-b7f6-3088333d062f.

Figure 8-18 illustrates the Microsoft Network Monitor conversation tree of the interaction between NetOnewayRelayClient.exe and NetOnewayRelayServer.exe. Note the TCP outgoing port 828 and SSL connection in the conversation tree.

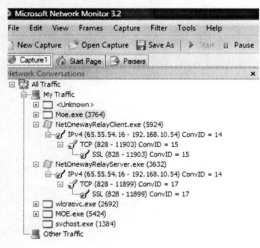

Figure 8-18. *Microsoft Network Monitor capture*

netEventRelayBinding

netEventRelayBinding extends the netOnewayRelayBinding by providing multicast messaging between multiple subscribers and publishers listening on the same rendezvous service endpoint. The netEventRelayBinding class inherits from netOnewayRelayBinding. This is the only binding that supports multiple receivers on the same service URI. Figure 8-19 illustrates the architecture of netEventRelayBinding.

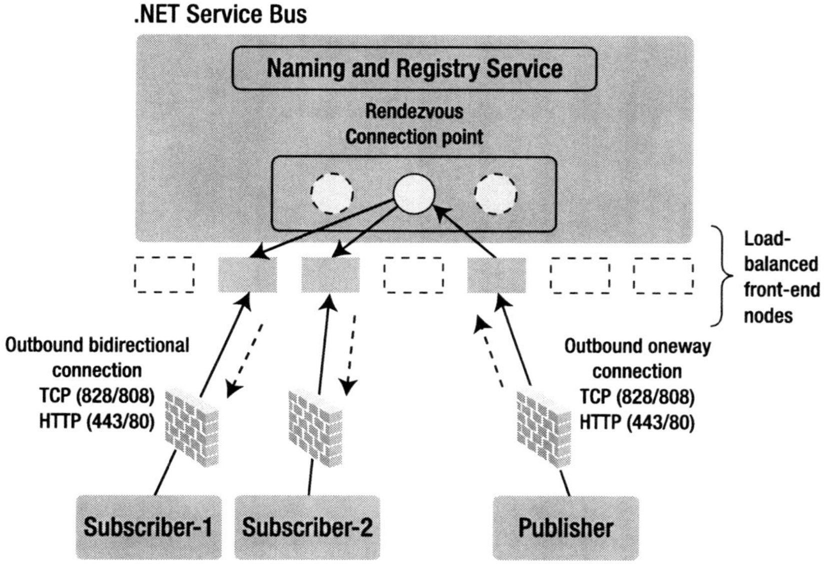

Figure 8-19. *netEventRelayBinding architecture*

In Figure 8-19, one publisher publishes messages on a defined endpoint URI, and two subscribers (Subscriber-1 and Subscriber-2) listen on the same endpoint URI. When the publisher sends a message to the endpoint URI, both receivers receive the message. The AppFabric Service Bus multicasts the message to all the subscribers of the URI. Internally, both the subscribers may be running on different front-end nodes. From the publisher and subscriber perspective, routing of the message to two subscribers is opaque and completely handled by the combination of netEventRelayBinding and the AppFabric Service Bus. Because netEventRelayBinding inherits from netOnewayRelayBinding, it supports the same connectivity modes and security features, as discussed for netOnewayRelayBinding.

You should use this binding if you require a publish-subscribe messaging system where a message needs to be sent to multiple receivers at the same time. netEventRelayBinding uses a multicast connection mode, whereas netOnewayRelayBinding uses a unicast connection mode.

In the ProAzure Energy service example, the control gateway needs to communicate with the head-end server about its availability and when it comes online and goes offline. This offers the head-end server better understanding of a gateway's online/offline pattern and can send scheduled commands to the control gateway only when it's online. The head-end server is a collection of small servers with dedicated specific roles. For example, there is a server instance that only sends scheduled commands to the control gateway when it's online. Another service checks for the required software upgrade on the control gateway and can upgrade the software on the control gateway when it's online. So, this example uses the netEventRelayBinding to send ONLINE/OFFLINE messages between the control gateway and the head-end server. When a control gateway is online, it periodically sends an ONLINE message to the head-end server. A control gateway also sends an OFFLINE message if it's shutting down gracefully. The service project for this example is NetEventRelayServer, and the client project is NetEventRelayGateway in the Ch8Solution. The NetEventRelayGateway project consists of netOnewayRelayBinding as well as netEventRelayBinding examples. The same application is used to send one-way as well as publish/subscribe messages.

AppFabric Contract

The AppFabric contract for the netEventRelayBinding example consists of two operations: Online() and GoingOffline(), as shown in Listing 8-14.

Listing 8-14. *netEventRelayBinding Service Contract*

```
[ServiceContract(Name = "IMulticastGatewayOperations.", Namespace =
"http://proazure/ServiceBus/energyservice/gateway")]
    public interface IMulticastGatewayOperations
    {
        [OperationContract(IsOneWay = true)]
        void Online(string gatewayId, string serviceUri, DateTime utcTime);
        [OperationContract(IsOneWay = true)]
        void GoingOffline(string gatewayId, string serviceUri, DateTime utcTime);

    }

    public interface IMulticastGatewayChannel : IMulticastGatewayOperations,
IClientChannel
    {
    }
```

The IMulticastGatewayOperations interface has two methods: Online() and GoingOffline(). Similar to the netOnewayRelayBinding, both methods must have the IsOneWay=true attribute and must not return any values. The gatewayID refers to the unique identifier of a gateway, and the serviceUri refers to the URI of the gateway service. I cover the URI of the gateway when I discuss netTcpRelayBinding.

Service Implementation

The implementation of the IMulticastGatewayOperations interface is shown in Listing 8-15.

Listing 8-15. *Implementation of the IMulticastGatewayOperations Interface*

```
[ServiceBehavior(Name = "MulticastGatewayOperations", Namespace =
"http://proazure/ServiceBus/energyservice/")]
 public class MulticastGatewayOperations :
EnergyServiceContract.IMulticastGatewayOperations
 {
```

```
public void Online(string gatewayId, string serviceUri, DateTime utcTime)
{
  Console.WriteLine(String.Format("{0}>ONLINE Uri:{1} @ {2}",
gatewayId, serviceUri, utcTime.ToString("s")));

}
public void GoingOffline(string gatewayId, string serviceUri, DateTime utcTime)
{
    Console.WriteLine(String.Format("{0}>OFFLINE Uri:{1} @ {2}",
gatewayId, serviceUri, utcTime.ToString("s")));
}
```

The implementation prints the name, URI, and the time values to the console.

Service Binding

The service binding for netEventRelayBinding is shown in Listing 8-16.

Listing 8-16. *netEventRelayBinding*

```
<netEventRelayBinding>
      <binding name = "OnewayMessageSecurity">

      </binding>
</netEventRelayBinding>
```

Relay Security

In the netOnewayRelayBinding example, you saw how to use shared-secret authentication with your ACS solution. This example explores the use of an SWT. Listing 8-17 shows the code segment required to authenticate using an SWT.

Listing 8-17. *SWT Authentication*

```
Uri address = ServiceBusEnvironment.CreateServiceUri("sb", serviceNamespaceDomain,
"Gateway/MulticastService");

TransportClientEndpointBehavior behavior = new TransportClientEndpointBehavior();
behavior.CredentialType = TransportClientCredentialType.SimpleWebToken;
behavior.Credentials.SimpleWebToken.SimpleWebToken =
SharedSecretCredential.ComputeSimpleWebTokenString(issuerName, issuerSecret);

ServiceHost host = new ServiceHost(typeof(MulticastGatewayOperations), address);
host.Description.Endpoints[0].Behaviors.Add(behavior);
```

The code creates an SWT from the issuer name and issuer secret key by calling the method SharedSecretCredential.ComputeSimpleWebTokenString(string issuerName, string issuerSecret) method from Microsoft.ServiceBus.dll.

Message Security

Similar to the netOnewayRelayBinding example, you can create specific configuration files for particular message security scenarios and then switch back and forth between these configuration files depending on the scenario you're executing. When you execute a particular security configuration, make sure you're switching the client security configuration consistently with the service configuration.

Service Endpoints

The service endpoint configuration of netEventRelayBinding in this example doesn't define the ACS authentication in the configuration file like netOnewayRelayBinding. The ACS authentication is handled in the code. Listing 8-18 shows the service configuration in of the NetEventRelayServer.

Listing 8-18. Service Endpoint Configuration

```
<services>
<service name="EnergyServiceContract.MulticastGatewayOperations">
        <endpoint address=""
                    binding="netEventRelayBinding"
                    bindingConfiguration="default"
                      name="RelayMulticastEndpoint"
                    contract="EnergyServiceContract.IMulticastGatewayOperations"
            />
        </service>
</services>
```

The relay authentication is handled in the code and therefore isn't visible in the configuration file.

Service Hosting

The netEventRelayBinding example uses SWT tokens for relay authentication instead of issuer name and issuer key as in the netOnewayRelayBinding example. So, the service host has to create an SWT from the issuer name and issuer key. The code for the service host is shown in Listing 8-19.

Listing 8-19. Service Hosting for netEventRelayBinding

```
string serviceNamespaceDomain = "{your service namespace}"
    string issuerName = "{ISSUER NAME}";
    string issuerSecret = "{ISSUER KEY}";
    ServiceBusEnvironment.SystemConnectivity.Mode = ConnectivityMode.AutoDetect;
    TransportClientEndpointBehavior relayCredentials = new
TransportClientEndpointBehavior();
    relayCredentials.CredentialType = TransportClientCredentialType.SharedSecret;
    relayCredentials.Credentials.SharedSecret.IssuerName = issuerName;
    relayCredentials.Credentials.SharedSecret.IssuerSecret = issuerSecret;
    Uri serviceAddress = ServiceBusEnvironment.CreateServiceUri("sb",
serviceNamespaceDomain,
```

```
            "Gateway/MulticastService/");
ServiceHost host = new ServiceHost(typeof(MulticastGatewayOperations), serviceAddress);
host.Description.Endpoints[0].Behaviors.Add(relayCredentials);
    host.Open();
```
One the service hosts are started, they listen on the endpoint URI
`sb://{your service namespace}.servicebus.windows.net/Gateway/MulticastService/`

Client Design

In this example, the client application performs both the netOnewayRelayBinding and the netEventRelayBinding operations. When a control gateway comes online, it sends online messages every 10 seconds by calling the Online() method on the head-end server's multicast URI:

`sb://proazure.servicebus.windows.net/Gateway/MulticastService/`

When you close the client application, it sends an offline message by calling the GoingOffline() method on the head-end server's multicast URI:

`sb://proazure.servicebus.windows.net/Gateway/MulticastService/`

Figure 8-20 illustrates the design view of the NetEventRelayGateway client application.

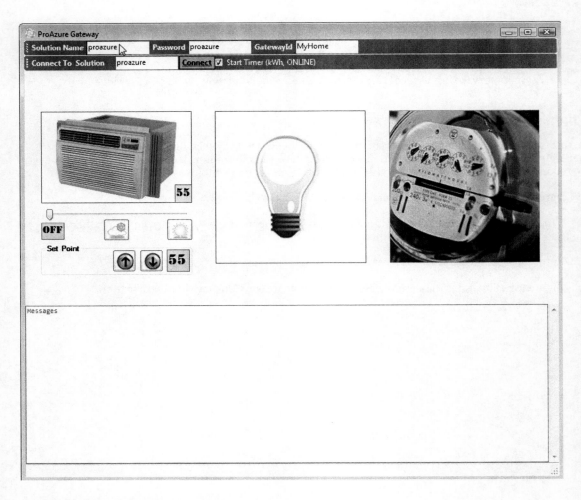

Figure 8-20. *NetEventRelayGateway design view*

The Start Time check box starts the timer to send an online message every 10 seconds.

■ **Note** I've combined the configuration of the netOnewayRelayBinding example and the netEventRelayBinding example in one project, NetEventRelayGateway.

Running the Application

The steps required to run the end-to-end application are as follows:

1. Open App.config for the NetEventRelayGateway and NetEventRelayServer and configure it to represent your service namespace and issuer credentials.

2. Open three command prompts as Administrator, and navigate two prompts to the bin\Debug directory of the NetEventRelayServer project and the third prompt to the bin\Debug directory of the NetOnewayRelayServer project. You do this because the client application also supports the netOnewayRelayBinding methods from the previous example.

3. Run NetEventRelayServer.exe in two prompts and NetOnewayRelayServer.exe in the third prompt.

4. Enter the solution name and solution password to start the service when prompted.

5. Open Windows Explorer, and navigate to the bin\Debug directory of the NetEventRelayGateway project.

■ **Note** Make sure the configuration for the server and the client match in terms of address and security.

---

6. Double-click NetEventRelayGateway.exe to start the client application.

7. Click the Connect button to connect to the relay service. If the connection is successful, the text box displays success messages to connect to two endpoints.

8. Check the Start Time check box if it isn't already checked.

9. If the configurations are correct, then you should see ONLINE messages in the two command windows of NetEventRelayServer.exe.

Thus you can build an Internet-scale publish/subscribe messaging service using netEventRelayBinding.

Figure 8-21 shows a running instance of the client application, and Figure 8-22 shows the messages received on the server command prompts.

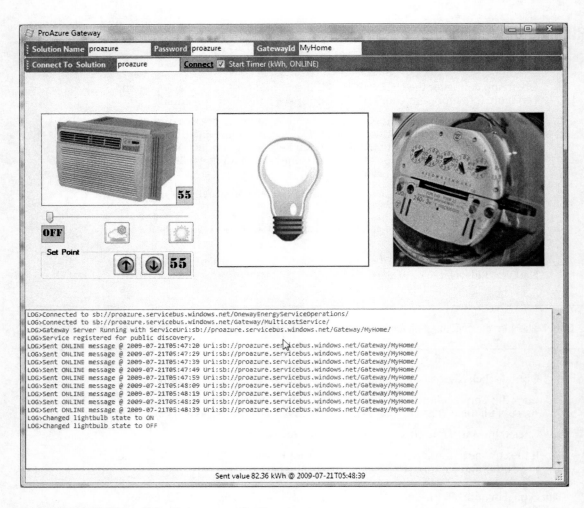

Figure 8-21. *NetEventRelayGateway application*

Figure 8-22. *NetEventRelayServer application*

NetTcpRelayBinding

netTcpRelayBinding is the recommended and most frequently used AppFabric Service Bus binding. It uses TCP as the relay transport and is based on the WCF netTcpBinding. It performs better than the HTTP bindings because it uses TCP for message delivery and the messages are encoded in binary format. NetTcpRelayBinding supports WS-ReliableMessaging, which is turned off by default. You can turn it on by setting reliableSessionEnabled to true. In WCF, you typically use netTcpBinding to create service endpoints reachable within the intranet, but with netTcpRelayBinding you can create service endpoints reachable over the Internet. This makes communication over the Internet faster than with HTTP bindings. Similar to netOnewayRelayBinding, netTcpRelayBinding establishes an SSL-protected control channel using outbound TCP port 828 and a non-SSL data channel using outbound TCP port 818.

■ **Note** netTcpRelayBinding is the only AppFabric Service Bus binding that supports WCF-style duplex callbacks through the relay service.

---

netTcpRelayBinding supports three different connection modes, as listed in Table 8-6 and defined in the AppFabric Service Bus API as the Microsoft.ServiceBus.TcpRelayConnectionMode enumeration.

Table 8-6. *TransportClientCredentialType Values*

Connection Mode	Description
Relayed (default)	In this mode, all communications between the service and the client are relayed via the AppFabric Service Bus relay service. If the message security (or security mode) is set to either Transport or TransportWithMessageCredential, the channel is SSL protected. The relay service acts a socket-forwarder proxy between the client and the service.
Direct	As of the November 2009 CTP, Direct mode has been removed from the API. Direct mode is supported only through Hybrid mode. In Direct Mode, first the service and the client connects to the relay service. The relay service then upgrades the connection to direct communication between the client and the service, enabling direct communication between them. Direct mode is capable of communicating when the client and the service both are behind firewall or NAT routers. In Direct connection mode, the service requires the opening of an additional TCP outbound port 819. Communication is aborted if the client and the service aren't able to establish a direct connection. Direct mode doesn't support Transport security mode; you have to use the Message security mode.
Hybrid	Hybrid is the most commonly used mode. First, the client and the service establish an initial connection to the relay service. The client and the service then negotiate a direct connection to each to each other. The relay service monitors the negotiation and upgrades the communication to Direct mode if possible, or continues with the relayed mode. Hybrid mode doesn't support Transport security mode; you have to use Message security mode.

Figure 8-23 illustrates Relayed mode communications between a client and a service.

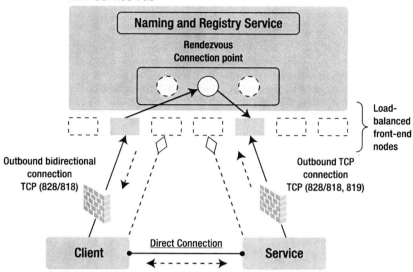

.NET Service Bus

Naming and Registry Service

Rendezvous
Connection point

Load-
balanced
front-end
nodes

Outbound bidirectional
connection
TCP (828/818)

Outbound TCP
connection
TCP (828/818, 819)

Direct Connection

Client

Service

Figure 8-23. *Relayed mode*

Figure 8-23 shows the following:

- The client and the service first communicate through the relay service.

- Communications begin in Relayed mode.

- Direct connection negotiation between client and service succeeds.

- The relay service keeps on probing for mutual port of communication between the client and the service.

- The probing succeeds, and the relay service provides the communication information to the client and the service to communicate with each other directly.

- The connection is upgraded to a Direct connection without any data loss.

- Future communications continue in Direct mode.

- If the probing of mutual ports fails or times out, the communication continues in Relayed mode.

In the ProAzure Energy Service example, the control gateway itself is a server that accepts commands from the head-end server. An end user can schedule a command to be executed on the gateway at a particular time or execute a real-time command on the control gateway, such as turning off all the lights in the building. The control gateway accepts the command and in turn sends the command to the lighting system on the control network. The control gateway also supports real-time retrieval of device values. For example, an end user can retrieve the current state of the HVAC set point or the lighting system in real time.

AppFabric Contract

The control gateway supports get and set operations on the back-end devices it supports. In the ProAzure Energy service example, it supports get and set operations on the lighting and HVAC systems but only get operation on the energy meter. Listing 8-20 shows the service contract for the control gateway service.

Listing 8-20. Control Gateway Service Contract

```
[ServiceContract(Name = "IEnergyServiceGatewayOperations",
Namespace = "http://proazure/ServiceBus/energyservice/gateway")]
    public interface IEnergyServiceGatewayOperations
    {
        [OperationContract]
        bool UpdateSoftware(string softwareUrl);

        [OperationContract]
        bool SetLightingValue(string gatewayId, string deviceId,
short switchValue);

        [OperationContract]
        short GetLightingValue(string gatewayId, string deviceId);

        [OperationContract]
        bool SetHVACMode(string gatewayId, string deviceId,
int hvMode);
        [OperationContract]
        int GetHVACMode(string gatewayId, string deviceId);

        [OperationContract]
        bool SetHVACSetpoint(string gatewayId, string deviceId,
int spValue);
        [OperationContract]
        int GetHVACSetpoint(string gatewayId, string deviceId);

        [OperationContract]
        int GetCurrentTemp(string gatewayId, string deviceId);

        [OperationContract]
        double GetKWhValue(string gatewayId, string deviceId);

    }

    public interface IEnergyServiceGatewayOperationsChannel :
IEnergyServiceGatewayOperations, IClientChannel
```

```
{
    }
```

As shown in Listing 8-20, the IEnergyServiceGatewayOperations support nine methods that the head-end server can call. Most of the operations are get/set methods, so the method signatures are self explanatory.

Service Implementation

The control gateway itself is the server, so the interface IEnergyServiceGatewayOperations is implemented in the control gateway application. The implementation of the IEnergyServiceGatewayOperations interface is shown in Listing 8-21.

Listing 8-21. *IEnergyServiceGatewayOperations Iimplementation*

```
public bool UpdateSoftware(string softwareUrl)
        {
         AddLog("UpdateSoftware:" + softwareUrl);
         return true;
        }

        public bool SetLightingValue(string gatewayId, string deviceId,
short switchValue)
        {
         ChangeLightBulbState(false, switchValue);
         AddLog("SetLightingValue:" + switchValue);
         return true;
        }

        public bool SetHVACMode(string gatewayId, string deviceId, int hvMode)
        {
         hvacMode = hvMode;
         trackBar1.Value = hvacMode;
         ChangeHVACMode();
         AddLog("SetHVACMode:" + hvMode);
         return true;
        }

        public bool SetHVACSetpoint(string gatewayId, string deviceId, int spValue)
        {
         ChangeSetPointValue();
         AddLog("SetHVACSetpoint:" + spValue);

         return true;
        }


        public short GetLightingValue(string gatewayId, string deviceId)
        {
```

```
        AddLog("GetLightingValue:" + lightBulbState);

        return lightBulbState;
    }

    public int GetHVACMode(string gatewayId, string deviceId)
    {
     AddLog("GetHVACMode:" + hvacMode);

     return hvacMode;
    }


    public int GetHVACSetpoint(string gatewayId, string deviceId)
    {
     AddLog("GetHVACSetpoint:" + txtSetPoint.Text);
     return int.Parse(txtSetPoint.Text);
    }

    public int GetCurrentTemp(string gatewayId, string deviceId)
    {
     AddLog("GetCurrentTemp:" + txtCurrentTemperature.Text);
        return int.Parse(txtCurrentTemperature.Text);
    }


    public double GetKWhValue(string gatewayId, string deviceId)
    {
     AddLog("GetKWhValue:" + kwh);

        return kwh;
    }
```

All the method invocations are logged to the Messages text box on the control gateway application.

Service Binding

The service binding for netTcpRelayBinding is shown in Listing 8-22.

Listing 8-22. *netTcpRelayBinding*

```
<netTcpRelayBinding>
<binding name="default" connectionMode="Hybrid">
<security mode="None" />
</binding>
```

Note that the connectionMode specified is Hybrid. You can specify the value as Hybrid or Relayed.

Relay Security

In the previous examples, you saw how to use different types of relay authentication. This example uses the ACS shared secret credentials to authenticate both the client and the service. Listing 8-23 shows the code from the NetEventRelayGateway project for setting the issuer and password for relay authentication.

Listing 8-23. *Shared Secret Relay Authentication*

```
TransportClientEndpointBehavior behavior = new TransportClientEndpointBehavior();
behavior.CredentialType = TransportClientCredentialType.SharedSecret;
behavior.Credentials.SharedSecret.IssuerName = issuerName;
behavior.Credentials.SharedSecret.IssuerSecret = issuerKey;
ServiceHost Host = new ServiceHost(serviceType);
Host.Description.Endpoints[0].Behaviors.Add(behavior);
```

Note The NetEventRelayGateway project implements the service contract because the control gateway itself is the server now and the head-end server is the client. Because the server instance implements the interface, you have to set the instance context mode to single, as shown here:

```
[ServiceBehavior(Name = "EnergyServiceGatewayOperations",
     Namespace = "http://proazure/ServiceBus/energyservice/gateway",
     InstanceContextMode=InstanceContextMode.Single)]
 public partial class EnergyManagementDevice : Form, IEnergyServiceGatewayOperations
```

Message Security

The netTcpRelayBinding uses Transport as its default message security if you don't explicitly configure it in App.config. This example doesn't use message security, to keep the example simple. Listing 8-24 shows the configuration of netTcpRelayBinding in the App.config file of the server in the NetEventRelayGateway project.

Listing 8-24. *Message Security in netTcpRelayBinding*

```
<netTcpRelayBinding>
<binding name="default" connectionMode="Hybrid">
<security mode="None" />
</binding>
</netTcpRelayBinding>
```

Service Endpoints

The service endpoint configuration is shown in Listing 8-25.

Listing 8-25. Service Endpoint Configuration

```
<services>
<service name="NetEventRelayGateway.EnergyManagementDevice">
<endpoint name="RelayTcpEndpoint"
contract="EnergyServiceContract.IEnergyServiceGatewayOperations"
binding="netTcpRelayBinding"
bindingConfiguration="default"
address="" />
</service>
```

Note that in the endpoint configuration, the address field is empty: the address is generated at runtime so you can run multiple instances of the same application representing difference control gateways. Each control gateway has its own service endpoint, which the head-end server accesses to call methods on each control device.

Service Hosting

The service is hosted in the control gateway, so NetEventRelayGateway contains the code to host the service. Listing 8-26 shows the code that hosts the service within the NetEventRelayGateway application.

Listing 8-26. Service Hosting

```
Uri address = ServiceBusEnvironment.CreateServiceUri("sb", solutionName, servicePath);
ServiceUri = address.ToString();
TransportClientEndpointBehavior behavior = new TransportClientEndpointBehavior();
behavior.CredentialType = TransportClientCredentialType.SharedSecret;
behavior.Credentials.SharedSecret.IssuerName = issuerName;
behavior.Credentials.SharedSecret.IssuerSecret = issuerKey;Host = new
ServiceHost(serviceType, address);
Host.Description.Endpoints[0].Behaviors.Add(behavior);
Host.Open();
```

In Listing 8-26, the URI for the service is generated dynamically by calling the ServiceBusEnvironment.CreateServiceUri() method. The servicePath contains the gatewayID, which makes the URI unique within the network of all the control gateways. The head-end server uses this URI to call methods on the control gateway.

Client Design

The head-end server acts as a client for all the control gateways. The client in this example is a simple console application that accepts a gateway ID, then creates the endpoint URI programmatically, and finally invokes multiple methods to turn off all the devices attached to the control gateway. The source code for the client application is in the NetTcpRelayBinding project. Listing 8-27 shows the code for the method (without exception handling) that turns off all the devices attached to the control gateway.

Listing 8-27. *TurnEverythingOff Source Code*

```
static void TurnEverythingOff(string solutionName, string password,
  string gatewayId)
    {
        ChannelFactory<IEnergyServiceGatewayOperationsChannel>
netTcpRelayChannelFactory = null;
        IEnergyServiceGatewayOperationsChannel
netTcpRelayChannel = null;

        Uri serviceUri = ServiceBusEnvironment.CreateServiceUri("sb",
solutionName, ServiceBusHelper.GetGatewayServicePath(gatewayId));
        netTcpRelayChannelFactory = new
ChannelFactory<IEnergyServiceGatewayOperationsChannel>
("RelayTcpEndpoint", new EndpointAddress(serviceUri));

        netTcpRelayChannel = netTcpRelayChannelFactory.CreateChannel();
        netTcpRelayChannel.Open();
        netTcpRelayChannel.SetLightingValue(gatewayId, "Lighting-1", 0);

        netTcpRelayChannel.SetHVACMode(gatewayId, "HVAC-1", 0);
        netTcpRelayChannel.SetHVACSetpoint(gatewayId, "HVAC-1", 78);

            netTcpRelayChannel.Close();
            netTcpRelayChannelFactory.Close();
    }
```

In Listing 8-27, a channel is created with the endpoint URI based on the gateway identifier. Then, the SetLightingValue(), SetHVACMode(), and SetHVACSetpoint() methods are called on the control gateway to turn off the devices attached to the control gateway. Because the URI is generated dynamically from the gateway identified, you can invoke these methods on any gateway that has an endpoint URI registered with the AppFabric Service Bus. The ACS shared secret is defined in App.config, and therefore you don't need to redefine it in the code. Listing 8-28 shows the definition of the shared secret in App.config of the client project NetTcpRelayBinding.

Listing 8-28. *Shared Secret Definition in the Client*

```
<behaviors>
    <endpointBehaviors>
      <behavior name="sharedSecretClientCredentials">
        <transportClientEndpointBehavior credentialType="SharedSecret">
          <clientCredentials>
            <sharedSecret issuerName="ISSUER_NAME" issuerSecret="ISSUER_KEY" />
          </clientCredentials>
        </transportClientEndpointBehavior>
      </behavior>
```

```
    </endpointBehaviors>
  </behaviors>
```

Running the Application

The steps required to run the end-to-end application are as follows:

1. Open Windows Explorer, and navigate to the bin\Debug directory of the NetEventRelayGateway project.

2. Double-click NetEventRelayGateway.exe two times to start two instances of the NetEventRelayGateway application.

3. Change the service namespace name, issuer name, and issuer key to your own values.

4. In the GatewayId field of the first application, enter MyOffice. Leave the default MyHome in the second application.

5. Click the Connect button on both the instances of NetEventRelayGateway to connect to the relay service. If the connections are successful, the text boxes display success messages with the URIs of the service endpoints. Note how the URIs are created based on the gateway identifier to make them unique.

6. Turn the light switch on, and turn the HVAC mode to HEAT or COOL.

7. Open a command prompt window with Administrator privileges, and navigate to the bin\Debug directory of the NetTcpRelayBinding project.

8. Start the NetTcpRelayBinding.exe console application.

9. Enter the service namespace name when prompted.

10. When prompted, enter the gateway ID MyHome.

11. Observe in the NetEventRelayGateway application that the light switch and the HVAC mode are turned off.

12. Perform the same operation on the gateway ID MyOffice to see similar results

Thus, you can dynamically register thousands of control gateway endpoints with the AppFabric Service Bus and execute methods on these control gateways at Internet scale

Figure 8-24 illustrates the two running instances of NetEventRelayGateway.exe, and Figure 8-25 illustrates the NetTcpRelayBinding.exe command prompt.

Figure 8-24. *NetEventRelayGateway application*

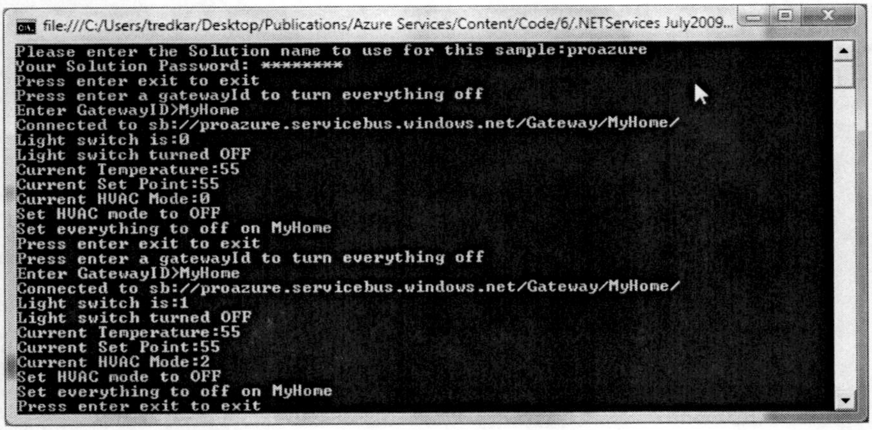

Figure 8-25. *NetTcpRelayBinding application*

You can catch the connection upgrade event when a Relayed connection is upgraded to a Direct connection by implementing the ConnectionStateChanged event on the IHybridConnectionStatus interface, as shown in Listing 8-29.

Listing 8-29. *Connection Upgrade Event*

```
IHybridConnectionStatus hybridConnectionStatus =
channel.GetProperty<IHybridConnectionStatus>();
        if (hybridConnectionStatus != null)
           {
                hybridConnectionStatus.ConnectionStateChanged += (o, e) =>
                {
                    //Do work
                };
           }
```

HTTP Relay Bindings

As discussed in Table 8-3 earlier, the AppFabric Service Bus supports the following HTTP relay bindings:

- BasicHttpRelayBinding

- WebHttpRelayBinding

- WSHttpRelayBinding

- WS2007HttpRelayBinding

This section covers only WS2007HttpRelayBinding and WebHttpRelayBinding because the concepts for using all these bindings are similar. When you use HTTP bindings, the AppFabric Service Bus uses

HTTP as the communication protocol instead of TCP as you saw earlier in the netOnewayRelayBinding and netTcpRelayBinding sections. HTTP bindings exchange plain XML, SOAP, WS-*, or raw text and binary messages, so they're preferred in non-WCF client environments.

At a higher level, all the HTTP bindings follow the same sequence of steps to communicate via the relay service, as shown in Figure 8-26.

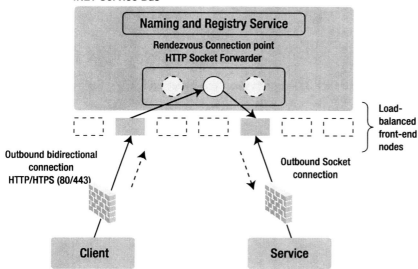

Figure 8-26. *HTTP bindings*

As shown in Figure 8-26, in an HTTP binding scenario, the service authenticates and registers its endpoint with the relay service. Then, a client authenticates and connects to the relay service to call a method on the service. The relay service routes the HTTP (REST), SOAP 1.1, and SOAP 1.2 calls to the service. Your business logic in the code doesn't change depending on the binding you use. As you saw earlier, you can configure bindings in the configuration file.

WS2007HttpRelayBinding

WS2007HttpRelayBinding supports SOAP 1.2 messaging with the latest OASIS standards for reliable message exchange and security. It's used to create SOAP over HTTP interfaces for your service. To demonstrate WS2007HttpRelayBinding, you use the same control gateway applications as the service, and the head-end server as the client application as you saw for netTcpRelayBinding. By modifying a few lines of code, you can easily convert netTcpRelayBinding to ws2007HttpRelayBinding.

The binding and service configuration for WS2007HttpRelayBinding is shown in Listing 8-30.

Listing 8-30. *WS2007HttpRelay Configuration*

```
<!--Define the binding -->
<ws2007HttpRelayBinding>
<binding name="default">
<security mode="None" relayClientAuthenticationType="None" />
</binding>
</ws2007HttpRelayBinding>

<!--Define end point -->
<endpoint name="RelayTcpEndpoint"
          contract="EnergyServiceContract.IEnergyServiceGatewayOperations"
          binding="ws2007HttpRelayBinding"
          bindingConfiguration="default"
          address="" />
```

The only difference between netTcpRelayConfiguration and ws2007HttpRelayConfiguration is the definition of the binding and replacing netTcpRelayBinding with ws2007HttpRelayBinding. Similarly, in the client application, you can make replacements as shown in Listing 8-31.

Listing 8-31. *WS2007HttpRelayBinding Configuration*

```
<!--Define the binding -->
<bindings>
 <ws2007HttpRelayBinding>
  <binding name="default">
   <security mode="None"/>
  </binding>
 </ws2007HttpRelayBinding>
</bindings>
<!--Define end point -->
<client>
<endpoint
name="RelayTcpEndpoint"
contract="EnergyServiceContract.IEnergyServiceGatewayOperations"
binding="ws2007HttpRelayBinding "
bindingConfiguration="default"
behaviorConfiguration="sharedSecretClientCredentials"
address="http://AddressToBeReplacedInCode/" />
</client>
```

The WS2007HttpRelayBinding client application authenticates itself with the AppFabric Service Bus using the ACS shared-secret authentication method. In the code, when you generate the URI in both client and the server, you must replace the "sb" protocol from netTcpRelayBinding to "http" for ws2007HttpRelayBinding:

```
Uri serviceUri = ServiceBusEnvironment.CreateServiceUri("http", serviceNamespace,
ServiceBusHelper.GetGatewayServicePath(gatewayId));
```

The steps required to run the end-to-end application are the same as running the netTcpRelayBinding example in the previous section.

Figure 8-27 shows the client and service applications using WS2007HttpRelayBinding.

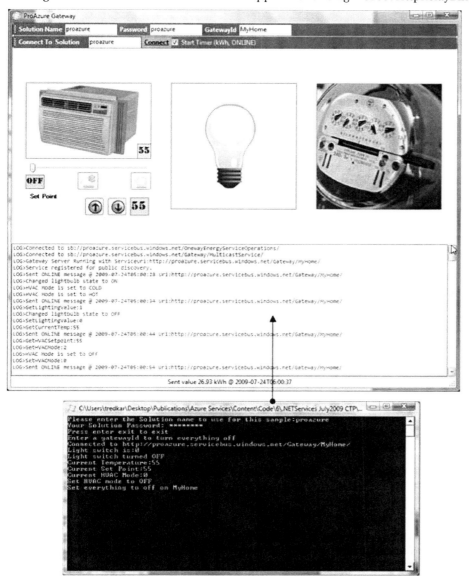

Figure 8-27. *WS2007HttpRelayBinding client and service applications*

While running the application, note the delay when using the WS2007HttpRelayBinding as compared to the netTcpRelayBinding. WS2007HttpRelayBinding polls the relay service for the message.

WebHttpRelayBinding

In the past few years, REST-style programming has becomes popular because it uses existing HTTP constructs to communicate messages and remote method invocations. As compared to SOAP, the REST interface is easier to use in manual and scripting interfaces. In the Windows Azure Storage chapters, you learned to use the REST interface exposed by the storage service to interact with storage objects like blobs, queues, and tables. WebHttpRelayBinding is used to create HTTP, XML, and REST-style interfaces for your service.

To demonstrate WebHttpRelayBinding, you create a simple service contract that represents a REST-style interface over the control gateway service. You can find the example for WebHttpRelayBinding in the project RESTGatewayServer in Ch8Solution.

Listing 8-32 shows the code representing two contracts: one for the lighting service (IRESTLightswitch) and the other (IRESTEnergyMeter) for the energy meter service.

Listing 8-32. *Lighting Service and Energy Meter Contracts*

```
namespace EnergyServiceContract
{

    [ServiceContract(Name = "IRESTLightswitch.",
Namespace = "http://proazure/ServiceBus/energyservice/gateway")]
    public interface IRESTLightswitch
    {
        [OperationContract(Action = "GET", ReplyAction = "GETRESPONSE")]
        Message GetLightswitchState();
    }
    public interface IRESTLightswitchChannel : IRESTLightswitch, IClientChannel
    {
    }

    [ServiceContract(Name = "IRESTEnergyMeter.",
Namespace = "http://proazure/ServiceBus/energyservice/gateway")]
    public interface IRESTEnergyMeter
    {
        [OperationContract(Action = "GET", ReplyAction = "GETRESPONSE")]
        Message GetKWhValue();
    }
}
```

You can combine both interfaces into one, but this example ties the simple HTTP GET operation to each method. The OperationContract.Action attribute property represents the HTTP action used to call this operation. This name must be unique within an interface. The System.ServiceModel.Channels.Message return type is a generic type of object to communicate information between the client and the service.

Listing 8-33 contains the implementation of both the service contracts.

Listing 8-33. *Service Implementation*

```
public class GatewayService : IRESTLightswitch, IRESTEnergyMeter
    {
        const string ON_FILE = "on.jpg";
        const string OFF_FILE = "off.jpg";
        Image on, off;
        static int LIGHT_BULB_STATE = 0;
        public GatewayService()
        {
            on = Image.FromFile(ON_FILE);
            off = Image.FromFile(OFF_FILE);
        }
        public Message GetLightswitchState()
        {
            Message m = Message.CreateMessage
(OperationContext.Current.IncomingMessageVersion, "GETRESPONSE", "ON");
            return m;
        }
        System.ServiceModel.Channels.Message IRESTLightswitch.GetLightswitchState()
        {
            Message response = StreamMessageHelper.CreateMessage
(OperationContext.Current.IncomingMessageVersion,
"GETRESPONSE", this.WriteImageToStream);
            HttpResponseMessageProperty responseProperty =
new HttpResponseMessageProperty();
            responseProperty.Headers.Add("Content-Type", "image/jpeg");
            response.Properties.Add(HttpResponseMessageProperty.Name,
responseProperty);
            return response;
        }
        public void WriteImageToStream(System.IO.Stream stream)
        {
            Image i = (LIGHT_BULB_STATE == 0) ? off : on;
            i.Save(stream, ImageFormat.Jpeg);
            if (LIGHT_BULB_STATE == 0)
            {
                LIGHT_BULB_STATE = 1;
            }
            else
            {
                LIGHT_BULB_STATE = 0;
            }
        }
        System.ServiceModel.Channels.Message IRESTEnergyMeter.GetKWhValue()
        {
            Random r = new Random();
            double kwhValue = double.Parse
(String.Format("{0:0.00}", (r.NextDouble() * 100)));
            System.ServiceModel.Channels.Message m =Message.CreateMessage
(OperationContext.Current.IncomingMessageVersion, "GETRESPONSE",
```

```
String.Format("{0:00}", kwhValue));
        return m;
    }
}
```

In Listing 8-33, the GatewayService class implements the IRESTLightswitch and IRESTEnergyMeter interfaces. The implementation of the methods is very simple because they're only simulating the call and not making any real calls to the devices. The GetLightswitchState() method returns an image representing the state of the lighting service. The GetKWhValue() method returns a text value representing a randomly generated kWh value. Note the use of the System.ServiceModel.Channels.Message object to transfer an image as well as a text value.

Because you can access the REST interface manually from the browser, you don't implement a client for the service. Listing 8-34 shows the configuration for the service.

Listing 8-34. *Service Configuration*

```xml
<?xml version="1.0" encoding="utf-8" ?>
<configuration>
  <system.serviceModel>
    <bindings>
      <!-- Application Binding -->
      <webHttpRelayBinding>
                    <binding name="default" >
                        <security
relayClientAuthenticationType="None" />
                    </binding>
      </webHttpRelayBinding>
    </bindings>

    <services>
      <!-- Application Service -->
      <service name="RESTGatewayServer.GatewayService"
                behaviorConfiguration="default">
        <endpoint name="LighswitchEndpoint"
                    contract="EnergyServiceContract.IRESTLightswitch"
                    binding="webHttpRelayBinding"
                    bindingConfiguration="default"
                    behaviorConfiguration="cardSpaceClientCredentials"
                    address=
"https://{your service namespace}.servicebus.windows.net/Gateway/MyHome/Lightswitch" />
        <endpoint name="EnergyMeterEndpoint"
                    contract="EnergyServiceContract.IRESTEnergyMeter"
                    binding="webHttpRelayBinding"
                    bindingConfiguration="default"
                    behaviorConfiguration="cardSpaceClientCredentials"
                    address=
"https://{your service namespace}.servicebus.windows.net/Gateway/MyHome/Meter" />
      </service>
    </services>
<behaviors>
```

```
    <endpointBehaviors>
      <behavior name="sharedSecretClientCredentials">
        <transportClientEndpointBehavior credentialType="SharedSecret">
          <clientCredentials>
            <sharedSecret issuerName="owner"
issuerSecret="wJBJaobUmarWn6kqv7QpaaRh3ttNVr3w1OjiotVEOL4=" />
          </clientCredentials>
        </transportClientEndpointBehavior>
      </behavior>
    </endpointBehaviors>
    <serviceBehaviors>
      <behavior name="default">
        <serviceDebug httpHelpPageEnabled="false" httpsHelpPageEnabled="false" />
      </behavior>
    </serviceBehaviors>
  </behaviors>  </system.serviceModel>
</configuration>
```

In Listing 8-34, the service is configured to use a shared secret to authenticate with the AppFabric Service Bus. The relayAuthenticationType=None value disables the user authentication so that users can access the service without authenticating themselves. You can start the service, and users should be able to access it through the browser.

The steps to run the RESTGatewayServer application are as follows:

1. Configure the service with your service namespace and shared secret information.

2. Open a command prompt as Administrator, and navigate to the bin\Debug folder of the RESTGatewayServer project.

3. Run RESTGatewayServer.exe.

4. When the service starts, it displays URIs for the Lightswitch and EnergyMeter endpoints. Write down the URI access points of Lightswitch and EnergyMeter, as shown in Figure 8-28.

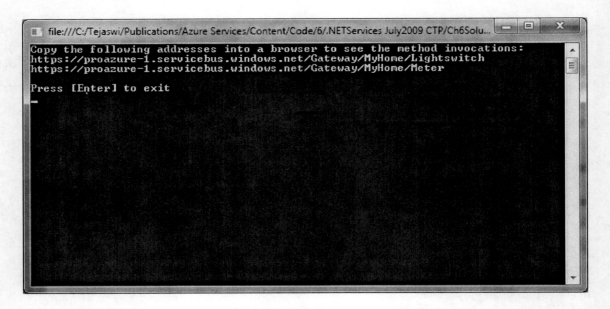

```
file:///C:/Tejaswi/Publications/Azure Services/Content/Code/6/.NETServices July2009 CTP/Ch6Solu...

Copy the following addresses into a browser to see the method invocations:
https://proazure-1.servicebus.windows.net/Gateway/MyHome/Lightswitch
https://proazure-1.servicebus.windows.net/Gateway/MyHome/Meter

Press [Enter] to exit
```

Figure 8-28. *Access URLs*

5. Open a browser, and navigate to each endpoint. The method is automatically
    invoked, and the result is displayed in the browser as shown in Figures 8-29 and
    8-30. Figure 8-29 illustrates the light switch state, and Figure 8-30 illustrates the
    energy meter value.

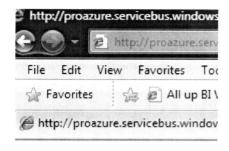

Figure 8-29. Light switch state

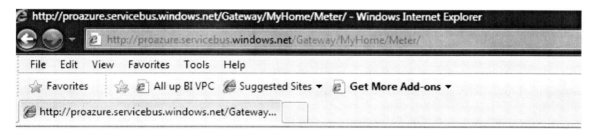

`<string xmlns="http://schemas.microsoft.com/2003/10/Serialization/">26</string>`

Figure 8-30. Energy meter value

6. You can also go to the AtomPub feed of the service to invoke methods. Navigate to the solution feed page `http://[solution name].servicebus.windows.net/`, as shown in Figure 8-31.

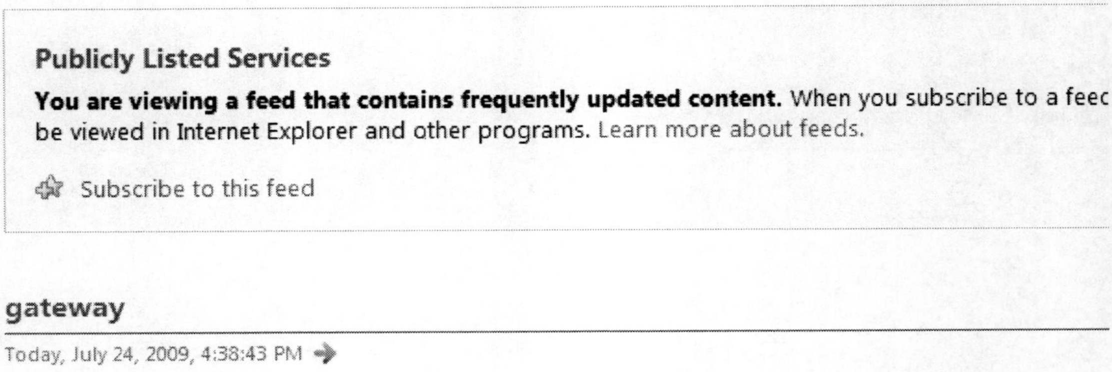

Publicly Listed Services

You are viewing a feed that contains frequently updated content. When you subscribe to a feed be viewed in Internet Explorer and other programs. Learn more about feeds.

 Subscribe to this feed

---

gateway

Today, July 24, 2009, 4:38:43 PM ➜

Figure 8-31. *Solution feed*

7. Click the gateway to go to the list of registered gateways feeds, as shown in Figure 8-32.

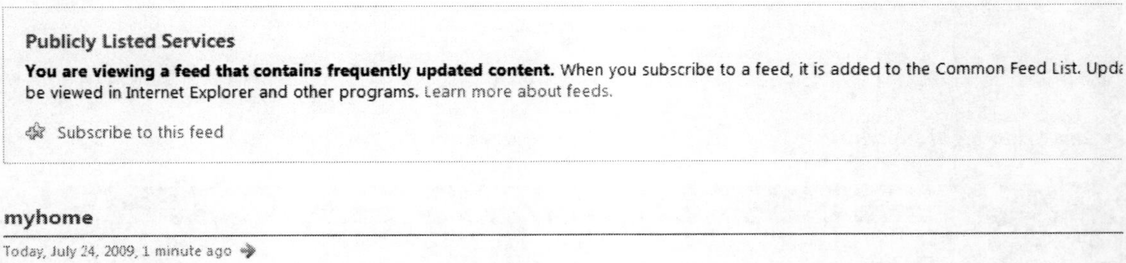

Publicly Listed Services

You are viewing a feed that contains frequently updated content. When you subscribe to a feed, it is added to the Common Feed List. Upda be viewed in Internet Explorer and other programs. Learn more about feeds.

 Subscribe to this feed

---

myhome

Today, July 24, 2009, 1 minute ago ➜

Figure 8-32. *Registered gateways*

8. Click the gateway (myhome) to go to the gateway operations feed page, as shown in Figure 8-33.

Publicly Listed Services

You are viewing a feed that contains frequently upda
be viewed in Internet Explorer and other programs. Lea

 Subscribe to this feed

lightswitch

Today, July 24, 2009, 4:41:44 PM ➡

meter

Today, July 24, 2009, 4:41:44 PM ➡

Figure 8-33. *Gateway operations*

9. Click any of the listed operations to invoke the remote method and see the response in the browser.

Message Buffer

A *message buffer* is a temporary cache you can create in the AppFabric Service Bus. I call it a temporary cache because the data in the cache isn't persistent and can't survive server reboots. Therefore, I recommend that you store only temporary data in message buffers and assume data loss while programming your applications.

A message buffer exposes operations through a REST API that you can use to create message buffers and execute CRUD operations on messages. The message buffer REST API integrates with ACS, and therefore you can share the authentication you use for other Service Bus application with the message buffer. Figure 8-34 illustrates the high-level architecture of the message buffer.

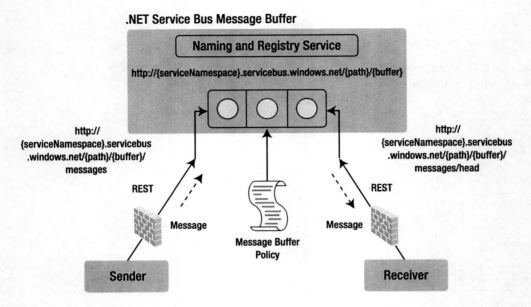

Figure 8-34. *Message buffer architecture*

As illustrated in Figure 8-34, the message buffer has three main components: a message buffer, a message buffer policy, and the message. The message buffer represents the actual buffer you use to store messages. The message buffer policy represents certain attributes of the message buffer such as the buffer lifetime, maximum message count, and message overflow policy. The message represents the message you send and receive from a message buffer.

The typical developer workflow in a message buffer application is as follows:

1. Create a message buffer policy.

2. Create a message buffer.

3. Send messages to the message buffer.

4. Receive or peek messages from the message buffer.

5. Delete messages.

6. Delete the message buffer.

The Service Bus SDK also provides a MessageBufferClient class in the Microsoft.ServiceBus.dll assembly for interacting with the message buffer. Figure 8-35 shows the class diagram of the MessageBufferClient and MessageBufferPolicy classes.

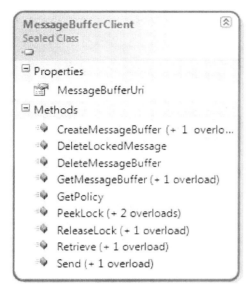

Figure 8-35. MessageBufferClient and MessageBufferPolicy class diagrams

As shown in Figure 8-35, the MessageBufferClient class includes all the basic operations like CreateMessageBuffer(), DeleteMessageBuffer(), Retrieve(), Send(), and Peek(), for interacting with the message buffer. The MessageBufferClient class abstracts the REST interface. You can call the MessageBufferClient methods from your code directly; the MessageBufferClient class translates the method invocations into REST API calls to the message buffer.

___

■ **Note** To learn more about the message buffer REST API methods, visit the AppFabric SDK at
`http://msdn.microsoft.com/en-us/library/ee794877.aspx`.

___

Programming Message Buffer Applications

Because of the REST API, a message buffer is available to any programming language, cross platform. You can write message buffer applications in any programming language that can make remote HTTP calls. This section goes over the typical developer operations on the message buffer using the MessageBufferClient class in the C# language.

Creating a Message Buffer Policy

A message buffer policy represents the runtime attributes of a message buffer. The policy is applied to a message buffer during its creation time. A message buffer policy is represented by the MessageBufferPolicy class, which is passed to the MessageBufferClient.CreateMessageBuffer() method. Listing 8-35 shows the code to create an instance of the MessageBufferPolicy class.

Listing 8-35. *Initialize MessageBufferPolicy*

```
private static MessageBufferPolicy GetMessagBufferPolicy(double bufferExpirationTime,
int maxMessageCount)
{
        MessageBufferPolicy policy = new MessageBufferPolicy
        {
            ExpiresAfter = TimeSpan.FromMinutes(bufferExpirationTime),
            MaxMessageCount = maxMessageCount,
            OverflowPolicy = OverflowPolicy.RejectIncomingMessage,
            Authorization = AuthorizationPolicy.NotRequired,
            Discoverability = DiscoverabilityPolicy.Public,
            TransportProtection = TransportProtectionPolicy.AllPaths

        };
        return policy;
}
```

In Listing 8-35, ExpiresAfter sets the lifetime of the message buffer. The lifetime of the message buffer is automatically renewed when you send a message to the buffer. MaxMessageCount represents the message capacity of the message buffer. OverflowPolicy represents the policy to be applied if there is a message overflow beyond the capacity of the message buffer. In the November 2009 release of the Service Bus API, the only overflow policy available was OverflowPolicy.RejectIncomingMessage. AuthorizationPolicy represents the authorization policy required to accesse the message buffer. The default policy is AuthorizationPolicy.Required, which means that authorization is required to send as well as receiving messages. Discoverability determines whether the message buffer is accessible from the AppFabric Atom Feed. If Discoverability isn't set to Public, then applications must know the explicit URI of the message buffer. The default Discoverability value is Managers, which means only the application that created the message buffer has access to it. TransportProtection represents the end-to-end security of the message that traverses from sender to the receiver.

Creating and Deleting a message buffer

When you've created the message buffer policy, you can create the message buffer by calling the MessageBufferClient.CreateMessageBuffer() method, as shown in Listing 8-36.

Listing 8-36. *Create Message Buffer*

```
private MessageBufferClient CreateMessageBuffer(
string serviceNamespace, string messageBufferName, TransportClientEndpointBehavior behavior,
MessageBufferPolicy policy)
```

```
{
MessageVersion messageVersion = MessageVersion.Default;
Uri messageBufferUri = ServiceBusEnvironment.CreateServiceUri
("https", serviceNamespace, messageBufferName);
return MessageBufferClient.CreateMessageBuffer(behavior, messageBufferUri, policy,
messageVersion);
}
```

Before you create a message buffer, you have to create an URI for the message buffer endpoint. You can create only one message buffer per endpoint; and when the endpoint is reserved for the message buffer, you can't register any other service on that endpoint. After the message buffer is created, you can get a reference to a message buffer (MessageBufferClient object) by calling the method

```
MessageBufferClient client =
MessageBufferClient.GetMessageBuffer(TransportClientEndpointBehavior behavior, Uri
messageBufferUri)
```

You can delete a message buffer by calling the method MessageBufferClient. DeleteMessageBuffer().

Sending Messages to a Message Buffer

To send messages to the message buffer, you can call the Send() method on the message buffer Client object that was returned either when the message buffer was created or when you called the GetMessageBuffer() method. Listing 8-37 shows the method call to send messages to a message buffer.

Listing 8-37. Sending Messages to a Message Buffer

```
private void SendMessage(string message, MessageBufferClient client)
{
        System.ServiceModel.Channels.Message msg =
System.ServiceModel.Channels.Message.CreateMessage(
                MessageVersion.Default,
                string.Empty,
                message);
            client.Send(msg, TimeSpan.FromSeconds(30));
            msg.Close();
}
```

The Send() method accepts a System.ServiceModel.Channels.Message object and optionally accepts a method execution timeout value. This is the time the method call should wait before timing out.

Retrieving Message from a Message Buffer

The message buffer client API provides two main methods for retrieving a message from the message buffer: PeekLock() and Retrieve(). The PeekLock() method is used to peek at the first message in the message buffer by locking the message before the buffer is instructed to release or delete the message. The PeekLock() method also provides overloads for specifying the method timeout to wait on message and the duration for which the message remains locked. You can lock a message for a duration between

10 seconds and 5 minutes, the default being 2 minutes. You can call the DeleteLockedMessage() or ReleaseLock() method to release a lock on the message.

The Retrieve() method retrieves the message from the message buffer and deletes the message from the message buffer. This kind of read is also called a *destructive read* and is the recommended method for high-performance applications to avoid round trips to the server. Listing 8-38 shows the code for retrieving messages from the message buffer.

Listing 8-38. *Retrieving Messages from a Message Buffer*

```
private string RetrieveMessage(MessageBufferClient client)
{
        System.ServiceModel.Channels.Message retrievedMessage;

        retrievedMessage = client.Retrieve();
        retrievedMessage.Close();

        return retrievedMessage.GetBody<string>();

}

private string PeekMessage(MessageBufferClient client)
{
        System.ServiceModel.Channels.Message lockedMessage = client.PeekLock();
        client.DeleteLockedMessage(lockedMessage);
        lockedMessage.Close();

        return lockedMessage.GetBody<string>();
}
```

Message Buffer Sample Application

I've created a message buffer sample application in the source code solution for this chapter. The MessageBuffer project in the chapter solution is a Windows application that creates a message buffer, sends messages to the message buffer, retrieves messages from the message buffer, and finally deletes the message buffer. Figure 8-36 shows the application in action.

Figure 8-36. *Message buffer sample application*

In the sample application, you can enter your own issuer credentials and service namespace and start interacting with the message buffer. From the application, you can create a message buffer, send messages, retrieve messages, peek and retrieve messages, and finally delete the message buffer. In this case, the message sender and the message receiver are the same application; but you can separate the message sender and message receiver functionality into different applications because the message buffer API is stateless and so the same instance of the message buffer is accessible to all authenticated applications.

Summary

Microsoft has built the AppFabric Service Bus as a foundation for cross-platform and cross-enterprise application integration. Services across the same or different enterprises can communicate with each other even if they're behind firewalls. Its integration with ACS and the security at the transport-level makes it secure to send encrypted messages over the Internet. The programming model is very similar to WCF, and you can utilize your existing WCF skills to build AppFabric Service Bus applications.

Message buffers are a different concept than WCF programming, but they're similar to the Windows Azure queues that you read about earlier in the book. You can use message buffers in nonreliable asynchronous store-and-forward scenarios.

In this chapter, you learned the concepts behind the AppFabric Service Bus that can help you built integration applications at Internet-scale. Early releases of the AppFabric Service Bus included another component called Workflow Services that is planned for a future release.

The next chapter covers Microsoft's database for the cloud: SQL Azure.

Bibliography

Lowy, J. (n.d.). Securing The .NET Service Bus. Retrieved from MSDN: http://msdn.microsoft.com/en-us/magazine/dd942847.aspx.

Microsoft Corporation. (2009). Windows Azure platform AppFabric November 2009 CTP. Retrieved from MSDN: http://msdn.microsoft.com/en-us/library/ee173584.aspx.

Microsoft Corporation. (n.d.). Windows Azure SDK. Retrieved from MSDN: http://msdn.microsoft.com/en-us/library/dd179367.aspx.

OASIS Standards. (n.d.). OASIS Standards. Retrieved from OASIS Standards: http://www.oasis-open.org/home/index.php.

Vasters, C. (n.d.). Azure: Microsoft .NET Service Bus. Retrieved from Clemens Vasters, Bldg 42: http://blogs.msdn.com/clemensv/archive/2008/10/27/azure-microsoft-net-service-bus.aspx.

CHAPTER 9

■■■

SQL Azure

SQL Azure is Microsoft's relational database service in the cloud. Any enterprise application, either cloud or on-premises, is incomplete without the support of a backend database. The database can be used to store business data, consumer data, or system data.

Applications are volatile, whereas databases are persistent. Front-end web applications usually depend on databases to persist business and system data. Therefore, databases usually are the bottleneck in a system and need careful attention when you're architecting scalability, high availability, and performance for a system. You can scale-out front-end web applications by adding more load-balanced nodes; but to scale-out database servers, you need to not only scale out the database servers but also the storage that these databases depend on. On top of that, you have to make sure you aren't jeopardizing the high availability of the database server and its storage. Typically, on-premises databases use clustering techniques to provide high availability. Thus, scaling-out databases is an expensive effort in terms of the costs involved in scaling-out storage and database servers.

SQL Azure provides high availability to your databases out of the box. At any point in time, SQL Azure maintains three replicas of your databases in the cloud. If one replica fails, SQL Azure automatically creates a new one to maintain three replicas available at any point in time.

SQL Azure is based on the Microsoft SQL Server relational database engine. SQL Server is Microsoft's relational database, which is used by enterprises in their on-premises systems and also offered as a hosted service by database hosting providers. With the launch of SQL Azure, Microsoft aims to offer a cloud relational database as a service for on-premises and cloud applications. When SQL Data Services (SDS) was launched at the Professional Developers Conference 2008, the service offering was an Entity-Attribute-Value (EAV) architecture with full scalability, fault tolerance, and high-availability features. Microsoft's vast partner and user community expressed the need for a relational database instead of a completely new EAV architecture because of the existing skill sets and applications that can be readily migrated to the cloud. Microsoft considered the feedback seriously and began the necessary work to replace the EAV architecture with traditional relational database features. In August 2009, Microsoft announced the availability of the Community Technology Preview 1 (CTP 1) version of the SQL Azure relational database. The EAV capabilities were removed from the product, and only the relational database was made available. SQL Azure doesn't provide all the features available in SQL Server, but it does provide the bare minimum features required to deploy and maintain a database. For example, features like the Service Broker, Common Language Runtime (CLR) stored procedures, and HTTP endpoints aren't available in SQL Azure. This may change in the future, depending on customer demand.

In future versions of SQL Azure, Microsoft plans to add features like data synchronization, business intelligence and reporting, and additional features from SQL Server that are missing from the SQL Azure platform.

■ **Note** This chapter assumes that you're familiar with SQL Server database concepts and that you can comfortably program TSQL SQL queries and data access using the ADO.NET API.

SQL Azure Architecture

SQL Azure is a scalable and highly available database utility service in the cloud. Like all other Windows Azure services, it runs in Microsoft data centers around the world. The data center infrastructure provides the SQL Azure service with load balancing, failover and replication capabilities. Figure 9-1 illustrates the high-level SQL Azure architecture.

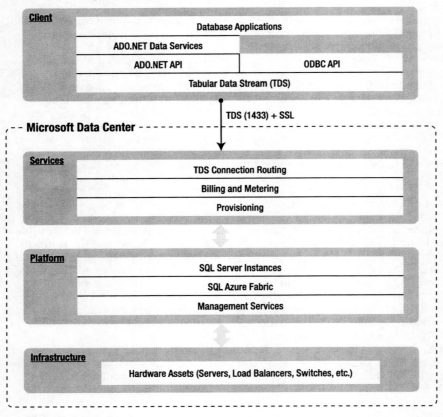

Figure 9-1. SQL Azure Architecture

As shown in Figure 9-1, the SQL Azure service is composed of four layers: infrastructure, platform, services, and client. All the layers except the client layer run inside a Microsoft data center.

Infrastructure Layer

The infrastructure layer is the supporting layer providing administration of hardware and operating systems required by the services layer. This is the core data center layer that is shared across multiple services in a data center.

Platform Layer

The platform layer consists of the SQL Server instances and the SQL Azure fabric, and Management services. The SQL Server instances represent the deployed databases, their replicas, and the operating system instances that host the SQL Server instances. The SQL Azure *fabric* is the underlying framework that automates the deployment, replication, failover, and load balancing of the database servers.

The SQL Azure fabric is responsible for creating three replicas of your database instance and provides automatic failover capabilities to these instances. As shown in Figure 9-2, if the primary instance of your database experiences a failure, the SQL Azure fabric designates one of the replicas as the primary instance and automatically routes all the communications to the new primary instance. In an effort to maintain three replicas at all times, SQL Azure also creates a new replica of the database.

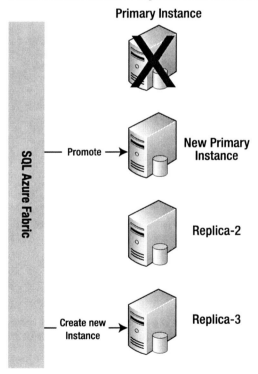

Figure 9-2. SQL Azure database replicas

The Management services are responsible for maintaining the health, upgrades, consistency, and provisioning of the hardware and software to support the SQL Azure fabric.

Services Layer

The services layer comprises external (customer) facing machines and performs as a gateway to the platform layer. It exposes the tabular data stream (TDS), billing, metering, and account provisioning services to customers.

■ **Note** TDS is the native Microsoft SQL Server protocol that database clients can use to interact with a SQL Server database. You can find the TDS protocol specification at `http://msdn.microsoft.com/en-us/library/dd304523(PROT.13).aspx`.

The services layer exposes the TDS protocol on port 1433 over Secure Sockets Layer (SSL). The services layer is also responsible for routing connections to the primary database instance in the platform layer. This layer maintains runtime information about your database replicas and routes the TDS coming from client applications to the appropriate primary instance. The services layer is also responsible for provisioning your database when you create a database in SQL Azure. The provisioning of databases involves communicating with the SQL Azure fabric in the platform layer to provision appropriate replicas of the database.

The billing and metering service is responsible for monitoring the runtime usage of your database for billing purposes. The billing and metering service tracks the usage of databases at the account level.

Client Layer

The client layer is the only layer that runs outside of the Microsoft data center. The client layer doesn't include any SQL Azure–specific components; instead, it uses all the existing features of SQL Server client components like ADO.NET, ODBC, Visual Studio.NET, SQL Server Management Studio, ADO.NET Data Services, and so on. The client API initiates a TDS connection to SQL Azure on port 1433, which is routed by the services layer to the platform layer to the appropriate database instance.

SQL Azure Limitations and Supported Features

Even though SQL Azure is based on SQL Server, it includes some limitations because of its Internet availability and cloud deployment. When you use SQL Server on-premises, the tools and client APIs have full access to the SQL Server instance, and communications between the client and the database are in a homogeneous and controlled environment.

The first release of SQL Azure has only limited functionality of the SQL Server database. One of the most important limitations in SQL Azure is that fact that the size of the database can't exceed 10GB. So, as a database administrator or an architect, you must plan the growth and availability of data accordingly. The supported and unsupported features of SQL Azure in version 1.0 are described in the following sections.

Database Features

SQL Azure supports the following database features:

- CRUD operations on tables, views, and indexes
- TSQL query JOIN statements
- Triggers
- TSQL functions
- Application stored procedures (only TSQL)
- Table constraints
- Session-based temp tables
- Table variables
- Local transactions
- Security roles

SQL Azure does *not* support the following database features:

- Distributes query
- Distributed transactions
- Any TSQL query and views that change or retrieve physical resource information, like physical server DDL statements,[1] Resource Governor, and file group references
- Spatial data types

Application Features

SQL Azure does *not* support the following application-level features:

- Service Broker
- HTTP access
- CLR stored procedures

---

[1] SQL Azure Team Blog: http://blogs.msdn.com/ssds/default.aspx

Administration Features

SQL Azure supports the following administration features:

- Plan and statistics
- Index tuning
- Query tuning

SQL Azure does *not* support the following administration features:

- Replication
- SQL profiler
- SQL trace flag
- Backup command
- Configuration using the sp_configure stored procedure

■ **Note** The SQL Azure SDK documentation lists all the other limitations that aren't covered in this section. See
`http://msdn.microsoft.com/en-us/library/ee336245.aspx`.

SQL Azure Data Access

SQL Azure allows you to connect to the cloud database only using the TDS protocol with limited
support, as described in the previous section. But because the TDS protocol is supported by most of the
SQL Server client APIs, all the features supported by SQL Azure work with existing client APIs. You can
use two common patterns to connect to SQL Azure databases: code near and code far.

Code-Near Connectivity

In *code-near* connectivity, your application is deployed in Windows Azure, which uses SQL Azure. You
geo-locate both of them in the same data center by configuring the geo-location features of Windows
Azure and SQL Azure. Figure 9-3 illustrates applications with code-near connectivity to a SQL Azure
database.

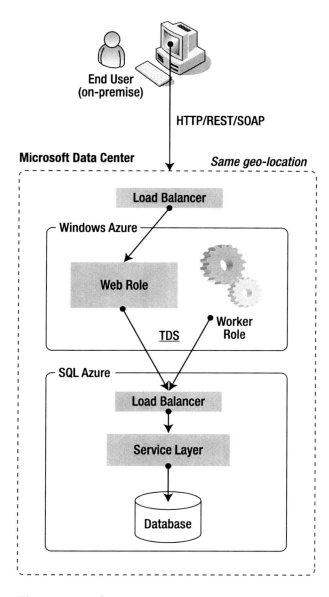

Figure 9-3. *Code-near connectivity to SQL Azure*

In a typical code-near architecture, the data access application is located in the same data center as the SQL Azure database. The end users or on-premises applications access the web interface are exposed via a Windows Azure web role. This web role may be hosting an ASP.NET application for end users or a web service for on-premises applications.

The advantages of the code-near approach are as follows:

- Business logic is located closer to the database.

- You can expose open standards–based interfaces like HTTP, REST, SOAP, and so on to your application data.

- Client applications don't have to depend on the SQL Server client API.

The disadvantage of this approach is the performance impact your application experiences if you're using Windows Azure as a middle tier to access the database.

Code-Far Connectivity

In *code-far* connectivity, your application is typically deployed on-premises or in a different data center than SQL Azure. In this pattern, the client application makes a SQL query using the TDS protocol over the Internet to the SQL Azure database. Figure 9-4 illustrates applications with code-far connectivity to a SQL Azure database.

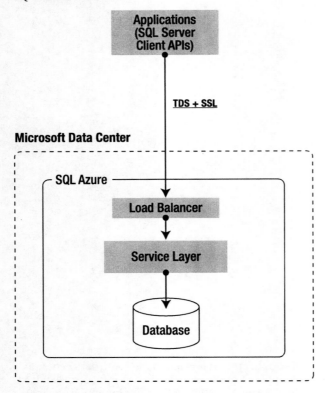

Figure 9-4. *Code-far connectivity to SQL Azure*

The biggest advantage of the code-far approach is the performance benefit your application can experience because of direct connectivity to the database in the cloud. The biggest disadvantage is that all the client applications must use the TDS protocol to access the database. Therefore, the data access clients must use SQL Server–supported client APIs like ADO.NET, ODBC, and so on, reducing data-access possibilities from APIs or platforms that don't support the TDS protocol.

Getting Started with SQL Azure

SQL Azure is a core component of the Windows Azure platform. Like all other Windows Azure components, it requires a Windows Live ID and a token for registration. Follow these steps to register for SQL Azure:

1. Create a Windows Live ID at www.live.com.

2. Register for SQL Azure at http://sql.azure.com.

3. When your registration is complete, log in to the SQL Azure portal at www.microsoft.com/azure/signin.mspx.

Next, create a new database server, as shown in Figure 9-5.

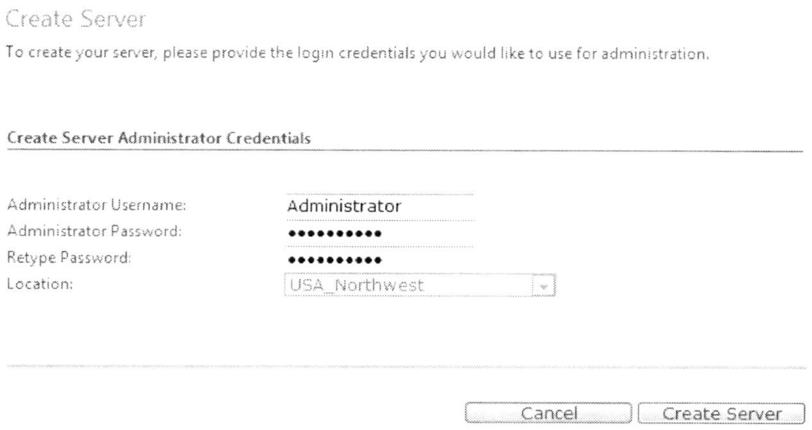

Figure 9-5. Create a new server

On the Create Server page, you're asked to create an administrator user name, administrator password, and geo-location. The geo-location represents the data center in which your databases are hosted. In a code-near configuration as discussed earlier, you can configure the geo-location to be the same as your Windows Azure project. The administrator is the super user of the database and should be used only to execute administrative queries on the database. You shouldn't use the administrator account to access application data from client applications; create a different user with lesser privileges (discussed later) in application connections.

After entering the administrator user name, password, and geo-location, click Create Server to create the server instance. You're taken to the My Projects page, shown in Figure 9-6.

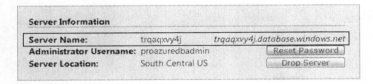

My Projects

These are all the projects you have created or for which you have been designated as a Service Administrator by your Account Administrator.

Project Name	Account Administrator	Service Administrator	Status
Microsoft Internal	tejaswi_redkar@hotmail.com	tredkar@microsoft.com	Enabled
SDS-only CTP Project	tejaswi_redkar@hotmail.com	-	Enabled

Figure 9-6. *My Projects*

Click the Manage link to navigate to the Server Administration page (see Figure 9-7). There, you can create and drop databases, view server information, reset the administrator password, and view connection strings.

Server Administration

Server Information

Server Name:	trqaqxvy4j	*trqaqxvy4j.database.windows.net*
Administrator Username:	proazuredbadmin	Reset Password
Server Location:	South Central US	Drop Server

Databases | Firewall Settings

Database Name	Size	Type	Available
master	80 KB	1 GB	Yes
silverlining	1016 KB	10 GB	Yes

Connection Strings | Test Connectivity | Create Database | Drop Database

Figure 9-7. *Server Administration*

To view the connection strings, select the Master Database radio button and click the Connection Strings button (see Figure 9-8).

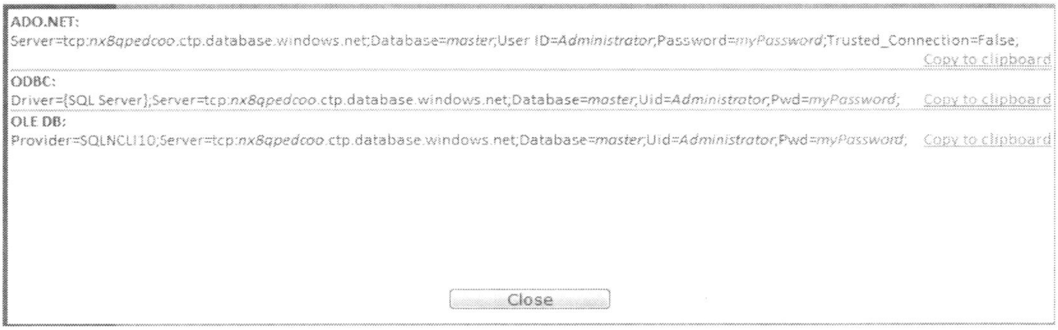

ADO.NET:
Server=tcp:*nx8qpedcoo*.ctp.database.windows.net;Database=*master*;User ID=*Administrator*;Password=*myPassword*;Trusted_Connection=False;
Copy to clipboard

ODBC:
Driver={SQL Server};Server=tcp:*nx8qpedcoo*.ctp.database.windows.net;Database=*master*;Uid=*Administrator*;Pwd=*myPassword*;   Copy to clipboard

OLE DB:
Provider=SQLNCLI10;Server=tcp:*nx8qpedcoo*.ctp.database.windows.net;Database=*master*;Uid=*Administrator*;Pwd=*myPassword*;   Copy to clipboard

Close

Figure 9-8. Connection Strings

The Connection Strings dialog box consists of the client connection strings for ADO.NET, ODBC, and OLE DB client connections. You have to replace the myPassword string with your own database password. With these connection strings, you can connect to the master database from any machine with Internet access and SQL client APIs installed.

■ **Tip** The recommended pattern is to build your database on-premises in SQL Express and then generate a script and execute the script on the cloud database either using SQL Server Management Studio or SQLCMD.

Creating a SQL Azure Database

To create a new database, follow these steps:

1. Click the Create Database button on the Server Administration page (see Figure 9-9).

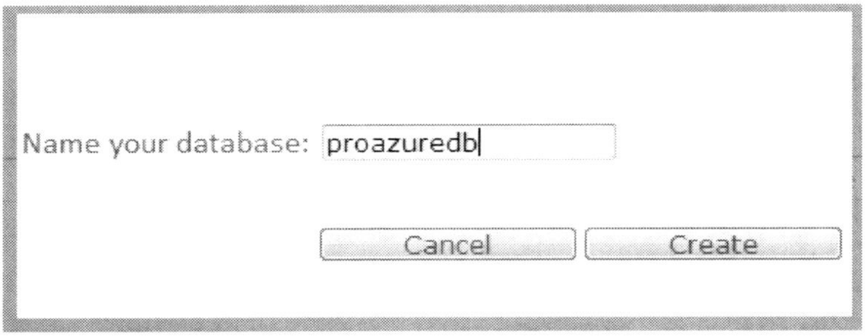

Name your database: proazuredb

Cancel   Create

Figure 9-9. Create Database

2. Name the database "proazuredb", and click Create. The proazuredb database shows up in the database list on the Server Administration page, as shown in Figure 9-10.

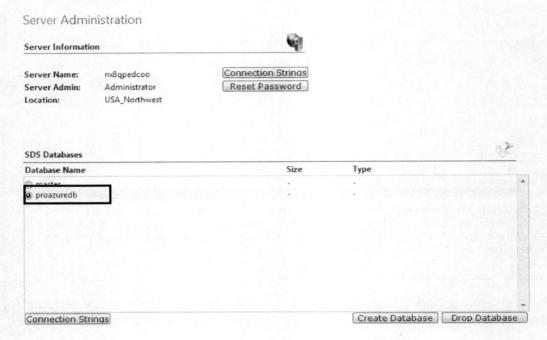

Figure 9-10. *Database list*

3. Select the proazuredb radio button, and click the Connection Strings button to view the connection strings for the proazuredb database (see Figure 9-11).

Figure 9-11. *proazuredb connection strings*

Note that all the databases in the same project have the same master database and administrator. If you want to drop the database, you can click the Drop Database button.

Connecting to a SQL Azure Database

After the database is created, you can connect to it from anywhere with SQL Server client capabilities. You can connect to the SQL Azure database three ways:

- SQL Server Management Studio
- SQLCMD
- ADO.NET

Connecting Using SQL Server Management Studio

The steps to connect to the SQL Azure database are as follows:

1. Open SQL Server Management Studio.

2. Choose Start ▶ All Programs ▶ SQL Server 2008 ▶ SQL Server Management Studio.

■ **Note** In the current CTP, click the Cancel button on the Login dialog box.

---

3. Click the New Query button in SQL Server Management Studio (see Figure 9-12).

Figure 9-12. New Query window

4. A new login dialog pops up (see Figure 9-13). Enter the SQL Azure server name and administrator username /password that you created while provisioning the database. The format for the server name is {your server name}.ctp.database.windows.net, where {your server name} is the name of the server assigned to your database during provisioning. You can get if from the Server Administration page on the SQL Azure portal.

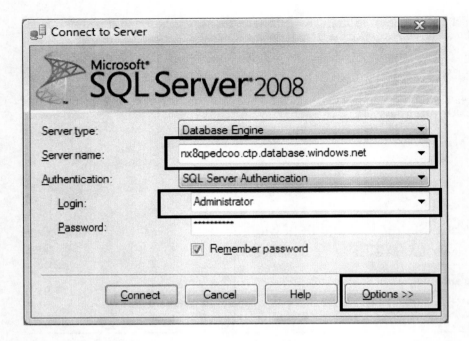

Figure 9-13. *Database login*

5. If you want to connect to a specific database, click the Options button and enter the database name (such as proazuredb) that you want to connect to (see Figure 9-14). If you don't choose a database name, you're connected to the master database by default.

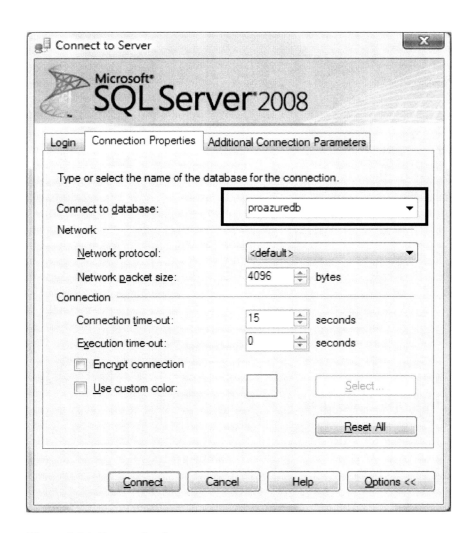

Figure 9-14. *Enter a database name*

6. Keep the database name set to default, and click Connect to connect to the master database. If the connection is successful, a new query window opens as shown in Figure 9-15.

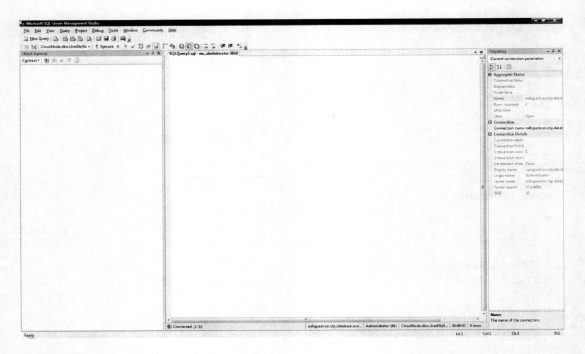

Figure 9-15. *New Query window*

7.   Now you're connected to the SQL Azure cloud master database. Type the
     following queries in the query window, and click Execute:

```
select * from sys.databases;
select @@version;
select @@language;
```

The first query returns the list of databases, @@version returns the version of the
database server, and @@language returns the database language currently in use.
As shown in Figure 9-16, the query returns two databases: master and proazure
db. The master database is created by the system during provisioning, but the
proazuredb is the usercreated database.

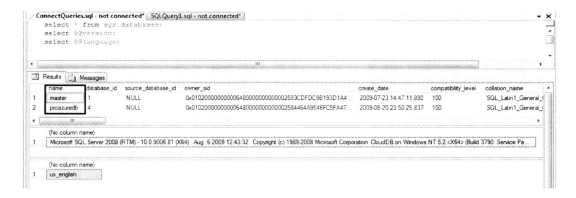

Figure 9-16. *Execute queries*

8. Create a new database named MyCloudDb. Execute the following query in the query window to create the MyCloudDb database:

```
CREATE DATABASE MyCloudDb;
```

When you execute the CREATE DATABASE statement, SQL Azure creates a new database in the cloud. Note that you don't have to worry about the location of the data files because SQL Azure abstracts the location of the data files from you.

9. Execute the "select * from sys.databases" query again. You see the new database in the list of databases returned by the query (see Figure 9-17).

Figure 9-17. *List the new database*

Creating Logins

From SQL Server Management Studio, you can execute common administration SQL statements like creating logins and users, and assigning users to database roles. To create a new login, you have to first create a new login in the master database, then create a new user for the login in the MyCloudDb database, and finally add the new user to one of the database roles using the system stored procedure sp_addrolemember:

1. Connect to the master database using SQL Server Management Studio. Make sure you set the database name to default in the Connection Properties tab, as shown in Figure 9-18.

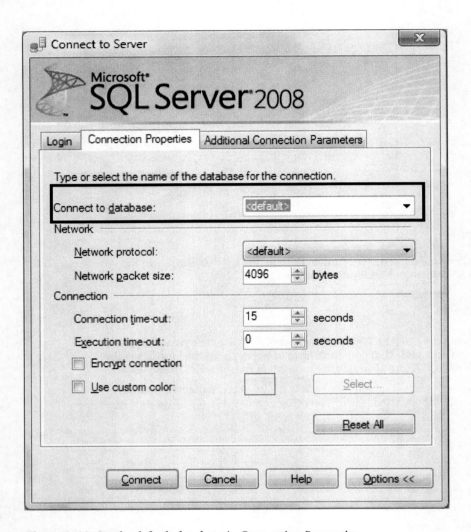

Figure 9-18. Set the default database in Connection Properties

2. Create a new login named testuser by executing the following query in the query window (see Figure 9-19):

■ **Tip** Use your own password in the query.

```
CREATE LOGIN testuser WITH PASSWORD = 'pas@word1'
```

```
    CREATE LOGIN testuser WITH PASSWORD = 'pas@word1'
```

📄 Messages

```
 Command(s) completed successfully.
```

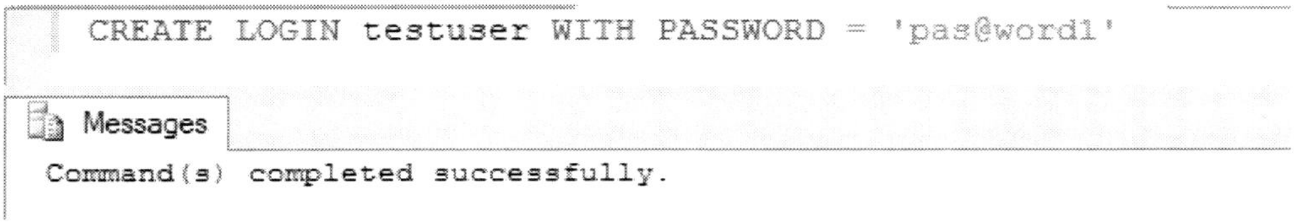

Figure 9-19. Create a new login

3. Connect to the MyCloudDb using your administrator account and by typing **MyCloudDb** in the Connection Properties tab, as shown in Figure 9-20.

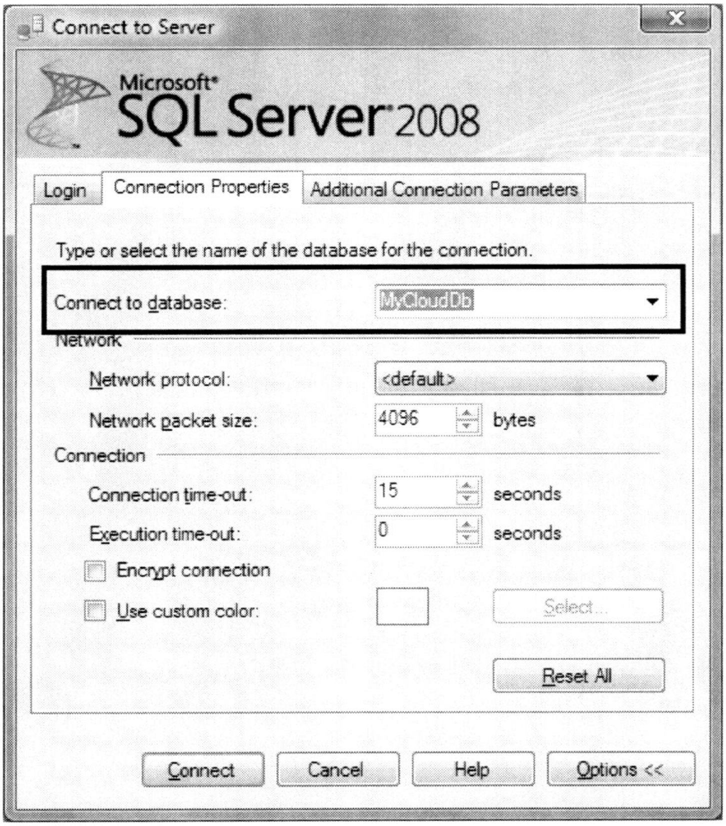

Figure 9-20. Set the database to MyCloudDb in Connection Properties

4. After the connection is successful, type the following query to create a new user testuser for the new login in MyCloudDb (see Figure 9-21):

```
CREATE USER testuser FOR LOGIN testuser;
```

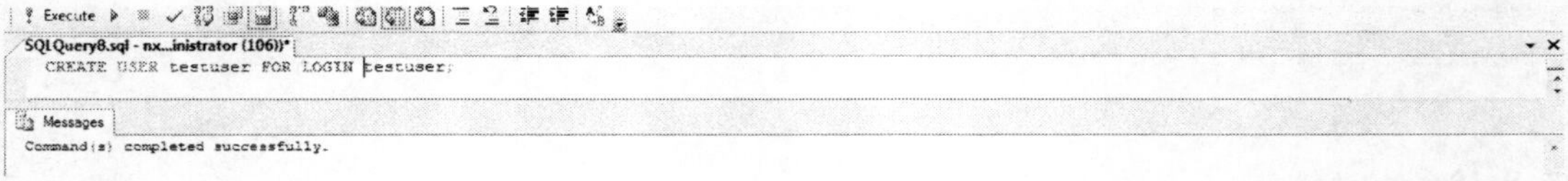

Figure 9-21. *Create a new user for the login*

5. After you add the user to the database, you have to add the user to a particular database role. Figure 9-22 illustrates the default roles in SQL Server.

Figure 9-22. *Default SQL Server roles*

6. Add the testuser to the db_owner group by executing the following query:

```
EXEC sp_addrolemember 'db_owner', 'testuser'
```

■ **Tip** In real-world applications, don't add users to the db_owner role because the db_owner role has extensive privileges to the database.

---

7. Connect to MyCloudDb using the newly created testuser, as shown in Figure 9-23.

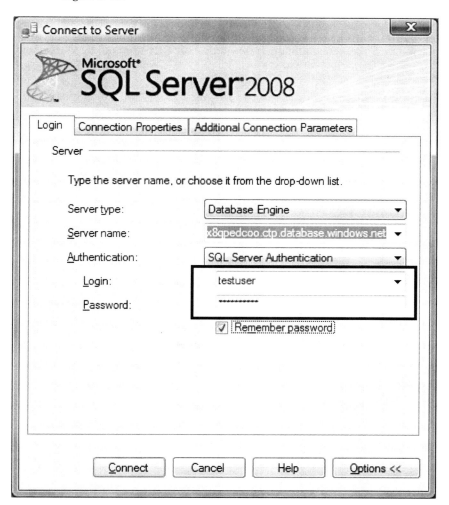

Figure 9-23. *Connecting to MyCloudDb as testuser*

Now you don't need to log in to the database with the administrator user; instead you can log in as testuser. From SQL Server Management Studio, you can also execute data definition (DDL) and data manipulation (DML) commands like CREATE TABLE, UPDATE TABLE, INSERT, DELETE, and so on. I cover DDL and DML in a later section with an example.

Connecting Using SQLCMD

SQLCMD.exe is a command-line utility used to execute commands on SQL Server. It comes with the SQL Server installation. SQL Server Management Studio is a good user interface tool to connect to SQL Azure; but in real-world production environments where automation is heavily used in administering SQL Servers, SQLCMD is the preferred tool. You can automate the execution of SQL command by scheduling SQLCMD. It accepts inline SQL as well as scripts files as input.

The steps to connect to SQL Azure using SQLCMD are as follows:

1. Open a command prompt as administrator, as shown in Figure 9-24.

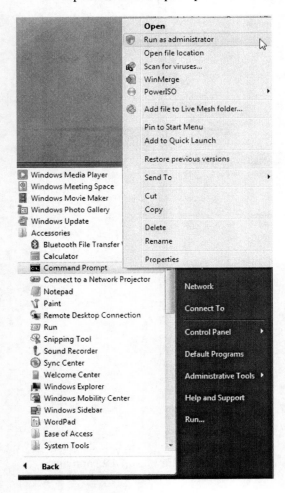

Figure 9-24. Open a command prompt.

The syntax to connect to a database using sqlcmd.exe is as follows (it should be entered as a single line):

```
sqlcmd -U <userlogin@servername>
  -P <password> -S <Fully Qualified ServerName> -d <database name>
```

userlogin is the user name you created for the database. In the previous example, it's either administrator or testuser, if you're connecting to the MyCloudDb database. *servername* is the server name from your Server Administration page in the developer portal. Don't provide the fully qualified server name. *password* is the password for the login. *Fully Qualified ServerName* is the servername appended by the fully qualified name of the SQL Azure server (servername.ctp.database.windows.net).

2. Execute the following command on the command line to connect to MyCloudDb (see Figure 9-25). Replace the server name with your own server name:

```
sqlcmd -U testuser@nx8qpedcoo -P pas@word1
  -S nx8qpedcoo.ctp.database.windows.net -d MyCloudDb
```

Figure 9-25. *Connect to MyCloudDb.*

If the connection is successful, you see "1)" displayed on the command prompt.

3. Execute the following command to create a table in MyCloudDb (see Figure 9-26):

```
CREATE TABLE CloudTable
  (ColNumber1 int primary key clustered, ColNumber2 varchar(50), ColNumber3 float);
```

Figure 9-26. *Create Table*

4. Execute the following command to get the information about the tables in the MyCloudDb database (see Figure 9-27):

```
SELECT * FROM sys.tables
```

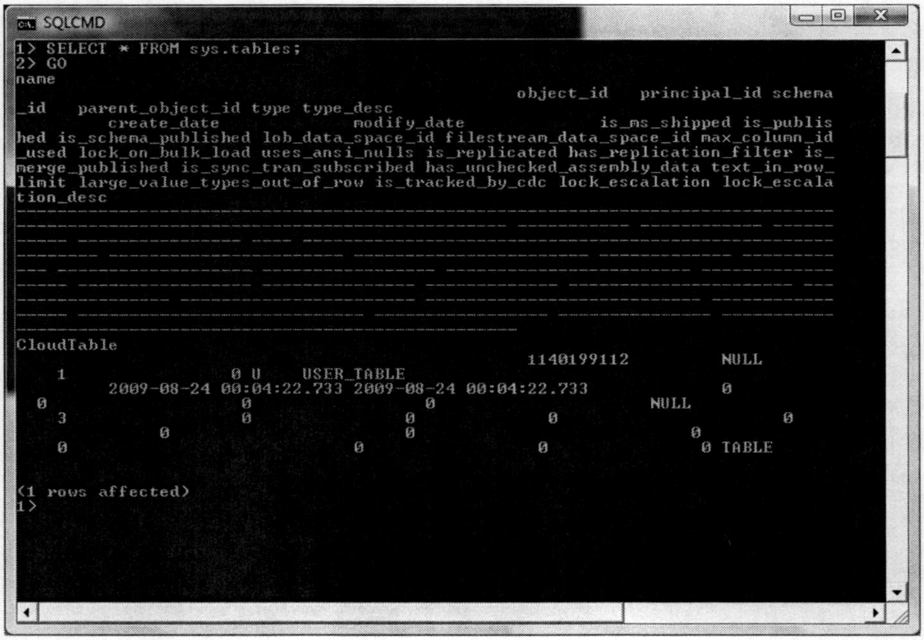

Figure 9-27. *Select all tables*

■ **Note** You can find more information about the SQLCMD command-line utility in SQL Server Books online at http://msdn.microsoft.com/en-us/library/ms162773.aspx. In this chapter, I use SQL Server Management Studio to connect to the SQL Azure database manually; but in an environment where you need scripting to automate SQL Server tasks, you should use SQLCMD.

Connecting Using ADO.NET

ADO.NET is the most popular method to connect to an on-premises SQL Server programmatically. SQL Azure supports ADO.NET connectivity similar to on-premises SQL Server. To open a connection to SQL Azure database using ADO.NET, you have to pass the connection string of the database acquired from the Server Administration page of the SQL Azure developer portal; or, you can programmatically build a connection string using the System.Data.SqlClient.SqlConnectionStringBuilder class, as shown in Listing 9-1.

Listing 9-1. *Build a Connection String Using SqlConnectionStringBuilder*

```
private string GetUserDbString()
  {
  // Create a connection string for the sample database
  SqlConnectionStringBuilder connString2Builder =
      new SqlConnectionStringBuilder();
  string server = "yourservername.ctp.database.windows.net";
  connString2Builder.DataSource = server;
  connString2Builder.InitialCatalog = "user database";
  connString2Builder.Encrypt = true;
  connString2Builder.TrustServerCertificate = true;
  connString2Builder.UserID = "userName";
  connString2Builder.Password = "pass@word1";
  return connString2Builder.ToString();
  }
```

The SqlConnectionStringBuilder class is used to build the string value of the SQL Azure database connection string. Note that the Encrypt and TrustServerCertificate properties are set to true, which is a best practice in general for connecting to databases in the cloud or in another domain.

After the connection string is constructed, you can connect to the SQL Azure database by opening a SqlConnection to the database. Listing 9-2 shows a series of database queries executed on a SQL Azure database after the connection is successfully established.

Listing 9-2. *SqlConnection and Query Execution*

```
using (SqlConnection conn = new SqlConnection(GetUserDbString()))
    {
     using (SqlCommand command = conn.CreateCommand())
     {
      conn.Open();
      // Create table
      command.CommandText =
"CREATE TABLE MyTable1(Column1 int primary key clustered, " +
"Column2 varchar(50), Column3 datetime)";
      command.ExecuteNonQuery();
      // Insert records
      command.CommandText = String.Format
("INSERT INTO MyTable1 (Column1, Column2, Column3) " +
"values ({0}, '{1}', '{2}')", 1, "TestData", DateTime.Now.ToString("s"));
      int rowsAdded = command.ExecuteNonQuery();
      DisplayResults(command);
      // Update a record
      command.CommandText =
"UPDATE MyTable1 SET Column2='Updated String' WHERE Column1=1";
      command.ExecuteNonQuery();
      AddText("UPDATED RECORD");
      DisplayResults(command);
      // Delete a record
      command.CommandText = "DELETE FROM MyTable1 WHERE Column1=1";
```

```
    command.ExecuteNonQuery();
    DisplayResults(command);
  }//using
}
```

Listing 9-2 shows the execution of CREATE, INSERT, UPDATE, and DELETE commands on a SQL Azure database in a sequential operation.

■ **Note** SQL Azure requires you to have a clustered index on the table to insert entries into the table.

Similarly, Listing 9-3 shows the code for the DisplayResults function, demonstrating SELECT command execution on the database table.

Listing 9-3. *SELECT Command*

```
private void DisplayResults(SqlCommand command)
  {
    command.CommandText = "SELECT Column1, Column2, Column3 FROM MyTable1";
    using (SqlDataReader reader = command.ExecuteReader())
    {
    // Loop over the results
    while (reader.Read())
    {
     AddText(command.CommandText);
     AddText(String.Format("Column1: {0}, Column2: {1}, Column3: {2}",
                    reader["Column1"].ToString().Trim(),
                    reader["Column2"].ToString().Trim(),
                    reader["Column3"].ToString().Trim()));
     AddText("\n");
    }
   }
 }
```

You can find the code for Listings 9-1, 9-2, and 9-3 in the ADONETConnection project in Ch8Solution located in the source code directory of this chapter. To run the ADONETConnection application, go to the bin\Debug directory of the ADONETConnection project and double-click ADONETConnection.exe. Figure 9-28 illustrates the user interface for the ADONETConnection.exe Windows application.

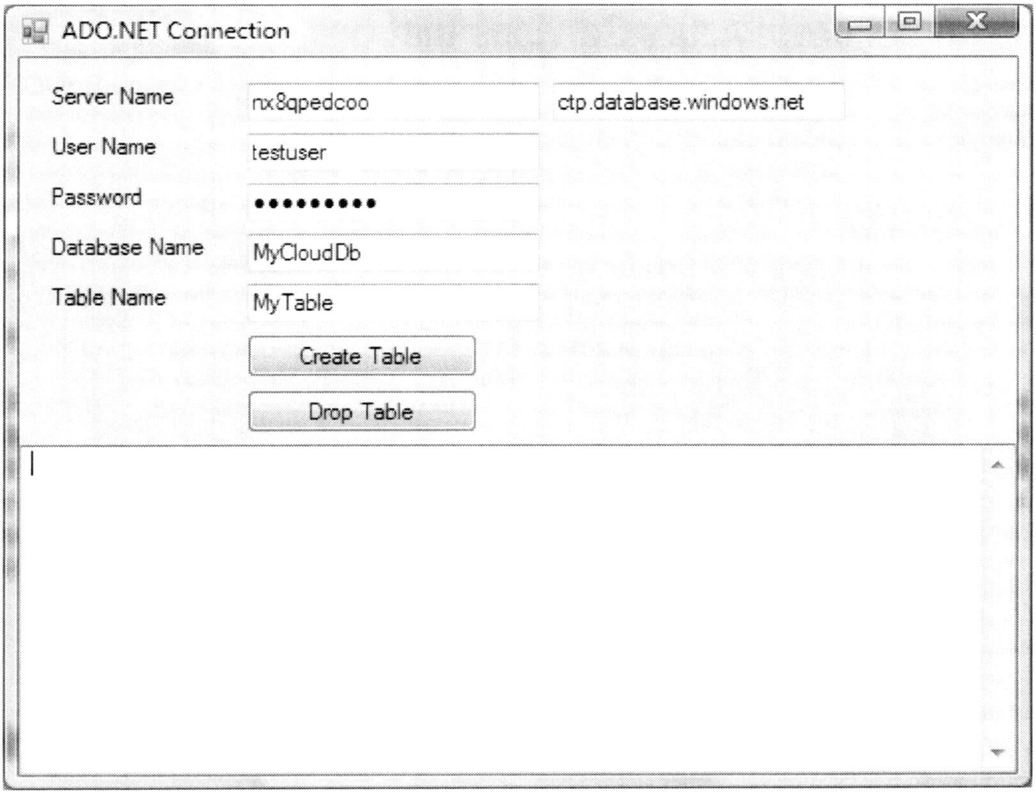

Figure 9-28. *ADONETConnection Windows application*

In the ADONETConnection application, you have to enter the server name, username, password, and database name of your database. Then, click the Create Table button to create a new table called MyTable1. Insert a record into that table, update the record, and delete the record. The results of the operation are displayed in the text box. To drop the table, click the Drop Table button. If the table already exists, the Create Table operation throws an exception. So, you may have to drop the table if you receive a "table already exists" exception.

■ **Caution** Here are a few important points to consider while designing SQL data access. Test your queries for SQL Injection. Use parameterized queries wherever possible. Encrypt your database connection string. And encrypt the username, password, and database information if you're constructing the connection string using the SqlConnectionBuilder.

Developing Windows Azure Services that Use SQL Azure

As an exercise to learn SQL Azure, in this section you develop an end-to-end application involving SQL Azure, Windows Azure, and AppFabric Service Bus. This example also helps you learn to integrate these three technologies seamlessly when building cloud applications.

Service Description

Consider a hypothetical company called SixFrogs Incorporated that offers a cloud-based demand-response service (Dem-Res) directly to utility companies and indirectly to consumers through utility companies.

A *demand-response (Dem-Res) system* is a popular pattern used by utility companies to curtail the electricity load during peak usage when the pricing for usage is very high. The cost savings are then passed on to consumers. The curtailment is determined in real time based on peak usage, pricing, and several other factors. In the interest of keeping the example conceptual, assume that the load reduction depends on peak usage and pricing.

Processes for Curtailment

The process flow for the Dem-Res system between SixFrogs, utility companies, and consumers is as follows:

1. Multiple utility companies subscribe to SixFrog's Dem-Res cloud system.

2. Consumers subscribe to the Dem-Res system through their utility company in return for a discount on their monthly electric bill.

3. Utility companies install their hardware (gateway) in consumers' houses and/or buildings and point those gateways to the Dem-Res system in the cloud.

4. Utility companies configure load curtailment for consumers for specific load devices (this example considers only HVAC).

5. Utility companies receive electric load-pricing information for a particular period of time. This pricing information is in dollars per kWh for a particular period of time. For example, a particular pricing entry may be represented as *$16/kWh between 1:00pm and 3:00pm on Monday August 24th 2009*.

6. Utility companies passes this pricing information to the Dem-Res system.

7. The Dem-Res system reads the pricing information and sends commands to the applicable gateways in buildings and houses to automatically curtail the load.

8. Periodically, the gateways communicate the energy usage to the Dem-Res system. The Dem-Res system checks the database for peak load and pricing information and sends curtailment commands to the gateways if required.

Figure 9-29 illustrates the high-level process for the Dem-Res system.

Utility Companies Subscribe to SixFrogs Dem-Res system

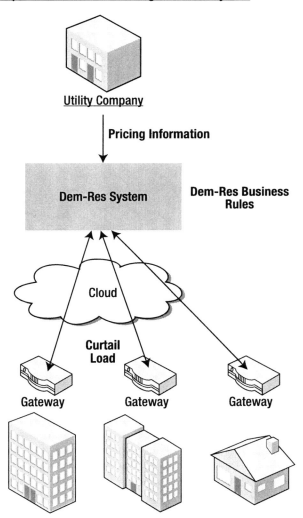

Figure 9-29. Dem-Res process

Technical Architecture

This section discusses the design of the Dem-Res system and its communication endpoints. The goal is to map the process architecture to the system architecture in the cloud representing Windows Azure components. From the earlier section and your knowledge of Windows Azure so far, it should be clear that you can build a complete Dem-Res system in Windows Azure. Figure 9-30 illustrates the technical architecture of the Dem-Res system.

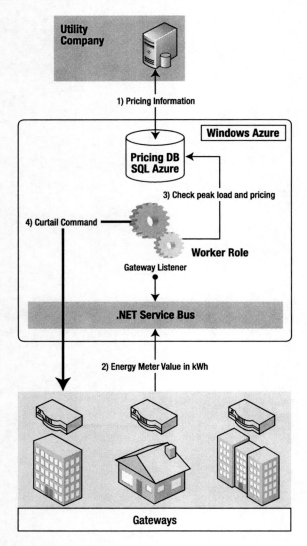

Figure 9-30. *Dem-Res system architecture*

As shown in Figure 9-30, the Dem-Res system consists of three core components:

- Pricing and Gateway database
- Gateway listener
- Gateway application

The flow of information within the components is as follows:

1. The utility company periodically sends gateway and pricing information to the pricing database in the Dem-Res system.

2. Periodically, the gateway sends an energy usage value to the gateway listener via the AppFabric Service Bus.

3. The gateway listener worker role queries the pricing database to check if the energy value is more than the peak load value.

4. If the gateway energy value is more than the peak load value, the gateway listener sends a curtail command to the gateway application. The gateway application in turn sends the control command to the appropriate device (such as HVAC in this example).

Pricing and Gateway Database Design

The Pricing and Gateway database is hosted in SQL Azure and is geo-located in the same region as the gateway listener worker role to keep the communications within the same data center. As the name suggests, the database consists of pricing and gateway information.

▨ **Tip** I recommend that y to design your SQL Azure database in SQL Server on-premises and then migrate the database to SQL Azure. When SQL Azure fully supports SQL Server Management Studio, you can work directly with the SQL Azure database.

The Pricing and Gateway database consists of four tables, as shown in Figure 9-31.

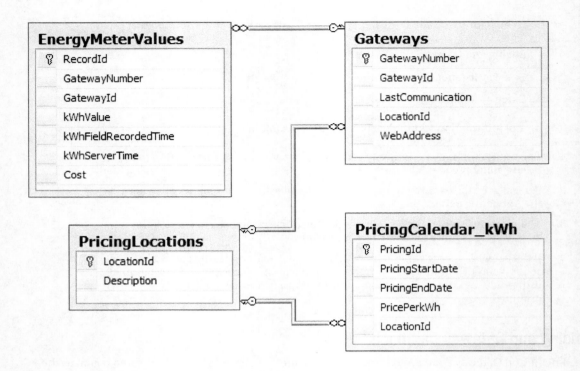

Figure 9-31. *Pricing and Gateway database design*

The Gateways table maintains the list of gateways in the field along with their location, which is referenced by LocationId from the PricingLocations table. The PricingLocations table consists of address locations that are mapped as pricing zones. Each zone has a price per kWh stored in the PricingCalendar_kWh table. The PricingCalendar_kWh table is updated periodically by the utility companies with the latest pricing. The EnergyMeterValues are the kWh values that gateways send periodically to the Dem-Res system.

The steps to create and testing the Dem-Res database system are as follows:

1. Create a database named proazuredemres.

2. Create table-creation scripts.

3. Create stored-procedure scripts.

4. Upload sample data into the tables.

5. Create data synchronization for the PricingCalendar_kWh table.

Creating the proazuredemres Database

To create this database, follow these steps:

1. Open SQL Server Management Studio.

2. Connect to the SQL Azure master database as an administrator, as shown in earlier sections.

3. Execute the following query in the New Query window to create the proazuredemres database:

```
CREATE DATABASE proazuredemres;
```

4. Create a new login named demresadmin in the db_owner role for the proazuredemres database. Follow the same procedure as shown in the "Creating Logins" section earlier in this chapter.

5. Log in to the proazuredemres database as the demresadmin user, and execute the following query to test if the login was created successfully:

```
select * from sys.databases;
```

Creating Database Tables

To create database tables, I recommend that you first create the tables and other database objects in your local SQL Server Express and then generate scripts to upload to the SQL Azure database. In this section, you directly create SQL Server objects in SQL Azure to keep the content relevant to SQL Azure only.

Listing 9-4 shows the script and schema to create the Dem-Res database tables.

Listing 9-4. *Dem-Res Table-Creation Script*

```
CREATE TABLE [dbo].[PricingLocations](
  [LocationId] [varchar](50) NOT NULL PRIMARY KEY CLUSTERED,
  [Description] [varchar](100) NOT NULL);
GO
CREATE TABLE [dbo].[PricingCalendar_kWh](
  [PricingId] [int] IDENTITY(1,1) NOT NULL  PRIMARY KEY CLUSTERED,
  [PricingStartDate] [datetime] NOT NULL,
  [PricingEndDate] [datetime] NOT NULL,
  [PricePerkWh] [float] NOT NULL,
  [LocationId] [varchar](50) NOT NULL);
GO
CREATE TABLE [dbo].[Gateways](
  [GatewayNumber] [int] IDENTITY(1,1) NOT NULL PRIMARY KEY CLUSTERED ,
  [GatewayId] [varchar](50) NOT NULL,
  [LastCommunication] [datetime] NULL,
```

```
    [LocationId] [varchar](50) NOT NULL,
    [WebAddress] [varchar](100) NOT NULL);
GO
CREATE TABLE [dbo].[EnergyMeterValues](
    [RecordId] [int] IDENTITY(1,1) NOT NULL PRIMARY KEY CLUSTERED,
    [GatewayNumber] [int] NOT NULL,
    [GatewayId] [varchar](50) NOT NULL,
    [kWhValue] [float] NOT NULL,
    [kWhFieldRecordedTime] [datetime] NOT NULL,
    [kWhServerTime] [datetime] NOT NULL,
    [Cost] [money] NOT NULL);
GO
ALTER TABLE [dbo].[EnergyMeterValues]
  WITH CHECK ADD  CONSTRAINT [FK_EnergyMeterValues_Gateways]
  FOREIGN KEY([GatewayNumber])
REFERENCES [dbo].[Gateways] ([GatewayNumber])
GO
ALTER TABLE [dbo].[EnergyMeterValues] CHECK CONSTRAINT
[FK_EnergyMeterValues_Gateways]
GO
ALTER TABLE [dbo].[Gateways]  WITH CHECK ADD  CONSTRAINT
[FK_Gateways_PricingLocations] FOREIGN KEY([LocationId])
REFERENCES [dbo].[PricingLocations] ([LocationId])
GO
ALTER TABLE [dbo].[Gateways] CHECK CONSTRAINT [FK_Gateways_PricingLocations]
GO
ALTER TABLE [dbo].[PricingCalendar_kWh]  WITH CHECK ADD  CONSTRAINT
  [FK_PricingCalendar_kWh_PricingLocations] FOREIGN KEY([LocationId])
REFERENCES [dbo].[PricingLocations] ([LocationId])
GO
ALTER TABLE [dbo].[PricingCalendar_kWh]
  CHECK CONSTRAINT [FK_PricingCalendar_kWh_PricingLocations]
GO
```

The first part of Listing 9-4 defines the tables, and then second part defines foreign key relationships between the tables.

To create tables in SQL Azure, follow these steps:

1. Connect to the proazuredemres database using SQL Server Management Studio.

2. Log in as the demresadmin user.

3. Open the createtables_proazuredemresdb.sql script file window from the DbScript folder of the Chapter 8 code directory in a NewQuery.

4. Click the Execute button to create the tables in the proazuredemres database.

5. Execute the following query to check if the tables and constraints were successfully created:

`select * from sys.objects`Creating Stored Procedures

One of the database design best practices is to locate data-processing logic closer to the database as much as possible. This is the reason stored procedures are recommended for data-processing logic rather than inline code. Stored procedures are also easier to modify and maintain than code because each stored procedure is an atomic unit containing data-processing logic that can be easily modified without having to recompile the code. For the Dem-Res system, I identified the stored procedures described in the following sections.

InsertPricingLocations

The InsertPricingLocations stored procedure inserts a new record in the PricingLocations table. This stored procedure is called by utility companies to add locations that are used to set energy prices. Listing 9-5 shows the create script for the InsertPricingLocations stored procedure.

Listing 9-5. InsertPricingLocations

```
CREATE PROCEDURE [dbo].[InsertPricingLocations]
  @locationId varchar(50),
  @description varchar(100)
AS
BEGIN
  -- SET NOCOUNT ON added to prevent extra result sets from
  -- interfering with SELECT statements.
  SET NOCOUNT ON;

  INSERT INTO PricingLocations(LocationId, [Description])
 VALUES (@locationId, @description);
END
```

The stored procedure consists of a simple insert statement. If you want to modify the stored procedure after it's installed in the database, replace CREATE PROCEDURE with ALTER PROCEDURE in the stored procedure body.

InsertPricingCalendar_kWh

The InsertPricingCalendar_kWh stored procedure inserts a new record in the PricingCalendar_kWh table. The stored procedure is called by the utility companies to update the kWh pricing for a particular period of time. Listing 9-6 shows the create script for the InsertPricingCalendar_kWh stored procedure.

Listing 9-6. InsertPricingCalendar_kWh

```
CREATE PROCEDURE [dbo].[InsertPricingCalendar_kWh]
  @pricingStartDate datetime,
  @pricingEndDate datetime,
  @pricePerkWh float,
  @locationId int
AS
BEGIN
  SET NOCOUNT ON;
```

```
 INSERT INTO PricingCalendar_kWh
(PricingStartDate, PricingEndDate, PricePerkWh, LocationId)
VALUES (@pricingStartDate, @pricingEndDate, @pricePerkWh, @locationId);
END
```

InsertGateway

The InsertGateway stored procedure inserts a new record in the Gateways table. This procedure is called when a new gateway is added to the Dem-Res database by the utility company or when the gateway communicates with the Dem-Res system for the first time. Listing 9-7 shows the create script for the InsertGateway stored procedure.

Listing 9-7. InsertGateway

```
CREATE PROCEDURE [dbo].[InsertGateway]
  @gatewayId varchar(50),
  @locationId int,
  @webAddress varchar(100)
AS
BEGIN
  SET NOCOUNT ON;

  INSERT INTO Gateways(GatewayId, LocationId, WebAddress, LastCommunication)
VALUES (@gatewayId, @locationId, @webAddress, getdate());
END
```

InsertEnergyMeterValues

The InsertEnergyMeterValues stored procedure inserts a new record in the EnergyMeterValues table. This stored procedure is called when the gateway sends the energy meter value to the Dem-Res server. Listing 9-8 shows the create script for the InsertEnergyMeterValues stored procedure.

Listing 9-8. InsertEnergyMeterValues

```
CREATE PROCEDURE [dbo].[InsertEnergyMeterValues]
  @gatewayId varchar(50),
  @kWhValue float,
  @kWhFieldRecoredTime datetime,
  @kWhServerTime datetime
AS
BEGIN
  SET NOCOUNT ON;
  DECLARE @gatewayNumber int
  DECLARE @cost float
  DECLARE @locationId int
  SELECT @gatewayNumber = GatewayNumber, @locationId=LocationId
FROM Gateways WHERE GatewayId = @gatewayId;
  SELECT @cost=PricePerkWh FROM PricingCalendar_kWh WHERE
LocationId = @locationId;
  SET @cost = @cost * @kWhValue;
```

```
  INSERT INTO EnergyMeterValues(GatewayNumber, GatewayId,
kWhValue, kWhFieldRecordedTime, kWhServerTime, Cost)
  VALUES (@gatewayNumber, @gatewayId, @kWhValue,
@kWhFieldRecoredTime, @kWhServerTime, @cost);
END
```

In Listing 9-8, PricePerkWh is retrieved from the PricingCalendar_kWh table to calculate the cost of energy for the kWh value at the location where the gateway is located. The cost is calculated by multiplying the kWh value by the price per kWh sent by the gateway. The cost value is then inserted into the record along with all the other fields of the table.

UpdateGatewayLastCommunication

The UpdateGatewayLastCommunication stored procedure updates the last communication time field in the Gateways table. This stored procedure is called when the gateway sends the energy meter value to the Dem-Res server. Listing 9-9 shows the create script for the UpdateGatewayLastCommunication stored procedure.

Listing 9-9. *UpdateGatewayLastCommunication*

```
CREATE PROCEDURE [dbo].[UpdateGatewayLastCommunication]
  @gatewayId varchar(50),
  @locationId int,
  @webAddress varchar(100)
AS
BEGIN
  SET NOCOUNT ON;
  UPDATE Gateways SET LastCommunication = getdate() WHERE GatewayId = @gatewayId
END
```

To install the stored procedures, open SQL Server Management Studio, connect to the proazuredemres database, and execute the CREATE PROCEDURE scripts as shown in Figure 9-32.

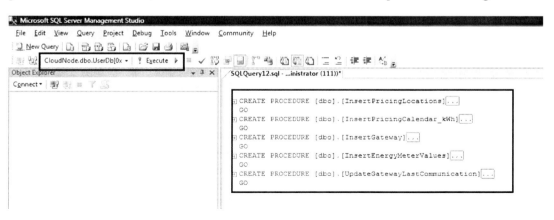

Figure 9-32. *Creating stored procedures*

Uploading Sample Data

In any database system design, you need sample data to test different scenarios and conditions that will affect the system in general. You also need sample data to test the business logic in application and stored procedures. In Ch8Solution in this chapter's source code directory, there is a Windows Forms project called ProAzureDemResDbApp that uploads sample data to PricingLocations, PricingCalendar_kWh, Gateways, and EnergyMeterValues in the SQL Azure Dem-Res database. The application calls the stored procedures discussed in the previous section to insert the data. The data is randomly generated based on some hard-coded parameters in the code. For example, the pricing locations are between the ZIP codes 95147 and 94583. Similarly, the gateway numbers are between 1 and 300. These values are also used to generate a web URL for the gateway, which is of the format `sb://proazure.servicebus.windows.net/gateways/{location_id}/{gateway_id}`.

Figure 9-33 illustrates the user interface of the ProAzureDemResDbApp application.

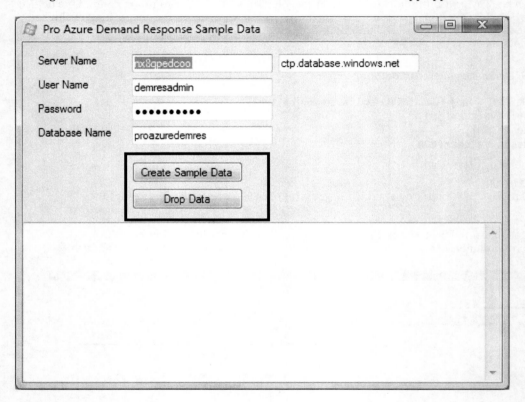

Figure 9-33. *ProAzureDemResDbApp user interface*

To upload sample data, follow these steps:

1. Run the ProAzureDemResDb application.

2. Enter your server name, username, password, and database name.

3.   Click the Create Sample Data button.

▨ **Note** It may take some time to run the query, depending on your network connection.

---

4.   To delete all the data in the tables, click the Drop Data button. Dropping data is useful if you want to re-create the sample data from scratch.

Listing 9-10 shows the code to insert data in the PricingCalendar_kWh table.

Listing 9-10. *Insert Pricing Calendar Data*

```
using (SqlConnection conn = new SqlConnection(GetUserDbString()))
{
 conn.Open();
  for (int j = START_LOCATIONID; j < END_LOCATIONID; j++)
  {
   using (SqlCommand command = conn.CreateCommand())
   {
     command.CommandText = "InsertPricingCalendar_kWh";
     command.CommandType = CommandType.StoredProcedure;
     string lid = j.ToString();
     Random r = new Random();
     double price = r.NextDouble();
     SqlParameter pricingStartDate = command.CreateParameter();
     pricingStartDate.ParameterName = "@pricingStartDate";
     pricingStartDate.Value = PRICINGCALENDAR_STARTDATE;
     command.Parameters.Add(pricingStartDate);
     SqlParameter pricingEndDate = command.CreateParameter();
     pricingEndDate.ParameterName = "@pricingEndDate";
     pricingEndDate.Value = PRICINGCALENDAR_ENDDATE;
     command.Parameters.Add(pricingEndDate);
     SqlParameter pricePerkWh = command.CreateParameter();
     pricePerkWh.ParameterName = "@pricePerkWh";
     pricePerkWh.Value = price;
     command.Parameters.Add(pricePerkWh);
     SqlParameter locationId = command.CreateParameter();
     locationId.ParameterName = "@locationId";
     locationId.Value = lid;
     command.Parameters.Add(locationId);
     command.ExecuteNonQuery();
   }//using

 }//for
}//using
```

Listing 9-10 demonstrates calling the InsertPricingCalendar_kWh stored procedure with parameterized values. In database programming, parameterized values are recommended over plain-text query strings, because there is a SQL injection risk when you use plain text queries. Parameterized queries reduce this risk because they don't append the value of the parameter to the SQL query, which gives a clear separation between the SQL query and its parameters. In Listing 9-10, note that the price per kWh is generated randomly. In the real world, the utility company provides the Dem-Res application with the price per kWh.

To test the creation of the data, you can login to proazuredemres database in your account using SQL Server Management Studio and execute a select * query on all the database tables.

Optimizing SELECT Queries

In the Dem-Res system, the most commonly used SELECT query selects PricePerkWh by LocationId from the PricingCalendar_kWh table, because for every message that comes in from the gateway, you have to calculate the cost. So, it's important that the performance of the SELECT query is optimized by appropriate indexes on the table. Depending on the other queries in the system, you may choose to create a clustered index on the LocationId field. But you can have only one clustered index on a table, which in this case is PricingId. In this example, you create a simple index on the LocationId field by executing this query:

```
CREATE INDEX INDEX_PricingCalendar_kWh_LocationId
  ON PricingCalendar_kWh(LocationId);
```

To test the index scan, you need sufficient data in the PricingCalendar_kWh table; otherwise, the SQL Server optimizer scans only the clustered index because the SQL Server optimizer may choose a different execution plan that yields better results. You can generate more test data by executing the stored procedure shown in Listing 9-11.

Listing 9-11. AddSampleData Stored Procedure

```
ALTER PROCEDURE AddSampleData
@NumRows int
AS
DECLARE @counter int
DECLARE @locationId int
DECLARE @locationIdStr varchar(50)
DECLARE @desc varchar(50)
DECLARE @pricingStartDate datetime
DECLARE @pricingEndDate datetime
DECLARE @pricekWh float
DECLARE @gatewayUrl varchar(100)
DECLARE @gatewayId varchar(50)
DECLARE @kWhValue float
DECLARE @now datetime


SELECT @counter = 1
WHILE (@counter < @NumRows)
BEGIN

SET @locationId = 10000 + @counter;
```

```
SET @locationIdStr = CAST(@locationId as varchar);
SET @desc = @locationIdStr + '-' + CAST(@counter as nvarchar)+'-description';
SET @pricingStartDate = DATEADD(m, 2, getdate());
SET @pricingEndDate = DATEADD(m, 3, getdate());
SET @pricekWh = CAST(@counter as float) * 0.00052;
SET @gatewayId = 'MyGateway' + @locationIdStr;
SET @gatewayUrl = 'sb://proazure.servicebus.windows.net/gateways/' +
 @locationIdStr + '/' + @gatewayId;
SET @kWhValue = @pricekWh * 5.2;
SET @now = getdate();

   EXEC InsertPricingLocations @locationId, @desc;
   EXEC InsertPricingCalendar_kWh @pricingStartDate, @pricingEndDate,
@pricekWh, @locationId;
   EXEC InsertGateway @gatewayId, @locationId, @gatewayUrl;
   EXEC InsertEnergyMeterValues @gatewayId, @kWhValue, @now, @now;

   SELECT @counter = @counter + 1;

END
```

The AddSampleData stored procedure creates sample data in all the database tables similar to the ProAzureDemResDbApp Windows application you saw earlier. Execute the stored procedure with the following query to enter 10,000 entries in the database tables:

```
EXEC AddSampleData 10001;
```

Note I demonstrate two different ways of creating sample data so you can choose the approach you feel comfortable with and understand the advantage of having the data-processing logic closer to the data. You can easily modify the AddSampleData stored procedure without recompiling any code as you would have to do with the Windows application shown earlier.

Next, to view the query execution plan, execute the query shown in Listing 9-12.

Listing 9-12. Show Query Plan

```
SET SHOWPLAN_ALL ON
GO
SELECT PricePerkWh FROM PricingCalendar_kWh WHERE LocationId = 95148;
GO
SET SHOWPLAN_ALL OFF
```

SET SHOWPLAN_ALL ON enables you to see the output of the query execution plan, as shown in Figure 9-34.

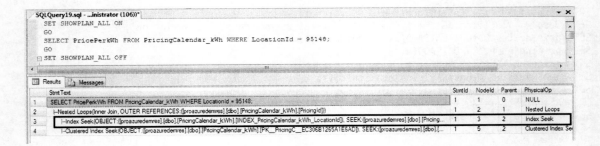

Figure 9-34. *Query plan output*

The query plan shows the steps followed by the SQL Server query optimizer to execute your query. The information shown in the plan is valuable for optimizing queries or debugging slow-running queries. Figure 9-34 shows the query optimizer using the index scan of the PricingCalendar_kWh_LocationId index you created earlier. To see the execution of the plan graphically, go to Query ▶ Display Estimated Execution Plan in SQL Server Management Studio.

Query 1: Query cost (relative to the batch): 0%
SET SHOWPLAN_ALL ON

Query 2: Query cost (relative to the batch): 100%
SELECT PricePerkWh FROM PricingCalendar_kWh WHERE LocationId = 95148;

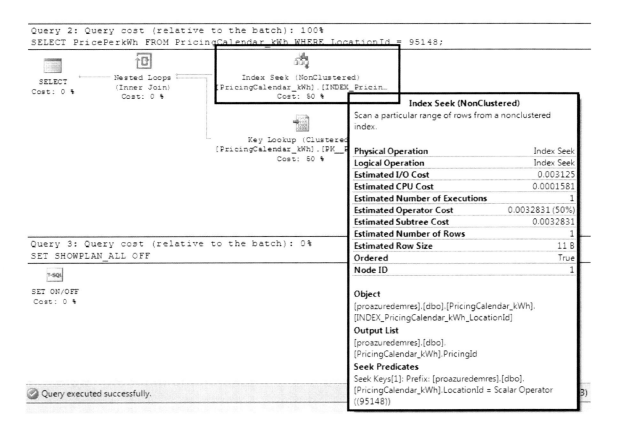

Query 3: Query cost (relative to the batch): 0%
SET SHOWPLAN_ALL OFF

Figure 9-35. *Graphical query plan output*

Pricing Table Synchronization

The values in the PricingCalendar_kWh table are provided by the utility companies. There are several ways to synchronize data in the cloud PricingCalendar_kWh table with an on-premises database table, such as creating a custom web service that can be called by utility companies, having an FTP server for data transfer between utility companies and the Dem-Res system, SQL Server Integration Services

(SSIS), and so on. This section shows you how to use SSIS to synchronize data between an on-premises database and the SQL Azure cloud database. SSIS is an Extract-Transform-Load (ETL) tool that comes with higher SQL Server editions. You can use SSIS to

- Extract data from a structured or unstructured data source
- Clean up the data or apply business rules to the data
- Upload the clean data to the destination database tables

SSIS is popular in business intelligence (BI) applications for extracting data from different kinds of sources and uploading the aggregated and clean data to a data warehouse for analysis and reporting. But the application of SSIS isn't limited to BI applications: many organizations use SSIS for simple cross-database data transfer. Figure 9-36 illustrates the use of SSIS in different kinds of applications.

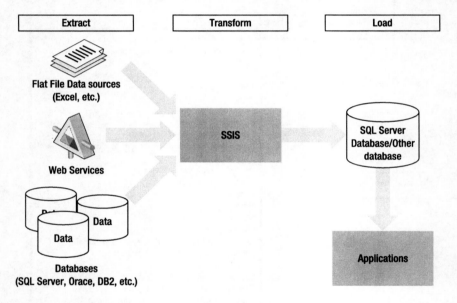

Figure 9-36. *SSIS applications*

As shown in Figure 9-36, SSIS extracts data from any kind of compatible source, transforms the data into an understandable format, and then loads the transformed data into the destination database. SSIS can be used in any kind of data-transfer application depending on the business needs. SSIS also offers the flexibility of developing custom components if the out-of-the-box features don't fulfill your requirements. SSIS is composed of *packages*, which are logical steps you design to execute an ETL operation. SSIS packages can be designed in Visual Studio; the programming environment is similar to a workflow environment.

In this section, you build an SSIS package to extract data from a pricing table in an on-premises SQL Server database and load it into the PricingCalendar_kWh table in your SQL Azure proazuredemres database. Figure 9-37 illustrates the simple architecture of the data transfer from on-premises SQL Server to SQL Azure.

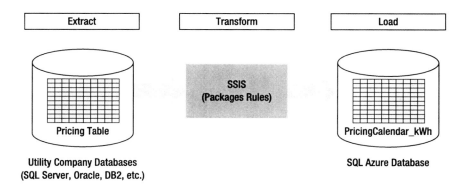

Figure 9-37. *PricingCalendar_kWh data synchronization architecture using SSIS*

Before creating an SSIS package, create a SQL Server database named utility_pricing on your local SQL Server instance; it represents a utility company's pricing database. Listing 9-13 shows the DDL script to create the database and all its associated objects, and the stored procedures AddSampleData and DropSampleData create and drop sample data, respectively.

Listing 9-13. *On-Premises DDL Database Script*

```
use [master]
CREATE DATABASE utility_pricing;
use [utility_pricing]
CREATE TABLE [dbo].[PricingLocations](
  [LocationId] [int] NOT NULL PRIMARY KEY CLUSTERED ,
  [Description] [varchar](100) NOT NULL)
  GO
CREATE TABLE [dbo].[PricingCalendar_kWh](
  [PricingId] [int] IDENTITY(1,1) NOT NULL PRIMARY KEY CLUSTERED ,
  [PricingStartDate] [datetime] NOT NULL,
  [PricingEndDate] [datetime] NOT NULL,
  [PricePerkWh] [float] NOT NULL,
  [LocationId] [int] NOT NULL)
GO

CREATE PROCEDURE [dbo].[InsertPricingLocations]
  @locationId int,
  @description varchar(100)
AS
BEGIN
  -- SET NOCOUNT ON added to prevent extra result sets from
  -- interfering with SELECT statements.
  SET NOCOUNT ON;

  INSERT INTO PricingLocations(LocationId, [Description])
VALUES (@locationId, @description);
```

```
END
GO
CREATE PROCEDURE [dbo].[InsertPricingCalendar_kWh]
  @pricingStartDate datetime,
  @pricingEndDate datetime,
  @pricePerkWh float,
  @locationId int
AS
BEGIN
  SET NOCOUNT ON;

  INSERT INTO PricingCalendar_kWh(PricingStartDate, PricingEndDate,
PricePerkWh, LocationId)
  VALUES (@pricingStartDate, @pricingEndDate, @pricePerkWh, @locationId);
END
GO

ALTER TABLE [dbo].[PricingCalendar_kWh]  WITH CHECK ADD  CONSTRAINT
  [FK_PricingCalendar_kWh_PricingLocations] FOREIGN KEY([LocationId])
REFERENCES [dbo].[PricingLocations] ([LocationId])
GO
CREATE PROCEDURE AddSampleData
@NumRows int
AS
DECLARE @counter int
DECLARE @locationId int
DECLARE @locationIdStr varchar(50)
DECLARE @desc varchar(50)
DECLARE @pricingStartDate datetime
DECLARE @pricingEndDate datetime
DECLARE @pricekWh float

SELECT @counter = 1
WHILE (@counter < @NumRows)
BEGIN

SET @locationId = 10000 + @counter;
SET @locationIdStr = CAST(@locationId as varchar);
SET @desc =  @locationIdStr + '-' + CAST(@counter as nvarchar)+'-description';
SET @pricingStartDate = DATEADD(m, 2, getdate());
SET @pricingEndDate = DATEADD(m, 3, getdate());
SET @pricekWh = CAST(@counter as float)* 0.00063;

    EXEC InsertPricingLocations @locationId, @desc;
    EXEC InsertPricingCalendar_kWh @pricingStartDate, @pricingEndDate,
@pricekWh, @locationId;


    SELECT @counter = @counter + 1;

END
```

```
GO
CREATE PROCEDURE DROPSAMPLEDATA
AS
BEGIN

 DELETE FROM PricingCalendar_kWh;
 DELETE FROM PricingLocations;

END
```

For simplicity's sake, I've kept the table schema for the pricing table the same for the proazuredemres and utility_pricing databases. To create sample data, execute the following stored statement:

```
EXEC AddSampleData 10001;
```

Designing an SSIS Package for Pricing Table Synchronization

The steps to create an SSIS package for synchronizing the on-premises pricing tables to the SQL Azure pricing tables are as follows:

1. Open SQL Server Business Intelligence Development Studio as an administrator.

2. Choose Start ▶ All Programs ▶ SQL Server Business Intelligence Development Studio.

3. Choose File ▶ New ▶ Project.

4. Select Business Intelligence Projects in the Project Types section to get a list of all the Business Intelligence Project types.

5. Select Integration Services Project in the Templates section.

6. Name the project "PricingUploadSSIS", as shown in Figure 9-38.

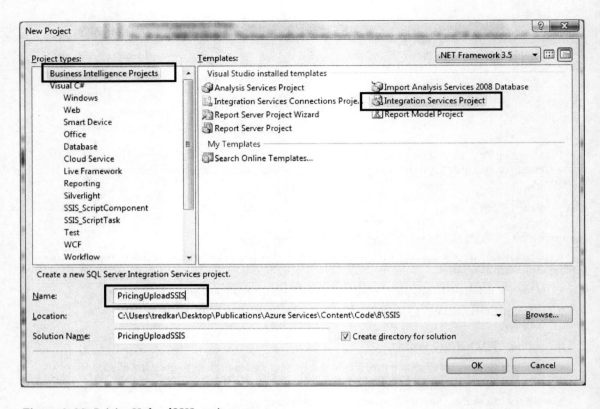

Figure 9-38. *PricingUploadSSIS project type*

7. Click OK to create the project.

8. On the Package.dtsx design page, drag and drop Execute SQL Task as shown in Figure 9-39.

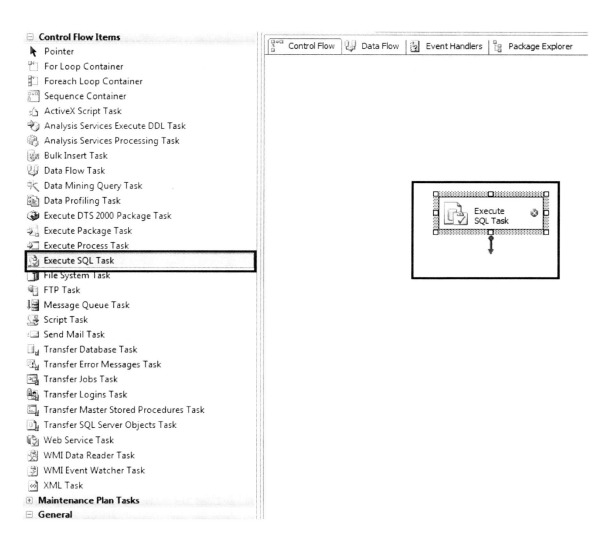

Figure 9-39. *Execute SQL Task*

9. Before you upload the data from the on-premises pricing tables to the SQL Azure pricing table, delete the existing data from the SQL Azure pricing table.

Note The pricing locations remain constant unless a new pricing location is added to the on-premises table. The only variable is the price per kWh from the PricingCalendar_kWh table.

---

10. Right-click the task on the designer surface, and click Rename to rename the task "Drop SQL Azure Pricing Data" (see Figure 9-40).

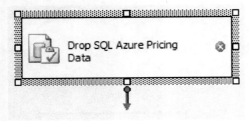

Figure 9-40. *Rename the execute SQL task.*

11. Right-click the task, and click Edit.

12. In the SQL Statement section, type the following query to delete all the records from the PricingCalendar_kWh table (see Figure 9-41):

```
DELETE FROM PricingCalendar_kWh
```

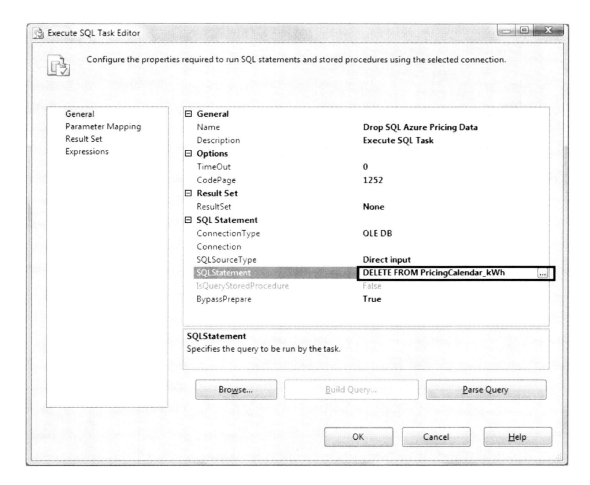

Figure 9-41. *DELETE SQL query*

13. In the Connection Type section, select ADO.NET from the drop-down list.

14. In the Connection section, select New Connection to open the Configure ADO.NET Connection Manager dialog box (see Figure 9-42).

Figure 9-42. *New Connection drop-down*

15. Click the New button to open the Connection Manager dialog box.

16. Enter the database server name.

17. Select the SQL Server Authentication type.

18. Enter the username and password of the login you've created to connect to the database.

19. Enter the name of the database: proazuredemres.

20. Click the Test Connection button to test your connection. A success connection dialog box opens on successful connection.

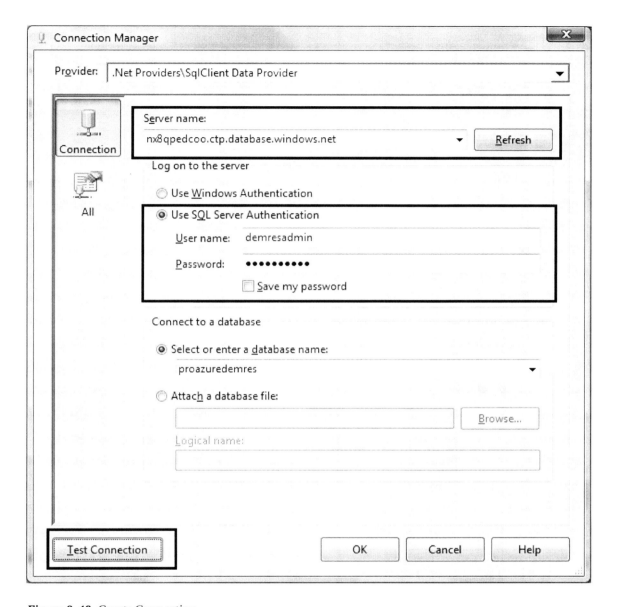

Figure 9-43. Create Connection

21. Click OK to close the Test Connection dialog box.

22. Click OK to save the connection.

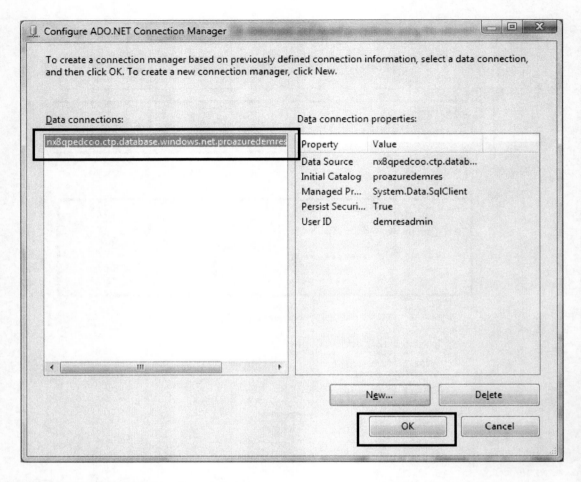

Figure 9-44. *Save SQL Azure Connection*

23. Drag and drop Data Flow Task from the Toolbox on the Package.dtsx design surface.

24. Rename the task to "Upload Pricing Data". Drag the end of the green arrow from the Drop SQL Azure Pricing Data task to the Upload Pricing Data task to let SSIS know the next logical step of execution. In this task. you upload the data from the on-premises PricingCalendar_kWh table to SQL Azure PricingCalendar_kWh table.

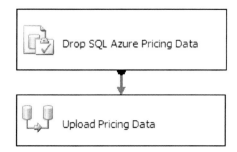

Figure 9-45. *Data Flow Task*

25. Right-click the Upload Pricing Data task, and click Edit to navigate to the Data Flow design surface (see Figure 9-46). Notice that the controls in the Toolbox change when you navigate to the Data Flow tab. The Toolbox only displays controls relevant to Data Flow tasks.

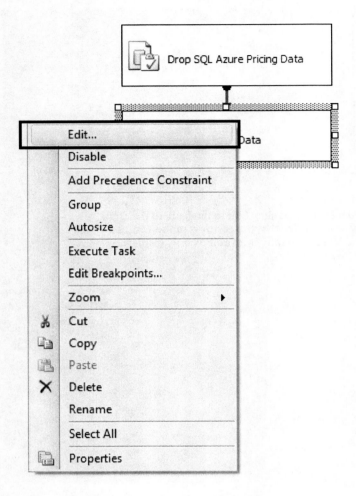

Figure 9-46. *Navigate to the Data Flow design surface.*

26. From the Data Flow Sources section on the Toolbox, drag and drop an ADO.NET Source onto the Data Flow design surface (see Figure 9-47. Rename the source "On-premises PricingCalendar_kWh". The ADO.NET Source represents the on-premises PricingCalendar_kWh data base table.

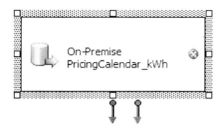

Figure 9-47. *ADO NET source*

27. Right-click the On-premises PricingCalendar_kWh task, and click Edit to open an ADO.NET Source Editor.

28. In the ADO.NET Source Editor dialog box, click the New button. By doing so, you create a new connection to the on-premises PricingCalendar_kWh database table.

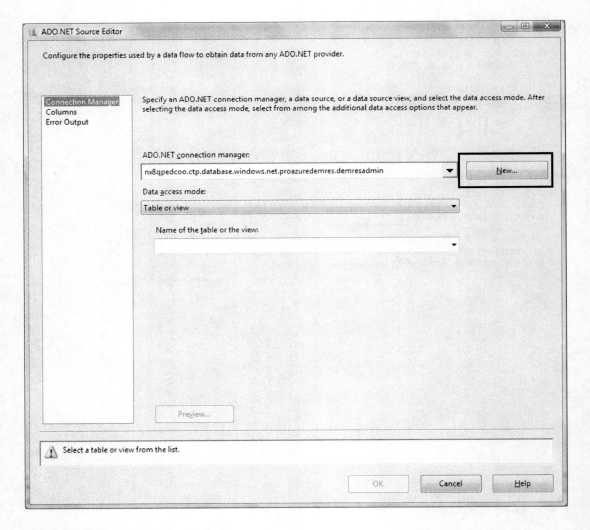

Figure 9-48. New Source Connection

29. In the Configure ADO.NET Connection Manager, click the New button to open the Connection Manager dialog box.

30. Fill in the on-premises database connection information.

31. Select the utility_pricing database from the database drop-down menu. and click OK.

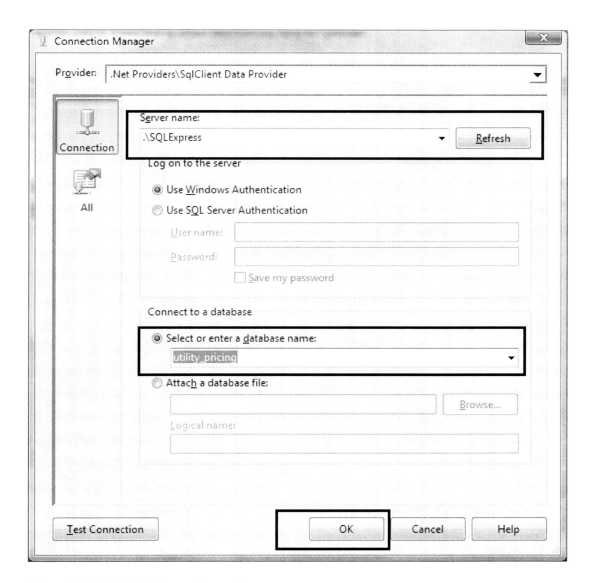

Figure 9-49. ADO.NET Source Connection

32. Click OK to go back to the ADO.NET Source Editor.

33. Select PricingCalendar_kWh from the Tables drop-down menu, and click OK (see Figure 9-50).

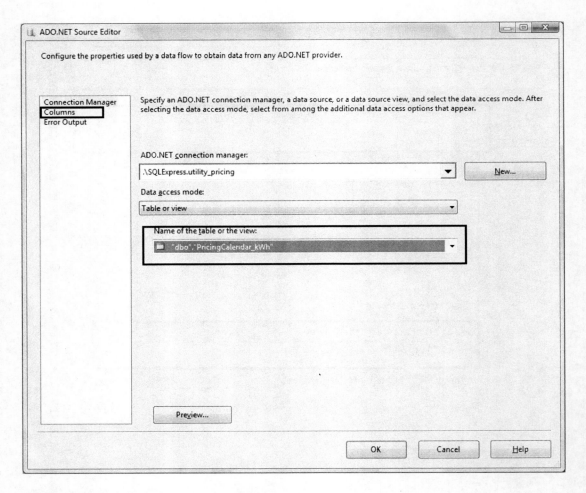

Figure 9-50. *Select PricingCalendar_kWh Table*

34. Drag and Drop ADO NET Destination from the Data Flow Destinations section of the Toolbox.

35. Rename the ADO NET Destination task to "SQL Azure PricingCalendar_kWH". The destination represents the PricingCalendar_kWh table in the SQL Azure database.

36. Connect the source and destination by connecting the green down arrow from the On-premises PricingCalendar_kWh task to SQL Azure PricingCalendar_kWh.

37. Right-click the SQL Azure PricingCalendar_kWh task, and click Edit to open the ADO.NET Destination Editor.

38. In the Connection Manager drop-down list, select the connection to the SQL Azure database. Select the PricingCalendar_kWh table from the Tables drop-down list, as shown in Figure 9-51.

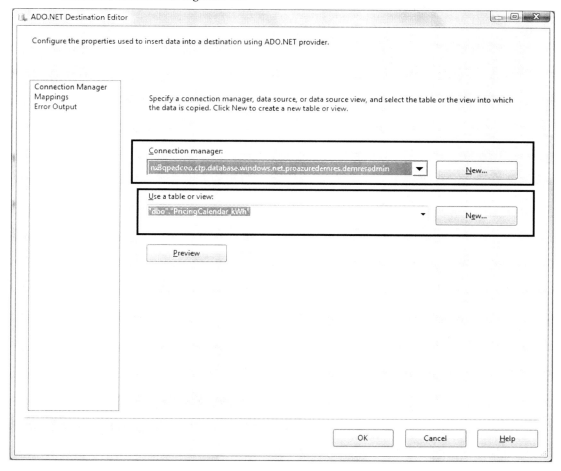

Figure 9-51. *ADO.NET Destination Editor*

39. Click the Mappings section to show the default mapping between the source and destination tables (see Figure 9-52). If the tables are similar as in this example, SQL Server does the default mapping for you.

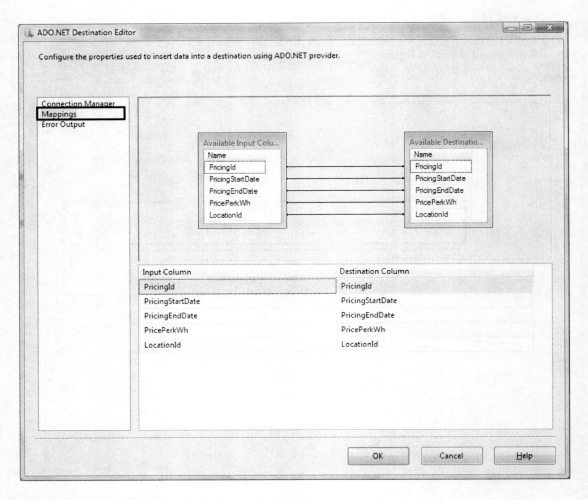

Figure 9-52. *Default source and destination mapping*

40. Select PricingId in the Input Column, and select Ignore to remove the mapping of the PricingId field (see Figure 9-53). The PricingCalendar_kWh table contains an identity field named PricingId that is auto-generated whenever a new item is inserted in the table. When a new record is inserted in the SQL Azure PricingCalendar_kWh table, a new PricingId is automatically generated. So, you don't have to synchronize the PricingId field to the SQL Azure database.

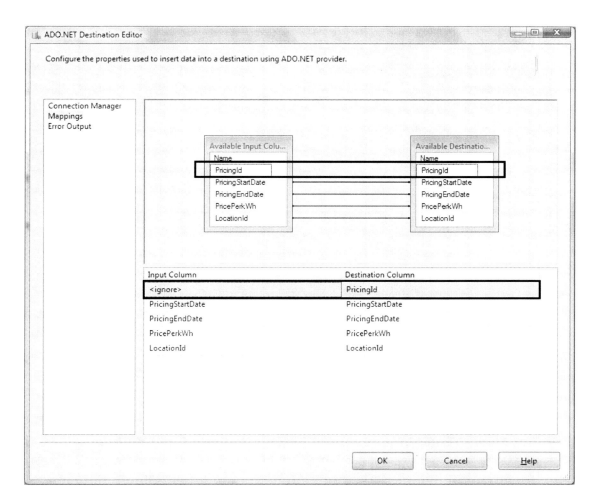

Figure 9-53. *Remove the PricingId mapping.*

41.   Click OK to close the ADO NET Destination Editor.

The Data Flow tasks are illustrated in Figure 9-54.

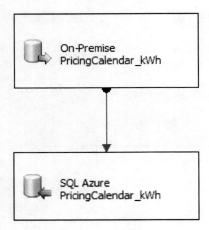

Figure 9-54. *Data Flow tasks*

The steps to test the PricingCalendar_kWh table synchronization between the on-premises utility_pricing database and the SQL Azure proazuredemres database are as follows:

1. Open SQL Server Management Studio.

2. Connect to the on-premises database utility_pricing.

3. Execute the following T-SQL statements in a New Query window to erase old pricing data and create new pricing sample data:

```
EXEC DROPSAMPLEDATA
EXEC AddSampleData 20;
select * from PricingCalendar_kWh;
```

The output from these statements is shown in Figure 9-55. You can keep existing data in the SQL Azure PricingCalendar_kWh table because the SSIS package deletes all the data from this table before uploading the on-premises data.

```
EXEC DROPSAMPLEDATA
EXEC AddSampleData 20;
select * from PricingCalendar_kWh;
```

	PricingId	PricingStartDate	PricingEndDate	PricePerkWh	LocationId
1	20	2009-10-31 11:21:17.693	2009-11-30 11:21:17.693	0.00063	10001
2	21	2009-10-31 11:21:17.693	2009-11-30 11:21:17.693	0.00126	10002
3	22	2009-10-31 11:21:17.693	2009-11-30 11:21:17.693	0.00189	10003
4	23	2009-10-31 11:21:17.693	2009-11-30 11:21:17.693	0.00252	10004
5	24	2009-10-31 11:21:17.693	2009-11-30 11:21:17.693	0.00315	10005
6	25	2009-10-31 11:21:17.693	2009-11-30 11:21:17.693	0.00378	10006
7	26	2009-10-31 11:21:17.693	2009-11-30 11:21:17.693	0.00441	10007
8	27	2009-10-31 11:21:17.693	2009-11-30 11:21:17.693	0.00504	10008
9	28	2009-10-31 11:21:17.693	2009-11-30 11:21:17.693	0.00567	10009
10	29	2009-10-31 11:21:17.693	2009-11-30 11:21:17.693	0.0063	10010
11	30	2009-10-31 11:21:17.693	2009-11-30 11:21:17.693	0.00693	10011
12	31	2009-10-31 11:21:17.693	2009-11-30 11:21:17.693	0.00756	10012
13	32	2009-10-31 11:21:17.693	2009-11-30 11:21:17.693	0.00819	10013
14	33	2009-10-31 11:21:17.707	2009-11-30 11:21:17.707	0.00882	10014
15	34	2009-10-31 11:21:17.707	2009-11-30 11:21:17.707	0.00945	10015
16	35	2009-10-31 11:21:17.707	2009-11-30 11:21:17.707	0.01008	10016
17	36	2009-10-31 11:21:17.707	2009-11-30 11:21:17.707	0.01071	10017
18	37	2009-10-31 11:21:17.707	2009-11-30 11:21:17.707	0.01134	10018
19	38	2009-10-31 11:21:17.707	2009-11-30 11:21:17.707	0.01197	10019

Figure 9-55. Create sample data in the on-premises database.

4. To run the SSIS package in Debug mode, click Debug ▶ Start Debugging. In Debug mode, Visual Studio steps through each task and color-codes it based on its execution status. First the task turns yellow, which means the operation is in progress. Then it turns either red or blue, depending on whether the task failed or succeeded, respectively. If both the tasks succeed, they turn green, as shown in Figure 9-56. If any tasks turn red, you can view the output window (View ▶ Output) to see output messages. You can also add breakpoints to the tasks to do detailed debugging of the package execution.

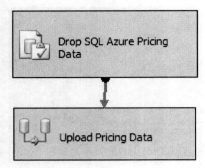

Figure 9-56. *PricingUpload SSIS package execution*

5.   Connect to SQL Azure database proazuredemres using SQL Management Studio, and execute the following command in a New Query window to view the new records uploaded from the on-premises database table:

```
select * from PricingCalendar_kWh;
```

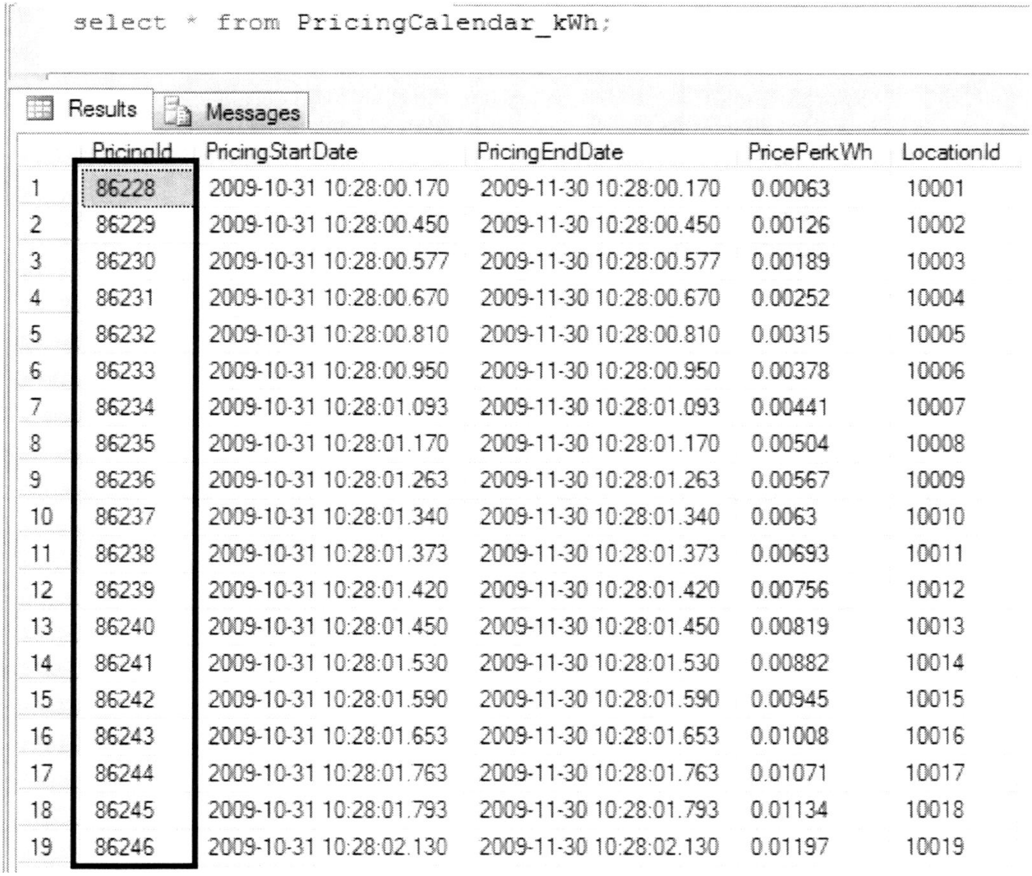

```
select * from PricingCalendar_kWh;
```

▦ Results ▣ Messages

	PricingId	PricingStartDate	PricingEndDate	PricePerkWh	LocationId
1	86228	2009-10-31 10:28:00.170	2009-11-30 10:28:00.170	0.00063	10001
2	86229	2009-10-31 10:28:00.450	2009-11-30 10:28:00.450	0.00126	10002
3	86230	2009-10-31 10:28:00.577	2009-11-30 10:28:00.577	0.00189	10003
4	86231	2009-10-31 10:28:00.670	2009-11-30 10:28:00.670	0.00252	10004
5	86232	2009-10-31 10:28:00.810	2009-11-30 10:28:00.810	0.00315	10005
6	86233	2009-10-31 10:28:00.950	2009-11-30 10:28:00.950	0.00378	10006
7	86234	2009-10-31 10:28:01.093	2009-11-30 10:28:01.093	0.00441	10007
8	86235	2009-10-31 10:28:01.170	2009-11-30 10:28:01.170	0.00504	10008
9	86236	2009-10-31 10:28:01.263	2009-11-30 10:28:01.263	0.00567	10009
10	86237	2009-10-31 10:28:01.340	2009-11-30 10:28:01.340	0.0063	10010
11	86238	2009-10-31 10:28:01.373	2009-11-30 10:28:01.373	0.00693	10011
12	86239	2009-10-31 10:28:01.420	2009-11-30 10:28:01.420	0.00756	10012
13	86240	2009-10-31 10:28:01.450	2009-11-30 10:28:01.450	0.00819	10013
14	86241	2009-10-31 10:28:01.530	2009-11-30 10:28:01.530	0.00882	10014
15	86242	2009-10-31 10:28:01.590	2009-11-30 10:28:01.590	0.00945	10015
16	86243	2009-10-31 10:28:01.653	2009-11-30 10:28:01.653	0.01008	10016
17	86244	2009-10-31 10:28:01.763	2009-11-30 10:28:01.763	0.01071	10017
18	86245	2009-10-31 10:28:01.793	2009-11-30 10:28:01.793	0.01134	10018
19	86246	2009-10-31 10:28:02.130	2009-11-30 10:28:02.130	0.01197	10019

Figure 9-57. *Uploaded Data in SQL Azure*

Note that other than PricingId, all the field values are exactly the same as the on-premises database. You specifically configured PricingId to be ignored while uploading the new records because it's an identity field that increments automatically on new data inserts.

As you learned in this exercise, SSIS is a very flexible tool for ETL operations, and it adds significant value when you're working with cloud databases. The out-of-the-box tasks in the SSIS Toolbox are rich in features that can help you synchronize, maintain, administer, and analyze data in SQL Azure from your on-premises infrastructure.

Gateway Listener Design

The Gateway Listener is a server that listens to the messages sent by gateways and updates the database with these messages. If required, it sends a curtail command to the gateway to curtail the load. In the Ch8Solution, the DemResWorkerRole project implements the Gateway Listener design. The DemResWorkerRole is a Windows Azure worker role project that registers itself as an AppFabric Service Bus endpoint and listens to messages using netTcpRelayBinding. The gateways send messages to the AppFabric Service Bus endpoint. Figure 9-58 illustrates the DemResWorkerRole design.

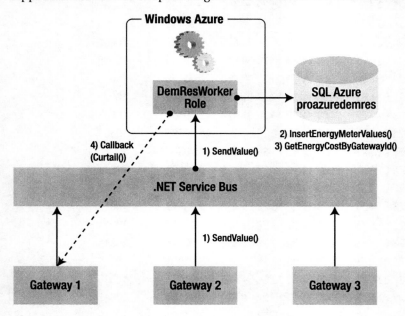

Figure 9-58. *DemResWorkerRole design*

The DemResWorkerRole is a typical AppFabric Service Bus service that uses a username and password for AppFabric Service Bus authentication. The Logging service runs on-premises as a separate AppFabric Service Bus service and receives log messages from the DemResWorkerRole.

■ **Caution** This example uses netTcpRelayBinding as the AppFabric Service Bus binding between the gateway and the DemResWorkerRole. The drawback with netTcpRelayBinding is that it doesn't have built-in load-balancing, and each endpoint can support only one service instance. In the real world, you should use either an AppFabric Service Bus Router or a WCF web service hosted in a web role. The purpose of this example is to demonstrate the integration between a Windows Azure worker role, the AppFabric Service Bus, and SQL Azure, so it uses simple bindings and configurations.

The logical steps of execution in the DemResWorkerRole are as follows:

1. Periodically, gateways call the SendValue() method on the DemResWorkerRole.

2. The DemResWorkerRole inserts a new record in the EnergyMeterValues database table in SQL Azure.

3. It then retrieves the kWh price for the location where the gateway is located and calculates the total unit cost of energy by multiplying the price per kWh by the kWh value.

4. If the total value exceeds one dollar, the DemResWorkerRole sends a curtail command to the gateway on a callback connection to the gateway.

Listing 9-14 shows the code for the contract and server implementation of the DemResWorkerRole.

Listing 9-14. *Contract and Implementation of the DemResWorkerRole*

```
[ServiceContract(CallbackContract = typeof(IDemResCallback))]
 public interface IDemResOperations
 {
  [OperationContract]
  void SendValue(string gatewayId, double value, DateTime gatewayTime);
 }
public interface IDemResCallback
 {
  [OperationContract]
  void Curtail(int setPointValue);
 }
[ServiceBehavior(ConcurrencyMode = ConcurrencyMode.Reentrant)]
 public class DemResService : IDemResOperations
 {

  public void SendValue(string gatewayId, double kWhValue, DateTime gatewayTime)
  {
   //Update the database table with the new value
   InsertEnergyMeterValues(gatewayId, kWhValue, gatewayTime);
   //Get the value from the database and curtail if total price > $1.0
   double cost = GetCostByGateway(gatewayId, kWhValue);

   if (cost > 1.0)
   {
    IDemResCallback callback = OperationContext.Current.
GetCallbackChannel<IDemResCallback>();
    callback.Curtail(70);
   }

  }

  private void InsertEnergyMeterValues
(string gid, double kWh, DateTime gatewayTime)
  {
```

```
try
{
  // Connect to the sample database and perform various operations
  using (SqlConnection conn = new SqlConnection(GetUserDbString()))
  {
    conn.Open();
    using (SqlCommand command = conn.CreateCommand())
    {
      // Insert records
      command.CommandText = "InsertEnergyMeterValues";
      command.CommandType = CommandType.StoredProcedure;
      SqlParameter gatewayId = command.CreateParameter();
      gatewayId.ParameterName = "@gatewayId";
      gatewayId.Value = gid;
      command.Parameters.Add(gatewayId);

      SqlParameter kWhValue = command.CreateParameter();
      kWhValue.ParameterName = "@kWhValue";
      kWhValue.Value = kWh;
      command.Parameters.Add(kWhValue);

      SqlParameter kWhFieldRecoredTime = command.CreateParameter();
      kWhFieldRecoredTime.ParameterName = "@kWhFieldRecoredTime";
      kWhFieldRecoredTime.Value = gatewayTime;
      command.Parameters.Add(kWhFieldRecoredTime);

      SqlParameter kWhServerTime = command.CreateParameter();
      kWhServerTime.ParameterName = "@kWhServerTime";
      kWhServerTime.Value = DateTime.Now;
      command.Parameters.Add(kWhServerTime);
      int rowsAdded = command.ExecuteNonQuery();
    }//using
  }
}
catch (Exception ex)
{
  throw ex;
}
}
```

Listing 9-15 shows the code for the GetEnergyCostByGatewayId stored procedure that retrieves the energy cost for the unit of energy sent by the gateway.

Listing 9-15. *GetEnergyCostByGatewayId Stored Procedure*

```
CREATE PROCEDURE [dbo].[GetEnergyCostByGatewayId]
  @gatewayId varchar(50)
AS
BEGIN
  SET NOCOUNT ON;
```

```
SELECT  PricingCalendar_kWh.PricePerkWh
FROM Gateways
INNER JOIN PricingLocations ON Gateways.LocationId = PricingLocations.LocationId
INNER JOIN PricingCalendar_kWh
  ON PricingLocations.LocationId = PricingCalendar_kWh.LocationId
WHERE (Gateways.GatewayId = @gatewayId);
END
```

The GetEnergyCostByGatewayId accepts gatewayId as the parameter and retrieves the price per kWh for the location of the gateway from the database. The DemResWorkerRole calculates the total cost and decides whether to curtail the load.

Gateway Application Design

A *gateway application* runs on gateways. This example builds it as a simple Windows application, but in the real world such applications are background processes that run on embedded operating systems like Windows CE. The gateway application calls the DemRes service in the cloud via the AppFabric Service Bus using the netTcpRelayBinding. In Ch8Solution, the DemResGateway project represents the gateway application. DemResGateway is a Windows application that implements the callback interface that the DemRes service can call to curtail the load. Figure 9-59 illustrates the DemResGateway architecture.

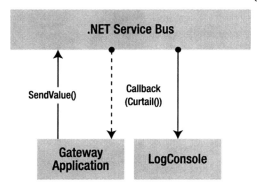

Figure 9-59. *DemResGateway application architecture*

Running the ProAzure Demand-Response Service

The steps required to run the Dem-Res system are outlined next. Begin by performing the following prerequisites:

1. Register for a Windows Azure account.

2. Create a project in the AppFabric portal.

3. Create a username and password in the AppFabric portal.

4. Create an InfoCard using Windows CardSpace on your local machine.

575

5. Upload the card as one of the AppFabric solution credentials. You need this card to call methods on the server from the gateway client.

6. Create a new SQL Azure database called proazuredemres.

7. Log in to proazuredemres using SQL Server Management Studio.

8. Open the proazuredemres_allobjects.sql file in a New Query window, and execute the script to create objects in the proazuredemres database.

■ **Note** Make sure you've chosen the correct database before executing the script. You may also use SQLCMD to execute the script from the command line.

---

9. Create sample data by executing the following stored procedure:

```
EXEC AddSampleData 10001;
```

10. Create a new on-premises database called utility_pricing.

11. Open the utility_pricing_allobjects.sql file in a New Query window, and execute the script to create objects in the utility_pricing database.

12. Create sample data by executing the following stored procedure:

```
EXEC AddSampleData 10001;
```

Now, follow these steps to run the application:

1. Open Ch8Solution in Visual Studio.

2. Add your own usernames, passwords, endpoints, SQL Azure connection strings, and other configuration parameters in the configuration files of the DemResWorker, DemResGateway, and LogReceiverConsole projects.

3. Build and deploy the DemResWorker cloud service project to Windows Azure.

■ **Tip** Run the complete end-to-end application locally in the development fabric before deploying it to Windows Azure.

---

4. Start the LogReceiverConsole application. This application receives log messages from the DemResWorkerRole.

5. Start the DemResWorker service in Windows Azure or in the development fabric.

6. Start the DemResGateway application on your local machine.

7. Click the Send kWh Value button to send a single kWh value to the DemResWorker service.

8. Click the button several times to get a value that results in a price greater than one dollar. If the cost of energy per unit is more than one dollar, the DemResWorker service sends a curtail command to the gateway using a callback interface. When this happens, you see a message box with the curtail value, as shown in Figure 9-60.

Figure 9-60. DemRes callback

Database-Migration Strategies

When you're creating a database from scratch, designing and deploying it in SQL Azure shouldn't be difficult. All the limitations and constraints in SQL Azure are published, and the database is a subset of your on-premises SQL Server database. So, any database you design for SQL Azure can be easily migrated to an on-premises SQL Server. But SQL Server is a mature database server used in enterprises of all sizes. Migrating these legacy databases to the cloud may require a complete redesign because of the wide range of rich features like Server Broker, CLR stored procedures, replication, mirroring, and so on that are supported by on-premises databases but aren't yet supported in SQL Azure.

A database migration involves migrating not only the data and its schema but also the business logic and applications that depend on that database. Thus the database-migration strategy to SQL Azure involves the following four actions:

1. Data definition migration

2. Data migration

3. Business logic migration

4. Application migration

Data Definition Migration

The *data definition* refers to the design of your database schema, which may include storage-specific objects like tables, views, indexes, constraints, and so on. The data definition is tightly coupled to the type of data stored in the database to achieve optimal performance.

A particular database's data definition can be easily represented by a script that can be automatically generated in SQL Server Management Studio. With minor modifications, these scripts can be executed on SQL Azure to migrate the data definition from on-premises SQL Server to SQL Azure. So, other than execution tools like SQL Server Management Studio and SQLCMD, you don't need any specific tools to migrate data definition from on-premises SQL Server to SQL Azure when you have the script representing the data definition. This is the recommended approach to migrate data definitions from on-premises to SQL Azure, because this approach gives you more control over the definition of the data.

You can also use SSIS to replicate data definitions on the fly between an on-premises database and SQL Azure. But this approach may require more work in designing, building, testing, and deploying packages.

Typical steps required to migrate data definition from on-premises SQL Server to SQL Azure are as follows:

1. Log in to your on-premises SQL Server database.

2. Generate a script for all the data definition objects, which include tables, views, indexes, and constraints (see Figure 9-61).

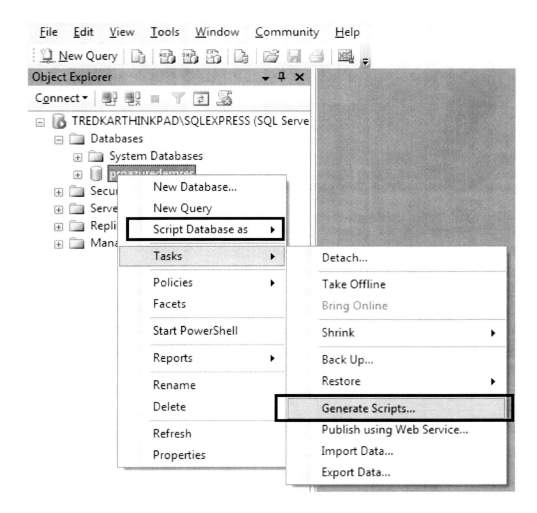

Figure 9-61. *Generate a script.*

3. Modify the script to remove the features or commands not supported by SQL Azure.

▨ **Note** For commands not supported in SQL Azure, please refer to the SQL Azure documentation.

---

4. Save the script as a SQL Azure database definition script.

5. Connect to the SQL Azure database to which you want to migrate the data definition.

6. Open a New Query window, and copy and paste the content of the SQL Azure database script into it.

7. Execute the script to install the data definition objects in the SQL Azure database.

Data Migration

Data migration refers to the actual data stored in SQL Server. An on-premises SQL Server supports several tools to migrate data across different SQL Server instances as well as heterogeneous databases like Oracle, DB2, Access, and so on. Some of the popular data-migration tools are as follows:

- *SQL Server BCP Utility:* Used for bulk copying data between SQL Server instances and/or file systems

- *SQL Server Management Studio:* Used to back up and restore SQL Server databases

- *Database mirroring:* Supports real-time data mirroring across SQL Server databases

- *Log shipping:* Used for real-time backup and restore functionality

- *Replication:* Supports real-time data mirroring across SQL Server databases

- *SQL Server Integration Services (SSIS):* Includes built-in backup and restore tasks that can be included in packages and executed in a standalone manner or coupled with other business logic

---

■ **Note** This isn't an exhaustive list but just the most commonly used tools that are included with SQL Server. Most companies use advanced data-replication and -migration tools built by Microsoft's partner companies. I discuss only the most popular out-of-the-box SQL Server tools that you can use for data migration.

Most of the tools from this list need both the source database and the destination database supporting the tool. As of this writing, other than SSIS and the BCP Utility (supported in future releases of SQL Azure), SQL Azure doesn't support any of these tools. Even within SSIS, some of the maintenance tasks aren't supported by SQL Azure, so your best option is to use tasks that support ADO.NET connections. The BCP tool is the simplest to use and the best option for quickly scripting and/or scheduling the data migration on a periodic basis. On the other hand, SSIS gives you the most flexibility because you can design workflows and/or data transformations within your data-migration package. The BCP Utility is the best option for simple, quick, no-code data migrations, whereas SSIS is the best option for data migrations involving workflows and/or transformations.

Business Logic Migration

In the simplest terms, the *business logic* refers to the logic that is applied to the data before it's stored in the database or retrieved from the database for viewing. The business logic may also consist of business rules applied to inbound as well as outbound data in specific conditions. In some distributed systems, the business logic is embedded in the middle tier; in other cases, it's embedded in stored procedures closer to the database. There are also some client/server systems where the business logic is embedded in the client tier. Microsoft Excel is a very good client example in which you can connect to a database and add business logic to the data retrieved in Excel.

When you're planning a database migration, migrating the business logic associated with the data is equally important. In cases where the business logic is programmed in stored procedures, you can follow the same procedure as in the data-definition migration discussed earlier. You can generate a script defining the stored procedures and execute the script in SQL Azure. SQL Azure doesn't support CLR stored procedures yet, so you have to reprogram the stored procedures in .NET middle-tier components and TSQL stored procedures.

When the business logic is embedded in the middle tier, you must identify the SQL Server–specific features used in the business logic and verify their supportability in SQL Azure. If they aren't supported, then you have to redesign an alternative.

Your business logic migration strategy will change depending on the tier that owns the business logic. Typically, in large scale enterprise systems, the business logic is programmed in the middle tier so multiple applications can share the same data and have their own business logic components. In these cases, migration may require a detailed analysis and planning exercise. In small- to medium-scale databases, the business logic tier is typically programmed in stored procedures and closer to the data. In these cases, if the business logic is in TSQL stored procedures, the process is easier—assuming the stored procedures access objects supported by SQL Azure. If the business logic is in CLR stored procedures, you need a detailed planning and analysis exercise similar to that used with middle-tier components.

Application Migration

All databases provide data-retrieval and -modification services to one or more applications that process inbound and outbound data from the database. Without applications, databases are simply silos of isolated data providing no value to the business. You don't need a database to create a silo of data; you can store the data in a file system, on tape, or on a storage area network in its raw format. Enterprises store data in databases to make it available to applications. Applications then retrieve data from the databases and present it to end users in a readable and business-friendly format.

When you're designing a strategy for a database migration to SQL Azure, you have to consider all the applications that are actively using the database and supporting business functions. In your migration strategy, you must design a business continuity plan in which the database is migrated to SQL Azure without affecting the business continuity of the applications and the database itself. In some cases, you may also have to migrate the applications to Windows Azure along with the database to SQL Azure. Business continuity is critical to enterprises, and all migration strategies must be designed so that application downtime is zero.

Database Growth-Management Strategies

When your data is on-premises, you can manage your SQL Server database's growth by adding more storage capacity. Typically, an on-premises storage area network is shared across multiple databases and applications, and it's only a matter of acquiring an extra block of storage from the company's storage-management team. Even though a cost is associated with the storage, you still have control over how you distribute your database growth.

When your data is in SQL Azure, there is a storage constraint of 10GB per database, and you don't have control over how the data files are stored or distributed across the storage area network. Microsoft's argument behind this constraint is that according to the company's analysis, 90% of the SQL Server databases in the world are less than 9GB in size.

With this constraint in mind, how do you architect your database for growth beyond 10GB? The following are a few strategies I have designed for SQL Azure customers:

- Partition data by location, and distribute it across multiple SQL Azure data centers.

- Partition data by date into multiple databases.

- Partition data by business functions into bucket databases.

- Partition data by tenant, with one configuration and one content database per tenant.

- Partition data between on-premises and SQL Azure databases.

■ **Note** Because of the SQL Azure size restrictions, all these strategies revolve around creating multiple SQL Server databases in SQL Azure and partitioning data across these databases.

In all the partitioning options, typically a centrally located or replicated configuration database maintains the references and boundary parameters of the content databases. The content databases contain the actual content partitioned by the appropriate boundary condition. These boundary conditions may be one of more of the following: location, date, business function, tenant, and premises. Figure 9-62 illustrates some of these partitioning strategies.

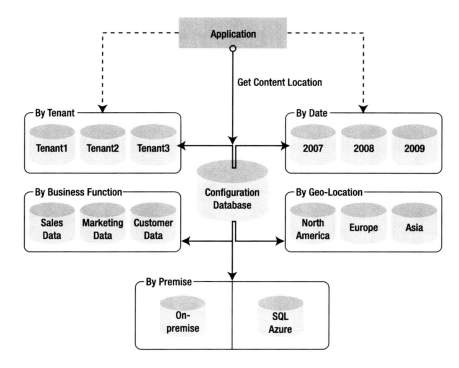

Figure 9-62. *Partitioning strategies*

In Figure 9-62, the configuration database contains the partition information of the content databases. The application queries the configuration database with query parameters and retrieves the list of content databases that fall within the specified parameters. For example, if your query is for dates in 2007, then the configuration database sends references to the 2007 database. The application can then connect to the appropriate database to execute the query.

Because of the two hops between the application and the databases, there is a performance impact on the data retrieval from the content databases. The configuration database isn't expected to change frequently because it depends on the partitioning parameters, which don't change often. Therefore, you can cache the configuration data in the application and synchronize only when it changes, bypassing an additional hop to the configuration database.

Summary

In this chapter, you learned to work with SQL Azure, the SQL Server database in the cloud. Because SQL Azure is based on SQL Server, you can use your existing SQL Server knowledge to work with SQL Server.

SQL Azure is a subset of SQL Server and supports only limited features specifically geared toward storage and retrieval of relational data. Many administration- and application-level features like mirroring, replication, the BCP Utility, Service Broker, CLR, replication, and so on aren't available in SQL Azure.

The biggest benefit of SQL Azure is its accessibility to any application from anywhere as long as the platform supports the TDS protocol. You can write cloud and on-premises applications to seamlessly query data in SQL Azure. In the Demand Response example, you saw the flexibility of accessing SQL Azure from Windows Azure, as well as seamless integration between SQL Azure, Windows Azure, and AppFabric.

Finally, I introduced some database-migration and database growth-management strategies for SQL Azure databases. SQL Azure is in its infancy and will evolve over time as the cloud infrastructure matures and customers demand more features.

Bibliography

Microsoft Corporation. (n.d.). *SQL Azure Team Blog*. Retrieved from SQL Azure Team Blog:
    `http://blogs.msdn.com/ssds/`.

Robinson, D. (2009). The Relational Database of the Azure Services Platform. *MSDN*, 71-74.

Index

▓ N

CPSIA information can be obtained at www.ICGtesting.com
Printed in the USA
236276LV00012B/10/P

9 781430 224792